Birds
of Nova Scotia

Birds
of Nova Scotia

Robie W. Tufts

Colour illustrations by
Roger Tory Peterson and John A. Crosby

Line drawings by John H. Dick

THIRD EDITION 1986
with revisions by members of the
Nova Scotia Bird Society under the
coordination of Ian A. McLaren

A co-publication
NIMBUS PUBLISHING LIMITED
THE NOVA SCOTIA MUSEUM

HALIFAX, NOVA SCOTIA

Co-published by Nimbus Publishing Limited and the
Nova Scotia Museum as part of the
Education Resources Program of the
Department of Education. Province of Nova Scotia

Minister The Hon. Thomas J. McInnis
Deputy Minister Gerald McCarthy

A product of the Nova Scotia Government
Co-publishing Program

Printed in Nova Scotia, Canada
Design by Graphic Design Associates, Halifax

Canadian Cataloguing in Publication Data
Tufts, Robie W.
    Birds of Nova Scotia

Co-published by the Nova Scotia Museum.
Bibliography: p. 458
Includes index.
ISBN 0-920852-64-5 (bound). — ISBN 0-920852-66-1 (pbk.)

1. Birds — Nova Scotia.   I. Peterson, Roger Tory,
1908-   II. Crosby, John A. (John Alexander),
1925-   III. Dick, John Henry, 1919-
IV. Nova Scotia Museum.   V. Title.

QL685.5.N6T83 1986   598.29716   C86-094283-X

Contents

List of Illustrations

Colour Plates

Illustrations by Roger Tory Peterson are part of the collection of the Newfoundland Museum and are reproduced with their kind permission.

Line Drawings   Page

Preface

Robie Tufts (1884-1982) had an enormous role in documenting Nova Scotian birdlife in technical and popular publications, in promoting the causes of conservation and in encouraging others, especially young people, to take up bird study, sometimes professionally (see the tribute by Godfrey 1984). One of his outstanding legacies is his original authorship of *The Birds of Nova Scotia* (1961, 1973), on which the present volume is based. The earlier editions can be found on the bookshelves of many Nova Scotians and enjoyed a wide readership elsewhere.

It has been clear for some years that the second edition was in need of reprinting or replacement. So many changes in the province's birdlife have been documented since that edition, which contains records to the end of 1969, that it would have been a disservice to have merely reprinted the book. However, a complete rewriting would entail much further research on published material, on scattered museum collections, on data in the Maritimes Nest Records Scheme (filed with the Canadian Wildlife Service, Sackville, New Brunswick) and on material from the Co-operative Breeding Bird Surveys carried out in Nova Scotia since 1966 (see Erskine 1978). Furthermore, the newly launched Maritimes Breeding Bird Atlas, to occupy hundreds of participants between 1986 and 1991, will undoubtedly expand our knowledge of the occurrence, distribution and abundance of breeding birds in Nova Scotia.

Fortunately, the wide and deep experience and knowledge of Robie Tufts is still a firm foundation for any account of the province's birds. Therefore our mandate for revision was more modest. The Nova Scotia Bird Society was asked by the Nova Scotia Museum to update those sections of the second edition on the status of occurrence of each species, using records accumulated and published by the society over the years. To do this, the current sub-editors of the seasonal bird reports in the society's periodical, *Nova Scotia Birds* (published since 1957, formerly as the *Newsletter* of the society), were asked to initiate revisions for birds for which they are responsible in that periodical. Charles R.K. Allen undertook the loons, grebes and waterfowl, Richard G.B. Brown the seabirds, J. Shirley Cohrs the passerines from flycatchers to starling, Phyllis R. Dobson the remaining passerines, Ian A. McLaren the herons and relatives, diurnal raptors, gallinaceous birds and the doves through woodpeckers, and Francis P. Spalding the shorebirds. I was asked to coordinate and standardize these efforts.

During the work it became clear that other changes were in order, some of which are explained in the Introduction. Many nomenclatural changes had to be made from the most recent *Check-list of North American Birds* (American Ornithologists' Union 1983). Geographical distributions of many species have changed or become better known in recent years. Some comments in the Remarks sections of the second edition are no longer appropriate and others had to be added. The Introduction was completely rewritten to reflect changed perceptions about birds, their environments and bird study.

It has been our aim in this third edition to preserve the organization and flavour of the previous editions. Robie Tufts' writing continues to enliven what would otherwise be a drier, more technical work. We have retained his first-person accounts in the sections on Breeding (which have not otherwise been modified essentially unless changes in breeding status have occurred since 1969) and in the Remarks sections, where his observations and anecdotes on common species are particularly illuminating. Of course, the illustrations that graced the previous editions were indispensable as well.

All this has involved a team effort extending beyond the contributions of the above-named sub-editors of *Nova Scotia Birds*. Deborah Burleson and John Hennigar-Shuh of the Nova Scotia Museum have been responsible for liaison among the various groups and individuals involved in the project. Fulton Lavender subdued the massive amount of material from the Nova Scotia Bird Society's records onto easily managed file cards. Our copy editor, Douglas Beall, has skilfully fished out ambiguities, obscurities, redundancies and infelicities. Fred Scott of the Nova Scotia Museum also cast a critical eye on technical and literary matters. Tony Crouch and Bonnie Baird of the Information Division of the Department of Government Services have made significant contributions to this project. We have had excellent word processing through numerous revisions by Barbara Colwell. Steven Slipp designed this edition, and Elizabeth Eve and Dan Sargeant of Nimbus Publishing shepherded the book to its final published form. Finally, we must all be grateful to those who over the years have supplied their observations on birds in Nova Scotia. Some contributers were singled out for acknowledgements in previous editions, but their ranks have swelled greatly in more recent years. Many are named in the sections on Status, Breeding and Remarks as authorities for unusual occurrences or noteworthy observations.

We hope that readers or, more precisely, users of this book will be pleased with our collective effort.

Ian A. McLaren
Halifax, Nova Scotia
April 21, 1986

Introduction

Nova Scotia Environments for Birds

Nova Scotia, the most southeasterly province of Canada, is a long and narrow peninsula extending some 650 km from Seal Island in the southwest to St. Paul Island off the tip of Cape Breton Island. Sable Island, a chain of sand dunes, lies some 140 km southeast of the Strait of Canso. At sea, the adoption by Canada of the 200-mile (322 km) limit allows us to claim birds seen beyond the limits of the Scotian Shelf in the offshore Atlantic and to the shared boundaries with the United States from the Gulf of Maine through Georges Bank, with New Brunswick in the Bay of Fundy and with Newfoundland in the Laurentian Channel.

This large area of land and water encompasses a great deal of geological and ecological diversity. The reader may find extensive information on the physiography and geology of the province in a monograph by Roland (1983) and also in a two-volume survey of the natural history of the province prepared by Simmons et al. (1984). A good summary of climate and weather in Nova Scotia is in Gates (1975). Here, only a brief discussion of environmental characteristics is made in the context of the birds that occur in the province. All significant place names and coastal areas in this section of the Introduction are shown on the regional map on pages 466-7.

The geographical setting of Nova Scotia has important effects on its birdlife. The province is virtually insular, thrusting out into the North Atlantic about halfway between the equator and the North Pole. Islands and peninsulas characteristically have a less diverse birdlife than is found on nearby mainlands (MacArthur and Wilson 1967). It is noteworthy that some birds nesting in Maine, southern Quebec and even nearby New Brunswick do not nest in Nova Scotia or do so rarely. However, the province is well situated to receive transient and vagrant birds from other parts of North America, offering a last landfall for birds coming from the west and a first landfall for birds migrating or displaced over the sea.

The weather in Nova Scotia is related to its geographical setting and influences its birdlife. The mean boundary between the tropical and arctic air masses passes northward in May and southward in September across the province. Airflow from much of the continent focuses on Nova Scotia; mean wind directions are southwesterly between spring and fall and more westerly in winter. Storm tracks from the southeastern and midwestern United States also converge on Nova Scotia, creating greatly variable weather conditions and frequent high winds. This convergence of windstreams on Nova Scotia has obvious consequences for migration and vagrancy of birds (see McLaren 1981b).

No part of the province is more than about 70 km from salt water, a considerable moderating influence on the climate. Thus average daily maximal and minimal temperatures at Halifax are about 0.5 and -6.6°C in January and 22.7 and 13.8°C in July. In comparison, temperatures at Kingston, Ontario, at almost exactly the latitude of Halifax, are more extreme: -3.6 and -12.3°C in January and 25.7 and 15.5°C in July. There is a temperature gradient within the province from Cape Breton Island to Yarmouth County, the latter averaging about 2°C warmer than the former in January, but the two differing little in July. There is also an offshore-inland gradient in temperature: Sable Island averages almost 2.5°C warmer and Kentville, in the sheltered Annapolis Valley, averages 2°C cooler than Halifax in January; Sable Island is about 2.7°C cooler and Kentville about 1.0°C warmer than Halifax in July. These differences affect birdlife. Spring comes late and breeding seasons are delayed in Nova Scotia, especially in coastal areas, compared with regions well inland in eastern Canada. Autumn migration is relatively protracted in Nova Scotia, and many half-hardy birds linger into late fall or early winter compared with other places in eastern Canada. Within the province such late birds are more likely to be found in Atlantic coastal regions than in inland localities or along the Bay of Fundy and Northumberland Strait.

Because it lies on so many storm tracks, Nova Scotia is rather wet. An annual average of 1100-1600 mm of precipitation spread rather evenly through the year is collected at most recording stations; this compares with about 870 mm at Kingston, Ontario. The proportion of this precipitation that appears as snow is greater inland and further northeast in the province—about 9 percent on Sable Island, 17 percent at Halifax, 21 percent at Kentville and 21 percent in Cape Breton Highlands National Park. During some winters on the Eastern and Southwestern shores, very little snow stays on the ground, and seed-eating birds may thrive. During winters with heavy snowfalls, many more of these birds depend on birdfeeders. Nearly all the province has cloudiness over 60 percent of the year; about 75 percent occurs on eastern Cape Breton Island. Coastal fog, especially along the Atlantic and Fundy shores, prevails from April through July. Even inland the amount of bright sunshine is limited: at Greenwood, Kings County, it is about 25 percent in January and 50 percent in July. In some years, rain, fog, and low temperatures may considerably reduce the reproductive success of birds that feed their nestlings on insects.

The geological history of Nova Scotia has shaped some aspects of present-day bird distributions in the province. Nova Scotia is part of the Appalachian Region of eastern North America, in a section where the land has been exposed to subaerial erosion since the Carboniferous period, some 280 million years ago. An uplift of the much-leveled landscape during the early Tertiary period led to some 50 million years of levelling and dissection of river valleys, accelerated during the Pleistocene epoch, with its succession of ice sheets. The present landscape is a result of deep erosion of the softer rocks of the old landscape. Hardrock areas have remained as hills and plateaus: the Cobequid and North mountains in central and south Nova Scotia, small areas in Pictou and Antigonish counties and in southern Cape Breton Island, and the extensive Cape Breton Highlands in the northeast. The maximum mainland elevation is Mount Nuttby in the Cobequids at 360 m, but the maximum overall is North Barren in Cape Breton Highlands National Park at 530 m. This relief is modest by world standards—

there are no alpine birds in Nova Scotia and no arctic or subarctic species lingering to nest on our hilltops, such as found in Newfoundland, southeastern Quebec and even New England (e.g., Water Pipits on Mount Washington). The ornithological significance of our hills is that they offer relatively inaccessible areas where shyer birds, such as raptors, may nest undisturbed.

Hardrock areas along the coast, particularly on the Eastern Shore and on Cape Breton Island, offer considerable opportunities for cliff-nesting or islet-nesting species. In such areas, cormorants and eiders breed in some numbers, and our only colonies of such birds as Black-legged Kittiwakes are to be found.

An important consequence of glaciation is the extensive deposits of till, forming large eskers and drumlins in many areas and supplying materials for redistribution by rivers and coastal currents. The sea level continues to rise relative to the rebound of the land unburdened of its Pleistocene ice, and parts of the coast are characterized by drowned estuaries with extensive salt marshes and often by unstable sandbars and dune beaches. These "softer" coastal landscapes, particularly along the Southwestern Shore, the inner Fundy Shore, and the Northumberland Strait offer many opportunities for marsh birds, shorebirds and waterfowl. On the Bay of Fundy side, the massive tides and greater rates of erosion have produced extensive salt marshes and mudflats in the Minas and Cumberland basins. These areas are major stopovers for migrating shorebirds, particularly Semipalmated Sandpipers, in eastern North America. At places where the lowlands meet the sea, particularly in the Minas and Cumberland basins, dykes were built by the French settlers, beginning in 1632. In time, former mudflats and salt marshes have become rich meadows which today attract open-country birds, particularly raptors in winter. In recent years, the creation of freshwater impoundments in former salt marshes has produced valuable habitat for marsh birds and waterfowl.

In general, however, the characteristics of birdlife in Nova Scotia are determined by the plant cover rather than geological circumstances. The province is largely forested and lies within the Acadian Forest Region (Rowe 1972). This region is transitional in nature, although the Red Spruce generally is confined to it. Thus many different plant associations occur in the forests, which may be purely coniferous, purely broad-leaved or various admixtures.

A narrow belt of largely coniferous forest extending 5-25 km inland along the Atlantic coast is characterized by poor growths of Balsam Fir and White and Black Spruce, with some Red Maple and birches. Characteristic birds in these forests include the Gray Jay, Boreal Chickadee and rarely Spruce Grouse and Black-backed Woodpecker. The plateau of northern Cape Breton Island was occupied by a forest of almost pure Balsam Fir which was largely killed by spruce budworm defoliation in the mid-to-late 1970s. Most of the dead forest has been clearcut and areas are being replanted with spruce, with unknown consequences for the birds that once nested there or may nest there in future. In very exposed coastal or highland forests where the spruce may form a dense, stunted krummholtz, northern or mountain species such as Gray-cheeked Thrush, Blackpoll Warbler and Fox Sparrow may be found nesting.

Within the coastal forest and also in the Cape Breton Highlands are extensive bogs and barrens, the barrens often with wide expanses of bedrock and massive glacial boulders (as in the well-known barrens around Peggy's Cove, Halifax County). Although these are arctic or alpine in appearance, this is a consequence of thin and often acidic soil, the result of the sweep of glaciation or sometimes soil-destructive fires, rather than severe climate. Thus, except for a few nesting Greater Yellowlegs on Cape Breton Island and the northern mainland, the avifauna of these barren landscapes is not particularly northern in flavour. Rather, such species as Palm Warbler, Savannah Sparrow and Swamp Sparrow are commonplace.

The largest portion of the province has forests typical of the Acadian Forest Region. Toward the south and southwest, conifers predominate, and hemlock, red spruce, and white and red pine are important. Red oak, sugar maple, and yellow and white birches are also present in varying admixtures. Deciduous trees are more abundant towards the north and east, along the slopes of the North and Cobequid mountains and on the mountain slopes of Cape Breton Island. Most forests in Nova Scotia have been cut over, burned or clearcut for farming, and the second-growth forests are often quite different in species composition from the original stands.

In the more coniferous parts of the forest, the Hermit and Swainson's Thrush, several wood warblers and the Dark-eyed Junco are conspicuous, together with a great number of species characteristic of boreal forests in southern and central Canada (Erskine 1977). Broad-leaved forests sustain a different assemblage of birds, depending on stage of succession (Nova Scotia examples in Freedman et al. 1981). Species such as the Common Yellowthroat, Chestnut-sided Warbler and White-throated Sparrow are common on clearcuts, and the Least Flycatcher, Red-eyed Vireo and Ovenbird are found abundantly in more mature stands.

Here and there glacial or riverine deposits have produced soils suitable for farming, although there are no Grade-1 agricultural soils in Nova Scotia. The most extensive agriculture is in the Annapolis Valley, a depression some 140 km long by 4-12 km wide, running from the Minas Basin in the northeast to St. Mary's Bay in the southwest. Extensive mixed farming in the valley, including the famed apple orchards, have produced habitats for birds (e.g., Eastern Meadowlark and, formerly at least, Eastern Bluebird) that have not nested elsewhere or do so rarely. The small old towns in the valley, which is more "summery" than the Atlantic coastal regions, have nesting birds such as the Northern Oriole that are uncommon elsewhere. In winter, waste grains in fields and around grain-storage facilities support large numbers of crows, flocks of blackbirds and the province's only substantial populations of Ring-necked Pheasants. Raptors are also more common, no doubt attracted by well-fed rodent populations.

Nova Scotia has a multitude of ponds, lakes and streams. Those of hardrock regions are highly acidic and generally have little or no emergent vegetation. Common Loons and some duck species nest on large lakes and smaller bodies of water, and bogs may have Common Snipe and a variety of water-associated landbirds, such as Rusty Blackbirds. However, in general these more acidic waters support little birdlife, and their productivity may have been impaired in recent years by the effects of acid rain (the earlier-mentioned wind patterns of eastern North America bring industrial pollution from points west and southwest). Birdlife is much richer on ponds and streams in the less acidic parts of the province, notably in the Annapolis Valley, near the New Brunswick border and in scattered localities elsewhere. In these waters, emergent vegetation, such as cattails, and sometimes the enhanced aquatic productivity resulting from urban or agricultural runoff, encourages a much greater variety of water and marsh birds; American Bitterns, teal species and Red-winged

Blackbirds are typical, and the first nestings of a number of waterfowl, as well as such birds as Black Tern and Common Moorhen, have occurred in such productive waters near the New Brunswick border.

The marine waters around Nova Scotia derive from the Gulf of St. Lawrence and the Labrador Current, a part of which curls south of Newfoundland and across the Scotian Shelf. The shallow Northumberland Strait warms considerably in summer, but the waters of the Scotian Shelf and the Bay of Fundy remain cold, especially the latter in which much tidal mixing with deep, cold water occurs. The warm Gulf Stream passes considerably to the south, outside territorial limits, although large, warm eddies detach at times and bring tropical waters over the Scotian Shelf.

The distributions of nesting inshore seabirds such as cormorants, Common Eiders, gulls and terns depend more on the availability of suitable nesting sites than on the character of the local waters, although the more turbid parts of the Bay of Fundy may be avoided. Wintering seabirds such as loons, grebes and sea ducks are widely distributed on all sorts of coasts.

The presence of truly pelagic seabirds almost defines our offshore waters. An extensive account of the distribution and seasonal abundances of such species in relation to the offshore environment is given by Brown et al. (1975). Our pelagic birds are mostly coldwater species that nest in the region, such as Leach's Storm-Petrel and Black-legged Kittiwakes, or come from further north, such as the Northern Fulmar and Dovekie. However, three subantarctic breeders, Greater and Sooty Shearwaters and Wilson's Storm-Petrel, predominate during summer. Our waters are not suitable for tropical or subtropical seabirds, which generally occur here as storm-driven vagrants; however, the outer limits of our pelagic zone have not been adequately explored, and some warmwater species may prove regular there.

Place Names in Nova Scotia

The authority for place names used in this book has been the *Gazetteer of Canada: Nova Scotia* (Queens Printer, Ottawa 1977). Generally, place names are accompanied by the names of the counties in which they occur, but names of major towns, prominent features and certain other places frequently referred to are shown on the map on pages 466-7 and are not designated by county in the text. For convenience, major lengths of coastline are often referred to in the text by their weather forecast designations (see map).

Among place names referred to without county in the species accounts, Seal Island, which lies off southwestern Shelburne County but is in Yarmouth County, should not be confused with several other Nova Scotia islands with that name. Cape Sable is a sandbar lying just off Cape Sable Island, the southern extremity of Shelburne County. Neither should be confused with Sable Island, technically in Halifax County, but lying well offshore.

The only place name for which the "official" gazetteer name is not used is Bon Portage Island, which lies 7 km west of Cape Sable Island and is given as Outer Island on current maps. Because there is an extensive literature on the island as Bon Portage Island, including some references to birds (Richardson 1965), this much more attractive name is retained here.

Names of Birds

The classification, sequence and names of birds in this book are according to the latest *Check-List of North American Birds* published by the American Ornithologists' Union (1983), the accepted authority on such matters.

Each species has a standard vernacular (English) as well as a scientific (Latin or Latinized) name. English names are traditionally capitalized to prevent the kind of confusion that would be caused by "I saw nothing today except a single black duck and a solitary sandpiper," when two species with those names are meant. Scientific names are printed in italics. The first word is that of the genus (plural genera) and is always capitalized. The genus is a group of closely related species, varying from a considerable number to only one. The second part of the name designates the species and is never capitalized. If, for example, we look at the names of certain thrushes, we see that the Hermit Thrush is *Catharus guttatus,* Swainson's Thrush is *Catharus ustulatus,* and the Veery is *Catharus fuscescens*—the genus name is the same, marking their close relationship.

With each scientific name, the original describer and namer of the species is given. Thus *Catharus ustulatus* (Nuttall) signifies that Thomas Nuttall, the English-born American naturalist, first named the Swainson's Thrush (in 1840). By convention, if the original genus name is changed, the describer's name is placed in parentheses. For example, Nuttall's name for the Swainson's Thrush was *Turdus ustulatus,* signifying (correctly) that it is related to the American Robin. *Turdus migratorius.* Later, other authorities decided that this and other small thrushes belong in a separate genus, *Catharus.* The species name, however, is not discarded or changed except to conform to rules of Latin grammar when its genus name is altered.

Many species have become slightly and sometimes substantially differentiated in different parts of their range into recognized subspecies (or races). In birds, subspecies are sufficiently closely related to be able to interbreed freely and often do so where their geographical ranges overlap. However, many birds considered to be of separate species may also interbreed (such as Black Ducks and Mallards in Nova Scotia), so the judgment on what constitutes a species or subspecies is somewhat arbitrary and subject to periodic revision. As an example, the subspecies of Veery nesting in Nova Scotia is *Catharus fuscescens fuscescens* (abbreviated as *C. f. fuscescens),* that nesting in Newfoundland is darker in colour and named *Catharus fuscescens fuliginosa,* and the olivaceous birds of western Canada are *Catharus fuscescens salicola.* Subspecies are not dealt with in the latest A.O.U. *Check-List,* although they were included in previous editions. In previous editions of this book each species was designated by the subspecies (if any) occurring in Nova Scotia. This is not common practice now in regional bird books, and only species names are given here in the headings of species accounts. However, when more than one subspecies of a bird is known or thought to have occurred in the province, these are noted in the text.

There have been substantial numbers of changes in the names of our birds since the 1973 edition of this book. English names have been changed to make them less parochial ("Common Gallinule" has become Common Moorhen, its older, British name), or more accurate ("Upland Plover" has become Upland Sandpiper, which it is); or because species have been "split" into two or more species ("Traill's Flycatcher" is now recognized as consisting of two closely related species, Alder and Willow Flycatcher); or because two or more species have been "lumped" into one species (our

"Ipswich Sparrow" is now recognized as a well marked subspecies of the widespread Savannah Sparrow). The scientific names of species have also been changed as a result of such "splitting" and "lumping," and also as a result of strictly nomenclatural decisions about the validity of previous names.

Bird Protection and Conservation

The first legislation for birds in Nova Scotia was enacted in 1794 to protect Black Ducks and Ruffed Grouse during their breeding periods; Indians and poor settlers were exempt. No further laws concerning game birds were introduced until 1900, when Spruce Grouse were given year-round protection; this is still in effect.

Subsequent legislation for protection of birds had its genesis in the United States where the extirpation of the Passenger Pigeon, great hunting pressure on shorebirds and waterfowl, and the commercial killing of seabirds and egrets for their feathers led to strong public sentiment for controls. The result was the Migratory Bird Law ("Weeks-MacLean Bill") in 1913, which took migratory birds out of desultory and disparate state controls and put them into federal hands. Immediately there was a ban on the sale of game birds and a proscription of spring shooting. The smaller shorebirds received complete protection, along with most non-game birds and songbirds.

In Canada protection of birds was the responsibility of the provinces. However, the argument that migratory birds do not know political boundaries resulted in the signing of the international Migratory Bird Treaty in 1916 and its ratification by the Act in 1917. This treaty extended protection, or jointly agreed-upon designations as game species, to most migratory birds in North America and has stood as a model of enlightened legislation which the rest of the world has yet fully to follow.

There are still some species or groups of species to which the treaty does not extend protection. It excludes non-migratory game birds, such as the Ruffed Grouse in Nova Scotia, which are managed under state or provincial laws. It also excludes species such as cormorants, hawks, owls, crows and blackbirds that were perceived in those days as inimical to human interests. Fortunately, the misguided hostility against most of these birds has largely gone, and now all non-treaty birds except the Rock Dove, American Crow, European Starling and House Sparrow are protected by various statutes in Nova Scotia.

Bird sanctuaries in Canada and the United States became established when conservationists in both countries recognized that the treaty alone could not restore diminishing populations of wildfowl. Thus large numbers of federal bird sanctuaries were established in Canada. Those in Nova Scotia are: the Amherst Point Bird Sanctuary in Cumberland County, Big Glace Bay Lake in Cape Breton County, Kentville Bird Sanctuary in Kings County, Sable Island, and four sanctuaries clustered in Queens and Shelburne counties, namely the Port Joli, Port Hebert, Haley Lake and Sable River sanctuaries.

Provincial game or waterfowl sanctuaries established primarily or initially for protection are at Brule Point in Colchester County, Blandford in Lunenburg County, Chignecto in Cumberland County, Liscomb in Halifax and Guysborough counties, Martinique Beach in Halifax County, Spectacle Island in Victoria County, Sunnybrae in Pictou County, and Waverley in Halifax County. The province also has a number of Wildlife Management Areas, most primarily for the maintenance of wildlife habitat and breeding sites, but some also closed to hunting and having the force of sanctuaries. The closed ones are at Abercrombie and Antigonish Harbour in Pictou County, Debert in Hants County, Kelly Lake in Halifax and Guysborough counties, Manganese Mines in Colchester County, Medford in Kings County, and Scatarie Island in Cape Breton County (only partly closed).

In addition, Cape Breton Highlands and Kejimkujik national parks, along with a large number of provincial parks, great and small, are closed to hunting.

Over the years it became clear that protection of birds from illegal or excess killing was not enough; thus the focus turned to protection of bird habitats for nesting and other activities. Although sanctuaries and parks often serve these ends, other areas in Nova Scotia have been set aside specifically to protect or manage habitats on behalf of wildlife, including birds, without proscription of hunting in season. Under the Canadian Wildlife Service, National Wildlife Areas have been established at Chignecto and John Lusby marshes in Cumberland County, on Boot Island in Kings County, Margaree Island in Inverness County, Sand Ponds in Yarmouth County, and at Wallace Bay in Cumberland County. Wildlife Management Areas, in addition to those noted in the previous paragraph, have been established by the province to protect breeding seabirds and Common Eiders on the Eastern Shore Islands in Halifax County, and on Pearl Island in Lunenburg County.

The work of Ducks Unlimited Canada has been very important in the improvement of wetlands as waterfowl nesting areas, and incidentally as habitat for many other water and marsh birds. As of 1985, this organization had undertaken 104 projects in the province, involving 128 different marshes totalling 7340 ha in area. Most are near the New Brunswick border, but other sites are found from Yarmouth to Cape Breton Island.

The Nova Scotia Bird Society owns a number of properties around the province established for protection of breeding birds. These are Hertford and Ciboux islands in Victoria County, Indian Island in Lunenburg County, three islands of the inner Tuskets off Yarmouth, Peters Island off Brier Island, and an 80 ha coastal site at Port Joli, Shelburne County.

In the last few decades there has been increased concern for particular species that are rated as "threatened" or "endangered" by national and international agencies. Thus government and organizations have become more involved in focused efforts to restore nesting habitats, protect from disturbance and in some cases reintroduce populations of depleted species. Examples of such efforts can be found in the species accounts on the Bald Eagle, Peregrine Falcon and Piping Plover.

The future well-being of birds in Nova Scotia will depend largely on an enlightened and caring public. It is hoped that this book will contribute to that end.

Suggestions for Beginners in Bird Study

In the introduction to the second edition, Robie Tufts describes his own approach to stimulating interest among young people: "If the boy were in his early teens, as was usually the case, he was advised, as an initial step, to procure a substantial note book. In this he was instructed to list, in the order in which they were encountered in the field, the names of the birds he already knew. When he met one he could not name . . . he was to study it well. He should write down an accurate description of its plumage markings; general notes concerning its comparative size (that of a sparrow, a robin, or a crow, for instance); its behaviour (was it feeding on the ground, in a tree, or what was it doing?); the type of habitat—woods, open field, swampland, garden, etc.; perhaps its song—and then in due course come to me in the hope that I might be able to identify it, thus enabling him to add a new member to his list. I found that as his list expanded so did his interest at even a greater rate." The "list" is of course a primary part of bird study, and systematic and extensive note taking, as described by Tufts, has much to recommend it.

Nowadays, there are many keen and expert bird-watchers (or "birders" as most now prefer) on whom beginners can depend for advice, although it is doubtful that any will have the impact of a Robie Tufts. However, birding is now a much more widespread activity, much better supported by organizations devoted to the hobby, better served by excellent field guides and other bird books, by superior optical equipment and by recordings of bird songs and calls.

Anyone with a developing interest in birds in Nova Scotia should join the Nova Scotia Bird Society (c/o the Nova Scotia Museum, Halifax B3H 3A6). Its periodical, *Nova Scotia Birds,* comes out three times a year, and it sponsors monthly meetings in Halifax in winter, and field trips around the province throughout the year.

For field identification of birds, at least one and preferably several guidebooks are indispensable. Among the recommended ones are *A Field Guide to the Birds* by Roger Tory Peterson (Houghton Mifflin Co., Boston, 1980), *A Field Guide to the Identification of North American Birds* by Chandler S. Robbins, Bertel Bruun and Herbert S. Zim (Golden Press, New York, 1980), *Field Guide to the Birds of North America* (National Geographic Society, Washington, 1983), and the three-volume *Audubon Society Master Guide to Birding* edited by John Farrand, Jr. (Alfred A. Knopf, New York, 1983). For details of measurements, plumages and much more information of great value, *The Birds of Canada* by W. Earl Godfrey (National Museum of Canada, Ottawa, 1986) is indispensable. *Birding Nova Scotia* (Allen and Dobson 1984) is useful for bird-finding in Nova Scotia. For more serious birders, or those who wish to become better informed, subscriptions to *American Birds,* published by the National Audubon Society (950 Third Ave., New York, 10022) will keep one abreast of the continental pattern of bird migration and distribution, and includes articles on identification and study of birds. Membership in the American Birding Association (P.O. Box 4335, Austin, Texas, 78765) will bring the bimonthly magazine, *Birding,* with many useful articles and features.

No definitive advice can be given here on optical equipment, for it is very much a matter of cost. In general, in purchasing a first pair of inexpensive binoculars (less than $100), it is best to buy simple, serviceable ones of 7-9 power and 35-50 objective diameter, and to avoid those designated "wide-angle," "zoom" or "quick-focus," as such optical or mechanical features often sacrifice optical quality. The ultimate in binoculars are the rugged, unitary, roof-prism types, which cost many hundreds of dollars. A telescope of 20-25 power is of great value for the study of water birds and shorebirds at a distance. There are several excellent makes available, and these should be tried for sharpness before purchase; again, "zoom" models tend to sacrifice optical qualities for mechanical advantages.

A portable tape recorder has become a feature of modern birding, used for recording bird sounds of interest and for playing calls and songs of species in order to attract them for observation. (This of course has to be done with due care not to excite the attracted bird to the point of harassment.) There are many excellent tapes available for the whole range of species that occur in Nova Scotia.

A Brief History of Ornithology in Nova Scotia

The first list of Nova Scotia birds was prepared by Samuel de Champlain (1922 edition) when he visited the outer Tusket islands off Yarmouth and Shelburne counties in the seventeenth century. He noted a surprising variety of identifiable birds, including nesting Northern Gannets, Atlantic Puffins and Common Murres, all since extirpated. These and other early French records of birds were summarized by Nicolas Denys in 1672 (see Allen 1939).

The nineteenth-century literature on Nova Scotia birds is summarized by McLaren (1985, 1986). The earliest substantial list was published by the industrious polymath, Thomas Haliburton (1825), and contains 79 species, including a few questionable ones. Abraham Gesner's (1842) list of specimens was the first to use the developing scientific nomenclature of the day, and almost all of his 33 species are readily identifiable.

The modern era might be said to have begun with the comprehensive lists of the British military naturalists, Blakiston and Bland (1856, 1857); these are merely replicated in the more-often quoted paper by Willis (1859). They included 204 species of birds, and their annotations have an air of accuracy and sophistication unmatched in most later nineteenth-century accounts. The annotated lists by J. Matthew Jones of 128 land birds (1879), and 105 water birds and shorebirds (1885), along with a number of notes by him on rare and commonplace species, bespeak a better grasp of the province's birds than held by his contemporaries. The works of J. Bernard Gilpin on waterfowl (1880), birds of prey (1881) and shorebirds (1882a), are anecdotal, ill-written and error-ridden. Although Andrew Downs' earlier contributions (Downs 1865, 1866) added little to the work of Blakiston and Bland, his later catalogue (1888) is the best-known nineteenth-century work on birds, and includes 234 species. Because he used the nomenclature of the then current check-list of the American Ornithologists' Union, a number of earlier puzzles on species identity were cleared up. But, perhaps because he restricted his account to "all the ones we have personally observed," a number of well-established earlier records were ignored or overlooked.

A number of ornithologists from Canada or the United States visited or received specimens from Nova Scotia during the late nineteenth century. Among them, Collins (1884) gives a fascinating account of seabirds in the offshore waters of Newfoundland and Nova Scotia. Chamberlain (1887a), in his *Catalogue of Canadian Birds,* includes numerous references to Nova Scotia. Jonathan Dwight (1895) visited Sable Island and stimulated a flow of specimens and several species lists of the birds of that remarkable island (see historical account in McLaren 1981a).

The most important figure in the late nineteenth and early twentieth centuries was Harry Piers (1870-1940), curator at the Provincial Museum (now the Nova Scotia Museum) from 1899 to 1940. In addition to publishing a series of papers (1890-1927) on unusual bird species in the province, he kept many notes, still on file at the Nova Scotia Museum, documenting the province's birds during his years of bird study. As museum specimens from earlier times were discarded or otherwise disappeared, his notes became the sole basis for some records. His friendship and support for younger bird students, including Robie Tufts, were of great importance to the future of ornithology in the province.

Harold Tufts, older brother of Robie Tufts, began publishing occasional notes on the birds of Nova Scotia before the turn of the century (1898, 1899), and others such as William Hickman (1896) and E. Chesley Allen (1915) produced early regional lists of value. However, the ornithological contributions of two men, Robie Tufts (beginning in 1915; bibliography in Godfrey 1984) and Harrison F. Lewis (beginning in 1913; bibliography in Solman 1974), were outstanding. Both men were employed by what later became the Canadian Wildlife Service, of which Lewis was chief, 1947-1952. Both combined enthusiasm for bird study with a strong concern for bird protection and conservation. Tufts' ornithological work culminated in *The Birds of Nova Scotia*. During his retirement years in Shelburne County, Lewis wrote a monthly column on natural history between February 1953 and December 1970 in the Shelburne *Coastguard,* in which many observations on birds were recorded.

Other useful contributions were made by professional ornithologists during the first half of the twentieth century, and some of these are referred to in the species accounts. However, the founding of the Nova Scotia Bird Society in 1955 consolidated and directed the activities of the many amateur bird enthusiasts in the province. Robie Tufts (president), Charles R.K. Allen (vice-president), Willett J. Mills (secretary-treasurer) and Harrison F. Lewis (editor) were among its first executive members. The society was incorporated in 1957 and its first (mimeographed) *Newsletter* was produced on 25 March 1959. In 1964, the first printed volume of the *Newsletter* was produced under the editorship of Phyllis R. Dobson, who single-handedly remained responsible for seasonal bird reports until 1974, when sub-editors were appointed for this purpose. The editorship passed to J. Shirley Cohrs in 1976, and in 1981 the periodical became *Nova Scotia Birds*. Thus, since 1957 there has been continuous documentation of the province's birdlife which has formed the basis for much of the present book.

Organization and Content of Species Accounts

The format used for each species is essentially that employed in previous editions. However, the contents of the species accounts, except for a few common ones, have been completely revised for this edition. Some explanations of the contents under each heading is in order.

Status By this is meant the status of occurrence of the species in the province. Records up to the end of 1984 are considered. An opening phrase summarizes the status.

For birds recorded fewer than 10 times in the province, all occurrences are documented; such species are all considered to be vagrants (see below).

For birds that occur here regularly, the seasons of occurrence are noted: *summer* for those that reside here in summer (almost always to nest), *winter* for those that arrive, generally from the north, for that season and stay until spring; *transient* for those that pass through the province in spring and fall (which here refer to the migration seasons, rather than astronomical seasons, as "spring" migrants may arrive well before 21 March and "fall" migrants may appear in July). Only a few species are designated as *resident,* i.e., present and largely or entirely non-migratory. A summer or winter species is noted in more than one category only if it occurs at other times in much larger or smaller numbers (see discussion of abundance categories below). Thus a bird that spends the summer here will obviously occur in spring and fall, but if its numbers are greatly swelled in migration, it might be given as "common transient, uncommon in summer." Birds that nest or have nested here are designated as *breeds,* with qualifications if they no longer do so.

Birds that occur here regularly without breeding but spend variable or unknown periods of time in the province are called *visitants.* Some seabirds and southern herons, which evidently routinely fly north after their breeding seasons and return south after a sojourn here, fall into this category.

Birds whose presence in the province is believed to be abnormal, because they are north and east of their geographical ranges in North America or perhaps from distant waters or even from Eurasia or South America are called *vagrants.* They are unlikely to find their way "home," although this is conjectural. A discussion of the phenomenon of vagrancy in Nova Scotia is given by McLaren (1981b). Some birds seem to "overshoot" their normal ranges during good weather in spring and reach Nova Scotia accidentally. There is a suggestion that some birds whose normal routes would take them northwest in western North America in spring instead fly northeast because of "mirror-image misorientation" and end up in Nova Scotia. In autumn, southern and southwestern birds appear to come here because of the phenomenon of "reverse migration," which has been well established by radar studies in Nova Scotia (Richardson 1982). Western species in fall seem to fly downwind when the autumn winds turn westerly. Some European birds (the 1984 Jackdaws, for example) have evidently arrived because of extraordinary easterly winds in the North Atlantic at times when hard weather was producing movements in western Europe. The word *straggler,* sometimes used elsewhere to mean vagrant, is here reserved for those individuals that remain beyond normal departure times to breeding or wintering grounds.

In previous editions, a number of species in the main text were designated as "hypothetical," usually when observations alone, unsupported by photographic or specimen evidence, were available, even though the sightings were considered acceptable. The phrase *sight records* in the species accounts in the present edition implies that no other evidence is available; the observations are then detailed in the text that follows. Birds considered to be *hypothetical* in the present edition are those for which observations or other evidence, although plausible enough to consider, do not entirely eliminate other possibilities or are lacking in information about circumstances, time or place. Such birds are listed with brief comments in Appendix 1.

Extinct and successfully *introduced* birds are included in the species accounts, but the few species that have been introduced without having established permanent populations are listed in Appendix 2.

Also in the initial phrase of the short status summaries, abundance categories are assigned for each species with more than 10 records in the province. Of necessity, these categories are somewhat subjective.

A *common* bird can be seen in numbers, a few to many, on any day at the right time and place. A *fairly common* one might be missed on some days but could be seen in numbers during a year. An *uncommon* one might be missed on most days but is certain to be seen by a persistent birder in the right places at some time during the year. A *rare* bird is generally one for which there are more than 10 but fewer than 100 records for the province, or even somewhat more if these have not been generally distributed (and are found mostly on the southwestern islands, for example). Any species may be designated as *very rare* at some seasons if there are fewer than 10 records for that season. Some species are listed as *locally* common, etc., if their habitats are particularly restricted in the province.

Following the prefatory statement after Status, an expanded analysis of records of occurrence is given. Where a bird's status has changed markedly in recent years, its earlier status is given. Except where such earlier records are mentioned, statements on seasonal occurrences in this edition are based largely on data published since 1957 in the Nova Scotia Bird Society *Newsletter* and its successor, *Nova Scotia Birds*. However, material from this source has been augmented by some otherwise unavailable records noted in previous editions of this book; by records from the newspaper column by Harrison F. Lewis in the Shelburne *Coast Guard*, 1953-1970; by extensive records from Sable Island summarized by McLaren (1981 a); and by records published in the journal *American Birds* and its predecessor, *Audubon Field-Notes*.

The *average* dates of first and last appearances used in the Status sections are the simple median, which is the middle of a series of numbers, with no corrections for ties. For example, if a bird was recorded in successive years as arriving on 16 March, 29 March, 3 April, 2 April and 28 March, the median date would be 29 March. For an even number of years, the middle two dates are averaged; thus the middle two dates 21 July and 28 July give a median of 25 July. It may be noted that the median, unlike the mean of a series of numbers, is less affected by extremes. In addition to such summaries of average dates of normal arrivals and departures, *earliest* and *latest* dates are given. However, if very early or very late dates are considered to represent abnormal occurrences, these are noted separately and are not included in the estimates of average (median) dates. Information is also given on times of major movements of more common species.

The status of species that are rare or irregular is dealt with variously, according to the amount of data available. For example, a species that has occurred only a few times in spring but more than 10 times in fall may have dates and places of all spring occurrences, but merely the total number of occurrences and extreme dates for fall.

Information on places of occurrence is given where appropriate and invariably for first records of rare species and for all records of species with fewer than 10 occurrences.

Description These are basically unchanged from previous editions, although many imprecisions were corrected. Vagrant species are not formally described, but field marks of these are generally noted briefly in the Remarks section when appropriate. In conjunction with the illustrations, the descriptions should help to identify adults and immatures where these differ from adults. However, they are not adequate for all plumages of all species and certain critical field marks and sources of possible confusion are referred to in the Remarks section. Readers should have other books available for critical identification problems (see books listed under Suggestions for Beginners in Bird Study, above).

Breeding In this section information is given only for those species that nest or have nested in Nova Scotia. The number and colour of eggs, and the structure and placement of nests are summarized. Then various details on specific nestings and aspects of breeding behaviour are given for most species. Here Robie Tufts' considerable achievements as a nest-finder and observer of birds are evident in his first-person accounts.

Range A brief description of geographical ranges, in both breeding and non-breeding seasons, is given for species that occur regularly in the province. These have been checked and updated using the current *Check-List of North American Birds* (American Ornithologists' Union 1983) and other sources but are not meant to be exhaustive. Brief statements about the ranges of vagrant species are given in the Remarks sections.

Remarks Although there is no set pattern for the contents of these sections, certain information is recurrent.

For regular and common species, the Remarks are largely unchanged from the second edition, and detailed observations and anecdotes in the first person are by Robie Tufts.

For vagrant, rare visitant, and rare transient species, this is the only section other than that on Status in which information is given. Because of the many changes since the second edition, the information on such species is all new.

With the elimination of subspecies designations from the headings of the species accounts, information is given in the Remarks sections on the scientific names, characteristics and distributions of subspecies where more than one is known or thought to have occurred in the province. In some cases, these represent well-marked birds that can be readily identified in the field and, indeed, some had been accorded full species status in the previous editions.

Accounts of the Bird Species of Nova Scotia

Order GAVIIFORMES

Family Gaviidae

Red-throated Loon   PLATE 1

Gavia stellata (Pontoppidan)

Status Fairly common transient, uncommon in winter, very rare in summer. The first southbound birds appear about mid-September (average 30 September, earliest 11 September), but the main fall movement is from mid-October to early November. They are frequently noted on Christmas Bird Counts but not often later in winter. Spring movements begin as early as mid-March and last for about a month (average of last sightings 1 May, latest 24 May). Several reports of birds in early June probably represent non-breeding laggards, and one on 13 August 1967 in Halifax County had presumably summered locally.

Description *Length:* 61-68 cm. *Adults in summer:* Head and sides of neck gray; back of neck streaked with white; front of neck has a triangular chestnut patch; rest of upperparts dark gray, marked with small white spots; abdomen white; bill blackish gray. *Immatures and adults in winter:* Mostly gray above and white below, and without chestnut throat patch. This bird resembles the larger Common Loon in winter, but the bill of the Red-throated is slightly upturned, a good field mark because the bill of the Common Loon is straight.

Range Breeds in arctic and subarctic parts of North America, Europe and Asia. In North America it winters mainly along the Pacific and Atlantic coasts.

Remarks This loon species is unique in being able to take off from land. In addition, it flies from water more quickly and easily than other loons. Its ability to manoeuvre in flight enables the bird to make effective use of small bodies of water which are in a sense out-of-bounds to other loon species, which require longer distances when taking to the air, especially when confronted with dead calm weather. The shore-hunters know this bird by the name "cape drake."

Pacific Loon

Gavia pacifica (Lawrence)

Status Eight sight records. Although some records are fully documented, there may be some uncertainty about the species involved (see Remarks). The first was studied at Three Fathom Harbour, Halifax County, on 27 November 1960 by Lloyd B. MacPherson and J. Alex McCarter, who compared it with nearby individuals of the other two loon species and supplied detailed descriptions. Subsequently, other well-described birds were reported in Halifax, Lunenburg and Digby counties, as early as 3 September and as late as 3 April, and in all months in between except February.

Remarks The Pacific Loon has recently been given species status separate from the Arctic Loon, *Gavia arctica,* of the Old World. The Pacific Loon breeds across northern Canada and winters mainly on the Pacific coast, rarely on the east coast of North America. Distinguishing Pacific Loons in immature or winter plumage from small Common Loons (which generally have white about the eyes) or from distant Red-throated Loons (whose bills do not always appear upturned) can be difficult. The identification problem is now compounded by the separation of the very similar Pacific and Arctic Loons into two species. The Arctic Loon has a darker hindneck in breeding plumage but is distinguishable perhaps only by its larger body and bill size in winter. Although the Pacific Loon undoubtedly predominates, the Eurasian species may occur in our waters. For these reasons, the occurrence of the Pacific Loon in the province cannot be fully confirmed until specimens are obtained or critical field marks developed for sight identification.

Common Loon PLATE 1

Gavia immer (Brünnich)

Status Common transient, fairly common in summer and winter. Breeds. After wintering on the sea, it appears on lakes as soon as they are free of ice, although a few non-breeders remain on salt water. Adults and juveniles begin to leave the lakes about mid-September. There are definite migrations along the coast: north largely between mid-March and late April, and south between mid-September and late November.

Description *Length:* 70-90 cm. *Adults in summer:* Head and neck blackish with greenish gloss; narrow patches of white on throat and sides of lower neck. Back black, conspicuously checkered with white. Underparts white. Bill black. *Adults in winter and juveniles:* Upperparts dark gray; underparts white. Winter adults have bills paler than those of summer adults; juveniles' bills are even paler; darkest on ridge of upper mandible.

Breeding *Nest:* On the ground, usually composed of coarse, decayed vegetable matter and placed near the edge of the water, although sometimes eggs are deposited on a bare gravel beach in a slight depression scraped out by the bird. As a safety measure against predators, islands are chosen as nesting sites. All 21 nests I have examined were located on islands in freshwater lakes, and all but one were close to the water's edge; the exception was placed about 4 m from the water at an elevation of 50 cm. *Eggs:* 1-3, usually 2; varying in colour from olive-brown to olive-green; sometimes plain but usually sparsely dotted with blackish brown spots. Some typical egg dates, all at Trout Lake, Annapolis County, are: 25 May 1925, two fresh eggs; 6 June 1927, two eggs slightly incubated; and 13 June 1928, two eggs about one-third incubated. Chicks leave the nest very soon after hatching. Usually not more than one pair occupies any given small lake. However, at Porters Lake, a small body of water in Digby County, I found two nests on 14 July 1922 less than 100 m apart. They were similarly located at the water's edge on the shores of two adjacent islands and faced each other across a narrow channel. One contained two heavily incubated eggs; the other, one egg and one newly hatched chick. The lake was said to contain unusually large numbers of yellow perch *(Perca flavescens),* which suggests that easy availability of food may have been a factor in inducing the two sets of parents to depart from the norm. On 14 August 1937 two half-grown young were seen at Trout Lake, Annapolis County, accompanied by an adult. As my canoe approached to within 150 m, the young dived and were not seen to resurface. The parent bird, feigning injury (even at that late date), flapped off over the surface but made no outcry as is the custom when the young are smaller. During August 1938 on three occasions the adults were seen at this lake, widely separated, each followed by one of the half-grown twins, which indicates the sharing of parental responsibility. A young loon perhaps ten days old was caught and banded at the same lake on 23 June 1923. Four months later on 27 October it was found dead, caught by the neck in a fisherman's seine at salt water off Gold River, Lunenburg County, approximately 70 km south of where it had been banded.

Range Breeds in North America from Alaska and southern Baffin Island, south to northern United States; also in Greenland and Iceland. Winters along the coast from southern parts of its breeding range south to the Gulf of Mexico, and in parts of Europe.

Remarks To observe this bird at its best, one should go in summer to its home on any one of the hundreds of picturesque lakes that grace the wilderness regions of the interior. Here, where dark evergreens mingle with white birch and aspen, and reflect their beauty on the clear waters, one will be sure to find a pair of loons. Many delightful hours may be spent watching them perform their daily routine, particularly when accompanied by their two dusky offspring, whose agility is as often surprising as it is amusing. Sometimes in the small hours of the night one may be startled when the stillness is broken by the birds' weird, tremulous calls; the long, wavering crescendos set the woodlands ringing with their echoes. When this wild cry was given on one occasion in broad daylight, a sleepy Barred Owl answered angrily from its seclusion as though protesting being awakened by the sound. I have always believed the loon's ecstatic vocal outpourings are a display associated with mating.

Because of the far-aft position of the loon's "propellers," the bird is extremely awkward on land and in fact unable to fly directly therefrom. It heads into the wind when taking off from the water, and its feet patter along the surface for some distance,

PLATE 1
all adults

Pied-billed Grebe, *winter*
Page 35

Red-necked Grebe, *winter*
Page 36

Horned Grebe, *winter*
Page 36

summer

winter

Red-throated Loon
Page 29

Common Loon
Page 30

winter

summer

Roger Tory Peterson

Roger Tory Peterson

PLATE 2
all adults

Parasitic Jaeger
Page 197
light phase

Sooty Shearwater
Page 42

Northern Fulmar
Page 39
light phase

Leach's Storm-Petrel
Page 45

Greater Shearwater
Page 41

Wilson's Storm-Petrel
Page 44

as though it were running, before it becomes fully airborne. Once in the air its flight is strong, swift and direct. When seen in flight it has a "hunchback" appearance that provides a good field mark.

Loons feed almost wholly on fishes they pursue and capture underwater, probably taking those species most easily caught. Their feeding destroys immense numbers of coarse fishes that are known enemies of young trout and salmon, and therefore any harm loons do is counterbalanced by this service.

It is illegal under both federal and provincial statutes to kill or injure a loon.

Common Loon and chicks.

Order PODICIPEDIFORMES

Family Podicipedidae

Pied-billed Grebe   PLATE 1

Podilymbus podiceps (Linnaeus)

Status Uncommon in summer, rare in winter. Breeds. It occurs throughout the province, generally arriving in April (average 16 April, earliest 31 March); a bird on 10 March 1974 may have overwintered. The main autumn migration occurs from late September through mid-October, but stragglers are regularly seen on Christmas Bird Counts and occasionally later in winter; there are four February reports, the latest up to 17 February on Sullivans Pond, Dartmouth.

Description *Length:* 30-37 cm. *Adults in summer:* Bill stout and chicken-like, with a black band around it. Upperparts blackish brown, throat black, sides of head and neck gray. Underparts silvery gray, dusky and barred on the sides. *Adults in winter and immatures:* Similar to adults in summer but the black throat patch and black band on the bill are lacking. Juveniles have heads streaked with whitish gray and throats streaked with brown. All grebes are practically without tails.

Breeding *Nest:* Usually placed on a bulky mass of decayed vegetable matter floating but anchored in shallow water amid or near aquatic vegetation. *Eggs:* 4-9; dull white, sometimes tinged with blue or green and often badly discoloured by nest stains. A clutch at Springville, Pictou County, contained four eggs on 4 June 1968 but was believed to be incomplete (H. Brennan). A nest near Brooklyn, Hants County, was seen by Charles R.K. Allen on 6 June 1965. It was floating near the shore of a weedy pond and was not examined for contents; the bird was sitting on the nest. At Falls Lake, Hants County, on 8 July 1940, H.H. Reid saw an adult with four chicks, two riding on their parent's back. W. Earl Godfrey observed an adult feeding a young bird on 19 July 1954 at Grande Anse, Richmond County.

Range Breeds across southern Canada, the United States, the West Indies and Central and South America. Winters from the central and southern United States southward, and on the Pacific coast north to southern British Columbia.

Remarks Look for this grebe on shallow fresh-water ponds margined with lush aquatic plant growth which provides food and shelter for the bird and its young. It is secretive, showing great aptitude for keeping out of sight, particularly during nesting season.

It has a number of calls, its most common being a loud *cow-cow-cow-cow-cow-uh cow-uh.* When in flight, having no tail worthy of the name, its legs trail behind as rudders for steering its course.

During the early twentieth century the dictates of hat fashion created a heavy demand for the breast feathers of grebes. Eventually the federal government, under pressure from bird-lovers, outlawed the commercial use of all wild-bird feathers, probably saving the grebes from premature extinction.

Horned Grebe   PLATE 1

Podiceps auritus (Linnaeus)

Status Fairly common transient, uncommon in winter, very rare in summer. Usually it does not appear until October (average 8 October, earliest 13 September), and considerable numbers may occur until year's end. Numbers somewhat diminish during winter, and a distinct spring migration occurs between mid-March and late April. Late birds are often seen into May (average 1 May, latest 15 May); two birds at Middle River, Victoria County, in July 1982 (H.E. Hopkins) and another at West Blanche, Shelburne County, on 18 June 1979 (P. Yankey) were unusual summer stragglers.

Description *Length:* 32-38 cm. *Adults in summer:* Head black with buffy orange tufts behind eyes; lower neck, chest and sides reddish. Upperparts brownish black. Wings have small white patch. Underparts silvery white. *Adults in winter and immatures:* Top of head, back of neck, and upperparts blackish gray; cheeks white. Underparts silvery white.

Range North America, Europe and Asia. In North America it breeds mainly from Alaska, the Mackenzie Delta, northern Manitoba and western Ontario, south to the north-central United States. Winters mainly on the Atlantic and Pacific coasts of the United States and southern Canada.

Remarks This grebe seems to be more gregarious than the larger Red-necked Grebe. It usually appears in small, scattered groups near the shore of a bay or inlet, but occasionally it is seen in much larger numbers in a more compact formation.

The diet of grebes is made up largely of small aquatic animal life; however, their stomachs almost invariably contain masses of grebe feathers, and parent birds have been seen feeding these feathers to their young, which swallow them avidly. This feather-eating remains unexplained, but appears essential to the grebes' well-being.

Red-necked Grebe   PLATE 1

Podiceps grisegena (Boddaert)

Status Fairly common transient, uncommon in winter. Autumn migrants are generally first noted in October (average 12 October, earliest 29 September). Counts of 40 or more have been made on Christmas Bird Counts around the province, but numbers diminish later in winter. Migrants gather at assembly points from mid-March to late

April and are occasional into May (average 3 May, latest 15 May). A bird on a freshwater pond on Sable Island on 3 July 1967 (C. Bell) was possibly an unseasonable migrant.

Description *Length:* 46-52 cm. *Adults in summer:* Top of head and back of neck black; throat and sides of head white; front and sides of neck brownish red. Back and wings brownish black; white patch in wing. Underparts silvery gray. Bill pointed and nearly as long as head; toes with individually scalloped webs. *Adults in winter and immatures:* The brownish red on the neck is lacking and the upperparts have more gray than adults in summer.

Range North America, Europe and Asia. In North America it breeds from Alaska and Yukon to Washington State and Minnesota. Winters mainly in coastal waters from southern Canada south to the southern United States.

Remarks An expert in underwater manoeuvres, it can dive in a leisurely manner, dive hastily in a flash or merely sink slowly in a sitting position. It is particularly shy, keen and ever watchful as though expecting danger at any moment.

It is slightly larger than the Horned Grebe. When flying, a second white wing area is often visible on the anterior edge.

It resembles the female Red-breasted Merganser, but mergansers have only one white patch in the wing. Its appearance in flight is different too: the merganser flies with head and neck extended straight out; this bird's head and neck seem to droop down from its body, an excellent field mark.

Grebes are unable to rise from land, and their take-off from water is slow and laborious.

Eared Grebe

Podiceps nigricollis (Brehm)

Status Two sight records. The first was seen at Sambro, Halifax County, on 1 January 1967 by Charles R.K. Allen, Benjamin K. Doane and other participants in the Halifax West Christmas Bird Count. It was minutely studied at ranges as close as 30 m and convincingly described. Another was seen by Betty June and Sidney Smith at Cape Sable on 7 January 1977.

Remarks The Eared Grebe on this continent is a western species whose range in winter is normally along the Pacific coast. A few, however, have been reported on the Atlantic coast from New England south.

Western Grebe

Aechmorphus occidentalis (Lawrence)

Status One sight record. A convincingly described bird was seen by Betty June Smith on a beach at Cape Sable on 6 February 1970. The bird was startled from the edge of the water at very close range.

Remarks Recently the "light morph" of the Western Grebe has been proposed as a species *(Aechmorphus clarkii),* so there is a remote possibility that the Cape Sable bird was not *Aechmorphus occidentalis.* The Western Grebe has been seen occasionally in New England waters.

Order PROCELLARIIFORMES

Family Diomedeidae

Black-browed Albatross

Diomedea melanophris Temminck

Status One sight record. A single bird, well-described, was sighted in Cabot Strait some 50 km northeast of Sydney on 15 July 1983 by David E. Wolf and Bret Whitney from the ferry between Sydney and Argentia, Newfoundland. An unidentified albatross skimming through Petit Passage, the narrow strait between Long Island and the peninsula of Digby Neck, was seen briefly by Wickerson Lent on 14 August 1970. It could have been this bird or a Yellow-nosed Albatross.

Remarks Albatrosses are birds of the trackless oceans, and most species are normally confined to the Southern Hemisphere. The huge adults of this species, with wingspans of 2.3 m, have white heads, necks, rumps and underparts, and dark upperparts. Their underwings are broadly bordered by black and their bills are largely yellow, differing in these respects from the Yellow-nosed Albatross. The nearest breeding grounds of the Black-browed Albatross are in the Falkland Islands, and there are only a few North American records, though it is more regular than the Yellow-nosed in the eastern North Atlantic.

Yellow-nosed Albatross

Diomedea chlororhynchos Gmelin

Status Two sight records. An albatross seen by Edward V. Thompson from MV *Bluenose* on 12 July 1968 about 50 km off Yarmouth had the field marks of this species. Another adult or near-adult was identified by Dan Salisbury and others on 20 August 1976 about 70 km west of Yarmouth.

Remarks This species is similar to but slightly smaller than the Black-browed Albatross. It has a black bill, yellow along the crest in adults, and narrower dark borders on the underwings than the Black-browed. The nearest breeding grounds to Nova Scotia are in the Tristan da Cunha group of islands in the South Atlantic. An individual of this species was collected on 1 August 1913 off Grand Manan Island, New Brunswick.

Family Procellariidae

Northern Fulmar   PLATE 2

Fulmarus glacialis (Linnaeus)

Status Common visitant. It is recorded throughout the year in offshore waters, rarely close to shore. In our area it is most common off southern Nova Scotia and at the entrance to the Bay of Fundy. No fewer than 1,100 birds were counted by Peter Vickery on a crossing of MV *Bluenose* on 4 July 1978. There was also a large movement between Shelburne County and Baccaro Bank on 20 May 1980 (R.G.B. Brown). By contrast, when Wickerson Lent saw a flock of 25-30 birds off Brier Island on 20 July 1959, he thought it unusual to see so many at one time. Observers here and in New England have the impression that Northern Fulmars have become more common since 1970. However, it is difficult to judge whether this is a genuine extension of the bird's range or a result of the greater number of observers and better opportunities for watching birds offshore.

Description *Length:* 48-51 cm. *All plumages:* Usually white everywhere except on back, rump and upper side of wings and tail, which are grayish brown; upper wings with pale patch at base of primaries; large, dark eye; bill stout, yellow and hooked. Some arctic birds are grayish or dark brown all over, but this form is rare off Nova Scotia.

Range Breeds from Franz Josef Land south to Brittany in the eastern Atlantic and in Greenland and the eastern Canadian Arctic. There are four small colonies in eastern Newfoundland and southeastern Labrador. Large numbers occur in winter on the Grand Banks and, to a lesser extent, on the Scotian Shelf. A different subspecies breeds in the North Pacific.

Remarks The Northern Fulmar is similar to a medium-sized gull in appearance, but its heavier head and neck, straight wings and gliding flight readily distinguish it in the field. Until recently the fulmar was virtually confined to the Arctic and was rare in temperate waters on either side of the Atlantic. However, a massive expansion in range began in Iceland in the eighteenth century, reaching northern Scotland by the 1880s, and Brittany and Norway by the late 1950s. The founding of small colonies in extreme southern Greenland in 1945, and in Newfoundland and Labrador in the late 1960s, probably represents continued western expansion. Fulmars feed extensively on the offal from fishing boats, and it has been suggested that the expansion of the fulmar's range is a result of food provided by an expanding fishing industry. However, more complex oceanographic factors probably played a part also.

Banding returns show that the fulmars that occur off Atlantic Canada are mainly immature birds from colonies in Greenland, Iceland and Britain. Fulmars breeding in the temperate North Atlantic tend to have longer bills than those from Greenland and the Canadian Arctic. Some taxonomists recognise these two subspecies as *Fulmarus glacialis glacialis* and *Fulmarus glacialis minor,* respectively. Birds of both forms have been collected off Nova Scotia; however, the validity of these subspecies is not generally accepted.

Black-capped Petrel

Pterodroma hasitata (Kuhl)

Status One sight record. A bird was reported to have been near the edge of the Scotian Shelf, some 140 km south by southeast of Cape Sable, on 14 July 1972 (Finch 1972).

Remarks This petrel's plumage pattern is similar to that of the larger Greater Shearwater, but the Black-capped Petrel's smaller extent of dark on the crown, broader wings, and swooping and soaring glides easily distinguish it.

It was thought to have been exterminated until a small colony was discovered in 1964 on inland cliffs on Haiti. It now occurs regularly in summer at the edge of the Gulf Stream off Cape Hatteras and occasionally north to Georges Bank. Our only sighting is consistent with this pattern of distribution.

Cory's Shearwater

Calonectris diomedea (Scopoli)

Status Uncommon summer visitant. It undoubtedly occurs with greater frequency than our few inshore records indicate. It is regularly seen off Sable Island, at the outer edges of the southern Scotian Shelf and on Georges Bank, all waters influenced by the Gulf Stream. However, on 29 August 1979 a flock of eight birds was observed close inshore as far north as Scatarie Island (R.G.B. Brown). Its usual season off Nova Scotia is from June to October (earliest 19 June; latest 19 October); the largest numbers off Sable Island occur in August and early September.

Description *Length:* 46-56 cm. *All plumages:* A large shearwater with broad wings and heavy body; medium brown above, white below; dividing line between brown and white on the face and neck blurred, not crisp as in the Greater Shearwater; often has white uppertail coverts; bill yellow, noticeably long and stout.

Range The subspecies *Calonectris diomedea borealis,* recorded off eastern North America, nests from Portugal and the Azores to the Canary Islands. Other subspecies breed in the Cape Verde archipelago and in the Mediterranean.

Remarks Adult Cory's Shearwaters dwell in colonies in the eastern Atlantic from May to October. The birds that visit us then are presumably immatures. Banding returns suggest that the birds winter off South Africa and Argentina, migrate up the west side of the Atlantic and pass through our waters en route to the eastern Atlantic.

Like all shearwaters, Cory's Shearwaters glide effortlessly over the sea, close to the surface of the water, on stiffly held wings.

Greater Shearwater   PLATE 2

Puffinus gravis (O'Reilly)

Status Common summer visitor. It is regular in offshore waters off eastern and southern Nova Scotia, from late May to early November, with later stragglers. Single birds seen southwest of Sable Island on 17 February 1975 (R.G.B. Brown) and 100 km southwest of Yarmouth on 30 March 1973 (P. Hope, R. Howie) were either overwintering birds or early spring migrants. Otherwise, the earliest record for summer is 21 May 1959 when Wickerson Lent counted 11 off Brier Island. In the early 1970s, very large numbers regularly occurred off Brier Island in late August and early September: 10,000 were reported on 1 September 1971, 3,000 on 3 September 1972, 4,000 on 26 August 1973 and 5,000 on 26 August 1976. These Greater Shearwaters, along with Sooty Shearwaters, Atlantic Puffins, and Herring and Great Black-backed Gulls (as well as humpback and finback whales), were feeding on dense swarms of krill (the euphausiid shrimp *Meganyctiphanes norvegica).* Numbers declined in the later 1970s despite the continued presence of the krill.

Description *Length:* 43-53 cm. *All plumages:* Upperparts dark brown; feathers on crown conspicuously darker than those on the back; uppertail coverts white-tipped and form a conspicuous white band across the base of the rump; underparts white, usually with a dark smudge on the belly; undertail coverts gray.

Range Breeds in the South Atlantic in the Tristan da Cunha group of islands and the Falklands. The total population of at least 5 million birds migrates to the North Atlantic during the Southern Hemisphere's winter. Their route takes them up the west side of the Atlantic to Georges Bank, the Scotian Shelf and the Grand Banks, where they disperse to the north and east.

Remarks These birds are called "hags" or "haglins" by our deep-sea fishermen, who meet them in summer far off the coast. At fish-cleaning time large numbers are sometimes attracted to the boats, where they mingle with Sooty Shearwaters to compete for the offal thrown overboard. The Greater Shearwater's wings are narrower than those of Cory's Shearwater, and are beaten more rapidly, and, when gliding, Greater Shearwaters stay closer to the water.

Sooty Shearwater   PLATE 2

Puffinus griseus (Gmelin)

Status Common summer visitor. Sooty Shearwaters are regular in offshore waters from late May to September, peak numbers being reached in August. An unusually early sighting was of three birds on Georges Bank on 12 April 1983; the latest were three off Sable Island on 26 November 1969. A bird observed a few hundred metres off Evangeline Beach, Kings County on 9 September 1956 was doubly unusual because the species is seen rarely in the upper Bay of Fundy and rarely so close to shore.

Description *Length:* 41-51 cm. *All plumages:* Sooty brown above and below, darkest on upper wings and tail; bill black and more slender than that of the Greater Shearwater; underwing linings are grayish white.

Range Breeds in New Zealand and adjacent islands, in the Falklands and on islands near Cape Horn. Outside the breeding season, it is widely distributed north to Labrador, southern Iceland, the Faeroes and western Norway in the Atlantic and also occurs widely in the Pacific.

Remarks These birds outnumber Greater Shearwaters when the two species first arrive here in May, but the ratio is soon reversed as the Sooty Shearwaters quickly pass on to the eastern Atlantic. Only a small portion of this species' total population migrates to the North Atlantic; the majority winters in the North Pacific or off Peru.

It is a graceful flyer. When seen skimming low over the waves, its long, narrow wings, colour and shape remind one of an oversized Chimney Swift, albeit with a decidedly different wing motion.

Manx Shearwater

Puffinus puffinus (Brünnich)

Status Uncommon summer visitant. Occurs regularly in small numbers on the Scotian Shelf and in the Bay of Fundy. The earliest spring report is of a bird seen on Browns Bank on 22 April 1976 (J.M. Laughlin); the latest fall sighting was off Sable Island on 1 October 1984. It would be unusual to sail out of Halifax in July or August without seeing at least one Manx Shearwater. In July 1978 it was the most common shearwater off Sable Island on calm days; no fewer than 125 birds were seen there on 24 July, and it occurred regularly up to 28 August. Numbers have increased significantly since 1970, when the species was placed on the provincial list on the basis of only one specimen and two sight records. The specimen, picked up on the beach at Sable Island on 23 June 1970 by A.R. Lock, had been banded the previous summer at a colony in Wales. Manx Shearwaters have colonized eastern North America since then—a single nest was discovered in Massachusetts in 1973 (Bierregaard et al. 1975), and a small but expanding colony was established in southern Newfoundland by Welsh birds in 1976 (Storey and Lien 1985). The species nests in burrows and visits its colonies at night only, so it is likely that other breeding sites remain undiscovered. The discovery of Manx Shearwaters breeding in Nova Scotia is probably only a matter of time.

Description Length: 31-38 cm. *All plumages:* The form usually seen off Nova Scotia is dark brown (black at a distance) above, with sharply contrasting white underparts.

Range The subspecies *Puffinus puffinus puffinus* nests on islands in the eastern North Atlantic from southwest Iceland to the Azores, in southern Newfoundland and, formerly, in Bermuda. The majority of the population breeds in the British Isles. Other subspecies are found in the Mediterranean and the Pacific.

Remarks This species is readily recognized as a medium-small shearwater with long, thin wings and a fast wing-beat interspersed with glides. The Sable Island specimen and almost all the birds seen off Nova Scotia have the crisply contrasting black-and-white plumage of the subspecies *P. p. puffinus*. However, single birds seen off Brier Island on 1 September 1978 and on the northeast tip of Georges Bank on 25 June 1980 had markedly brownish underparts (R.G.B. Brown) and possibly belonged to the eastern Mediterranean subspecies *Puffinus puffinus yelkouan*.

Little Shearwater

Puffinus assimilis Gould

Status One record. The only confirmed Canadian record of this species (*Puffinus assimilis baroli* subspecies) was a dead bird picked up on Sable Island on 1 September 1896 by Superintendent R.J. Bouteillier (Dwight 1897). In addition, small black-and-white shearwaters thought to be this species or Audubon's Shearwaters were seen off Sable Island on 27-28 August 1978 (A. Sheppard) and off eastern Cape Breton Island on 29 July 1982 (two birds, S. Zendeh). The birds off Cape Breton Island were evidently blown into Nova Scotian waters by a storm; their description suggests Little Shearwaters rather than Audubon's Shearwaters.

Remarks This and the next species resemble miniature Manx Shearwaters with a very rapid wing-beat interspersed with glides. The Little Shearwater has a shorter tail than Audubon's Shearwater, and the *P. a.baroli* subspecies from breeding grounds in the eastern Atlantic has white on its face extending above the eye.

Audubon's Shearwater

Puffinus lherminieri Lesson

Status Two sight records. The first Nova Scotian (and second Canadian) record was of a bird seen southwest of Sable Island on 7 October 1979 in an area of very warm water (Brown 1980). A second bird was well observed from MV *Bluenose* on 27 August 1980, some 30 km southwest of Yarmouth (B. Curry).

Remarks This small shearwater resembles the Little Shearwater in its auk-like wing-beat tempo but has a longer tail and dark undertail coverts. It breeds in the Bahamas and throughout the Caribbean, wandering northward in the Gulf Stream.

Family Hydrobatidae

Wilson's Storm-Petrel   PLATE 2

Oceanites oceanicus (Kuhl)

Status Common summer visitant. These storm-petrels are regular in offshore waters from April to October, and numbers peak between early June and late August. The earliest record is a bird seen on Georges Bank on 11 April 1983 (R.S. d'Entremont) and the latest was observed close to shore "in a tearing gale and rough seas" at Scots Bay, Kings County, on 11 November 1975 (J. and J.S. Cohrs, M. and R. Anderson). This bird is far more frequently seen during its relatively short sojourn here than Leach's Storm-Petrel. It is found along the entire Scotian Shelf on the Atlantic side of Nova Scotia, and a few birds enter the Gulf of St. Lawrence. The largest numbers, however, occur in the south, at the entrance to the Bay of Fundy and in the region of Browns and Georges banks. On 25 June 1980, R.G.B. Brown counted over 2,500 Wilson's Storm-Petrels at the northeastern edge of Georges Bank, some 220 km south of Cape Sable. At least 2,000 birds were counted off Yarmouth from MV *Bluenose* on 26 September 1975 (D.W. Finch).

Description *Length:* 18-19 cm. *All plumages:* The basic plumage pattern is the same as in our other two storm-petrels, but the white rump patch is larger than in Leach's Storm-Petrel and extends further onto the flanks. The tail is not notched and the feet protrude beyond it.

Range Breeds in enormous numbers in the Falklands, and on islands in Tierra del Fuego and around the coasts of Antarctica. Migrates northward into the Pacific and Indian oceans, and in the North Atlantic as far as Labrador. The majority of Atlantic birds winter off New England and southern Nova Scotia.

Remarks Wilson's Storm-Petrel follows ships more readily than does Leach's Storm-Petrel. It also has the feeding habit of hovering just above the surface of the water, maintaining its position by paddling with its feet. At such times, the distinctive yellow webs on the feet may be seen. Its shorter, more-rounded wings and swallow-like flight, less erratic than that of Leach's Storm-Petrel, are useful field marks.

British Storm-Petrel

Hydrobates pelagicus (Linnaeus)

Status One record. On the evening of 10 August 1970 a strange storm-petrel was trapped in a mist net employed for banding shorebirds on Sable Island (McNeil and Burton 1971). The specimen was subsequently presented to the National Museum of Canada; it was the first authenticated record of the species for North America.

Remarks *Length:* 14-19 cm. This is a small storm-petrel with a square tail and a weak, fluttering flight interspersed with short glides. It is sooty black or brown, with a white rump. The small patch of white feathers at the base of the underwing is a diagnostic field mark. It breeds in the eastern North Atlantic from Iceland to Spain and the Mediterranean and winters off South Africa. There have been one or two supposed sightings of the species from the MV *Bluenose* between Yarmouth and Maine, but the details are not wholly satisfactory.

Leach's Storm-Petrel   PLATE 2

Oceanodroma leucorhoa (Vieillot)

Status Common in summer. Breeds. Our breeding birds arrive off Nova Scotia in early April and remain until early November, and there may be later stragglers. The earliest sighting was off Cape Sable on 6 April 1972; the earliest reported arrival at a colony, on Pearl Island, Lunenburg County, was 11 April 1938 (M.B. Pearl). However, dead birds found in oil from the tanker *Arrow* on Sable Island on 1 March 1973 (Brown et al. 1973) must have been alive somewhere in the region. Fairly large numbers occur locally about the many coastal islands where they breed but are seldom seen because of the bird's nocturnal habits. Daylight hours are spent in nest burrows or at sea in search of food. However, in the gray dawn of 8 November 1913 a dozen or more were found near the mouth of the Cornwallis River, where it enters Minas Basin. They seemed to be asleep among the sedges at the edge of the tidal waters and several were caught by hand. Another unusual exception was a large flock feeding in broad daylight on 15 July 1969 at the windward (northwest) side of the Canso Causeway. Charles R.K. Allen writes: "Water dotted with them as far as the eye could see—must have been several hundred at least. Many groups and singles flying low across the Causeway." Late sightings are usually of birds driven inshore or inland by winter storms. The latest definite record was the bird found at Port Philip, Cumberland County, on 29 December 1964 (A. Schurman), which was much emaciated and died the next day. However, it is likely that a flock of storm-petrels observed off Sable Island on 3 January 1966 (C. and N. Bell) were of this species.

Description *Length:* 20-23 cm. *All plumages:* A blackish brown bird with a small white rump patch that extends only a little way onto the flanks; dark gray wing coverts; forked tail; bill, legs and feet black.

Breeding *Nest:* Bare earth at the end of a horizontal burrow up to 1 m long. Leach's Storm-Petrels nest in colonies; most are on coastal islands, but a small colony near Louisbourg in 1954 was located on a peninsula. *Egg:* 1; creamy white, with a faint wreath of lavender around the larger end. The incubation is surprisingly long, 40-50 days, and is performed by both parents. On 8 June 1907 Harold F. Tufts examined two burrows on Seal Island, and found two adults but no eggs. My earliest date for a fresh egg is 12 June 1937 at Indian Island, Lunenburg County. Other egg dates are: 17 June 1944, several fresh sets; 17 July 1930, of three eggs examined, two were fresh; 28 September 1934, several burrows examined, all contained young.

Range Most of the North Atlantic population breeds in eastern Newfoundland. Its range extends from Massachusetts to southeastern Labrador, and small colonies exist in Iceland, the Faeroes, Scotland and Norway. It also breeds in the North Pacific. It winters at sea, probably in the tropics.

Remarks The forked tail and black (not yellow) webs to the feet are often cited as field marks that separate Leach's Storm-Petrel from Wilson's Storm-Petrel, but these are of little use at sea. However, the long, almost tern-like wings of Leach's Storm-Petrel and its erratic, bounding flight are distinctive.

Storm-petrels, better known to many as "Mother Carey's chickens" or "careys," were sometimes disliked by the keepers of island lighthouses, who were often wholly dependent on rain water for domestic use. They stored the water in hogsheads placed to catch it as it ran off the roofs of their buildings. The petrels, flying about in numbers at night, dropped excrement on the roofs, which seriously contaminated the water. To remedy this situation, house cats were turned loose to kill large numbers of the defenceless birds at night about the entrances to their burrows. Fortunately for the birds, most of these islands are now automated and no longer occupied by lightkeeping personnel.

Order PELECANIFORMES

Family Phaethontidae

White-tailed Tropicbird

Phaethon lepturus Daudin

Status Rare vagrant. Ten records since 1870, five of which were collected. Several are known to have been victims of heavy gales; probably all were. Briefly, they are: 6 September 1870, Shubenacadie, Hants County (Jones 1885); 27 August 1927, Wolfville (R.W. Tufts); August 1957, Brier Island (W. Lent); 26 July 1959, Hillsborough, Inverness County (Hawley); August 1959, Brier Island (Lent); September 1959, Brier Island (Lent); 7 October 1962, Brier Island (Lent); 9 October 1962, Cape Sable (S. Smith); August 1963, Brier Island (Lent); and 13 July 1964, Hillsborough (Hawley).

Remarks The name of this beautiful, largely white bird with long tail streamers is proper, for it nests on tropical and subtropical islands and does not voluntarily wander far from these places. The nesting colony nearest the North American mainland is in Bermuda. The bird lays a single egg in a crevice or hole of a steep white coral cliff.

In size it approximates that of a crow, but it flies like a pigeon, with quick wing beats. It feeds in the manner of our terns, by diving for the small fishes it has spotted from the air with its keen vision.

Family Sulidae

Brown Booby

Sula leucogaster (Boddaert)

Status One record. It was found more or less stranded on a rocky ledge known as the Salvages, at Blanche, Shelburne County, on 28 July 1941 by Albert Dixon Summers. The bird was very much alive but so tame it permitted being handled. Efforts to feed it were unsuccessful, suggesting a state of near-starvation. The bird remained in the immediate vicinity of the ledge for several days, after which it was not reported again. Mr. Simmons obtained an excellent close-up photograph that authenticates his species identification.

Remarks This gannet-like bird occurs widely in tropical waters. Both sexes have a chocolate-brown head, neck and upperparts, and white underparts. The breeding colonies nearest to Nova Scotia are in the Bahamas, from which this stray may have come.

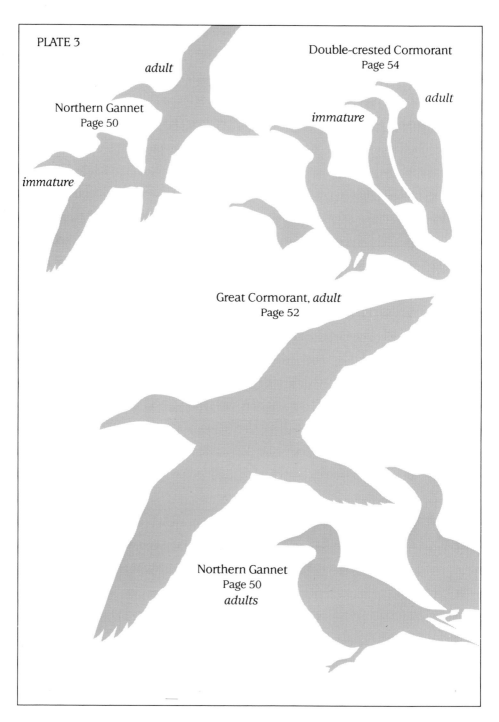

PLATE 3

adult

Double-crested Cormorant
Page 54

Northern Gannet
Page 50

adult

immature

immature

Great Cormorant, *adult*
Page 52

Northern Gannet
Page 50
adults

PLATE 4

Black-crowned Night-Heron
Page 66
immature

American Bittern
Page 56

adult

Great Egret
Page 61

Great Blue Heron
Page 59

male

female

Bufflehead
Page 102

Greater Scaup
Page 90

male

female

female   *male*

Wood Duck
Page 75

male

female

Brant
Page 71

Mallard
Page 80

American Wigeon
Page 86

Northern Gannet   PLATE 3

Sula bassanus (Linnaeus)

Status Common transient, uncommon in summer. Formerly bred. In the nineteenth century there was a small colony on Gannet Rock off Yarmouth (Bryant 1857). Today it is common in spring and fall off southwestern Nova Scotia and along the Atlantic coast, as migrants pass to and from their nesting grounds in Newfoundland and the Gulf of St. Lawrence. The first spring birds arrive in March (average 22 March, earliest 7 March), and the peak of their migration extends from mid-April to mid-May. The relatively small but regular summer population is largely made up of immatures. The return migration begins in early September and reaches its peak between mid-October and early November. However, stragglers are regularly reported in December, occasionally even in early January (latest 9 January 1959, off Bon Portage Island).

Description *Length:* 87-100 cm. *All plumages:* Bill longer than head, stout at base and tapering to a point. *Adults:* White with black wing-tips; yellowish orange suffusion on the head; blackish bare skin in front of eye and on throat. Bill bluish gray. *Immatures:* In first-year plumage, the juveniles are dark grayish brown, spotted with white. Molts produce various intermediate stages of whiteness. Adult plumage is attained after three years.

Range The Northern Gannet breeds only in the North Atlantic, in Britain, Ireland, Brittany, Norway, Faeroe, Iceland and Atlantic Canada. Our birds winter off the southeastern United States from Virginia to the Gulf of Mexico. Immature birds migrate further south than adults.

Breeding *Nest:* Made of seaweed placed on cliff ledges or the tops of rocky offshore islands. Usually found in large colonies, the nests frequently so close together the birds can touch one another. *Egg:* 1, bluish white. The present world breeding population of the Northern Gannet is about 213,000 pairs. Some 32,800 pairs breed at six colonies in Canada: Bonaventure and Anticosti islands and Bird Rocks, in the Gulf of St. Lawrence, and Cape St. Mary's and Funk and Baccalieu islands in eastern Newfoundland. The Canadian population is only a fraction of its former size. Bird Rocks was the largest gannet colony in the world in the early nineteenth century, with over 100,000 pairs. However, the cumulative effects of persecution, the loss of nesting habitat resulting from erosion and the erection of a lighthouse had reduced this population to less than 1,000 pairs by 1900. It now stands at some 5,300 pairs. Three colonies were completely exterminated during the nineteenth century: Perroquet Island, near the Strait of Belle Isle, and the two "Gannet Rocks" on the New Brunswick and Nova Scotia sides of the Bay of Fundy. Recent attempts to nest at two sites in southwestern New Brunswick have been unsuccessful. Some 20 km off the coast from Cape Forchu, Yarmouth County, lies a barren rock shown on the chart as "Gannet Rock." On 9 August 1935 I visited this bleak spot to check on a report that gannets still nested there. Not one was seen. On 7 December 1943, E. Chesley Allen sent me excerpts from his records: "Ben Doane recollects being on Gannet Rock and seeing the eggs of Gannets. The year would be about 1865. He estimates the number of birds at

200. Horace Rankin, of Arcadia, and L.B. Wyman, of Yarmouth, two gunners, claim that about 1880 there were about 20 Gannets nesting on this rock. Wyman remembers going on the rock and catching an old bird on the nest. He placed it in his boat and brought it half way to land when it got over the side and escaped. Amos Baker, an aged resident of Yarmouth South, said he could remember the rock white with them. Henry Baker, born on Cape Forchu in 1850, says when he went fishing as a boy with his father between 1860 and 1870, gannets were very common off shore and Gannet Rock was white with them. He says they disappeared soon after the erection of lobster fishermen's shacks on Green Island." Green Island lies about 7 km landward from Gannet Rock; the disappearance of the colony was caused by the persistent egging carried on by the Green Island fishermen.

Remarks These large, white birds with their conspicuously long black-tipped wings, beating tirelessly up and down the coasts in quest of fish make an arresting sight. Having spotted from a considerable height its prey near the surface, it drops headlong with wings half folded like an Osprey. Unlike the Osprey, which strikes the water breast first, the Gannet strikes head first, sending the spray in all directions. It disappears below the surface for only a moment but long enough to swallow the fish, for it usually reappears "empty-handed."

Family Pelecanidae

American White Pelican

Pelecanus erythrorhynchos Gmelin

Status Rare vagrant. Chamberlain (1887a) refers to a specimen from Nova Scotia without giving details. Between 27 September and 15 October 1948, about 50 of these spectacular birds were seen in small groups or alone within a very limited area in Kings County. A hurricane from the south that had raged along the coast was believed to have been responsible for their sudden appearance (Tufts 1949). There were two subsequent records of this bird in Nova Scotia: a single bird stayed at West Bay, Inverness County, between 19 and 31 October 1977 (several observers, photographs); and another was at Merigomish, Pictou County, on 21 August 1981 (R. Baker et al.), probably the same bird seen and photographed at Wallace Bay, Colchester County, in early September (S.I. Tingley).

Remarks These very large white birds with black wing-tips, broad wings and ungainly beak are unmistakable. They breed in the interior of North America and winter along the Gulf of Mexico, California and both coasts of Central America, so their occurrence here is quite accidental.

The 16 birds seen at Port Williams, Kings County, in 1948 were in muddy tidal water close to the bridge. They seemed bewildered as they swam aimlessly about in close formation, showing little if any interest in the group of bird-watchers that had gathered along the bridge to view the novelty. The turbid water prevented the pelicans from even attempting to feed, and it was believed none would survive. A number were collected for specimens, all of which showed evidence of emaciation.

Brown Pelican

Pelecanus occidentalis Linnaeus

Status Rare vagrant. This species was first recorded in Nova Scotia by Piers (1894), who listed two from Pictou County: one taken at River John on 31 May 1885 was mounted and later acquired by the museum at Pictou Academy; the other, an adult male, was shot on 1 June 1893 on Pictou Island by lightkeeper J.W. Hogg. John Macoun (1903) mentions a third specimen from Pictou Island, shot by J.W. Hogg on 15 May 1895. In his notes Piers mentions two other occurrences: one taken in 1896 at Prospect, Halifax County, and the other shot by William Graham during June 1899 at Three Fathom Harbour, Halifax County. A male was taken at Louisbourg on 4 May 1904 and is now in the Nova Scotia Museum. The seventh specimen was shot by Forman Atkinson at Clarks Harbour, Shelburne County, during June 1924; E.B. Smith reported that the bird was sitting on a mackerel trap with nearly one half a bucket of herring in its pouch. Individuals of this unmistakable bird were seen: on 26 June 1963 on Sable Island (C. and N. Bell); off Seal Island, gorged with herring, on 18 September 1976 (E. and G. Crowell); off Long Island, Digby County, on 26 June 1982 (several observers); and with an injured wing on 15 February 1983 southwest of Cape Sable on Browns Bank (M. Potvin).

Remarks This pelican breeds on Caribbean and Atlantic coasts from Georgia to Brazil; and in the Pacific from Washington State to Ecuador. Its manner of fishing is spectacular and quite different from that of its larger cousin, the White Pelican, which scoops fish from shoal water. The Brown Pelican dives headlong for its food from an altitude of 30 m or more, like the gannet.

It is noteworthy that almost all Nova Scotia occurrences were within May and June.

Family Phalacrocoracidae

Great Cormorant   PLATE 3

Phalacrocorax carbo (Linnaeus)

Status Fairly common resident. Breeds. Great Cormorants are common in summer along the coast but only in the region of their breeding rookeries, most of which are on eastern Cape Breton Island; elsewhere they are uncommon to rare. Fall migration to the south begins in September and reaches a peak in late October and early

November. A substantial part of the population winters off New England. Remaining winter birds are seldom seen far from their established roosts on rocky ledges along the coast. The migratory birds return from mid-March onwards.

Description *Length:* 80-101 cm. *All plumages:* Bill 6.3-7.6 cm., hooked at the tip; tail with 14 feathers; feet black and fully webbed. *Adults in breeding plumage:* Body looks black with a bluish or greenish gloss; back feathers bronze-gray with dark borders; numerous hair-like feathers scattered over the head and neck; throat pouch yellow with wide, white hind border; patch of white on each flank, developed by early March and shed during May. *Adults in winter:* Similar but without the hair-like feathers on head and neck and without flank patches. *Immatures:* Sooty brown with whitish brown breast and belly.

Breeding *Nest:* In colonies on cliff ledges on islands or the mainland. Composed of twigs and other coarse vegetable matter, usually including fresh seaweed; sometimes composed entirely of seaweed. *Eggs:* 3-7, usually 4-5; bluish white, overlaid with a chalky deposit. Laying begins during the latter part of April. Colonies of this cormorant in Nova Scotia are believed to have been established relatively recently. The first observed colony was at Crystal Cliffs, Antigonish County, where in June 1940 H.S. Peters found about 60 pairs nesting; by 12 May 1944 the colony had some 80 pairs. On 18 June 1940, I visited Bird Islands, Victoria County, and made a count of 39 occupied nests of this cormorant. A small colony I visited at Monk's Head, on the south side of Antigonish Harbour, had about 60 pairs, all appearing to be of this species; I was told by a local farmer that the colony was of very recent origin. Harrison F. Lewis visited Monk's Head on 11 June 1966 and found that the Great Cormorant colony there had ceased to exist because of erosion of the site by the sea. A Canadian Wildlife Service survey in 1971 (Lock and Ross 1973) estimated some 398 pairs of Great Cormorants on Bird Islands but only 33 pairs at Crystal Cliffs; the total population breeding in Nova Scotia was put at some 2,000 pairs out of a total Canadian population of about 2,700 pairs. The Nova Scotian population had increased about 1.5 times by 1982 (Milton and Austin-Smith 1983).

Range In North America, breeds locally in the Gulf of St. Lawrence, southern Newfoundland and along the Atlantic coast of Nova Scotia; most common in Cape Breton Island. Found as far south as North Carolina in winter. Other populations breed in western Greenland; the eastern North Atlantic from Iceland to the Cape Verdes; Eurasia; and Australasia.

Remarks Cormorants usually swim with their bodies submerged and only their head and neck visible—I have never seen one swim with its lower back and tail above the water line. When I visited the Crystal Cliffs colony on 12 May 1944, the birds were losing their hair-like flank patches, wisps of which were lodged in the grass along the edge of the cliff; some birds had completely lost this adornment, and others retained only traces of it.

Over short distances, cormorants fly low and often in line, one behind the other, but during prolonged flights they often fly rapidly at considerable heights in V formation and are frequently mistaken for wild geese, which have a similar wing motion.

In other parts of its range, the Great Cormorant breeds and winters on both inland and coastal waters. However, the North American population appears to make little use of freshwater habitats.

Double-crested Cormorant   PLATE 3

Phalacrocorax auritus (Lesson)

Status Common in summer, very rare in winter. Breeds. First spring migrants often appear in late March (average 4 April, earliest 26 March); three on the Gaspereau River, Kings County, on 15 March 1948 (L. Duncanson) were exceptional. The peak of migration is mid-April to late May. In summer it is common along the coast and on many rivers and lakes inland. Although the species nests on freshwater lakes in the interior of North America and the majority of our sites are along the Atlantic coast, a small population also breeds in the Minas Basin. The fall migration begins in August, but the main movement takes place between mid-September and late October. A few Double-crested Cormorants have been reported on Christmas Bird Counts in recent years. Some probably overwinter in southern Nova Scotia, but the majority migrates to New England and further south.

Description *Length:* 74-89 cm. *All plumages:* Bill similar to that of the Great Cormorant. *Adults:* Smaller than but similar in appearance to Great Cormorant adults, but lack white hind border to throat pouch and never have white flank patches or conspicuous white anywhere on head or neck; possess only 12 tail feathers; throat pouch is orange. Tufts of narrow and curved black feathers found on its head during breeding season are referred to in the bird's name. *Immatures:* Similar to those of the other species but markedly smaller, and usually with their necks paler than their bellies.

Breeding *Nest:* Seaweed and other coarse vegetable matter placed on a rude foundation of small sticks. They nest in colonies, and the sites commonly chosen are of three types: on projecting shelves on the sides of steep cliffs; on level surfaces above the sea wall and preferably near its edge; and in trees 2-10 m or more in height. The trees chosen are usually on islands with low shores without cliffs and quickly die from exposure to the cormorants' excreta. An unusual nesting site was established by a small colony many years ago in the Town of Pictou on the piles of an old causeway, where it may be readily observed from a nearby bridge. *Eggs:* 3-6, usually 4-5; bluish white with overlay of chalk-like substance. Laying begins in late April or early May. On 21 June 1933 at Cape Split, Kings County, about 40 pairs were nesting on "Squaw Rock." Some nests contained partly incubated eggs and others held half-grown young. According to a 1971 Canadian Wildlife Service survey (Lock and Ross 1973), the Nova Scotian population of Double-crested Cormorants numbered about 4,400 pairs, out of some 10,600 pairs breeding in Atlantic Canada and the Gulf of St. Lawrence. There were about 12,100 pairs in Nova Scotia in 1982 (Milton and Austin-Smith 1983).

Range Breeds locally from southwestern Alaska and the interior of North America to the Gulf of St. Lawrence and southern Newfoundland, south to the southern United States and the Bahamas. Most of the birds in Atlantic Canada breed in the western Gulf of St. Lawrence and on the Atlantic coast of mainland Nova Scotia. Winters from the southern parts of its summer range south to Florida and the Gulf of Mexico.

Remarks Some commercial and sport fishermen consider both species of cormorants to be "bad birds." They are often condemned as killers of trout and other fishes of importance to man, but data acquired from studies of the food habits of the Double-crested Cormorant (Lewis 1929, 1957) tend to refute these charges.

   Both species of cormorants are protected throughout the year by provincial statute in Nova Scotia.

Family Fregatidae

Magnificent Frigatebird

Fregata magnificens Mathews

Status Six records. The first bird was taken near the entrance to Halifax Harbour on 16 October 1876 (Deane 1879). A male specimen was taken near Devil's Island, Halifax County, during June 1891; and George Little shot a male at Terence Bay, Halifax County, on 5 December 1932 (R.W. Smith 1938); both of these birds are now at the Nova Scotia Museum. One appeared on tuna fishing waters near Lower Wedgeport, Yarmouth County, on 14 July 1949 and remained in the vicinity for ten days or more (I.J. Pothier). Frank Brennan saw one swooping to take a small fish on 4 August 1949 from a wharf at Freeport, Digby County. Finally, a female frigatebird was seen at Matthew's Lake, Shelburne County, on 1 September 1980 by Russel J. Crosby.

Remarks These huge, fork-tailed seabirds are strays from the tropics probably carried here by gales. Their long, hooked bills enable them to catch the near-surface fish that form the major portion of their diet. Israel Pothier writes of the Lower Wedgeport bird: "Along with a hundred or more people, I watched this bird above the Tuna Wharf. It is a graceful flyer. It hardly ever moved its wings and there was a 20 to 25 mile wind blowing at the time. It took one herring but would not come closer than 50 feet. From about 1:30 to 7 p.m. it stood (in air) looking more like a Chinese kite than a bird."

Order CICONIIFORMES

Family Ardeidae

American Bittern PLATE 4

Botaurus lentiginosus (Rackett)

Status Uncommon in summer, very rare in winter. Breeds. Regular in freshwater or brackish marshes from time of spring arrival, generally in April (average 17 April, earliest 29 March). An unusually early spring sighting was on 16 March 1949, when one was seen flying low over Halifax (H.G.F. Morgan). Late birds are often recorded in November and a number have been reported in late December, evidently attempting to winter. On 31 January 1949 one "was standing close to the fish-ladder where the dammed waters of the Milo Lakes, near Yarmouth, discharge into the harbour. The water at this point is open all winter. The bird seemed to be in good condition" (I.J. Pothier, letter to R.W. Tufts). A weakened individual captured near Wolfville on 12 February 1974 was restored to health on a diet of smelts and frogs.

Description *Length:* 58-84 cm. *Adults:* Upperparts finely marked with various shades of brown and buff. Underparts whitish, broadly streaked with brown. A broad black streak extends along the sides of the neck. *Immatures:* Similar but more buff and without black streak down sides of neck.

Breeding *Nest:* On the ground, usually in wet places; composed of reeds and other coarse vegetable matter. Cattail swales are favoured sites. *Eggs:* 3-5; pale olive or buff. On 12 June 1923 a nest that held three newly hatched young was discovered near Barrington, Shelburne County. It was little more than a soggy mass of rotting vegetation in swampy land among alders and there was no attempt at concealment. Harry Brennan found a nest near his home in Springville, Pictou County, under a small bush on marshy ground near the shore of a lake. On 5 May 1965 it contained two eggs; when visited on 30 May it held five; on 20 June there were four young and one infertile egg in the nest. On 2 June 1968 Mr. Brennan found two bitterns' nests. They were poorly concealed among short reeds and low deciduous bushes in wet land near Moose River, which runs into Eden Lake, Pictou County. The nests were not over 5 m apart, each being occupied by a sitting bird; visited again on 22 June each contained four young. He further reports having found a nest on 31 May 1969 that held five eggs. Its placement and construction were similar to those just described, but the behaviour of the sitting bird seems noteworthy: it was so loath to leave the nest that it permitted being touched by hand without moving. From 9 July to 16 August in recent years, I have examined six juvenile bitterns picked up along roadsides near Wolfville and brought to me for identification. All showed traces of natal down about their heads and necks and, though seemingly full-grown, none had acquired the power of flight.

Range Breeds from central British Columbia, southern Mackenzie Valley, northern Manitoba and Newfoundland, south to southern United States. Winters from southwestern British Columbia and Delaware south to Guatemala and Panama.

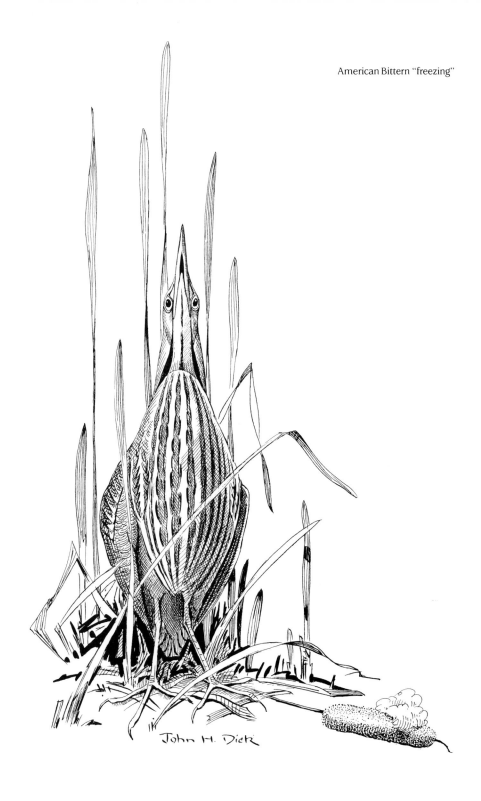

John H. Dick

Remarks A common trait of the bittern is to evade detection by standing motionless with its bill pointing skyward. If the bird is surrounded at such moments by stands of last year's cattails, as is usually the case, the camouflage is excellent.

When cornered, bitterns defend themselves ably with their javelin-like beaks. On one occasion I banded and released a juvenile in a field where cattle were pastured, near a cattail swamp. Drawn by curiosity, a large steer that had been watching the operation at fairly close quarters drew near with head lowered, sniffing audibly, as though to investigate. Instead of beating a hasty retreat to cover, as it could well have done, the bird stood its ground and, with head drawn in close to its body, glared menacingly at the steer. Finally, with a suggestion of timidity, the beast's nose came within inches of the poised bird. Suddenly the sharp beak shot out and upward, stabbing the animal viciously on the tender part of its nostril, whereupon, with a loud snort and tail held high, the steer turned and went galloping across the field. The bird, after gaining its composure, slowly strode off in a dignified manner and soon disappeared among the cattails.

Bitterns might be confused with the young of Black-crowned or Yellow-crowned Night Herons, but the latter have no black streak on the sides of the neck, and the coarse white spots on their wings are very different from the finely vermiculated pattern of bittern wings. Furthermore, bitterns are decidedly tawny in contrast to the grayer plumage of the night herons.

The vocal performance of the male bittern, heard chiefly during mating season, is unique and weird. The notes, uttered between short intervals of silence, are produced or accompanied by grotesque contortions of the neck. Some say they sound like the working of an old-fashioned pump. Others liken them to the sound produced when one drives a stake into wet boggy land, hence the name "stake-driver" by which the bird is known to many. To me its note suggests neither of these. It is more like a low gulp, which under favourable conditions can be heard for a considerable distance.

Least Bittern

Ixobrychus exilis (Gmelin)

Status Rare in summer. Breeds. Although listed by Blakiston and Bland (1857) as "accidental," the first concrete report was of a very early bird taken on 16 March 1896 at Prospect, Halifax County (Piers 1898). Another was found alive, tangled in eelgrass, on Cape Sable Island on 25 April 1907. The earliest of the 14 individuals recorded since 1960 were seen on 19 May 1980 and 1984, the latest on 11 November 1973. A specimen in the Nova Scotia Museum was collected from Upper Musquodoboit, Halifax County, on 28 November 1906. In recent years the bird has been heard and seen regularly in the Amherst Point Bird Sanctuary, where Mark Forbes in 1982 discovered and photographed the first and only nest in the province. Two birds reported near Sydney in early June 1924 (I.A. Bayley) and another at Truro on 23 June 1949 (S.A. Elliot) suggest that they may occasionally nest elsewhere.

Description *Length:* 28-35 cm. *Adult male:* Crown, back and tail glossy black; sides of head, hindneck and area on wings chestnut; outer wing coverts buff and flight feathers slaty. Throat and underparts white, washed with buff. There is a blackish patch on either side of breast. *Adult female:* Similar, but black on back and crown is replaced by glossy umber.

Breeding *Nest:* In dense cattails or other emergent marsh vegetation; made of both dry and living plant material. *Eggs:* 2-7; pale blue or greenish. The nest discovered by Mark Forbes in the Amherst Point Bird Sanctuary contained six eggs. Unfortunately, the chicks were killed by a heavy rain in late June.

Range Breeds from Oregon and extreme southern Ontario, Quebec and New Brunswick, south to the West Indies, Paraguay and Brazil. Winters from northern Florida and southern California southward.

Remarks These little acrobats of the cattail swales have long since learned, in the eternal struggle for survival, that instead of taking wing when danger threatens, it is usually safer to run and hide—and when migrating, to do so under cover of darkness.

Great Blue Heron   PLATE 4

Ardea herodias Linnaeus

Status Common in summer, rare in winter. Breeds. Abundant in the neighbourhood of its breeding colonies from the time of arrival in spring (average 28 March, earliest non-wintered bird on 18 March) until early August, when its young have begun to be self-reliant. From then until late October, distribution is much more general and the bird is common throughout Nova Scotia. Large departures over the sea to the southwest have been observed from Seal Island and Cape Sable in late September through October. In recent years, a small but increasing number have attempted to winter, mostly in the southern parts of the province, but sometimes on Cape Breton Island. Few appear to have survived until spring.

Description *Length:* 107-132 cm. *All plumages:* Bill rather long, tapering to a sharp point. Very long legs and neck. *Adults in breeding plumage:* Forehead, sides of head, and throat white. Sides of crown and back of head black with slender black nape plumes. Neck mainly ashy brown with double streak of black in front. Feathers of lower foreneck narrow and much elongated. Back, wings and tail mainly slaty gray, with scapulars lengthened and plume-like. Breast and belly streaked black and white. *Immatures:* Similar to adults but with forehead and whole top of head bluish black; no plumes; and breast and belly streaked ash and white.

Breeding *Nest:* Of rude construction, composed largely of sticks with lining of coarse vegetable matter; usually placed high in deciduous or evergreen trees. One exception was that of a small colony numbering perhaps 20 pairs, located on a small rocky islet in Haley's Lake, Shelburne County, visited on 14 July 1944. The nests there were mostly in low, stunted trees, and a few were placed on the ground. *Eggs:* 4-7; pale blue. Laying begins about the middle of April. On 22 May 1913 a colony at Scragg Lake, Annapolis County, comprised of about 25 pairs, was located in old-growth yellow birches. Almost all the nests were placed at the greatest height consistent with safety, among the smaller top branches at 23-25 m above ground. Eggs of well-advanced incubation were collected, one set of five and one of four. Over the edges of most nests young herons could be seen extending their long necks when the parents came in with food. A dozen or more young ones of varying stages of development were noted dead on the ground beneath the trees, apparently having fallen from their nests. Several parents came in carrying small fish held crosswise in their beaks. About 1960, Great Blue Herons established a breeding colony on Boot Island, near the mouth of the Gaspereau River, in Kings County. The nests were placed in dense spruce woods, 3-6 m up. Some were close to the trunks, but more were saddled well out on heavy branches. On 1 July 1968 there were about 20 pairs in the colony, plus many half-grown young ambling precariously about the branches close to their nests. Others were still too young to leave home. On 26 April 1970 this colony had increased markedly to approximately 40 pairs. Three nests were examined and found to contain seven, five and four eggs respectively.

Range Breeds from southeastern Alaska and across southern Canada to the Magdalen Islands and Nova Scotia, south to southern Mexico and the West Indies. Winters from southern British Columbia and the northern United States south to Central America.

Remarks The use of the erroneous name "crane" when referring to this bird is far less general here than it was two decades ago. Cranes are birds that breed in the northwest, and few have been recorded in Nova Scotia. When flying, herons invariably fold their long necks in an S formation; cranes extend theirs forward to full length. This heron's two worst enemies are the lumberman's axe and the vandals who visit colonies during the breeding season to shoot defenseless parent birds. It is not unusual for a colony to be broken up by lumbering operations, but in most instances the birds merely re-establish themselves farther back in the forest. A man with a rifle or shotgun, however, is a more serious matter. The fact that the heron is protected throughout the year in both Canada and the United States under international treaty regulations is not much of a deterrent, because the shooting is done in remote areas where chances of apprehension are slight. Fortunately, this brutal practice has become more infrequent over the years.

The food of the Great Blue Heron is small fishes, frogs, snakes, mice and other animals.

Great Egret   PLATE 4

Casmerodius albus (Linnaeus)

Status Rare visitant. The first record was of a bird collected near Halifax in September 1867 (Jones 1868). Only a few more were recorded prior to 1960, but since then it has been almost annual, with 21 individuals sighted in April, 18 in May, 6 in June, 5 in July, 7 in August, 4 in September, 13 in October and 5 in November. A very early bird was recorded near Sydney between 19 and 26 March 1981, and two very late birds were near Fourchu, Richmond County, on 13 December 1975, and near Yarmouth until 4 December 1977.

Description *Length:* 90-107 cm. *Adults in breeding plumage:* All white with plumes from the back which extend beyond the tail. Legs and feet black. Bill yellow or orange. *Adults after breeding season, and immatures:* Without plumes.

Range Found widely throughout the world. In the Western Hemisphere, breeds from New Jersey to Oregon and south to Patagonia. Individuals, like many others of the heron family, wander northward after their breeding season.

Remarks Early in the present century, this bird and its close relative, the Snowy Egret, were killed by hunters gathering aigrettes (plumes), which were sold to the millinery trade. Plumes are at the peak of perfection during breeding season, and it was then that the slaughter took place, the parent birds being shot from ambush as they returned to their nests carrying food for their young. The species was saved from probable extinction by the timely enactment of laws that forbade women to wear the plumes on their hats. With no market for the feathers the killing ceased and now the species has made a satisfactory recovery.

Snowy Egret

Egretta thula (Molina)

Status Uncommon visitant. The earliest reference to it is by Blakiston and Bland (1857), who regarded it as "very rare." Jones (1868) mentions a specimen. Only a few more were recorded prior to 1960, but since then it has become the most frequent of "southern" herons. Three individuals have appeared in March, 63 in April, 90 in May, 12 in June, 7 in July, 8 in August, 21 in September, 17 in October and 5 in November. The earliest was on Sable Island on 24 March 1977, and the latest seasonable bird was on 23 November 1962 on Bon Portage Island. More unusual was a bird on 15-16 December 1979 at Cole Harbour, Halifax County (J.C. and J.S. Cohrs et al.), and another on 6 January 1963 on Bon Portage Island (B.J. and S. Smith).

Description *Length:* 50-70 cm. *Adults in breeding season:* Plumage pure white. About 50 cm. long, recurved plumes grow from the egret's back and extend slightly beyond its tail. Bill black, yellow at base of upper mandible; legs black; feet yellow. *Adults after breeding season, and immatures:* Without plumes.

Range Breeds from Maine and California south locally to Argentina and Chile.

Remarks This dainty little heron is one of the most charming of our marsh birds. The beauty of its snowy plumage, especially when enhanced by long, waving plumes, and the exquisite, graceful, darting movements characteristic of its feeding, provides a picture not soon forgotten by the nature lover. Like other egrets this bird nearly met early extinction because of the commercial value of its lovely plumes.

The white plumage of immature birds resembles that of the immature Little Blue Heron; however, the black bill, black legs, and yellow feet of the Snowy Egret readily distinguish it from this heron, which has a paler bill and greenish legs.

In 1984, about six birds summered in the Black-crowned Night Heron colony on Bon Portage Island (although no nests were found). Groups have summered in other parts of western Nova Scotia and in Halifax County, and it is probable that the species will soon be on the province's list of breeding birds.

Observers should be alert to possible occurrences of the very similar Little Egret, *Egretta garzetta,* a wanderer from the Old World that has appeared twice in Newfoundland and once in Quebec. It has blue-grey rather than yellow at the base of the bill, never shows yellow up the back of the legs, and adults have two narrow head plumes instead of the shaggy mass of the Snowy Egret.

Little Blue Heron

Egretta caerulea (Linnaeus)

Status Rare visitant. The first report was of an immature white bird "shot at Cole Harbour, lately" (Jones 1885). There were about 15 subsequent records up to 1960, and it has become almost annual since, mostly in southern counties. Of these, 16 were reported first in April, 11 in May, 3 in June, 5 in July, 17 in August, 10 in September, 9 in October and 1 in November. The earliest was on 1 April 1972 and the latest on 17 November 1962. White immature birds and dark adults are reported in similar numbers.

Description *Length:* 50-74 cm. *Adults:* Head and neck dull maroon. Rest of plumage dark slaty blue. Bill black at tip, shading to bluish toward its base. Legs and feet blackish. *Immatures:* Mainly white with more or less slate colour on the tips of the primaries and sometimes traces of this colour elsewhere. Legs and feet greenish yellow.

Range Breeds from Maine and Missouri south through the West Indies and Mexico to South America. Wanders northward irregularly into Canada.

Remarks The white immatures are sometimes mistaken for egrets, but the greenish legs of this bird are unlike those of Snowy and Great Egrets, which have black legs. Furthermore, the dark bill of the Little Blue Heron contrasts with the yellowish bills of Great and Cattle Egrets. It is rather shy and retiring by nature and when feeding seems to favour river margins and shallow ponds inland from the coast. It is a day feeder, retiring at nightfall to its well-established rookeries.

Tricolored Heron

Egretta tricolor (Müller)

Status Rare visitant. The species was first recorded by Thomas F.T. Morland, who studied one in full breeding plumage at Crescent Beach, Lunenburg County, on 13 June 1957. Since then, 14 individuals have been reported, including several confirmed by photograph and one by specimen. An extraordinarily early individual was seen in Cole Harbour, Halifax County, on 28 February 1975 and for some weeks thereafter (F.L. Lavender). Another early arrival was seen on 29 March 1969. Three have appeared in April, six in May, one in July, and two in August.

Description *Length:* 50-70 cm. *Adults:* White belly and foreneck contrast with slaty blue upperparts. White throat tinged with chestnut. Two short white plumes on head. *Immatures:* Chestnut hindneck and wing coverts.

Range Breeds in Baja California, along the Gulf Coast (rarely inland), and north on the Atlantic coast to Maine. Also in South America.

Remarks This is the most coastal of the "southern" herons. Increasing in numbers and spreading northward, it can be expected to be seen more often in the province.

Reddish Egret

Egretta rufescens (Gmelin)

Status Two sight records. On 5 September 1965, John Comer found what he took to be a Reddish Egret feeding in a marsh at Clam Bay, Halifax County. He studied it for about three-quarters of an hour, at distances as close as 50 m. Next day, he and four others observed it for more than two hours. Noted were the shaggy, dull brick-red head and neck, slate-blue body, particoloured (flesh, with black tip) bill, and restless shuffling and prancing motions "as though [it were] climbing through a wire fence." Mr. Comer was familiar with the species in Florida, and he and the others felt able to exclude the Little Blue Heron as a possibility. Another bird believed to be of this species was reported by Eileen Armsworthy and June Jarvis, who studied it closely at a range of approximately 30 m as it stood by a pond near Canso, Guysborough

County, on 5 November 1966. It was observed under favourable light conditions, aided by binoculars. It was in white-phase plumage. They noted the black tip of its otherwise flesh-coloured bill and its "drunken shuffle when feeding." A strong gale had lashed the shore the previous day.

Remarks In spite of the foregoing, this species is included with a measure of hesitancy because of its similarity in certain important respects to the uncommon Little Blue Heron, the immatures of which are also white and which it approximates in size. Furthermore, the Reddish Egret has never been definitely recorded in Canada, and its normal range is restricted to the extreme southern parts of the United States and much farther south.

Cattle Egret

Bubulcus ibis (Linnaeus)

Status Rare visitant. It was first recorded in Nova Scotia on 23 November 1957 at East Sable River, Shelburne County, by Mrs. Frank Craig, who reported it to Harrison F. Lewis. On 10 December 1957, Benjamin Smith found one dead on Cape Sable and submitted the specimen to the Nova Scotia Museum. The species has become almost annual among the "southern" herons. There are reports of 8 individuals appearing in April, 41 in May, 9 in June, 18 in July, 1 in August, 3 in September, 17 in October and 2 in December, sometimes in small groups. A remarkable flight of about 25, along with a like number of Great Blue Herons, descended on the oceanographic research vessel CSS *Dawson* about 600 km east of Halifax on 30 March 1984. The latest seen was at Centreville, Shelburne County, on 14 December 1967.

Description *Length:* 48-58 cm. *Adults in breeding season:* White with orange-buff plumes on crown, foreneck, and back. The stout, yellow bill becomes reddened. *Non-breeding adults and immatures:* Dark legs and yellow bills, and stouter heads and shorter necks than other small white herons.

Range Now nesting from northern California, southern Saskatchewan, southern Ontario, and Maine, south to South America.

Remarks Somewhat smaller than our Little Blue Heron. In spring and summer its plumage is white with buff on crown, nape, back, and breast. These buff areas are lacking in autumn when the bird is all white. During all seasons the bill varies from yellow to orange. Legs are black in juveniles, changing to bright yellow in adults. It customarily associates with cattle, hence its name. Why it does so is not definitely known, but an acceptable theory is that the browsing animals disturb insects on the ground, making them readily available to the hungry birds. Abundant in Africa and elsewhere in the Old World, it is not known how the species became established in this hemisphere. It is generally believed that it crossed over from Africa by natural means, as evidenced by the fact that one banded in Spain as a nestling was recovered one year later in Trinidad. The species was first noted in Suriname, South America, between 1877 and 1882. From there it gradually spread northward and by 1952 had reached Newfoundland, even before it was recorded in Nova Scotia. Its spread seems to have become checked somewhat in recent years.

Green-backed Heron

Butorides striatus (Linnaeus)

Status Uncommon visitant. The first record was of several in a "remarkable flight of birds" to Brier Island on 15 April 1881 (Chamberlain 1881). Although there were only about a dozen subsequent records up to 1960, it has become more regular, with annual occurrences since 1964, mostly in the southern counties. Among these, there were 7 in April, 45 in May, 18 in June, 5 in July, 24 in August, 12 in September, 11 in October and 2 in November. The earliest was on 9 April 1981 and the latest on 13 November 1981.

Description *Length:* 39-56 cm. *Adults:* Top of head and crest dark blackish green; sides of head and neck chestnut or maroon; white streak from chin to breast; back and wings glossy green, the wing coverts narrowly margined with buff; underparts ashy; legs and feet greenish yellow. *Immatures:* Similar, but neck and breast are streaked with black.

Range The North American subspecies breeds from southwestern British Columbia, southern Nevada, central Arizona, Kansas, central Michigan, southern Ontario and southern New Brunswick, south through the West Indies and Panama. Winters from southern United States southward. Other races occur in South America and the Old World.

Remarks Unlike most herons, which nest in colonies, this bird usually nests singly, far removed from others of its kind. The nest, usually in a bush or low tree, is a mere platform of twigs without lining.

A characteristic of this species is the partial web between its middle and outer toes. This enables the bird to swim with a measure of assurance. A dislodged nestling will swim with ease, even grace, to safety. Like many other species not strong in flight, the Green-backed Heron migrates under the protective cover of darkness.

Chapman (1934) mentions it as breeding in Nova Scotia but cites no evidence. Its recent pattern of occurrence suggests that it may have done so or soon will.

Black-crowned Night-Heron   PLATE 4

Nycticorax nycticorax (Linnaeus)

Status Uncommon visitant, rare in summer. Breeds. Although it was evidently occasional earlier in the nineteenth century (Jones 1885), the first concrete specimen records are given by Piers (1892a). To 1960 there were only about 25 records, but since then it has become almost annual in increasing numbers. Among those that appeared to be merely visitors, 10 were first noted in April, 37 in May, 18 in June, 15 in July, 36 in August, 7 in September and 7 in October. The earliest spring report in recent years was from Brier Island on 6 April 1961, but an earlier one was shot in Yarmouth County on 26 March 1928. The latest was on Sable Island on 20 October 1984. On 1 June 1977 three active nests were discovered in a Great Blue Heron colony on Bon Portage Island (Quinney and Smith 1980). A fledged young was noted at a later date. By 1984 there were approximately 15 night heron nests in this colony. An incompletely feathered juvenile with two adults seen on Seal Island in July 1984 and other sightings of young summer birds in western Nova Scotia suggest that it will be found more widely.

Description *Length:* 60-70 cm. *Adults:* Forehead white, crown and back black with a greenish or bluish gloss. Two, three or four long narrow white plumes on hindneck. Sides of head, neck and underparts white with grayish wash; rest of plumage gray. Bill black, legs and feet yellow, eyes ruby-red. *Immatures:* Very different. Upperparts mainly light brown, spotted and streaked with white. Underparts whitish, streaked with grayish brown. Outer flight feathers usually lightly tinged with rust. Tarsus about equal to middle toe and claw.

Breeding *Nest:* Made of coarse twigs and branches, with finer lining. Usually in trees, up to 40 m high. Nests on Bon Portage Island in spruces, virtually the only trees available. *Eggs:* 3-5; pale blue-green.

Range Breeds from central Washington, southern Manitoba and New Brunswick south to Paraguay; winters as far north as southern New England. Also occurs in Europe, Asia and Africa.

Remarks Night herons lack the characteristic long necks and legs so conspicuous in other herons. In flight their necks are not S-folded like the others but appear short and drawn in, somewhat crow-like. At rest they present a rather short, stocky appearance.

As its name suggests, the night heron feeds largely at night, spending the daylight hours with others of its kind in dense cover. However, occasionally it will be found on its marshy feeding grounds in broad daylight.

Yellow-crowned Night-Heron

Nycticorax violaceus (Linnaeus)

Status Rare visitant. The first record was of one killed on Cape Sable Island in March 1902 and purchased in the Boston market (Kennard 1902). Up to 1960 there were only a dozen records and it is still among the less common of the "southern" herons. Since 1960 sightings included 1 in March, 3 in April, 3 in May, 11 in July, 27 in August, 11 in September, 9 in October and 1 in November. The earliest landed on CSS *Dawson* 600 km east of Halifax on 30 March 1984; the latest was on Sable Island on 4 November 1968.

Description *Length:* 56-71 cm. *Adults:* Crown and broad streak on sides of head white, stained with rusty or yellow tinge; rest of head black. Remainder of plumage dark gray, back streaked with black. Legs greenish. Eyes orange. *Immatures:* Similar to Black-crowned Night-Heron of same age but darker and more finely streaked and spotted. No rusty wash on outer flight feathers. Bill stouter and legs longer. Tarsus longer than middle toe and claw.

Range Breeds from Massachusetts, Ohio, Kansas and Baja California south to the West Indies, Brazil and Peru.

Remarks It is difficult to distinguish this bird from the Black-crowned Night-Heron when both are in immature plumage, but the Yellow-crowned Night-Heron has less prominent white spotting, a thicker neck, a stouter all-dark bill, darker flight feathers and in flight its legs extend well beyond its tail. It is said to be less nocturnal in feeding habits than the preceding species.

Family Threskiornithidae

White Ibis

Eudocimus albus (Linnaeus)

Status Four records. An adult was found on Bon Portage Island on 13 July 1959 by Evelyn Richardson, possibly brought by a hurricane that grazed the province two days earlier. Becoming progressively weaker, it was collected on 15 July by Morrill Richardson for the Nova Scotia Museum. Subsequently there was a well-described sighting of an immature bird at Amherst Point Bird Sanctuary on 9 June 1976 (C. Desplanque). In the same year, an adult was seen in mid-June and an immature in mid-July, both on Cape Sable, Shelburne County (B.J. Smith et al.).

Remarks Slightly larger than the Glossy Ibis; white with black outer primaries; legs, long curved bill, and face are orange-red. *Immatures:* Dark wings and dusky head and neck. It is a native of tropical and subtropical America, breeding as far north as Virginia and Texas. There are few Canadian records.

Glossy Ibis

Plegadis falcinellus (Linnaeus)

Status Uncommon visitant. About 1865, according to McKinlay (1885), several appeared near Pictou, one of which was collected. Up to 1960 there were a further seven records; most of these birds were collected. Since then it has been almost annual, with 64 first seen in April, 127 in May, 7 in June, 3 in July, 7 in August, 1 in September and 5 late birds at Wallace Bay, Colchester County, on 1 October 1981. Many of these have come in groups. In 1974 they arrived as early as 7 April, and there were flocks of up to 37 in Kings County and 15 in Digby County, in May.

Description *Length:* 50-65 cm. *All plumages:* Distinctive downward-curved bill. *Adults in breeding plumage:* Chestnut, with glossy green and purple on head and wings. *Adults after breeding season:* Duller and flecked with pale spots on head and neck. *Immatures:* Duller still.

Range Worldwide in warmer climates. In North America it breeds from Maine south to Florida and along the Gulf Coast to Louisiana, casually in inland regions.

Remarks The species has been expanding its breeding range northward through the eastern United States and may some day nest in the province.

Order PHOENICOPTERIFORMES

Family Phoenicopteridae

Greater Flamingo

Phoenicopterus ruber Linnaeus

Status One record. On or about 13 October 1969, one of these exotic birds was seen near the roadside at Cape John, Pictou County, by a number of local residents. On the afternoon of the fifteenth Alvin Holmes found it dead on the beach nearby—it had been shot that day. The specimen was acquired by the Nova Scotia Museum.

Remarks The flamingo may have been a victim of a hurricane which came from the region of the Bahamas (where a breeding colony of flamingos has long been established) early in October and reached Cape Race, Newfoundland, about October 17. That this was a wild bird rather than an escapee is suggested by its rich pink plumage (captive birds are duller). Its occurrence here represents the first record of the species for Canada, and possibly the first further north than New Jersey.

Order ANSERIFORMES

Family Anatidae

Fulvous Whistling-Duck

Dendrocygna bicolor (Vieillot)

Status Two records. A bird of this species, identified from a wing sent to the Canadian Wildlife Service, was shot on Bon Portage Island on 15 January 1976. Two flocks, one of 14 and the other of about 25 individuals, appeared on Bon Portage Island during January and February of that year. Most, if not all, were shot by local gunners, and one specimen was presented to the Nova Scotia Museum.

Remarks Although these birds nest in the southwestern United States and in Latin America, they are prone to wander, and there are several records for southeastern Canada and the northeastern United States.

Tundra Swan

Cygnus columbianus (Ord)

Status Rare transient. Apart from a casual reference (Downs 1888) to "one or two instances" in earlier times, the first concrete record was of a specimen taken at Musquodoboit Harbour, Halifax County, on 6 January 1900 (Piers' notes). The next record was of two seen, one shot, in Richmond County in late fall 1919. In 1932 there were two early spring records: two very weak birds, one of which was captured alive, appeared on the barrens near Louisbourg on 10 March, and a very thin bird was shot from a small flock at Little River, Yarmouth County, on 21 March. Four were seen on Brier Island on 9 November 1966 (W. Lent), three were seen there on 10 November 1973 (E.L. Mills, W. Lent) and seven appeared around Port Hebert, Shelburne County, in late December 1975 (R. Widrig et al.). Three were seen at Seaforth, Halifax County, on 28 November 1978; one illegally shot the next day was secured for the Nova Scotia Museum. In 1983, groups of 4-12 birds visited at Island Pond, Yarmouth County, in late November; on Sable Island during the first week of December; and at Bissett Lake, Halifax County, between 5 and 9 December.

Remarks The Tundra Swan, formerly known as the "Whistling Swan" in North America, nests in arctic and subarctic regions of the Old and New Worlds. Among North American waterfowl this magnificent white bird ranks in size only second to its slightly larger cousin, the Trumpeter Swan, which is decidedly more western in its range. A normal, healthy swan is extremely shy and hence difficult to approach, a trait which has contributed in no small way to its ability to maintain its numbers.

Like some of our other large wild birds, swans pair for life, and it is customary for the young to remain with their parents during the first year. The swan seen in our parks is the Mute Swan and is not a native bird but one brought here from Europe.

Tundra Swans migrating to and from the east coast do not normally appear north of Massachusetts. When migrating, they fly at great altitude. Some of those found here show evidence of severe exhaustion, suggesting a forced landing after a prolonged but unsuccessful struggle against strong winds.

Greater White-fronted Goose

Anser albifrons (Scopoli)

Status Three records. The species was first recorded here in 1926, when T.S. Pattillo shot one at Oak Island, near Wallace, Cumberland County, on October 26 (specimen now in the Nova Scotia Museum). The next one, feeding with a flock of Canada Geese, was shot near Debert, Colchester County, on 12 November 1949 by Carl Adshade. It had been wounded previously, as evidenced by a scar on the base of its lower mandible, and was heavily infested with lice. The species was not reported again until 3 November 1961, when one was shot at Paradise, Annapolis County, by Donald Bailey. He took the strange specimen to Walter E. Whitehead at Round Hill, Annapolis County, who was able to identify it.

Remarks The subspecies *Anser albifrons flavirostris,* to which the 1926 and 1949 birds belonged, breeds on the west coast of Greenland. In winter it migrates to the western parts of the British Isles and, rarely, to the Atlantic coast of North America.

Snow Goose

Chen caerulescens (Linnaeus)

Status Rare to uncommon transient. There are several nineteenth-century records, and it has been occasional since in nearly all parts of the province, perhaps more regularly in recent years. Nearly all reports are for spring (5 March to 23 May) or autumn (26 September to 25 November), generally one to a few birds, often with Canada Geese. Exceptional numbers occurred on 2 May 1978 at St. Esprit, Richmond County, where more than 300 were seen. St. Esprit was also the site of two out-of-season visitations of 40 Snow Geese on 20 June 1975, and 30 on 28 June 1976 (R. and

S. Meyerowitz). These birds should normally have reached even the most northerly nesting areas by early June. Two (one in "Blue" phase) shot at Cole Harbour, Halifax County, in early January 1974, and two more shot at Lingan Bay, Cape Breton County, on 2 January 1979, may have been attempting to winter, and one near Yarmouth between 27 February and 16 March 1984 may have wintered in the region. (For occurrences of the two subspecies of this goose and also of the "Blue Goose" colour phase, see Remarks.)

Description *Length:* 60-93 cm. *Adult white phase:* Pure white, sometimes with rusty stains on head, with black primaries (thus distinct from various white domestic geese); pink bill. *Immature:* In first autumn, dusky brown head and neck, pinkish gray legs and dark gray bill. *Adult blue phase:* Head and neck mostly white, otherwise largely grayish brown; grayer on back, with dark gray wing coverts; black flight feathers. *Intermediates:* Regular, like the "blue" phase with white bellies and wing coverts.

Range Breeds from northeastern Siberia across arctic Canada to northwestern Greenland, south along both coasts of Hudson Bay. Winters from British Columbia and New York State south to Mexico.

Remarks Birds nesting in the southern and western Canadian Arctic and migrating largely through the continent's interior belong to the smaller subspecies *Chen caerulescens caerulescens.* The "Blue Goose," a phase interbreeding with white birds, occurs extensively (and apparently exclusively) in this smaller subspecies. The larger *Chen caerulescens atlantica* nests in the high Arctic and winters largely in the middle Atlantic states.

Most Nova Scotian birds are presumably "greater" Snow Geese, *C. c. atlantica.* A specimen of this subspecies, shot near Yarmouth on 11 March 1932 (Smith 1938), is in the Nova Scotia Museum. A bird taken about 11 November 1911 at Comeau's Hill, Yarmouth County, was recorded by Allen (1916) as a "greater" Snow Goose, but measurements taken later clearly establish it as *C. c. caerulescens.*

The "blue" phase of *C. c. caerulescens* was first recorded in October 1950 near Barrington, Shelburne County (M. Rawding; motion pictures of two "Blue Geese" and one Snow Goose confirmed by W.E. Godfrey). Since then there have been four reports of this phase in fall and four in spring, in addition to the aforementioned bird shot at Cole Harbour in early January 1974.

Brant   PLATE 4

Branta bernicla (Linnaeus)

Status Fairly common transient, rare in winter. Although it congregates in some numbers on long-established feeding grounds in the province, it is rarely seen in some parts, including Cape Breton Island and the Eastern Shore. Fall concentrations are regular along the shores of Northumberland Strait where the first flocks arrive in early September. They occur in smaller numbers irregularly at many other points along the coast. For reasons not understood, they largely bypass Cape Breton Island in spring and fall. On their main feeding grounds their numbers build up to a peak in early November but by late November most move on, although the time of departure varies somewhat from season to season. Stragglers formerly occurred rarely in winter, two having been taken on the Grand Pré meadows on 31 December 1929 (W.E. Godfrey) and one in Halifax Harbour on 12 January 1925 (P.A. Taverner). In recent years, a few have wintered regularly on Brier Island, and flocks of spring migrants return to that island and to feeding grounds on Cape Sable in late winter (since 1960, average 6 March, earliest 28 January). Later they appear on Northumberland Strait; and "thousands" congregated off Wallace Harbour, Cumberland County, on 9 April 1927 (C.I. Macnab). Their spring migration is prolonged—it is usual to see flocks of 100-200 birds about the shores of Minas Basin as late as early June; these loiterers may be immature non-breeders.

Description *Length:* 64-79 cm. *Adults:* Head, neck and upper breast black; narrow patch of white on each side of neck; back and wings dark grayish brown; uppertail coverts white; tail black; lower breast and sides brownish gray, fading to white on belly and toward tail; bill, legs and feet black. *Immatures:* Similar but with little or no white on sides of neck.

Range Circumpolar. Breeds on the islands of the Arctic. Winters on the coast from Massachusetts to North Carolina and from British Columbia to Baja California.

Remarks This small goose is essentially a saltwater bird. The virtual disappearance of eelgrass *(Zostera marina)* from the Atlantic coast about 1931 affected it more adversely than it did the Canada Goose, whose feeding habits are more varied. Although Brants still return to their old feeding grounds, where the eelgrass has made a partial if not complete recovery, their numbers are significantly reduced in comparison to the great flocks that swarmed over the same feeding grounds prior to 1931.

Wickerson Lent has observed that when they first arrive at Brier Island on their way north they invariably congregate on Pond Cove, on the southwest side of the island, to eat mainly sea lettuce *(Ulva linza)* and Irish moss *(Chondrus crispus)*, but later, when eelgrass is available, they spread along the shore.

The subspecies visiting Nova Scotia is *Branta bernicla hrota.* An individual of the "Black Brant", *Branta bernicla nigricans,* which nests in the western Canadian Arctic and in Alaska and migrates along the west coast of North America, was identified among the Brant on Cape Sable on 12 March 1970 (B.J. and S. Smith).

Barnacle Goose

Branta leucopsis (Bechstein)

Status One sight record. Late in the afternoon of 20 November 1969, Game Warden Edward Turner was on patrol along the west bank of Port Hebert harbour, Shelburne County. There he saw a flock of seven unusually tame geese standing by themselves on the marsh by the edge of the harbour. Early the following day, they allowed him to approach within 50 m and study them with binoculars. They were noticeably smaller than Canada Geese, had small bills, black breasts, and conspicuous white foreheads, a feature that ruled out the possibility that they might be Brant. After studying them as long as he cared to, he was convinced they were Barnacle Geese.

Remarks This sighting was detailed in his "Outdoors" column in the Shelburne *Coast Guard* by Harrison F. Lewis, who considered Mr. Turner well qualified to make this identification Kortright (1942) states that the Barnacle Goose is less inclined to associate with other geese than is any other goose species and so readily approachable that it is known as the "fool" among geese. These characteristics were noted by Mr. Turner, lending further credence to his identification.

The Barnacle Goose is an Old World species that breeds in Greenland. Most records in North America have been dismissed as escapees from captivity, but our small group (perhaps a family) seems not to have had such an origin.

Canada Goose   PLATE 5

Branta canadensis (Linnaeus)

Status Common transient, locally fairly common in winter, rare in summer. Breeds. Southbound migrants appear in September (average 16 September, earliest 2 September). Segments of these migrant flocks remain as winter residents in sheltered bays and harbours where, under normal conditions, food is available throughout the winter; such locations are found in Queens, Shelburne, Halifax and Cape Breton counties. When winters are not too severe, Canada Geese will be found in smaller numbers in other parts of the province. At Port Joli, Queens County, on 13 January 1927 approximately 2500 were feeding on the eelgrass beds that are usually exposed or within reach of the birds at low tide. Although some wintering flocks may move earlier within the province, there is a clear swelling of numbers in March and April. Most are gone by May, but in recent years nesting has occurred in Annapolis, Colchester and Halifax counties.

Description *Length:* 85-110 cm. *Adults:* Head and neck black, with contrasting white throat and cheeks; back and wings grayish brown; uppertail coverts white, forming a band across the black rump and tail; underparts white, washed and barred with ashy gray; bill, legs and feet black. *Immatures:* Similar.

Breeding Prior to 1965, reports were received of pairs of wild Canada Geese in Nova Scotia with downy young. One such report came from the marshlands near Amherst in June 1930. Because so many of these birds were kept on farms at that time, wing-clipped or pinioned, the possibility that the pair in question were semi-domesticated birds that had escaped from captivity cannot be ruled out. During the late 1960s, numbers of pen-raised Canada Geese were released by various agencies, and these birds have established small nesting populations in the Musquodoboit and Stewiacke river valleys and, to a lesser extent, on the Annapolis River.

Range Breeds from Alaska and southern Baffin Island to northern California and across the United States to Tennessee and Maine. Winters from southeastern Alaska, the Great Lakes region and the Atlantic coast of Newfoundland, south to southern California, Mexico and Florida.

Remarks At the approach of spring, wintering flocks become restless and noisy as the compelling urge to return to northern nesting grounds awakens. On 21 March one year, from the shore of Port Joli Harbour, Queens County, I watched detached flocks rise from the water and mill about in the air, calling vociferously as though urging others to follow. The first to leave in spring are the old breeders, some long mated. We have all seen and sensed the mystery of these migrating flocks of wild geese high overhead, flying in long, wavering V formations, or heard their musical notes drifting down from the heavens after dark as "High through the drenched and hollow night their wings beat northward hard on winter's trail," to quote from *The Flight of the Wild Geese* by Sir Charles G.D. Roberts. Sometimes in spring they proceed too hastily and encounter ice conditions that cause them much physical hardship from lack of available food. Others loiter behind on lush feeding grounds as they wander slowly northward—these are undoubtedly birds that have not attained breeding status.

During winter 1931-32, a mysterious blight struck the eelgrass *(Zostera marina)* beds along the Atlantic coast, causing a serious food shortage for the geese on their ancestral wintering grounds and many died of starvation. This disease prevailed over the entire range of this marine plant along the Atlantic coast, the cause of it never determined. It persisted for several years before the plant recovered, greatly diminishing the size of wintering flocks.

Very cold weather sometimes temporarily seals feeding grounds, preventing the geese from reaching their food. On 8 March 1932, I heard that a flock of some 150 geese was in trouble at Cole Harbour, long a winter refuge for Canada Geese about 15 km east of Halifax. Through the sympathetic and generous co-operation of the owner of a private plane, 70 kg of corn in 5 kg paper bags was dropped onto a frozen marsh. Then, by skilful manipulation of the plane, the weakened birds were herded to the marsh. Before we left, we enjoyed watching the flock, through binoculars, feeding on the corn.

Spring migrants frequently resort to upland clover fields to feed on the roots which they relish greatly. In the early days of migratory bird law enforcement, many complaints were received from farmers who believed the geese were damaging their crops of clover. On one occasion, I co-operated with a farmer to stake off an area of field on which the geese were concentrating. Some months later at mowing time, I visited this section of the field with the owner and was much relieved to find a luxuriant growth of clover, which proved to the farmer's satisfaction that the alleged damage of which he had complained a few months earlier was imagined and not real. The fact that we had plenty of rain that particular spring may have helped.

Our transients belong to the subspecies *Branta canadensis canadensis,* which breeds in eastern Quebec, Labrador and Newfoundland. Four occurrences in Nova Scotia of the very small *Branta canadensis hutchinsii,* which nests in the eastern and central Canadian Arctic, are mentioned by McAtee (1945).

Wood Duck PLATE 4

Aix sponsa (Linnaeus)

Status Rare to locally uncommon in summer, very rare in winter. Breeds. The present population has recovered through protection from severe overhunting and has been much augmented by restocking and escapes from captive flocks. Spring migrants (not birds that have overwintered) first appear usually in April (average 9 April, earliest 18 March). It was recently successfully introduced to Cape Breton Island and thus it nests in small numbers throughout the province, most regularly in the border region. Latest migrants are normally seen in November (average 9 November, latest 29 November), and a few stragglers routinely occur on Christmas Bird Counts. One was shot on Brier Island on 5 February 1967, and since 1975 individuals or small groups have regularly wintered among wild birds fed by the public at Sullivans Pond in Dartmouth.

Description *Length:* 43-53 cm. *Adult male:* Top of crested head iridescent green and blue. Two lines of white extend into crest, one from base of bill and one from behind eye; cheeks purple; chin and throat contrasting white, this extending as a forked stripe, one branch going up side of head and the other towards back of neck; white band between breast and flank, bordered behind with one of black; breast and patch on each side of the base of tail reddish chestnut; back dark green with bronze and purple iridescence; wings mixed iridescent blue and purple, with narrow white line along hind edge; tail rather long, black with green iridescence; belly white; sides buff; speculum steely blue; eyes red; legs dull yellow. *Adult female:* Head dark gray with slight greenish gloss; crest shorter than in male; throat, chin and eye ring white; upperparts brownish gray with weak bronze reflections; wing similar to male's; underparts streaked with buff and white; belly paler, almost white.

Breeding *Nest:* In a hollow tree, the old nest of a large woodpecker or manmade nest-box; height from the ground 1-15 m or more, availability of site being the determining factor; I know of no nest located far from fresh water. *Eggs:* 8-15, pale buff or creamy white. They are deposited on rotten wood mixed with down from the female's breast. I have seen only one occupied nest of this species. It was located in a live maple growing in swampy woods within a metre of the shore of Moose Lake, near Italy Cross, Lunenburg County. The entrance to the natural cavity was an opening, about 3.5 m up, and the nest proper was about 60 cm perpendicularly below it. On 10 June 1960 the female was on the nest but refused to leave when the tree trunk was heavily pounded from below. She could be seen dimly, as could the down used in nest construction, through a small natural aperture in the trunk at nest level. The contents of this nest were not determined and the male was not seen.

Range Breeds from southern Canada south to the southern United States and Cuba. Winters largely in southern sections of its breeding range.

Wood Duck—female and ducklings.

Remarks Wood Ducks were hunted relentlessly after the Europeans arrived on this continent. Relatively tame and unwary, they were easily killed from ambush. The drakes are at the peak of their plumage perfection during the breeding season and many were killed about their nests and mounted for home adornment. Later, their brightly coloured feathers were in demand for artificial trout flies. It is probable that the species was saved from extinction by the protection afforded it under the Migratory Bird Convention in 1916, because the species has shown a marked recovery since then.

Wood Ducks frequently have difficulty in finding suitable nesting sites. One spring in Cumberland County, a female Wood Duck came to a chimney carrying a stick in her beak, obviously with the intention of building a nest therein, and had to be discouraged before giving up her plan. If a nest-box is suitably constructed and erected in natural habitat, Wood Ducks will often take possession. The entrance hole, if round, should not exceed 9-10 cm in diameter; and diamond-shaped holes, 7.5 by 10 cm, are best for reducing raccoon predation. If the nest-box is fastened to the top of a pole driven into the bottom of a shallow pond or lagoon near a wooded bank, a measure of safety from furred predators will be provided; such nests can be placed by cutting a hole in the ice before the spring breakup.

Soon after hatching the young "jump for it" from their nest sites, their fall being broken by their tiny, extended feet and their small, flapping wings. But how does a little one reach the entrance of the cavity, some 30 cm straight up from the nest, to make this jump? It is born with unusually sharp toenails and a sharp, hooked nail (soon to be shed) at the end of its tiny bill which enable it to climb the perpendicular wall.

Wood Ducks may use the same nest site year after year, and it was long presumed that the same pair returned together. More recently, through banding, it has been found that it is the female that comes back, but invariably with a new mate. Pairing occurs on the wintering grounds and, when the northward migration begins, she leads him to the nest site of the year before. In some species, such as the Yellow Warbler, it is the male that returns each year; but in these cases pairing does not occur until nest construction is about to commence.

Green-winged Teal   PLATE 5

Anas crecca Linnaeus

Status Common transient, fairly common in summer, rare in winter. Breeds. Spring migrants normally arrive in late March or early April (average 28 March, earliest 22 March, earlier birds having probably overwintered), with a peak usually about the second week in April. The bird nests widely in the province, especially in freshwater marshes in the Annapolis Valley and near the border, but also in coastal salt marshes. Considerable concentrations occur during September and October in coastal ponds and marshes, where they are also found routinely in small numbers through winter.

Description *Length:* 30-38 cm. *Adult male:* Head and upper neck mostly chestnut; patch from eye to back of head glossy green; chin black; back, sides and flanks brownish gray, finely barred with black lines; a white crescent usually present between breast and flank; wings gray; wing patch bright green, edged in front with cinnamon and white and with black bordering; breast buff, with round black spots; underparts white; undertail coverts and bill black; legs bluish gray; webs black. *Adult female:* Top of head, back, wings and tail dark brown with buff or white edges to the feathers; underparts paler, lightest on belly; wings similar to those of male but often with little or no cinnamon on wing bar. *Immatures:* Similar to adult female.

Breeding *Nest:* On the ground, made of grass and lined with down, sometimes in dry places but usually on or near marshy ground. *Eggs:* 9-13; creamy buff. A nest at Grand Pré found by Ralph L. Mosher on 30 June 1950 was partially concealed in a patch of cultivated strawberries growing near a cattail marsh and contained 13 eggs.

Range Breeds from Alaska, the Mackenzie Valley, James Bay, northern Quebec, and Newfoundland, south to northern Maine, Minnesota and central California. Winters from southeastern Alaska, Nova Scotia and New England, south to Honduras and the West Indies. Also occurs widely in the Old World.

Remarks This is the smallest North American duck. The drake in full breeding regalia is handsome, considered by many to rate second only to the elegant male Wood Duck. If confronted with danger during flight, it is able to accelerate its speed dramatically. On a marsh near Amherst many years ago, a small flock came in, attracted by our floating decoys. After circling a few times, they came almost within shooting range still showing suspicion and suddenly detected the deception. Instead of turning off, which would have afforded us a shot, they put on a burst of speed and "zoomed" low over the blind. By the time we reversed our shooting positions, they had flown beyond range.

It is a hardier bird than its relative the Blue-winged Teal, arriving earlier in spring and remaining much later in fall. Its numbers in the 1960s compared favourably with those of my boyhood recollections.

The subspecies that occurs regularly in Nova Scotia is *Anas crecca carolinensis*. However, the Eurasian subspecies, *Anas crecca crecca* (formerly designated as a separate species), is a rare vagrant here. The drake of this subspecies lacks the white crescent carried on each side of the breast by the North American form which, in turn, lacks the white stripe along each side of the back above the wing that the Eurasian drake displays. The females of the two subspecies are practically indistinguishable. A male of the Eurasian subspecies was collected in September 1854 (Jones 1885), and another was taken at Minesville, Halifax County, on 14 February 1913. It was not reported again until 26 April 1955 at the Amherst Point Bird Sanctuary. Since 1971, there have been seven spring occurrences of one or two birds in the Amherst region as early as 25 March 1979 and as late as 6 May 1976. They were also seen at the Glace Bay Bird Sanctuary on 3 April 1971 (2 birds), and on the West Lawrencetown Marsh, Halifax County, on 14 April 1983 (2 birds) and 28 April 1984 (1 bird). A drake appeared on Sullivans Pond, Dartmouth, on 3 January 1980 and was last seen on 30 March of that year.

American Black Duck   PLATE 5

Anas rubripes Brewster

Status Common resident. Breeds. Its distribution is fairly general except in winter, when concentrations occur at coastal areas, particularly along the Southwestern Shore where feeding conditions are more favourable.

Description *Length:* 53-61 cm. *Adults:* Head and body mainly dark brown, the feathers bordered and marked with buff; underparts paler; crown, nape, and line through the eye dark brown; rest of head and neck noticeably paler than body; purple wing patch bordered in front and behind with black, usually with a thin, white line on the edge of the outer border; legs greenish yellow, orange or red-orange, the season, sex and age being determining factors; bill greenish yellow in the male, olive-green in the female. A good distinguishing mark of the Black Duck in flight is the contrast of its white wing linings with its darker body.

American Black Ducks in spruce pond

Breeding *Nest:* Composed of grass and coarse vegetation, with a lining of down taken from the breast of the parent bird. The nest is usually on the ground, well concealed by protective plant growth, but on rare occasions it is located in a hollow tree or even in an old nest of a hawk or crow—perhaps such unusual sites are chosen to avoid loss of nests from flooding. Laying begins in late March and continues for several weeks. *Eggs:* 7-12, usually 8-10; pale greenish blue or creamy buff. A nest containing 11 practically fresh eggs was found at Gaspereau, Kings County, on 10 April 1932; and another containing 12 slightly incubated eggs was discovered at Albany, Annapolis County, on 17 May 1930. A female followed by downy young was seen near Wolfville on 17 May 1951. The nest is usually placed near water but one found on Wolfville Ridge on 18 April 1929 was approximately 1.5 km. from water.

Range Breeds from northern Saskatchewan, northern Ontario, northern Quebec, Labrador and Newfoundland, south to South Dakota and North Carolina. Winters from southern Ontario and the Maritime Provinces to the southern United States.

Remarks American Black Ducks usually feed on the surface or by tipping. An exception was noted at the Kentville Bird Sanctuary on 4 October 1940, when one dived repeatedly and remained underwater for 10-20 seconds. In autumn they consume grain lost at harvest time, and seeds of many kinds of aquatic plants, as well as the plants themselves. One shot on Boot Island, Kings County, on 15 December 1941 contained 100 or more amphipod shrimps identified as probably *Orchestia grillus* by Francis M. Uhler of the U.S. Fish and Wildlife Service.

If a mother is killed or forcibly separated from her brood, another Black Duck with ducklings of her own, regardless of their age, will quickly adopt the orphans. To effect such an adoption, locate a mother with a brood and simply turn the orphans loose in the vicinity, on the water if feasible. When their sharp, piercing calls are heard, the response is likely to be immediate as the foster mother goes straight to them, answering their appeals with a series of low, seductive quacks. I have had the pleasure of effecting three such adoptions.

Formerly, two races of this species were recognized by ornithologists. The "Red-legged Black Duck" was supposed to range further north in summer than the other. It was later found that the red legs and yellow bill of this supposed northerner were merely a matter of age and season, so the two subspecies were merged (Shortt 1943).

Mallard   PLATE 4

Anas platyrhynchos Linnaeus

Status Locally common in summer, uncommon in winter. Breeds. Formerly occurred as a rare stray in autumn. A beautiful drake taken on the Grand Pré meadows in October 1900 by D.R. Munro was mounted and displayed as a curiosity. There are a few records of Mallards, all believed to have strayed from their western range, that were shot at widely separated points in Nova Scotia during the early twentieth century. Beginning about 1930, attempts were made to establish this bird in Nova

Scotia. In 1941, George W. Tingley released 92 adults on the Amherst Marsh, and during 1953 and 1954 approximately 200 young Mallards were turned loose in the Amherst Point Bird Sanctuary by local sportsmen. There has been a steady increase in numbers since the late 1950s, and birds have now become established remote from places of release. In the late 1970s and early 1980s, more than 50 occurred on successive Halifax West Christmas Bird Counts. Although a few are found in winter among the hardy American Black Ducks on coastal marshes, wintering birds are common only where they are fed artificially—at Glace Bay Bird Sanctuary, Sullivans Pond in Dartmouth and the Shubenacadie Wildlife Park, for example.

Description *Length:* 53-69 cm. *Adult male:* Head and neck glossy green, a white ring around neck; breast chestnut; upper back dark grayish brown, becoming black on rump and uppertail coverts; wing patch purple, bordered by white and black; tail feathers gray, outer ones paler, the four middle ones recurved; belly pale gray, finely marked with black lines; undertail coverts black; bill greenish yellow; legs orange. *Adult female:* Top and sides of head pale brown, streaked with dark brown or black; upperparts brown, feathers edged with buff; wing patch as in male; breast and belly buff, mottled with dark grayish brown.

Breeding *Nest:* On the ground, usually in marshy places near open water. Composed of coarse grasses and reeds and lined with down. Usually well concealed but occasionally exposed. *Eggs:* 8-14; greenish to olive-buff in colour. Several nests have been reported during May and June in recent years.

Range In North America, breeds mainly from the Aleutian Islands and northwestern Alaska, northwestern Mackenzie, northern Manitoba and northern Ontario, south to northern Baja California, northern Kansas and northern Virginia; also on the coast of Greenland. Winters from southern and western Canada south to Mexico. Widely distributed in Europe and Asia.

Remarks I recount the following incident as an example of the reluctance of imported Mallards to act like normally wild ducks: During winter 1968-69, an overwintering flock at Tannery Swamp, Kings County, attracted much attention because a highway bisects this wet habitat to which the birds cling during the lean months. On 21 January, while motoring on this strip of highway, I was obliged to come to a complete stop behind a row of cars. The Mallards had decided to cross this busy road by foot and succeeded in holding up traffic until the last bird slowly waddled to safety.

Because they interbreed freely with the American Black Duck, the introduction of this species is a mixed blessing—in much of its range, the American Black Duck is being replaced by Mallards and hybrid forms. The Mallard tends to occur in more productive marshes and breed later than the black duck, so Nova Scotia remains a stronghold of relatively pure American Black Duck populations.

Females might be confused with female American Black Ducks, but the Mallard is paler, has a white bar on both sides of the purple wing patch, instead of one thin, white line, and its tail feathers are paler.

Northern Pintail PLATE 5

Anas acuta Linnaeus

Status Fairly common transient, uncommon in summer and winter. Breeds. Evident spring migrants generally arrive in March (average 19 March, earliest 2 March), although some first spring records may represent movements of birds that had wintered in the province. Larger numbers build up during April. It nests throughout the province in salt and freshwater marshes, occasionally on Sable Island and most frequently in the Amherst region. Concentrations of local breeding birds and transients are seen from about mid-September to early November. Generally, only small numbers remain among the wintering waterfowl flocks, but an unusual observation of 110 birds on 10 January 1966 at Pictou Harbour was reported by Eric Holdway.

Description *Adult male:* Length 66-76 cm; head, throat and upper foreneck rich brown; back of neck blackish brown, separated on sides from foreneck by a white line which extends to breast; back and forewings gray, with black scapulars; iridescent wing patch varying from glossy green to bronze-purple, with a bar of cinnamon-brown in front of it; secondaries tipped with white; flanks white, marked with fine, wavy black lines; breast and belly unmarked white; tail white, with black middle feathers long and pointed; legs and bill slate-blue. *Adult female:* Length 53-62 cm; crown reddish brown, streaked with blackish brown; rest of head and neck paler; upperparts and sides dark brown, the feathers edged and marked with buff or light gray; wing patch much duller than in male; in flight wing shows a single white line along hind edge; legs and bill slate-blue.

Breeding *Nest:* On the ground, composed of coarse vegetable matter, with a lining of down from the breast of the parent. *Eggs:* 7-12; pale olive-green to olive-buff. The species was not known to breed in Nova Scotia in the nineteenth century. It is uncertain when breeding was first recorded, but John Tingley reported in 1940 that he had frequently seen nests and broods in the Amherst area; since then, others have been found widely in the province.

Range In North America breeds from northern Alaska, the Mackenzie Delta, Southampton Island and northern Quebec, south to California, Illinois and Massachusetts, sporadically beyond. Winters from southern Alaska, Missouri to Panama, casually further north. Also found in the Old World.

Remarks The drake of this species ranks among the most beautiful of ducks and has a similar rating as a table bird. It is most frequently found on fresh water where it feeds largely by "tipping," its longer neck enabling it to feed at greater depths than those reached by the other freshwater ducks with which it competes.

The female might be confused with the female Mallard, but her neck is longer and more slender, and her tail is longer and pointed.

Blue-winged Teal   PLATE 5

Anas discors Linnaeus

Status Common transient, fairly common in summer. Breeds. Widespread in freshwater marshes and ponds, less so in salt marshes. Migrants generally arrive in late March or early April (average 1 April, earliest 24 March), and in numbers by mid-April to early May. Large gatherings are seen from late August, and last sightings are routine to late October and occasional in November. Individuals or small groups have occurred on Christmas Bird Counts (latest 25 December 1972 on the Halifax West count), but there are no later winter reports.

Description *Length:* 37-41 cm. *Adult male:* Forehead and crown blackish brown; large white crescent in front of eye; sides of head and neck lead-gray, glossed with faint purple sheen; upperparts dark brown; wing coverts pale blue and separated from green speculum by a bar of white; patch on either side at base of tail white; underparts brown, evenly spotted or barred with black; undertail coverts black; legs yellow or orange. *Female:* Mainly dark brown, the feathers bordered with buff or white; much paler underneath; wing similar to that of male, but white bar in front of speculum is much reduced.

Breeding *Nest:* On the ground, seldom far from marshy areas, always well concealed. Composed of fine dry grasses and usually lined with down. *Eggs:* 10-13; buff. A nest containing 13 fresh eggs was found on 21 May 1953, on the bank of the Kentville Bird Sanctuary. Although the female flushed at a distance of only about 3 m, it took some time to locate the nest, so well was it concealed. It was cup-shaped and hidden in a depression prepared by the bird at the base of a thick clump of tall, coarse grass. The edge of the nest was about level with the ground surface and, apparently by a flick of her wing when she flushed, the mother had concealed the eggs with a light covering of grass and down, making the eggs invisible even when looking straight at the nest. The female fluttered off weakly and dropped in the marsh reeds nearby and was not seen again; the male was not in evidence. A female followed by seven downy young was seen in a slough on the Grand Pré meadows on 8 August 1944; the late date and small brood suggest a deferred nesting attempt.

Range Breeds from east-central Alaska, Great Slave Lake, Manitoba, southern Quebec and southwestern Newfoundland, south to northern California and North Carolina. Winters from the southern United States to Brazil and Peru.

Remarks On 4 October 1940 at the Kentville Bird Sanctuary, I watched two of these birds actively feeding. Instead of surface feeding, with occasional "tipping" as is their custom, they both resorted to diving and stayed under for 10-20 seconds. They were accompanied by an American Black Duck feeding in the same manner.

This bird shows a strong preference for freshwater ponds or sloughs and is seldom seen on tidal waters. It is one of the first of our native ducks to leave its summer habitat and one of the latest to return in spring. It has shown a notable increase in

Nova Scotia during the past 50 years but is still less common on Cape Breton Island than on mainland Nova Scotia.

The female Green-winged Teal is similar but lacks the conspicuous blue patch on its upper wing.

Northern Shoveler

Anas clypeata Linnaeus

Status Uncommon locally in summer, rare transient elsewhere. Breeds. The bird was a very rare vagrant in the nineteenth century; Gilpin (1880) and Jones (1885) give specimen records for April 1879. Other old records are of individuals shot near Digby in December 1916 and on Bon Portage Island on 15 September 1919. None was reported again until 24 November 1955, when two appeared on Bon Portage Island, one of which was shot (H.F. Lewis). Since the early 1970s it has become quite regular in the province, possibly because of augmentation by birds that have escaped from the Shubenacadie Wildlife Park. However, it behaves as a normal migrant, arriving generally in April (average 11 April, earliest 2 April), and departing before winter (average of last sightings 22 October, latest 22 November).

Description *Length:* 43-53 cm. *All plumages:* Spatulate bill longer than head. *Adult male:* Head and upper neck dark iridescent bluish green; back white with middle area dark brown; lower neck and breast white; belly and sides rufous; undertail and uppertail coverts dark green; lesser wing coverts light blue; greater wing coverts dark gray, tipped with white; speculum green. *Adult female:* Throat buffy white; head and neck streaked with light brown and black; above is dark brown, the feathers margined and spotted with light buff; wing coverts and speculum as in male; rest of underparts washed with buff, spotted all over with brown except middle part of belly.

Breeding *Nest:* On the ground, well concealed, usually near water. *Eggs:* 6-11; pale buff to greenish gray. The first evidence of breeding was recorded by Alan D. Smith, who found a brood on the Missaguash River marsh, Cumberland County, on 27 July 1968. Since then nests or broods have been reported in that area, the Annapolis Valley and Three Fathom Harbour, Halifax County.

Range In North America, breeds from Alaska, east to Manitoba and sporadically to Nova Scotia, and south to California, Iowa and Delaware. Winters from coastal southern British Columbia southward, and along the Atlantic coast from South Carolina, south to the Gulf Coast, Costa Rica and the West Indies, casually as far north as Maine. It is also found in Europe and Asia.

Remarks The name of this bird refers to the peculiar shape of its bill, which is longer than the bird's head and broader at the end than at the base. It is known to some duck-hunters as the "spoonbill." Slightly smaller than our American Black Duck, the drake in breeding plumage is strikingly handsome, showing more white than any other member of the dabbling duck group. The drably coloured female is polyandrous, a trait not commonly found in ducks. In North America the Northern Shoveler is primarily a western species.

Gadwall

Anas strepera Linnaeus

Status Rare in summer, very rare in winter. Breeds. It was listed by Blakiston and Bland (1857) as "in winter: rare," which is plausible, as early collectors tended to know their waterfowl. However, it was not recorded again until one was shot on the Grand Pré meadows on 14 November 1931 by Lemuel Morine; another was shot there on 11 November 1947 (M. Frankson); and a female, now in the Nova Scotia Museum, was taken at Wallace, Cumberland County, on 3 November 1953. In 1966, Cyrus S. Eaton released a few near Hollahan Lake, Lunenburg County, and some evidently nested in the vicinity. Since 1970 the species has become much more regular with numbers summering in the Amherst region. Birds arrive in April (average 9 April, earliest 2 April) and are generally last seen in October or November. However, a bird was shot in Pubnico on 16 January 1978; another wintered on Sullivans Pond, Dartmouth, in 1979-80; and one was seen at Green Bay, Lunenburg County, on 28 January 1984.

Description *Length:* 48-58 cm. *Adult male:* Head and neck buff with fine dusky brown streaks; body gray, with strong black scaling on breast; sides finely barred with gray; uppertail and undertail coverts black; tail pale grayish brown; wings gray, with some chestnut in coverts, outer secondaries mostly black, inner ones white. *Adult female:* Mottled brown, with white secondary patch as in male.

Breeding *Nest:* Usually on a well-drained site but sometimes afloat, and well concealed. *Eggs:* 5-14, creamy or greenish buff. The first brood in the Amherst Point Bird Sanctuary was in 1978, and frequent broods or nests have been recorded annually in that region since. A brood was recorded on Bon Portage Island in 1981 (P. Barkhouse et al.).

Range In North America, breeds from southern Alaska, the Yukon and the MacKenzie Valley to southern Ontario and Quebec, sporadically in the Maritimes, locally to southern California, Wisconsin, Ohio and on the Atlantic coast to North Carolina. Also in Eurasia, from Iceland to northern China and Sakhalin. Withdraws from northern parts of its range in winter.

Remarks The Gadwall is nowhere abundant, although it is widely distributed. It is essentially a freshwater species and has a low rating as a table bird. Although formerly a stray to Nova Scotia from the centre of the continent, it is clearly becoming established here as a nesting bird.

Eurasian Wigeon

Anas penelope Linnaeus

Status Rare vagrant. Downs (1888) stated merely that it was "rare," but Piers (1915) discounted this vague reference and concluded that a bird on 9 January 1912, near Yarmouth, was a first record. Another dozen were taken or observed prior to 1970. These included a bird shot on Cape Sable Island, in early December 1926, wearing a leg-band put on the bird in Iceland on 2 July of the same year (Lloyd 1927). Since 1970 there have been some 21 records of 27 birds (maximum of three at the Amherst Point Bird Sanctuary, 25 April to 8 May 1982). By county, 15 birds have occurred in Colchester (all near Amherst), 9 in Halifax, 5 in Cape Breton, 4 in Yarmouth, 3 in Cumberland, 2 in Kings and 1 in Shelburne. By month of first appearance, there have been 10 in April, 8 in November, 5 in May, 4 in October, 3 each in December and January, 2 in February and September, and 1 each in March and June. Most unusual was a drake seen in Lusby Marsh, Colchester County, between 29 June and 12 July 1975 (C. Desplanque, D.W. Finch).

Remarks This medium-sized duck resembles the American Wigeon. The drake of the Eurasian Wigeon, however, has a bright cinnamon-brown head with a creamy buff crown, while that of the male American Wigeon has a conspicuous green facial patch and a white crown. The underwing surfaces of both male and female Eurasian Wigeon are ashy brown, mottled with dark gray, but those of the American bird in both sexes are white with little or no mottling. These are distinctive characteristics more useful for identification with the birds in the hand than in the field.

It has long been presumed that these travellers reaching Nova Scotia come from Iceland, and the recovery of a band from the leg of one of them tends to confirm this theory.

American Wigeon PLATE 4

Anas americana (Gmelin)

Status Uncommon in summer, rare in winter. Breeds, but was considered rare in the nineteenth century (Blakiston and Bland 1857, and others) but has increased markedly since about 1950 in Nova Scotia, as elsewhere in eastern North America (Palmer 1976). Some of the Nova Scotian breeding population could have originated as escapees from the Shubenacadie Wildlife Park during the 1950s and 1960s. First spring arrivals (where wintering birds have not been noted) may arrive in March (average 2 April, earliest 8 March). They are most frequently found in summer in the Amherst area and around the Debert sanctuary, but scattered pairs occur more widely. Peak fall numbers occur in September and October (an estimated 500 were seen in the Amherst Point Bird Sanctuary on 19 September 1978). They are occasional on Christmas Bird Counts around the province, and rare but regular later in winter. Several have overwintered among waterfowl fed by the public at Sullivan's Pond, Dartmouth.

Description *Length:* 46-56 cm. *Adult male:* Crown and forehead white; sides of head from eye to nape glossy green; cheeks and throat gray, finely streaked with black; breast and sides reddish brown; belly white; back brown, barred with fine black lines; prominent white patch on forewing; speculum green, bordered with black. *Adult female:* Similar but lacks white crown and green facial patch of the male; much smaller white area in the wing; speculum mainly black, with or without green.

Breeding *Nest:* Composed of dry coarse vegetable matter, with the usual lining of down. Placed on the ground, usually near water. *Eggs:* 8-12; buffy white. The first breeding record was of a brood of six seen following the female at Amherst Point Bird Sanctuary on 25 August 1957 (Bartlett 1960). Nests and broods have been noted annually in the Amherst region since the mid-1960s and have been discovered in the Debert sanctuary and elsewhere in the province.

Range Breeds mainly from Alaska to Manitoba (locally further eastward), south to northeastern California, northern Colorado, and Nebraska. Winters from southern Alaska, Ohio and southern New England to the West Indies and Central America.

Remarks The characteristic field marks of the male are a shiny white crown that contrasts with a dark green cheek patch, a pale gray neck, and a conspicuous white patch on each flank near the base of the tail. The female, on the other hand, is nondescript and might be confused with the female Gadwall.

It is a wary bird, quick to take alarm. Its flock formations are usually compact and the whistling sound made by the wings can be heard for a considerable distance. Its food, which it obtains by tipping, is made up almost wholly of vegetable matter, but it ranks far below average as a table bird.

In some parts of its range it is known to wildfowlers as a "poacher" or "baldpate." Its well-known habit of waiting on the surface to snatch wild celery and other aquatic plant food from the mouths of other duck species as they emerge from foraging in deep waters explains the origin of the first of these nicknames. The second name obviously refers to the white crown displayed by the drake.

Canvasback

Aythya valisineria (Wilson)

Status Rare transient, very rare in winter. Gilpin (1880) and Jones (1885) mention three collected birds, one taken in 1881; Allen (1916) reported one taken on 29 October 1905; and three were shot on 29 November 1927. Since 1950 there have been records from coastal areas in all parts of the province. About as many of these are for spring (six reports totalling 13 birds, 4 March to 26 April) as for autumn (five reports of 14 birds, 23 September to 18 December, plus 10-12 shot at Little Harbour, Shelburne County, in late December 1951). Winter records are: one shot in the Medway River, Queens County, in January 1953; four seen near Riverport, Lunenburg County, on 24 February 1974; and two at Annapolis Royal on 2 February 1975.

Remarks The Canvasback has long been recognized as the best table bird among wild ducks—this is commonly attributed to the fact that the succulent roots of wild celery *(Valisneria americana)* are prominent amongst its food.

To identify it, one should note its peculiar-looking, flattened head, its relatively long bill and its light, canvas-coloured upperparts.

It is found in sloughs and grain fields of the North American prairie regions and occurs here as a stray, well north of its winter range on the east coast of the United States.

Redhead

Aythya americana (Eyton)

Status Rare in summer, very rare in winter. Breeds. The first record of this species was of one shot near Sambro, Halifax County, late in the nineteenth century (Jones 1885). Piers (1894) noted another Redhead taken near Dartmouth in February 1894. Another four were recorded prior to 1960, but since then it has been seen more frequently, possibly partly as a result of releases of pen-reared birds in the eastern United States. Birds were also released by Cyrus S. Eaton in Lunenburg County. Redheads are found in small numbers in summer in the Amherst area and at Wallace Bay, Cumberland County. Transients have been seen elsewhere between 4 April and mid-May in spring (three reports, five birds) and between 23 September and 18 December in autumn (seven reports, 16 birds); these have been found widely, from Cape Breton Island to Yarmouth County. Winter records, other than the above-mentioned bird from Dartmouth, are all for Yarmouth County: a male shot in winter 1901 (Allen 1916), another killed in February 1901 (Piers' notes) and a bird seen in Argyle Sound on 22 February 1976.

Description *Length:* 45-58 cm. *Adult male:* Back and sides gray, finely barred with black; breasts, uppertail and undertail coverts black; head rounded and rufous. *Adult female:* Dull brown, paler beneath, with an indistinct light patch below and behind base of bill. *Both sexes:* Gray secondaries, and gray bill with an indistinct pale grayish white ring around the tip.

Breeding *Nest:* A cupped mound of old vegetation, usually in shallow water but sometimes on dry ground. *Eggs:* about 10; greenish to olive-gray; often lays in nests of other ducks. The first brood in Nova Scotia was seen in the Wallace Bay National Wildlife Area in 1978, and other broods have been found annually since. A brood was noted in the Amherst Point Bird Sanctuary in 1981.

Range Breeds in Alaska, and from northern Saskatchewan and central Manitoba, south to southern California, Kansas and Iowa, sporadically in eastern North America. Winters from British Columbia, the Great Lakes and New England to southern Mexico.

Remarks Highly prized as a table bird, the Redhead ranks close in this regard to its larger cousin, the Canvasback, to which it bears a general resemblance. Redheads of both sexes are darker, and the shapes of their necks and heads are quite different from those of the Canvasback: this bird's head is more rounded, giving it a puffy appearance; that of the Canvasback has a peculiar, flattened appearance.

Ring-necked Duck   PLATE 5

Aythya collaris (Donovan)

Status Fairly common transient, uncommon in summer, rare in winter. Breeds. There are indications that it was earlier extirpated as a breeding bird from Nova Scotia, as elsewhere in eastern North America (Palmer 1976). Blakiston and Bland (1857) stated that it was "rare" but "breeds inland." Gilpin (1880) thought that live birds kept by Andrew Downs were taken as young in the province, although Downs (1888) did not mention breeding. The first report in recent times was of a bird shot at Port Joli, Queens County, in 1935 (the wing sent to R.W. Tufts). It has become widely established as a breeding species since then. Birds generally arrive in early April (average 4 April, earliest 16 March) and are widespread by mid-April, especially in the Amherst region. Larger gatherings occur in September and October, and stragglers are regular on Christmas Bird Counts. Small numbers have been reported in January in Halifax, Hants and Lunenburg counties, and a few have survived the winters recently among hand-fed waterfowl on Sullivans Pond, Dartmouth.

Description *Length:* 40-45 cm. *Adult male:* Head, neck, chest, back and tail black, with purplish, greenish or bluish reflections on head; tiny white triangle patch on chin; narrow, inconspicuous chestnut ring around neck; wing patch gray; belly mostly white; a white spur extending up in front of the flanks provides a good field mark; flanks and lower belly finely marked with wavy black lines; bill blackish slate with band of white or bluish white across it. *Adult female:* Upperparts brown, darkest on crown and nape, many feathers bordered with lighter brown; cheeks and throat gray and brown, much paler on throat and at base of bill; narrow white eye ring; upper belly whitish gray; sides and lower belly grayish brown; bill slaty black with faint band of pale bluish gray near end.

Breeding *Nest:* On the ground, well concealed among grass and weeds, near water. Composed of coarse vegetable matter, with the usual lining of down. *Eggs:* 6-14, creamy buff. The first definite breeding record was supplied by Peters (1941), who found two broods near the New Brunswick border. Many broods and nests have been seen since.

Range Breeds across southern Canada from British Columbia to Newfoundland, and south to Massachusetts, Nebraska and northeastern California. Winters from British Columbia, the northern and central United States to the West Indies and Guatemala.

Remarks Hunters are likely to mistake this bird for the Greater Scaup ("blue-bill"), the males of the two species being quite similar in general appearance. The back of the male ring-neck is black, but that of the male scaup is gray. Furthermore, this bird's wing patch is gray and that of the scaup is white.

According to Kortright (1942) it is in no way a shy bird, but in my limited experience with that species, I have found it to be particularly wary and most difficult to approach during the breeding season (I have had little experience with it at other times of year).

It might more appropriately have been called by its popular name of "ring-billed" duck because the rings that cross the bills of both sexes are far more conspicuous than the obscure chestnut ring present around the neck of the male only.

It obtains its food mainly from the bottom by diving but unlike most diving ducks is able to spring vertically into the air when taking off, with its wings making a pleasing whistling sound.

Greater Scaup   PLATE 4

Aythya marila (Linnaeus)

Status Fairly common transient, uncommon in winter. Autumn arrivals are generally first reported in October (average 18 October, earliest 16 September). It may remain abundant until the end of the year, when large flocks are sometimes seen during Christmas Bird Counts (1500 were seen on 16 December 1973 off Cape Sable Island). In winter it occurs in reduced numbers along the coast from Yarmouth to Sydney in waters where food is available. The spring migration begins along the Eastern Shore and elsewhere during February and reaches its peak during March or early April. Last spring sightings generally occur in late April (average 21 April, latest 8 May). The foregoing extreme dates probably represent under-reporting of the species, which may at times occur well offshore in larger bays.

Description *Length:* 43-53 cm. *Adult male:* Head, neck, breast, rump, tail and tail coverts black, the head with greenish reflections; back, sides and belly white; back and sides finely marked with wavy black lines; wing patch white; bill dull blue with black tip; legs dark gray. *Females:* Area around base of bill white; head, neck, breast and back dark brown; sides grayish brown; wing patch and belly white; legs dark gray; bill dull bluish gray with black tip.

Range Breeds in Alaska, northwestern Canada, around Hudson Bay and James Bay, the Magdalen Islands, Anticosti Island and Newfoundland. Winters from the Aleutian Islands, the Great Lakes and the coasts of southern Canada as far south as the Gulf Coast. It also occurs in the Old World.

Remarks Among duck-hunters this bird is popularly known as a "blue-bill" or "greater blue-bill." Its proper name is probably derived from the bird's infrequent call, *scaup scaup*. It is a particularly hardy duck, capable of withstanding severe cold and rough weather in winter along the coast where it "rafts" in the vicinity of its feeding grounds.

If it is shot over water, the bird is seldom retrieved by hunters unless killed or severely wounded because it swims quickly underwater and keeps most of its head below water when it does rise to the surface.

There is a report that a Greater Scaup followed by a brood was seen during summer 1968 in the Red River Lakes area of Inverness County, where the elevation is about 425 m. This was reported at Cape Breton Highlands National Park headquarters by a visiting tourist who seemed to know his birds (W. Neily).

Lesser Scaup

Aythya affinis (Eyton)

Status Uncommon transient, very rare in winter. Gilpin (1880) referred to a mounted specimen without giving details, and Piers (notes) examined a bird collected on 18 February 1898. Downs (1888) mentioned a very doubtful "brood of young ones at Grand Lake." It was thought, perhaps more reliably, to be uncommon on Sable Island in winter at the turn of the century (McLaren 1981a). A specimen taken on 27 October 1917 near Truro is in the Nova Scotia Museum. In more recent years, it has been occasional in autumn, the earliest on 15 September 1944, with most records from October and November, and a few during Christmas Bird Counts from Cape Breton Island to Lunenburg County. A group of seven at Pictou on 16 January 1975 was well studied by Stuart Tingley, and another was reported at Lingan, Cape Breton County, on 18 January 1980 by Hedley Hopkins. There have been some 18 reports of about 45 birds in spring, between 23 March and 31 May.

Description *Length:* 38-46 cm. *All plumages:* Similar in general appearance to the Greater Scaup, but the area of white in the wing of this bird is more restricted than in that of its larger relative and does not extend far onto the primaries. *Adult male:* The head shows mainly purplish reflections instead of the mainly green ones of the Greater Scaup.

Range Breeds from Alaska to the west coast of Hudson Bay, south to southern British Columbia, northern Wyoming and North Dakota, casually further south and east. Winters from southern British Columbia, the Great Lakes and New England, south to Mexico, the Gulf States and the West Indies.

Remarks The "little blue-bill," as this duck is known to some, is a more inland species than the Greater Scaup. It is exclusively a North American species with a wide distribution. Because it is not always readily identified, some supposed records may be in error. On the other hand, it may be more regular than the records suggest. In all plumages, the crown of this bird is more peaked, differing from the more rounded head of the Greater Scaup.

Common Eider   PLATE 7

Somateria mollissima (Linnaeus)

Status Common transient, fairly common in summer. Breeds. Nests on numerous islands along the coast. Winters in large numbers, estimates of up to 1500 having been recorded on some Christmas Bird Counts. In addition, many large flocks pass by in spring, when enormous "rafts" may be seen generally between mid-March and mid-April. Large fall movements are generally from late September to mid-October.

Description *Length:* 56-66 cm. *Adult male:* Cheek, throat, neck, back and breast all white; crown, flanks, belly, centre of rump, uppertail and undertail coverts black; patch on either side of rump white; black crown divided posteriorly by a white median line; green on back and sides of head; legs, feet and bill greenish yellow; frontal processes from base of bill yellowish green. *Adult female:* Mostly brown, barred with black; belly sooty brown; legs, feet and bill greenish gray.

Breeding *Nest:* On the ground, composed of grass and vegetable debris, lined with down from the bird's breast. Sometimes it is well concealed but at other times it is in the open. Usually in colonies of various sizes and, in the writer's experience, always on islands. *Eggs:* 4-6, usually 5; greenish olive.

Range Breeds from Alaska, the Canadian Arctic islands and Greenland, south to James Bay and along the Atlantic coast to Maine; also widely distributed in northern parts of the Old World. Winters along coast in the southern parts of its breeding range and somewhat further south.

Remarks Eiders are strong, heavily built ducks that live along our coasts throughout the year. Seeming to scorn the protection afforded by inland bays and harbours, they resort in fall and winter to the waters off the outer islands and exposed headlands, where they feed by diving. Although their food is made up largely of marine animal life, they are, nevertheless, highly esteemed as a table bird by the shore-hunters who endure severe hardships in winter in order to shoot what they call "sea ducks."

Over water, they usually fly low and in long line-formation with slow wing-beats. When undertaking extended flight overland, as in migration, they fly high and often form an uneven semicircle, the front ranks massed with long wavering lines trailing at the ends. Such flocks pass over Wolfville with marked regularity during October, coming from Minas Basin and taking a southwesterly course, at heights of about 200 m.

Only at nesting time are they likely to be seen about the inshore islands where they come to rear their young. Soon after the young are strong enough, they are led to the outer shoals. At such times it is not unusual to see one or more females followed by a group of young made up of several broods, suggesting that the care and responsibility for their safety is being shared.

Two subspecies occur here seasonally and are common. *Somateria mollissima borealis,* the more northern subspecies, arrives along our coast in late autumn, lingering until at least late March. The race that breeds and summers here is *Somateria mollissima dresseri,* but stragglers probably remain throughout the winter and mingle with those of their northern relatives. The frontal processes of the bill are pointed at the inner ends in *S. m. borealis* and rounded in *S. m. dresseri.*

Common Eiders courting female

King Eider   PLATE 7

Somateria spectabilis (Linnaeus)

Status Rare in winter, very rare in summer. Its occurrence was first noted by Jones (1868), who recorded a specimen taken in March 1863. Later nineteenth-century accounts added a few more specimens. About a dozen more were recorded prior to 1960, and since then there have been about 21 reports of 26 individuals. These have occurred rather evenly throughout the winter, between 3 October and 14 March, except for two evident non-breeders off Brier Island on 23 July 1971 (E.L. Mills) and a drake in courtship display in a group of Common Eiders off Seal Island on 21 May 1972 (B.K. Doane et al.). According to shore-hunters, it may be more common in winter than our records suggest.

Description *Length:* 53-60 cm. *Adult male:* Neck, shoulders and breast white; back and belly black; top of head bluish gray; cheeks greenish white; bill orange to red; large yellow-orange shield extending from bill onto forehead; legs and feet yellowish orange. *Adult female:* Similar to Common Eider but feathers on side of bill do not reach to nostril.

Range Breeds in the Canadian Arctic, Greenland, Alaska and Siberia. On the Atlantic coast, it winters south to Massachusetts but rarely beyond.

Remarks Gunners who regularly pursue the offshore diving ducks in winter occasionally take this species from flocks of Common Eiders, but as a rule King Eiders range further offshore. To the hunters along the Southwestern Shore it is known as the "comb duck" because of the strange formation of its bill. Even at long distances, the adult male of this eider can be distinguished from adult male Common Eiders by the larger amount of black on its wings and back.

Labrador Duck

Camptorhynchus labradorius (Gmelin)

Status Extinct. Formerly a regular visitor along our coast in winter. According to Audubon (1839), Professor McCulloch of Pictou procured several in his neighbourhood. Later, a male and female from the McCulloch collection were said to have been presented to the Dalhousie University Museum (Downs 1886), where they were on display for many years. According to Lloyd (1920), who examined both specimens, the female was an American Scoter, but whether it had been originally misidentified or subsequently exchanged is not known. The male, still the property of Dalhousie University, is in the National Museum of Canada, having been loaned to that institution in 1968 as the only extant specimen of the species in Canada. Other specimens from around Halifax are rather confusingly discussed by Gilpin (1880, 1882b), Jones (1885), Downs (1886, 1888) and Dutcher (1891, 1894). According to McLaren (1985) it seems that only two birds (not the three or four inferred by Gilpin 1880) were actually collected: one purchased in the Halifax market in 1852 that ended up in the Brewster Collection at Cambridge, Massachusetts, and another taken at about the same time and sent to a Colonel Drummond in Scotland.

Remarks Very little is known of the life history of this bird, and the causes that led to its extinction are not understood. Possibly it was a colonial nesting species and therefore particularly vulnerable. Perhaps never abundant, the colonies may have been raided systematically year after year by natives and fishermen who took the eggs for food, thus seriously interfering with normal reproduction. It is generally believed that its extinction was not the result of overshooting. The last definite record is on 12 December 1878, when one was shot at Elmira, New York.

Harlequin Duck   PLATE 6

Histrionicus histrionicus (Linnaeus)

Status Rare winter resident. Although widely distributed in small numbers from the lower Bay of Fundy around the coast to Cape Breton Island, its occurrence has been most regular at a few localities such as Brier Island; Port Hebert, Shelburne County; near Broad Cove, Lunenburg County; and Cranberry Head, Yarmouth County. The earliest fall occurrence was on 22 September and the latest in spring was on 16 May.

Description *Length:* 38-45 cm. *Male:* Mainly dark bluish gray (looks black at a distance), with contrasting spots and narrow patches of white, and rich chestnut flanks. *Females:* Dusky brown, with three round white spots on the side of the head; no white in the wing.

Range Breeds in central Quebec, Labrador, southern Baffin Island, Greenland and Iceland; in western North America from Alaska south, in the mountains, to central California. Also breeds in Siberia. In North America, winters on both coasts south to New York State and California.

Remarks Known widely as "lords and ladies," a name appropriately bestowed in an attempt to describe the elegance of the drake, these are perhaps the most beautiful of the sea ducks. Another local name is "rock duck," inspired by the bird's habit of feeding on inshore waters off rocky coastlines.

Oldsquaw   PLATE 6

Clangula hyemalis (Linnaeus)

Status Common in winter, very rare in summer. Formerly very common, its numbers have shown a marked decrease from those of a few decades ago. It appears along the coast in October (average 19 October, earliest 5 October). Estimates of over 200 have been made on Christmas Bird Counts around the province, but large numbers are not generally seen again until late March or early April. The last are generally seen in late April or early May (average 1 May, latest 6 June). Non-breeding stragglers sometimes have been reported in July and August.

Description *Length:* (male) 53-55 cm; (female) 41-43 cm. *Male in winter:* Sides and front of head pale grayish brown; a dark brown patch covering cheek and upper neck on each side; crown, neck, belly and sides white; breast and a line extending along back dark brown; tail pointed, central feathers black and much elongated; bill gray, with a pale yellow-orange or pink band across end. *Male in summer:* Head, neck, breast and upperparts dark brown; belly, flanks and mask-like face patch white; bill as in winter. *Female in winter:* Dark brown above; sides of head and neck white, with brown crown

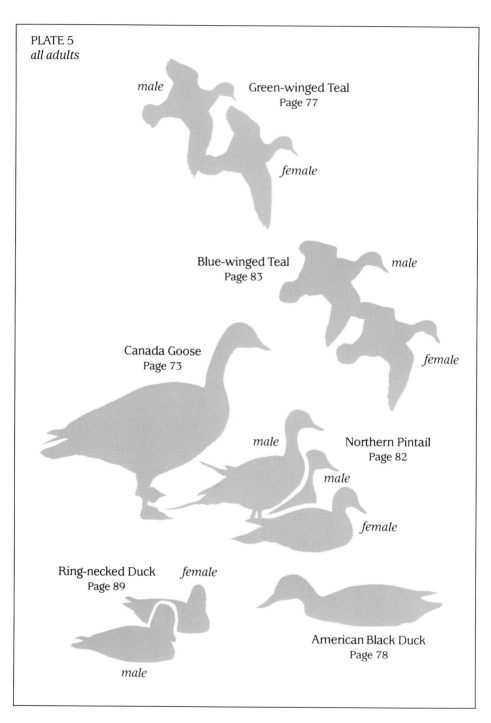

PLATE 5
all adults

male   Green-winged Teal
         Page 77

         female

Blue-winged Teal   *male*
Page 83

                   female

Canada Goose
Page 73

        male   Northern Pintail
                 Page 82

                 male

                 female

Ring-necked Duck   *female*
Page 89

                   American Black Duck
                   Page 78

        male

96

Roger Tory Peterson

PLATE 6
all adults

Oldsquaw
Page 95

female, winter

female

male, winter

male

Red-breasted Merganser
Page 106

male

female

male

Common Merganser
Page 104

female

Common Goldeneye
Page 100

female

Harlequin Duck
Page 95

male

and upper neck patches; breast gray; belly white; tail pointed but lacking the long feathers of the male. *Female in summer:* Similar to winter female but sides of head and throat darker; feathers on upperparts margined with light brown.

Range Breeds in the arctic and subarctic regions of North America, Europe and Asia. In North America, winters south to the Great Lakes and along the coasts to central California and South Carolina, and irregularly further south.

Remarks The Oldsquaw, also known as the "cockawee," is a diving duck still common along our shores in winter. It seems to be as much at home along the bleak, precipitous and rockbound coastlines as along sheltered inshore waters protected by headlands, but it will not normally be found frequenting muddy tidal waters such as those of Minas Basin. It is an expert diver and a strong and speedy underwater swimmer. Hunters have learned it is useless to pursue one that has fallen slightly wounded and dives, because when it does surface, as it must do for air, only its bill is exposed momentarily, too briefly for the hunter to see it in the first place, much less react. Its food is marine animals obtained sometimes at considerable depths— numbers of these birds have been caught and drowned in gill nets at depths of 50 m or more.

It has a wide range of calls. Its Latin name, *Clangula hyemalis,* means "noisy winter duck," and is quite appropriate.

Black Scoter   PLATE 7

Melanitta nigra (Linnaeus)

Status Common transient, uncommon in winter, rare in summer. All three scoters tend to migrate well offshore, and times of arrival and departure are often not discerned. The southward flight of the Black Scoter may be earlier than those of the other two scoters; several flocks were observed passing Cape Sable during 8-15 August 1968 (B.F. Smith). However, the peak of movement is in October. Estimates of 100-200 birds come from some Christmas Bird Counts but generally few are reported during winter. There is a distinct movement in April and early May, and the latest reported in recent years were 20 at Pictou on 20 May 1967. A later bird was taken on Trout Lake, Annapolis County, on 22 May 1938. Several at Aspy Bay, Victoria County, on 19 August 1941 (Godfrey 1959b) were probably summering non-breeders.

Description *Length:* 43-53 cm. *All plumages:* No white on wing. *Adult male:* Solid coal black with base of bill enlarged and coloured bright yellow-orange. *Adult female:* Dark brown, paler on abdomen; sharply defined, pale grayish brown patch covering cheeks, throat and sides of upper neck, contrasting with the dark brown cap and back of neck.

Range In North America, breeds from Alaska locally to Newfoundland. Winters on the Atlantic coast from Newfoundland to Florida, and on the Pacific coast from the Aleutian Islands to California. Another subspecies is found in Europe and Asia.

Remarks This species is the least abundant of the three scoters. It is commonly known to hunters by the names "black coot" and "butter-nose coot"—the former because of the colour of its plumage and the latter because of the strange butter-coloured protuberance at the base of the male's bill. It takes off from water more abruptly than most other "diving ducks," a feature which is helpful in field identification.

Surf Scoter   PLATE 7

Melanitta perspicillata (Linnaeus)

Status Common transient, fairly common in winter, rare in summer. The southward flight may begin in August but larger numbers are seen in late September and October. Estimates of 50-100 birds or more have been made on Christmas Bird Counts on the Eastern Shore. The spring flight appears to peak during May, but summer occurrences, generally of immature-plumaged birds, are regularly reported. In winter, it is rarely found on fresh water, usually near the coast.

Description *Length:* 45-50 cm. *All plumages:* No white on wing. *Adult male:* An all-black scoter with greatly enlarged and highly coloured bill; two sharply defined white patches, one on the forehead and the other on the nape. *Adult female and immature:* Whitish gray patches at base of bill and behind eye; upperparts dark brown; underparts lighter brown; belly grayish white, more or less mottled with brown.

Range Breeds from Alaska and central British Columbia to the Ungava Peninsula. Winters on the Atlantic coast from Newfoundland to Florida, and on the Pacific coast from the Aleutian Islands to Baja California.

Remarks The bird's name is derived from its habit of diving through breaking surf when feeding near the shore in rough weather. This is obviously done to avoid being thrown about by the tumbling waters which follow the wave crests when they break. About 90 percent of its food consists of various forms of marine animal life, and it has a low rating as a table bird.

The three scoters are commonly but erroneously called "coots," and because of the black and white head of the drake, the Surf Scoter is commonly called the "skunk-head coot."

White-winged Scoter   PLATE 7

Melanitta fusca (Linnaeus)

Status Common transient, fairly common in winter, uncommon in summer. The main fall movement occurs in October and November, and estimates of 100-300 birds are regular on Christmas Bird Counts around the province. Large numbers are seen at times in later winter, and major northward movements occur in late March or early April. A congregation of many thousands on the Northumberland Strait ferry route on 18 June 1934 was said by a ship's officer to have been unique during his many years of service. They are reported more regularly during summer than the other two scoters and are occasionally seen on fresh water.

Description *Length:* 50-58 cm. *Adult male:* Mostly black; small white spot under eye; white wing patch, conspicuous in flight; bill orange with prominent black enlargement at base. *Adult female and immature:* Grayish brown above, lighter below; light grayish brown patches at base of bill and behind eye; white patch on wing.

Range Breeds from Alaska to the Ungava Peninsula and Newfoundland, south to North Dakota in the interior. Winters on the Atlantic coast from Newfoundland to South Carolina, and on the Pacific coast from the Aleutian Islands to Baja California.

Remarks This is the largest and most plentiful of the three North American scoters, and the only one with a white patch on the wing.
   Kortright (1942) states that the grinding power of its gizzard is almost unbelievable. Oysters and other molluscs are swallowed whole and many shells that would require a hard blow of a hammer to break are readily ground and chemically disintegrated in its gizzard. The gullet of one bird, collected over an oyster bed, contained no less than 10 oysters, one measuring over 5 cm in length. The remains of 46 oysters were found in the gizzard of another.

Common Goldeneye   PLATE 6

Bucephala clangula (Linnaeus)

Status Common transient, fairly common in winter, uncommon and local in summer. Breeds. By late October a heavy influx of birds from northern breeding grounds augments our sparse summer population. Estimates of 100-500 birds are regular on Christmas Bird Counts along the Atlantic coast. Large numbers remain throughout the winter, when they favour broad shallow bays and inlets, particularly along the Southwestern Shore where food is more readily available. At that season it is not unusual to find them in small numbers also along the lower reaches of swift-flowing streams that remain open. Major spring movements are evident in March and early April. Only on Cape Breton Island do some numbers remain to breed.

Description *Length:* 45-66 cm. *Adult male:* Head dark green with circular white patch between eye and bill; neck, breast, much of wing coverts, wing patch and belly white; rest of plumage black; bill dark gray; eye golden yellow; legs and feet orange-yellow. *Adult female:* Head brown; foreneck white, tinged with gray; breast, back and sides ashy gray; wing coverts tipped with white; wing patch and belly white.

Breeding *Nest:* In a hollow tree or stump, or manmade box, sometimes at great heights, and usually near water in wooded areas. *Eggs:* 6-12 or more; pale bluish green, unlike those of any other duck except Barrow's Goldeneye. During 1961-67 the Maritime Nest Records Scheme listed 37 breeding records: 31 of broods of varying sizes and ages, and 6 of nests with eggs located in manmade nest-boxes. Godfrey (1958) reports having seen 11 broods from 15 June to 3 August 1954. All of the above breeding records were on Cape Breton Island; although goldeneyes have not been found breeding on the mainland, they may do so.

Range Breeds from Alaska, across the wooded parts of northern Canada to Newfoundland, and south to northern Washington, northern North Dakota, northern New York State and Maine. Winters from the southern limits of its breeding range to the Gulf States. Occurs also in the Old World.

Remarks The goldeneye has a low rating as a table bird, particularly when shot about fresh water in winter, no doubt the result of the food they take at that season. One shot by Cyril Coldwell in winter on the Gaspereau River had recently devoured nine eels, one about 20 cm long.

The name "whistler," by which it is known to many duck-hunters, is appropriate because its fast-moving wings produce a vibrant, sweet, whistling note.

Goldeneye ducklings, like young Wood Ducks, reach the ground or water by jumping from their nests high up in hollow trees. They are about two days old before they attempt this feat. It appears that the location of the nest is determined by the availability of a suitable cavity. It may be a metre from the ground or water, or high up. Brewster (1909a) examined a nest with a rough-edged entrance so narrow that it would barely admit his flattened hand, and Bent (1925) says the bird will desert its nest if the eggs are handled by humans.

Barrow's Goldeneye

Bucephala islandica (Gmelin)

Status Rare in winter. As Jones (1885) noted, the two goldeneyes were probably not distinguished in Nova Scotia before the discussion of their differences by Gilpin (1880). These and other nineteenth-century sources considered Barrow's Goldeneye as rare. Prior to 1960 very few were reported. Since then, there have been some 45 records involving about 110 individuals, all between 2 November at earliest and 20

April at latest (there are October and late-April records from earlier years). They have been particularly regular at the head of Bedford Basin near Halifax, at Sydney and in Pugwash Harbour, Cumberland County.

Description *Length:* 50-58 cm. *Adult male:* Very similar to the Common Goldeneye but head has a purple rather than green gloss, and the white patch in front of eye is crescent-shaped instead of circular. *Adult female and immatures:* In life it is difficult to distinguish females and immatures of this species from those of the Common Goldeneye, but the rounder, darker heads of the Barrow's females and, in late winter and spring, their completely yellow bills, are good field marks. Birds in the hand can be distinguished by a comparison of their respective bills, that of Barrow's Goldeneye being narrower and its "nail" smaller.

Range Breeds in western and eastern parts of North America; from Alaska and the Yukon, south to Washington State, and southwestern Alberta; in northeastern Quebec and Labrador; also in southern Greenland and Iceland. On the Atlantic coast it winters from the Gulf of St. Lawrence to New York State but rarely further south.

Remarks Two Barrow's Goldeneyes shot on 3 January 1933 were among three taken from a small flock of goldeneyes. The third bird was a drake Common Goldeneye. Because Barrow's Goldeneyes sometimes mingle with their more common relatives, to which they bear a marked resemblance, and because so few hunters distinguish one species from the other when shot, it may be that this species occurs here in winter more frequently than the relatively few records indicate.

Bufflehead   PLATE 4

Bucephala albeola (Linnaeus)

Status Fairly common transient, uncommon in winter. Autumn migrants generally appear in the second half of October (average 23 October, earliest 15 October). Estimates of up to 100 birds have been made on Christmas Bird Counts on the Atlantic coast, but larger numbers have been seen around the Bay of Fundy (over 200 birds on several counts from Digby). It remains through winter in diminished numbers about bays and inlets wherever feeding conditions are favourable. There is a buildup of numbers in late March to mid-April and a few may linger into May (average of last sightings 4 May, latest 16 May).

Description *Length:* 30-37 cm. *Adult male:* Head dark green with purple or bronze iridescence, with a large triangular white patch extending from below and behind the eye up over top and back of head; back and primaries black; tail gray; rest of plumage white; Bill lead-coloured, yellowish gray along edge of upper mandible; legs and feet pinkish gray. *Adult female:* Sooty brown with white patch on cheeks and on wings; belly white; bill and legs similar to those of male.

Range Breeds from central Alaska, the southern Mackenzie Valley and northwestern Ontario, south to northern Washington, northern Montana, southern Saskatchewan, southern Manitoba and locally in southern Ontario. Winters from Alaska, the Great Lakes and Newfoundland, south to the Gulf States and California.

Remarks Among the rather large group known as "diving ducks," this drake is one of the most handsome. Its name is derived from its disproportionately large head, which provides an excellent field mark. Most diving ducks, such as eiders, scoters and Oldsquaws, are very slow to take wing, having to patter over the surface for a considerable distance before leaving the water, but this bird rises directly and quickly. It is one of the few ducks that nest in holes in trees; the female is so small she is able to pass through the entrance of an unoccupied flicker nest. When tree sites are not available, Buffleheads have been known to nest in sandbanks, in the manner of kingfishers.

Hooded Merganser

Lophodytes cucullatus (Linnaeus)

Status Uncommon transient, rare in summer, very rare in winter. Breeds. It was listed as rare in the nineteenth century by Blakiston and Bland (1857) and Jones (1885), the latter referring to a bird taken at Lawrencetown, Halifax County, in November 1884. The next specimen was taken at Petpeswick, Halifax County, on 21 March 1907, and there were only 17 more records between that year and 1960. It has become more regular since. It prefers freshwater ponds and still waters until freeze-up, after which the few that remain favour shoal waters of bays and inlets, mostly along more southern coasts. Evident fall migrants generally appear first in September (average 14 September, earliest 25 August), and numbers build up in October. A few are recorded annually on Christmas Bird Counts and occasionally through the winter. There is a less pronounced migration in spring, with new birds usually appearing in late March or early April (average 2 April, earliest 15 March) and remaining in non-breeding areas into May (average 10 May, latest 16 May). A few remain to nest, largely in the southwestern end of the province.

Description *Length:* 40-48 cm. *Adult male:* Prominent crest, front of which is black, remainder white narrowly edged with black; rest of upperparts black to very dark gray, lighter on tail; underparts white, with black band extending from back and coming to a point on sides of breast; sides cinnamon-brown, with fine transverse black barring. *Adult female:* Upperparts dark brown; throat white; head, neck and upper breast grayish brown; crest rufous.

Breeding *Nest:* In a hollow tree, stump or manmade nest-box, usually near water, height from the ground determined by available nest site. Nest is lined with dry vegetable debris mixed with down from the bird's breast. *Eggs:* 8-16; buffy white. The first evidence of breeding in Nova Scotia was given by Richard Cain and William

Woodworth (in the employ of the Provincial Department of Lands and Forests at the time) who encountered a female and brood of four on 29 August 1962 on the Shelburne River near the border of Queens County; one of the young was collected. Other broods have been recorded since in the southwestern end of the province. The first nest for Nova Scotia, reported by Norman D. Phinney, was about 3 km from the headquarters of Kejimkujik National Park. The pair was first seen near his cottage on 29 April 1968 at a nest-box erected near the water's edge to attract Wood Ducks. Presumably the same pair nested in this box in 1969 and 1970, and was successful every year, with broods of 8-12 young. When the female returned to her nest and saw Mr. Phinney sitting on his verandah at close range, she would circle cautiously several times before entering the nest-box. The male was seldom seen and only during the early part of the season.

Range Breeds from extreme southern Alaska to Oregon and from Manitoba to Nova Scotia and the lower Mississippi Valley. Winters from as far north as open fresh water can be found, south to the Gulf States, Mexico and Cuba.

Remarks Native to North America, it is one of the most beautiful of our waterfowl. For this distinction, the full-plumage drake is in close competition with the drake of the Wood Duck, and the two species may be found in close association in summer. When erected, the conspicuous, fan-like crest of the drake is its outstanding adornment and serves as an excellent field mark, but when this crest is depressed or laid back, as is often the case, identification in life is surprisingly more difficult.

When wounded it is seldom retrieved because of its skill in hiding along the shoreline when resurfacing for air. Unlike the other two mergansers, this bird rises quickly and is particularly swift in flight. I flushed a flock of about 25 from Lumsdens Lake, Kings County, in October 1966 and was impressed with how quickly they gained altitude.

A specimen in the hand can be readily distinguished from other kinds of ducks by noting its "saw-bill," typical of all mergansers, and from the other two mergansers by its smaller size and general appearance.

Common Merganser   PLATE 6

Mergus merganser Linnaeus

Status Common transient, uncommon in winter and summer. Breeds. It arrives on fresh water in numbers in late March or early April, when the ice breaks up. Small numbers remain to breed throughout the province. This summer population is augmented by transients in fall and early winter, particularly on the Bay of Fundy, the North Shore and on Cape Breton Island, with fewer on the South Shore. In the depth of winter it can be found on swift-running streams which remain open, where it has been said to prey heavily on eels.

Description *Length:* 53-68 cm. *All plumages:* Slender, toothed bills like other mergansers. *Adult male:* Head and upper neck dark glossy green; back black; rump and tail gray; underparts white, tinged with salmon pink; lower neck white; bill and feet red. *Adult female:* Head cinnamon-brown with prominent crest; throat white; upperparts grayish blue; underparts creamy white; bill and feet duller red than in spring male. Males in midsummer and early autumn resemble females.

Breeding *Nest:* In natural cavities in trees or on the ground, well concealed by vegetation; usually near water. *Eggs:* 6-10; creamy white. A nest found on a small island on the Northumberland Strait held six eggs on 28 May 1929. It was well concealed under the low branch of a spruce growing close to the edge of the bank. When disturbed, the sitting female flew directly to join her mate who was near the edge of the tidal water, about 30 m from the nest site. A nest found by Anthony J. Erskine on 3 June 1961 on the Margaree River, Inverness County, contained 10 eggs and was located in an open-top stump, about 3 m up. Many broods have been seen on inland waters, usually accompanied only by the female, though sometimes by both parents. Eight seen on open water near the head of Lumsdens Lake, Kings County, on 18 February 1945 were divided into four well-segregated pairs whose manner strongly indicated they were already mated at this early date.

Range Breeds from central Alaska, the southern Mackenzie Valley, central Quebec, and Newfoundland to the northern and southwestern United States. Winters from southern Canada to northern Mexico. It is also found in Europe and Asia.

Remarks Kortright (1942) says the male deserts his mate when she begins to incubate, leaving the family responsibilities entirely to her. Although this trait is common among many duck species including, in my experience, the Red-breasted Merganser, it is not always true of this bird. On at least two occasions I have seen the drake in attendance: once while the female was incubating (as cited above) and once on a small stream near Antigonish when both birds were with the brood.

The food of mergansers is largely small or medium-sized fishes which they capture underwater by swift pursuit. Many anglers and commercial fishermen have complained that these birds are highly destructive to fishes of economic value, but these birds take those kinds of fishes that are most readily captured. Along with the trout and small salmon they are accused of destroying, such fishes include perch, minnows, eels and other so-called "coarse" fishes that are enemies of trout and salmon. By destroying these predators which are of no economic value, the mergansers undoubtedly assist the valuable species. It is reasonable to assert that if these birds were seriously destructive, trout would have been long extinct because mergansers have been preying on fish since time immemorial. The fact that good trout can still be found in the hinterlands provides additional proof that the birds are not responsible for the overfishing of trout, because they have ready access to such places.

As already stated, the plumage of the male in summer and early autumn is similar to that of the female, both having cinnamon-brown heads with crests. By late October some drakes have begun to acquire their breeding plumage, but the date when this molt is complete varies considerably with individuals. For instance, on 26 October

1950 one shot at Black River, Kings County, had a salmon-pink breast but the head was merely speckled with brown and green; on 13 November 1951 three males seen in the same waters had bright green heads; but on 20 December 1943, one taken near Wolfville, perhaps an immature, still had a brown, crested head, though its breast was pink; on 29 December 1942, four seen at Black River were all in full breeding plumage. The delicate salmon-pink breast of the adult male fades to white soon after death.

Among hunters the Common and the Red-breasted Merganser are often known as "shell-drakes" or "shell-ducks."

Red-breasted Merganser   PLATE 6

Mergus serrator Linnaeus

Status Common transient, fairly common in summer and winter. Breeds. This is one of the most common ducks of our coastal waters and estuaries in autumn, winter and spring. During summer it is regular on coastal ponds and inland waters, particularly on Cape Breton Island.

Description *Length:* 50-63 cm. *Adult male:* Head black with strong green gloss and conspicuous crest; neck white; back black; breast pale cinnamon-brown, heavily mottled and streaked with black; sides white, finely barred with gray; belly creamy white; bill and feet red. *Adult female:* Head and crest dark cinnamon-brown fading to white on throat, but contrasting less sharply than in Common Merganser; upperparts bluish gray; underparts creamy white; bill and feet dull red. *Adults in autumn and immatures*: Resemble the female as above.

Breeding *Nest:* Always on the ground, near water and well hidden among protective vegetation. Composed of vegetable debris and lined profusely with down plucked from the parent's breast. When the female leaves the nest, the eggs are usually well covered with down as a protective measure against predators. *Eggs:* 8-10 or more; creamy buff. Anthony J. Erskine found a nest containing 10 eggs near Margaree Forks, Inverness County, on 6 June 1961, and Townsend (1922) found a pair nesting in July 1921 near the small pond on Isle Haute, a high, wooded island in the Bay of Fundy. During 4-28 July 1954, Godfrey (1958) counted 10 broods in various parts of Cape Breton Island. Two mated pairs were seen on Trout Lake, Annapolis County, on 23 May 1923, and later in June both females were seen there followed by their respective broods.

Range Breeds from northern Alaska, the Mackenzie Delta and northern Baffin Island, south to northern British Columbia, Alberta, southern Manitoba and the northern tier of the eastern United States. Winters from southern Alaska, the Great Lakes and Newfoundland south through the United States. It also occurs in Greenland, Europe and Asia.

Remarks Slightly smaller than the Common Merganser. Specimens of each can be readily distinguished in all plumages, sexes and ages by bill examination: the nostril of the Common Merganser is placed half way between the eye and the tip of its bill, but the Red-breasted Merganser's nostril is considerably nearer the eye.

On 6 August 1933 a mother was seen at Trout Lake, Annapolis County, escorting her brood. The youngsters were about a week or ten days old. Half flying and half swimming, they pattered over the surface at such speed that two able paddlers in a canoe were unable to overtake them.

Townsend states that both parents care for the young (Bent 1923). In my experience with this species, this is not the case. During 1923-49, I observed one to three pairs of these birds during May and June each year from my cabin on Trout Lake. Early in May the drakes were in company with their mates daily. Then, abruptly, the males disappeared and from then on the females were alone or, in due course, alone with their broods. A flock of 25-30 drakes of this species in full breeding regalia was seen off the Bay of Fundy shore at Margaretsville, Annapolis County, on 24 May 1931; these were obviously birds free of any domestic responsibilities.

The remarks concerning the feeding habits of the Common Merganser are equally applicable to this species.

Ruddy Duck

Oxyura jamaicensis (Gmelin)

Status Uncommon transient, rare and local in summer, very rare in winter. Breeds. The status of this species has changed during the past century. According to Jones (1885) it was "formerly rare, but in late years somewhat common," and Downs (1888) states that "a good many are shot in fall migration." Although it remained largely a rare fall transient in subsequent years, in the 1970s it was increasingly reported earlier in late summer and fall at the Amherst Point Bird Sanctuary, and nesting began there in 1978. Birds on Sable Island on 25 June 1971 and in Cape Breton County on 4 August 1979 and 14 August 1982 were unusual. Away from the Amherst region, it usually first appears in October (average 29 October, earliest 5 October) and can be more common in November. Winter stragglers were on Cape Sable Island on 5 January 1909 (Allen 1916), in Yarmouth Harbour on 12 January 1969, and in Dartmouth from mid-November 1979 to mid-February 1980. There are few spring reports, the earliest on 4 April 1975 on Sable Island, and others scattered in April and May.

Description *Length:* 36-42 cm. *Adult male in summer:* Upperparts, including neck, rich rusty brown; top of head black; cheeks and chin white; underparts silvery white; bill sky-blue. *Male in winter:* Mostly brownish gray with white cheeks; darker gray on crown. *Female:* Resembles male in winter plumage but has dark brownish gray stripe across cheek.

Breeding *Nest:* Usually in dense cattails on a floating platform; some down added. *Eggs:* 5-15; dull white, stained. The first report of breeding in Nova Scotia came when

Stuart Tingley and Stephen Young photographed a duck with four downy young on 18 July 1979 at Amherst Point Bird Sanctuary. Broods have occurred there annually since but not elsewhere (P. Barkhouse, Canadian Wildlife Service). Concerning the eggs laid by this bird, Kortright (1942) states: "The female, though one of the smallest of the ducks, weighing about one pound, lays enormous eggs, the average size of which is 2.45 by 1.79 inches. The Mallard and Canvasback, ducks three times the size of the little Ruddy Duck, lay substantially smaller eggs. A clutch of 14 eggs of the Ruddy Duck weighs approximately three pounds, or about three times as much as the little mother herself."

Range An exclusively North American species, breeding from Alaska, the southeastern Mackenzie Valley and western Ontario, south to southern California, Texas and Louisiana, with scattered or sporadic breeding in the east.

Remarks When seen swimming, this comical-looking, plump little duck can be identified by its characteristically upturned tail. When danger threatens it usually resorts to diving, but when hard pressed it takes off with apparent difficulty, pattering along over the surface for some distance and using legs as well as wings in its struggle to become airborne. In full flight its wing-beats are rapid. It occurs more frequently on fresh water and along the coast will usually be found in sheltered inlets with shoal water.

Order FALCONIFORMES

Family Cathartidae

Black Vulture

Coragyps atratus (Bechstein)

Status Four records. One killed at Pugwash, Cumberland County, on 12 January 1896 was sent to taxidermist T.J. Egan, in Halifax where it was examined by Piers (1897). Another killed at Owl's Head, Halifax County, on 1 December 1918 was sent to taxidermist L.A. Purcell, in Dartmouth (Piers' notes). The third was seen at Linacy, Pictou County, on 22 July 1936 by Alban Brown, who became familiar with this species and the following one when he lived in Florida before coming to Nova Scotia. The fourth was well studied by Betty June and Sidney Smith at Cape Sable one autumn in the early sixties.

Remarks The Black Vulture is similar in appearance to the somewhat larger Turkey Vulture, but distinguished by its black (instead of red) head and neck, its squarish tail and the lighter colour near the ends of its wings, conspicuous in flight.
    The bird has a more southern range in the United States, breeding north to New Jersey on the eastern seaboard, and rarely wandering to southern Canada.

It is a more aggressive bird than the Turkey Vulture and any rivalry over the ownership of a carcass usually results in the dominance of the former.

Vultures very rarely attack living animals, and then only if they are small or injured. Vultures are given protection throughout the year by law as well as by public sentiment.

Turkey Vulture

Cathartes aura (Linnaeus)

Status Rare visitant. Although there are no published nineteenth-century records, Piers' notes refer to museum specimens (not extant) taken from Clarks Harbour, Shelburne County, in fall 1892 and from Pugwash, Cumberland County, about 1899. Prior to 1960, a further dozen or so wandered to the province, and since then it has been more regular. Among the visitants after 1960, which generally appeared but briefly, two were noted first in January; three each were noted in February, March and April; five in May; three in June; five in August; two in September; four each in October and November; and one in December. These reports have come from nearly every county, from Yarmouth to Victoria. Since 1974 adult birds (along with an occasional immature in autumn) have been seen regularly over Brier Island and further up Digby Neck. From late December 1982 to early February 1983 up to seven were noted around Yarmouth, subsisting on offal from slaughtered cattle. These occurrences suggest that the Turkey Vulture may soon be found nesting in the province.

Description *Length:* 66-81 cm. *Adults:* Head and upper neck bare, skin crimson; rest of plumage blackish, paler on flight feathers; bill stout and hooked, grayish white. *Immatures:* Similar but head and neck are covered with dark, fur-like feathers.

Range Breeds from southern British Columbia, southern Manitoba, southern Quebec and central Maine, south throughout the United States and Central and South America.

Remarks Although classified as a bird of prey, its claws and beak are comparatively weak for its size and quite ineffective for capturing living prey and tearing fresh meat. Its food is confined wholly to carrion—for this reason it is not only harmless but beneficial. When gliding it holds its wings somewhat above horizontal—a good field mark. Wheeling lazily in the summer sky, its effortless, graceful flight is equalled by few other birds.

Family Accipitridae

Osprey PLATE 8

Pandion haliaetus (Linnaeus)

Status Fairly common in summer, very rare in winter. Breeds. Ospreys first arrive in late March or early April (average 5 April, earliest 15 March) and are widespread by May. They are most common in summer around shallow bays and estuaries, nesting on islands, shorelines, and occasionally far from water. There are distinct movements from mid-August through September, but last sightings of the year may be much later (average 22 October, latest 8 December). One on Brier Island was hovering over a trout-stocked pond on 13 January 1969 and next day was seen near the lighthouse (W.L. Lent). During January and February 1975, a bird was seen several times in the vicinity of Cole Harbour, Halifax County, by Fulton Lavender; he saw another in the same area the following January. Several other winter reports have come from inexperienced observers or without details. Such winter stragglers are very rare in the northern part of the Osprey's range.

Description *Length:* 53-61 cm. *Adults:* Upperparts dark brown; head and neck white, with a wide black stripe running from the eye down the side of the neck; crown slightly streaked with black. Underparts white except breast, which bears faint streaks of dark brown, especially in female. Cere, legs and feet bluish gray.

Breeding *Nest:* Of coarse sticks; usually in trees from 6-20 m up, occasionally on rocky cliffs, and very rarely on the ground. Nests are usually placed in dead trees, frequently in burned-over areas where they may be seen from a considerable distance. Nests generally are used from year to year until blown down or until the birds are driven elsewhere by human interference. *Eggs:* 2-4, usually 3; dull white, heavily blotched with various shades and densities of rich brown, chiefly around the larger end. Sometimes they are so heavily pigmented that little of the white ground colour can be seen. Repair of old nests begins soon after arrival and egg laying starts two weeks later and continues over several weeks. Hatching commences in June, fledging as early as late July. A study in Antigonish County found that, on average, slightly more than one young was fledged per nest in 1975 and 1976 (Prevost et al. 1978). In recent years, Ospreys have taken to nesting on electric power poles and towers, endangering themselves and threatening power failures. They can be encouraged to use nearby nest platforms instead (Austin-Smith and Rhodenizer 1983), and these are being made more widely available, with much success. Unlike most other members of the hawk family, Ospreys are not bold in defence of their nests when they contain eggs, but they do become more belligerent as their offspring develop.

Range Breeds from northwestern Alaska, northern Manitoba, central Quebec and central Labrador, south to Mexico and Cuba. Winters in the Gulf States, Mexico, Baja California, and Central and South America. Additional races occur in other parts of the world.

Remarks It is probable that the Osprey lives entirely on live fish, which it catches by spectacular diving. Watchfully winging its way 30 or more metres above the water, it pauses to hover when a fish is sighted near the surface. Having marked its prospective victim, it drops like a bolt out of the blue with wings half-folded, striking the water with its breast (rather than head first), sending the spray in all directions. Sometimes it disappears momentarily below the surface. Taking off once again, it soon pauses in flight to shake the water from its plumage. A small fish is held by one talon, a larger fish by both. All are carried off in streamlined position, head first. Usually the bird is rewarded the first time for its diving effort, but not infrequently it misses the target and the fish escapes. On a small saltwater inlet in Mahone Bay, Lunenburg County, on 10 August 1938, I watched one dive three consecutive times before it was successful.

In some places Ospreys are known to nest in colonies, some of considerable size. However, in Nova Scotia nests are generally isolated.

In many parts of North America this species declined in number due to increased concentrations of poison found in the fishes it eats, accumulated as a result of the indiscriminate use of pesticides. However, the decline was not as apparent in Nova Scotia. With the restriction and elimination of some responsible pesticides, the bird has increased in recent years. It is estimated that there are more than 250 active nests in the province (P.J. Austin-Smith).

American Swallow-tailed Kite

Elanoides forficatus (Linnaeus)

Status One record. In August 1905, Adelbert Wilson found one by the roadside near his home in Lower East Pubnico, Yarmouth County, so weak from injury or starvation that it was unable to fly and died soon thereafter. The specimen was mounted by Yarmouth taxidermist Benjamin Doane, and remained in the Wilson home until 1945. A casual reference to "fork-tailed hawks" by Gilpin (1881) lacks substance.

Remarks These elegant birds of prey breed locally in South Carolina, Florida and Louisiana, south to South America. A few have wandered as far north as southern Canada, and there are recent records from New England.

Bald Eagle   PLATE 8

Haliaeetus leucocephalus (Linnaeus)

Status Uncommon resident. Breeds. Most of our Bald Eagles are found on Cape Breton Island during summer. In 1984, of 238 nest sites in a nearly complete survey, 136 were occupied by eagles; of these, 195 (108 occupied) were on Cape Breton Island (Austin-Smith and Dickie 1985). During the winter, they are more widespread, especially in coastal areas, and some leave the province. More adults than immature birds appear

PLATE 7
all adults

Black Scoter
Page 98

female

male

male

female

Surf Scoter
Page 99

male

female

White-winged Scoter
Page 100

male

Common Eider
Page 92

female

male

female

King Eider
Page 93

male

Roger Tory Peterson

PLATE 8

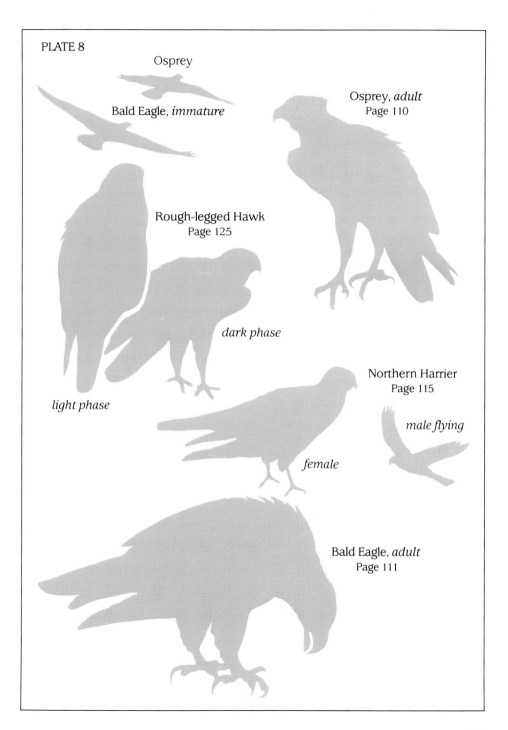

Osprey

Bald Eagle, *immature*

Osprey, *adult*
Page 110

Rough-legged Hawk
Page 125

dark phase

light phase

Northern Harrier
Page 115

male flying

female

Bald Eagle, *adult*
Page 111

to stay in Cape Breton Island, especially around the shores of Bras d'Or Lake. On the mainland, there are winter concentrations in Kings County (where up to 66 have been counted), along the Shubenacadie River, Hants County (up to 20), and the Tusket River, Yarmouth County (up to 14).

Description *Length:* 78-110 cm. *Adults:* Dark brown, nearly black, with white head and tail; bill and tarsus yellow, the tarsus bare for half its length. *Immatures:* Dark brown, usually showing some whitish gray in their wing linings and breast; bill blackish.

Breeding *Nest:* Composed of large sticks with lining of coarse, decayed vegetable debris; usually in very large trees at heights of 10-25 m and often visible against the skyline for long distances. The actual nest is relatively small and cup-shaped with a wide verandah-like platform of coarse sticks extending out around it. *Eggs:* 2, rarely 3; dull white, often badly nest-stained. Laying begins about mid-April. Of 11 nests visited during the period from about 1920 to 1945, five were in pine trees, and six in old, wind-wracked, gnarled beeches. Eight of them held two eggs, two held three, and one was not reached. The earliest date for eggs is 7 April 1940 at Narrows Lake, Halifax County. The young are cared for many weeks after hatching. A nest at Black River Lake, Kings County, was visited on 22 August 1928, when one of the eaglets made its initial flight. If not unduly disturbed, the pair will return year after year to the same nest, adding new material each season.

Range Breeds from northwestern Alaska, Mackenzie Delta, Ungava Peninsula and Newfoundland, south to the Gulf Coast.

Remarks Although the Bald Eagle is a powerful bird, I have never seen one attack live prey. Two instances of such behaviour, however, have come to my attention. Both victims were gulls, one a Herring Gull and the other a Greater Black-backed Gull, both adults. The first was attacked and killed at Black River Lake when it passed too close to a nest containing half-grown eagles (E. Mullen). The other incident was related by Charles R.K. Allen, who watched the kill at Bedford Basin, Halifax County, on 15 February 1968.

Formerly a target for every gun within range of which it chanced to come, the eagle was persecuted on all sides by the public, the result of prejudice handed down over many generations. I heard a back-country farmer boast of how he had destroyed an eagle's nest located far back on his property. Waiting till he knew the nest contained young, he journeyed back armed with gun and axe. He told of felling the tree, killing the little ones and wounding one of the parent birds, but the other was too wary to come within range. When asked why he had done it, he replied, "Well, I don't know, eagles are bad birds aren't they?" When asked what harm they do he was unable to mention any but kept reiterating that he had always thought they were bad birds. It is pleasing to note that in more recent years, there is a strong public sentiment in favour of protecting this rare and majestic bird. It was in 1872 that the Bald Eagle was adopted as the national symbol of the United States of America but not until 1940 that the federal "Bald Eagle Act" was passed, by which full protection was afforded to the eagle. In Nova Scotia it is also illegal to kill or to injure an eagle.

During recent decades, populations of this bird decreased alarmingly throughout much of its range, evidently as a result of pesticides such as DDT which were ingested by the eagles from their fish diet. Fortunately, with the banning of the most damaging pesticides, the decline appears to have been stemmed. The Nova Scotia eagle population appears to have been largely unaffected by these pesticides and is now sufficiently healthy to supply small numbers of young for restocking of depleted populations elsewhere. Four eaglets were sent to New Jersey in 1983 and six to Massachusetts in 1984 (Austin-Smith and Dickie 1985).

Our breeding birds are of the subspecies *Haliaeetus leucocephalus alascanus.* *Haliaeetus leucocephalus leucocephalus* (the southern form) occurs here as a non-breeding wanderer, six birds having been collected since 1942. Four were taken in Halifax County, and the other two in Yarmouth County. The origin and identity of these birds were determined through bird-banding, all having been tagged in Florida as nestlings. These six birds were all immature, none having carried its leg band for a longer period than one year and 129 days. This fact suggests that young eagles of this race are more prone to wander than adults.

Northern Harrier   PLATE 8

Circus cyaneus (Linnaeus)

Status Uncommon in summer, fairly common transient, rare in winter. Breeds. Once common, its numbers have diminished during the past quarter century. It remains widely distributed but is more common during summer near the New Brunswick border. Birds believed to be spring migrants (rather than overwintered birds) arrive generally in late March or early April (average 3 April, earliest 14 March). Larger numbers occur during fall migration, especially on our southern islands (for example, 30 were reported on Seal Island on 10 October 1982). A few birds regularly remain into early winter and occasionally throughout the winter, mostly in coastal areas.

Description *Length:* 45-60 cm. *Adult male:* Light slate-blue above; white below, sparsely spotted with rusty brown. Black wing tips. *Adult female:* Mostly reddish brown above, underparts buffy with narrow streaks of dark brown. *Immatures:* Like adult female but darker and more reddish. All three plumages have a conspicuous white rump patch.

Breeding *Nest:* Invariably placed on the ground, usually in wet meadows or near their margins; composed of coarse reeds and decaying vegetable matter; a flat, rather slovenly affair. *Eggs:* 3-6; dull white or bluish white; rarely with brownish markings distributed sparsely, mostly about the larger end. An extensive study of the behaviour and breeding biology of this species in the Amherst area was carried out by Acadia University graduate student Robert Simmons in 1980-83. He found up to 20 nests each year in the area with, as usual in this species, some strongly territorial males mated to more than one female.

Range Breeds north to northern Alaska, northwestern Mackenzie, northern Manitoba, central Quebec and probably Newfoundland, south to middle and southwestern United States. Winters from British Columbia, southern Ontario and Nova Scotia to Colombia and the West Indies. Additional races occur in Europe and Asia.

Remarks Although the food of this hawk consists largely of mice and other small rodents, it eats a variety of other animals. While canoeing on the Cornwallis River above Kentville in August 1942, I twice flushed Northern Harriers from among marginal reeds, so close it was apparent they had been disturbed while feeding. Investigation revealed a small salmon, long dead, half-devoured, and a freshly killed frog that had been neatly and adeptly skinned.

On 2 September 1949 I saw one at Canard, Kings County, sitting on the ground with its wings slightly extended, obviously holding its prey. When approached, the hawk carried its victim a short distance, but finding it too burdensome soon dropped it. Proceeding to the spot, I found a Gray Partridge the hawk had just killed by strangulation, the victim's neck bearing the only marks of violence. Further examination of the bird showed it had been sick, its body cavity filled with an offensive yellowish fluid. Had the partridge been healthy, the hawk probably would have known instinctively not to attack prey of that size and weight.

On a third occasion, while duck hunting on the Grand Pré in early November 1933, I disturbed a Northern Harrier at mealtime. It flushed from a thick growth of cattails on the edge of a slough within a few feet of me. Investigation revealed the remains of an American Black Duck lying on top of a muskrat's house, its breast half-eaten. Examination of the carcass revealed a shattered wing, the gangrenous condition of the wound proving beyond doubt that this duck had escaped from a hunter earlier in the season. Had the hawk not finished it off, its doom would have come with the first heavy frost.

With further reference to the food habits of this bird, the United States Fish and Wildlife Service (1940) received a complaint from a group of sportsmen resident in the southern states that this hawk was preying heavily on local quail. They demanded steps be taken to reduce the number of Northern Harriers. An investigation followed and "of 1100 'pellets' that were collected and analyzed, it was found that quail parts were present in four only, and cotton rat remains in 925." Because cotton rats are known to be highly destructive to quail eggs, the maligned hawk was shown to be in fact beneficial to the quail, and thus the wholesale destruction of hawks by well-meaning but misinformed hunters was fortunately prevented.

Sharp-shinned Hawk   PLATE 9

Accipiter striatus Vieillot

Status Fairly common in summer, common transient, uncommon in winter. Breeds. One of our most common hawks. Its range in summer is largely restricted to second-growth evergreen woods, where it breeds and manages to keep well out of sight. In winter it is frequently seen about towns and villages where it comes in pursuit of small birds, mainly House Sparrows and starlings—not by preference but because of their availability. Migration, largely along the coast and on our southwestern islands, is well underway by early September, but the peak of migration usually occurs in late September through mid-October. For example, over 600 were reported on Seal Island on 8 October 1980, and over 1000 on Brier Island on 26 September 1982. These birds, mostly immatures, leave the province in large numbers and cross the Gulf of Maine. Spring migration is not as spectacular, but small groups of birds are sometimes seen on the move between early April and mid-May.

Description *Length:* 25-35 cm. *Adult male:* Upperparts bluish gray; underparts white, barred heavily with rufous; legs and feet slender and yellow. *Adult female:* Similar to male but upperparts are browner, less bluish. *Immatures:* Dark brown above; white below, streaked with pale rufous brown.

Breeding *Nest:* Made of small sticks lined with finer twigs. Usually placed at low (4-10 m) heights and, in my experience, invariably in conifers, spruce being chosen most often. The selected nest tree is usually growing on the edge of a path or roadway in the woods or on the edge of a clearing. The bird usually will leave the nest if the tree is tapped gently, but at times it will not respond to even vigorous pounding. *Eggs:* 3-6, sets of 4 being more commonly laid than those of 5. They are bluish white to buff, distinctly blotched or sometimes washed with rich chocolate-brown or cinnamon-rufous. Occasionally considerable time lapses between nest completion and commencement of egg laying. For instance, a nest discovered near Wolfville on 27 April 1924 contained no eggs although complete and the bird was scolding nearby. Visited a number of times later, it was still empty on 20 May. On 26 May, however, the bird was sitting on a set of four eggs. If a first nest is destroyed, this hawk will usually try once more. A nest containing four slightly incubated eggs on 2 July 1933 was undoubtedly a second nesting. Another found on the Wolfville Ridge on 9 July 1966 contained two young about ready to leave the nest, and three infertile eggs. One young flew when an attempt was made to climb the tree. It landed on the ground about 4.5 m from the take-off. Before leaving I placed it on a low branch of the nest tree. Revisiting the site two days later I found both young in the nest.

Range Breeds from Alaska across Canada to Newfoundland, north to the tree limit, and south over much of the United States. Additional races occur in the West Indies and South America.

Remarks Not infrequently, complaints are received from persons who maintain winter feeding stations for birds during these lean months. They report that a small hawk of sorts is hanging about the garden premises; the birds are terrified, leave the feeder, and duck into thick shrubbery the moment the hawk arrives. More than likely this will be a "Sharp-shin." The bird-lover is placed in a rather awkward position. Now that all hawk species are protected throughout the year by provincial statute, it is illegal to shoot the marauder. In fact, few in these enlightened days feel disposed to resort to such harsh measures even if they are equipped with a gun, as many of them are not. What we are witnessing at such times is natural and, distressing though it is, our feathered friends must take their chances for survival as their forebears have been compelled to do since time immemorial.

On one occasion I happened to see a Sharp-shinned Hawk kill a House Sparrow in my garden. It was bitterly cold, the snow was deep, and all wild birds were in need of food. As I watched, three hungry, covetous crows suddenly attacked and so harassed the little hawk that the latter was forced to flee for its life, leaving the crows to fight among themselves for possession of the spoils.

As another example of the predatory habits of this bird, I once saw one pursuing a flock of about 40 starlings. The sagacious birds, flying in close formation, evidently knew the hawk could strike only from above and they seemed determined not to give it that advantage, for they suddenly began to spiral upwards, the hawk close on their heels but always just below. Higher and higher climbed the starlings, still maintaining tight formation, until the hawk, seeming to realize the futility of its effort, turned and volplaned to earth. Immediately the smaller birds were seen to relax and glide downward, but I noted they chose a different direction than that taken by their erstwhile pursuer.

Cooper's Hawk

Accipiter cooperii (Bonaparte)

Status Rare resident. Breeds. Nineteenth-century specimens mentioned by Gesner (1842) and Gilpin (1881) are suspect. The only concrete evidence of breeding in the province was provided by Harold F. Tufts, who found a nest containing four eggs at Black River, Kings County, on 18 May 1906. The eggs were collected and later acquired by the National Museum of Canada. Belief that the bird occurs regularly, although uncommonly, is strengthened by the number of times it has been reported by cautious observers from widely separated localities. Most have been recorded in September and October, especially during hawk flights on our southernmost islands. Reports of adults during the breeding season include two seen by Harold F. Tufts at Albany, Annapolis County, in mid-May 1929; and birds near Whycocomagh, Inverness County, in July 1946 (J.E.V. Goodwill), in Kejimkujik National Park on 29 June 1968 (E.L. Mills), and in Cumberland County on 25 and 30 June 1980 (C. Desplanque).

Description *Length of male:* 35-46 cm. *Length of female:* 42-50 cm. *Adult male:* Upperparts blue-gray; underparts white, heavily barred with bright cinnamon; tail long and rounded at end. *Adult female:* Similar to adult male but upperparts more brownish, less bluish, and underparts paler. *Immatures:* Similar in colouring to immature Sharp-shinned Hawks.

Breeding *Nest:* Made of sticks; usually in deciduous trees in woodlands remote from human habitation. It is very similar to but smaller than that of the Goshawk, and smaller calibre sticks are used. The nest found by Harold F. Tufts was built about 6 m up a hardwood tree in open woodland. *Eggs:* 4-5, usually 4; dull white and rounded ovate.

Range Breeds from southern British Columbia, central Alberta, western Ontario, southern Quebec and Nova Scotia, south throughout much of the United States. Winters north as far as the northern States and southern Ontario, and south to Costa Rica.

Remarks The paucity of acceptable records of this bird in Nova Scotia arises from the fact that it closely resembles its smaller close relative, the Sharp-shinned Hawk, and its larger one, the Goshawk. In adult plumages the Goshawk and the Cooper's are readily distinguishable, but the immatures of both in their first-year dress are brownish gray and striped and look very much alike. In all hawk species the female is considerably larger than her mate—and that is where the confusion lies. The Cooper's female averages only slightly smaller than the male Goshawk, and a smaller male Cooper's is about the same size as a larger female Sharp-shin. In addition, the plumages of the Sharp-shin and the Cooper's, both adult and immature, are very similar. When comparing specimens in the hand, however, certain distinctions are readily noticeable. The tail of the Sharp-shinned Hawk is squarish across the end, but that of the Cooper's is longer and rounded. In adults, the top of the head of the latter is considerably darker than that of the former. Cooper's and the Goshawk both have long, rounded tails, but immature birds can be distinguished by noting the whitish superciliary eyebrow line found in the Goshawk but lacking in the Cooper's. The belly of the immature Cooper's is often unstreaked, unlike the other two species. However, even at fairly close range, these differences are not always easily observed. Needless to say, no records of this species should be accepted without the reporting of the above-mentioned details.

Northern Goshawk PLATE 9

Accipiter gentilis (Linnaeus)

Status Uncommon resident. Breeds. Most frequently seen during fall migration. Favours heavily wooded areas, and does not fly high.

Description *Length:* 50-66 cm. *Adults:* Upperparts bluish gray; head blackish gray, a white line over and behind the eye; underparts grayish white, evenly marked with fine wavy bars and streaks of dark gray. *Immatures:* Upperparts fuscous, feathers margined with rufous; primaries and tail barred with dark brown; underparts white to buff, streaked with dark brown.

Breeding *Nest:* Seldom more than 10 m from the ground in trees, a marked preference being shown for deciduous varieties. Composed of coarse sticks with a lining of smaller sticks; bits of dry bark; and usually tips of evergreen, a preference being shown for pine and hemlock—these green twigs are added or perhaps renewed after the eggs have hatched. When viewed from below, an occupied nest will show small flecks of white down sticking to the outer structure. Heavy, old-growth hardwoods are most favoured at nesting time, but nests frequently may be found in woods of mixed growth. It is customary for a pair to return year after year to an established nest site and it is not unusual to find a bird in adult plumage mated with one wearing immature dress. Of 44 nests examined, yellow birch was selected 12 times; beech, 7; maple, 6; poplar, 6; pine, 5; white birch, 5; hemlock, twice; and spruce, once. Repair of old nests commences early in March and laying begins about the middle of April. *Eggs:* 2-4, usually 3; white or very pale bluish white. Of 47 nests where laying of eggs had been completed, 16 were found to contain two; 23 held three; and 8 had sets of four. Much variation in behavior is shown by individual birds when an occupied nest is approached. Usually extreme aggressiveness is shown, the female being bolder than her mate. Such birds, particularly when the nest holds young, will dive-bomb ferociously, sometimes striking a human intruder severely with their talons. On rare occasions, birds will leave their nests when an approaching intruder is still 50 m away and fly off silently into the woods, calling intermittently from long range as long as danger threatens.

Range Breeds from northwestern Alaska across forested Canada and south to the northern United States. Other races occur on the western coast of North America and in the Old World.

Remarks The early European settlers were largely dependent upon the produce of their lands. Every farm had its own flock of hens, which was allowed to roam at large, making easy prey for natural predators. The first large hawk (probably a Goshawk) caught in the act of killing a hen initiated a long and vicious campaign aimed at the extinction of all hawks. This hatred was handed down from father to son for many generations. No attempt was made to distinguish one hawk from another—all were bad. Larger hawks were known as "hen-hawks" and smaller varieties, not having the strength to kill hens, were called "chicken-hawks." Exaggerated stories of their destructiveness were told and even those with no poultry of their own were activated through sympathy to join in the crusade.

A change in public sentiment against this barbaric and unwarranted treatment of hawks began to appear a number of decades ago and continued to gain ground. Enlightenment comes hand in hand with education and much was accomplished through that channel. Another reason for the decline in hostility towards these birds was the reduction in the number of farmers with poultry yards, probably because these became unprofitable. Poultry raising today is big business. The private individual with no hens to lose has lost his bitterness towards hawks. Legislators, ever mindful of the wishes of their constituents, have been bold or enlightened enough to enact laws protecting all species of hawks and owls in Nova Scotia throughout the year.

Only at nesting time have I heard these birds use their vocal organs. The usual note, uttered in protest as the nest is approached, is a strident, staccato *cac-cac-cac* which carries a piercing, menacing tone. (Two other notes seldom heard are mentioned by Tufts in Bent [1937].)

Red-shouldered Hawk

Buteo lineatus (Gmelin)

Status Rare transient, very rare in summer. Occurrences recorded by Blakiston and Bland (1856), Downs (1865), H.F. Tufts (1899) and Townsend (1906) all lack supporting evidence. The first modern sighting was reported by D.F. Rupert (of Sarnia, Ontario), who gave good details of an adult soaring over Wallace, Cumberland County, on 15 July 1966. An emaciated corpse found in a snowbank at Louis Head, Shelburne County, on 1 March 1975 was forwarded to the Nova Scotia Museum as the first confirmed occurrence of the species. Otherwise, sightings have been reported by reliable observers almost annually since 1973, somewhat more frequently of late. Only six individuals have been seen in spring (28 April-27 May), but there have been 12 reports totalling about 30 individuals for fall (25 August-23 November), mostly during hawk flights on Brier Island. There are June reports from Cape Breton Highlands National Park and Yarmouth and Kings counties. Most surprising were well-documented stragglers on Christmas Bird Counts at Brier Island in 1974, 1976 and 1979.

Remarks Although immatures of this bird can be confused with those of Red-tailed and Broad-winged Hawks, the more slender Red-shouldered Hawk has darker underwing coverts, is uniformly streaked below (the red-tails have unstreaked breasts, and broad-wings have unstreaked bellies), and usually has a distinctive pale "window" at the base of the primaries when seen overhead. As the normal range of the Red-shouldered Hawk lies only slightly south and west of Nova Scotia, its occasional presence here is not unexpected and the recent summer reports suggest that it might nest here rarely.

Broad-winged Hawk   PLATE 10

Buteo platypterus (Vieillot)

Status Uncommon in summer, fairly common transient, very rare in winter. Breeds. First migrants are generally sighted in late April or early May (average 2 May, earliest 10 April), and they are seen in small numbers throughout the province during summer. Small groups of non-breeding birds in immature plumage are sometimes seen on Brier Island in early summer, but autumn flights begin in late August. The peak of movement in the fall generally occurs between mid-September and early October, with occasional stragglers until late November. Noteworthy concentrations on Brier Island have included an estimated 3000 on 3-4 October 1968 and 1500-2000 on 26 September 1983; five immature birds have been reported in mid-to-late December since 1967. One of these was later found dead near River Philip, Cumberland County, on 2 January 1979; another was photographed during the Halifax East Christmas Bird Count on 17 December 1983; and an injured bird was captured near Sydney on 16 December 1983 and subsequently restored to health. Most unusual was an immature bird that resided in and around Wolfville between 23 January and 4 February 1983 and was well studied and photographed by many observers. The source of the sometimes abundant migrants in the province, especially along Digby Neck and on Brier Island, is presumably from farther west, perhaps from beyond New Brunswick, where the species is said to be an "uncommon summer resident" (Squires 1976). North Mountain, beginning at Blomidon, Kings County, producing thermal air currents to sustain these hawks in their soaring migrations, may guide them to the southwest, ultimately concentrating them on Brier Island, whence they depart across the Gulf of Maine when the weather is suitable.

Description *Length:* 35-47 cm. *Adults:* Upperparts dark brown without bluish tinge. Tail dark brown with two light bands across it. Underparts dull rufous brown irregularly barred with white, the rufous being more uniform towards the breast. *Immatures:* Dark brown above and whitish below; striped on sides of breast, flanks and abdomen with dark brown. Tail grayish brown, usually crossed by several dark brown bars.

Breeding *Nest:* Made of sticks, at low elevation in trees of both soft and hardwood growth. *Eggs:* 2-4; dull buffy white, blotched and washed with cinnamon-brown; occasionally unmarked. Harry Brennan has supplied the following accounts of three nests he examined in Pictou County: on 17 May 1964, 5 m up in a yellow birch in woods of mixed growth, three eggs. On 8 May 1965, about 6 m up in a medium-sized maple, birds scolding but nest empty; on 22 May it contained four eggs. On 10 May 1965, a nest at Irish Mountain was about 6 m up in a yellow birch; not examined until 23 May when it contained three eggs. The only other nest of the species in Nova Scotia that has come to my attention was one containing two eggs found near Halifax on 23 May 1952 by Kenneth Beanlands, situated about 5 m up a dead tamarack tree.

Range Breeds from central Alberta east to Nova Scotia, south to the Gulf Coast and Texas. Winters from southern Florida through Central America to Peru. Additional races occur in the West Indies.

Remarks This rather sluggish, slow-flying hawk is endowed with an unsuspicious nature. These unfortunate traits too often led to its untimely end by the gun of an uninformed hunter who shoots all hawks indiscriminately. This hawk's diet of insects and small rodents makes it beneficial to man.

Swainson's Hawk

Buteo swainsoni Bonaparte

Status One sight record. A light-phase adult bird was identified by Wickerson Lent and Barry Kent MacKay during a hawk flight on Brier Island in September 1964.

Remarks Because the bird was perched quite close, facing the observers, and allowing them to see the distinctive dark upper breast and undertail banding, and because both observers were experienced, the record is very plausible. Although there are no other records from Atlantic Canada, this prairie hawk occasionally appears in autumn in the northeastern United States.

Zone-tailed Hawk

Buteo albonotatus Kaup

Status One record. One of the most unusual bird finds in recent years was an adult of this southern hawk seen in the vicinity of Musquodoboit Harbour, Halifax County, between 24 September and 4 October 1976. It was discovered by Andrew MacInnis, who alerted others, a number of whom were able to see the bird. All field marks were well documented, including its resemblance to a Turkey Vulture when soaring, and confirming photographs (National Museum of Canada, on file) were obtained by Eric Crowell.

Remarks The species breeds from northern South America to Arizona, Texas and New Mexico, where it is partially migratory. It has strayed to California and Nevada, but evidently not elsewhere in North America. Further discussion of this record, including the probability of its being a true vagrant rather than an escaped bird, is given by McLaren and MacInnes (1977).

Red-tailed Hawk   PLATE 10

Buteo jamaicensis (Gmelin)

Status Uncommon in summer, fairly common in winter. Breeds. In summer it normally frequents heavily timbered regions more or less remote from settlement but in winter is often found in the vicinity of farms and settled districts, and around poultry plants, where it may become a scavenger. Large numbers have been tallied during Christmas Bird Counts at Wolfville in recent years (89 in 1982). The peak of fall migration occurs in October; over 60 were recorded in passage along Digby Neck on 27 October 1984.

Description *Length:* 48-64 cm. *Adults:* Upperparts brown or grayish brown, often with some reddish brown about head and neck. Tail chestnut above (paler below) with narrow black band near tip. Underparts whitish with narrow dark streaks on chin, throat and breast. A more or less well-defined band composed of broad blackish streaks across upper belly. *Immatures:* Upperparts dark brown with white spots and streaks intermingled. Tail grayish brown, crossed by narrow blackish bars. Underparts whitish streaked with brown much like adults.

Breeding *Nest:* In tall trees, a marked preference being shown for white and yellow birches; occasionally well hidden in a tall spruce; composed of sticks and similar in general construction to that of the Goshawk but usually situated at considerably greater heights. *Eggs:* 2-4, usually 3; dull white, irregularly washed and sometimes blotched about the larger end with various shades and densities of rich chocolate-brown. A nest located 18-20 m up a giant yellow birch at White Rock, Kings County,on 30 April 1928 contained four eggs. A pair was seen nest-repairing at Gaspereau Mountain on 30 March 1919 and two other pairs were similarly engaged in the same general area on 6 and 10 April 1944. On 12 May 1968, Cyril Coldwell found a nest that was noteworthy, placed about 15-17 m up a large tree in a thick clump of spruces growing in open woodland, segregated from other large trees. The nest was so well hidden that its location was only discovered by patient waiting at considerable distance to watch the bird return to it. Within a quarter mile stood a growth of solid hardwoods of the type usually acceptable to the species for nesting. The young were successfully reared. This hawk is far less pugnacious in defence of its nest than the Goshawk, though some individuals are bolder than others.

Range Breeds in most of southern Canada (except Newfoundland) north to near the tree limit and south through much of the United States and West Indies. Several races are recognized.

Remarks This is the hawk usually seen high overhead soaring in great circles with wings and tail spread widely. Its usual call, sometimes heard intermittently when soaring, is a prolonged, wheezy whistle which has been likened to the sound of escaping steam.

Stomach analyses of hundreds of specimens provide indisputable evidence that this hawk is of high economic value to the agriculturist. John B. May (1935) mentions the examination of 850 stomachs of the Red-tailed Hawk: 86 percent held small mammals; less than 10 percent held poultry and game birds; and the rest contained small birds, reptiles and insects. One shot at Gaspereau on 17 November 1935 by Cyril Coldwell was found to have devoured three field mice and one Red Squirrel; and the stomach of an adult male collected by Godfrey near Baddeck on 13 July 1954 contained three Cinerous Shrews *(Sorex cinereus),* two Smoky Shrews *(Sorex fumeus)* and one Wood Frog *(Rana sylvatica).* One hawk flushed on Wolfville Ridge on 27 December 1933 by Ronald W. Smith left a freshly killed Common Snipe on the blood-stained snow. Frequently the food of this hawk consists of dead or crippled birds. This may account for at least a portion of the poultry or game birds found in their stomachs— it is not correct to assume that every bird eaten has been killed by the hawk itself.

Rough-legged Hawk   PLATE 8

Buteo lagopus (Pontoppidan)

Status Uncommon in winter, very rare in summer. Formerly of irregular occurrence, in recent decades it has been seen more routinely but seldom in the large incursions that occur in inland parts of North America. The birds normally arrive from their northern nesting grounds between mid-September and mid-October (average 2 October, earliest 27 August). An exceptional invasion occurred in 1899-1900, when it was not unusual to see 20-25 at one time foraging over the Grand Pré meadows of Kings County. They were not again seen in pronounced numbers until 1951 when 12-15 birds occurred at the same location. Large numbers (10 or more) have been recorded on Christmas Bird Counts at Brier Island, Amherst or Wolfville, in 1960, 1964, 1976, 1977, 1980, 1982 and 1983. Last sightings are usually in April or May (average 2 May, latest 25 May). However, a few stragglers, evidently immature birds, have been seen in summer. Erskine (1968) reported summer occurrences around the Amherst marshes in 1965 and 1966, and on Cape Breton Island on 24 July 1966. More recent reports have been of a molting bird near Tusket, Yarmouth County, on 4 July 1977 (C.R.K. Allen), and one near Amherst on 18 July 1981 (C. Desplanque).

Description *Length:* 50-60 cm. Legs (tarsi) are feathered to the toes, giving them a rough appearance—hence its name. It occurs in light, dark, and intermediate colour phases. The light phase is most common. *Adults:* In pale phase, brown above, interimposed with cream and ochre; whitish streaks on head and neck broader in adult female. Breast streaked with brown and white. Abdomen of female blotched with dark brown, forming a band; abdomen of male usually merely barred with dark brown. Tail white basally with broad dark terminal band in female (usually several narrow bars in male). Thighs barred in both sexes. *Immatures:* In pale phase, resemble adult female but buffier below; thighs unbarred, a more extensive and better defined abdominal band, and the terminal half of the tail is unbarred dark brown. Dark-phase birds are uniformly brownish black with some white on inner webs of the primaries and at base of tail. Tail usually has some light barring.

Range Breeds in Alaska and across northern Canada north to the southern arctic islands and south to northern Manitoba and Ontario, the north shore of the Gulf of St. Lawrence and Newfoundland. Winters from southern Canada to the southern United States. It also occurs in Europe and Asia.

Remarks This is one of our largest and most beneficial hawks. Despite its size, its talons are comparatively weak but admirably suited for picking up small rodents from their grassy runways, so commonly seen in our meadowlands. These small mammals make up a very high percentage of its food.

On 28 February 1954, I watched one on the Grand Pré meadows kill four mice in a matter of a few seconds. With wings held high, it hopped about as though performing some sort of dance. Watched through a 20-power telescope, it was then seen to devour the mice one after another in quick succession, swallowing them whole, head first. That birds of prey sometimes, if not always, refrain from killing beyond their immediate food requirements, is clearly exemplified by the behaviour of this particular bird. Having disposed of the four mice, it alighted on a fence post nearby and assumed a posture of sleepiness. Traces of snow on the ground enabled me to notice a large Norway Rat *(Rattus norvegicus)* wandering aimlessly along the fence line towards the hawk. When the rodent reached a point 5-6 m away, the bird suddenly became alert, probably aroused by sound rather than sight. With apparently intense concentration, it slowly shifted its position on the post and, with head lowered in a menacing attitude, faced the oncoming rat, which, unaware of its perilous circumstance, continued to draw near. When it reached the base of the hawk's perch, the bird leaned forward as though poised to strike. But it refrained from striking, and the rat, oblivious to the close call it had just had, continued on its way. Gradually the hawk resumed its former state of composure, settled down, and appeared to sleep.

With reference to the food of this bird, Taverner (1934) states: "Of 45 stomachs examined, 40 contained mice; 5, other mammals and a lizard. A record like this is enough to condemn the indiscriminate killing of hawks. The Rough-leg is a mouse-hawk par excellence. It also feeds on grasshoppers and has been known at times to do excellent work controlling plagues of these destructive insects."

Rough-legged Hawk eating mouse

Golden Eagle

Aquila chrysaetos (Linnaeus)

Status Rare visitant. There are a few nineteenth century specimen records, and Gilpin (1872) and Jones (1885) suggest that it may have bred in the eastern counties. One was shot in Shelburne County about 1930 and ultimately acquired by the Nova Scotia Museum. This eagle was not reported again until 1965, when well-documented sightings occurred at Louisbourg on 28 September (J. Lunn) and in Pictou County on 27 November (Mrs. W. MacInnis). Since then, there have been reports of 25 sightings of about 30 birds: one sighting each in January, May and June; two in September, October and November; three in February, March, July and December; and four in April. Summer sightings include two adults on 29 July 1984 at Martinique Beach, Halifax County (R.B. Dickie), where others had been seen during winter and spring.

Remarks The natural haunts of this swift-flying, powerful predator are wild mountainous regions far removed from the abode of man. Unlike the heavier and more sluggish Bald Eagle, this bird is accustomed to killing to satisfy its food requirements.

In the hand it can be readily distinguished from the Bald Eagle by noting that its tarsi are covered with feathers to the toes, those of the Bald Eagle being mostly bare. In the immature bird, light areas at the base of the tail and primaries are rather conspicuous in flight and help to identify it at a distance. Unlike the young Bald Eagle, the adult Golden Eagle is all dark except for faintly paler tail bands.

It is gratifying to see an upsurge in reports of this fine species, which may yet be found nesting in Nova Scotia, as it has been in eastern Canada and nearby Maine.

Family Falconidae

American Kestrel   PLATE 10

Falco sparverius Linnaeus

Status Common in summer, uncommon in winter. Breeds. This is by far our commonest hawk. It usually first arrives in late March or early April (average 1 April, earliest 20 March), and numbers appear by mid- to late April. During summer it is widespread, especially in agricultural regions. Fall migration is noticeable by mid-August, and, on Brier and Seal islands, daily counts of 25 or more have been recorded between early September and late October (exceeding 100 on several occasions between 21 September and 10 October). Infrequent winter birds are usually seen in coastal localities.

Description *Length:* 23-30 cm. *Adult male:* Top of head and nape bluish gray with large chestnut-brown patch. Two black patches on each side of head, one extending downward from in front of eye, the other down from the ear. Back chestnut, more or

PLATE 9

Peregrine Falcon, *adult*
Page 132

Northern
Goshawk
Page 119

Gyrfalcon
Page 134
gray phase

immature

immature

adult

Merlin
Page 131

adult

Sharp-shinned Hawk
Page 116

adult

Roger Tory Peterson

PLATE 10
all adults

American Kestrel
Page 127

Broad-winged Hawk
Page 121

Red-tailed Hawk
Page 123

Ring-necked Pheasant
Page 136

Spruce Grouse
Page 138

male

female

female

male

Ruffed Grouse
Page 140

Gray Partridge
Page 134

less barred with black. Tail chestnut with black subterminal bar. Wing coverts bluish gray, barred or spotted with black. Primaries black, barred with white on inner webs. Chin and throat white. Underparts buffy white and more or less spotted with black. *Adult female:* Head similar to that of male but duller and with feather shafts blackish brown. Back, wing coverts and tail reddish brown, conspicuously barred with black. Breast and belly streaked with reddish brown.

Breeding *Nest:* In a tree cavity, usually one bored by a flicker, from 3 to 15 or more metres up. There is no lining to the nest, the eggs being deposited on chips of decayed wood. *Eggs:* 4-7, usually 5; creamy white, heavily marked and washed with bright cinnamon-brown. A nest containing five fresh eggs was found in an open grove at Port Williams, Kings County, on 10 May 1905, a typical date for first laying.

Range Breeds from Alaska, northwestern Mackenzie Valley, northern Ontario, southern Quebec and Nova Scotia, south to the West Indies and South America. Winters from southern Canada southward.

Remarks The smallest of North American hawks. Its usual call is a high-pitched, pleasing, rapidly repeated *killee, killee, killee,* most frequently heard during breeding season. Its former name of "Sparrow Hawk" was a misnomer, for though it does prey on small birds of sparrow size, particularly during migration, its menu is made up largely of insects, especially grasshoppers, mice, and reptiles. "Of 427 stomachs examined, mammals occurred in 147; poultry or game, none; small birds, 69; other vertebrates, 13; insects, 269; miscellaneous, 30; and 29 were empty" (J.B.May 1935). On 25 July 1937, I saw one at Albany, Annapolis County, carrying a small, wriggling green snake in its talons. C.R.K. Allen tells of one in August 1955 feeding on flying insects (probably flying ants) by "hawking" about and seizing them in its mouth.

Further evidence that hawks kill only to satisfy their immediate food requirements (see Rough-legged Hawk) was provided by a tame, recently fed American Kestrel which on several occasions showed not the slightest interest in a live House Sparrow that had been released in its pen. Only some hours later (more than 10 hours on one occasion) did it kill and eat the sparrow.

Its small size (slightly larger than a robin), its conspicuous chestnut markings, its common habit of hovering on rapidly beating wings when prey is sighted below, and its slender, pointed wings (typical of all falcons) provide good field marks for easy identification. It is one of the most beneficial of our hawks and well merits the protection provided to all hawks by provincial statute.

Merlin PLATE 9

Falco columbarius (Linnaeus)

Status Rare in summer, fairly common transient, uncommon in winter. Breeds. Most frequently seen in September and October, especially along the coast and on our southernmost islands. On Seal Island, peak counts of 10-30 individuals have been obtained almost annually between mid-September and mid-October in the past two decades. Often they are seen leaving the island to the south or southeast, evidently prepared to undertake long over-water flights. A few are reported most winters, especially around towns or cities, sometimes preying on small birds around bird feeders. An increase in reports during late March or early April appears to represent first returning migrants, which continue to be seen through May.

Description *Length:* 25-35 cm. *Adult male:* Upperparts pale slate-blue, dark slate-gray or bluish black, shaft streaked with black. Tail barred with black and similar blue in varying proportions. Below, white or cream, more or less heavily streaked with ochre and brown, heaviest and darkest on flanks. Throat white, immaculate or sparsely streaked. Thighs strongly tinged with warm buff, more or less heavily streaked with dark or sandy brown. *Adult female:* Similar but larger, with brownish upperparts. *Immatures:* Similar to female.

Breeding *Nest:* Usually in trees, sometimes on a cliffside and not infrequently on the ground. Rarely in a tree cavity. When tree sites are chosen, the old nest of a crow is sometimes used as a base. *Eggs:* 2-5, usually 4-5; creamy, heavily blotched with various shades and densities of reddish brown. Only a few nests have been recorded in the province. The first was discovered on the "Edmunds Grounds" on the outskirts of Halifax by Lloyd Duncanson on 1 August 1955. It was in a spruce tree about 8 m up, placed in a nest formerly used by crows. Two fully fledged young were perched on a limb near the nest, and a parent bird scolded vociferously. The second nesting pair, discovered by Howard G. Scott near his home in New Glasgow, afforded him an excellent opportunity to watch between early June and early August 1967 as their brood of two fledged. Mr. Scott graphically described the falcons' persistent harassment of every raven that came within range of their little kingdom, a trait typical of Merlins. Though the raven is a powerful bird, strong on the wing, and at least three to four times larger than the Merlin, it is no match for the latter in aerial maneuvering. On several occasions he saw the pair attack their enemy, one from beneath and one from above. He watched the bird below suddenly assume an inverted position, momentarily flying upside down with its talons extended to strike the raven, forcing the intruder on one occasion to make a headlong crash landing in an attempt to escape its attackers, "croaking dismally" as it disappeared into a thicket of spruce. When Mr. Scott entered the woods to assess the damages, the raven fled from its hideout, apparently unharmed. Among more recent nestings, were those in Point Pleasant Park, Halifax, in 1980 and 1981, evidently successful despite the summer throngs of people frequenting the park.

Range In North America, breeds from Alaska to Newfoundland, north to the tree limit and south to the northern United States. Winters from the United States (rarely southern Canada) south to the West Indies and northern South America. Widely distributed in the Old World.

Remarks This species was once known as the "Pigeon Hawk" in North America, a name derived from its resemblance in flight to the extinct Passenger Pigeon. Unlike its larger relative, the Peregrine Falcon, it is not a wary bird, often allowing humans to approach within easy gunshot. This misplaced confidence far too often led to its destruction in the past.

Peregrine Falcon   PLATE 9

Falco peregrinus Tunstall C 000

Status Rare transient, very rare in summer and winter. Formerly bred. After World War II, Peregrine Falcon populations declined drastically in various parts of the world from egg losses caused by DDT and other pesticides. By the mid-sixties no known breeding pairs remained in eastern North America south of the subarctic. With the almost complete ban of DDT in North America, survival of the species became possible, but its recovery remained in doubt until restocking programs were initiated. Since 1960, almost all sightings of birds in Nova Scotia have been during autumn migration, doubtless from the less troubled Arctic populations (about 210 individuals, average of first sightings 17 September, earliest 12 August). There have been a few sightings in winter (13 individuals) and in spring (13 individuals; average date of last sightings 13 May, latest 30 May). By contrast, only four birds were reported for the months of June and July between 1960 and 1979. However, beginning in 1982, the Canadian Wildlife Service began to release young falcons in Fundy National Park, New Brunswick, and near Advocate, Colchester County; a total of 19 had been released in Nova Scotia up to 1984. Summer sightings since 1980, including a banded young bird from such a release seen on Sable Island in late August 1982, give hope that the species will again become established in the province.

Description *Length:* 38-50 cm. *Adults:* Top of head, cheeks, and "moustache" very dark slate-gray; upperparts mainly dark bluish ash, barred and spotted with dark slate-gray, lightest on rump; tail marked with six or more narrow black bands and broader subterminal blackish bar, and edged with white; throat and upper breast dirty white; underparts buff, regularly barred with dark brown; bill horn-coloured; legs and feet greenish yellow. *Immatures:* Upperparts dark brown; underparts lighter brown, heavily streaked with dark brown.

Breeding The following details concerning what is known of its former nesting activities in the province are given as a matter of record: during many years of field work only two instances of nesting have come to my attention. The first was on the cliff side of Diamond Island, one of the Five Islands group in Colchester County. I had been informed of its location by a resident of the village of Five Islands who told me the birds had been nesting there as far back as he could remember, but he did not know what kind they were. I visited the island on 13 June 1942 and while watching from the beach below soon saw a parent bird enter the eyrie with food for the young, whose cries were clearly heard following its arrival. This nest was practically inaccessible to humans, being approximately 30 m above the beach and probably that far down from the top of the cliff. To my knowledge this nest was not visited again until the summer of 1964 at which time Daniel D. Berger found no evidence of even recent occupancy. The other nest was near Advocate, Cumberland County. It was on a ledge of a perpendicular cliff, about 45 m up and equally far down from the top. This nest was reached by Lloyd Duncanson by means of a rope on 13 July 1955. It contained two young about ready to fly, and another near the nest had been dead for a week or longer.

Range Formerly bred throughout much of North America wherever there were mountains or cliff faces, south to northern Georgia in the east and the Mexican border in the west, but now extirpated except in the Arctic and subarctic, in scattered western parts and, with restocking, in a few parts of eastern North America. Other populations are found throughout much of the world.

Remarks Like a true sportsman, the Peregrine Falcon takes its game on the wing, striking it down with a spectacular blow of its powerful talons. There are times when it appears to enjoy pursuing prey only for sport. For instance, at Evangeline Beach, Kings County, on 12 August 1927, I watched one chasing a flock of small sandpipers out over the water. The hawk was in pursuit for longer than it would have taken it to make a kill. As the approximately 500 terrified birds twisted and turned in frenzied effort to elude their pursuer, the hawk dashed through their midst. After some moments, during which its aerial manoeuvres were obviously activated by play rather than ferocity, the falcon suddenly turned off empty-handed towards the wooded shore.

Most migrant birds are of the northern subspecies, *Falco peregrinus tundrius,* whereas formerly breeding (and restocked) birds belonged to the eastern *Falco peregrinus anatum.* The latter are darker than the northern birds and have been tentatively identified among northern migrants in recent autumns.

Gyrfalcon PLATE 9

Falco rusticolus Linnaeus

Status Rare in winter. Although there were only three records in the nineteenth century (first mentioned by Blakiston and Bland 1855) and only 7 more up to 1960, it has become more regular with some 35 individuals reported since that year. The earliest fall arrival was "playing" with a Northern Raven near Tusket, Yarmouth County, on 1 September 1981 (C.R.K. Allen). The latest in spring was a white-phase bird that stayed around Amherst, until at least 20 May 1979 (C. Desplanque et al.). They have been seen most frequently in recent years on the Grand Pré meadows, near Wolfville, around the Amherst marshes, and on Brier Island. Only two have been reported on Cape Breton Island.

Remarks This powerful predator from the north occurs in varying colour phases which range from near-white to almost black, intermediate shades being much more common. It is by far the largest of the four falcons that occur in Nova Scotia.

Order GALLIFORMES

Family Phasianidae

Gray Partridge PLATE 10

Perdix perdix (Linnaeus)

Status Introduced. Uncommon local resident. Breeds. These birds, commonly called "huns" or "Hungarian partridges," were first brought to Nova Scotia by a group of Halifax sportsmen, headed by the late R.B. Willis, who imported them from Czechoslovakia in the spring of 1926. On 7 April of that year 40 pairs were liberated near Elderbank, Halifax County, and later that month 20 pairs were released near Nappan, Cumberland County. A number of broods were seen, and soon other importations followed. On 1 November 1927, Chief Justice R.E. Harris liberated ten pairs near his home in Clementsport, Annapolis County; and the following spring, on 23 March, twenty pairs were released on the Perkins Farm near Shubenacadie, Hants County. On 28 March 1928, John W. Piggott liberated 10 pairs on his farm at Bridgetown and at least some of these nested successfully that year. On 31 March 1934, the Kings County Fish and Game Association imported a shipment from England, placing 27 birds at New Minas and 20 at Lakeville. Notable local increases occurred and reports indicated the birds were spreading satisfactorily. By 1940 an open season (October 15-31) was granted by the province; it has remained open for a period each fall since then. In the Annapolis Valley they appeared to reach their population peak from 1940-44. In recent years most reports have come from the Wolfville/Canning area of Kings County, although smaller numbers have been seen elsewhere in the Annapolis Valley and around Economy, Colchester County.

Description *Length:* 30-35 cm. *Adult male:* Upperparts finely marked with black, browns and grays, becoming more rufous on lower back; throat and sides of head rich buff; a conspicuous chestnut-brown patch on underparts at junction of breast and belly; breast gray, finely pencilled with black; flanks barred with chestnut. *Adult female:* Similar but tones duller and sometimes showing no patch on underparts or only a trace of it. The best mark by which the sexes can be separated is found on the crown. In the female the background is dark brown, profusely dotted with tear-shaped, light tan spots; in the male the ground colour is ashy or bluish gray and instead of spots the markings are fine, silk-like lines of pale straw or buff, becoming more pronounced on the nape. It must be borne in mind that these distinctions are valid only when examining adults; there is chance for confusion among immatures.

Breeding *Nest:* On the ground, well concealed in long grass or other protective vegetation and composed wholly of dry grass. *Eggs:* 15-27 or perhaps more; olive-buff, unmarked. Laying begins during the second half of May and only one brood is raised, but if the nest is lost there will usually be a second attempt. Two nests, both at North Grand Pré, Kings County, have been examined. On 14 June 1937 one contained 23 eggs, and on 27 June 1937 the other held 27. In both cases the birds were incubating, an indication that laying had been completed. Both parents care for the brood and remain with it until about the middle of March following, when the coveys break up and disperse.

Range Europe and west-central Asia; first brought to Canada about 1908 and liberated in Alberta. Nova Scotia introductions as described.

Remarks When coveys are seen following the nesting season, it is correct to assume that these are family groups. However, rarely there is a departure from this custom. On 12 February 1937, I was informed by a farmer that a "huge flock of huns" was feeding on the dykelands near his farm at North Grand Pré. Investigation revealed that this congregation numbered 250-300 birds. They were exceedingly wary, flushing at long range and flying a mile or more before alighting. The foregoing is the only instance of its kind in Nova Scotia that has come to my attention, but similar concentrations of huns have been recorded in Alberta.

Concerning their food habits in winter, one with the appearance of a strong, healthy bird picked up dead by the roadside on 3 February 1948—the victim of an overhead wire—had a full crop containing 142 wheat kernels, 28 barley kernels, 928 oat kernels and 235 pieces of quartz-like grit. Other stomach analyses have shown quantities of fine, tender green grass, evidently procured from warm, spring-fed bogs that remain open all winter. As evidence of the resourcefulness of this bird at times of food shortage, the following incident is recounted: at Avondale, Hants County, William Webb's two children, accompanied by the family dog, were trudging across farmlands covered with deep snow. They were startled when four Gray Partridges burst from the powdery depths like miniature bombs, one after the other in quick succession. A fifth while struggling to free itself was caught by the dog, which made short work of it. Later their father visited the spot and found numerous tunnels running in various directions. These, plus the amount of "droppings," provided evidence that the birds had been there for some time—sheltered from inclement weather and natural enemies, and well provided with sustenance by the lush, green clover that appeared unaffected by its covering of snow. The bird killed by the dog had been plump and in good condition. This expedient may be practised by huns in winter more commonly than realized.

Ring-necked Pheasant   PLATE 10

Phasianus colchicus Linnaeus

Status Introduced. Uncommon to common local resident. Breeds. After a number of unsuccessful attempts to introduce this bird into Nova Scotia, it is now uncommon to fairly common over parts of the more settled areas of the province. Although the present population of pheasants is of recent origin (1935), an unsuccessful attempt to establish them was made over a hundred years ago. Documentary evidence is provided by an extract taken from the *Christian Messenger* of 24 September 1856, which reads:

Official Notice.

Provincial Secretary's Office
Halifax, August 22, 1856

An Act for the Preservation of Pheasants.
Passed the 18th day of April 1856.

Be it enacted by the Governor, Council and Assembly, as follows:

1.   It shall not be lawful for any person to take or kill, within this Province, any Pheasant, or to buy, sell, or have in possession any dead Pheasant that has been so taken or killed. . . .

The second attempt to bring them here was made about 1890, when the Mic-Mac Club of Halifax liberated a number near the Northwest Arm. It too failed. The next effort took place in Yarmouth County early in the present century when a number of sportsmen released about 50. Of this introduction E. Chesley Allen (1916) writes: "A number of pheasants, fifty or more, have been liberated here during the past five years and are said to be multiplying rapidly. The mating call of the male is heard as early as 26 March and is becoming one of the spring sounds of the woods, while reports of young broods come in from all over the western part of the county at least." Although they may have done well at first, their numbers gradually diminished, for by 1922 they were considered a rarity there. In 1924 a further effort was made by A.G. Bremner, who liberated 50 young birds on 7 September near his home in Clementsvale, Annapolis County. A report received from him in the spring of 1926 indicated that he had met with success, but in subsequent years nothing further was heard of pheasants in that neighbourhood. Finally, in 1935, the Kings County Fish and Game Association procured 1,000 eggs. These were allotted to certain interested farmers in the district who, in a cooperative spirit, agreed to place them under domestic setting hens. This outlay netted the association about 85 birds, which were subsequently released in

Kings County under favourable conditions. During the following decade they increased substantially and an open season for hunting them was granted in 1943 (25-31 October, three cocks only). They continued to prosper, finally reaching a peak about 1953. From then on, however, their numbers declined sharply. Whether the decline was the result of excessive hunting pressure or other factors less obvious is not known. A short open season has continued nevertheless, and in order to help the species maintain its numbers, additional pen-raised birds have been released from time to time in widely separated districts. After several easy winters, numbers in Kings County had again built up by the late 1970s; 632 were noted on the Wolfville Christmas Bird Count in 1980. However, the bird continues to be scarce in most other parts of the province where it occurs.

Description *Adult male: Length:* 90 cm. Strikingly coloured, with a long, narrow, gracefully pointed tail 30-45 cm long. The back is marked in a beautiful complicated pattern, with deep maroon, cream, ochre, black and metallic emerald-green. Breast is a solid, rich copper-bronze with violet reflections, each feather tipped with black; abdomen black; rich ochre on flanks; head and neck, except crown, brilliant steely black with a more or less complete white collar (sometimes lacking entirely) around neck. Face is largely bare red skin; crown is metallic green-ochre with narrow, white superciliary line. Short, steely black ear tufts. *Adult female:* Entirely unlike the male; her tail is considerably shorter and her plumage is variegated browns and grays with underparts pale fawn.

Breeding *Nest:* On the ground, composed of dry grass and usually well concealed by vegetation, often placed in the open or along marginal growth. *Eggs:* 12-20 or more, greenish buff and unmarked. There are indications that, at times, more than one hen will lay in a single nest. Only one brood is raised, but if the first nest is lost another attempt will be made. The males are highly polygamous and the females alone care for the brood.

Range Mongolia and eastern China. Introduced and widely established in various parts of the world.

Remarks One of the greatest hazards to pheasants is the mowing-machine, for a female very frequently chooses a hayfield as her nest site. Evidence points to the loss of a high percentage of these nests and not infrequently mothers are killed or seriously maimed.

The pheasant's food is highly diversified. During the season of plenty its diet consists mainly of grain, weed seeds, fruits and insects. The crop of one I examined on 26 November 1968 was completely filled with the blue-gray fruit of the bayberry *(Myrica pensylvanica)*. At other times of year, when the snow lies deep and the cold is severe for protracted periods, near-starvation will drive them to extremes. For instance, a few years ago at Lower Wolfville a farmer had disposed of 40-50 crow carcasses late in November by tossing them under some heavy, low-growing spruce boughs that flanked a hillside bordering his orchard. During the ensuing winter months he frequently flushed pheasants from under these spruces as he happened to be passing. He naturally assumed they had gathered there for shelter. It was not until the following spring that the truth was revealed, whereupon I was invited to see at first hand his macabre discovery: crow skeletons all over the place, picked clean to the bone, and pheasant droppings numerous enough to suggest a well-used hen yard.

Of the many and varied locales in Nova Scotia where pheasants have been released in the hope that the species might become established, perhaps the most inappropriate is Sable Island, that treeless, windswept strip of sand which lies in the Atlantic about 160 km from the mainland. A number were liberated there in the summer of 1961 but remained scarce until 1964, when they began to increase with winter feeding. Numbers of nests and broods were seen in subsequent years, but they all died in winter 1970-71 with the cessation of chicken-rearing and the associated incidental food supply for the pheasants.

Spruce Grouse   PLATE 10

Dendragapus canadensis (Linnaeus)

Status Uncommon resident. Breeds. In its restricted habitat it may be fairly common, its population being subject to irregularly recurring fluctuations. This bird is normally found only in nonarable regions, mainly on huge land tracts in the interior, remote from settlement. Large portions of these areas were burned-over many years ago, resulting in the destruction of much of the humus, as evidenced by the sparse and stunted new growth which now covers much of the land. There are innumerable wet sphagnum bogs thickly studded with a poor growth of spruce and tamarack. In such places these birds will be found throughout the year.

Description *Length:* 31-43 cm. *Adult male:* A small grouse, coloured black, gray and white, with a small area of featherless red skin above each eye. It is always recognizable by its black chin, throat, lower neck and breast. *Adult female:* Irregularly barred and mottled with grays, blacks and whites, and with a large admixture of rusty brown, particularly on the upperparts and breast. Bars across nape and upper back are lacking in the Ruffed Grouse.

Breeding *Nest:* On the ground in open, sunlit clearings bordered by wet sphagnum bogs which provide food and shelter for the birds. It is usually placed at the base of a small evergreen seedling, and is often concealed by low-growing vegetation but perhaps just as often is rather exposed. The nest is merely a slight depression scraped out in the turf, lined with vegetable debris and a few feathers from the bird's breast. *Eggs:* 4-10, usually 5-6; beautifully marked with spots and blotches of various shades of dark brown and chestnut over a ground colour of buff or pale brown. Of 39 egg clutches examined, all complete, 5 contained four eggs; 11, five; 14, six; 8, seven; and 1, ten. Laying normally begins about the middle of May and continues for about 10 days. The earliest complete set, six fresh eggs, was found on 17 May 1923, and the latest, again of six, on 27 May 1926. A set of four examined at Albany, Annapolis County, on 26 May 1938 was heavily incubated. A nest that contained 10 eggs was discovered on 9 May 1942 at Black River, Kings County, when it held 6, making it apparent that laying had started on or about 3 May. On 13 May it contained 10 eggs; and the same number on the following day gave evidence that laying was completed. The nest was located on high ground fairly remote from swampland and unusually well concealed in a thick clump of juniper *(Juniperus communis),* making it exceptional in (1) its location, (2) the date laying began, (3) the number of eggs it contained, and (4) the habitat in which it was placed. The fact that "dustings" were never found near any of the occupied nests is evidence that the female flies a considerable distance from the nest before alighting and returns to it by flight rather than on foot. This wise provision of nature safeguards the nest from trailing predators.

Range The coniferous forests across Alaska and Canada (except Newfoundland), in the east extending as far south as Maine and southern Quebec.

Remarks This bird is commonly called "fool hen." In some respects the name is appropriate, for it often will permit a person to approach within a metre before moving away. On 26 May 1926 at Albany, Annapolis County, a male was caught by dropping a shoe-string snare over its head. It was placed in a bag and taken to a cabin on an island a mile or so away, where it was banded and gently placed on the ground in the hope that it might remain on the island and become a sort of pet. Having other ideas, it immediately sprang into the air and was last seen swiftly heading up the lake in a bee-line toward the spot where it had been captured.

Occasionally one of these birds will suddenly appear in a town or other settled district, some distance from its normal habitat. Such an event occurred in Wolfville on 5 October 1940, when a female was caught by some small boys who brought it to me alive, with no visible mark of injury. It was kept in an enclosure until 17 October when it was taken to a typical habitat and released. During its captivity it was offered various types of food, of which it seemed to prefer apples and fir needles.

The young of the Spruce Grouse, like those of its "ruffed" relative, are able to fly briskly when only a few days old.

Willow Ptarmigan   PLATE 11

Lagopus lagopus (Linnaeus)

Status Introduced, rare local resident. Breeds. An attempt to introduce Willow Ptarmigan into Nova Scotia was made by a group of Halifax sportsmen in 1933. Fourteen birds imported from northern Manitoba were liberated in Waverley Park, near Halifax, all soon passing into oblivion. Later it was thought more consideration had been given to sportsmen's convenience than to the physical requirements of the birds when the site for liberation had been chosen. In 1968 another effort to bring this bird to Nova Scotia was made by the provincial Department of Lands and Forests, under the supervision of Neil VanNostrand. On 26 July of that year, 20 chicks, three adult hens and a cock were imported from Newfoundland and liberated on Scatarie Island, 2 km or more off the coast of Cape Breton County. In 1969 additional birds were imported, four adults and 60 chicks having been procured from the same source.

In spring 1970 two broods and a nest of 13 eggs were found on Scatarie. Annual visits to this island by Lands and Forests personnel have confirmed that the species is established there. A white ptarmigan, presumably a Willow Ptarmigan, was observed at Cape Canso, Guysborough County, in early December 1969 by June Peters and others. This bird could have been an emigrant from Scatarie Island, some 100 km to the northeast. A male Willow Ptarmigan closely observed on Sable Island by Christel and Norman Bell on 12 August 1966 must have come from outside the province, probably from Newfoundland.

Remarks Scatarie Island is a lonely spot, uninhabited except for those who operate the lighthouse located at a point quite remote from the area of liberation. The island is slightly less than 20 km square, a third of which is said to provide ideal habitat for the ptarmigan.

Rock Ptarmigan PLATE 11

Lagopus mutus (Montin)

Status One record. An adult in full winter plumage was taken at Elmsdale, Hants County, on 20 April 1922 by Malcolm Lucas (Piers 1927). The specimen was acquired by the Nova Scotia Museum and remained in its collection of mounted birds for many years. The black loral mark, a characteristic of the Rock Ptarmigan in winter, removed any doubt in Piers' mind with regard to the species, but he was unable to determine to which race it belonged.

Remarks Some years ago a thief stole a number of mounted specimens from the Nova Scotia Museum's collection, and this ptarmigan unfortunately was among them. It has not been possible, therefore, to establish this bird's subspecific identity.

Ruffed Grouse PLATE 10

Bonasa umbellus (Linnaeus)

Status Rather uncommon to common resident. Breeds. Its populations are heavily reduced periodically by cycles of disease which strike, roughly, at intervals of seven to ten years and occur regionally rather than uniformly over the province; recovery from a low takes approximately three years.

Description *Length:* 40-48 cm. *Adult male:* Colours mainly browns and grays; broad, black feathers making "ruffs" on sides of neck; tail long and fan-shaped, with unbroken subterminal band of black. *Adult female:* Similar but smaller and "ruffs" less conspicuous; cinnamon-rufous breast marking; tail shorter with subterminal band usually broken in centre.

Ruffled Grouse drumming

Breeding *Nest:* On the ground, usually in open second-growth woodlands, often placed at the base of a deciduous tree trunk. The depression is rather deeply cup-shaped and copiously lined with dead leaves and a few feathers from the sitting bird. *Eggs:* 9-13, usually 10; plain buff, sometimes sparsely marked with dots of dark brown. Of 25 nests examined, all with laying completed, 6 contained nine eggs; 16, ten; 2, eleven; and 1, thirteen. Walter E. Whitehead examined a nest of this species on 20 May 1963 near his home at Round Hill, Annapolis County. It had been placed at the base of a spruce in open woodland and contained 18 eggs, half plain and unmarked, and the others with small dark brown dots unevenly distributed over their surface. The size of the clutch and the difference in the colour of the shells strongly indicate that the eggs were the product of two females, a rare incidence in any species of wild bird. Laying normally begins late in April and continues for about two weeks. The earliest complete set of eggs examined was one of 13 at Margaretsville, Annapolis County, on 6 May 1919, and the latest was a set of 10 at Black River, Kings County, on 22 May 1917. The young leave the nest very soon after hatching and are well able to fly up to perch in trees when only a few days old. When danger threatens the brood, the crafty mother feigns injury, squealing pathetically as though in distress—a trick that never seems to fail to lure the enemy away from the little ones.

Range The wooded regions of Canada (except Newfoundland) and the northern United States.

Remarks Many hunters of upland game birds consider the Ruffed Grouse or "birch partridge," as it is commonly called, the finest of them all. In districts close to settlement where considerable hunting pressure has been exerted, it has become extremely wary, taking off in a burst, at the distant approach of its arch-enemy and flying at an angle that quickly puts a screen of vegetation between itself and the hunter, testing the sportsman's skills and powers of coordination to their utmost.

Species of birds belonging to different genera rarely interbreed, but there are several known instances in Nova Scotia of breeding between this bird and the Spruce Grouse, an example of which may be seen in the Downs collection of mounted birds at Acadia University in Wolfville. This male hybrid shows characteristics of both parents, with those of the Ruffed Grouse predominating. Concerning this subject Piers (1894) says: "A hybrid between the 'Spruce' and 'Birch Partridges,' shot about three or four years ago, is said to be in the collection of Mr. Scott Dawson of Pictou. Mr. McKinley says he has observed only one other such specimen from that neighbourhood. I have seen one in Down's possession. He bought it at a butcher's shop in Halifax."

The old theory handed down for many generations that grouse sometimes die trapped under crusted snow is believed to be without foundation. That they dive into soft, deep snow when blizzards are raging or during periods of extreme cold is an established fact, but there is no proof they are ever unable to free themselves from subsequent crust formations. The dead birds sometimes found exposed on the melting snows in wooded areas in late winter probably died from disease.

In addition to the above-cited ruse, the mother bird uses other methods to safeguard her young from enemy attack. Harold F. Tufts was working in his woodlot at Port Mouton, Queens County, in June 1955. His little dog, a timid animal, was nosing about nearby when suddenly an ear-splitting *ki-ki*-ing and a rustling among the bushes was heard. Suspecting his dog had encountered a porcupine, my brother hastened to the rescue. There was no porcupine; instead his pet was fleeing a wrathful mother grouse fluffed up to double her normal size, hissing menacingly and in hot pursuit. When the dog reached the protection of its master's heels the bird quickly disappeared.

In autumn we sometimes find a Ruffed Grouse in settled districts, even in towns or cities. They may crash through windows or be found sitting stupidly in a cellar or barn. For a time it was commonly believed that these "crazy grouse" were diseased birds suffering from an infestation of parasites or some other affliction. More recently, research workers have come to explain this strange behaviour as merely a manifestation of Nature's insistence that individuals disperse to avoid overcrowding. This theory does not explain, nor is it known, why a few grouse in late fall behave in this "crazy" manner. Natural dispersal is one thing but self-destruction is something else.

Of 157 birds examined during my late hunting days, 80 were females and 77 males, an indication that the ratio between the sexes is practically even.

Order GRUIFORMES

Family Rallidae

Yellow Rail   PLATE 13

Coturnicops noveboracensis (Gmelin)

Status Rare transient, very rare in summer. Considered rare by several nineteenth-century authors, but only Jones (1885) refers to a specimen, collected at Cole Harbour, Halifax County. Another was caught by hand near Wolfville by Harold F. Tufts on 19 September 1895. Other specimen records include one shot near Little River, Yarmouth County, on 14 December 1904 (Allen 1916) and another collected at Grand Pré on 9 October 1933 by W. Earl Godfrey, who also sighted one there on 9 October 1937. Since 1960, migrants have occurred: near Canso, where Eileen Armsworthy examined two birds in the hand, one on 7 December 1966, which had been killed by a cat, and another on 17 October 1968 brought to her alive; on Sable Island on 16 September 1973 (D. Welsh); and on Seal Island on 23 October 1976 (B. Mactavish, S.J. Tingley) and 22 October 1977 (E. Cooke). Summer records in earlier years suggest it may have nested. During June 1924 and July 1925, I.A. Bayley observed two in residence near North Sydney. Colin Faulkner heard another calling repeatedly during summer 1938 near Noel, Hants County.

Description *Length:* 15-19 cm. *All plumages:* A short-billed rail, smaller than the Sora. *Adults:* General colour buff or yellowish; back streaked with black, many feathers with narrow white margins giving scaled effect; shows a white wing patch in flight; centre of belly white; sides washed with buff and barred with lighter buff; flanks gray, narrowly barred with white; legs and feet greenish yellow.

Breeding Though no indisputable evidence of nesting is available, Colin Faulkner's account of the Noel bird (see Remarks) strongly suggests that it breeds here. It nests on the ground in wet, grassy marshes, rather than in swamps among tall reeds where most members of its family dwell.

Range Breeds from southern Mackenzie Valley, Manitoba, Ontario, Quebec and New Brunswick, south to North Dakota and other northern states, including Massachusetts and Connecticut. Winters in the southern states.

Remarks This is probably the most elusive of our rails. At the approach of an enemy, it seeks safety by hiding rather than flying, even when the grass cover is so short that little protection is afforded. It is probably safer for it to depend upon its protective colouring at such times than it is to take wing.

A vivid recital of a calling Yellow Rail near Noel in 1938 comes from Colin Faulkner (letter to R.W. Tufts, 30 July 1938): "Many people in this countryside, both nature-lovers and the superstitious, are interested at present in a weird sound moving about on the surface of a swamp or salt marsh and nearby uplands. No one has been able to see the bird or insect or what-not that produces the sound. The noise resembles that made if dry bones were knocked together. In intensity it can be heard on still nights about 100 yards or even farther. The sound is located on the surface of a swamp or salt marsh; it is *not* up in the air at all. It recedes when approached, returns when let alone, stops momentarily when a pebble is thrown near it. It keeps the *click, click, click, click* up continuously for ten minutes or longer, when after a brief pause it begins again. It was also in the same swamp about 70 years ago. . . . Because of the sound, those interested call it the 'bone-knocker.'"

Corn Crake

Crex crex (Linnaeus)

Status One record. McKinlay (1899) reports on the province's only specimen (whereabouts now unknown), taken near Pictou "nearly a quarter century ago in the month of October." The mounted bird remained unidentified until it was examined by Frank M. Chapman, who visited Pictou in 1898.

Remarks There are a number of early records of this Old World rail in eastern North America. There have been no occurrences since 1928, perhaps because it became much less abundant in Europe, especially in Britain.

Clapper Rail

Rallus longirostris Boddaert

Status Very rare vagrant. Two specimens mentioned by Piers (1894) were taken near Lawrencetown, Halifax County: one about 10 May 1892 and the other during October 1893. Subsequent records, all of single birds, are: at Sable River, Shelburne County, on 2 September 1957 (S.M. Chivers); on Brier Island on 24 September 1957 (J. Comer, W. Lent and W.J. Mills); at Glace Bay Bird Sanctuary on 2 December 1967 (A.J. Erskine); on Cape Sable on 17 December 1970 (B.J. and S. Smith); at Grand Desert, Halifax County, on 5 December 1971 (photographed by D.W. Finch); in Dartmouth on 20 November 1973 (R. Melanson); on the Broad Cove, Lunenburg County, Christmas Bird Count on 30 December 1973 (several observers); a very tame individual foraging in debris around the docks on Seal Island, from 26 October to 5 November (photographed by B. Mactavish and S.J. Tingley); and on the Broad Cove Christmas Bird Count on 31 December 1976 (I.A. McLaren).

Remarks It is noteworthy that some of these birds were found around the margins of salt marshes during high tides after a period of sharp freezing; this combination of events may provide the best opportunity for finding this wanderer from the eastern seaboard of the United States.

King Rail

Rallus elegans Audubon

Status One sight record. On 15 September 1957 Betty June and Sidney Smith observed a large rail which they identified as this species on the open terrain of Cape Sable Island.

Remarks The Smiths were able to study this rail at close range with binoculars and noted its much richer, rusty coloration in comparison with the Clapper Rail. The species nests locally as far north as Massachusetts and southern Ontario, and its occasional occurrence here as a vagrant is not unexpected.

Virginia Rail   PLATE 13

Rallus limicola Vieillot

Status Uncommon and local in summer, very rare in winter. Breeds. Our few spring records (first arrivals average 8 May, earliest 20 April) are probably not representative, and the species is probably more common in summer than records indicate. It is most often seen in autumn, with first reports away from breeding sites (average 12

September, earliest 24 August) suggesting that migration begins quite early. It often lingers through December and is sometimes found during Christmas Bird Counts around the province. Individuals on 19 February 1958 at West Middle Sable (H.F. Lewis), on 19 March 1967 near Wolfville (R.W. Tufts) and on several occasions through February 1975 at Russell Lake, Dartmouth (F. Lavender) probably wintered successfully, but others have been found dead during this season. A bird in juvenile plumage (apparently entirely black) was seen at Hillaton, Kings County, on 11 and 18 November 1968 (R.W. Tufts). Immatures customarily do not carry their blackish plumage beyond late summer.

Description *Length:* 25-27 cm. *Adults:* Foreneck, breast and sides cinnamon-rufous; back brownish black, the feathers broadly margined with a clay-coloured shade similar to that of breast; flanks grayish black, barred with white; cheeks slaty gray, almost black in front of eye; a buffy white line from bill over eye; bill largely red; legs reddish brown. *Juveniles:* Largely dull blackish gray, but wings and tail similar to adult; whitish gray chin and breast; white mixed in the underparts.

Breeding *Nest:* On the ground in marshlands. Composed of coarse vegetation with lining of softer materials, and usually attached to the stalks of reeds, just above the water level. *Eggs:* 6-12; light buff, heavily spotted with bright rufous brown. The first breeding record for Nova Scotia comes from Fred Payne, a biologist with the Department of Lands and Forests, who found a nest in Cumberland County on the Missaguash River marsh about 2 km from the New Brunswick border. It contained five well-incubated eggs on 21 June 1962. Since then, other nests or young birds have been found in the same border region; at Russell Lake, Dartmouth; and at Black River, Kings County.

Range Breeds from southern Canada south to California and North Carolina. Winters in the United States and Mexico. Additional races occur in South America.

Remarks Its call is a guttural *cut-cut-cutta-cutta-cutta,* repeated over and over again. This sound is likely to be heard after nightfall, coming from freshwater marshes where lush reeds predominate. Although capable of sustained flight, when startled or pressed into flight it will flutter weakly a short distance, with legs dangling, before dropping out of sight. On the ground it may be seen moving slowly along the muddy margin of a pool bordered by rushes or running lightly over the weedy surface, enabled by its amazingly long toes.

Sora PLATE 13

Porzana carolina (Linnaeus)

Status Uncommon in summer, very rare in winter. Breeds. This is the most frequently encountered rail in Nova Scotia. It normally first appears in April (average 26 April, earliest 8 April). One killed by a cat on 11 March 1942 on Heckman's Island, Lunenburg County, and another found emaciated and recently dead on 4 March 1984 on Chebucto Head, Halifax County, were abnormally early. The Sora is widespread in summer but fairly common only in the border region. Fall migration, evidenced by birds appearing in places where they do not breed, is underway in August (average 23 August, earliest 21 July). Latest reports are generally for October or November, but a few linger into early winter (for example, sightings were made during the Halifax East Christmas Bird Counts of 1975, 1976 and 1978). One bird lived through winter 1978-79 at Russell Lake, Dartmouth, where it was last seen on 7 April (F.L. Lavender).

Description *Length:* 20-23 cm. *All plumages:* A short-billed, chunky little rail without any rufous. *Adults:* Region about base of bill, throat and line through centre of crown black; upperparts dark brown, streaked with black, some feathers with whitish gray edges; breasts and sides of head pale gray; flanks dark gray, barred with white; bill yellow. *Juveniles:* Similar but buffier and without black facial marks.

Breeding *Nest:* Always in marshy places, usually fastened to the stalks of reeds, just above the water level. It is composed of coarse dead reeds and a lining of soft grass. *Eggs:* 8-15; creamy or buffy white, spotted profusely with rich browns. The first Sora nest recorded for Nova Scotia was found near the New Brunswick border by George Boyer on 1 June 1954. It contained 12 eggs, some fresh, others with soft embryos, indicating that the bird had begun to incubate before laying was completed. Since then, nests have been found in the same area and other scattered localities.

Range Breeds from southeastern Mackenzie Valley, southern Quebec and southwestern Newfoundland, south to northern Baja California, Oklahoma and Pennsylvania. Winters from southern United States to northern South America.

Remarks At home in freshwater marshes, the Sora is best located by a high-pitched whinney believed to be its note of alarm. Another common note is a clear, whistled *ka-wee*. To see this performer, one requires patience and a measure of good luck.

Purple Gallinule

Porphyrula martinica (Linnaeus)

Status Rare vagrant. The first occurrence was a specimen taken near Halifax on 30 January 1869 (Jones 1870); Piers (1897) mentions three other nineteenth-century specimens. Three more were reported to 1960, and 21 since then. Nine have turned up in May, five in January, four in July, two each in March, April and June, and one each in February, August, September and October. They have occurred in various parts of the province, including Sable Island (four records) and on a ship off Cape Breton Island on 10 January 1984.

Remarks With head, neck and breast a rich metallic purple, it is equipped with long legs for efficient wading in shallow waters. A bird of tropical and subtropical America, its occurrence in Nova Scotia reflects the species' tendency to wander north of its normal range.

Common Moorhen PLATE 13

Gallinula chloropus (Linnaeus)

Status Uncommon transient, rare and local in summer. Breeds. The "Water Hen" of Haliburton (1825) could be this species or the American Coot, but Gilpin's (1882b) report of one taken near Halifax on 23 May 1880 is the earliest reliable reference. Although there were only about a dozen records prior to 1960, it has been reported regularly since. In Nova Scotia, at the fringes of its range, it arrives rather late (average 12 May, earliest 4 April). It is most widespread and frequent in autumn; away from its localized nesting areas, most have occurred in October. One arrived on Sable Island as early as 19 August 1966, and a very late bird was found during the Halifax East Christmas Bird Count on 27 December 1980.

Description *Length:* 30-37 cm. *Adults:* An almost evenly slate-coloured bird; darker on the head, becoming brownish olive on back and slightly lighter below; conspicuous white flank streaks and white edging under tail; bill and frontal plate bright red, the bill with a greenish yellow tip; legs with red "garters" just below the feathering; toes long and without scallop-shaped lobes.

Breeding *Nest:* A bulky mound composed of reeds and rushes, placed in thick vegetation in or at the edge of shallow water. *Eggs:* 6-17, buff irregularly marked with fine, dark brown speckling. Two broods of young in the Amherst Point Bird Sanctuary in summer 1976 (C. Desplanque) were the first firm evidence of nesting. Since then, one to four broods have been seen there in most summers, and two nests were found by Mark Forbes in 1982. It now nests regularly near the New Brunswick border and a few summer reports from the Northumberland Strait area and from Kings and Halifax counties suggest it may nest elsewhere.

Range In North America it breeds from central California, Arizona, Oklahoma, Nebraska, Minnesota, southern Ontario, Quebec and New Brunswick, south to Baja California and the Gulf States. Winters from southern United States southward. It is also found in Europe, Asia, Africa, South America, the West Indies and other parts of the world.

Remarks These large members of the rail family are far less elusive than their smaller relatives. They spend more time in the open, about the water edges of the marshes in which they live. It is not unusual for them to swim on shallow, open ponds in the manner of coots, which they closely resemble. The species was formerly known as the "Common Gallinule" or "Florida Gallinule."

American Coot   PLATE 13

Fulica americana Gmelin

Status Locally fairly common in summer, uncommon transient, rare in winter. Breeds. In recent years it has arrived in April (average 16 April, earliest 1 April) at its regular nesting grounds near the New Brunswick border, but elsewhere in the province it is rare in spring and summer. Gatherings of up to 75 birds have occurred in the Amherst Point Bird Sanctuary during recent autumns. It routinely appears in coastal regions in December and a few have overwintered in Sullivans Pond, Dartmouth, in recent years, competing with ducks for bread and other offerings.

Description *Length:* 33-44 cm. *Adults:* Slaty gray all over; bill whitish gray; small red spot at base of frontal shield; head and neck somewhat darker than rest of body; white patch under tail; legs greenish gray; toes heavily scalloped.

Breeding *Nest:* Composed of reeds and grasses and placed among the rank vegetation bordering freshwater ponds and marshes. *Eggs:* 8-12; buffy white, uniformly speckled with dark brown or black. Although Hickman (1896) thought it might have nested near Pictou, the first firm evidence of nesting was a flightless young banded by Alan D. Smith at Missaguash River marsh, Cumberland County, in 1969. Since then, several broods have been reported most years at the Amherst Point Bird Sanctuary, where Mark Forbes of the Canadian Wildlife Service found 11 nests in 1982.

Range Breeds from central British Columbia, the Prairie Provinces, southern Ontario, southern Quebec, and Nova Scotia, south to Central America, northern South America, the West Indies and Hawaii. Winters from southern British Columbia and much of the United States southward.

Remarks Rails typically spend most of their time well concealed among marsh reeds, but this member of the family is an exception, for coots are commonly seen swimming on open water with the ease and grace of a swan, their heads bobbing slightly as they move. Their toes are not webbed but equipped with scallop-like flaps which serve their purpose admirably. Coots are locally known by the name "mud hen." They are killed for food by pot-hunters in parts of their range, but their slow and laboured take-off makes them of little appeal to the skilled marksman.

Family Aramidae

Limpkin

Aramus guarauna (Linnaeus)

Status Three sight records. A bird was closely observed on Sable Island by Christel and Norman Bell on 12 September 1964, and another was seen there briefly by them on 27 November 1967 (McLaren 1981a). An injured bird was captured under wharves on Brier Island in the mid-1950s and examined in the hand by Wickerson Lent who identified the bird only retrospectively.

Remarks Although this southern species otherwise has not been recorded on the Atlantic coast north of Maryland, these sightings by knowledgeable observers are convincing evidence of its occurrence in the province.

Family Gruidae

Sandhill Crane

Grus canadensis (Linnaeus)

Status Nine records. The first was discovered on 30 October 1976 by Sherman Bleakney as it fed warily in cornfields near Port Williams, Kings County, and it was seen by several others during the next three days. Later that year, on 18 December, census-takers on the Halifax East Christmas Bird Count were thrilled to see one of these great birds circling overhead, calling loudly and then heading southeast over the sea (photographed by B. Mactavish). On 2 May 1977, one appeared near Great Village, Colchester County (E. Cooper). A most unusual series of events occurred in 1981. On 24 July, William Crins, a knowledgeable birder from Ontario, observed a Sandhill Crane soaring and calling over barrens and bogs inland from Chezzetcook, Halifax County. Another appeared at Grand Pré, Kings County, on 30-31 August (B.F. Forsythe), and one spent some time in autumn on Cape Negro, Shelburne County (E. Turner). Finally, in early September a wild bird appeared at the Shubenacadie Wildlife Park, Hants County, evidently attracted by the captive flock of Sandhill Cranes there. It became attached to one (already mated) crane in particular, and when that crane died in summer 1983, the wild bird departed. A bird near Smelt Brook, Victoria County, in late May 1982 (J. and R. MacKinnon), and two near Middle Musquodoboit, Halifax County, on 9 October 1983 (W. Owen et al.) complete our records.

Remarks The Nova Scotia occurrences appear to be part of a larger pattern of expansion by the species. In June 1982 a pair occurred near St. John's, Newfoundland, and two trans-Atlantic wanderers appeared over Fair Isle, in the Shetlands, in April 1981.

Unlike the pinioned captives, which are of the subspecies *Grus canadensis tabida,* the wild individual at Shubenacadie Wildlife Park was clearly of the small northern form, *Grus canadensis canadensis* according to Eldon Pace, the park director (personal communication, November 1982).

Order CHARADRIIFORMES

Family Charadriidae

Northern Lapwing

Vanellus vanellus (Linnaeus)

Status Rare vagrant. There are eight records of this stray from Europe having occurred in Nova Scotia. The first appearance was at Ketch Harbour, Halifax County, where one dead from starvation was picked up on 17 March 1897 (Piers 1898). The next one was seen at Upper Prospect, Halifax County, where it was shot by a local hunter on 12 December 1905 and later acquired by the Nova Scotia Museum. Late in 1927 a remarkable visitation of Northern Lapwings arrived along our shores, with Newfoundland the focal point. Several seen near Lower L'Ardoise, Richmond County, from early December until about Christmas 1927 were trying to feed about swampy places (A.J. Matheson), and late in December 1927 one was shot at Pleasant Valley, Antigonish County (P.A. Taverner). It was next reported from Little Dover, Guysborough County, where Mrs. S.K. Jarvis saw one about Christmas-time 1964. In 1966 there was a similar but smaller invasion. Of these, one of the birds was observed on 10 January by Murdoch Digout near his home in St. Peters, Richmond County, and picked up nearly dead on 2 February. Two others were seen on 20 January near Round Island, Mira Bay, Cape Breton County, by George Spencer, and another was heard calling during a snow storm at Halifax on 26 February 1966 by Christopher Helleiner, who was familiar with the species in England. In all, 32 Northern Lapwings were reported during the 1966 flight as having been seen in Nova Scotia, Prince Edward Island, New Brunswick and Newfoundland, and at St. Pierre and Miquelon (Bagg 1967).

Remarks One of the birds of the 1927 invasion, killed at Bonavista, Newfoundland, on 27 December, was wearing a band placed on its leg as a nestling at Ullswater, Cumberland, England, in May 1926. Bagg (1967) has described the circumstances under which the 1966 invasion and others like it were impelled to North America by bad weather in western Europe and unusual easterly winds in the North Atlantic.

Black-bellied Plover   PLATE 12

Pluvialis squatarola (Linnaeus)

Status Common transient, rare in summer and winter. It is fairly common in spring, with first arrivals in early to mid-April (average 18 April, earliest 4 April) and most sightings from mid-May to early June. There are also records of small numbers of non-breeders through June, but evident migrants (perhaps failed breeders) may appear in early July (average 7 July, earliest 4 July). They are abundant from late July through mid-October, with small numbers through November and stragglers into January. A few have succeeded in wintering along the Eastern and Southwestern shores, notably on Cape Sable.

Description *Length:* 26-34 cm. *All plumages:* Axillars black; hind toe small. *Adults in spring:* Above checked black and white, giving overall gray effect at a distance; face, throat, breast, sides and belly (to about the thighs) solid black; undertail coverts white; forehead and sides of head above the eye white; uppertail coverts and tail white, finely barred with black; legs dark bluish gray to black; front toes webbed at base. *Immatures:* Crown, back and tail mottled brownish gray and speckled with whitish or pale yellow; below grayish white, finely streaked with brownish gray on breast and flanks. *Adults in winter:* Similar to immatures; back and crown dark ashy brown, finely speckled with creamy or yellowish white; belly white; flanks, breast, foreneck and face softly streaked with grayish brown.

Range In the Western Hemisphere it breeds on arctic coasts and islands and winters in coastal areas from southern British Columbia and New Jersey, rarely to Nova Scotia, south to Chile and Argentina. Also found in the Old World.

Remarks Although most common on sand beaches and tidal mudflats, it regularly makes short flights inland to recently mown hayfields. Here, small flocks attracted by earlier arrivals build up to fairly large numbers, some individuals actively feeding on insect fare while others appear to sleep. These short flights inland occur when rising tides drive the birds off the adjacent mudflats where they usually feed.

Prior to 1928, when it was legal to hunt them, gunners in some districts considered the light-breasted immatures that arrived later in the season to be of a different species and called them "silver-backs."

The Black-bellied Plover is the largest of our plovers and in life may readily be distinguished from the Lesser Golden-Plover, which approximates it in size, by its conspicuous white tail, that of the second bird being uniformly dark. Another good field mark is the Black-bellied Plover's black axillars, which show conspicuously in flight, the underwing of the Lesser Golden-Plover being light gray.

Its mellow, slightly melancholy call of three syllables carries far and is easy to recognize. The species has increased in numbers in recent decades.

Black-bellied Plover and Semipalmated Sandpipers in rain — winter plumage

Lesser Golden-Plover PLATE 12

Pluvialis dominica (Müller)

Status Common transient. It is occasional in spring, with three occurrences of one or two birds each between 29 March and 7 April, the rest during May. It is generally uncommon but sometimes numerous as a fall migrant generally appearing in early August (average 16 August, earliest 21 July). It is most commonly seen in September but regularly noted until late October with stragglers well into November (latest 27 November).

Description *Length:* 24-28 cm. *All plumages:* No hind toe. *Adults in summer:* Upperparts dark gray, strongly speckled with golden yellow; crown nearly unspeckled; cheeks, throat and underparts black, including undertail coverts; forehead white, extending in band above eye and down side of neck to edge of belly, where it is suffused with gray. *Adults in autumn:* Traces of black on underparts.

Range Breeds from the arctic coast of Alaska, eastward to northern Baffin Island, south to northern Manitoba. Winters from Bolivia, Paraguay and Brazil south to east-central Argentina and Uruguay; casual in winter in the southern states.

Remarks Somewhat smaller than its close relative the Black-bellied Plover, the species with which it is most likely to be confused, it may be distinguished by its generally darker appearance. The Black-bellied Plover, particularly when in flight, shows a conspicuously white or nearly white tail and black axillars. The underwing of the Lesser Golden-Plover is uniformly light grayish brown, and the bird has no white on its tail.

Most northbound migrants travel a course far to the west of Nova Scotia, coming overland from their wintering grounds in South America through the Mississippi Valley and the Prairie Provinces. However, this bird's migratory route in autumn is quite different. After nesting in the far north is completed, the main flocks gather at points in Atlantic Canada and New England before beginning an arduous, 4000 km trans-Atlantic flight to Brazil. Fairly large numbers leave Nova Scotia about mid-September, though stragglers are seen much later. These laggards probably fly southward overland through the Atlantic states.

During the late nineteenth century this bird was abundant here in the fall, but soon afterwards its numbers began to decline rapidly. This decline was brought about by an overshooting of spring migrants (chiefly in the United States) and for some years the bird was thought to be marked for early extinction. In spite of this, legal hunting was permitted in both Canada and the United States through 1927. Since then it has been given year-round protection in both countries and is believed to be making a slow recovery.

The Greater Golden-Plover *(Pluvialis apricaria)* of Eurasia has occurred in Newfoundland and might turn up here. Among other field marks, its white underwings, which contrast with the gray underwings of the Lesser Golden-Plover, are conspicuous in flight.

Wilson's Plover

Charadrius wilsonia Ord

Status Eight or nine records. A summer adult from Halifax is mentioned in the *Catalogue of Birds of the British Museum* (1896, Vol. 24, p. 216). The first well-documented record is of a female taken at Brier Island on 28 April 1880 (Goss 1885). There are no twentieth-century records until 1971, when one was tentatively identified on Cape Sable Island on 12 September (B.K. Doane). The next year, one was photographed by Ian A. McLaren on Sable Island on 2 April, and two more were well studied by Benjamin K. Doane on Cape Sable Island on 8 October. One was found on Seal Island on 17-19 May 1975 (photographed by S.I. Tingley), another was at Beach Meadows Beach, Queens County, on 14 May 1977 (F.L. Lavender), one was on Seal Island on 26-28 May 1984 (E.L. Mills et al., photos), and another was at Conrad Beach, Halifax County on 13-14 July 1984 (F.L. Lavender, D. Currie).

Remarks Slightly larger (at 18-20 cm) than the Semipalmated Plover, it has a much heavier, longer black bill and pinkish gray legs. This bird breeds coastally from New Jersey and Baja California southward, wandering north casually. Conservation measures and a growing number of competent observers account for the recent increase in records; even so, most records are from islands at the extremities of the province.

Semipalmated Plover PLATE 12

Charadrius semipalmatus Bonaparte

Status Common transient, rare in summer. Breeds. It is an uncommon spring migrant, with a few arriving in late April (average 9 May, earliest 19 April; a bird on Sable Island on 11 April 1972 was abnormally early). Most are seen in mid-May and, in diminishing numbers, to the end of the month. It breeds sparingly from southwestern Nova Scotia to Halifax County, on the North Shore from Cumberland to Pictou County, and on Sable Island. It is a familiar fall migrant along all shores, first appearing in early July (average 11 July, earliest 3 July) and abundantly from late July through mid-September. It remains fairly common until early October, with stragglers still present in November and even December. Individuals on Christmas Bird Counts at Brier Island on 20 December 1973, and Halifax West on 18 December 1976, were very late.

Description *Length:* 16-19 cm. *Adults:* Back and crown grayish brown; forehead white; line from bill to eye and single band on breast black; underparts white; legs yellowish gray or flesh-coloured; toes webbed at base.

Breeding *Nest:* On the ground, usually on a pebbly beach, well above high water. The depression is usually lined sparsely with dry eelgrass. *Eggs:* 4; creamy buff, blotched with dark brown chiefly about the larger end. If the first nest is destroyed, there will be a second one, but the second is more likely to contain three eggs than four. First laying begins in early May and continues until mid-June. A nest found at Cook's Beach, Yarmouth County, on 6 June 1923 contained four eggs about ready to hatch, and three nests found in the same area on 19 June 1923 each held four fresh eggs. Between 1922 and 1928, in the general area of Cook's Beach, I discovered 21 nests. It was not unusual to find complete sets of fresh eggs in early June, on the same day that the downy young of other pairs were in evidence. On 24 June 1922, two nests presumed to be second attempts were found; one contained three eggs, and the other held two eggs. Stony beaches flanked by extensive salt or brackish marsh areas are the preferred terrain.

Range Breeds across low arctic and subarctic North America, south along the Pacific coast to southern British Columbia and, in the east, south to Nova Scotia. Winters as far south as Patagonia in South America.

Remarks This plover frequents sandy beaches and mudflats during migration and, although it mixes to some extent with swarms of its many relatives, it shows an inclination to remain aloof, particularly at high tide when it is resting on beaches.

Two colloquial names for this shorebird are "ox-eye" and "ring-neck." It can be readily identified by the single black band (brown in young birds) across an otherwise pure white breast.

The Killdeer, which this bird resembles, is about twice as large and has two black bands across its breast. The Piping Plover is much like the Semipalmated Plover in size and plumage pattern but is much paler.

Piping Plover   PLATE 12

Charadrius melodus Ord

Status Rare summer resident. Perhaps 50-60 pairs still breed along the Atlantic shore and along the Northumberland Strait. Early arrivals appear in late March and early April (average 5 April, earliest 21 March, an abnormally early bird was at St. Esprit, Richmond County, on 7 March 1982); most are here by mid-April. Migrants are seen in early August and most are gone by September (average 17 September, latest 9 October); late stragglers were on Sable Island on 24 November 1967 and 17 November 1969. There is a most unusual winter record of one on Sable Island on 25 January 1967 (C. and N. Bell). Human disturbance of the white sand beaches where it breeds accounts for the continued decline of this species.

Description *Length:* 15-19 cm. *All plumages:* Forehead and underparts white; feet rich yellow. *Adults:* Above pale sandy brown; no black bar through face but a black band across front of crown; forehead and underparts white; the single black breast band may be broken in middle. *Juveniles:* Breast band very poorly defined or lacking.

Breeding *Nest:* A mere depression scraped in the sand, well above the highest tides, sometimes lined sparingly with bits of broken seashells or a few wisps of dry eelgrass. *Eggs:* 4; creamy white, evenly speckled with fine spots of dark brown or black. Laying begins about mid-May. On 23 May 1930, a nest at Summerville Beach contained four slightly incubated eggs. On 14 May 1943, on the same beach, a nest contained one egg, laying having just begun. If the first nest is destroyed, there will be another but it will probably contain only two or three eggs. On 13 June 1928, two nests at Summerville Beach each held one egg, evidence that these were second nestings.

Range Breeds on the Atlantic coast from the Gulf of St. Lawrence south to northern North Carolina and locally in central North America. Winters from South Carolina to the Gulf States and casually further south.

Piping Plover and nest

Remarks There is something ethereal about these ghost-like birds on their nesting grounds. This is particularly noticeable on a cloudless day in June when the sun, accentuating the dazzling whiteness of the sand, and the ocean surf pounding incessantly on the beach combine to impair one's ability to see and hear clearly. Invading their sanctum at such times, one is likely to be made aware of their presence not by sight but by sound, hearing a soft, flute-like *pipe-pipe-pipe-pipe* repeatedly at short intervals. The note is both sad and sweet, and one finds it difficult to determine the direction from which it comes. This is because the performer is an accomplished ventriloquist. When standing still, it is almost invisible. After scanning all directions of the beach, one detects motion as the bird makes one of its characteristic short runs. One is often startled to realize that the well-camouflaged bird was so close at hand.

When its nest is approached, the sitting bird will leave when the intruder is still some distance away, run to meet him and circle widely, all the while calling plaintively, soon to be joined by its mate. Not until the intruder comes very close to the nest do the birds resort to the ruse of feigning injury to lure him away. On windless days the nest may be located by looking for trails in the soft sand, the nest being their focal point. However, so fine is the sand that even a slight breeze quickly erases the birds' footprints.

In 1985 this bird was placed on the list of endangered Canadian species by the Committee on the Status of Endangered Wildlife in Canada. Its decline on the east coast is discussed by Cairns and McLaren (1980). Efforts to increase public awareness with signs placed on Nova Scotia beaches where it nests have apparently enhanced breeding success in some places.

Killdeer   PLATE 13

Charadrius vociferus Linnaeus

Status Fairly common transient, uncommon in summer, rare in winter. Breeds. It generally appears first in March (average 23 March, earliest 1 March, assuming early March birds to be normal migrants). It is an increasingly regular breeding bird, especially in the southwestern half of the province. Migrants are most frequent in September and October with regular stragglers to November and December. Late fall individuals are thought to be reverse migrants from further south. Birds have wintered in all parts of the province from Cape Breton Island to Yarmouth County, and others have appeared through the winter, sometimes in association with storms.

Description *Length:* 23-28 cm. *Adults:* Back and crown grayish brown; rump and upper tail bright rufous; forehead, throat, ring around neck, patch above and behind eye, and underparts white; double band of black crosses breast; legs usually flesh-coloured, but variable.

Breeding *Nest:* On the ground; a depression scraped out in an open pasture, cultivated field or gravel pit usually a considerable distance from the coast; lined sparsely with dry grass. *Eggs:* 4; buffy white, spotted and irregularly marked with chocolate-brown chiefly around the larger end. A nest found at Gaspereau, Kings County, on 7 May 1968 contained the usual four eggs. The sitting bird ran from the nest when I was not closer than about 35 m, indicating that the eggs were fresh or nearly so. The nest was in an open, stony pasture inland from the coast. Another that year, at Black River, Kings County, was similarly located in an open field. It held four eggs in which incubation was, presumably, well advanced because the bird sat "close" when the nest was approached. A nest at Chebogue Point, Yarmouth County, contained two eggs on 7 July 1967, obviously a second nesting attempt. I have never known this bird to select a concealed nest site.

Range Breeds from southeastern Alaska, southern Mackenzie Valley, and central Quebec to western Newfoundland and south to the West Indies and southern Mexico; also in Peru and northern Chile. Winters from southern British Columbia, the Ohio Valley and Nova Scotia, southward to Colombia and Peru.

Remarks Although it is sometimes seen along our beaches during migration, mingling in the flocks of others of its close relatives, the Killdeer is essentially a bird of the interior, frequenting wet fields, sloughs and pasturelands.

Its name is derived from its call, a sharply enunciated *kill-dee kill-dee,* often heard when the bird rises in alarm. The distinctive black double band across its otherwise white breast provides an excellent field mark.

It has apparently expanded its former range in recent years.

Family Haematopodidae

American Oystercatcher

Haematopus palliatus Temminck

Status Three records. Blakiston and Bland (1857) state that "it has been seen here," without providing details. Audubon claimed to have found it nesting along the shores of the Bay of Fundy about 1833 (Forbush 1916). The location as cited does not rule out the possibility that he saw it on the New Brunswick side of the bay. It was not recorded again until 20 July 1907 when W.H. Osgood saw a flock of about 20 at Digby (Cooke 1910). A more recent sight record is provided by Charles R.K. Allen, John Comer and Thomas F.T. Morland, who saw an oystercatcher at Grand Desert, near Chezzetcook Inlet, Halifax County, on 19 May 1957; whether the bird was an American Oystercatcher or its European counterpart, *Haematopus ostralegus,* was not determined. One at Matthew's Lake, Shelburne County, on 28 April 1983 was confirmed from a photograph by Robert Turner.

Remarks The American Oystercatcher is a large (43-53 cm), brown-backed shorebird with a black head and throat, a white belly and white wing patches, which are conspicuous in flight. The large bill is bright red. It occurs normally on beaches and is particularly wary.

Along the Atlantic coast it breeds locally from Massachusetts to the Gulf States and the Caribbean. The very similar European Oystercatcher, *H. ostralegus* (which has not been recorded in North America), has a black rather than dark brown back.

Family Recurvirostridae

Black-necked Stilt

Himantopus mexicanus (Müller)

Status Two records. The first was the sighting of four by Nettie Moore at Canning, Kings County, on 23 September 1965 (Bagg and Emery 1966). On 27 May 1979 two at Cape Sable were filmed by Betty June and Sydney Smith.

Remarks Black above, white below with a long slender bill and extremely long red legs, this large shorebird (33-43 cm, or about the size of the Greater Yellowlegs) is not

PLATE 11

Willow Ptarmigan
Page 139

male, changing plumage

female, summer

Rock Ptarmigan
Page 140

male, summer

male, summer

Rock Ptarmigan
Page 140
two birds, winter

Willow Ptarmigan
Page 139
winter

Roger Tory Peterson

PLATE 12

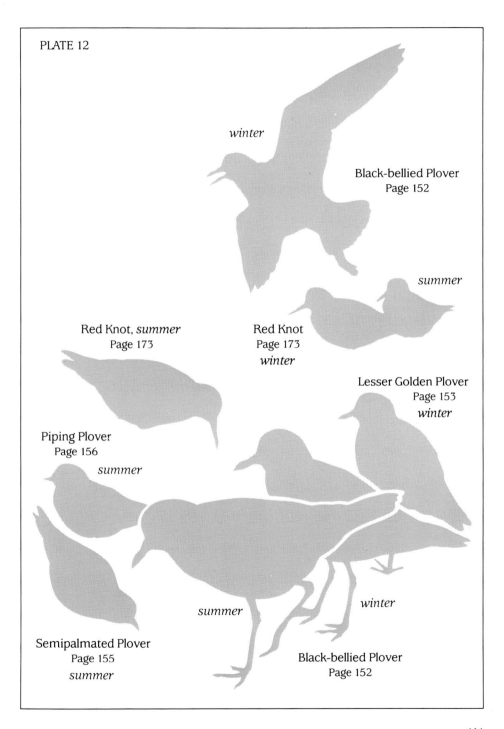

winter

Black-bellied Plover
Page 152

summer

Red Knot, *summer*
Page 173

Red Knot
Page 173
winter

Lesser Golden Plover
Page 153
winter

Piping Plover
Page 156
summer

summer

winter

Semipalmated Plover
Page 155
summer

Black-bellied Plover
Page 152

apt to be confused with any other. The species has also been recorded in Newfoundland and New Brunswick, but in eastern North America it does not nest north of Delaware. It seems to be expanding its breeding range.

American Avocet

Recurvirostra americana Gmelin

Status Six records. Constance and Roswell Gallagher discovered and photographed the first individual on Cape Sable Island on 28 August 1969; another was seen shortly after on Sable Island on 16 September (C. and N. Bell). An early wanderer was found at Three Fathom Harbour, Halifax County, by Eric Cooke on 5 July 1970 and was photographed the next day by Ian A. McLaren. Other individuals were on Seal Island on 22-23 September 1970 (several observers); at Cole Harbour, Halifax County, on 4 September 1974 (B. Mactavish, S. Tingley) and near Canning, Kings County, for a week in mid-September 1976 (O. Moorehouse et al.).

Remarks Breeding in the Prairie Provinces and the western United States, these wanderers were far from home in Nova Scotia. This species is one of the largest (40-50 cm) and most showy of the shorebird group. Its outstanding characteristics are an exceptionally long, slender, upcurved bill, long legs, and contrasting buff, white and gray plumage, all of which combine to make the bird unmistakable.

Family Scolopacidae

Greater Yellowlegs   PLATE 15

Tringa melanoleuca (Gmelin)

Status Common transient, rare in summer. Breeds. Only a few first arrivals have been noted before mid-April (average 17 April, earliest 28 March), and it is normally most numerous about mid-May. It breeds in the Cape Breton Highlands and probably in Guysborough and Halifax counties. Non-breeders are found in small numbers elsewhere on the coast. It is an abundant fall migrant: a few arrive in early July; it is most common from mid-August to early September, when numbers gradually decline. Last sightings are routine in November (average 15 November, latest 7 December). Very late birds have been recorded on Christmas Bird Counts: eight around Chezzetcook (Halifax East count) on 20 December 1969, two at Glace Bay on 26 December 1973, and three at Glace Bay on 26 December 1979.

Description *Length:* 33-38 cm. *All plumages:* Legs and feet bright yellow. *Adults in summer:* Upperparts dark gray, spotted and streaked with black and pale gray; uppertail coverts and tail white, more or less barred with black; breast white, thickly spotted with black; sides barred with black; belly white. *Adults and immatures in winter:* Similar but upperparts brownish gray edged with whitish gray; wing coverts dark gray, sides only slightly barred.

Breeding *Nest:* A depression in the ground, well concealed and lined with grass and other dry vegetable debris. *Eggs:* 4; dark buff, irregularly spotted and blotched with rich chocolate-browns of varying densities. The male shares the domestic responsibilities. The species has long been known to occur during summer on the barrens of Cape Breton Highlands National Park at elevations of about 400 m. John S. Erskine saw a young bird swimming there in a weed-infested pond (as though trying to escape) on 20 July 1956 while a pair of adults protested the observer's intrusion. The first nest, with four eggs, was found near Twin Island Lakes, Victoria County, on 27 June 1974 (Majka et al. 1976). There have been summer reports from suitable habitats in Guysborough and Halifax counties.

Range Breeds from Alaska to Newfoundland and, in the east, as far south as northern Nova Scotia. Winters on both coasts from Oregon and New York State, south through Mexico, Central America and the West Indies to southern South America.

Remarks It is one of our larger shorebirds, being readily identified in life by its conspicuously long yellow legs, its dark back and its lightly barred tail and white rump, being very noticeable when the bird takes flight. Its usual call is distinctive: three or four rapidly repeated, whistled notes on a descending scale, *whew-whew-whew,* given excitedly when the bird is flushed. In spring its scolding note, heard when its breeding territory is invaded, is more like *oodle-oodle-oodle.* (For further distinctions see Lesser Yellowlegs.)

Lesser Yellowlegs

Tringa flavipes (Gmelin)

Status Common transient. It is rather uncommon in spring, generally first appearing after mid-April, with a few reliably identified birds reported earlier (average 20 April, earliest 1 April). Last spring sightings are usually in late May (average 23 May, latest 7 June). A few probable non-breeders have occurred in late June, but first migrants generally appear in early July (average 11 July, earliest 1 July). Peak numbers are found from late July through early September; stragglers are routine in November (average 6 November, latest 28 November).

Description *Length:* 25-28 cm. *All plumages:* Like the Greater Yellowlegs but noticeably smaller when a direct comparison is possible. The bill is proportionally shorter, straighter and more slender.

Range Breeds from Alaska to Quebec, mostly north of cultivation. Winters from the Gulf States to the West Indies, Chile and Argentina.

Remarks Its call is distinctively different from that of the Greater Yellowlegs, and this simplifies field identification when the two species are not seen together for comparison of size difference. The call of the Greater Yellowlegs consists of three or four high-pitched, rapidly repeated, whistled notes with a slightly descending cadence, but the Lesser Yellowlegs' call is two sharp, whistled notes that suggest alarm, quickly repeated several times and usually given at the moment the bird is flushed.

This bird is usually seen singly or in small numbers about the brackish pools which are common in low-lying marshy areas along the coast, but it sometimes occurs in large flocks early in the season.

As evidence of their power of flight, a Lesser Yellowlegs banded on Cape Cod, Massachusetts, was recovered six days later on the island of Martinique in the southern Caribbean Sea, about 3,000 km away.

Solitary Sandpiper   PLATE 13

Tringa solitaria Wilson

Status Uncommon transient. Small numbers have been reported for 12 springs since 1960, between 28 April and 8 June. It is a rather uncommon fall migrant: although a few normally appear after mid-July (average 20 July, earliest 6 July), most are noted from mid-August through early September. They are last seen in October most years (average 16 October, latest 9 November).

Description *Length:* 20-23 cm. *Adults:* Back almost black, finely speckled with white or buff; centre feathers of tail black, outer ones white, conspicuously barred with black; sides of head, neck and breast white, streaked and speckled with black; belly white; legs and feet olive-green.

Range Breeds in the wooded northland of Canada and Alaska. Winters from the southern states and the West Indies south to central South America.

Remarks This shorebird is rarely seen in salt marshes and almost never on beaches, nor does it consort with its relatives. It shows a decided preference for the swampy margins of brackish pools, freshwater ponds and woodland streams, frequently being seen far from the coast. Its name is most appropriate, for during its migration it often is seen alone.

Good field marks are its dark wings and white outer tail feathers, barred with black and conspicuous in flight.

For many years, naturalists were puzzled at being unable to learn the secret of this bird's nesting habits. Finally it was discovered that, unlike most sandpipers, practically all of which nest on the ground, this one uses the old nests of birds that build in trees in the Canadian northland.

Willet   PLATE 13

Catoptrophorus semipalmatus (Gmelin)

Status Fairly common in summer. Breeds. Generally first arrives in late April (average 22 April, earliest 9 April; see Remarks for earlier individual on Sable Island). It now breeds in coastal areas provincewide, having become increasingly common and widespread in the past 20 years. Most depart in August, with last sightings regular in October, rarely later (average 7 October, latest 29 November). On Sable Island, two very late stragglers were noted on 21 December 1973 (P. Dunning). In light of these records, Robert Turner's convincing report of one near Lockeport in January 1984 is perhaps a little less surprising. (See Remarks for discussion of probable racial status of these late birds.)

Description *Length:* 35-43 cm. *Adults:* Upperparts gray, the head and neck streaked with dusky brown; back barred with blackish brown; uppertail coverts mostly white; basal half of primaries and greater part of secondaries white; rest of wings blackish brown; underparts white, streaked and spotted with dusky brown on foreneck and breast; flanks barred with dusky brown; axillars and underwing coverts blackish brown; bill blackish brown, paler at base; legs and feet bluish gray.

Breeding *Nest:* On the ground, usually well concealed among low-growing bushes in open fields or bushy pastures and usually, if not always, in the vicinity of salt marshes. The nest is a shallow depression with a lining of dry vegetable matter. *Eggs:* 4 (one record of 5); olive or buff, thickly spotted with chocolate-brown, mostly about the larger end. They sometimes nest in loose colonies, perhaps 8-10 pairs scattered over 40 ha. A nest containing four fresh eggs was found at Chebogue, Yarmouth County, on 25 May 1930, concealed under a clump of blueberry bushes about 100 m from a salt marsh. Another at Chebogue contained four eggs on 19 June 1923. The bird sat so "close" that I was able to place a metal band on its leg without causing it to leave the nest (undoubtedly the eggs were about to hatch). On 5 August 1920 at Grosses Coques, Digby County, about 20 young showing traces of natal down were observed feeding along brackish pools.

Range In the east, breeds along the coast in Nova Scotia, recently in New Brunswick and southwestern Newfoundland, and from (rarely) southern Maine to Florida and other Gulf Coast states to Texas. Also in the central United States and the Prairie Provinces. Winters from British Columbia and Virginia, south to South America and the West Indies.

Remarks These large, showy shorebirds are quite spectacular, especially when encountered on their nesting grounds. At first approach, an intruder is met by the excited and protesting members of the scattered colony which unite, often circling low overhead or alighting on treetops or other convenient perches, all scolding vehemently:

pill-will-willet pill-will-willet, given in rapid succession. This barrage continues until the enemy retreats, followed by the birds for some distance as though being chased away.

The large white marks on its wings, conspicuous in flight, have led to its being called "white-wings" by countryfolk throughout much of its breeding range.

Our nesting birds are *Catoptrophorus semipalmatus semipalmatus.* Birds of the prairie subspecies, *Catoptrophorus semipalmatus inornatus,* are regular on the U.S. coast in fall migration, usually after eastern birds have departed. They are larger, longer-billed, longer-legged and recognizably paler and grayer than eastern birds. The first sight record of a western Willet in Nova Scotia was on Sable Island on 30 August 1969 (D.W. Finch). Since then, several have been reported (one collected, two photographed) after 25 August. It is possible that most of our late Willets are from this western population. More surprising was a bird, evidently of this race, on Sable Island on 2 April 1972 (photograph in McLaren 1981a).

Willet on spruce top

Spotted Sandpiper   PLATE 14

Actitis macularia (Linnaeus)

Status Summer resident. A few arrive in late April (average 3 May, earliest 15 April, apart from one exceptionally early bird on 8 April 1979). More are present by mid-May, late May on Cape Breton Island. It breeds along streams and lakes, and locally along coasts provincewide. Because it does not congregate in migratory flocks, its departure in August and September goes relatively unnoticed, but stragglers are regular in October (average 20 October, latest 7 November). A bird on 29 November 1970, another on 11 December 1968, and four late-December individuals, the latest on 31 December 1968 at East Bay, Cape Breton County (W.P. Neily et al.), were exceptional.

Description *Length:* 18-20 cm. *Adults in summer:* Brownish gray above with slight greenish lustre, more or less marked and barred with blackish brown; grayish white line through eye; underparts white, profusely marked with round, black spots; legs greenish yellow. *Adults in winter:* Breast unspotted. *Immatures:* Similar to winter adults; breast slightly washed with gray.

Breeding *Nest:* On the ground, usually concealed by low plant growth but sometimes wholly exposed; a shallow depression sparsely lined with dry vegetable matter. *Eggs:* 4; creamy buff, thickly spotted and blotched with dark or chocolate-brown, more profusely around the larger end. Laying begins during late May. Two sets of four fresh eggs were found: one on 30 May 1898 at Gaspereau, Kings County, and the other on 16 June 1949 at Port Mouton, Queens County. A remarkable nesting location was the bleak rocky ledge known as Gannet Rock about 4 km off Cape Forchu, Yarmouth County. The only birdlife there on 9 August 1935 was a pair of Spotted Sandpipers, one of which was followed by a half-fledged youngster. The rock was bare of vegetation and its highest part so low that during heavy storms the spray must be thrown over most, if not all, of the surface.

Range Breeds throughout Canada from the limit of trees south to California and Virginia. Winters from southern British Columbia and South Carolina to South America.

Remarks Like all members of the family Scolopacidae, the young leave the nest soon after hatching. I once attempted to catch a day-old chick as it ran ahead of me along the shore of a pond. When hard pressed, it took to the water and swam with ease. When further pressed, it actually dived but bobbed to the surface within a second or two. When placed by hand on the beach, it scampered off, apparently none the worse for its ducking. If an adult is attacked by a winged predator while in flight over water, it will dive below the surface to escape its pursuer. If still harassed after surfacing, it will dive again (Tothill 1918).

Upland Sandpiper

Bartramia longicauda (Bechstein)

Status Rare transient. The first record was a bird collected on Sable Island in 1868 (Gilpin 1882a), and there were only five more reports up to 1957. Since then, one or two and occasionally several have appeared each spring (earliest 3 April, latest 13 June), mostly in May. In summer 1976 a pair spent 15-23 June in courtship display at Canard, Kings County, but did not stay. In the same year one was on Sable Island between 22 and 27 June. Fall migrants have been recorded in like numbers almost every year between 14 July and 19 November (both dates for Sable Island), but generally between late August and mid-September. Most records are from Seal, Sable, Brier and Cape Sable islands.

Remarks About robin-sized or slightly larger (30 cm), it is predominantly buffy brown, evenly marked with dark brown above, and with a white belly. Its head is comparatively small and rounded, suggesting that of a pigeon. Its neck is noticeably slender and its tail is slightly elongated.

It frequents low-lying meadows rather than beaches and mudflats, and is more at home in the prairie regions of the continent than in the east.

Its manner of flight is strikingly similar to that of the more common Spotted Sandpiper and provides a good field mark.

Eskimo Curlew

Numenius borealis (Forster)

Status Formerly common transient, no recent records. Latest definite record of occurrence in Nova Scotia is a fragmentary specimen from Sable Island marked " ? fall of 1902" (McLaren 1981a). Another was on sale in the Halifax Public Market on 11 September 1897 (Piers' notes). Hickman (1896) recorded one on 24 May 1895 at Pictou and stated that the species was a common transient there in autumn but not in spring; this is suspect as he does not mention the Whimbrel. Other nineteenth-century authors considered the bird uncommon; Jones (1885) noted that "this species, which was formerly very common, has now become exceedingly rare." A mounted specimen, without date, in the Nova Scotia Museum collection was probably taken in Nova Scotia; it was mounted by Downs about 1846 (Piers' notes).

Remarks This bird provides a striking example of the havoc that can be wrought in a relatively short period by uncontrolled slaughter inspired by human greed. Before the 1880s this species was abundant and virtually unmolested during its breeding season on the low arctic tundra of the northwest. On its southward migration route in autumn it had little to fear from humans—well coated with fat, it took off from Nova Scotia in a direct over-water course for South America, covering some 4000 km or more, non-stop. It spent our winter months on the broad pampas of Argentina and

Patagonia. On its return in the spring it passed up the Mississippi Valley and northward across Canada. It was during this period of its travels that its annihilation was accomplished, apparently by excessive shooting, although climatic factors may also have been involved (Banks 1977). The birds travelled in immense flocks of close formation, making them particularly vulnerable. These birds had survived the long and hazardous over-water flight and other dangers incident to migration and were now close to their nesting range. Particularly unwary at that season, bewildered flocks, devastated by gunshot, would often return to decoys only to receive a second broadside. The last recorded bird collected in Canada was at Battle Creek, Labrador, on 29 August 1932. The appearance in recent years of several of these birds in Canada and the United States, and the deplorable killing of one in Barbados, the West Indies, on 4 September 1963, furnish evidence that the Eskimo Curlew is still extant.

In life it is best distinguished from its close relative the Whimbrel by its smaller size, but both birds have to be seen together to make the comparison. A curlew in the hand can best be identified by noting the colour pattern on the underside of the outer primaries. In the Eskimo Curlew these are unmarked buff, but in the Whimbrel they are buff, barred with darker brown.

Whimbrel   PLATE 15

Numenius phaeopus (Linnaeus)

Status Uncommon transient. It is a rare spring migrant, with most records between 29 April and 2 June. Early individuals were on Sable Island on 6 April 1972 and at Cherry Hill Beach, Lunenburg County, on 6 April 1981. Birds seen on 21 June 1976, 20 June 1980, and 23 June 1983 may have been non-breeders. First migrants have otherwise appeared in early July (average 9 July, earliest 30 June). It is generally an uncommon fall migrant, although locally common in some years. Last sightings are generally in October (average 11 October, latest 26 November). One of the European race (see Remarks) remained until late December.

Description *Length:* 38-48 cm. The long, down-curved bill varies in length from 7-10 cm, depending upon age and sex. *Adults:* Upperparts dull brown more or less marked with buff; crown blackish brown with a central buffy gray stripe; buffy gray line above and a dark brown line through eye; underparts buff, lightening to nearly white on throat and cheeks; brown bars on flanks and faint stripes on breast up to neck and face; legs and feet bluish gray.

Range Breeds from Alaska to the west side of Hudson Bay. Migrates southward, chiefly along both coasts; wintering in southern states (rarely) and south to parts of South America. Other populations are found in the Old World.

Remarks For many years before the Migratory Bird Treaty between Canada and the United States was signed in 1916, Whimbrels were hunted relentlessly in Cape Breton and Richmond counties in particular, where they loitered in autumn to fatten on the rich berry-laden barrens. Gorged with food, they gathered in the late afternoon to fly to rocky islets along the coast to roost for the night. Aware of these roosting places, groups of hunters waited for the unsuspecting birds. As the flocks streamed in to alight, the slaughter was heavy, the bewildered survivors flying off into the gathering darkness in screaming confusion and alarm.

In 1920 I discussed the Whimbrel situation with some of the older hunters of the general area about Scatarie Island, off the Cape Breton County coast. They told me that a marked diminution in the number of Whimbrels had taken place during the preceding two decades, adding that the thousands of earlier days had been reduced to a few hundred. From more recent reports it appears that there has been little if any improvement.

Whimbrels from Europe (*Numenius phaeopus phaeopus*), which have a distinctive white rump, are very rare visitants. The first, taken aboard ship near Sable Island on 25 May 1906 (Brewster 1909), was ascribed to *Numenius phaeopus islandicus* of Iceland, now considered indistinguishable from *N. p. phaeopus*. More recently, individuals have been identified at Cherry Hill Beach, Lunenburg County, lingering from 13 October to 28 December 1974 (S. Fullerton et al.); at Matthews Lake, Shelburne County, on 20 August 1976 (G. Perry); at Martinique Beach, Halifax County, on 19 August 1977 (A.R. MacInnis); and at Hartlen Point, Halifax County, on 23 June 1983 (F.L. Lavender et al.).

Eurasian Curlew

Numenius arquata (Linnaeus)

Status One sight record. Shirley and Lisë Cohrs reported seeing this large curlew at Cherry Hill Beach, Lunenburg County, on 6 May 1978.

Remarks The bird's large size (50-60 cm) and huge bill (based on comparison with a nearby Willet), white rump, uniformly marked head and two-syllable call were noted. There are only four confirmed North American records of this Old World species.

Long-billed Curlew

Numenius americanus Bechstein

Status One old sight record. Blakiston and Bland (1857) list it as "very rare" and Jones (1885) states that "this species, which was formerly very common, has now become exceedingly rare." There is other evidence that this species regularly visited northeastern North America in the first half of the nineteenth century. The only explicit report is by Gilpin (1882a), who stated that in September 1870 he saw one at Windsor. There are no twentieth-century records.

Remarks Larger than the Whimbrel (50-65 cm vs. 38-44 cm), its bill is proportionately much longer and more strongly down-curved than the Whimbrel's. It is cinnamon-brown above, streaked with dark brown, and ashy buff below, with pale, unmarked cinnamon-brown wing linings. Its call is a musical *curlee*. Primarily a bird of the western plains, it is still an occasional visitor to the east coast of the United States.

Hudsonian Godwit PLATE 13

Limosa haemastica (Linnaeus)

Status Uncommon transient. Fall migrant individuals and small flocks begin to arrive in July (average 18 July, earliest 1 July), and larger numbers occur in August and early September. Stragglers are fairly regular in October but very rare in November (average 8 October, latest 8 November). Birds on Sable Island on 6 June 1965 and at Sunday Point, Yarmouth County, on 2 June 1974 were far from their normal northward route through the Great Plains.

Description *Length:* 33-40 cm. *All plumages:* White uppertail coverts form a broad white band across base of tail. *Adults in spring:* Upperparts mottled dark brown and buff, with broad band of white across uppertail coverts; tail black, tipped narrowly with white; underparts rufous, narrowly barred with black and narrowly tipped with white; bill long, slender and slightly upcurved; legs and feet slaty blue. *Immatures and adults in winter:* Upperparts brownish gray; belly whitish gray; breast gray, tinged with buff.

Range Breeds locally from the Mackenzie Valley eastward to western Hudson Bay. Winters in South America.

Remarks Recent studies of this bird during summer have revealed that it is still quite common in its breeding range. It has also been learned that in late July and early August large concentrations gather on the extensive mudflats bordering the west coast of James Bay. A few birds continue their migration through the Maritimes, but the main body, not showing up here or elsewhere in large numbers, is believed to take off from the James Bay concentration area on a direct transoceanic flight to a point in South America. This hypothesis would explain why the Hudsonian Godwit is not seen anywhere along its way southward in North America in numbers comparable to those known to breed in our northland.

This bird is one of our largest shorebirds. Its size, general dark colouring, long dark legs, conspicuous white rump patch, and slightly upturned bill readily distinguish it from all others.

Marbled Godwit

Limosa fedoa (Linnaeus)

Status Rare transient. The species was first recorded for Nova Scotia on 15 April 1915 by Louis B. Bishop who received a specimen from taxidermist Robert P. Searle of Halifax, who told him that the bird had been taken at Sambro Light, Halifax County, but gave no date (Piers' notes). It was next reported by Harrison F. Lewis who saw two near the Sable River estuary, Shelburne County, on 8 September 1953, the day following hurricane "Carol." Since then, there have been 15 more sightings, almost all of single birds and all but four occurring in August or September. The earliest were four near Pictou on 1 August 1961 (E. Holdway); late individuals were on 17-24 October 1964 at Cole Harbour, Halifax County, and on 14 November 1964 at Glace Bay. On 29 September 1962 the remarkable number of about 25 of these birds was seen on Cape Sable by Betty June and Sidney Smith. Although it is possible that the 1915 specimen should be referred to as a bird of the previous fall, there is a definite spring record of one on 8 June 1979 on Sable Island.

Remarks A large (40-50 cm) brown godwit, this species has cinnamon-brown wing linings, is uniformly buffy gray above, evenly marbled with black, and has no white rump patch or wing stripe. It breeds in the northern Great Plains and on James Bay and normally migrates primarily through western North America to Central and South America, with some birds wintering in the southern United States. It is quite regular on the east coast of the United States in fall.

Ruddy Turnstone   PLATE 16

Arenaria interpres (Linnaeus)

Status Common transient, rare in winter. It is an uncommon spring migrant generally seen during May (earliest 28 April, latest 2 June). Birds in early April on Cape Sable during 1978 had probably overwintered locally. A few late-June birds during three years may have been non-breeders. It generally appears around mid-July (average 16 July, earliest 1 July) in migration and remains common through September. It can still be found locally in November and has occurred on a dozen Christmas Bird Counts around the province. Individuals and small groups have successfully wintered several times at Louisbourg and have been seen on Sable Island and Cape Sable during January or February.

Description *Length:* 20-25 cm. *All plumages:* Legs short, giving the bird a squat appearance. *Adults in summer:* A sturdy orange-legged shorebird with striking contrasting colour pattern; upperparts variegated with black, bright rufous and white; tail with broad black band, white at base and tipped with white; throat and belly white. *Adults in winter:* Dark grayish brown above, with white eyebrow, throat and underparts; lower breast black with a faint gray patch on each side.

Range Breeds throughout the Arctic. In North America, most winter from the southern United States south to Brazil and Chile.

Remarks Turnstones are found feeding along bleak coastlines among kelp-covered rocks, or on sand beaches. On occasion they will resort to inland pastures and mown hayfields. On 12 September 1921, a bird was collected from a flock of 20 or more that was circling a pasture at Chebogue, Yarmouth County; the flock finally alighted and appeared to be feeding. It is not unusual to see small numbers, mixed with much larger numbers of Black-bellied Plover, on the meadowlands at Grand Pré, Kings County, after the hay has been cut.

It is unusual to see large concentrations of turnstones. When the adult is seen in flight with a flock of the smaller sandpipers, as so often happens, its sharply contrasting plumage makes it stand out.

The name "turnstone" refers to the bird's habit of turning over small stones and other objects in search of food along the shore. Their custom of feeding among the kelp at low or half tide has caused them to be known by some shore folk as "seaweed-birds."

Red Knot   PLATE 12

Calidris canutus (Linnaeus)

Status Fairly common transient, rare in winter. It is an uncommon to rare spring migrant from mid-April through May (earliest 17 April, latest 8 June; a bird on Sable Island on 2 April 1972 was abnormally early). It is much more common as a fall migrant, first appearing in July (average 16 July, earliest 6 July), most frequent in August and September, with stragglers to year's end. There are a few reports for late January and February, including about 100 on Sable Island on 30 January 1978, indicating occasional attempts to winter here, especially in the southwest of the province.

Description *Length:* 25-28 cm. *Adults in spring:* Above finely mottled with grays, black and light ochre, running into stripes on crown; throat, breast and sides of head cinnamon-brown; dark gray line through eye; abdomen and undertail coverts white; uppertail coverts white, barred with black. *Adults in winter:* Pale ashy gray above, from crown to rump, with feathers on back narrowly edged with white; underparts white, the breast lightly streaked and speckled, and the flanks narrowly barred with gray. *Adults in autumn:* Underparts of some individuals show traces of the "red" of spring.

Range Breeds on arctic islands in both the New and Old Worlds. In the New World, it winters in coastal regions from California and Massachusetts, south to Chile and Argentina.

Remarks The Red Knot is a medium-sized, rather short-legged and chunky sandpiper. Look for it on sand beaches with adjacent mudflats, where it feeds, and on low-lying meadows after the hay has been cut. Small flocks frequently consort with larger flocks of Black-bellied Plover on the meadows at Grand Pré, Kings County.

In the old days when shorebird shooting was legal, the Red Knot was highly regarded as a table bird; and because the flocks, in close formation, came readily to decoys, its numbers were alarmingly reduced. Much of the shooting in those days was done during spring migration, particularly in the United States. Although the species has recovered somewhat under protective legislation, which came late, it is no longer abundant in our region.

Sanderling   PLATE 14

Calidris alba (Pallas)

Status Common transient, rare in winter. It is an uncommon spring migrant (although some of these had probably wintered locally) from early April through May, with some last sightings in June (average 29 May, latest 8 June). A bird on Cape Sable on 17 June 1971 was probably a non-breeder. It is a very common fall migrant, a few arriving as early as mid-July (average 17 July, earliest 11 July), and it is most abundant from mid-August through September. It is still fairly common in late October and early November; laggards are regular until early January, especially on Sable Island and in the southwest, where they regularly succeed in overwintering.

Description *Length:* 18-20 cm. *Adults in spring:* Upperparts variegated with black, rusty ochre and white; below white; throat, neck and upper breast overwashed with variable amounts of reddish ochre spotted with brown; bill, legs and feet black. *Adults and immatures in winter:* Above pale brownish gray variegated with black; below pure white.

Range Breeds in the Arctic of both the New and Old Worlds. In the eastern part of the New World it migrates southward along the Atlantic coast, wintering from Nova Scotia to the West Indies and southern South America.

Remarks Typically birds of the beaches seldom seen elsewhere, these hardy little sandpipers seem to be in their element when heavy waves pound the shoreline. With nimble feet they follow the backwash down, to scamper back quickly before the rush of incoming waves, gleaning particles of food from the sea. After the great congregations of their numerous relatives have left our shores for warmer climates, some of these little beachcombers often will be found still searching diligently for food along our beaches, which by then seem to us bleak and forbidding.

Semipalmated Sandpiper   PLATE 14

Calidris pusilla (Linnaeus)

Status Common transient. It is an uncommon spring migrant, generally appearing by mid-May (average 13 May, earliest 23 April). A few non-breeders are found through June so the beginning of fall migration is difficult to discern. Groups begin to arrive by early July, and from mid-July to late August the bird is abundant, remaining common through mid-September. It is still present in smaller numbers in October, and stragglers are sometimes seen in November (average 30 October, latest 23 November). A bird on Cape Sable on 31 December 1975 may have been a Western Sandpiper.

Description *Length:* 14-16 cm. *All plumages:* Legs black, bill stout, not strongly decurved. *Adults in summer:* Dark grayish brown above, white below, sides of head, neck and breast suffused with light grayish brown. *Adults in winter:* Uniformly gray above. *Juveniles:* Brownish gray above.

Range Breeds in the lower Arctic, and in subarctic regions from western Alaska to Labrador. Migrates through the interior and along the Atlantic coast to reach its wintering grounds, which extend from the southern United States to South America.

Remarks Towards the end of the nineteenth century, the future welfare of these sparrow-sized "game birds" seemed grim, for they were being massacred wholesale over a wide area by men and boys armed with shotguns. But before hunting had gone too far, protective international legislation, though belated, was enacted in 1918 and was strongly supported by public sentiment fostered through educational channels.

In Nova Scotia, perhaps no sand beaches or mudflats are more attractive to these birds than those found about the Minas Basin. One of these, Evangeline Beach, is the centre of immense congregations of shorebirds in autumn, perhaps 90 percent of which are of this species. Locally known as "peeps," they begin to arrive in early July and are augmented steadily by new arrivals from the north until about mid-August when a peak is reached. To see these immense flocks to the best advantage, one should visit Evangeline Beach during the peak period when the incoming tide is nearing its height. At such times, gradually forced off the mudflats where they feed, they gather in vast numbers on the beach, where they rest in dense formations. When disturbed, the roar of wings and the chorus of peeps is impressive. Sometimes the flock is strung out over the water in long lines extending several hundred metres or more; sometimes it is closely packed. It is thrilling to watch them as they turn and twist in perfect unison. Flashing a momentary gleam that suggests a silver sheet as their white breasts and underwings are exposed, they suddenly create a dark cloud as they wheel to show their mottled gray upperparts. Dewar (1912) suggests that this behaviour of shorebirds in flight is protective, enabling the flock to foil attacks from birds of prey. He points out that these aerial evolutions resemble wave movement or sea spray from above and thus might confuse a predator.

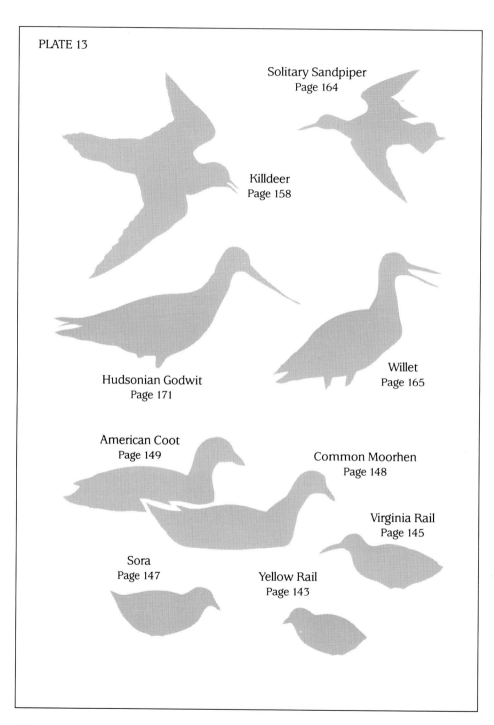

PLATE 13

Solitary Sandpiper
Page 164

Killdeer
Page 158

Hudsonian Godwit
Page 171

Willet
Page 165

American Coot
Page 149

Common Moorhen
Page 148

Virginia Rail
Page 145

Sora
Page 147

Yellow Rail
Page 143

Roger Tory Peterson

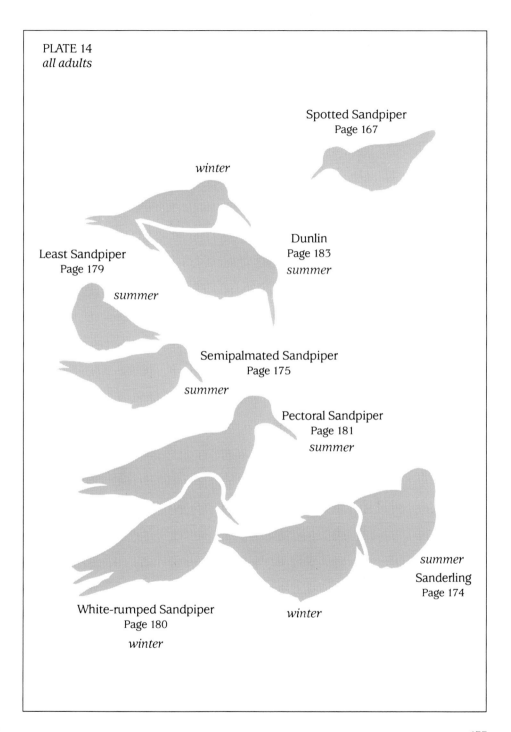

PLATE 14
all adults

Spotted Sandpiper
Page 167

winter

Least Sandpiper
Page 179

summer

Dunlin
Page 183
summer

Semipalmated Sandpiper
Page 175

summer

Pectoral Sandpiper
Page 181
summer

summer
Sanderling
Page 174

White-rumped Sandpiper
Page 180

winter

winter

I am pleased to say that the flocks of shorebirds which gather at Evangeline Beach in late summer had not dwindled in size by 1970 and were as impressively large as when I watched them as a boy.

Western Sandpiper

Calidris mauri (Cabonis)

Status Rare transient. At least some of a large flock of small sandpipers seen by Christel and Norman Bell on Sable Island on 23 December 1963 were believed to be this species. The first fully documented observation was by Davis Finch, who picked out two, possibly three, among Semipalmated Sandpipers on Brier Island on 4 September 1969. On 9 September 1970 Jean Burton collected a juvenile on Sable Island (Ouellet et al. 1973). Since then, fall migrants have been reported in most years, at least six documented by photographs. Most have occurred between mid-August and late September, with a few in October and one sighting of four at Conrad Beach, Halifax County, on 16 November 1980. A well-described early migrant was at John Lusby Marsh, Cumberland County, on 16 July 1980 (S.I. Tingley).

Remarks The recent change in status is probably more a tribute to advances in techniques of field identification than to any change in the range of the species. However, it is possible that some have been misidentified. On average the bill of the Western Sandpiper is heavier, thicker at the base and more drooping than that of the Semipalmated Sandpiper. There is, however, considerable overlapping of bill size in the two species, and this is particularly true of birds seen in the northeast. Juvenile Western Sandpipers typically show more chestnut in the scapulars and mantle but, again, there is considerable variation. In short, it is not always possible to distinguish fall juveniles; winter adults present an even more difficult problem. A common call of the Western Sandpiper, a thin *cheet,* is quite different from the rather harsh *chir-rup* of the Semipalmated Sandpiper. Western Sandpipers breed in northeastern Siberia and Alaska, and most migrate down the west coast. However, there is a regular flight to the east coast in autumn, and the bird is much more regular in the southeastern United States during winter than is the Semipalmated Sandpiper.

Little Stint

Calidris minuta (Leisler)

Status The only record of this species for Nova Scotia is of a juvenile discovered by Ian A. McLaren at Hartlen Point, Halifax County, on 23 October 1983. Many others saw this bird during the next three days, and its identity was confirmed by photographs.

Remarks A close Old World relative of our Semipalmated and Least Sandpipers, it very rarely reaches North America; ours was the third Canadian record. The size of our Least Sandpiper (15-16 cm), it has black rather than yellowish gray legs, but in certain plumages it is very difficult to distinguish from another Old World species, the Rufous-necked Stint *(Calidris ruficollis)*. Juveniles show a considerable amount of chestnut about the head and mantle and have white lines at either edge of the mantle in a distinctive V pattern.

Least Sandpiper   PLATE 14

Calidris minutilla (Vieillot)

Status Common transient, rare and local in summer. Breeds. It is a rather uncommon spring migrant, generally appearing in May (earliest 25 April, except for one abnormally early bird on Sable Island on 11 April 1972) and gone by month's end (latest apparent migrants 1 June). It nests regularly on Sable Island and has nested on Cape Sable Island, as well as in Halifax County and perhaps elsewhere. Migrants first appear in early July (average 6 July, earliest 1 July), after which the species becomes abundant until late September. Stragglers are frequent in October, rare in November (average 23 October, latest 6 December). A very late bird was found by Russel Crosby on the Christmas Bird Count at Port l'Hebert, Shelburne County, on 23 December 1976.

Description *Length:* 13-16 cm. *Adults in spring:* Upperparts brown, the feathers with blackish brown centres and gray, white or buff margins; white eyebrow line; wing coverts grayish brown; flight feathers blackish gray; underparts mostly white, with throat and breast suffused with brown and lightly streaked with gray; bill black; legs and feet greenish gray; toes showing no traces of webs. *Immatures:* Similar to adults but markings less distinct; feathers of upperparts show traces of rufous with white margins; breast less distinctly streaked than in adults.

Breeding *Nest:* On the ground, a slight depression sparsely lined with dry vegetable matter. *Eggs:* 3-4, usually 4; pale buff, thickly speckled with dark chestnut-brown and purplish gray. Dwight (1895) found Least Sandpipers nesting on Sable Island, where they still nest in numbers (Miller 1985). On 4 June 1907, Harold F. Tufts saw downy young accompanied by parent birds on a small marsh on Cape Sable Island, and other evidence of breeding there has been obtained from time to time since. A nest with four eggs was found on Conrad Beach, Halifax County, on 3 June 1971 (I.A. McLaren), and other nests and fledglings have been found there and in nearby areas in subsequent years. Suggestions of breeding have also come from Guysborough and Richmond counties.

Range Breeds across the northern parts of continental North America from Alaska to Labrador and, in the east, south to Nova Scotia and, recently, Massachusetts. Winters from the southern United States to central South America and the West Indies.

Remarks During migration this little sandpiper is as much at home on sandy beaches and exposed tidal flats as it is on salt marshes and along pools near the coast. Although it does mingle with the other sandpipers when resting on the sand beaches at high tide, it tends to remain somewhat aloof from the others. Many times I have noted flocks of 40-50 or more segregated from the others, resting higher up on the beach where the pattern of their plumage tends to blend with the pebbles.

It is most likely to be confused with the Semipalmated Sandpiper, which is slightly larger and has a grayish rather than brownish cast to its upperparts. The legs of the Least Sandpiper are greenish gray, but those of the Semipalmated Sandpiper are black. Smaller sandpipers are commonly called "peeps," and none may legally be killed in Canada or the United States.

White-rumped Sandpiper   PLATE 14

Calidris fuscicollis (Vieillot)

Status Common transient. It is only occasional as a spring migrant, mostly in late May (extreme dates 24 April-10 June). It is a common fall migrant, with a few arriving during July in some years (average 1 August, earliest 6 July); its numbers are highest in late August and during September, but stragglers regularly persist until early November. There are half a dozen late December records and one for 20 January 1977 at Louisbourg (R. Burrows). In addition, there was a remarkable sighting of two birds, which had presumably overwintered, at Sydney Harbour on 23 March 1974 (H. Hopkins).

Description *Length:* 18-20 cm. *All plumages:* White stripe over eye. *Adults in spring:* Upperparts dark brown, variegated with feather edges of buff, rufous or white; breast and flanks narrowly streaked with dark brown; rump always white; legs dark greenish gray; toes not webbed. *Adults in autumn:* Breast streaking often suffused with a vague breast band of light ashy gray or even pale buff; upperparts much grayer and less variegated than in summer.

Range Breeds along arctic coasts and southern arctic islands from Alaska to Baffin Island. Migrates through interior of continent and along the Atlantic coast. Winters in southern parts of South America.

Remarks It is found on sand beaches and mudflats, mingled with hosts of other small shorebirds, and also on the margins of brackish pools just at the shoreline. In view of the fact that numbers of these birds loiter along our shores until late November, it is surprising to read that others of the species, seemingly impatient to reach their distant wintering grounds, have been seen along the coast of Brazil in August and as far south as Cape Horn by September 6 (Wetmore in Bent 1927).

This shorebird is readily identified by its white rump, which can best be seen in flight—a mark it does not share with any of its small relatives that occur regularly in Nova Scotia.

Baird's Sandpiper

Calidris bairdii (Coues)

Status Rare transient. Although Gilpin (1882a) mentions it, the first concrete record is of a bird collected by Harold F. Tufts at Grand Pré, Kings County, on 7 September 1899. Only five more were recorded prior to 1966, but since then fall migrants have been seen in small numbers every year. Most have occurred from late August through mid-September, with extreme dates of 12 July and 24 October. Two at Summerville Beach, Shelburne County, on 16 May 1983, well studied by Roland Chaisson, were highly unusual, as the species is almost unknown outside the central interior of North America during spring migration.

Description *Length:* 18-19 cm. *Adults in summer:* Upperparts dark brownish gray, feathers inconspicuously margined with pale buff or brownish gray; central tail feathers dark gray, outer ones brownish gray; throat white; breast buff, lightly streaked with dark brown; belly white; legs black. *Adults in winter:* Plumage paler.

Range Breeds in the Arctic from eastern Siberia and Alaska to northwestern Greenland. Winters in South America, migrating mostly through the interior of North America, being uncommon on both the Atlantic and Pacific coasts.

Remarks This small sandpiper resembles the Least, Semipalmated and White-rumped Sandpipers. Its larger size and black legs, however, distinguish it from the Least; the absence of a white rump distinguishes it from the White-rumped; and its buff breast contrasts with the grayer breast of the Semipalmated.
 The Pectoral Sandpiper, though similarly marked, is larger and has greenish gray, not black legs. Another good mark of Baird's Sandpiper is the length of its folded wings which extend beyond its tail.

Pectoral Sandpiper   PLATE 14

Calidris melanotos (Vieillot)

Status Fairly common transient. It has been occasionally recorded in spring since 1963, between 7 April and 23 May. It is a fairly common fall migrant, with a few first birds often occurring before mid-July (average 17 July, earliest 5 July); one on Sable Island on 26 June 1977 may have been a non-breeder. It is more regular from mid-August on, with greatest numbers usually present in September, sometimes in October, and with a very few remaining some·years until November. There is a later record of two on 17 December 1979 at Port l'Hebert, Shelburne County.

Description *Length:* 20-23 cm. *Adults in spring:* Upperparts dark brown striped with buff, with buff feather edges; dark brown stripe through eye is bordered above by white; below, breast and foreneck marked with buff band, heavily and evenly striped with brown; belly white, contrasting sharply with lower breast; bill greenish yellow, lighter at base, darker toward end; legs greenish yellow. *Adults in autumn:* Similar but buff on upperparts replaced by rufous; breast heavily washed with buff.

Range In North America, breeds in the low Arctic and subarctic from Alaska to Hudson Bay. Winters in South America.

Remarks This sandpiper is seldom found on sand beaches. It much prefers salt marshes after the hay has been cut, or freshwater marshes where one might expect to flush Common Snipe. It is because of a general similarity to the snipe in appearance and its choice of habitat that it has been given the colloquial name "grass snipe." Larger than our smallest sandpipers, it is distinguished by its broad and strongly striped buff breast band.

Purple Sandpiper PLATE 16

Calidris maritima (Brünnich)

Status Locally fairly common in winter. It occurs in flocks along the rocky shores on the Atlantic and Fundy coasts, and even in the sheltered Minas Basin. Usually it is first reported in early November, occasionally in October; most are gone by the end of April, but laggards are regular in May (latest 4 June 1957). There have been only five records between 31 July and the end of September, but since its rocky habitat is not searched by birders as thoroughly as are beaches and salt marshes during late summer, it may actually arrive here earlier than our records show.

Description *Length:* 20-23 cm. *Adults in spring:* Dark slaty brown and black above with slight purplish gloss, feather edges and tips being broadly marked with buff or white, or sometimes a pale ochre; wing coverts and secondaries tipped with white; underparts mainly white, the breast heavily washed with ashy gray and with indefinite brown spots extending along flanks; rump black; inner secondaries with much white; chin whitish gray; legs dull orange to olive-ochre. *Adults in autumn and winter:* Upperparts nearly black with purple iridescence, feathers edged with pale gray; below white, with broad breast band of ashy gray.

Range Breeds in arctic regions of eastern North America and the Old World. In North America, winters on the eastern seacoast south to Maryland.

Remarks My most interesting contact with this bird occurred on 14 January 1925 at the mouth of Port Joli Harbour, Queens County, on the open Atlantic coast. The temperature was hovering around -18°C, the waves were pounding the kelp-covered rocks and the spray flew freely. There I found 50-60 of these little sandpipers blithely running about as though it were a day in June, seemingly oblivious of the restless and icy waters that all but engulfed them. I particularly recall the ease with which they were approached, the result, perhaps, of their lack of familiarity with humans.

Dunlin   PLATE 14

Calidris alpina (Linnaeus)

Status Fairly common transient, rare in winter. It is a rare spring migrant, with scattered records between 12 April and 30 May. It is a rather common fall migrant, with a few reports for July (earliest 5 July), but is rarely noted before mid-August. It is usually most numerous in September and early October but in some years is still plentiful in early November; stragglers are regular through December. A few have evidently overwintered on the Southwestern Shore; at Martinique Beach, Halifax County; and near Glace Bay.

Description *Length:* 20-23 cm. *All plumages:* Bill slightly down-curved; legs and feet black. *Adults in summer:* Back and crown predominantly rich red-brown, marked with black streaks; breast, neck and face gray, streaked with white; throat white; large black patch on abdomen. *Adults in autumn:* Soft uniform gray above, suffusing across breast; remainder white; light eyebrow line; occasionally fall adults retain a few of the red feathers of summer on their backs and some individuals show traces of the black abdominal patch.

Range In North America, breeds across the Arctic, migrating down both coasts and through the interior. Winters on the coasts from Alaska and Massachusetts (rarely Nova Scotia) south to Mexico. Occurs also in the Old World.

Remarks This stocky, short-legged bird shows a strong preference for sandy beaches with their adjacent mudflats, where it feeds during receding tides. It is generally seen in small flocks of occasionally 100 birds or more. When the Dunlin is seen in autumn, its long, slightly down-curved bill is its best field mark; in breeding plumage, the black abdominal patch and the reddish brown upperparts are unmistakable.

Curlew Sandpiper

Calidris ferruginea (Pontoppidan)

Status Rare vagrant. In spite of some confusion in the literature, it seems that there were two nineteenth-century specimens, one killed in autumn 1864 (McLaren 1985). There are 11 modern records. The first bird was found on Sable Island by Christel and Norman Bell on 26 January 1968; they also saw two birds in breeding plumage there that year, one on 26 July and the other on 10 August. In 1971, one was seen on Brier Island on 10 July (E.L. Mills) and another at Three Fathom Harbour, Halifax County, on 31 October (E. Cooke et al.). Elizabeth Reid found one at Port Morien Bar, Cape Breton County, on 26 October 1969, and Daniel Welsh saw another on Sable Island on 22 November 1970. In 1978, three impeccably described birds were seen: on Sable Island on 24 August (many observers); on Cape Sable on 24 September (B.J. Smith); and at

Matthews Lake, Shelburne County, on 22 October (G. Perry, R. Turner). The only photographically confirmed bird was an adult in breeding plumage at Cherry Hill Beach, Lunenburg County, on 2 July 1983 (J. and S. Cohrs).

Remarks This Old World shorebird occasionally wanders to North America. In breeding plumage, its rich chestnut-brown underparts distinguish it from the Dunlin. Otherwise, its strongly decurved bill and its white rump, conspicuous in flight, are distinctive.

Stilt Sandpiper

Calidris himantopus (Bonaparte)

Status Uncommon transient. Dwight (1903) recorded an adult female collected on Sable Island on 18 August 1902. It was not reported again until 1950, when there were two sightings, and 1959, when one was collected on 13 August. Since 1965 the bird has been seen annually in small numbers. Spring reports are of individuals on Mud Island, Yarmouth County, on 14-15 May 1974 and on Sable Island on 13 June 1967, 8-11 May 1968, and 8 June 1979. The June birds on Sable Island could have been displaced spring migrants, but one at Three Fathom Harbour, Halifax County, on 22 June 1978 was possibly an early fall migrant. Otherwise, these have first appeared generally after mid-July (average 27 July, earliest 30 June), somewhat earlier in recent years. The largest groups (10-15 birds at times) have come in August and early September, and latest sightings are usually in September or October (average 1 October, latest 13 November). Most remarkable was the individual closely observed from time to time by Betty June and Sidney Smith on Cape Sable from 22 February to 26 March 1979.

Description *Length:* 19-23 cm. *All plumages:* Long greenish gray legs; long, slightly drooping bill. *Adults in spring:* Upperparts grayish brown; underparts heavily barred with dark brown; white eyebrow stripe; chestnut ear patch. *Adults in autumn:* Plumage dull gray above, with varying remnants of spring plumage; white below; distinct, nearly white eyebrow stripe.

Range Breeds from northeastern Alaska to northeastern Manitoba and northernmost Ontario. Winters in South America and casually north to Florida and southern California.

Remarks It bears some resemblance to the Lesser Yellowlegs, but when first seen it is more likely to be confused with the Short-billed Dowitcher, with which it often associates. It probes sand or mud with its distinctive, long, slightly drooping bill, its long legs submerged in water.

It frequents brackish pools in marshy areas, such as are found behind sandy or rocky beaches along the coast. It migrates mainly through the Prairie Provinces to and from its wintering grounds in South America.

Buff-breasted Sandpiper

Tryngites subruficollis (Vieillot)

Status Uncommon transient. Gilpin (1882a) mentions a specimen, and Downs (1888) considered it as an uncommon fall migrant but may have confused it with the Red Knot (McLaren 1985). Sightings of numbers on Sable Island on 2 September 1901 (R. Bouteillier 1901) and of one on 12 September 1905 (J. Bouteillier 1906) are plausible, and the first bird collected was brought to a Truro taxidermist on 10 September 1910 (Piers' notes). The next record was of three observed by Michael Anketell-Jones at Hartlen Point, Halifax County, on 26 September 1965. Since then it has appeared annually in small numbers. Two spring records are most unusual: a bird on Conrad Beach, Halifax County, on 8-9 April 1976 (R. Connor et al., photographs) and another on Sable Island on 20 May 1978 (I.A. McLaren). Apart from an early bird on Brier Island on 6 August 1972, fall migrants have rarely appeared before late August (average 27 August, earliest 18 August), and the latest are very rarely seen after September (average 16 September, latest 16 October, apart from one lingering at Hartlen Point until 16 November 1983).

Remarks With a blackish gray bill and greenish yellow legs, this species averages slightly smaller (19 cm) than the Pectoral Sandpiper and larger than the Semipalmated Sandpiper. It is pale buff over much of its body and nearly unmarked below. It breeds in Alaska and the western Canadian Arctic, migrating through the Midwest and occurring rarely on the Atlantic or Pacific coasts.

Ruff

Philomachus pugnax (Linnaeus)

Status Rare vagrant. One was collected at Cole Harbour, Halifax County, on 27 May 1892 (Piers 1894, 1915), and another at New Minas, Kings County, on 1 October 1928 (Smith 1938). Since 1959 Ruffs have appeared during 13 of 25 years. There have been seven spring birds, between 19 April and 30 May. A total of 17 fall migrants has appeared between 2 July and 25 October. All have been single birds, apart from a male and female on Sable Island between 19-25 July 1978.

Remarks In size the Ruff falls between the Lesser and Greater Yellowlegs, with which it frequently associates. Its legs are shorter, and its bill is shorter and stouter than either of the yellowlegs. It is perhaps more likely to be confused with the Pectoral Sandpiper. The legs of the Ruff vary from dull yellowish green to olive-green or flesh-coloured. The male Ruff is considerably larger than the female (called a Reeve), 30 cm vs. 23 cm.

Short-billed Dowitcher PLATE 15

Limnodromus griseus (Gmelin)

Status Common transient. It is uncommon in spring, generally first appearing in late April or early May (average 7 May, earliest 18 April; one on Sable Island on 8 April 1972 was abnormally early). Small flocks are sometimes seen in May, but the bird is seldom seen after month's end (latest 3 June). A bird on Sable Island on 13 June 1975 may have summered in the region, but 14 on Cape Sable on 21 June 1979 were presumably early migrants. Fall migrants otherwise appear routinely in early July (average 5 July, earliest 30 June). They are most numerous in late July and August and are still present in small numbers in October. Later birds, including one on Cape Sable on 28 December 1968, have not always been critically distinguished from possible Long-billed Dowitchers.

Description *Length*: 26-30 cm. *All plumages:* Legs and feet yellow or greenish yellow. *Adults in spring:* Upperparts dark brown to black with feather edges of various shades of reddish ochre; tail and rump white, more or less spotted or barred with black; underparts, including throat and breast, strongly brick-red, finely spotted across breast with black. *Adults in autumn:* Dull gray on back, more or less interspersed with brown and ruddy ochre, as worn in summer; head, neck, breast and flanks lighter gray; chin lighter than breast or face; often show the red-breasted summer plumage, but it is worn, faded and interspersed with gray.

Range Breeds in southern Alaska, southern Mackenzie Valley, northern Alberta, northeastern Manitoba and the interior of northern Quebec. Winters from the southern United States south to Brazil.

Remarks This bird is partial to the muddy shorelines and margins of brackish pools so frequently found behind beaches along the coast. Its straight bill, which in length rivals that of the Common Snipe, and its white tail and rump narrowly banded with black, are good field marks. It is locally called the "spot-rump."

The regular subspecies here is *Limnodromus griseus griseus,* which nests in northern Quebec. A few adult *Limnodromus griseus hendersoni,* which breed in the far northwest, have been distinguished in recent years among early fall migrants. When still in breeding plumage, they retain more extensive rufous on the belly, are almost unspotted on the upper breast and have much brighter feather edgings above, compared with adult *L. g. griseus* at the same stage.

Long-billed Dowitcher

Limnodromus scolopaceus (Say)

Status Rare transient. A bird collected on Sable Island and labelled 4 October 1897 was identified as this species by Pitelka (1950). There were no further records until 20 September 1969, when Charles R.K. Allen and Ian A. McLaren saw and heard two near Musquodoboit Harbour, Halifax County. Since then autumn migrants, generally in ones and twos, have been reported every year except 1972, between 12 August and 11 November. A number of later dowitchers could have been this species, and four early ones, identified near Amherst as Long-billed Dowitchers on the basis of their calls on 1-10 July 1977 (C. Desplanque) could have been failed breeders.

Remarks This bird breeds in Alaska, northwestern Canada and eastern Siberia and migrates largely down the west coast. It is similar to the Short-billed Dowitcher, especially in winter plumage, but its bill is longer, sometimes markedly so. White barring on the tail is narrower, giving it a darker appearance. Juveniles can be distinguished from those of the Short-billed Dowitcher by the narrower rusty edgings on their back feathers and by the lack of barring on the tertial wing feathers. The surest aid to identification is the call, a sharp *keek* as opposed to the Short-billed Dowitcher's *tu-tu-tu.*
  It seems likely that the greater acumen of observers accounts for the almost annual records in recent years, because it is improbable that the species has only recently begun to visit the province more regularly.

Common Snipe   PLATE 15

Gallinago gallinago (Linnaeus)

Status Common in summer, very rare in winter. Breeds. Snipe first arrive in late March and the first half of April (average 8 April, earliest 16 March); a "tired" bird on Chebogue Point, Yarmouth County, on 8 March 1982 (E. Ruff) was abnormally early. Most depart in October, but stragglers are regular until January and attempts at overwintering are occasionally successful (Tufts 1915).

Description *Length:* 26-29 cm. *All plumages:* Bill long and straight. *Adults:* Upperparts mottled brown of various shades striped and flecked with buffy white; breast buffy gray, spotted with grayish brown; belly white; flanks barred with black; legs and feet greenish gray; tail black with broad, brick-red subterminal bar.

Breeding *Nest:* On the ground in wet meadows; a slight depression in a small mound slightly above normal water levels, lined with dry grass. *Eggs:* 4; olive-green to light brown or buff, heavily blotched with dark or chocolate-brown chiefly around the larger end. Laying begins in early May and continues for about ten days. Two nests at Black River, Kings County, each contained four fresh eggs; one nest was found on 10 May

1906, the other on 4 May 1938. In each case the sitting bird flushed close underfoot and was soon joined by its mate. Mousley (1939) records the incubation period as 20 days.

Range In North America, breeds from Alaska to Newfoundland, south to the middle states. Winters regularly in restricted areas from southern limits of its breeding range, south to northern South America. Widely distributed also in the Old World.

Remarks Known as "jack-snipe" to many sportsmen, it is little hunted in Nova Scotia and its numbers vary only slightly from year to year. Although classified as a shorebird, it is practically never seen on exposed beaches or tidal mudflats, its natural habitat being the wet meadows and bushy swamps that provide it with food and protective cover.

Unlike the woodcock, to which it is closely related, the snipe may perform its courtship flight by night or by day and remains aloft much longer, particularly on moonlit nights and cloudy or rainy days. The hollow, tremulous notes, best described as *who-who-who-who-who-who,* which come from high overhead with increasing and decreasing volume or intensity, are referred to as "winnowing" or "drumming." Some writers say this weird sound is caused by the passage of the air through the stiff feathers of the bird's tail, but others believe that both the tail and wing-beats are involved. I have often noted that the sound begins at the precise moment the flying bird suddenly swerves upward. When the slanting, downward course begins, the normal wing motion suddenly changes to a pulsating, fluttering movement, ending abruptly when the bird starts to rise to its former flight level. Although we commonly associate these flight performances with the nesting season, a snipe was heard winnowing as late as 5 November 1951 over a swampy meadow near Cambridge, Kings County.

The snipe has at least three vocal sounds. Two calls, which I have only heard during the nesting season, are given when the bird is perched on the ground, a fence rail or taller tree stump. One is pleasing, like the piping of a frog, and the other is a harsh *kuk-kuk-kuk.* Both are repeated slowly, often for quite long periods. The third is a harsh, raspy *scaip-scaip,* repeated excitedly two or three times, chiefly when the bird is flushed from its feeding. This suddenly given and sometimes disconcerting note, heard at any season, is the one best known to hunters.

Twice during late summer, I have seen flocks of snipe flying high in close formation. One flock of about 40 birds alit on a mudflat at Black River Lake, Kings County, where the water was very low at the time. When flushed, they arose and flew off in formation as before. The other flock, of about 25 birds, dropped into a swamp on Wolfville Ridge. When flushed, they too flew off in a close flock. The only other record I have concerning snipe flocking in this way comes from Charles R.K. Allen, who saw 23 flush in unison at Cole Harbour, Halifax County, on 31 October 1964.

Rural people living near meadows where snipe are nesting have long known this bird as the "meadow-hen." Many know it only from its strange sound produced in spring and summer high up over the meadows and have little idea what the bird looks like.

American Woodcock   PLATE 15

Scolopax minor Gmelin

Status Common in summer, very rare in winter. Breeds. First arrivals are noted from early March to month's end (average 21 March, earliest 27 February). During summer it occurs throughout the province in swampy thickets. Major movements have been noted in October, and a few stragglers remain until January, rarely later. One successfully overwintered on Brier Island, 1963-64 (W. Lent).

Description *Length:* 28 cm. *All plumages:* A chunky bird with large eyes set high in a large head; neck thick and short; bill long and straight. *Adults:* Upperparts mostly cinnamon, with intricate pattern of various shades of rich browns, ashy grays, and blacks; below, a soft uniform rich cinnamon-buff; legs short and flesh-coloured. Females are considerably larger than males.

Breeding *Nest:* On the ground in open wooded areas such as pastures with low birches and alders, and often without any attempt at concealment, the bird depending at such times on its remarkable protective colouring; a shallow depression scraped out and then lined with dead leaves and other debris. *Eggs:* 4; olive-brown, flecked and blotched lightly with various shades of rufous and lavender. Laying begins in early April. Only a single brood is raised, but if the first nest is destroyed there will be another. The earliest date for a complete set is 9 April 1936, found by Israel J. Pothier near Lower Wedgeport, Yarmouth County. On 22 May 1943 I found a nest containing four fresh eggs at Black River, Kings County; the abnormally late date indicates that it may have been a second attempt. Three newly hatched young were found in a nest with one infertile egg at Black River on 14 May 1943. A nest reported by John W. Piggott near Bridgetown, Annapolis County, held four young just hatched on 29 April 1928. A half-grown young still showing much natal down was banded at Black River on 17 May 1944.

Range Breeds in eastern North America north to Newfoundland, west to southeastern Manitoba and south to the Gulf States. Winters in the southern parts of its breeding range.

Remarks The general behaviour of this bird is as erratic as its take-off when flushed, a fact to which every experienced woodcock hunter will attest. When approached, it will sometimes jump at 5-10 m distance or sometimes be nearly underfoot before taking flight. A hunting dog will usually catch the bird's scent at long range and make its characteristic "point," but sometimes the bird flushes virtually under the dog's nose, startling the dog and baffling the hunter.

Woodcocks normally migrate at night, moving across the countryside in loose, scattered congregations at low altitudes, but on 31 October 1931 I saw one in broad daylight at Black River flying overhead at an altitude of perhaps 100 m, passing out of view in a general southwesterly direction.

Evidence that they return annually to the same nesting grounds is furnished by Jack Mayer of Moncton, New Brunswick, who has had considerable experience in banding woodcock. He tagged a downy young on 9 June 1940 in a copse near his home and located a nest there the next year. As the bird flushed under his feet, he noticed she was wearing a red band. He later netted the bird on her nest and determined it was the same bird he had banded a year earlier. On 1 October 1941, he shot the banded bird while it loitered about its nest site.

Three abnormally plumaged "golden woodcock" have been taken over the years, two by myself many years ago and one by Merrill Rowding of Liverpool in early November 1949; the last bird was sent to Austin Rand, who published a detailed description (Rand 1950).

American Woodcock and chicks

Wilson's Phalarope

Phalaropus tricolor (Vieillot)

Status Uncommon transient. A sight record of a bird on 9 June 1905 (Bouteillier 1906) was the first for the province. This western species was again recorded by Gross (1937), who observed ten birds "critically for a positive identification" off the Nova Scotia coast on 19 June 1934. The next sighting was on 4 November 1955 by Morrill Richardson, who saw one offshore from Bon Portage Island. There were two separate reports of individuals in September 1959, three birds together in September 1961, and one in September 1969; the species has occurred annually since 1969 in ones and twos, sometimes in small groups of up to six. Most have been on Brier, Cape Sable, Sable and Seal islands, with other scattered reports from throughout the province. There have been ten spring individuals, all between 13 and 27 May, except for one female on Sable Island on 13 June 1976. A female was seen on John Lusby Marsh, Cumberland County, on 5 July 1980, and a male and two juveniles were repeatedly observed there that year between 16 July and 9 August. However, most of our records are clearly of fall migrants, of which about 110 have been seen since 1969, mostly from mid-August to mid-September, with extreme dates of 19 July to 15 November.

Description *Length:* 20-24 cm. *Adult female in summer:* A conspicuous black eyestripe extends down the sides of the neck to the upper breast, where it becomes rich brick-red and extends onto back; head, upper neck and back are pale gray; upper wings dark brown with paler striations; rump white; tail gray, tipped with white; underparts mostly white. *Adult male:* Similar but duller. *Adults in winter:* Head, upper neck, back and tail gray; dark stripe on the face and neck is absent; wings brownish gray, striated; underparts white.

Range Breeds in the interior of North America east of the Rockies, principally on the prairies but recently extending east to southern Quebec and the New Brunswick-Nova Scotia border. Winters on the pampas of southern South America.

Remarks Wilson's Phalarope may be distinguished from the other two phalaropes by its white rump, the absence of white in the wing and its longer, thinner bill. Unlike the others, this species occurs at sea only on passage between its summer and winter quarters. One route passes along the Pacific coast; the other runs by way of the southeastern United States and the West Indies. The bird's normal range in the Atlantic is thus well south of Nova Scotia. Our offshore sightings in June, at sea and on Sable Island, are puzzling.

Although there is no proof of breeding in the province, the 1980 observations near the New Brunswick border and subsequent late July sightings in that area suggest that breeding has occurred.

The three phalaropes are unique among North American birds, the females being larger and more brightly coloured than the males. The females are the more dominant sex, defending territories and pursuing the males ardently when courtship is underway on the nesting grounds. She lays the eggs in a nest the male has prepared. When the last egg has been deposited, however, he immediately takes over the monotonous task of incubation; when the young appear, their welfare is his responsibility. On rare occasions, the female will assist him, showing motherly interest in her young ones.

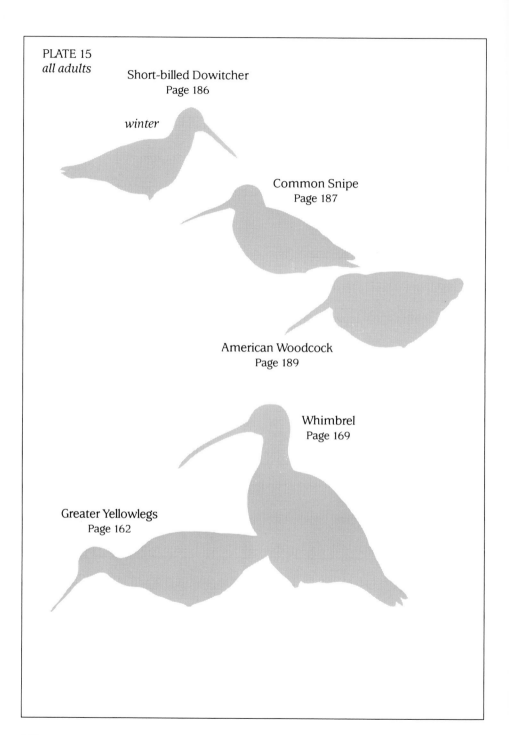

PLATE 15
all adults

Short-billed Dowitcher
Page 186

winter

Common Snipe
Page 187

American Woodcock
Page 189

Whimbrel
Page 169

Greater Yellowlegs
Page 162

Roger Tory Peterson

Roger Tory Peterson

PLATE 16
all adults

male, winter   Red-necked Phalarope
Page 194

female, summer

male, winter

Red Phalarope
Page 195

female, summer

Purple Sandpiper, *winter*
Page 182

Ruddy Turnstone
Page 172

winter

summer

Red-necked Phalarope   PLATE 16

Phalaropus lobatus (Linnaeus)

Status Common transient, rare in summer. They are common during migration, but because they travel far offshore, our records are incomplete. Our earliest reported spring arrival was on Cape Sable on 29 April 1977. Large numbers were passing Brier Island between 12 and 21 May 1979, and 300-500 birds were there on 23 May 1969. The birds' passage lasts until the first week of June; the latest spring reports were of over 100 birds near Pictou on 5 June 1967, and of four females in breeding plumage off Bird Islands, Victoria County, on 8 June 1974. Non-breeders may remain offshore; small numbers were seen through summer 1969 around the *Lurcher Lightship* off Yarmouth. The fall migration begins earlier than does that of the Red Phalarope and extends from early July to early September, with stragglers later. Some early observations (R.W. Tufts) in the Bay of Fundy off Digby Neck are: approximately 1500 on 8 July 1930, several hundreds there on 9 July 1931, and approximately 1000 on 20 July 1935. Only three were identified as Red Phalaropes, and all others near enough to see clearly were Red-necked Phalaropes. In August during more recent years, however, the Red, not the Red-necked Phalarope has been by far the commoner species on the Nova Scotian side of the Bay of Fundy. The situation is reversed on the New Brunswick side, where the numbers of Red-necked Phalaropes off Deer and Campobello islands have been put at over 250,000 birds and Red Phalaropes are scarce. An unusual inland bird was observed at Sheffield Mills, Kings County, some 16 km from Minas Basin on 23 September 1977. Few Red-necked Phalaropes are seen in Nova Scotia after the end of September, although there are several late October sightings and one very late straggler appeared at Cherry Hill Beach, Lunenburg County, on 21 November 1971.

Description *Length:* 18-20 cm. *All plumages:* Bill more slender and pointed than that of the Red Phalarope. *Adult female in summer:* Upperparts dark gray; back and scapulars with two buff lines forming a V on back; sides of neck and foreneck rufous; greater wing coverts tipped with white; flanks gray; rest of underparts white. *Adult male in summer:* Similar to female but upperparts duller, showing more light brown or buff; rufous on neck more restricted. *Adults in winter:* Upperparts mostly gray; gray stripe from eye to region about ear; greater wing coverts tipped with white as in Red Phalarope; underparts white, mottled with gray on breast.

Range Circumpolar. In North America, breeds in the Arctic south to James Bay, the Aleutians and the southern tip of Greenland. Winters off Peru, the southern Arabian Peninsula and Indonesia. Unlike the Red Phalarope, it is not known to winter in the Atlantic; the birds we see in the Maritimes probably move inland across the continent later and winter off the Pacific coast of South America.

Remarks In breeding plumage, the Red-necked Phalarope, formerly known as "Northern Phalarope", is readily distinguished from the Red Phalarope by its darker upperparts and pale underparts. However, both species are in winter plumage by the time they reach Nova Scotia in July. At this season, Red-necked Phalaropes are best identified by their strongly striped scapulars and by their more slender bills and necks.

Although the Red Phalarope is often seen at sea during the fall, Red-necked Phalaropes are for the most part reported only from the Bay of Fundy region. Birds which breed in the eastern Arctic probably migrate over land to reach us. The tide-rips at the mouth of the Bay of Fundy are as important a feeding area for the Red-necked Phalarope during fall migration as the mudflats at the head of the bay are for the Semipalmated Sandpiper.

Red Phalarope   PLATE 16

Phalaropus fulicaria (Linnaeus)

Status Common transient. The earliest reported spring occurrences are of single birds at Cape Sable on 27 April 1981 and at Broad Cove, Lunenburg County, on 1 May 1983. Most birds, however, arrive in mid-May, and large numbers have been observed off southern Nova Scotia during the last week of that month. For example, very large flocks were reported by White (1891) off the Southwestern Shore between 27 and 30 May 1890. In spring 1980, a flock of 1200 birds was seen off Cape Sable on 20 May, one of 3000 some 25 km south of Seal Island on 27 May, and there were flocks of over 100 off Sable Island on 31 May and 2 June. The birds' northward passage is very rapid; several killed by collision with the light on Cape Sable on 9 June 1968 are the latest to be reported in the spring. An interesting record is provided by Harding P. Moffatt who found a bright female "in spring" 1969 feeding on "floating May-flies," on Five Island Lake, Halifax County, about 18 km from salt water. Southbound birds begin to appear offshore in July and continue passing through until September, the peak being reached at the end of August. The earliest were 13 seen on 12 July 1985 in Cabot Strait, some 50 km northeast of Glace Bay. The species becomes very common off Brier Island in late August and early September; as many as 20,000 birds have been estimated in some years. Fairly large numbers remain there until the end of September, but counts of 100 are typical in early October. Unusual were 1500 Red Phalaropes off Brier Island on 7 November 1973 and 40 observed from the ferry *Princess of Acadia* (Digby to Saint John, New Brunswick) on the same day. On 12 November 1983, five were seen from Chebucto Head at the mouth of Halifax Harbour, and on 21 December 1973 a straggler appeared at Cape Sable.

Description *Length:* 20-23 cm. *All plumages:* As in all phalarope species, front toes lobed, and webbed at base; legs and feet dull yellow. *Adult female in summer:* Back striped with black and light ochre; cap black; cheeks white; underparts brownish red. *Adult male in summer:* Similar but crown streaked; less white on face. *Adults in winter:* Slate-blue mantle; white head, with poorly defined dark spot about eye extending back over ear region; a stripe down nape; mainly white underparts.

Range Circumpolar, along the coasts and islands of the High Arctic. In North America, breeds as far south as west Greenland, Hudson Strait and northern Alaska. Migrates down both coasts of the continent, being rare inland. Winters at sea, off western and southwestern Africa, and off Peru.

Remarks Except at nesting time these diminutive members of the sandpiper family are at home on the open sea where they wander about, far from land, often in very large flocks. They are especially common along the outer edges of major ocean currents, such as those off the coasts of Peru and Senegal, where the zooplankton on which they feed is abundantly concentrated at the sea surface.

To some mariners they are known as "whale-birds" or "sea-geese." The first name refers to the fact that baleen whales often feed on the same concentrations of zooplankton as do the phalaropes. The second name is an onomatopoeic rendition of their twittering calls.

Family Laridae

Subfamily Stercorariinae

Pomarine Jaeger

Stercorarius pomarinus (Temminck)

Status Uncommon transient, rare in summer. Reliable early records are few. One was shot near Digby by W. Gilpin, following the heavy gale of 4 October 1869 (Piers' notes), and an immature bird was taken off Brier Island by D.R. Munro in November 1900. Three immature females were collected on 8 August 1916 off the coast of Dover, Halifax County, by a fisherman who sent them to Louis B. Bishop (Piers' notes). However, Pomarine Jaegers, the two other jaeger species and the Great Skua have been reported regularly over the past 15 years. This apparent change of status must be ascribed to the increase in seagoing ornithologists rather than to expansions of these birds' ranges. In spring, Pomarine Jaegers usually reach Nova Scotian waters at the end of April (earliest 18 April 1984). A few spend the summer here, but most have passed through our area by the end of May. Fall migrants reappear during the second half of August, and birds are regularly seen all through September and October. The latest stragglers were seen on 6 November 1979 and 1982.

Description *Length:* 65-78 cm, including elongated central tail feathers. Occurs in two colour morphs or phases, and various intermediate ones. *All plumages:* Bill hooked, feet webbed. *Adults in dark morph:* Generally dark brown, slightly lighter below and on cheeks; black cap. *Adults in light morph:* Underparts, breast, neck and face white; cheeks, and throat in some cases, tinged with yellow; cap black; rest of upperparts dark brown; dark barring may occur on flanks, breast and underparts; bases of the primary feathers are white, providing a fairly conspicuous white "wing-flash"; tips of the central tail feathers are spatulate and twisted, and project several centimetres beyond the outer ones. *Juveniles:* grayish brown, heavily barred on upperparts and underparts with blackish brown; central tail feathers are little elongated.

Range Circumpolar. Breeds on the Arctic islands and mainland across North America. Winters mainly at sea from the Virginia coast south to the West Indies, from California to Peru, and off the western coast of Africa.

Remarks Jaegers are freebooters of the open sea, preying on other forms of marine birdlife; they are known to fishermen as "sea hawks." This plucky member of the jaeger subfamily has been known to attack the much larger Great Black-backed Gull and successfully steal its prey.

Parasitic Jaeger   PLATE 2

Stercorarius parasiticus (Linnaeus)

Status Uncommon transient, rare in summer. Reliable early records are few. There are two specimens in the American Museum of Natural History collected in 1894 and 1898 on Sable Island; one collected at Three Fathom Harbour, Halifax County, in late April or early May 1897 is in the Nova Scotia Museum; and one taken at Cape Sable on 30 April 1907 by Harold F. Tufts is in the National Museum of Canada. Allan Brooks collected five specimens off Brier Island on 28 September 1930. Parasitic Jaegers have been seen fairly regularly off Nova Scotia in recent years. The earliest spring record is off Yarmouth on 18 April 1983; however, most birds do not arrive until the second week in May or later. The northward migration of this species is largely completed by early June, but, like the Pomarine Jaeger, some spend the summer in our area. Fall migrants return during the last 10 days of August, and their passage continues until mid-October. Late stragglers have been observed on 3 November 1979, on the same date in 1983 and on 4 November 1982.

Description *Length:* 46-67 cm, including central tail feathers. Two colour morphs and many intermediate stages. *All plumages:* Central tail feathers project beyond the others a short distance and are pointed, not rounded and twisted; bill hooked; feet webbed. The colourations of the Parasitic Jaeger and the other two jaegers are distinguished only with difficulty. (See preceding species for general description.)

Range Circumpolar. Breeds in the Arctic across North America. Winters offshore from Maine to the east coast of South America, and to the west coast of Africa.

Parasitic Jaeger chasing tern

Long-tailed Jaeger

Stercorarius longicaudus Vieillot

Status Rare transient. The paucity of available records suggests that this jaeger occurs off our shores less frequently than the two preceding species. Chamberlain (1891) says it is common in the Bay of Fundy during spring and fall, but subsequent observations do not bear this out. Six immature specimens in the American Museum of Natural History were taken near Sable Island on 15 August 1896. Allen (1916) recorded an immature specimen from the vicinity of Yarmouth taken late in summer 1910. Recent records from Sable Island were of two harrying some terns on 9 June 1968, one on 12

June 1977 and two on 4 June 1979. There are only five other reports of individuals: 19 May 1978 in the Northumberland Strait; 10 September 1979 on Georges Bank; 30 April 1980 near Seal Island; 30 May 1979 on the Scotian Shelf about 170 km south of Halifax; and 10 November 1980 off Brier Island. In the last two cases, and perhaps in some of the others, the identification was by no means certain.

Description *Length:* 50-58 cm, including the long tail streamers. Only one (light) colour morph usually occurs in this species, though dark birds are known. In colouration, it is hardly distinguishable from the two preceding jaegers (see Pomarine Jaeger for description). Decidedly smaller than the Pomarine; slightly smaller and lighter in build than the Parasitic. The very long tail feathers of the adult are narrow and attenuated, instead of broad and twisted as in the Pomarine, and project well beyond the tail, instead of only a little way as in the Parasitic. Unfortunately, these feathers are often broken or missing in birds seen in autumn. The white wing-flashes are poorly developed in this species, and breeding light-morph birds never have a dark band across the breast. Legs bluish gray; toes webbed.

Range Circumpolar. In North America, breeds from Alaska to Greenland and south to the northern Ungava Peninsula. Winters off the coasts of the southern United States and South America.

Remarks The breeding of the Long-tailed Jaeger on arctic tundra is closely related to the abundance of lemmings and mice, its principal summer food. These rodents undergo regular cycles of abundance and scarcity, and in years of scarcity the jaegers often do not breed at all.

Great Skua

Catharacta skua (Brünnich)

Status Rare visitant. Although there were several nineteenth-and early twentieth-century sightings, the first known specimen, killed in Shelburne County and consigned to a dealer in Boston, was intercepted by a game warden in Yarmouth on 25 May 1910 (Allen 1916). On 7 June 1957, Scott (1959) collected a female about 5 km south of Lockeport, and he saw another about 15 km south of Lockeport on 22 August of that year; Eric Holdway saw one off Caribou Harbour in the Northumberland Strait on 2 October 1962; and two were seen by Robert Smart from the deck of the ferry *Bluenose*, which runs between Yarmouth and Bar Harbour, Maine, on 6 July 1969. Since 1970 it has been reported regularly, though in small numbers, from the offshore waters east and south of Nova Scotia in every month except December, the majority of records occurring between June and October. It is probable that the Great Skua may be found off Nova Scotia at any time of year. However, some sightings could be the closely related South Polar Skua (see Remarks). Banding returns suggest that only second-winter immature Skuas migrate to the western Atlantic; birds of other ages winter off western Africa.

Description *Length:* 51-66 cm. *Adults:* Dark brown to cinnamon, streaked ochre or rufous, more uniform on the underparts; indistinct blackish brown cap; white wing-flashes are large and conspicuous; central tail feathers are pointed but project hardly at all past the rest of the tail feathers. *Juveniles:* Similar but duller; underparts more tawny. The Great Skua resembles a dark-morph jaeger but may be distinguished by its broader wings, larger white wing-flashes, ponderous wing-beat and heavy body.

Range In the North Atlantic, the Great Skua breeds in Scotland, Iceland and the Faeroes. It winters off western Africa and to a lesser extent in the western Atlantic. Other subspecies breed in New Zealand, Antarctica, the subantarctic islands and southern South America.

Remarks The closely related South Polar Skua, *Catharacta maccormicki,* breeds in Antarctica and migrates north into the Atlantic and Pacific. Although it has not yet been definitely recorded in Canadian waters, there can be little doubt that it occurs here. Specimens have been collected recently off New England and west Greenland, and on Flemish Cap, some 700 km east of Newfoundland. It can only be a matter of time before the South Polar Skua is added to the Nova Scotia list. It resembles the Great Skua but is smaller overall, with a smaller head and more slender bill. Plumages are highly variable, and it is most easily identified in its light morph, in which the blackish brown upperparts contrast sharply with the pale head and underparts. There is usually no hint of rufous in any plumage.

Subfamily Larinae

Laughing Gull

Larus atricilla Linnaeus

Status Uncommon visitor. Formerly bred. It was last recorded as a breeding bird on 18 June 1941, when a visit to the Bird (or Halibut) Islands off Harrigan Cove, Halifax County, revealed a colony of about 25 pairs just beginning to nest (R.W. Tufts). Horton Beaver, long-time resident and fisherman of the area, stated that these birds were abundant there when he was a boy. This colony, he believed, was the last in that area. In 1960 there were no Laughing Gulls to be seen there or anywhere else in the vicinity. How long this colony persisted after 1941 is not recorded. The only other possible recent colony was at Quoddy, Halifax County, where R. Dicks suspected they were breeding on 23 August 1958. Evidence that Laughing Gulls once nested throughout Nova Scotia is provided by Bryant (1857), who collected two pairs in summer 1856 on Green Island, Yarmouth County, the females with enlarged oviducts. Langille (1892) observed "some eight or ten Laughing Gulls, among clouds of terns" and found one nest with two fresh eggs of this species on Flat Island, near Tancook, Lunenburg County. Residents of Seal Island told Louis B. Bishop in August 1909 of a breeding colony on one of the small islands nearby (Piers' notes). Today the species is a regular summer visitor in small numbers to southern parts of the province. Most recent records—almost all of single birds—fall between mid-May (earliest 14 May) and early October. Some late fall and winter sightings are: 27 January 1972 on Sable Island; 17 December 1972 and 15 December 1979 during Halifax East Christmas Bird Counts; 20-29 December 1963 on Bon Portage Island; and 16 January 1971 at Yarmouth. In 1968, immediately following the arrival of hurricane "Gladys" on 21 October, thousands of Laughing Gulls were dumped along our shores. Many were distressed and are believed to have died, but judging by their suddenly reduced numbers early in November it is also believed that substantial numbers were able to reorient themselves and return south; nonetheless, birds were reported in the Halifax area as late as December 21.

Description *Length:* 40-43 cm. *Adults in summer:* Dark leaden gray on back and wings; wings with white border on hind edges; primaries black with small white tips; head and throat with a hood of slaty black; rest of plumage white; bills and legs dark red. *Adults in winter:* Similar to above but head and throat are white, spotted and streaked with grayish brown. *First-winter birds:* Resemble winter adults but the upper surfaces of the wings are mainly brown or blackish brown, the breast and neck are flecked with brown and the tail has a blackish sub-terminal band.

Breeding *Nest:* On the ground in colonies; composed of coarse, dry vegetable matter lined with fine grass. Nests are neatly built and deeply cup-shaped. On 18 June 1941 a few nests on Bird Island contained the usual three eggs, others held incomplete sets and some were empty. *Eggs:* 3; buff to greenish olive, irregularly spotted and blotched with dark brown or black.

Range Breeds along the Atlantic and Gulf coasts from southern New England (occasionally New Brunswick) to Texas, the West Indies, Yucatan and northern Venezuela. Winters in the southern states, occasionally farther north, south to northern South America.

Remarks It is slightly larger than the Common Black-headed and Bonaparte's Gulls, with which it may be confused in its various plumages. However, the adult bird has a dark gray mantle which blends into the still darker wing-tips, and the border of the hind part of the wing is conspicuously white. The other two species have pearly gray mantles, and the ends of their wings are white, narrowly bordered with black.

The Laughing Gull's name is derived from its call. When I visited the aforementioned colony on Bird (or Halibut) Islands in 1941, the birds circled low overhead, calling vociferously. They were protesting our intrusion but their chorus of rapidly repeated *ha-ha-ha*'s made them seem highly amused. According to Horton Beaver, my boatman on that occasion, they were known locally as "black-polls."

Franklin's Gull

Larus pipixcan Wagler

Status Six records. A single bird was seen on Sable Island between 26 May and 2 June 1973 by Jean Boulva, whose photographs confirmed the identification. This was the first record for the province. Since then, single birds have been reported on Cape Sable on 8 January 1973 (B.J. and S. Smith); on Sable Island between 23 August and 13 September 1978 (several observers, photographs); 13-14 May 1981 on Brier Island (W. Lent et al.); on Seal Island (photographed by I.A. McLaren) on 18-20 July 1983; and at Grand Pré dyke, Kings County, on 3 September 1983 (J. Timpa et al.).

Remarks Adults in breeding plumage resemble Laughing Gulls but smaller, and more white on the tips of the primaries, with the black of the wing-tips divided from the gray of the upper wing by a broad white band. Immatures are also like Laughing Gulls, but more extensively dark on face and nape. Although many Franklin's Gulls migrate to Peru by way of the Caribbean from their breeding grounds on the western prairies, they reach the Atlantic coast well south of the Maritime Provinces, and we are unlikely to receive more than an occasional vagrant.

Little Gull

Larus minutus Pallas

Status Seven records. It was first reported by Eric Holdway, who saw one off Caribou, Pictou County, on 10 October 1960. The second record is based on diagnostic photographs taken by Wayne Neily of a bird in flight at Glace Bay on 25 November 1967. Since then, immature birds have been observed in Digby Gut on 1 November 1972 (C. Johnston); on Sable Island on 10 June 1975 (two birds, photographed by D.W. Finch), 27 August 1978 (P. and R. Christie) and 4 June 1983 (M. Malone); and at Round Bay, Shelburne County, on 28 August 1981 (photographed by I.A. McLaren).

Remarks Adults of this, the world's smallest, gull have pearly gray backs and wings, dark brown "hoods," small black bills and dusky underwings. Immatures resemble young kittiwakes but are much smaller and lack a hindneck bar. Little Gulls breed mostly in the Old World, from the Netherlands to Mongolia. The first nest in the New World was discovered in Ontario in 1962, and the species now breeds in central North America in very small numbers.

Common Black-headed Gull

Larus ridibundus Linnaeus

Status Uncommon winter visitant. Records of this small, Old World gull have increased markedly in recent decades. It was first recorded for the province during late winter 1921-22 by Charles R.K. Allen, who saw an immature on Halifax Harbour. Lloyd B. Macpherson saw numbers of them at the same location during winter 1929-30. It became regular during the 1950s. Since 1970 it has arrived regularly in August (average 28 August, earliest 3 August). During winter it is locally fairly common along Atlantic coastal areas, with the Halifax and Sydney areas perhaps the focal points, but it remains rare along the Bay of Fundy. Most have gone by mid-April, but some late stragglers are seen in May (average 16 May, latest 30 May).

Description *Length:* 36-38 cm. *Adults in breeding plumage:* Back and upper wings pearly gray; outer primaries white, tipped with black; outermost primary has a black leading edge; underside of primaries dusky; front of the head has a chocolate-brown mask or hood which extends back to the ear; there is a prominent white eye ring; remainder of plumage white, tinged with pink on the breast in spring; bill and legs red. *Adults in winter:* Most of the black on the hood gone, though a prominent spot remains behind the eye. *Immatures:* Also lack the hood; upper wing mottled with brown; brown band near the tip of the tail; the bill is yellowish or flesh-coloured, tipped with blackish brown; legs are yellowish flesh.

Range This is an Old World species which breeds in Iceland, northern Europe and northern Siberia. However, it colonized southwestern Greenland in the 1960s. Newly fledged young were observed in western Newfoundland in 1977, and a small colony was discovered on the Magdalen Islands in the Gulf of St. Lawrence in 1982.

Remarks Common Black-headed Gulls in full breeding plumage are now so regularly reported in Nova Scotia in the spring and late summer that it is only a matter of time before they will be found breeding here. This should be looked for on islets, coastal salt marshes, or marshy lakes in the interior of the province.

Bonaparte's Gull

Larus philadelphia (Ord)

Status Uncommon transient, rare in summer and winter. Most spring records occur between the beginning of April and mid-May, but first sightings are routine in March (average 28 March, earliest 3 March). The few seen during the summer are probably non-breeding immature birds. The species is much more common in the fall. The first migrants generally arrive at the beginning of August (average 4 August, earliest 22 July), and their passage extends well into November, with stragglers as late as 21 January 1964 at Bon Portage Island, 30 January 1967 at Cape Sable, and all winter in the Halifax area in several recent years. Unlike the Common Black-headed Gull, the majority of our Bonaparte's Gulls are reported from the Northumberland Strait and the Bay of Fundy, on western coasts of the province.

Description *Length:* 30-36 cm. *Adults in summer:* Head has a slaty black hood sharply defined against the rest of the plumage; back and wings pearly gray; primaries mostly white, the outermost with a black web and all with black tips, giving the effect of a white wing end bordered with black; rest of plumage white; bill black; legs and feet orange-red. *Adults in winter:* Similar but head white; shading to gray on sides and back. *Immatures:* Top of head and nape gray; spot on auriculars dark gray; back pearly gray mottled with grayish brown; rest of wing similar to adult but black of primaries more extensive; tail white, with a narrow, black subterminal band; rest of plumage white; bill mostly dark brown; feet dully flesh-coloured.

Range Breeds from central Alaska and Mackenzie Delta south to central British Columbia and Alberta, and east to James Bay. Winters from Massachusetts to the Caribbean and also along the west coast of Central America.

Remarks This small gull closely resembles the Common Black-headed Gull, from which it may be distinguished by its black (instead of dark red) bill, and by the black markings on the underside of the primaries, which are confined to a narrow black border along the tips of those feathers.

The immediate destination of most fall migrants in our area is Head Harbour Passage in southern New Brunswick, where very large numbers of Bonaparte's Gulls are to be found from August to October, feeding on swarms of euphausiid shrimps. These birds reach the Maritime Provinces after a long overland migration from their nearest breeding area, in northwestern Ontario. The shrimps eaten after breeding season replenish the gulls' fat reserves before the birds continue on their southward journey.

Mew Gull

Larus canus Linnaeus

Status Five records. On 9 March 1969 Christel and Norman Bell saw a gull consorting with Herring Gulls at close range about their yard on Sable Island. They noted its conspicuous greenish legs and its unmarked and unbanded, small yellowish bill and were convinced that the bird was either the western Mew Gull or its European counterpart, the Common Gull, *Larus canus canus.* On 7 February 1976 a first-year bird of the European subspecies was seen by Ian A. McLaren at Lawrencetown River, Halifax County. In the same year single adult birds were seen off Brier Island on 19 August and at Canning, Kings County, on 3 October (several observers); the second bird stayed for over a month, and its identity was confirmed photographically. A second-year bird in very battered plumage found by Fulton Lavender in Dartmouth on 12 March 1984 remained for at least two weeks. It too was photographed and appeared to belong to the European subspecies.

Remarks The Mew Gull takes its name from its mewing, cat-like cry. Adults resemble those of the slightly larger Ring-billed Gull, except that the Mew Gull has a shorter, thinner, unbanded bill; a rounder forehead; and larger, darker eyes. Compared with young Ring-billed Gulls, first-winter and year-old individuals of the European subspecies have a more sharply demarcated tail band, with no mottling on the white base; those of the western North American *Larus canus brachyrhynchus* have more heavily marked tails. Both the European and the North American subspecies have been recorded on the East Coast, but only *L. c. canus* has been confirmed in Nova Scotia.

Ring-billed Gull   PLATE 17

Larus delawarensis Ord

Status Common transient, uncommon in winter, rare in summer. It was considered rare to uncommon in the nineteenth century but has become regular in recent years. The peak of spring migration occurs during the second half of April and the first week in May. Birds are occasionally seen in June and a few probably spend the summer in the province. Thirty were seen at Argyle Head, Yarmouth County, on 26 July 1983, but first fall migrants generally appear at the beginning of August and the main movement takes place between September and early November. It is regular in small numbers during winter, especially where mudflats continue to be exposed and around sewer outlets in towns and cities.

Description *Length:* 46-51 cm. *Adults in summer:* Pearly gray mantle over back and wings; outer primaries black with white spots on outer two, others tipped with white; rest of plumage pure white; bill yellow with black ring or band near end; legs and feet greenish yellow. *Adults in winter:* Similar to those in summer but head and neck streaked with grayish brown. *Immatures:* Mottled dark brown and gray, becoming lighter with age; tail marked with wide black band near end, with some mottling on the white parts.

Range Breeds locally: east of the Rockies, across southern Canada and the northern states; in eastern North America from Northern Ontario, central Quebec, northeastern Newfoundland and southeastern Labrador, south to the Great Lakes and northern New Brunswick. Winters from Nova Scotia, the lower Great Lakes and (rarely) the Gulf of St. Lawrence, south to Florida and Cuba.

Remarks This bird closely resembles the Herring Gull in general habits and appearance and could readily be mistaken for it, but it is considerably smaller. If at close range, the observer will note that the adults of this bird have greenish yellow legs unlike those of the Herring Gull, which are flesh-coloured; and the band or "ring" on the bill of adult birds will also be seen. At distant range, the greater black on the outer primaries is a good field mark. Immatures of the two species are similar, but this bird is smaller, has a more buoyant flight, and has a black band on the end of its tail.

Herring Gull   PLATE 17

Larus argentatus Pontoppidan

Status Common resident. Breeds. Abundant along the coast throughout the year, particularly in the vicinity of its many breeding colonies. Frequents many rivers and lakes in summer, breeding on islands in some lakes. Banding has shown that many Herring Gulls move south to New England in the winter. Those that remain are scavengers, often gathering in huge assemblies about sewer outlets and garbage disposal sites. During the past 70 years, its numbers increased greatly, initially because its persecution became illegal but more recently because the growing abundance of garbage provides it with a secure winter food supply.

Description *Length:* 58-66 cm. *Adults in summer:* Back and upper surface of wings pale gray; outer primaries black, tipped and spotted with white near the ends and gray basally, the gray extending closest to the tips on the inner webs; rest of plumage white; bill yellow with red spot on lower mandible; legs and feet flesh-coloured. *Adults in winter:* Similar but head and neck streaked with brownish gray. *First-year immatures:* Generally grayish brown; upperparts mottled with light gray or buff; head streaked with dirty white; tail and primaries plain blackish brown. Various transition plumages occur between the first-year immature bird and the adult.

Breeding *Nest:* Usually on the ground, in dense colonies. Sometimes located on cliffsides, on rocks in lakes, and infrequently in trees (spruce only, in my experience). Nests are composed of coarse weeds and decaying vegetable matter in variable quantities. *Eggs:* 2-3, usually 3; grayish to olive-brown, with heavy, chocolate-coloured blotches scattered over the surface. Frequently individual eggs, sometimes all, in a set are plain ashy blue or olive-gray without the usual markings. Some most unusual Herring Gull eggs resemble the reddish eggs of the Peregrine Falcon. I have seen only two such sets, both laid by the same bird on Kent Island, New Brunswick. One of these sets is in the Nova Scotia Museum. Egg laying begins in early May but it is not until late May that all members of most colonies are so engaged. If the first and second nests are destroyed, a third attempt is customary.

Range Breeds across northern North America from southern Alaska to south-central British Columbia, and from southern Baffin Island to New York State; this includes the interior of the continent south to the Great Lakes. Winters from southern parts of its breeding range to Panama and Barbados. Different subspecies breed in the Old World.

Remarks The Herring Gull is by far the most abundant of our gulls, its great numbers creating a significant impact on man's economic interests.

It is valuable as a scavenger, keeping our beaches and shorelines free from decaying fish and similar refuse, and on occasion from rats which infest our harbours. Large congregations often gather on meadowlands and mown fields to eat meadow voles, grasshoppers and other insects. Large flocks at sea direct fishermen to schools of herring by screaming excitedly and hovering in dense formation above the fish. The loud clamorous cries of Herring Gulls about their breeding rookeries have warned mariners of the dangerous proximity of land in dense fog. The gull also adds to the aesthetic quality of our coasts.

These birds have a negative impact on human interests. At times they seriously damage blueberry crops; they carry off fish placed on fields for fertilizer; and their method of breaking open mussels by dropping them from heights onto hard surfaces has damaged the roofs of automobiles. The roofs of fishhouses and other outbuildings along the shore have been damaged by the chemical action of the excrement dropped by the hundreds of gulls that resort to the ridgepoles of these buildings at roosting time. The gulls also devour fish that fishermen leave exposed for brief periods.

Herring Gulls have greatly increased in number during recent decades, unquestionably the result of protection given under the international Migratory Bird Convention between Canada and the United States, which went into effect in Canada in 1917. Previously, it had been killed indiscriminately to supply a heavy commercial demand for its feathers. An unforeseen result of protection is that the species is now so plentiful that it has become a serious threat to terns.

Iceland Gull   PLATE 17

Larus glaucoides Meyer

Status Fairly common in winter, very rare in summer. Iceland Gulls generally arrive from the north in October (average 15 October, earliest 30 September). Large numbers are found around Halifax and Sydney harbours in particular; an estimated 740 were recorded on the Glace Bay-Sydney Christmas Bird Count in 1965. Most have departed by late April, but they are routine in June on Sable Island (McLaren 1981a) and one was seen on Cape Sable on 15 August 1968. Some birds probably spend the summer in our area.

Description *Length:* 58-64 cm. *Adults:* About the size of the Herring Gull, with pale, pearly gray mantle across back and wings; rest of plumage white; wing-tips sometimes marked with pale to dark gray, resembling a paler version of the Herring Gull; bill yellow, with a red spot at the tip of the lower mandible; legs and feet flesh-coloured, with leaden tint. *First-year immatures:* Plumages white with dusky or cinnamon markings; wing-tips white or dusky; bill all dark.

Range Breeds in southern Greenland, southern Baffin Island, northwestern Quebec and on islands in northern Hudson Bay. Winters in Europe, Iceland and eastern North America south to New Jersey.

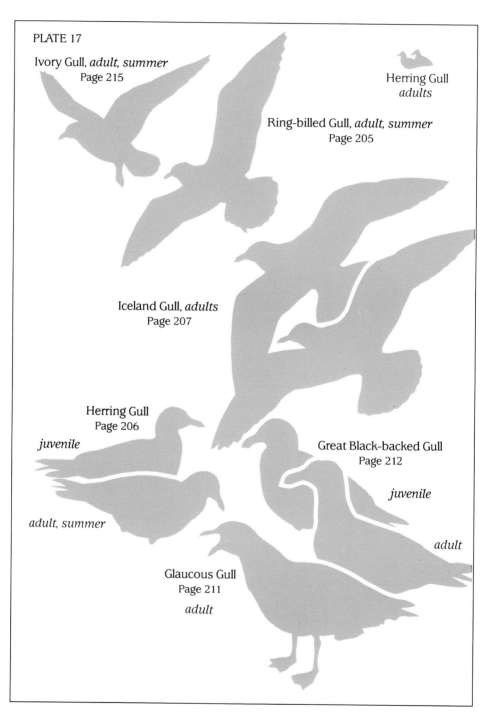

PLATE 17

Ivory Gull, *adult, summer*
Page 215

Herring Gull
adults

Ring-billed Gull, *adult, summer*
Page 205

Iceland Gull, *adults*
Page 207

Herring Gull
Page 206

juvenile

Great Black-backed Gull
Page 212

juvenile

adult, summer

adult

Glaucous Gull
Page 211

adult

208

PLATE 18

adult

Black-legged Kittiwake
Page 213

immature

Common Tern
Page 218

adult, summer

immature

Arctic Tern, *adult summer*
Page 220

immature

Caspian Tern
Page 216

adult, summer

Remarks Most birds seen in Nova Scotia belong to the subspecies *Larus glaucoides kumlieni,* which breeds in arctic Canada and is generally distinguishable by its dusky wing-tip markings. The subspecies *Larus glaucoides glaucoides,* breeding in Greenland, has pure white primaries. However, some birds nesting among "Kumlien's gulls" on Baffin Island also have pure white primaries, so it is by no means certain that Greenland birds can be distinguished here.

Adult Iceland and Glaucous Gulls are similar in appearance but the Iceland Gull is considerably smaller, especially in its head and bill. The immatures of the two subspecies may be difficult to distinguish in life, although "Kumlien's gull" generally has dusky primaries. Both may be studied about docks in winter, but the number of "white-winged" gulls that winter here varies considerably from year to year.

Thayer's Gull, *Larus thayeri,* once regarded as a subspecies of the Herring Gull but now recognized as being closely related to the Iceland Gull, nests in the Canadian Arctic and migrates to the Pacific coast and occasionally to inland and eastern North America. It resembles the Iceland Gull in body size, head shape and bill size, but adults may have darker backs than our Herring Gulls and usually do have darker eyes and wing-tips than "Kumlien's gulls." Immature Thayer's Gulls are much duskier than most young "Kumlien's gulls," with the upper wing-tips even darker. There have been several sightings of possible Thayer's Gulls in the Halifax region, but in view of the great variability among "Kumlien's gulls" seen here, such records need more confirmation, perhaps by specimens. Some authorities believe Thayer's Gull is another subspecies of the Iceland Gull.

Iceland Gull

Lesser Black-backed Gull

Larus fuscus Linnaeus

Status Rare winter visitant. The first record for Nova Scotia was a third-winter bird photographed in Digby by Davis Finch on 25 March 1970. Up to the time of writing (January 1986), this bird has returned to Digby every autumn since (earliest arrival 19 September 1976); two adults were seen there on 4 April 1980. In January 1979 a first-year and a third-year bird were reported in the Dartmouth-Halifax area, and the older bird has returned to the same site annually since. Another bird appearing first in winter 1981-82 has also become a regular visitant to the Halifax waterfront. A Lesser Black-backed Gull was seen over Sable Island on 6 September 1979 and in June 1981 a third-year bird was found lingering on Cape Breton Island (R. Stymeist). In 1982, single adults were observed: at Petit de Grat, Richmond County, on 13 March; at Port Philip, Cumberland County, on 18 April; on 17 September at Bon Portage Island. The species colonized Iceland in the 1920s, and there can be little doubt that our birds are the forerunners of a further westward expansion in range.

Remarks Adults resemble miniature Great Black-backed Gulls but are smaller than a Herring Gull, have a more delicate bill and their legs are yellow, not flesh-coloured. First-winter birds are darker than those of the other two species. They may be distinguished from young Herring Gulls by their darker wing coverts, which form a broader dark margin on the trailing edge of the wings in flight.

This gull breeds in northern Europe and Iceland and normally winters from Europe to southern Africa. Wanderers are regularly recorded in eastern North America from Labrador to Florida, and it is likely that some breed here, perhaps mated to Herring Gulls if they cannot find others of their own kind.

The ancestors of the Lesser Black-backed and Herring Gulls probably inhabited the North Pacific and spread into Eurasia and North America at the end of the Ice Age. The backs of the Eurasian populations become progressively darker as one travels west, culminating in the Lesser Black-backed. The backs of the Herring Gulls of North America remain pale, and that species has crossed the Atlantic to establish a breeding range which overlaps with that of the Lesser Black-backed Gull. The two forms are distinct and normally do not interbreed, yet they are part of a circumpolar ring of intergrading and interbreeding subspecies.

Glaucous Gull PLATE 17

Larus hyperboreus Gunnerus

Status Uncommon in winter. During some winters it is fairly common along the coast but is seen more frequently about harbour docks and sewage outlets. This species has been seen on all of Nova Scotia's coasts but it is most common on Cape Breton Island. It generally first appears in October (average 14 October, earliest 2 October);

individuals on Sable Island in mid-September 1979 (W. Stobo) and on 10 September 1984 (R. Pocklington) were exceptional. Stragglers remain into May (average 16 May, latest 31 May), especially on Sable Island.

Description *Length:* 66-76 cm. *Adults:* Light pearly grey mantle across back and wings; wings without black tips; rest of plumage pure white. *Immatures:* Vary from barred, pale ashy brown to brownish cream and have pink bills with dark tips.

Range Circumpolar. In North America, breeds on the coasts of northern Alaska, the Canadian Arctic islands and Greenland. In eastern North America, winters from southwestern Greenland south to New York State.

Remarks Approximating the Great Black-backed Gull in size, this bird is powerful and predatory, robbing other seabirds of their food and at times raiding their nests. It is distinguished from the Iceland Gull by its larger size, heavier bill and relatively short wings at rest.

Great Black-backed Gull   PLATE 17

Larus marinus Linnaeus

Status Common resident. In summer it is common to abundant near its breeding grounds and widely found along the coast. In winter it is less common except around cities, towns and garbage disposal areas, where it scavenges, often in large numbers, with Herring Gulls, crows and ravens, all clamouring for food during these lean months when competition is keen. It is found in greater numbers well offshore at all seasons. One of the largest colonies of this species in North America is located at Lake George, a few kilometres from Yarmouth.

Description *Length:* 71-79 cm. *All plumages:* Legs and feet flesh-coloured. *Adults:* Back and upper surface of wings dark (almost black) slate; flight feathers tipped with white; rest of plumage white; bill yellow with red spot on lower mandible. *Immatures:* Mottled with dusky browns and grays, varying in density and pattern according to age.

Breeding *Nest:* On the ground, usually on an island and in colonies. Single nests remote from others are sometimes placed in the crevices of large granite boulders protruding from lakes far in the interior of the province. I have no record of this species nesting in trees. The nests are composed of various quantities of coarse, decaying vegetable matter. Some nests are neatly and solidly constructed; others are crude affairs with little if any material being used. *Eggs:* 2-3, usually 3; light brown or buff, spotted evenly with dark brown or black. An egg without spots or blotches is sometimes laid, the ground colour being shades of light ashy blue or greenish olive. Such an egg may be one of three, the other two being normal; sometimes all three eggs are unspotted. Laying begins in the first part of May. Of nine sets of eggs examined on 20 May 1928, seven were fresh and the other two were slightly incubated.

Range Breeds from Greenland east to northern USSR and from Labrador south to North Carolina, with a small population in the Great Lakes.

Remarks The Great Black-backed Gull is the largest gull in the world. It can be distinguished from the more common Herring Gull when both are seen in subadult plumages by its size and its paler head and neck. After about four years it wears its adult mantle of sombre, non-lustrous black, which contrasts sharply with its glistening white plumage. These colours explain why in many localities it is known as the "coffin-carrier" or "minister bird."

Except around its nesting colonies where it will circle low overhead, this gull is extremely wary. I vividly recall an incident on the Grand Pré meadows: I was sitting on the edge of a drainage ditch, well concealed by a thick clump of rose bushes and wearing the prescribed duck-hunter's coat and cap. Scanning the horizon for ducks, I noted a Great Black-backed Gull winging its way across the dykelands and coming head on. Having been told the visual powers of gulls are far superior to those of ducks, I remained motionless in my well-camouflaged hideout, eyeing the on-coming gull, in an attempt to test the proposition. When it reached a point about 100 metres from me, I was amazed to see it suddenly flare up, pause momentarily, flapping its wings in reverse, and quickly change course to pass me, well out of the range of my gun. Wild ducks and Canada Geese would have come into the decoys without hesitation.

Black-legged Kittiwake   PLATE 18

Rissa tridactyla (Linnaeus)

Status Common in winter, uncommon in summer. Breeds. Occurs widely in large numbers from October to April, mainly on offshore waters, but it occasionally comes inshore and even inland as a result of storms at sea. On 20 October 1968 large numbers moved into Halifax Harbour just ahead of hurricane "Gladys." During fall and winter the bird can be seen in huge numbers off Digby Neck and Brier Island; an estimated 48,000 were recorded during the Brier Island Christmas Bird Count on 27 December 1978. It is seldom seen in summer, except far offshore or in the immediate vicinity of its small colonies in northeastern Nova Scotia.

Description *Length:* 41-46 cm. *All plumages:* Hind toe absent or very short. *Adults in summer:* Wings and back pearly gray; ends of primaries are black; rest of plumage white; bill yellow without red spot; feet black. *Adults in winter:* Similar but crown and nape are suffused with pale gray, and eye has a small dark area behind it. *Immatures:* Similar to winter adults, but with blackish band across back of neck, white secondaries and inner primaries, and black on outer primaries and lesser wing coverts; tip of tail and bill black; feet brownish.

Breeding The first Nova Scotian colony was discovered on 7 June 1971, by Anthony R. Lock of the Canadian Wildlife Service, on Green Island, a short distance off the coast from Gabarus, Cape Breton County. He estimated it to have 90 to 100 pairs. *Nests:* The nests were constructed of grasses and seaweeds in typical kittiwake fashion, plastered with mud and guano onto narrow rocky ledges 3-8 m above the ocean surface. *Eggs:* He examined 14 nests: six contained clutches of three eggs, pale brown with darker blotching; seven held two; and the last held but one egg, undoubtedly an incomplete laying. Lock believed this colony had been long established. Since then, four small kittiwake colonies have been discovered in northeastern Nova Scotia, and the total breeding population probably amounted to over 500 pairs in 1983 (A.R. Lock).

Remarks The pattern of the adult kittiwake's plumage is superficially similar to that of the Herring Gull, but it is a smaller bird with black, not flesh-coloured, legs and a lighter, more buoyant flight. The immature bird's plumage is not easily confused with that of any other species, except perhaps Sabine's Gull.

Bird-banding has revealed that this bird is a great wanderer. One captured on a trawl off the LaHave Islands, Lunenburg County, on 13 January 1943 had been banded in Iceland on 27 May 1938. Another, killed at Little Fogo Island, Newfoundland, on 20 September 1937 had been banded near Murmansk, USSR, on 19 June 1937. A young bird banded on the nest at North Shields, England, on 26 June 1956 was found dead about 200 km east of Halifax on 1 January 1959.

The name "kittiwake" is derived from the bird's peculiar cry. Fishermen off southern Nova Scotia know it as the "fall gull."

Sabine's Gull

Xema sabini (Sabine)

Status Rare transient. The first record, not fully confirmed, was at Cape Sable on 4 and 12 March 1961 (B.J. and S. Smith). Two adults seen on 5 February 1965 and one seen on 19 December 1966 at Sable Island (C. and N. Bell) were unseasonable. In 1969 an adult, well-described by Davis Finch, was seen on Sable Island on 27 August; another bird was observed from MV *Bluenose*, 16 km off Yarmouth on 30 September. Other Sable Island sightings were on 12 September 1974, 12 June 1977, 26 May 1978 (photographed) and 19 June 1979; and a bird was seen some 70 km southeast of the island on 13 April 1976. There were two birds at Cape Sable on 28 December 1977, later confirmed by Christmas Bird Count observers on 2 January 1978. Finally, three were seen on the Nova Scotian side of Cabot Strait on 8 August 1980, and single birds were seen at Brier Island on 4-7 June 1981 and at Seal Island on 16 October 1983.

Description *Length:* 34 cm. *Adults in breeding plumage:* Hood dark gray, bordered with black; bill black, with yellow spot at tip; feet black; outer primaries black, tipped with white; secondaries and inner primaries white; back and upper wing coverts gray;

remaining plumage white; tail weakly forked; the forepart of the hood is lost in winter. *Juveniles:* Nape, upper neck, upper wing coverts and back medium brown, striated with dark brown; tip of tail black.

Range Breeds in the North American and Eurasian Arctic; winters off the northwestern coast of South America and off western Africa.

Remarks The striking wing pattern of adults is unmistakable, and immature birds only superficially resemble young kittiwakes. Most Sabine's Gulls that breed in the Canadian Arctic travel directly across the Atlantic to the Bay of Biscay in the fall, well north of our area, and similarly return well offshore to the north. Our spring and fall birds were at the fringe of their migration routes, but our few winter birds are quite unexpected.

Ivory Gull   PLATE 17

Pagophila eburnea (Phipps)

Status Rare in winter. As one might expect with this arctic species, most of our records come from the winter months. The first was a bird reported from Halifax in 1849 (Jones 1885). One collected at Chezzetcook, Halifax County, on 15 October 1889 and one taken on Cape Breton Island on 26 October 1892 were brought to Halifax to taxidermist T.J. Egan, for mounting (Piers 1894). On 9 December 1905, one was shot near Sable Island (Allen 1916). More recently, single birds were seen at Cape Sable on 31 January 1961 and 15-17 January 1964, and two birds were there late in 1977. Other birds were seen during Christmas Bird Counts at the Sydneys on 28 December 1977 and 1982. In 1979, two were at Sambro, Halifax County, on 7-9 February; two at Glace Bay on 10 February, and another there on 1 March; and one at Digby on 15 April. There was a late sighting at Glace Bay on 5 May 1982, but the most unusual record, because it occurred in early summer, was of a bird in full breeding plumage on Sable Island, well studied by Christel and Norman Bell on 20 June 1969.

Description *Length:* 41-48 cm. *Adults:* Entire plumage white. Legs and feet black; bill black, with yellow tip. *Immatures:* Mainly white; gray suffusion on sides and front of head; sparse, sharply defined dark feather edges and flecks on some wing coverts and the tips of flight feathers; legs and bill black.

Range Breeds in the Canadian Arctic islands, northern Greenland and the Eurasian high Arctic; normally winters south to Newfoundland.

Remarks Ivory Gulls are associated with pack ice at all times of year. Their winter occurrence in Nova Scotia probably depends on the southerly extent of winter ice off Newfoundland.

Subfamily Sterninae

Gull-billed Tern

Sterna nilotica Gmelin

Status Rare vagrant. In an interview with Harry Piers in 1902, Richard Bouteillier reported this tern on Sable Island as "rare, sometimes rather plentiful . . . . breeds." McLaren (1981a) viewed this as "tantalizing", since Bouteillier certainly knew the three usual terns. However, it occurs today only as a rare visitor. The first recent record is of two well-described birds at West Lawrencetown Beach, Halifax County, on 2 August 1963 (C.R.K. Allen, L.B. Macpherson). The remaining records are all of single birds: at Conrad Beach, Halifax County, on 29 October 1967; at Cherry Hill Beach, Lunenburg County, on 17 August 1975; at Three Fathom Harbour, Halifax County, between 24 July and 1 August 1979 (photographed); at Pinkneys Point, Yarmouth County, on 28 May 1980; at East Lawrencetown, Halifax County, between 19 and 24 June 1980; at Cherry Hill on 20 September 1980; on 1 May 1982 at Crescent Beach, Lunenburg County; and on 17 July 1984 at Cow Bay, Halifax County.

Remarks This nearly white, short-tailed, stout-billed tern is at home in warmer waters, breeding north to New York State on the east coast, and occasionally wandering northward.

Caspian Tern   PLATE 18

Sterna caspia Pallas

Status Rare transient. Three nineteenth-century reports are mentioned by Jones (1885) and Piers (1894). This bird has sometimes reached our shores as a storm-borne casualty. The storm which wracked our coast on 26 August 1924 was responsible for dead birds found near Prospect, Halifax County, on 28 August and at Cape Sable on 27 August. Hurricane "Gladys," which reached Nova Scotia on 21 October 1968, brought with it at least eight of these birds, reported from Chebucto Head, Halifax County, to Canso and on Sable Island. However, recent reports from all parts of the province suggest that Caspian Terns are regular spring and fall transients in small numbers. Since 1968 there have been nine reports of 17 birds between 20 April and 17 June and 14 reports of 17 birds between 29 June and 31 August.

Description *Length:* 48-58 cm. *Adults in breeding plumage:* A large white tern with a stout, red bill tipped with black; the complete black cap is retained for most of the breeding season and the forehead remains dusky in all plumages.

Range In North America, breeds inland from Great Slave Lake south to California, and in the Great Lakes, and on the coasts of the Carolinas and the Gulf of Mexico. A small population breeds in the Gulf of St. Lawrence and Newfoundland. Widely distributed in the Old World.

Remarks This large tern can be distinguished from the Royal Tern by its stouter bill, darker forehead and duskier underwing tips. Most of our sightings are probably of birds going to and coming from colonies in the Gulf of St. Lawrence or Newfoundland.

Royal Tern

Sterna maxima Boddaert

Status Five records. The first was a female taken on Brier Island by Wickerson Lent on 1 October 1958 following a heavy gale which had lashed the coast a few days earlier. He collected another there on 13 September 1960 from a flock of four that appeared about four hours after hurricane "Donna" struck Digby Neck. Both specimens were presented to the Nova Scotia Museum. The third occurrence was reported in the aftermath of hurricane "Gladys" by Eric Mills, who saw three on 22 October 1968 "hurrying south" past Chebucto Head, Halifax County. Five birds on Sable Island were brought by storm-force winds on 16 August 1971 (D. Welsh). One at Three Fathom Harbour, Halifax County, on 20 July 1979 (J. Kearney, E.L. Mills) evidently was not associated with a tropical storm.

Remarks This large tern is very similar to the Caspian Tern (see Remarks for that species). It breeds from the Caribbean north to Maryland, and in western Mexico and western Africa.

Roseate Tern

Sterna dougallii Montagu

Status Rare in summer. Breeds. Never recorded as common in the province, its numbers have decreased since 1962. Evidence that it was formerly more plentiful is found in some earlier records. For instance, on 9 June 1906 Harold F. Tufts visited Noddy Island, one of the Mud Islands group lying off the coast from Yarmouth, where he found a thriving colony of Roseate Terns (but he does not mention its size). Brooks (1933) tells of visiting Indian Island, Lunenburg County, on 20 August 1930, where he found an estimated 125 pairs of Roseates nesting in a colony with Common and Arctic Terns; on 12 June 1937 there were only about 20 Roseate Terns in the colony, and on 8 July 1938 there were none, the site having been taken over by a horde of Herring Gulls (R.W. Tufts). In 1956 Marie Henry banded a Roseate Tern chick near Yarmouth on Little Bald Island where a few were nesting. They have long been known to nest among other terns on a few islands in Shelburne, Queens, Lunenburg and Halifax counties, but these colonies have not been systematically visited. On 4 June 1957 a small colony was found on Thrum Cap, an islet off Barren Island, Guysborough County. Dwight (1895) and Saunders (1902) found it breeding on Sable Island. In 1971 Anthony R. Lock estimated 125 pairs there; in recent years these have dwindled to a few pairs (A.R. Lock). Roseate Terns reach Nova Scotia in mid-May (the earliest report is of a bird on Sable Island on 13 May 1971). The fall migration takes place between mid-July and late August (latest sighting, from Sable Island, on 27 September 1970).

Description *Length:* 36-43 cm. *Adults in summer:* Pearly gray mantle across back and wings; crown black; underparts white, tinted with a delicate suffusion of pink; tail entirely white, more deeply forked and longer than in Common Tern; bill black, often more or less reddish base; feet red. *Adults in winter:* Similar but forehead is streaked with white or mottled with black; underparts entirely white. *Juveniles:* Distinctly black legs and scaly backs.

Breeding *Nest:* A depression in the ground sometimes lined sparsely with dry grass or other vegetable matter; in colonies, usually mixed with Common and Arctic Terns. *Eggs:* 2 normally, not readily distinguished from those of Common and Arctic Terns.

Range Breeds mainly on warm-water coasts in the Atlantic, Indian and Pacific oceans. In North America breeds along the Atlantic seaboard from Nova Scotia to the Caribbean. Winters from the West Indies to Brazil.

Remarks It can be distinguished in flight from the Common and Arctic Terns by its longer and more deeply forked tail, its more slender appearance, its black or nearly black bill and its grating call.
   The decline of the species in Nova Scotia since 1962 was part of a general decline over the North Atlantic, which came about through the depredations of gulls, the destruction of beaches on which it nests and human persecution on its wintering grounds. At present, there are conflicting opinions on whether the Roseate Tern continues to decline in numbers.

Common Tern PLATE 18

Sterna hirundo Linnaeus

Status Common in summer. Breeds. As a rule, Common Terns arrive in early May (average 3 May, earliest 27 April). They are common to abundant in summer in the vicinity of breeding colonies, particularly those along the Southwestern and Eastern shores. Because Common Terns fly at relatively low levels to dive for small fishes near the surface, they avoid water muddied by tidal action like that along the Minas Basin. The main fall migration takes place between late August and the end of September, and stragglers are seen in October. The latest fall record is of a bird seen near Pictou on 11 November 1963 (E. Holdway). Later sightings could involve confusion with Forster's Tern.

Description *Length:* 33-40 cm. *Adults in summer:* Mantle of pearly gray across back and wings; whole top of head black; sides of head, throat and tail white; breast and belly very pale gray; tail forked; outer web of outer tail feathers gray; bill red at base, black at tip; feet red. *Adults in winter:* Similar but only hind part of crown is black; forehead white. *Juveniles:* Similar to winter adults but back somewhat mottled and buffy, tails much shorter, and distinctive dark mark on the inner forewing.

Breeding *Nest:* A mere depression scraped out in the turf or sand, sometimes with a lining. In my experience, nests always occur in colonies numbering from a few to many hundred pairs, usually on coastal islands but sometimes on mainland beaches remote from human intrusion or on islets in freshwater lakes. On 5 August 1966 Marie Henry found one newly hatched young being fed by a parent on a small, bare island in Kejimkujik Lake. The species breeds extensively on lakes elsewhere in its range. *Eggs:* 3; olive-green to olive-brown, heavily marked with dark brown blotches, usually heaviest around the larger end. On 12 June 1937 about 100 pairs of terns were nesting on Indian Island, Lunenburg County. Perhaps 60 pairs were Common Terns and the rest were Arctic and Roseate Terns; none of the many eggs had yet hatched.

Range Breeds from Great Slave Lake east to southern Labrador and Newfoundland, south to the northern tier of the United States, and southward along the Atlantic coast locally to the Caribbean. Winters from South Carolina southward and on the Pacific coast. Widely distributed in the Old World, from the British Isles to eastern Siberia.

Remarks Our three breeding terns—the Common, Arctic, and Roseate—are known to those who live along the shore as "mackerel gulls." In life it is difficult to distinguish between them. Generally, in summer the bill of the Common Tern is reddish with a black tip, that of the Arctic is blood-red and the Roseate's may be all black or have a small reddish area about the base. The Roseate has a longer tail than the other two, and the experienced field observer will detect its whiter, more slender and elongated appearance. The legs of the Arctic Tern are slightly shorter than those of the other two, and its squatty appearance on the ground may be helpful. In flight, the broad, sooty trailing edge on the underside of the Common Tern's primaries contrasts with the narrower, sharper edges of the Arctic and the whiter underwings of the Roseate. The grating quality of the Roseate Tern's call is also distinctive. At rest, juvenile Common Terns can be distinguished from the other two by their darker "shoulder" mark which appears as a dark bar on the upper forewing in flight.

A visit to a colony of nesting terns, particularly a large one, is an experience long remembered. As the nesting ground is approached, the angry birds come to meet the intruder scolding vociferously. When the nests are reached, the harsh, screaming *tearr, tearr, tearr* reaches its highest pitch, and is accompanied by savage dive-bombing, as with folded wings the birds drop at terrific speeds to within centimetres of the intruder, sometimes spraying him with highly odoriferous, regurgitated fish.

Arctic Tern   PLATE 18

Sterna paradisaea Pontoppidan

Status Common in summer. Breeds. This species arrives in Nova Scotia in the second week of May, a little later than the Common Tern. The earliest report is of two birds collected near the Tusket Islands, Yarmouth County, on 3 May 1956. In summer it is common along the coast where the water is clear and the tidal reach is extensive rather than abrupt but is uncommon to absent in areas where tidal mudflats cause muddy waters. The return passage begins in mid-July and is largely completed by mid-September. The latest sighting is of a group of birds at Sable Island on 1 October 1976.

Description *Length:* 36-43 cm. *Adults in summer:* Similar to Common Terns; tarsi considerably shorter; legs red; bill red, without black tip. *Adults in winter:* White fore-crowns, black on the head being largely confined to nape; bills darker. *Immatures:* Similar to winter adults but tails shorter.

Breeding *Nest:* A depression in the turf or sand, sometimes scantily lined with bits of dried eelgrass or other rubbish, and sometimes without a lining; in colonies, usually mixed with Common Terns. In my experience, islands are selected for nesting rather than mainland beach sites. *Eggs:* 1-2, usually 2; not readily distinguishable from those of the Common Tern.

Range Circumpolar. In North America, breeds across the Arctic from Alaska to northern Greenland, south to northern British Columbia, Lake Athabaska, James Bay and along the Atlantic coast to Massachusetts. It is known to nest within 850 km of the North Pole (Cooke 1915). Winters off southern Africa and in the Antarctic.

Remarks The Arctic Tern is one of the greatest avian travellers. It leaves our shores in autumn for a trans-Atlantic flight to Europe, where it follows the coast southward to its wintering grounds off southern Africa; juveniles continue south to the edge of the Antarctic pack-ice. The recovery of bands from these birds tells amazing stories. A juvenile banded in Maine on 3 July 1913 was found dead on the Niger River Delta in West Africa in August 1917. Another, banded in Labrador as a downy chick on 22 June 1927 was recovered in France on 1 October that year; only three months old, it had flown across more than 5,000 km of ocean. Another banded in Labrador as a chick on 23 July 1928 was found less than four months later on the beach at Margate, Natal, South Africa.

It closely resembles Common and Roseate Terns (distinguishing field marks are cited under those species).

Forster's Tern

Sterna forsteri Nuttall

Status Rare vagrant and transient. An immature female was collected on 4 September 1924 by L.A. Purcell at Maynard Lake, Dartmouth; a severe southerly gale had lashed the province on 26 August. A second bird was reported by Charles R.K. Allen and Lloyd B. Macpherson from Lawrencetown, Halifax County, on 19 October 1958. A third was seen by Mr. Allen at West Chezzetcook, Halifax County, on 11 September 1960. Between 27 October and 1 November 1968, following the wake of hurricane "Gladys," six birds were seen in the area of Cole Harbour and Cow Bay, Halifax County, and one was seen near Port Felix Harbour, Guysborough County. An immature bird was well documented on 23 May 1970 at Seal Island (B.K. Doane). In 1984, there were several reports: on 15 July and 14-15 September at Conrad Beach, Halifax County; at Eel Lake, Yarmouth County, on 17 November; and at Crescent Beach, Lunenburg County, on 29-30 December (photographed). Other fall or early-winter terns that have been reported may have been this species. These include individuals (some reported as Common Terns) on the Halifax East Christmas Bird Counts of 1981 and 1983, and near Cape Sable on 10 February 1975.

Remarks Adults in breeding plumage resemble the Common Tern but have heavier bills, longer legs and, in flight, the bases of the inner primaries are distinctly silvery white. Winter adults and immatures have a distinctive dark bar behind their eyes.

Forster's Tern breeds on the North American prairies, along the east coast from New York State to North Carolina, and on the Gulf of Mexico. Birds in Nova Scotia may be vagrants from the south (especially after storms) or transients from the centre of the continent, which normally migrate to the east coast further south.

Least Tern

Sterna antillarum (Lesson)

Status Rare vagrant. Andrew Downs obtained a specimen from Alton, Colchester County, on 1 September 1879 (Jones 1885), and the bird appears to have been a frequent stray to Sable Island at the turn of the twentieth century (McLaren 1981a). One was taken at Barrington, Shelburne County, on 28 August 1924 immediately following a heavy southerly gale. Three birds were seen and one collected at Grand Desert, Halifax County, on 13-15 August 1970, and two more were observed on 26 August 1970 at Big Island, Pictou County. In 1971, single birds were reported from Three Fathom Harbour, Halifax County, on 16 August and from Seal Island on 25 August. Individuals were seen at Brier Island on 9 May 1980; at Caribou Island, Pictou County, on 10 July 1983; and at Seal Island on 1-7 September 1983; and two birds were seen on Sable Island on 11 September 1984.

Remarks These tiny terns resemble our larger nesting species, but the adults have white foreheads and yellow bills and feet. Hurried flight regularly interspersed with hovering is characteristic. They are widespread in temperate and tropical regions; in eastern North America they breed from the Caribbean north to southern Maine.

There once was a commercial demand for its plumage to satisfy the millinery trade, which resulted in a marked diminution in its numbers over North America. Despite subsequent protective legislation, the population has never regained its former size.

Sooty Tern

Sterna fuscata Linnaeus

Status Five records. The first record for Canada was recently dead at Gaspereau, Kings County, on 28 August 1924 (Tufts 1925); a gale from the south had passed over the province on 26 August. This specimen is in the Nova Scotia Museum. Local reports suggested that other Sooty Terns reached Yarmouth County in the wake of the same storm. Hurricane "Gladys" ravaged our coast on 21 October 1968 and brought at least one Sooty Tern, found by Eric Cooke at Three Fathom Harbour, Halifax County, on 23 October. Our three other records are well-described: an immature bird at Sable Island on 4 July 1972 (D.A. Welsh); a bird at Green Bay, Lunenburg County, on 28 July 1975 (J.S. and L. Cohrs); and a dying bird picked up on Melmerby Beach, Pictou County, on 7 September 1979 (A. McKay).

Remarks The Sooty Tern is about the same size as our three breeding terns but markedly different in appearance. Adults are sooty black above and white below, and juveniles are largely sooty brown. Colonies of this species are very large, and the Sooty Tern is thought by some to be the most abundant seabird in the world. The nearest colonies to Nova Scotia are in Florida and the Bahamas.

Black Tern

Chlidonias niger (Linnaeus)

Status Uncommon transient, rare and local in summer. Breeds. Black Terns arrive in May (average 27 May, earliest 12 May) and transients or non-breeding birds may appear through June. Small numbers nest in the marsh of the Missaguash River and at Amherst Point Bird Sanctuary, Cumberland County. Numbers have occurred widely (including at Sable Island) in July; but the main fall migration is in August. Latest sightings are normally in September (average 5 September, latest 24 September), but very late birds were at Johnstons Pond, Shelburne County, on 26 October 1976, at Cape Sable on 20-23 November 1977 and (two birds, one collected) at Brier Island on 26 December 1966.

Description *Length:* 21-24 cm. *Adults in breeding plumage:* Black head, neck, breast and belly; back and wings dark gray; tail pale gray; undertail coverts and underside of flight feathers white. *Adults in non-breeding plumage:* Pale gray above and white below, with black on crown and nape only. *Juveniles:* Resemble winter adults but browner.

Breeding *Nest:* A shallow depression in a low mound of water weeds, usually floating, in shallow freshwater or brackish marshes. *Eggs:* 2-4, usually 3; pale brown with darker brown blotches. The first nest recorded for the province was found on 12 June 1975 by William Barrow of the Canadian Wildlife Service about 100 m from the New Brunswick border in the Missaguash River marsh. Nesting in the Amherst Point Bird Sanctuary was first indicated by recently fledged young in 1977 (C. Desplanque).

Range The interior of North America from Nova Scotia west to the Rockies and north to Great Slave Lake, wintering in northern South America. In the Old World, it breeds from Spain to the Urals.

Remarks This bird nests commonly in reedy ponds and lakes in the interior of North America. It has recently spread to Nova Scotia by way of New Brunswick, where it first nested in 1937 (Squires 1976).

Subfamily Rhynchopinae

Black Skimmer

Rhynchops niger Linnaeus

Status Rare vagrant. Not including the large numbers brought to our shores in 1924 and 1968 by hurricanes, there have been only two reported, neither apparently associated with storms: at Cape Sable on 20 July 1964 (S. Smith) and another on Sable Island on 14 August 1965 (C. and N. Bell). Following the hurricane that struck our coast on 26 August 1924, many Black Skimmers, along with numbers of other southern species, were scattered along our Southwestern and Eastern Shores. Many were dead and others were emaciated. Hurricane "Gladys" passed over Cape Breton Island on 21 October 1968 and brought several species of southern birds, including hundreds of Black Skimmers. The first one was seen near Three Fathom Harbour, Halifax County, on 22 October and many others were seen in the same general area on 27 October. From then on they were reported from widely separated points, in numbers ranging from one to the estimated 200 seen at Jeddore, Halifax County, on 1 November; the latest were two near Dartmouth on 8 December. Some were said to be dying—not surprising because, given their specialized manner of feeding (see Remarks), it is unlikely that these storm-borne waifs had been able to obtain food on their journey to Nova Scotia.

PLATE 19
all adults, summer plumage

Razorbill
Page 229

common form

Common Murre
Page 227

"bridled" form

Atlantic Puffin
Page 232

Black Guillemot
Page 231

Roger Tory Peterson

Roger Tory Peterson

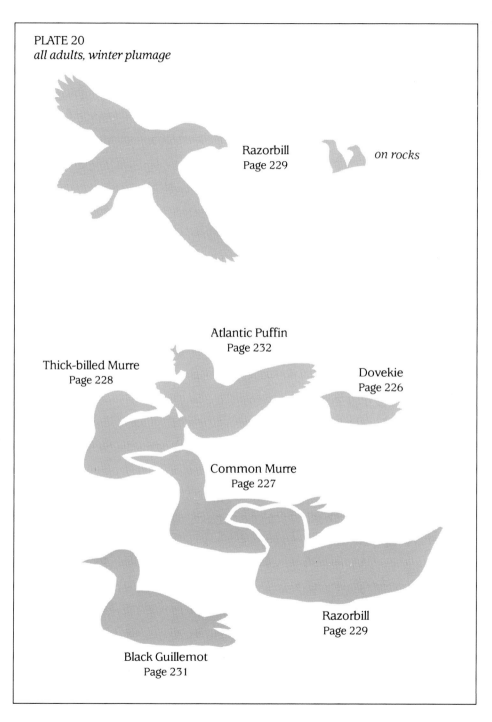

PLATE 20
all adults, winter plumage

Razorbill
Page 229

on rocks

Atlantic Puffin
Page 232

Thick-billed Murre
Page 228

Dovekie
Page 226

Common Murre
Page 227

Razorbill
Page 229

Black Guillemot
Page 231

Remarks Black Skimmers are unmistakable: black above (dusky in immatures), white below, with large red, black-tipped bills, the lower mandible longer than the upper. They breed on the warm-water coasts of North and South America, north to Massachusetts on the Atlantic. Their name is derived from the peculiar manner by which they obtain their food: they skim over the water with their beaks tipped downward, cutting the surface of the water with the sharp edges of their lower mandibles to scoop up small fishes.

Family Alcidae

Dovekie PLATE 20

Alle alle (Linnaeus)

Status Common in winter, very rare in summer. The first sightings of Dovekies are generally in late October (average 1 November, earliest 15 October). They are abundant offshore from November to April, especially along the edge of the Scotian Shelf southwest of Sable Island, but are rarely seen inshore in numbers except during large "wrecks" of weakened birds during late fall (see Remarks). However, hundreds of evidently lively birds are regularly seen on Christmas Bird Counts at Brier Island — about 500 were reported there on 31 December 1966 and again on 20 December 1973. They are rarely recorded in spring, although many were seen off Sable Island as late as 15 May 1977. There are few records for summer. One collected by Scott (1959) about 2 km south of Ram Island, Shelburne County, on 18 June 1957 was a female without enlarged ovarian follicles. Others were reported on 16 July 1968 at Broad Cove, Victoria County, and near the *Lurcher Lightship* off Yarmouth on 3 and 26 July 1969.

Description *Length:* 19-23 cm. *Adults in summer:* Upperparts glossy black; neck and breast sooty brown; lower breast and belly white; stubby, sparrow-like bill. *Adults in winter:* Similar but throat and breast white, the breast often tinged with gray.

Range Breeds on the coasts of Greenland and on the high Arctic islands east to western Siberia; there are also very small populations on Baffin Island and Iceland and in the Bering Sea. The bulk of the world population of more than 14 million birds nests in northwestern Greenland and winters off Newfoundland and Nova Scotia, and occasionally further south.

Remarks This little black and white, web-footed, robin-size bird with "no neck" is often picked up near the coast or even well inland in a weakened condition or dead. The following cases are typical: an estimated 1,000 were seen in Sydney Harbour on 25 October 1930, some of which, when picked up and tossed into the air, were able to fly away (A.A. Bayley); one caught by hand on a freshwater lake at Albany, Kings County, approximately 30 km from salt water, on 19 November 1941 was too weak to take off or even dive when approached; and between 11 and 23 December 1932 no fewer than 22 Dovekies, dead or very weak, were brought to me, having been picked up at various points in Kings County.

Dovekies are notoriously liable to being driven, often in large numbers, far outside their normal winter range by storms; one such bird reached Cuba! Theories advanced by ornithologists to explain this tendency are linked to storms and high gales at sea, and to the food shortages that directly result. Murphy and Vogt (1933) have written a detailed account of this spectacular phenomenon.

Quite at home on the broad ocean, Dovekies drift about in winter, feeding on the plankton that is everywhere abundant when weather conditions are favourable. However, when very rough weather strikes, this minute marine life sinks to low, inaccessible levels, causing a serious food shortage for the Dovekies when storms are prolonged.

The Dovekie is known to residents along the coasts of Nova Scotia by the name "bull-bird," or "ice bird."

Common Murre PLATES 19 & 20

Uria aalge (Pontoppidan)

Status Common in winter. Formerly bred. Bryant (1857) found them nesting off Yarmouth on Gannet Rock and Green Island. Bayley (1925) mentioned about a dozen pairs of murres nesting on Bird Island, Victoria County, but did not identify the species; he was told by a local resident that murres had been very common there in the past. However, Percy Taverner visited the islands in 1929 and recorded only two Common Murres, and Thomas F.T. Morland found only one there on 24 July 1965. No breeding murres were discovered in Nova Scotia in 1971 during the course of Anthony R. Lock's survey for the Canadian Wildlife Service. Despite its name, this species is less commonly seen than the Thick-billed Murre. Most reports are from between December and April, with stragglers into May. A late bird at Sable Island on 20-25 June 1974 was apparently injured. Oiling has become a serious problem for these birds: the skeletal remains of a Common Murre that washed up near Margaretsville, Annapolis County, on 6 March 1946 showed evidence of oil contamination; on 28 February 1967 at Morden, Annapolis County, and again on 5 and 8 March 1967 at Harbourville, Kings County, a number of these birds were found dead or dying, all victims of oil; and Wickerson Lent found 31 oil-contaminated individuals on inshore waters near Brier Island during the first week of February 1960. However, the Thick-billed Murre was the principal victim of the oil spilled from the tankers *Arrow* and *Kurdistan* off Cape Breton Island in February 1970 and March 1979, respectively. This suggests that most Common Murres winter off southern Nova Scotia or further south.

Description *Length:* 40-43 cm. *Adults in summer:* Head and neck dark seal-brown; back and wings black; sometimes a narrow white ring around the eye with a line extending back; underparts entirely white. *Adults in winter:* Front and sides of neck are white and narrow dark line extends back from the eye.

Range In the Atlantic, breeds along steep, rocky coasts from Portugal to Iceland and Spitsbergen, and from New Brunswick to southwestern Greenland. A separate population breeds in the North Pacific. The eastern North American population is about 570,000 pairs, of which 550,000 breed in Newfoundland and Labrador, and almost all the rest breed in the Gulf of St. Lawrence. There is a small colony of fewer than 100 pairs on Yellow Murre Rock, off southwestern New Brunswick. Western Atlantic birds winter at sea from Newfoundland southwards, especially off New England.

Remarks Murres seen on the water may be distinguished from ducks by their short, thick necks and sharp-pointed black bills. Their name is derived from their call, a deep, bass *murre*. They are called "turr" in Newfoundland and "scribe" along some sections of the Nova Scotian coast. The two murre species are difficult to distinguish, except at close range. Its longer, more slender bill and, in winter, the dark line extending from its eye across a white cheek distinguish the Common Murre.

In game-law parlance, murres are "migratory non-game birds" protected throughout the year in both Canada and the United States—except in Newfoundland, where a winter "turr" hunt is permitted, the Thick-billed Murre being the species principally affected.

Johnson (1940) mentions three records of banded Common Murres recovered in Nova Scotia but only gives the details of one banded in the Cape Whittle region on the north shore of the Gulf of St. Lawrence on 11 August 1926 and recovered in Lunenburg County on 14 December 1926.

Thick-billed Murre   PLATE 20

Uria lomvia (Linnaeus)

Status Common in winter. Occurs regularly from early December to April, occasionally both earlier and later. Single birds at Brier Island on 20 September 1972 and at Cherry Hill, Lunenburg County, on 6 October 1979 were unusually early arrivals. The main spring passage takes place during the second half of April, although there are a few May records and an active bird was seen off Sable Island on 14 June 1979. They are more common on offshore waters than near the coast, except when driven ashore by storms, when they may be picked up dead or exhausted, sometimes at a considerable distance inland. Large numbers are regularly seen near Brier Island during Christmas Bird Counts—the highest estimate was 20,000 birds on 20 December 1973. Banding has shown (Tuck 1961) that Thick-billed Murres from colonies in Greenland, and from Lancaster Sound and Hudson Strait in the Canadian Arctic, all winter off southern Newfoundland; the birds visiting Nova Scotia are probably from all three areas.

Description *Length:* 43-48 cm. *Adults in summer:* Head and neck dark seal-brown; back and wings black; entirely white below. *Adults in winter:* Upperparts same as in summer but front and sides of neck white.

Range Breeds on rocky cliffs around the Polar Basin and south to Newfoundland, southern Greenland and Iceland, and in the North Pacific. In eastern North America, winters at sea off Newfoundland, western Greenland and, to a lesser extent, Nova Scotia. The eastern Canadian population is about 1,300,000 pairs, of which only 11,000 breed at the southern edge of the range, in Newfoundland and the Gulf of St. Lawrence.

Remarks (For further notes on the Thick-billed Murre, see the Common Murre.) Irregularly, in late autumn or winter, numbers of murres are found dead or in weakened condition along the coast or inland, victims of heavy gales with which they were unable to cope successfully, presumably because they were too close to shore when overtaken by the storm. In my experience, surprisingly, all such casualties are of the Thick-billed species. One of these unfortunates was found lying helpless on a lawn at Coldbrook, Kings County, on 14 December 1969, weak from starvation. It was soon released in the Cornwallis River at Port Williams, the nearest salt water. A passing Great Black-backed Gull, detecting the disability, attacked almost immediately, but the murre adeptly dived. The muddy water of the receding tide favoured the murre because the gull was unable to follow the weakened bird's course. After several unsuccessful attempts to catch it when it would briefly surface, the gull gave up and the murre was last seen heading downstream for the open coast.

Razorbill PLATES 19 & 20

Alca torda Linnaeus

Status Uncommon transient, rare in summer and winter. Breeds. Most common in summer in the immediate vicinity of its principal breeding colony at Bird Islands, Victoria County, where, in 1971, it numbered 50-100 pairs. Bayley (1925) estimated about 500 pairs there around 1925, and John R. Gallagher found 200-300 birds there on 3 July 1964. Smaller numbers also nest on St. Paul Island in Cabot Strait, and on Pearl Island, Lunenburg County (two pairs in 1975), and once nested on Gannet Rock and Green Island off Yarmouth (Bryant 1857). A small bird in down-like juvenile plumage was taken by V.E. Gould on Dingwall Bay, Victoria County, on 24 August 1935 (Godfrey 1958). In spring and fall the Razorbill is a regular transient along the Atlantic and Fundy coasts, where it is less common in winter. It arrives in mid-October and, except in the vicinity of its colonies, is rarely seen after mid-May.

Description *Length:* 40-47 cm. *Adults in summer:* Upperparts sooty black; sides of head and throat tinged with brown; breast, belly and a line from eye to bill white; bill laterally compressed, black, crossed by a white band. *Adults in winter:* Similar but with sides and front of neck white, and white line in front of eye lacking. *Immatures:* Similar to adults in winter but bill is smaller and lacks white band.

Breeding *Nest:* None worthy of the name; a single egg is laid on bare rock or ground on the rocky cliffsides of coastal islands. *Egg:* 1; varies from greenish blue to creamy white, all spotted and streaked with dark brown. Laying begins in late May or early June.

Range In eastern North America, breeds mainly in southeastern Labrador, but its range extends south to Maine, and it also breeds in western Greenland. Winters off New England and southern Nova Scotia. It is also found in the Old World, from Brittany to Iceland and northwestern Russia. The world population of the Razorbill is over 100,000 breeding pairs; about 25,000 nest in Atlantic Canada.

Remarks The Razorbill may be distinguished from murres by its bill, which is blunt-ended and fairly deep, rather than pointed or crow-like. Furthermore, it usually swims with its tail cocked up, whereas murres do not. It is known locally as a "noddy" or "tinker."

Great Auk

Pinguinus impennis (Linnaeus)

Status Extinct. The former status in Nova Scotia of this large, flightless relative of the Razorbill is now difficult to determine. The only evidence of its having occurred here is provided by a number of bones which John S. Erskine discovered in shell heaps, the first during 1957 at Scotch Point, Port Joli, Queens County. There he found many bird bones, one later identified by Godfrey (1959a) as the left humerus of a Great Auk. The formation of this shell heap was provisionally dated by Erskine to about the fourteenth century. He subsequently made two more discoveries in shell heaps at St. Margaret's Bay, Halifax County, and at Mahone Bay, Lunenburg County. Among the many bird bones found at both locations, Dr. Pierce Brodkorb of the University of Florida has identified some of the Great Auk. Dr. Brodkorb dated both heaps as having been formed during the thirteenth century. The last record of living Great Auks is that of two killed in Iceland on 3 June 1844. Downs (1888) supposed that the species was formerly common here, but the only definite information he presented refers to Newfoundland. Some ornithologists have considered the birds killed with sticks by Champlain's men on the Mud Islands, Yarmouth County, about 20 May 1604 to have been Great Auks; however, as Godfrey (1959a) has pointed out, these were probably Northern Gannets. Grieve (1885), on his distribution chart, indicated Cape Breton Island as a breeding place for the Great Auk. This was based, however, on the rather flimsy evidence of Fisher (in Hakluyt 1600), whose party landed on Cape Breton Island in summer 1593 but, harassed by Indians, remained only briefly. They "saw divers beastes and foules, as black Foxes, Deers, Otters, great Foules with redde legges, Pengwyns, and certain others." In his account of the natural resources of Acadia (the Maritime Provinces and southern Newfoundland) in the middle of the seventeenth century, Nicholas Denys reported seeing the species far offshore but made no mention of colonies (Allen 1939).

Remarks So much has been published regarding the wholesale slaughter of these flightless, hence helpless, birds on their breeding grounds that it seems needless to retell the sad tale here. Those who wish to read of the barbarous methods that eventually resulted in the bird's extinction may consult Bent (1919).

Black Guillemot   PLATES 19 & 20

Cepphus grylle (Linnaeus)

Status Common resident. Breeds. In summer it is common only around its widely distributed nesting colonies on the coast; elsewhere it is rare. In late fall and winter it is fairly common along inshore coastal waters, perhaps being seen most frequently along the Eastern and Southwestern shores. In spring it begins to arrive in breeding plumage at its nesting grounds about mid-April.

Description *Length:* 30-36 cm. *Adults in summer:* Coal-black with large white wing-patches and red feet. *Adults in winter:* Underparts white; upperparts black, feathers broadly tipped with white; wings have the same white mark as in summer.

Breeding *Nest:* None worthy of the name. *Eggs:* Usually 2; dull white, heavily marked with spots and blotches of dark brown; laid under cover, on bare gravel or earth, often under large boulders or driftwood on the beach about 1 m above high water and sometimes at the end of a burrow in peaty soil at the top of a steep embankment on islands. Laying begins early in June. Fresh eggs were examined on 19 June 1922 in nest sites under boulders at Seal Island, Yarmouth County. Three nests in burrows about 3.5 m above the rocky beach were discovered on Little Half Bald Island (locally called "Inner Bald"), off Wedgeport, Yarmouth County, on 19 July 1956 by Marie Henry. One of these nests contained the usual two eggs and the others each held well-developed young. The burrows were excavated to a depth of about 35 cm; one was found to have two entrances. Nesting colonies ranging in size from 10 to 40 pairs were visited: at Cape Split, Kings County, in 1933; on Bird (Ciboux and Hertford) Islands, Victoria County, in 1940; on Bird (Halibut) Islands off Harrigan Cove, Halifax County, in 1941; and on Seal Island in 1922 and 1938.

Range In eastern North America, breeds along rocky coasts from the Arctic south to Maine. Winters as far north as open water permits and southward to New York State. Also breeds all around the Polar Basin, and in Europe as far south as Ireland and the Baltic Sea.

Remarks Most people living along the shore know this bird as the "sea pigeon." Its colour pattern in summer somewhat resembles that of the drake White-winged Scoter, but this bird is much smaller than the Scoter. Generally seen on inshore waters, it feeds on small fishes, seeming to show a strong preference for Rock Eels *(Pholis gunnellus),* which it procures by diving.

It is classified as a migratory non-game bird and as such is completely protected throughout the year, both in Canada (including Newfoundland) and the United States, by international treaty.

Atlantic Puffin   PLATES 19 & 20

Fratercula arctica (Linnaeus)

Status Uncommon transient, rare in winter and summer. Breeds. It is common in summer in Nova Scotia only around its remaining breeding colonies, which, at the time of the 1971 Canadian Wildlife Service survey, were located on Bird Islands, Victoria County (50-70 pairs), and Pearl Island, Lunenburg County (where up to 12 pairs nested unsuccessfully in 1975). The Bird Islands are unusual because puffins there are forced to nest in holes in the sides of the cliffs, their preferred habitat in the turf on top of the islands having been taken over by gulls. During a visit to the Bird Islands on 27 June 1933 the breeding population was estimated at several hundred pairs (R.W. Tufts). On 3 July 1964 John R. Gallagher estimated it at 800-1000 individuals. There can be little doubt that the decline in numbers is largely the result of predation by Herring and Great Black-backed Gulls. Puffins formerly bred on several islands off Yarmouth (Bryant 1857). Harold F. Tufts (1907) found "a few" nesting on Seal Island in mid-June 1907, and Harrison Lewis found only one pair there on 14 July 1912 but did not find their nest. On 19 June 1922 no puffins were breeding there, nor were any seen (R.W. Tufts); the many predatory house cats that roamed there unchecked in 1922 were probably responsible. Seven puffins off Brier Island on 24 May 1969 were possibly late transients, but summer birds occasionally reported near Sable Island and two birds seen by Thomas F.T Morland on 8 July 1962 some 8 km off Sable River, Shelburne County, were probably non-breeding wanderers. During fall the species occurs as a transient along the coast but is less common there in winter and spring. The birds arrive at the end of September and remain at least until December.

Description *Length:* 29-34 cm. *Adults in breeding plumage:* Throat and upperparts glossy black; white below; face pale gray; its large and absurdly shaped bill, nearly as high as it is long and brightly coloured with red, blue and yellow, is most conspicuous; legs and feet reddish. *Adults in winter:* Most of the horny plates on the outside of the bill have been shed; sides of head are darker gray. *Juveniles:* Resemble adults in winter but their bills are even smaller.

Breeding *Nest:* At the end of a burrow in the ground or in a crevice among boulders, sometimes, if not usually, lined with soft nesting material. *Egg:* 1; dull white, sometimes showing delicate traces of fine markings about the larger end. Laying begins in late May or early June.

Range Breeds along coasts from Greenland to Maine, and from Iceland and Spitsbergen to Brittany and northeastern Russia. The world centre for the Atlantic Puffin population is Iceland, where many millions breed. In our area it nests from the

Maine-New Brunswick border north to southeastern Labrador, rarely in the Hudson Strait. The North American population is about 330,000 pairs, most of which occur in southeastern Newfoundland. In winter, some migrate along the coast as far south as Massachusetts.

Remarks The puffin or "sea parrot," as it is commonly called by fishermen, is readily identified by its parrot-like beak, its bright orange legs and its exceptionally rapid wing-beats. From a boat, I have watched them bringing in food for their young and, as they whirred by overhead, their orange legs conspicuously straddled far apart, have noted that the fare invariably consisted of small, slender eel-like fishes which trailed or dangled from their beaks. It seemed that these fishes were captured a considerable distance seaward from the colony, which suggests they were not available nearby.

Atlantic Puffins

Order COLUMBIFORMES

Family Columbidae

Rock Dove

Columba livia Gmelin

Status Introduced, common resident. Breeds. Brought over from Europe as a domestic bird, it is now sedentary and common to abundant about cities, towns and farm buildings when tolerated.

Remarks Details of the domestic pigeon's importation are unrecorded, but the present population is believed to have sprung from birds that escaped or were liberated from captivity. Although living in a semiwild state for over 100 years, it still clings to areas close to habitation, never having become wholly independent of man.

It lays but two white eggs and breeds most of the year. John Doyle saw one carrying nesting materials to a building on the waterfront in Halifax on 19 February 1969, and Mark Elderkin saw one carrying a twig in its bill to a nest under construction in one of the public school buildings in Wolfville on 20 October 1970. These observations suggest a breeding season covering at least eight months. Several instances have been reported of these birds having chosen nesting sites in trees. Small twigs are used in nest construction and I have noted the bird carries only one at a time.

Probably few persons realize that the various fancy forms of pigeons, such as the pouter and the carrier, are all descendants of a single species, the Rock Dove. The changed forms have been produced by artificial selection. That all are descendants of a single species is proven by the fact that when hybrid offspring of the diverse races are bred together, the result are Rock Doves typical in form and plumage (Townsend 1915).

Three banded birds (one with a message container) and four unbanded ones have reached Sable Island (McLaren 1981a), suggesting that "domestic" birds are prone to wandering.

Band-tailed Pigeon

Columba fasciata Say

Status Two records. A bird discovered on 23 September 1974 on Seal Island by Richard G.B. Brown, Ian MacGregor, Bruce MacTavish, and Stuart Tingley (who also photographed it) was seen subsequently by many others up to 19 October. The second bird, a female, was captured in a duck-banding trap set at the Shubenacadie Wildlife Park, Colchester County, on 1 December 1981 and remained captive until released the following June (E. Pace).

Remarks A few individuals of this far-western bird have been recorded elsewhere in eastern North America, generally in autumn. There is no reason to assume they are anything other than true vagrants.

White-winged Dove

Zenaida asiatica (Linnaeus)

Status Five records. The first was closely observed by Alban Richard on Sable Island on 10 August 1979. On 27 August of that year another was photographed on Seal Island (I. and J. McLaren). Subsequent birds have all been seen at bird feeders. One stayed from mid-September to 10 October 1982 near Sambro, Halifax County (G. Patrick). Two more were photographed: at Stellarton, Pictou County, 18-23 May 1982 (L.F. McKay), and at North Sydney, 26-29 May 1984 (L. Maclean).

Remarks This southwestern species has wandered to the northeast more regularly in recent years.

Mourning Dove   PLATE 23

Zenaida macroura (Linnaeus)

Status Uncommon in summer, fairly common transient, uncommon in winter. Breeds. A pair from Nova Scotia is listed in Gesner's (1842) catalogue. Blakiston and Bland (1856) and Downs (1865) do not include it, whereas Jones (1879) found it "not uncommon" in autumn. Downs (1888) thought that "it appears to be becoming rather common," although it "once was rare." Evidently it became less common in the interim. When the first edition of this book was published in 1962, it rated as a rare summer resident and uncommon fall visitant. Although still uncommon in summer, it has become regular in some numbers in fall and winter. It first appears in spring, generally in late March or early April (average 31 March, earliest 12 March) but overwintering flocks may still be associated with grain-storage facilities or bird feeders into May. The bird is most common in summer in the Annapolis Valley but is found in agricultural and urban areas throughout the province. Its numbers are augmented in the fall, especially in October, and counts of 25 or more have been made during Christmas Bird Counts in the Halifax area, in Yarmouth County, Wolfville and sometimes elsewhere. Such large groups may remain in these areas through winter, subsisting at feeders or grain-storage sites.

Description *Length:* 30-33 cm. A long-tailed, small-headed, pigeon-like bird. *Adult male:* Back olive-brown; a small black dot on the sides of the head below the ear; four middle tail feathers are black to the tip, the outer ones mostly broadly tipped with white. Breast faintly purplish pink; sides of neck showing iridescence; head pale fawn with bluish crown. Bill blackish gray, feet reddish gray. *Adult female:* Similar but shows less iridescence. *Immature:* Much like female but shows even less iridescence.

Breeding *Nest:* A rude, flat affair put together loosely with small twigs, placed on a horizontal branch at low heights. *Eggs:* 2; white. Although its breeding was suspected for many years, breeding was first confirmed on 12 July 1964, when Cyril Coldwell discovered two weakly flying fledglings at Gaspereau, Kings County. The first reported nest was found by Eva Urban on her property at Avonport, Kings County, on 16 June 1979. Since then, nesting has been more widely noted.

Range Breeds from southeastern Alaska, middle British Columbia, across southern Canada to Nova Scotia, south to the West Indies and Mexico. Winters from extreme southern Canada to Panama.

Remarks Its name is derived from the sad and mournful call of the male: *coo-coo-coo-coo*, uttered softly and heard most frequently during mating season. In general appearance the Mourning Dove resembles the now-extinct Passenger Pigeon, but it is considerably smaller. When flying, its rapid wing-beats produce a whistling sound like that made by the Common Goldeneye. In some states of the United States and in certain restricted management areas in British Columbia, it is hunted in open season as a game bird. But in other states and throughout the rest of Canada, it is classified as a "song bird," receiving protection.

It is a ground-feeder whose fare in late fall and winter consists largely, if not wholly, of waste grain, weed seeds and what it may gather at bird feeders.

Passenger Pigeon

Ectopistes migratorius (Linnaeus)

Status Extinct. Formerly bred.

Remarks It scarcely seems fitting to dismiss this bird with the single word "extinct." Little is now known about this one-time member of our avifauna.

Among the records so meticulously prepared by the late Harry Piers there are some references with dates concerning the Passenger Pigeon in Nova Scotia which merit inclusion here lest they be lost forever. One reads: "James P. Kelly (son of Pat J. Kelly, who mounted birds) told me, August 28, 1919 that when he was a boy, say about fifteen years old, (which would be about 1857) about the end of August, he and Tom J. Egan, on returning from shooting across the North West Arm, Halifax, saw a bird near Kenny's at foot of South Street, on east side of the Arm. Kelly shot it and it proved to be a Passenger Pigeon—not a Carolina Dove. It was the only Passenger Pigeon that Kelly ever saw, although his father had told him that they used to be common about Halifax."

In another passage Piers writes: "W.A. Purcell, taxidermist of Halifax, tells me that about 1846 or 1847 Passenger Pigeons were abundant and his father, at Purcell's Cove, used to shoot large numbers of them. He says they disappeared about 1850."

A last record for Annapolis County came from John F. Tufts, based on recollections of his early life at Albany, where he was born in 1843. In the autumn of 1855, while working on his father's farm, he saw a flock of about 20 "wild pigeons" alight on the branches of a tall, dead pine tree. Though he had seen wild pigeons before, they were none too common. As he stood watching them, a shot rang out, fired from the thick underbrush beneath the tree, and three birds were seen to fall. He ran over to investigate and found an Indian trapper sitting on the ground with a wounded pigeon in each hand and a third lying dead beside him.

To Blakiston and Bland (1856), it was still "sometimes very abundant; arrives about the end of July." This suggests that it no longer nested extensively by the middle of the nineteenth century. Jones (1879) states that "this bird some thirty or forty years ago was extremely abundant in fall but has now apparently forsaken the province." McKinlay (1885) details its abundance and refers to nestings in Pictou County in pioneer times. The report of one on Sable Island in 1903 (McLaren 1981a) should probably not be taken seriously.

The last Passenger Pigeon died in captivity in a Cincinnati zoo on 1 September 1914.

Common Ground-Dove

Columbina passerina (Linnaeus)

Status One record. A report of this readily identified species in Shelburne County in October 1966 was convincingly referred to by Harrison Lewis in his column in the Shelburne *Coast Guard:* "On October 10, as Mr. and Mrs. [Donald] Robertson and two friends were driving through Middle Ohio, they saw a Ground-Dove standing beside the road and stopped to watch it. Soon it flew across the road into a tree. Thus the observers, all of whom knew this species in Florida, had a good view of this stray individual as it stood on the ground and flew. They noted its small size, rufous wings, and stubby black tail."

Remarks This species occasionally has occurred north of its normal range in the southeastern United States, at least to New York and Ontario, so its appearance here is not extraordinary.

Order CUCULIFORMES

Family Cuculidae

Black-billed Cuckoo   PLATE 23

Coccyzus erythropthalmus (Wilson)

Status Uncommon in summer. Breeds. Formerly fairly common but in recent decades much less so. Usually first seen in May (average 23 May, earliest 6 May). Numbers are augmented during fall migration. Wanderers, sometimes singing birds, appear in July in areas where not seen previously; a bird on Sable Island on 16 July 1976 was in juvenile plumage. The peak of movement generally occurs in late September or early October, but birds may linger (average date of last reports 18 October, latest 22 November).

Description *Length:* 28-33 cm. *Adults:* Similar to the Yellow-billed Cuckoo, but bill is all black, and tail feathers are more narrowly margined with white.

Breeding *Nest:* A slovenly arrangement of twigs, often little more than adequate. Sometimes a few green leaves are found in a nest; it is believed these are added about the time the eggs are hatching. Nests are sometimes placed in a clump of deciduous bushes or on a low branch of an apple tree in an orchard, rarely in an evergreen, and always at low elevations. *Eggs:* 2-4, usually 3; pale greenish blue, rounded ovate, the surface being rough rather than glossy. Sometimes, perhaps usually, the first egg is partially incubated before the final ones appear. Individual pairs may initiate nesting at any time during the summer, showing characteristic irregularity in that respect too. A nest in North Aylesford, Kings County, examined on 22 June 1945, contained four young, the smallest of which was only about one-half the size of the largest. This nest was in a small fir tree growing in a thick clump of deciduous bushes, and about 2.5 m from the ground. Another was discovered in the same locality on 2 July 1949 containing three eggs, one fresh, the others partially incubated. A late nest reported by John Betts, located in River Hebert, Cumberland County, contained two eggs on 6 August 1939.

Range Breeds across southern Canada from southeastern Alberta to Nova Scotia and south to the southern states. Winters in South America.

Remarks There is some evidence, though inconclusive, that large numbers of these birds have been poisoned in recent decades by devouring caterpillars that were victims of the arsenical sprays formerly used by orchardists. It is largely insectivorous, showing a marked preference for tent caterpillars. Its call, a hollow, plaintive *coo-coo-coo coo-coo-coo,* is believed by some to forecast rain, hence the name "rain-bird" by which it is commonly known in parts of its range.

Yellow-billed Cuckoo

Coccyzus americanus (Linnaeus)

Status Uncommon vagrant. Although Blakiston and Bland (1856) thought it nested in the province, and Downs (1888) made vague references to a nest, these reports are not supported by other nineteenth-century accounts. Up to 1960 it had been reported some 30 times, but many more records have accumulated since. A few occur in spring (earliest 29 April, latest 22 June); more appear as reverse migrants in autumn, sometimes in numbers suggesting a widespread incursion. First appearances are generally in August or early September (average 4 September, earliest 14 July). Peak numbers are usually reported for September or October, and some appear or remain quite late (average 27 October, latest 18 November). A corpse at Wolfville on 1 January 1955 had been dead for some weeks.

Description *Length:* 20-33 cm. *Adults:* Light cinnamon-brown above; all white below; long tail with outer feathers black, broadly tipped with white. Bill curved, the lower mandible yellow.

Range Breeds from southern British Columbia, North Dakota, southern Ontario, Quebec and New Brunswick, south to Mexico and the West Indies. Winters from Central America to parts of South America.

Remarks In size, shape and general habits, this long, slender, slow-moving bird closely resembles its near relative the Black-billed Cuckoo, the only species in Nova Scotia with which it might be confused. The yellow on the lower mandible, the chestnut in the wings seen in flight and the conspicuous white trimmings on the tail of this bird are field marks that help distinguish it. It shows a marked preference for thick shrubbery and when seen is usually skulking about silently at low levels.

Order STRIGIFORMES

Family Tytonidae

Common Barn-Owl

Tyto alba (Scopoli)

Status Five records. The first specimen was found dead at Tusket, Yarmouth County, on 16 December 1910 by W.H. Robbins (Allen 1916). Two were taken at Canso, Guysborough County, one shot by Appleton Roberts on 28 December 1928 and the other by Robert Keating on 10 December 1933. Both birds were mounted and the second was acquired by the Nova Scotia Museum. On 29 May 1971, workmen found a barn owl sheltering in an industrial building in Amherst. As it appeared to be injured, it was taken by Evelyn Lowerison to the Canadian Wildlife Service offices in nearby Sackville, New Brunswick. There the bird was photographed and, when unrestrained, flew strongly back toward Amherst. The fifth bird was found dead in mid-January 1977 in a lobster pot in Lower Argyle, Yarmouth County, by Larry MacKenzie.

Remarks The common Barn-Owl approximates the Short-eared Owl in size. Highly nocturnal, it spends the daylight hours well concealed, often in the hayloft in a barn, where it will sometimes nest.

It is resident from British Columbia, southern Ontario, and New England south, and widely elsewhere in the world.

Barn owls prey very heavily on mice and other small rodents but unfortunately are so rare in Nova Scotia that they are of no economic importance here.

All 11 species of owls known to occur in Nova Scotia are protected by provincial statute.

Family Strigidae

Eastern Screech-Owl

Otus asio (Linnaeus)

Status One specimen record. Concerning one taken in Halifax County, Piers (1894) writes: "About the last week in September, 1892 Purcell stuffed a specimen which was killed by 'Josh' Umlah, who lives on Prospect Road, near Indian Lake, to the S.W. of Halifax. It presented the red phase of plumage. The mounted specimen now belongs to Mr. George Beamish of this city." Fishermen reported to Ian McLaren that a small reddish owl with distinct ear tufts was killed on Seal Island in late winter 1973-74.

Remarks The Eastern Screech-Owl is about the size of the Northern Saw-whet Owl, from which it can readily be distinguished by its conspicuous "ear tufts," wholly lacking in the Saw-whet. It has red and gray phases. Its normal range lies to the south and west of Nova Scotia.

Great Horned Owl   PLATE 21

Bubo virginianus (Gmelin)

Status Uncommon resident. Breeds. Once one of our common owls, it has become scarcer in recent decades. The considerable fluctuation from year to year in numbers during late fall and winter may be brought about by irregular visitations by members of the same species from farther north wandering in search of food.

Description *Length:* 50-60 cm. *Adults:* Upperparts mottled with various shades of brown, gray, and black; prominent ear tufts; facial discs grayish white to buffy white; eyes yellow. White patch on throat sometimes extends down in narrow line to feet but is occasionally absent; underparts otherwise buff and gray, finely marked with black and white bars. Legs and feet feathered to ends of toes.

Breeding *Nest:* Usually a rude platform of sticks, the remnant of a nest originally built by a crow, a hawk or even an eagle, sparsely lined with dead leaves and other rubbish which may well have been placed there by the caprice of autumn winds rather than by the birds themselves. The top of an old, long-dead pine broken off squarely about 5 m from the ground was selected for one nest. The decayed wood of the interior exposed by the break had been scraped out to a depth of about 13 cm, leaving the strong outer shell as a low protective wall about the nest. Another unusual nest site was a large cavity in a huge dead pine, about 10 m up. The entrance, probably the result of a large limb breaking away many years before, was just large enough for the bird to go through. The two eggs were placed on soft, rotted wood matted with owl's feathers about 30 cm below the base of the entrance. Of 30 nests I examined, all others were originally nests of other large, tree-nesting species. Another nest worth mentioning was that of a pair attracted to an artificial site prepared by Cyril Coldwell in his woodlot of heavy growth at Gaspereau, Kings County. Late in the fall of 1964 he constructed a basket-like nest, using chicken wire heavily padded with moss, in an old hemlock. Visiting the nest in March 1965 he found it occupied by a pair of "great horns," which successfully raised twins. *Eggs*: 2, rarely 3; dull white and rounded ovate. Laying begins the first week in March. Of the 30 nests already mentioned, the contents of only 21 were ascertained: in 18, two eggs had been laid; in the others, three eggs. The earliest date for a complete set is 8 March 1947, when a nest containing two slightly incubated eggs was found in Kentville (J. Kelsall). Other dates are: 24 March 1927, two eggs almost fresh; 20 March 1932, three eggs slightly incubated; 22 March 1946, three eggs (from which young were emerging on 2 April); 2 April 1924, two eggs heavily incubated; and 1 May 1930, two eggs about ready to hatch. The last-mentioned late nesting suggests either a wide divergence in laying dates or, more likely, a second attempt, the first having failed.

Range Breeds throughout the forested parts of both North and South America but does not occur in the West Indies.

Remarks In referring to the terrain preferred by this species at nesting time, Bent (1938) says: "I find only 13 local nests recorded in my notes . . . all were in the heaviest timber available and as far as possible from human habitations." Of the 30 nests of this species I have seen in Nova Scotia, 21 were in woodlots near farms; 2 were near settlements in non-farming sections; 6 were in remote heavy timberlands far removed from the likelihood of human intrusion, while the last (Tufts 1954) was in an ornamental deciduous tree, some 6 m above the main thoroughfare in a residential section of Amherst. This comparison shows a marked difference in behaviour patterns between Bent's Great Horned Owls and those observed in Nova Scotia, a difference not readily explained.

It seems probable that the birds which selected the unusual Amherst nest site were influenced by the proximity of the town dump, heavily infested with Norway Rats. Analyses of pellets found under the nest tree showed the pair had preyed heavily on those rodents.

A Great Horned Owl taken on 15 March 1935 near Wolfville had numerous porcupine quills protruding from its face. Some were broken off, giving the impression they had been there for some time, but the bird showed no ill effects.

The usual call of this owl is a series of four or five low-pitched *hoo* notes. It is quite different from the highly distinctive call of the Barred Owl.

Bubo virginianus virginianus is the resident breeding race. Gilpin (1881) described a nearly white specimen taken at Digby in February 1876 and "thought it might have been of the Arctic variety." Indeed, it appears to have been *Bubo virginianus subarcticus* of the Hudson Bay drainage, which sometimes occurs well southward. Another very pale bird was seen on Seal Island on 16 October 1980 (B. Hinds et al.). Piers, in his unpublished notes, mentions a specimen taken near Halifax in 1915 attributed to the dark, sooty Labrador subspecies, *Bubo virginianus heterocnemis.*

Snowy Owl PLATE 21

Nyctea scandiaca (Linnaeus)

Status Rare to uncommon winter visitor, very rare in summer. Nova Scotia appears to be on the fringe of its periodic southward excursions. During its stays in Nova Scotia, the Snowy Owl is generally found in coastal barrens and meadows, rarely far inland. Recent noteworthy numbers have appeared during the winters of 1934-35, 1937-38, 1941-42, 1945-46,1960-61, 1964-65 and 1981-82. During other winters since 1960-61, only 1 to 10 birds have been reported. Birds do not generally first appear until mid-November (average 28 November, earliest 16 October). There are fewer records for mid-winter; and birds in spring often appear to be on their way north—the latest was near Glace Bay on 26 May 1975. However, occasional birds linger in summer. Nineteenth-century reports from Sable Island, along with one on 5-6 August 1964, are mentioned by McLaren (1981a). Other individuals occurred on Ciboux Island on 26 August 1962 (H.F. Kuch et al.), the Cabot Trail on 1 August 1964 (S. MacLean) and Seal Island between 22 and 28 July 1973 (B.K. Doane). Erskine (1968) documents other summer reports from the Maritimes.

Description *Length:* 58-69 cm. *Adult male:* White, more or less marked and barred with black; legs and feet feathered to ends of toes; eyes yellow; no ear tufts. *Adult female:* Larger than male and plumage more heavily barred. *Immatures:* Even more heavily barred than females.

Range Circumpolar. In North America breeds across the Arctic and winters from the arctic coast south, sporadically well into the United States.

Remarks Unlike some owls, these large white birds are day hunters, well able to see in broad daylight. The belief is general that the presence of Snowy Owls here in winter denotes a shortage of its food supply in the northland, and that the volume of the flight of these south-bound owls as winter comes to the Arctic is in direct ratio to the extent of the food shortage there.

It lays 3 to 10 eggs to a clutch. The difference in the size of sets is striking but the explanation is simple: when food is in normal supply the fertility of the female increases and more eggs are laid, but during lean years, egg production decreases in direct ratio to the availability of food for offspring.

Northern Hawk-Owl   PLATE 21

Surnia ulula (Linnaeus)

Status Rare visitant. There are indications that this owl was more common in the nineteenth century. Blakiston and Bland (1856) thought it "common," and Jones (1879) had it as "not uncommon throughout the year." Downs (1888) and Piers (1892a) both state "now . . . very rare," and the latter gives several specimen records. The reference to year-round presence by Jones (1879) is curious; it is perhaps relevant that a specimen was collected on Sable Island on 10 June 1902 (McLaren 1981a). The only notable invasions in the present century (more numerous in regions further inland in North America) occurred in 1913 when 15 were recorded around Halifax (Piers) and in 1923 when three were shot and a few others seen around Wolfville. Since 1960, only a few have occurred. During winter 1963-64, one was collected near Mooseland, Halifax County, and single individuals were seen in Colchester and Lunenburg counties. On 10 March 1972, one was photographed near New Glasgow by Gillian and James Elliot. On 7 January 1973, two were seen near Bridgetown, Annapolis County, and on 2 May 1973, one appeared at St. Esprit, Richmond County (R. and S. Meyerowitz). Perhaps the most tantalizing report (again by the Elliots) was of one perched on a tree in stunted growth along Highway 3 near the Shelburne County barrens (in many ways like its northern breeding terrain) on 4 July 1977. A bird discovered by Edgar Spalding and Stuart Tingley on Brier Island on 8 May 1982 was subsequently seen by several others up to 16 May.

Remarks About crow-size, with yellow eyes and no ear tufts, this is one of our few diurnal owls, well able to see its quarry in broad daylight. Like the Northern Shrike and the American Kestrel, it habitually perches alert and upright, often for long periods, overlooking an open meadow or barren land, ever watchful for the small birds and rodents upon which it preys.
   Like the Snowy Owl, it is a bird of the northern regions. Those seen here are believed to have been driven south by the scarcity of food at "home." As it has nested in the Gaspé Peninsula and in recent years in southeastern Ontario, New Brunswick and southern Quebec, its nesting in Nova Scotia is not impossible.

Barred Owl   PLATE 24

Strix varia (Barton)

Status Uncommon resident. Breeds. Our most common owl. Occurs in woods of old growth and is seldom seen elsewhere. It is more common some years than others, but whether this results from a shifting or fluctuation of the local population or from an influx of wanderers from outside has not been determined. The appearance of birds on Seal Island on 12 October 1975, Sable Island on 10 November 1975 and Brier Island on 3 September 1977 seem to reflect such movements, but an individual on Sable Island on 31 July 1966 was seasonally anomalous.

Northern Hawk-Owl in blizzard

Description *Length:* 50-56 cm. *Adults:* No ear tufts. Eyes nearly black. Upperparts grayish brown, the feathers mottled with light gray. Underparts white, barred with dark brown across the breast and similarly striped below and on sides. Bill yellowish brown; legs and feet feathered to the ends of toes.

Breeding *Nest:* Usually 4 to 12 m up in a hollow hardwood tree in mixed hard and soft growth. No lining is used other than owl feathers and rotted wood matted together. *Eggs:* 2-3, usually 3; dull white and rounded ovate. Laying begins early in April, as indicated by a nest at Black River which contained three heavily incubated eggs on 17 April 1925. Another, examined on 24 May 1926 at Albany, Annapolis County, contained one very young owlet and a pipped egg. A nest at Jordan Falls, Shelburne County, contained three downy young on 12 June 1910. It was in a beech tree about 9 m up, in what appeared to be the dilapidated, long-unused nest of a Goshawk (H.F. Tufts). Of 21 nests I have recorded, all were in hollow trees except this last-mentioned one. A most unusual nesting location was brought to my attention on 17 May 1968. In the front yard of Fenwick Wood's residence at Coldbrook, Kings County, not over 20 m from the front door, a pair of these owls had chosen a natural crevice in an aged elm, where they successfully raised three husky owlets.

Range Primarily an eastern bird, it now ranges in Canada as far west as the Pacific Coast, and south to Florida, the Gulf Coast and Mexico.

Remarks This owl and the very rare Common Barn-Owl are the only two of Nova Scotia's 11 owls that have dark blue-black eyes instead of the yellow ones so typical of the family. It is largely a nocturnal hunter, spending the daylight hours in comparative seclusion among thick evergreens. Like all owls it has a variety of calls, but the usual and most distinctive one may be written as *whoo-whoo-whoo-who-whoo to-whoo-ah,* with strong accent placed on the final *whoo.* This call is most often heard just prior to and during the nesting season, and on calm nights it can be heard for a kilometre or more. When a human intruder approaches the vicinity of an occupied nest, the parents, together or singly, usually appear on the scene and often show anxiety and hostility by viciously snapping their beaks.

The Barred Owl is not easily confused with any other of our owls, with the possible exception of the Great Gray, which is considerably larger, has yellow eyes and is so rare in Nova Scotia that even one is not likely to be encountered in a lifetime.

Great Gray Owl

Strix nebulosa (Forster)

Status Three records. One specimen was shot at Northport, Cumberland County, in June 1903 and another taken in Pictou County before 1882 (Gilpin 1881). The only recent record was of a bird well studied near Berwick, Annapolis County, on 26 March 1976 (G.R. Boyd et al.).

Remarks Its normal range lies far to the north and west of Nova Scotia. Although its periodic invasions southward have brought it in recent years to New Brunswick and Maine, Nova Scotia has not been reached by significant numbers. In general appearance it suggests an overgrown Barred Owl, but its eyes are typically yellow, whereas those of its smaller counterpart are dark brown or black.

Long-eared Owl   PLATE 24

Asio otus (Linnaeus)

Status Rare resident. Breeds. Although other nineteenth-century authors had rated it "rare" or "not common," Harold F. Tufts (1899) designated it "common except in winter" in Kings County. Apart from one report each from Annapolis, Digby, Queens and Shelburne counties, all summer reports since 1960 have come from Kings County, where all but one of reported nestings also have occurred. Scattered reports from southwestern counties and nocturnal mist-netting on Bon Portage Island by bird-banders from Acadia University in recent years have revealed a distinct outbound migration in October and November. An individual on Sable Island on 29 July 1966 suggests such movements may begin even earlier. Some remain in winter; roosts of 3-12 individuals have been found regularly by Bernard L. Forsythe in mixed woods in Kings County, but only a few have been recorded in other parts of the province at this season. Birds on Cape Sable on 10 May 1972 and 29 March 1981 were presumably returning migrants.

Description *Length:* 35-42 cm. *Adults:* Similar in general appearance to the Great Horned Owl but much smaller, having conspicuous ear tufts. Upperparts are mottled with varying shades of brown, black and white; facial disc is buffy brown, blending into a dark brown border; underparts buffy white, streaked and barred with light and dark shades of brown; tail barred. Eyes yellow; feet and toes feathered.

Breeding *Nest:* Seldom, perhaps never, builds its own nest. Usually eggs are laid in an old crow or hawk nest; sometimes they are placed on top of the thick, parasitic growth of mistletoe *(Arceuthobium pusillum)* locally known as "witch's broom," commonly found on spruce trees. Nests are located in thick, evergreen woods, usually if not always near the edge of a cleared space. They are lined with soft grass matted with feathers from the parent bird. *Eggs:* 4-5; white and rounded ovate. Laying begins during the second half of April. A nest lined with grass at Greenwich, Kings County, examined on 1 May 1955 contained four eggs freshly laid in what had been a crow's nest. A nest found by R.W. Smith on Wolfville Ridge on 17 May 1930 contained five slightly incubated eggs in a depression the bird had scraped in a growth of mistletoe and lined with soft dry grass mixed with feathers. The nest was 6 m up a spruce and the bird refused to leave until the climber came within a metre or two. Three young in juvenile plumage, out of the nest only a few days, were seen at dusk at Oak Island, Kings County, on 16 July 1943.

Range Breeds from southern Mackenzie River, central Manitoba, central Ontario, southern Quebec, and Nova Scotia, south to Arizona, Arkansas and West Virginia. Winters from its northern breeding range south to the Gulf States and Mexico. Found also in the Old World.

Remarks Among our "beneficial" owls this species ranks near the top. According to Bent (1938) its food, on a seasonal average, is 80-90 percent injurious rodents, and he knows not a single instance of one having attacked domestic poultry. Of 16 stomachs examined by Mendall (1944), mice were found in 14, shrews in 2, a bat in 1 and insects in 1. It is obvious the bird merits the year-round protection afforded it under provincial statute.

A highly nocturnal hunter, its daylight hours are spent in marked seclusion in deep evergreen woods, which suggests it may be present in larger numbers than records indicate.

The terms "long-eared" and "short-eared" are confusing because they are not descriptive of the owls' ears but refer to tufts of feathers which are erectile on the tops of their heads. Sometimes the tufts are laid back and quite inconspicuous, particularly in the case of the Short-eared Owl.

Short-eared Owl PLATE 21

Asio flammeus (Pontoppidan)

Status Uncommon in summer, rare in winter. Breeds. A few sightings between 13 March and 17 April in areas where it had not wintered represent spring arrivals; birds on Sable Island on 25 May 1966 and 20 May 1977 were also probably northward bound. Virtually all nesting-season reports are from Grand Pré, Kings County, and the New Brunswick border region. An early migrant was on Sable Island on 3 August 1964. This species is most often seen in autumn and especially during Christmas Bird Counts, in all parts of the province. Small numbers have been seen in winter, mostly in the southwestern counties.

Description *Length:* 35-42 cm. *Adults:* Entire body streaked with various soft shades of light and dark browns; darker on upperparts; stripes broader and more sharply defined on breast, finer on belly and flanks; tail barred; back and wings mottled; wing linings brownish white with black patch near base of primaries; ear tufts inconspicuous; eyes yellow.

Breeding *Nest:* On the ground, composed of coarse grass and weed stems, with lining of fine grass and owl feathers matted together. Sometimes the nest is concealed by low-growing bushes, but it is always in open country. An open hayfield is often chosen as a nest site, with little if any attempt at concealment. *Eggs:* 4-8; white and slightly rounded ovate. Laying starts about the middle of May. A nest found on the meadows below Wolfville on 17 June 1924 contained four slightly incubated eggs. The fact they were partly incubated indicates a complete set, and the small number suggests a second nesting attempt. Another nest located on the Grand Pré meadows, Kings County, held three eggs and five newly hatched young on 23 June 1935.

Range Breeds from Alaska, Baffin Island and Greenland south to New Jersey, Kansas and southern California; also in South America and the Old World. In North America, winters from southern Canada southward.

Remarks This bird is an excellent mouser. According to the times of day when their normal hunting activity reaches its peak, owls are classified as being nocturnal (night hunters), diurnal (day hunters) or crepuscular (twilight hunters). This owl has crepuscular feeding habits. No owl can see in utter darkness, but they can see much better than humans can when light conditions are minimal.

At dusk on 1 December 1934 on the Grand Pré meadows, I observed one whose behaviour was most unusual. I first noticed it circling me at a range far too close for its own safety. Its manner suggested anxiety or curiosity, I couldn't tell which. After a few moments it retired to a nearby mound of earth from which it began to call intermittently with a strange, raspy, cat-like meow.

Boreal Owl   PLATE 21

Aegolius funereus (Bonaparte)

Status Rare winter visitant. Although Blakiston and Bland (1856) rated it as "resident inland," this status is unsupported by other nineteenth-century authors. However, it may have been more regular in early days, for Jones (1879) states that it was "becoming very rare." Available records in the present century are few, ranging from October to March. A minor invasion occurred in 1922-23, when two were collected in Kings County, two in Colchester County and one in Cumberland County. A large female taken near Wolfville on 3 January 1932 had eaten a White-winged Crossbill. Since then there have been only seven reports: early March 1968 in Pictou County (H. Brennan); 23 December 1968 on Sable Island (see Remarks); 12 October 1969 on Brier Island (I. McLaren, R. Hughes); early January 1978 at Homeville, Cape Breton County (C. Ferguson); 23 December 1978 in Halifax (the photograph by Freeman Patterson was published in a bird calendar); 21 December 1980 on the Cape Breton Highlands National Park Christmas Bird Count; and a dead bird on 15 February 1982 at Malagawatch, Inverness County (J. McNicol).

Description *Length:* 23-30 cm. *Adults:* Above, chocolate-brown, mottled with white spots; below, white striped with brown; forehead flecked with small white spots; facial disc light gray with dark borders; eyes yellow; bill yellowish gray; no ear tufts.

Range Northern forested parts of the Northern Hemisphere. In Canada its breeding range extends across the continent from the northern coniferous forests south (in the east, to southern New Brunswick). Wanders irregularly farther south in winter to the northern United States.

Remarks This bird's highly nocturnal ways and secluded, heavily wooded habitat make one suspect that it may have occurred here in summer but escaped observation. I found it nesting regularly on nearby Grand Manan (New Brunswick) and thus it would not be wholly surprising if someone were to find it nesting here.

Here is the story of a Boreal Owl I kept in captivity for about 10 months. On 23 December 1968, in bleak weather, Norman Bell found a very tired, hungry and utterly dejected Boreal Owl sitting on the ground near the West Light on Sable Island. Weak from exhaustion, the bird offered no resistance when he picked it up. It was fed House Sparrows, which it accepted with eagerness, but these were not numerous on Sable Island and so it was decided that the little waif would be flown to the mainland and delivered to me. It arrived in splendid condition, alert and most friendly, on 18 January 1969 and soon became the centre of ornithological interest, for few had ever seen one of these birds alive. While in my care it was given one House Sparrow daily. On two occasions it was offered a choice between a sparrow and a mouse—both times, to my surprise, it spurned fur in favour of feathers. It seemed to be in perfect physical condition, always evincing a markedly friendly interest bordering on excitement when I approached. It was kept in a large, roomy cage, replete with two spruce stumps, which it flew between and perched upon. Late in the summer it became listless. I often found it sitting on the floor rather than on its tree stump. Sometimes the sparrow was only partly devoured. On the morning of 13 October it showed only slight interest in its daily offering; late that afternoon I found it dead. A post-mortem revealed nothing except that it was a female, which I had always suspected because of its large size. Whence it came to Sable Island and how the long flight of 150 km or more was accomplished, and ever undertaken in the first place, will never be revealed, but one can theorize that while foraging along a coastal woodland at night it was blown offshore by heavy winds. Owls are not particularly strong fliers. Unable to return to land it had been carried off helplessly and, lured by the gleaming beacon of Sable Island, had steered its course in that direction.

Northern Saw-whet Owl   PLATE 24

Aegolius acadicus (Gmelin)

Status Uncommon resident. Breeds. Seldom seen but probably not as rare as it seems to be. It normally inhabits wooded areas remote from settlement and, being nocturnal, spends the daylight hours in seclusion, often hidden in dark thickets or tree cavities. Sometimes in winter, particularly during periods of extreme cold, small numbers appear suddenly, one here and one there, about farmyards, villages and even in towns or cities; whether these are residents forced from their normal habitat by hunger or wanderers from farther north is not known, but generally they are found weakened from starvation or dead. Parties from Acadia University have shown that some of these owls migrate out of or through the province, with observations gathered by nocturnal mist-netting and banding on Bon Portage Island; 72 were banded during October 1981. One owl on Sable Island on 16 August 1963 suggests movement earlier in the season. Sightings between 8 March and 19 April in places where Saw-whets do not nest may have been of returning migrants.

Description *Length:* 19-22 cm. *Adults:* Dark cinnamon-brown on back, flecked and mottled with white; forehead and crown light or dark brown about evenly divided, giving the impression of stripes; facial disc light gray with radiating brown streaks; eyes yellow; bill black; feet and toes light gray, almost white; and breast and belly white, streaked with rufous. *Juveniles:* Chocolate-brown with white "eyebrows" and rufous lower breast and belly.

Breeding *Nest:* In a hollow tree, usually the old nest of a flicker. Sometimes the usual lining of decayed wood fibre matted with owl's feathers is supplemented with a small quantity of soft, dry grass. It is placed at heights usually ranging 2-12 m, site availability being the determining factor. *Eggs:* 4-7, usually 5; dull white and rounded ovate. Laying begins in early April. Seven nests have been examined, five of which I shall describe in detail: one was 12 m up a dead pine at Albany, Annapolis County. On 27 May 1919 it contained six young about ready to fly. The old bird refused to leave and was removed manually. The nest tree was on open, burned land remote from settlement, and the nest cavity had apparently been excavated by a flicker. On 31 May 1943 a second nest was discovered at Greenfield, Kings County, in a very rotten spruce stub 2.5 m from the ground, in a semi-cleared woodlot surrounded by evergreen woods. It contained four well-fledged young, and a fifth was perched on a log nearby. When the nest was discovered neither parent was in evidence, but when it was visited a few hours later at twilight, both adult birds were present, showing normal anxiety. The location of the third nest was exceptional: it was placed in a partially dead maple, 3 m above the sidewalk in a residential section of Wolfville, occupying a hole originally used by flickers. On 25 May 1954 the young were about ready to fly and, in spite of their vulnerable position, at least some got off safely. The fourth nest was examined on 26 May 1966 at Springville, Pictou County. It was located in a very decayed yellow birch, in a cavity originally used by a pair of Pileated Woodpeckers, and contained two young. The late date and the small size of the clutch indicated a second nesting. The fifth nest, also at Springville, contained seven eggs early in April 1967. The birds had used a wooden box constructed by Harry Brennan, which he had erected in a clearing near his home.

Range Breeds across North America, from southern Alaska to Nova Scotia, and in the east as far south as Maryland. In winter some wander considerably south of the breeding range.

Remarks The Saw-whet is the smallest owl in Nova Scotia. Its name is derived from the sound of one of its calls, which is said to be like a saw being filed, or "whetted." I have never heard this owl give any call but one, and it did not sound like a saw being filed but like *tang-tang-tang-tang,* with a metallic quality. The calls were deliberate, continuing monotonously for a considerable time. After a brief pause it would start again. I have heard it at all hours of the night and at evening twilight. At dusk on 8 March 1950 one was heard calling at Gaspereau, Kings County, from an orchard of old apple trees. A flashlight was used to locate the performer. As the light drew near, the owl stopped calling as though suspicious of danger. However, after much searching I discovered it sitting on the low, dead branch of a large spruce on the edge of the orchard. When focused in the centre of the beam at a distance of about 3 m, it drew in its feathers until it seemed mostly head, with a very slender body attached, its facial expression like that of an inquisitive miniature monkey.

Northern Saw-whet Owl

Order CAPRIMULGIFORMES

Family Caprimulgidae

Common Nighthawk   PLATE 23

Chordeiles minor (Forster)

Status Uncommon in summer, fairly common transient. Breeds. Usually arrives in May (average 18 May, earliest 22 April). Birds are sometimes reported as heard much earlier, but this undoubtedly represents confusion with the American Woodcock (see Remarks). During breeding season, only a few are found in urban areas; most seem to prefer clearings and barren outcrop areas in forested land. Much larger numbers occur during fall migration, probably augmented from outside the province, generally beginning in late July (average date of first flocks 30 July, earliest 20 July). Flocks of hundreds are sometimes reported in August and Sarah MacLean observed an estimated 10,000 or more over Highway 4 on Cape Breton Island on 25 August 1968. The latest sightings generally occur in September or early October (average 22 September, latest 20 October).

Description *Length:* 22-25 cm. *Adult male:* Upperparts and breast irregularly patterned with black, brown, buff and white; primaries blackish, each with a transverse white bar conspicuous in flight; tail black with bars of creamy buff and a white band near the end; prominent white patch on throat; belly white, barred with black, often with buffy tinge. *Adult female:* Similar but throat patch is cinnamon instead of white, and white marks on tail are lacking.

Breeding *Nest:* None worthy of the name. Formerly, eggs were laid usually on the bare ground, with a preference being shown for freshly burned-over areas. In recent decades there has been a growing tendency to resort to the gravelled roofs of flat-topped buildings. For instance, during the summer of 1955 the roofs of six such buildings in Wolfville—all that were suitable—were used as nest sites by nighthawks. Only one pair to a roof is customary. *Eggs:* 2; white, evenly and thickly marked with fine grayish-brown speckles. Laying begins during the first part of June. A set of eggs examined on 20 June 1918 was fresh; another on 15 June 1915 showed slight traces of incubation. A parent with two well-developed young was seen on the roof of a local bank in Wolfville on 6 July 1942.

Range Breeds from the Yukon east to Nova Scotia, and in the east as far south as Georgia, southern Florida and the West Indies. Winters in South America as far south as Argentina.

Remarks About the turn of the present century, it was common practice to use these birds as targets during the fall migrations and large numbers were shot each year. Protective legislation, supported by growing public sentiment in favour of bird protection, soon brought this wanton killing to an end.

John H. Dick

Common Nighthawks feeding

When it perches on a limb or fence rail, its position is almost invariably lengthwise, supposedly because its feet are too weak to maintain a balance were it to attempt to perch as other birds do. On 22 June 1963, however, I saw one perched cross-wise on a large elm limb 6-8 cm in diameter. Another nighthawk suddenly appeared and swooped down at the perched bird, which quickly changed its position to normal, raising its head as though to counter the hostile gesture of the bird in flight. Watching this "play," it seemed as though the perched bird were being reprimanded for having violated the parking custom common to the species. Charles R.K. Allen tells of once having seen a nighthawk trying to alight on a telephone wire.

Its common call is a short, harsh *peent,* suggesting to some listeners the ground note of the woodcock. This call usually is given in flight but not uncommonly when perched. In the latter case it is heard only intermittently, with marked irregularity. The loud booming sound characteristic of the species is produced by air rushing through the stiff outer primary feathers of its wings as it abruptly swerves upward following a sudden downward swoop when flying at higher altitudes.

It should be mentioned that this bird, despite its name, is not in any way related to hawks. Its feeding habits are similar to those of swallows and swifts, for its fare is made up wholly of insects it captures while flying. It does often fly at night, making the first part of its name quite appropriate. It is also sometimes called a "mosquito hawk."

Chuck-will's-widow

Caprimulgus carolinensis (Gmelin)

Status Six records. Surprisingly, Haliburton's (1825) list includes "Great Bat, or Chuck-will's Widow, or Goatsucker" along with "Whip poor Will" and "Night Hawk," but he gives no evidence. Late in October, about 1890, one was found barely alive near Pictou. It died shortly afterward and was given to the museum of Pictou Academy, a first record for Canada (Piers 1894). A bird was shot on 1 June 1905 at Canso, Guysborough County, and mounted (H. Piers); another was found dead at Freeport, Digby County, in early May 1963; on 15 May 1975 a moribund individual was found at Wedgeport, Yarmouth County, by William Boudreau and identified by Israel J. Pothier; all three were sent to the Nova Scotia Museum. On 1 November 1981, one blundered into a mist net set for owls by a bird-banding team from Acadia University and was banded, photographed and released. Finally, a goatsucker flushed repeatedly near Pubnico, Yarmouth County, on 20 May 1984 by R.S. D'Entremont, although not identified at the time, uttered the distinctive grunting calls produced by this species but never by Whip-poor-wills.

Remarks This southern species regularly occurs north of its normal range during migration, but its nocturnal habits may prevent it from being recorded here more often.

Whip-poor-will   PLATE 23

Caprimulgus vociferus Wilson

Status Rare in summer. Breeds. It has occurred in all mainland counties, but the only Cape Breton Island report is of one at Port Hawkesbury in late May 1975 (F. Robertson). It first arrives in May (since 1960, average 16 May, earliest 7 May; an earlier arrival was on 4 May 1942). Reports after the breeding season are rare as it generally does not sing then. The latest fall sighting was on 11 October 1974; anomalously, one was heard singing at Wilmot, Annapolis County, on 31 October and 1 November 1971 (T. Hawkins) and another was found recently dead at Pubnico, Yarmouth County, on 1 November 1979.

Description *Length:* 22-25 cm. *Adult male:* Top of head dark grayish brown with fine black stripes; back similar but mottled as well; primaries black, barred with cinnamon; tail mottled and barred with black and light gray or buffy; three outer tail feathers on each side are white halfway out to ends; narrow white band across upper breast; face tawny; breast dark, finely mottled with light buff; belly light buff, barred with dark brown or black; stiff bristles at base of bill. *Adult female:* Similar but band on upper breast is more cinnamon than white, and there is no white on three outer tail feathers, these being narrowly tipped with light brown.

Breeding *Nest:* None worthy of the name, eggs being laid on the ground among dry leaves in woods or thickets. *Eggs:* 2; dull white, faintly marked with pale lilac or brown spots. The first nest recorded in Nova Scotia, containing two eggs, was discovered by Clarence Mason in the Waverley Game Sanctuary, Halifax County, in late June 1930. On a second visit on 30 June, he found the eggs just hatching. Another nest was found by Hugh Bigg on 9 June 1942 at La Have Lake, Annapolis County. The bird was sitting on the usual two eggs and did not flush until underfoot.

Range Breeds from the southeastern part of the Prairie Provinces east to Nova Scotia and south to the northern parts of the Gulf States and Mexico. Winters from the southern states to Central America.

Remarks Many have heard this bird in Nova Scotia, but relatively few have actually seen it. Its day begins as darkness approaches and, unlike its cousin the nighthawk to which it bears a close resemblance, it prefers low elevations for feeding and perching. Its favoured haunt is a bushy pasture or open woodland where, having chosen a suitable boulder or other low perch, it gives forth its familiar call, *whip-poor-will,* in rapid and clearly enunciated repetitions.

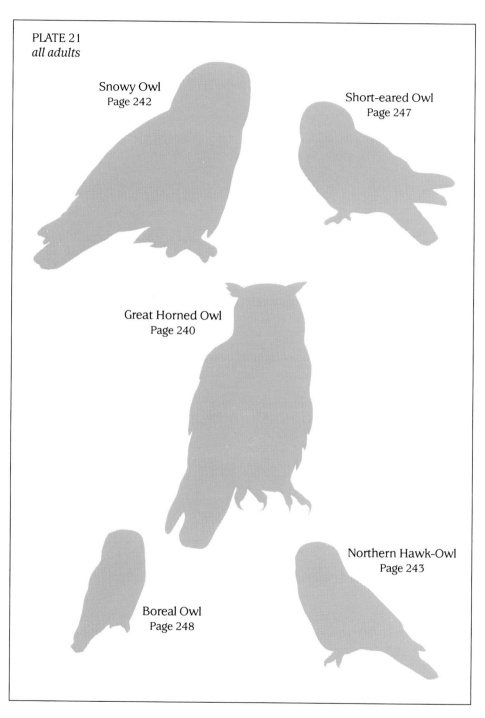

PLATE 21
all adults

Snowy Owl
Page 242

Short-eared Owl
Page 247

Great Horned Owl
Page 240

Northern Hawk-Owl
Page 243

Boreal Owl
Page 248

Roger Tory Peterson

PLATE 22
all adult males

Downy Woodpecker
Page 266

Black-backed Woodpecker
Page 268

Hairy Woodpecker
Page 267

Northern Flicker
Page 269

Yellow-bellied Sapsucker
Page 264

Order APODIFORMES

Family Apodidae

Chimney Swift   PLATE 23

Chaetura pelagica (Linnaeus)

Status Uncommon in summer. Breeds. It generally arrives in early May (average 6 May, earliest normal date 29 April; five on 22 April 1977 were three weeks ahead of next arrivals). Although there are scattered colonies in artificial structures from Yarmouth to Cape Breton Island, the only major one is in Wolfville, where 382 were counted entering a large, unused chimney on the campus of Acadia University at dusk on 22 May 1983. However, Helen and Hubert Hall note that Yarmouth County in 1984 had "many this summer, always on backwoods roads, far from chimneys," and this may be true in other localities. First migrants may appear in late July in areas where they had not nested, but the peak of movement occurs in late August or early September. An estimated 2,000 were over Brier Island on 24 August 1965 (W. Lent). Most are gone by the end of September, but stragglers occur later (since 1960, average 4 October, latest 1 November; the latest ever was over Wolfville on 10 November 1948).

Description *Length:* 13-14 cm. *Adults:* Sooty brown above and below; lighter on throat and breast; black spot in front of eye. Shafts of tail feathers extend beyond vanes.

Breeding *Nest:* A cup-shaped bracket of fine twigs securely fastened together with the bird's glue-like saliva; always unlined. It was customary for them to glue these bracket nests to the perpendicular inside walls of large hollow trees, and in some parts of their breeding range they still do, but more recently they have largely forsaken tree sites for man's evil-smelling chimneys. Occasionally they resort to old, abandoned shacks standing in remote areas, where they fasten the nest to the inside wall. One nest I discovered at Albany, Annapolis County, was placed in an unused, rock-lined well. It was glued to the side of a protruding rock about 1 m below ground and about 1 m above water. *Eggs:* 4-6; white. In fresh eggs the albumen has a peculiar glue-like texture that makes it difficult for an oologist to prepare specimens. They are rather late nesters. One seen breaking a twig from a tall dead branch on 29 May 1943 near Wolfville was engaged in nest construction, but laying does not usually begin until late June. On 24 July 1924 at Black River Lake, Kings County, a nest containing four fresh eggs was examined. The nest was stuck to the inside wall of an abandoned mill about 2 m above the floor, entrance having been made through an unglazed window. On 15 August 1940 a fledgling that had fallen from a nest in a chimney was picked up alive on the hearth below.

Range Breeds from eastern Saskatchewan east to southern Quebec and Nova Scotia and south to the Gulf States. Winters in the upper Amazon drainage.

Remarks These little speedsters racing across our summer skies have until recent years kept their winter homes secret. In 1944, through bird-banding, the mystery was solved. Thirteen, marked with numbered leg-bands that were attached in previous summers while the birds were in North America, were caught by Indians living in a wild, remote district of northeastern Peru, some 350 km south of the equator.

Bird-banding has also given us factual information regarding how long Chimney Swifts live. One adult banded at Kingston, Ontario, on 7 June 1929 was recaptured at the same place 11 years later, on 19 May 1940.

Here is a bird that never voluntarily touches the ground. Its food is taken on the wing; it sleeps clinging to a perpendicular wall of wood or stone; it gathers nesting material while hovering by snapping off small, brittle twigs from high, dead branches; and when thirsty it flies close to the surface of the water, skimming it lightly with its open bill. Charles R.K. Allen tells of having seen a pair copulating while in flight.

Its manner of flight is so characteristic that it is not likely to be confused with any other Nova Scotia bird.

Family Trochilidae

Ruby-throated Hummingbird   PLATE 23

Archilochus colubris (Linnaeus)

Status Fairly common in summer. Breeds. Distributed throughout the province in urban and wild areas, generally arriving by mid-May (average 12 May, earliest normal date 1 May). An untimely individual in a Yarmouth garden from 17 to 19 April 1977 was almost three weeks ahead of the next reported. It routinely has been last recorded in October (average 3 October, latest normal occurrence 6 November). However, it should not be assumed that all very late hummingbirds, like the female in Halifax on 1 December 1979 (M. Verpoorte), are in fact Ruby-throated Hummingbirds (see next two species).

Description *Length:* 7.5-9.5 cm. *Adult male:* Top of head and back bright glossy green; tail dark grayish brown and forked. Throat patch iridescent, showing coal-black at one moment and ruby-red the next; breast whitish, sides dark with greenish tinge. Bill long and needle-like. *Adult female:* Upperparts similar to male, but outer ends of her feathers are beautifully and broadly tipped with satiny white, and tail is not forked. Underparts whitish with no throat patch.

Breeding *Nest:* About the size of half a walnut shell; composed of plant down, covered externally with bits of gray lichen held in place by spider's web and delicate plant fibres; saddled on a horizontal twig and seldom more than 9 m from the ground. It nests in gardens and orchards, but as often in wooded areas far from human abode. *Eggs:* 2; white, elliptical ovate in shape. A nest containing two fresh eggs was found at Caledonia, Queens County, by Harold F. Tufts on 12 June 1909. It was about 6 m up on a horizontal limb of a tamarack in a remote wooded area. Another at Greenwich,

Kings County, contained two fresh eggs on 2 July 1918. It was situated about 9 m up a large spruce growing near a flower garden. On 16 July 1930 a nest in an apple tree contained two well-developed young, one of which flew that day and the second the day following. A nest at Berwick, Kings County, on 10 July 1940 containing two eggs was about 2 m from the ground, saddled typically on the twig of an apple tree. The eggs in this nest hatched on 21 July; by noon on 12 August the second young one had flown. A nest at Newport, Hants County, contained two half-grown young on 30 June 1943. It was situated about 3 m up an apple tree and was a "double-decker," the nest of that year having been built on top of the previous year's, the line of demarcation clearly visible. About six days are required to construct a nest and the female does all the work. When the eggs are laid the male leaves his mate and normally does not see her again.

Range Breeds from Alberta east to Nova Scotia and south to the Gulf States and Florida. Winters from Florida and Louisiana south to Panama.

Remarks Poets and naturalists struggle to find adequate phrases to describe the fairy-like elegance of this tiny bird. To attempt a description of the jewel-like iridescence of its plumage is difficult, for the colours, like those of a prism, change with every movement. When a hummingbird hovers over a flower, it looks as if standing on air.

This tiny species twice has been seen chasing larger birds, in one case a robin and in the other a nighthawk. On each occasion the pursuer, close on the tail of the larger bird, appeared to be flying along at leisurely speed while the pursued was exerting full wing power to free itself from its spiteful tormentor.

Gillian Rose tells of watching a ruby-throat closely following a Yellow-bellied Sapsucker which in its characteristic manner was boring holes in the bark of an old apple tree. The "hummer" was poking its needlelike bill into one hole after the other to drink the sweet sap as the larger bird progressed, not an uncommon practice for hummingbirds.

The metabolism of hummingbirds is very rapid. They must eat often to keep their "engines" humming, and this they do during daylight hours. From "bedtime" to the break of day they must fast. In order to conserve their energy during this period of no food intake, they not only sleep but become torpid, their body organs barely functioning. I have seen this only once. A neighbour phoned to say he had a hummingbird that must be "sick." It had been perched on a low, dead twig since dark and had refused to fly when he touched it. On arrival I found a male ruby-throat perched on an ornamental shrub close to the verandah. I tried to pick it off gently, but it would not relax its grip. I snapped off the twig, placed the bird in a box, and brought it home to administer to its ailment, whatever it might be. Thinking the bird might be cold, I wrapped it in warm cotton wool and left it in the box still clinging to its twig. Next morning I was much relieved to find it had fully recovered, for it buzzed off quite normally. It was not until some months later I chanced to read that hummingbirds become torpid at the approach of darkness to conserve energy.

There are over 300 species of hummingbirds and the range of most of them is limited to tropical regions. The ruby-throat is the only one that normally comes to eastern Canada. All species of hummingbirds are confined to the New World, none occurring outside the Americas.

Black-chinned Hummingbird

Archilochus alexandri (Bourcier and Mulsant)

Status One sight record. Michael Gochfeld, an experienced birder from New York, observed a male, evidently of this species, at Salt Springs, Antigonish County, on 30 May 1964, and submitted an extensive description (Gochfeld 1964). He repeatedly established that its throat was black regardless of light angle, but iridescent violet on the lower border.

Remarks Although the throat of the male Ruby-throated Hummingbird may appear blackish at virtually all angles if the bird is perched high, the lower throat is never violet. There are no other eastern records of adult male Black-chinned Hummingbirds at any season. Birds in female or immature plumage, distinguishable from ruby-throats only in the hand, are occasional in Florida, and one turned up in Massachusetts in the late autumn of 1979.

Rufous Hummingbird

Selasphorus rufus (Gmelin)

Status Two sight records. A hummingbird was seen by three observers in the Bedford, Halifax County, garden of M.A. Christie on 8 August 1967. Several ruby-throats, a species with which the Christies had been familiar for many years, had been about the garden all summer. This different bird stayed about the garden for two days, giving them ample opportunity to establish that its colouring was definitely that of an adult male Rufous Hummingbird. Another hummingbird at Hebron, Yarmouth County, on 21 August 1983 was described by Annie Saunders as being larger than a ruby-throat, having a back the colour of a dark robin breast, broken streaks on the throat, and white tips on some tail feathers. These marks in combination appear to exclude anything but a young male Rufous Hummingbird.

Remarks Of all North American hummingbirds, this one is most prone to wander from its normal range. Most records in the East have been of immature birds, difficult to identify to species. For example, a bird with a bright green back and rufous sides seen briefly by Steven Manuel on Seal Island on 10 September 1983 could have been this species or some other member of the genus *Selasphorus*. Observers should be particularly alert in late autumn, the season when most exotic hummingbirds have appeared in the East.

Order CORACIIFORMES

Family Alcedinidae

Belted Kingfisher   PLATE 23

Ceryle alcyon (Linnaeus)

Status Common in summer, rare in winter. Breeds. Migrants generally first appear in early to mid-April (average date of first appearance 9 April, earliest 29 March; other earlier reports probably of overwintering birds). It occurs in summer mainly along the shores of inland streams where its nesting requirements are met. Although outbound migrants are most common in September and October—for example on offshore islands where they have not nested—stragglers are frequent through December, especially on Christmas Bird Counts. Although most that stay beyond this month probably perish, a few have successfully wintered in areas from Yarmouth County to Cape Breton.

Description *Length:* 30-38 cm. *Adult male:* Head bluish gray with ragged crest; white spot in front of eye; bold white band around neck, not quite meeting behind; back, wings and tail bluish gray; wings and tail flecked with rows of small white dots; bluish gray band across breast; underparts otherwise white; bill heavy and bluish black. *Adult female:* Similar but, in addition to a breast band like that of the male, has a bright cinnamon band across lower breast extending down sides of belly.

Breeding *Nest:* In a tunnel in a sandbank or sawdust pile where undermining has created a perpendicular wall. There is considerable variation in depth of tunnels, 120-160 cm perhaps being average. The chamber (or nest proper) at the end of the passageway is sometimes lined sparingly with grass or feathers. The nest site is usually near a lake shore or stream, but sometimes it is a considerable distance from water. *Eggs:* 6-10, usually 7 or 8; white. A nest found on 26 May 1918 in a sandbank at White Rock, Kings County, contained six eggs; one in a sawdust bank examined on 5 June 1918 at Little River Lake, Kings County, contained eight. The eggs in both were fresh and laying may not have been completed. On 23 June 1915 a nest at White Rock contained young that were large enough to come to the tunnel entrance, where they were seen taking food from one of the parent birds.

Range Breeds from Alaska east to middle Labrador and Newfoundland, south to the Gulf States and southern California. Winters from southeastern Alaska, southern British Columbia, and occasionally in other parts of extreme southern Canada, south to the West Indies and Panama.

Remarks If given an opportunity, this bird can be destructive to trout and young salmon in fish hatcheries and rearing ponds, and provision has been made in our statutes whereby control measures may be applied under these abnormal conditions. In its natural habitat the bird takes those fishes most readily caught; and it is fair to assume that in the process of feeding it destroys enough sluggish, coarse, and enemy fish to offset the few fast-swimming young trout and salmon it may be able to capture. Formerly legal targets for gunners at all seasons, kingfishers are now protected by law throughout the year.

The bird's haunts are lake shores and the margins of woodland streams. There it will be found perched on a limb overhanging the water, silently watching for a chance to plunge headlong for unsuspecting prey that venture too near the surface. If disturbed it will fly off ahead, giving its familiar "rattle" as it goes. Its very presence adds to the beauty and charm of the surroundings.

Order PICIFORMES

Family Picidae

Red-headed Woodpecker   PLATE 24

Melanerpes erythrocephalus (Linnaeus)

Status Rare vagrant. Downs (1888) referred to it as "a mere straggler" and Piers (1894) stated that one was collected at Ketch Harbour, Halifax County, "about ten years ago," which may be the basis for Downs' reference. The next record was not until 1928. One each appeared in 1949, 1952 and 1953, but since 1962 the birds occurred more regularly, with reports every year except 1977. Clearly there has been a change in status. Among these visitors, 21 first appeared in October; 13 appeared in May, 11 each in September and November, 3 in June, 2 each in May and July, and 1 in April. One adult spent winter 1978-79 at feeders in Bedford, Halifax County, and another overwintered in Amherst in 1982-83. When noted, immatures have outnumbered adults by about two to one.

Remarks The normal range of this woodpecker lies to the west and south of Nova Scotia. It is a bird of the open countryside, seeming to avoid woodland areas. Adults are unmistakable, and the large, white wing patches of immatures are diagnostic. Concerning the habits of this bird, Godfrey (1966) says: "It takes insects on the wing, flycatcher fashion, more frequently than do most other woodpeckers. It eats also fruits and nuts in some quantities and is not above taking eggs and young of other birds on occasion. Except in extreme southern Ontario, it is nowhere a common bird in Canada."

Red-bellied Woodpecker

Melanerpes carolinus (Linnaeus)

Status Nine records. The first report was of one that made visits to the birdfeeder of Mrs. G. Vye of Middleton, Annapolis County, between 15 November 1961 and 5 May 1962. Its presence was documented on film which was subsequently sent to the National Museum of Canada. Other individuals appeared at Digby on 9 February 1962 (P.D. Weir); at a Kentville feeder between 8 January and 21 March 1968 (B. Eaton, photos); at the feeder of Mrs. Nellie Snyder, Crousetown, Lunenburg County, between 4 December 1968 and 2 March 1969 (many observers, photos); on Brier Island on 24 June 1969 (W. Lent, collected); in Halifax on 14 November 1974 (J. and S. Cohrs); in Barrington, Shelburne County, on 2 November 1975 (V. Sperka); at a feeder in Hampton, Annapolis County, on 28 October 1982 (S. Macdonald et al., filmed); and near Bridgewater on 14 May 1983 (C. Naugler).

Remarks The Red-bellied Woodpecker is a southern species, normally occurring in Canada only in southernmost Ontario, where it is rare. The colour pattern of its plumage is quite striking, and unlike that of any other woodpecker in Nova Scotia.

Yellow-bellied Sapsucker   PLATE 22

Sphyrapicus varius (Linnaeus)

Status Fairly common summer resident. Breeds. Distributed throughout woodlands, arriving in April (average 22 April, earliest 4 April). The peak of fall movement is generally late September and it is seldom seen after mid-October (average 12 October, latest 28 October). One at Centreville, Shelburne County, on 21 December 1970 (W. Smith) was late, and one taking suet at the feeder of Eunice Stevenson at Sheffield Mills, Kings County, on 10 January 1969 is our only true winter record.

Description *Length:* 20-22 cm. *Adult male:* Forehead and crown scarlet, bordered with black; nape white; back black, barred with white; tail black, centrally barred with white; white line extending back from above eye separates crown from broad black stripe extending from eye down neck and along sides of back; white line beginning at base of upper mandible runs down sides of neck to breast; throat scarlet, bordered with black; sides of belly marked with blackish gray; belly pale yellow; upperwing with conspicuous white patch along coverts. *Adult female:* Similar but throat white; crown usually scarlet, rarely black.

Breeding *Nest:* An excavation in a tree, usually a live poplar, about 3-10 m from the ground, in woodland areas. It is unlined, the eggs being laid on bare chips. *Eggs:* 4-6; glossy white. Excavating starts about the middle of May and egg laying begins during the second half of the month. A nest containing four fresh eggs was found 28 May 1905 about 3 m up in a live poplar at Black River, Kings County, and on 15 June 1916

Yellow-bellied Sapsucker

another in the same area, also in a live poplar, contained five partially incubated eggs. On 17 May 1919, birds were seen excavating in three localities at Albany, Annapolis County; one of these nests, visited on 6 June, contained one runt egg. On 12 June it contained six fresh eggs, two of which were runts.

Range Breeds from southeastern Alaska, Yukon Territory, the southern Mackenzie Valley, southern Quebec, and Newfoundland, south to the northern United States and, in the mountains, to California. Winters from southern British Columbia and central United States to Central America and the West Indies.

Remarks The name "sapsucker" is appropriate for this bird because it habitually drills holes in the bark of trees, causing sap to run. It appears to gain a measure of sustenance from the sap and is said to over-indulge in it at times to the extent of becoming groggy. It also eats insects attracted to the sap. Excessive drilling operations sometimes cause a tree, or parts of it, to die. Whether these birds have any preference in trees is not known, but maple, wild apple, birch, poplar and alder are most frequently pock-marked.

The sound woodpeckers produce by tapping rapidly on dead branches is called "drumming" and is believed to be a method of communication with others of their kind. According to Charles R.K. Allen, the sound produced by sapsuckers is distinctive because the long "roll" ends with two or three more widely spaced blows. One of the

Yellow-bellied Sapsucker's calls is similar to the mewing note of a catbird and can easily be mistaken for it.

Although similar in size to other woodpeckers, its distinctive colour pattern should preclude its being confused with them.

Downy Woodpecker   PLATE 22

Picoides pubescens (Linnaeus)

Status Common to fairly common resident. Breeds. It is found throughout the province at all seasons but perhaps is more evident in winter, when it comes to feeding stations. It is partially migratory and appears in augmented numbers on our southern islands in fall. It is believed to be less common now than during the early years of this century.

Description *Length:* 16-18 cm. *Adult male:* Considerably smaller and with a shorter bill than the Hairy Woodpecker but otherwise practically the same in colour and pattern, with the exception that its white, outer tail feathers are barred with black, those of its larger relative being all white. *Adult female:* Similar to male but lacks red bar on head.

Breeding *Nest:* An excavation in a tree; those trees in which drilling is less difficult are apparently favoured. The height at which the nest is built is usually lower than those of the Hairy Woodpecker. *Eggs:* 3-6, usually 4-5; glossy white. As a rule it nests about 10 days later than the Hairy Woodpecker. A nest in a dead maple contained four fresh eggs on 4 June 1898; and a set of three eggs in a nest at Black River, Kings County, were one-half incubated when examined on 20 June 1916.

Range Breeds in wooded areas from southern Alaska to Newfoundland and south through Florida, the Gulf Coast and southern California. Winters over most of its breeding range.

Remarks A marked change in the public mind has taken place over the years regarding the role of woodpeckers in man's economic pursuits. At the beginning of the twentieth century, woodpeckers were considered injurious to trees, but gradually their worth as destroyers of tree-damaging insects was realized. Winter predation on the codling moth, for example, by Hairy and Downy Woodpeckers was described by C.R. MacLellan (1958): "The Hairy Woodpecker and the Downy Woodpecker are both important in control of the codling moth in Nova Scotia. In the years 1950 to 1956 these birds reduced the over-wintered larval population on tree trunks by 52 per cent. Woodpeckers find codling moth larvae by sight and touch. Searching is done at random, with the woodpecker looking for likely spots for cocoons or locating the exact spot by tapping with the beak. After finding the cocoon, the woodpecker either flicks the bark off with its chisel-shaped beak and feeds on the exposed larva or drills a hole through the bark into the cocoon and withdraws the larva with its barbed tongue."

This is the smallest of our woodpeckers. Except for its close resemblance to the Hairy Woodpecker, it is not easily confused with other Nova Scotia woodpeckers.

Hairy Woodpecker PLATE 22

Picoides villosus (Linnaeus)

Status Fairly common resident. Breeds. One of our most common woodpeckers. Though usually found nesting in wooded regions, it is commonly seen in settled areas, particularly in winter when it is often a patron at feeding stations. Its numbers may have increased slightly during the past several decades, but it is still reported less frequently than the Downy Woodpecker.

Description *Length:* 24-25 cm. *Adult male:* Back black with white stripe down centre; wings black, speckled with white; small scarlet patch on back of head; crown black; white patch above and below the eye, separated by a black patch; underparts white; tail black centrally, outer feathers white. *Adult female:* Similar but lacks the scarlet patch on head.

Breeding *Nest:* A cavity excavated by the bird in a tree. As is common practice with some of its relatives, it very often chooses a live poplar for its nest site, 3-12 m above ground. No lining other than wood chips is used. *Eggs:* 3-6, usually 4-5; glossy white. There is considerable irregularity in the date when nesting begins. For instance, on 12 May 1943 a female was seen busily excavating a nest at Black River, Kings County, but on 3 May 1924 a nest at East Margaretsville, Annapolis County, contained four eggs about one-half incubated. On 28 May 1905 two nests were located, one containing four eggs partly incubated and the other with young large enough to come to the entrance for food. A nest in a dead beech stub was one-half excavated on 10 April 1918 but the female did not finish laying her four eggs until 10 May.

Range Breeds from southern Alaska to Newfoundland and south to Panama. Winters throughout most of its nesting range.

Remarks It is very similar in appearance to the Downy Woodpecker, from which it can be distinguished by its larger size and by its white tail feathers, which lack the small transverse black bars that mark those of the smaller bird. Another good field mark at close range is length of the bills, that of the Hairy being noticeably longer than that of the Downy.

The nest I found at East Margaretsville was located within 50 m of a Great Horned Owl's nest containing two half-grown owlets. The presence of these fierce predators had not deterred the woodpeckers from selecting their own nest site even though the owls had been long established before the woodpeckers arrived.

Three-toed Woodpecker

Picoides tridactylus (Linnaeus)

Status Rare visitant. Morrell (1899) reported seeing two males and a female near River Hebert, Cumberland County, in winter 1897-98, and his bird list is otherwise plausible. McLeod (1903) mentioned having a specimen from Queens County. The next was a male seen near Upper Musquodoboit, Halifax County, on 8 September 1954 (H.S. Cruikshank). There have been several reports since: one on Brier Island on 29 September 1957 (W. Lent); one in Halifax on 13 March 1960 (W. Mills, W. Bird); two at Green Bay, Lunenburg County, on 3 June 1970 (S. Cohrs); one in early February at Ingonish, Cape Breton Highlands National Park (I. Gettas, photographed by W. Neilly); one near Glace Bay on 8 August 1975 (S. MacLean, G. Spencer); two discovered in Amherst Point Bird Sanctuary on 11 November 1978 (C. Desplanque) and seen by others in following weeks; one on the Halifax West Christmas Bird Count on 23 December 1975 (D. Gray); and one photographed at Shad Bay, Halifax County, in March 1984 (M. Almon).

Remarks The range of this species lies further north than that of the Black-backed Woodpecker, a close relative. The adult males of both species have a yellow crown patch, but both male and female Three-toed Woodpeckers have backs conspicuously barred with black and white; those of the Black-backed are plain glossy black. Summer records suggest that some Three-toed Woodpeckers may nest in the province.

Black-backed Woodpecker   PLATE 22

Picoides arcticus (Swainson)

Status Uncommon resident. Breeds. Most often found in areas remote from settlement. These restless birds may favour the dead and blackened trees left standing in burned-over woodlands, or stands of old-growth spruce in damp, mossy woods. Distribution is general but spotty throughout the province. These birds sometimes invade areas south of their normal range in large numbers, but we do not receive these major incursions. A few occur sometimes in spring and fall on our offshore islands, implying some local migratory movement.

Description *Length:* 24-25 cm. *Adult male:* A woodpecker with three instead of four toes. Back glossy black; underparts white with black bars on sides; outer tail feathers white; yellow crown patch. *Adult female:* Similar but lacks the yellow crown patch.

Breeding *Nest:* An excavation in a tree, usually at relatively low heights. A preference is shown for locations in stands of old-growth evergreens. *Eggs:* 3-5; glossy white and indistinguishable from those of the Hairy Woodpecker. A nest discovered by Robert Gibbon near his home in Stewiacke, Colchester County, was being excavated by the male on 10 May 1959; on 19 May the male was seen sitting on two eggs—laying was probably incomplete. The nest was about 2.5 m from the ground in a live spruce that appeared to have a decayed core. The tree was growing on the edge of a clearing in damp, mossy woods of solid evergreen growth. Gibbon found a number of nests in the same area and gives a detailed account of the bird's breeding behaviour (Gibbon 1964). It has since been found nesting in Annapolis, Guysborough, Halifax and Shelburne counties.

Range Breeds in coniferous woodlands from Alaska to Labrador and Newfoundland, and south to New Hampshire, northern New York, northern Michigan and, in the mountains, to central California. It winters over much of its breeding range.

Remarks Except when encountered on its nesting grounds, this bird seems to be a restless creature, usually on the move as though dissatisfied with its present lot and seeking better feeding grounds further afield. The rather conspicuous yellow crown patch worn by the male and the solid, glossy black back common to both sexes readily distinguish it from the other woodpeckers that occur in Nova Scotia.

Northern Flicker PLATE 22

Colaptes auratus (Linnaeus)

Status Common in summer, rare in winter. Breeds. It arrives in early April (average 5 April, earliest 27 March), but large numbers are not seen usually until later in April. Large numbers are seen from mid-September to mid-October, especially on our southwestern islands; thousands were present on Brier Island during September 1984 (R.B. Stern). Flickers present after mid-November probably will attempt to winter. Some have been recorded during Christmas Bird Counts around the province, but few have been seen in late winter, suggesting that most do not survive.

Description *Length:* 30-33 cm. *Adult male:* Crown ashy gray with red bar across nape; back grayish brown with broken bars of black; rump white; undersurface of wings and tail brilliant yellow; throat and face cinnamon; short, black "moustache" mark extending down from gape; underparts light fawn, boldly marked with round black spots; black crescent-shaped band across breast. *Adult female:* The same but she lacks the black facial mark below the cheek.

Breeding *Nest:* A cavity excavated by the bird in a tree or post, at heights of 1-15 m or more. The nest has no lining other than chips of rotten wood. Nesting locations vary from garden premises to remote woodlands. Usually dead stumps are used, but it is not uncommon to find nests in live trees, especially poplars—probably because so many have decayed hearts which simplify excavation. Sometimes a low tree stump is used, the entrance being not more than a metre from the ground. *Eggs:* 8-10; glossy white. Laying begins about the middle of May. Both sexes share the incubation and feeding of young, the males doing most of the incubating. In 1951 a pair nested in my garden. From 26 May to 13 June, while incubation was in progress, I tapped the tree

100 times; the male appeared at the opening 60 times and the female 40 times. On 24 June 1935 the first young bird left the nest, but the last did not leave until 28 June. A complete set of eight fresh eggs was found on 25 May 1914, and a set of nine about one-half incubated was examined on 5 June 1904; both nests were in the vicinity of Wolfville.

Range Breeds from central Alaska east to southeastern Labrador and Newfoundland, south (east of the Rockies) through much of the United States. Winters from South Dakota, southern Ontario, and Maine (casually in Nova Scotia) south to the Gulf Coast.

Remarks The greatest hazard for the flicker at nesting time is the European Starling. Unless assistance by humans is rendered when competition begins, the builders and rightful owners of the nest will likely be driven out by the smaller but more aggressive and persistent aliens.

Though it feeds largely on the wood-boring ants and beetles it finds in dead trees, the flicker often alights on the ground to prey on smaller, terrestrial ant species. One on 2 August 1946 and another on 29 July 1949 were seen in cherry trees competing with hordes of gluttonous robins and starlings, looking quite ungainly and out of place. On 2 September 1949, one was seen eating rowanberries. Perhaps the strangest behaviour at feeding time was recounted by Rand: a flicker came regularly to his feeding station in February 1923 for suet but occasionally left it to glean a few tasty morsels from the frozen carcass of a cat exposed nearby.

One spring I erected a flicker's nest stump in my garden. I cleaned it thoroughly and placed a quantity of fine sawdust in the bottom to add to its attractiveness. When the birds returned in proper season, I was disappointed to find my efforts were not appreciated, for immediately they began to remove the sawdust a beakful at a time, working in alternate shifts for the better part of two days. This chore having been completed, there was much tapping inside as they picked off chunks of dead wood of approved size from the interior of the rotten stump, allowing the chips to fall to the bottom and form a lining to their liking.

Though I have seen flickers come to my birdbath to drink many times, only once, on the hot day of 15 August 1966, did I witness one taking a thorough bath like other birds.

Our subspecies is the "Yellow-shafted Flicker" (*auratus* subspecies group). An individual with bright salmon-red underwings and undertail and a red "whisker" stripe, evidently a "Red-shafted Flicker" (one of the *cafer* group of subspecies), spent several days in June 1971 around the house of Warden and Mrs. Black of Pleasant Bay, Inverness County (J. Timpa).

Pileated Woodpecker Plate 24

Dryocopus pileatus (Linnaeus)

Status Uncommon resident. Breeds. Generally restricted to old-growth woodlands remote from settlement. Though sedentary by nature, it shows a tendency to disperse over the countryside in late autumn. It is becoming more common and has been seen near settlements more often in recent years.

Description *Length:* 43-50 cm. *Adult male:* Top of head has a bright scarlet crest; a scarlet mark extends back from lower mandible; rest of head boldly marked with contrasting black and white, the white extending down sides of neck to wings; back and underparts sooty black; wings black with white bars seen only in flight; bill is horn-coloured. *Adult female:* similar but lacks red mark behind base of lower mandible and on forepart of her crown.

Breeding *Nest:* An excavation in a hole 3-20 m or more up a large tree. The entrance hole is sometimes round but at other times elliptical, the vertical diameter always being greater. *Eggs:* 3-4; glossy white, as though highly polished. A nest discovered at Black River Lake, Kings County, on 14 May 1922 contained four fresh eggs. It was in a white birch tree stub about 18 m up, in open hardwoods; the male only was in attendance. The eggs were deposited on dry chips 40 cm below the base of the entrance hole. On 10 June 1915 at Albany, Annapolis County, two young were seen which, by their appearance, had been out of the nest about 10 days. A nest in the Sable River area of Shelburne County visited on 30 May 1955 by Harrison F. Lewis was in a large stump of Yellow Birch about 8 m up and had a circular entrance hole. Harry Brennan found a nest near his home in Springville, Pictou County, on 15 May 1968 not over 4.5 m up a large, dead Yellow Birch; it contained two eggs and one newly hatched young.

Range Breeds in forested areas from the southern Mackenzie Valley east to Nova Scotia, south to central California, the Gulf Coast and southern Florida. Mainly resident.

Remarks Those who have travelled in heavily timbered woodlands may have noticed dead stumps riddled and deeply furrowed over parts of their surface, the work of a Pileated Woodpecker searching for wood-boring ants.

It is by far the largest of our woodpeckers. When seen in its natural habitat for the first time, it is an impressive sight not soon forgotten. Its unusual call is very much like that of the Northern Flicker but differs somewhat in quality of tone. Its flight is sometimes direct but more often undulating, with its bold, white wing patches conspicious.

All of our woodpeckers are protected throughout the year by federal and provincial laws.

PLATE 23

Chimney Swift
Page 258

Purple Martin
Page 289

female

male

Cliff Swallow
Page 295

Ruby-throated Hummingbird
Page 259

male

female

Belted Kingfisher, *male*
Page 262

Mourning Dove
Page 235

Black-billed Cuckoo
Page 237

Whip-poor-will
Page 255

Common Nighthawk
Page 252

Crosby '61

PLATE 24

Eastern Wood-Pewee
Page 275

Eastern Phoebe
Page 282

Alder Flycatcher
Page 278

Least Flycatcher
Page 280

Pileated Woodpecker
Page 271

Barred Owl
Page 243

Long-eared Owl
Page 246

Red-headed Woodpecker
Page 263

Northern Saw-whet Owl
Page 249

Order PASSERIFORMES

Family Tyrannidae

Olive-sided Flycatcher   PLATE 25

Contopus borealis (Swainson)

Status Fairly common in summer. Breeds. Usually arrives in the second half of May (average 20 May, earliest 5 May); birds on Sable Island on 25 April 1975 and in Shelburne County on 30 April 1973 were very early. Numbers during breeding season have decreased markedly in the past 50 years for no known reason. Before 1940 it was customary to find pairs occupying groves of mixed deciduous and coniferous trees in settled areas and forested regions. Migration is well underway again during mid-August, with peak movements towards the end of the month. Last sightings are normally in September, with stragglers much later (average 16 September, latest 8 November).

Description *Length:* 18.5-20.5 cm. *Adults:* Dark olive above, darker on wings and tail; no wing bars; white throat and broad white stripe down centre of breast and belly; rest of underparts dark olive; tufts of fluffy white feathers sometimes show on upper flanks, but often are concealed by closed wings.

Breeding *Nest:* Made of twigs, and weed or grass stems, lined with rootlets or beard lichen, the choice of lining obviously based on availability. Most nests are strong and compact, but a minority are loosely built and sometimes barely adequate. Of 43 nests examined, all but one were saddled on horizontal branches 2-15 m off the ground; the exception was in a hemlock, about 6 m up, placed close to the trunk and well concealed by thick-growing sprouts. This last tree was in an open sunny glade, with insects readily available, but without a preferred type of nesting tree in the immediate vicinity, which probably explains the deviation. All other nests were exposed. The trees selected by the 43 flycatcher pairs were: spruce, 24; apple, 8; fir, 6; elm, 3; locust, 1; and hemlock, 1. *Eggs:* 2-4, usually 3; creamy white, spotted (sometimes beautifully wreathed) chiefly around the larger end, with various shades and densities of lavender and chocolate. Of the 43 nests, 32 held three eggs; 8 held four; and 3 contained two. Laying was completed in all, the sets of two being second attempts. Nesting begins early in June, two sets of three fresh eggs having been examined on 11 June 1914. If the first nest is destroyed, the pair will try again, but I have no evidence that a third nest is ever attempted.

Range Breeds from central Alaska to Newfoundland and southward; in the east, to the mountainous regions of North Carolina. Winters in South America as far south as Peru.

Remarks On his return in spring, the male selects a territory for nesting and all rivals are immediately challenged. Sitting on the topmost dead branch or the highest tree in his little kingdom, with an unobstructed view in all directions, he remains alert and upright, like a sentinel on duty, for hours at a time. During the nesting period the male is practically never absent from his chosen domain. His clear, whistled call, which permits several equally euphonic translations, can be heard far off as he orders his listener with *come right-here* or *quick more-beer*. There is the story of a trapper in the back country who, finding his bear trap empty, claimed he was taunted by a very impudent bird perched overhead that kept jeering at him with *what no-bear*. The first word is shorter and weaker than the other two where emphasis is placed, and the final note is usually drawn out and slurred downward.

When the safety of the nest is menaced, both birds will join in an attack upon the intruder. I once saw a red squirrel knocked off a nest limb by one of two irate parents; so intense was their combined fury that the squirrel chose to escape further punishment, scurrying away across the ground with both birds in hot pursuit. The presence of young in this particular nest probably increased the parents' aggressiveness. Their note at such times is a low-pitched, angry *tip-tip-tip,* uttered rapidly and repeated incessantly while danger threatens.

Eastern Wood-Pewee   PLATE 24

Contopus virens (Linnaeus)

Status Fairly common in summer. Breeds. First spring arrivals generally occur in May (average 11 May, earliest 21 April in two years); a bird on Brier Island on 14 April 1977 (W. Lent) was abnormally early. It is widespread in summer, except along the Eastern Shore and on Cape Breton Island, where it is uncommon to rather rare. Major movements have been recorded in late August and early September, and it is routinely last seen in October (average 6 October, latest 9 November).

Description *Length:* 15-16.5 cm. *Adults:* Dark grayish or brownish olive above, darker on crown and tail; wings marked with two bars; no eye ring; underparts grayish white, darker on breast; chin white; upper mandible black, lower mandible grayish yellow.

Breeding *Nest:* Extremely neat and symmetrical, suggesting a larger version of a Ruby-throated Hummingbird's nest. It is a shallow affair composed of plant down, fine grasses, vegetable fibres and other soft material, with an exterior finish of bits of gray lichens attached by spider's web, apparently for camouflage. The nest appears too small for the size of the bird. It is saddled on a horizontal limb, usually of a deciduous tree—with apparent preference being shown for elm, although apple, locust and white birch are also frequently selected as nest sites—at heights of 3-12 m or more. Though the bird is often found in remote wooded areas at nesting time, a preference is shown at that season for shady, ornamental groves where elms predominate near human habitation. *Eggs:* 3-4, usually 3; white to creamy white, marked with blotches of dark brown and lavender, in various degrees of density, chiefly around the larger end. Laying begins about mid-June. A set of three fresh eggs was examined on 20 June 1918 at Port Williams, Kings County, 13 m up and 4.5 m out on the limb of a large locust tree in an ornamental grove. An exceptionally late nest was found by W.A. Brown on 5

Eastern Wood-Pewee and nest

September 1945 at North Aylesford, Kings County, which contained three young about ready to leave; this was probably a second nesting attempt, the first having failed, rather than a second brood.

Range Breeds from southeastern Saskatchewan to Prince Edward Island and Cape Breton Island and, in the east, as far south as central Florida. Winters from Central America to Peru.

Remarks The bird's name is derived from a song given by both sexes, a long drawn-out whistle, clear and plaintive, in two or three slurred phrases: *pee-wee*, or *pee-ah-whee* with a rising inflection on the *whee*. Most songbirds stop singing soon after their nests contain young, as though they were too burdened with parental responsibilities to indulge in song. But this bird's song may be heard here from the time it arrives in spring until it departs in autumn.

Like other flycatchers, its food consists almost wholly of winged insects taken in the air. My notes read: "September 4, 1949: Many Wood Pewees in my garden today. Migration is in full swing. Noticed they appear to show a preference with regard to which insects they take. Saw one that was perched near me refuse to take several insects that buzzed by at close range and then suddenly take a longer flight to snap one up."

Several of our flycatchers bear a close resemblance to one another in size, shape and plumage markings. In distinguishing them, consideration should be given to their respective habitat preferences, which are characteristically different. This bird is similar in size to the Eastern Phoebe, but that bird is an inveterate tail wagger that lacks the conspicuous white wing bars of the Eastern Wood-Pewee.

Yellow-bellied Flycatcher   PLATE 25

Empidonax flaviventris (Baird and Baird)

Status Fairly common in summer. Breeds. This is generally the latest *Empidonax* flycatcher to arrive in spring (average 22 May, earliest 8 May), and northbound transients continue to appear in numbers in coastal areas and on islands into June. It is widespread in suitable habitats in summer. Peak movements have been noted in early September, and last reports are usually during that month (average 13 September, latest 23 October). Very late birds have been recorded on Sable Island on 16 November 1969 (C. Bell) and on Seal Island on 8 November 1976 (B. Mactavish).

Description *Length:* 12.5-14 cm. *Adults:* Olive-green above; wings and tail dark brown, wings showing distinct bars; underparts sulphur yellow, denser on belly; upper breast and sides washed with olive-green; upper mandible black, lower mandible flesh-coloured.

Breeding *Nest:* On the ground, usually well concealed in the mossy bank of a woodland stream, or among the roots of an upturned tree in wet, well-shaded woods; it is beautifully constructed of mosses and fine grasses. *Eggs:* Usually 4; creamy white with numerous pale cinnamon-brown markings, chiefly around the larger end. W. Earl Godfrey examined a nest with four eggs near Baddeck on 30 June 1954. It was on the ground in damp, shady woods of mixed growth, concealed by overhanging moss. Another nest found at Moore's Falls, Kings County, by John T. Erskine on 10 July 1955 contained four eggs and was in a similar location.

Range Breeds from northern British Columbia and southeastern Mackenzie Valley east to Newfoundland, and south to New Hampshire, northern Minnesota and central Alberta. Winters from Mexico to Panama.

Remarks In summer, you are not likely to find this bird far from the wet, mossy, well-shaded woods of coniferous or mixed growth for which it shows a strong preference. It is a timorous bird, always flitting behind a bush or thicket as though determined to keep just out of sight. Its song is a sweet, sad and plaintive whistle, suggesting to some the call note of the Semipalmated Plover with less volume.

The identification of small flycatchers of the genus *Empidonax* outside the breeding season, when habitat and song are diagnostic, is an evolving art. The Yellow-bellied Flycatcher, with its greenish back and yellowish underparts, including the throat, is generally easy to distinguish from the Least and Alder Flycatchers. In spring there is a possibility of confusion with the similarly greenish and early migrating Acadian Flycatcher (see Remarks under that species) but late fall records should eliminate the possibility of the very similar Western Flycatcher, *Empidonax difficilis,* for which there are few records in the eastern United States. There are times when *Empidonax* flycatchers are best reported as "*Empidonax* species (?)."

Acadian Flycatcher

Empidonax virescens (Vieillot)

Status Three sight records. Nineteenth century references to this bird undoubtedly represent confusion with other species of the genus. Full descriptions have been filed on only three sightings of apparent Acadian Flycatchers: two on Sable Island, 23 May 1977, seen by Ian A. McLaren; one on Seal Island, 9 October 1979, seen by Ian A. McLaren, Eric Mills and others; and one on Brier Island, 14 May 1984, seen by Ian and Bernice McLaren. Other occurrences have been suspected.

Remarks Adults of this large *Empidonax* flycatcher are generally even brighter green on the back than the Yellow-bellied Flycatcher, lack its yellowish throat and have larger, broader bills. Nevertheless, our sight records can only be tentative evidence of the species' occurrence here until specimens, measurements of captured birds, or voice recordings are obtained.

The breeding range of this species is in the eastern United States as far north as southern New Hampshire and Vermont.

Alder Flycatcher   PLATE 24

Empidonax alnorum Brewster

Status Fairly common in summer. Breeds. Spring migrants are generally silent, but birds identified as this species usually appear in the second half of May (average 20 May, earliest 4 May). Other earlier *Empidonax* flycatchers, not identified to species, have been noted on 26 April 1969 and 1 May 1975 on Sable Island. The species is evenly distributed throughout the province in summer. After nesting is over, it is practically silent; this fact, coupled with its adroitness in keeping out of sight, add to the difficulty of determining dates of actual departure. Movements of this species and Least Flycatchers are conspicuous in late August, but stragglers are occasional into October (19 October 1973 on Seal Island; 11 October 1981, Halifax County; and 30 October 1982 on Sable Island).

Description *Length:* 13.5-15 cm. *Adults:* Olive-brown above with a tinge of greenish; often indistinct whitish gray eye ring; wings and tail dark brown, wings showing two bars; underparts grayish white on breast, pale yellow on sides and belly; throat white; bill blackish gray above, flesh-coloured below.

Breeding *Nest:* In low bushes in thickets, often in alders, and never more than 1-2 m from the ground. It is made wholly of grass, with coarser grasses used for the framework and finer grasses used for the lining. Sometimes plant down is added to the outside, apparently for decoration. A common characteristic is the addition of several long grass stems attached to the nest proper and allowed to hang down loosely over the sides of the nest. *Eggs:* 3-4; white, delicately marked with cinnamon spots scattered chiefly around the larger end. Laying begins about 15 June and continues to the end of the month. The earliest date for a complete set is 23 June 1904; the latest date is 7 July 1917, when a partially incubated set of three was examined at Gaspereau, Kings County. Two nests, each containing four fresh eggs, were found near Wolfville on 30 June 1915.

Range Breeds from central Alaska to Newfoundland, and as far south as Tennessee in the Appalachians. Its precise winter range is still undetermined, but presumably it winters widely in South America.

Remarks Unlike its close relative, the Yellow-bellied Flycatcher, this bird frequents alder, blackberry, wild rose and other types of low-growing shrubbery that occur in drier places. It is a restless little creature, flitting here and there in a nervous manner and managing to keep out of sight most of the time.

The song, if such it may be called, is a short, wheezy, *wee-bee-o* difficult to trace to its source because the bird seems constantly to change its location in the thicket. When an intruder approaches an Alder Flycatcher on its nest, it slips off unobtrusively and, keeping well hidden behind a canopy of leaves, utters its scolding note, a soft, low *p-r-e-t,* given as if by a ventriloquist.

Outside the breeding season, the Alder Flycatcher can be differentiated from Least Flycatchers by the brownish rather than grayish cast to its back, especially the nape. The proportionately larger head of the Least Flycatcher, its more conspicuous eye ring, shorter extension of primary wing feathers, sharper call note and, at least at times, more "vibrant" tail flick, are also helpful distinctions. Nevertheless, sight records of migrants, especially of birds late in fall when stray western species are a possibility, should be dealt with cautiously.

Willow Flycatcher

Empidonax traillii (Audubon)

Status One record. On 22 June 1980, Ian McLaren found a singing male of this species at Indian Point, Lunenburg County, which was subsequently seen and heard by many others. A tape recording by McLaren was accepted as evidence of its occurrence by W. Earl Godfrey of the National Museum of Canada. On 24 July of that year, Fulton Lavender saw a pair feeding young at the same place.

Remarks The song of this species is an emphatic *fitz-bew,* quite different from the *wee-bee-o* of the Alder Flycatcher. Willow Flycatchers are perhaps impossible to distinguish with certainty from Alder Flycatchers on appearance alone. They are the brownest of the genus and may virtually lack an eye ring. Flycatchers with these field marks have been reported on occasion, and it is probable that this species is an occasional vagrant here during migration seasons. They breed across the northern and central United States, into southern British Columbia, Ontario and Quebec.

Least Flycatcher   PLATE 24

Empidonax minimus (Baird and Baird)

Status Fairly common in summer. Breeds. This species arrives a little earlier than the Alder Flycatcher (average 14 May, earliest 4 May; see earlier occurrences of unidentified *Empidonax* under the Alder Flycatcher). It is found throughout the province during breeding season, perhaps more frequently in the Annapolis Valley than elsewhere. Movements of this species with the Alder Flycatcher are conspicuous in late August and early September, with stragglers reported on Seal Island on 19 October 1973 and at Glace Bay on 20 October 1981.

Description *Length:* 12.5-14.5 cm. *Adults:* Grayish olive above; wings and tail dark brown, wings showing two white bars; underparts light gray, which is somewhat darker on breast, with a suggestion of sulphur-yellow on sides and belly; conspicuous white eye ring.

Breeding *Nest:* Compact and symmetrical; constructed of grasses, plant down and other fine vegetable matter, and usually placed in the crotch of a deciduous tree (rarely saddled on a horizontal limb) at heights of 1-8 m or more. In the apple belt of the Annapolis Valley, probably the majority of nests are built in apple trees; I have never known one to be placed in a conifer. *Eggs:* 3-5, usually 4; white. Laying begins late in May and continues well into June. A set of four slightly incubated eggs was examined on 3 June 1894 in a nest about 3 m up in an apple tree in an orchard. Another nest containing four eggs was found on 26 June 1913 about 3.5 m up in an elm tree. A nest containing five nearly fresh eggs was seen on 20 June 1922 at Wolfville; the location was unusual because the nest was not more than 1 m off the ground and was saddled on the low bough of a large apple tree. I have no evidence that this bird attempts to raise more than one brood each year—a nest found on 22 August 1929 containing young about ready to fly suggests the possibility but may simply have been a second nesting attempt, the first attempt having failed.

Range Breeds from west-central Mackenzie Valley to northern Nova Scotia and, in the east, south to the mid-eastern United States. Winters from northeastern Mexico to Panama.

Remarks This bird is usually seen in orchards, shady groves and open woodlands, sitting erectly on a dead twig in the open with its tail pointed slightly inward. From this perch it makes frequent sallies after winged insects that pass within its range. Having snapped up its victim, it returns immediately to the same twig, jerks its head back and, with fluttering wings, says *che-bec* repeatedly and with such earnestness and clear enunciation that the watcher cannot fail to be impressed. It resembles its larger cousin, the Eastern Wood-Pewee, in shape and colour but is not readily confused with any other of our garden birds. When seen in remote wooded areas, as it is less frequently, its voice and small size will identify it. Other field marks, useful for silent migrating birds, are mentioned in Remarks under the Alder Flycatcher.

Least Flycatcher singing

Eastern Phoebe   PLATE 24

Sayornis phoebe (Latham)

Status Uncommon transient, rare in summer. Breeds. The first record of a phoebe in Nova Scotia was reported by C.R. Harte (Macoun 1903), who saw a pair near Sydney on 30 August 1901. The bird was not recorded again until 1932, when W. Earl Godfrey saw one near Wolfville on 30 May. The first specimen was collected by Cyril Coldwell at Gaspereau, Kings County, on 15 April 1945. It was considered a great rarity at that time. Since then it has been widely seen with numbers of nests observed. The species generally first arrives before mid-April (average 10 April, earliest 25 March). During summer it has been found nesting widely but sparsely on the mainland, but not yet on Cape Breton Island. It is the last of our breeding flycatchers to depart. Peak movements have been recorded in October, with a few stragglers in November (average 18 October, latest 12 November). An amazing individual wintered at Ralph Johnson's feeder at Liverpool up to at least 4 February 1974, at times eating small seeds.

Description *Length:* 16.5-18 cm. *Adults:* Above brownish gray, distinctly darker on crown; wings and tail brownish black, wings without conspicuous bars; underparts white, washed with gray; bill black.

Breeding *Nest:* Bulky, composed largely of moss and mud, and lined with soft grass; placed on a beam or rafter in an abandoned building or in a culvert under a bridge. *Eggs:* 4-6; white, rarely with faint dots of cinnamon-brown. The first record of breeding was reported by Mrs. C.W. Dean, who found a nest at Carleton, Yarmouth County, in 1963. The next record was of a youngster being fed by a parent at Steam Mill Village, Kings County, on 15 July 1967. Since then it has been found nesting in all mainland counties except Antigonish and Guysborough.

Range Breeds from west-central Mackenzie Valley, southern Quebec, and Nova Scotia, southward to northern Georgia, Arkansas and eastern New Mexico. Winters from the southern edge of its breeding range to the Gulf Coast and Mexico.

Remarks It is called a "phoebe" because that is what it seems to say when it sings. The word is enunciated in a short, explosive *fee-be,* with a strong accent on the first syllable. Its call note is a sharp *chip.* It has a characteristic habit of tail wagging, which is helpful in identifying it in the field. Any flycatcher seen here in April is very likely of this species and sure to be if it wags its tail.

Say's Phoebe

Sayornis saya (Bonaparte)

Status Five records. The first was identified on Seal Island on 24 September 1966 by Chris W. Helleiner and collected by Charles R.K. Allen. On 7 September 1972 one was seen at Ingonish, Victoria County, by Irving Cantor. The third bird was found and photographed by Ian A. McLaren on Sable Island on 18 September 1974. Another fall vagrant was seen on 27 August 1980 on Brier Island by C. Henry Barnett and C. William McCormick. An individual well seen and photographed on 20 May 1980 on Seal Island (M. Litchfield, R. Veit, B. Mactavish) was a first spring record for eastern North America.

Remarks This bird of the far west is readily recognized as a large phoebe with a rusty belly and lower breast. It is an occasional fall vagrant along the Atlantic seaboard.

Vermilion Flycatcher

Pyrocephalus rubinus (Boddaert)

Status Two sight records. Evelyn Richardson (1965) reported two apparent occurrences of this species: the first was a female sojourning aboard the fishing boat of Arthur Wickens off Seal Island on 25 May 1955 (Tufts 1955), and the second was a male feeding on tideline kelp flies on Bon Portage Island at the feet of Carroll Crowell on 29 May 1960.

Remarks The only other Canadian records of this species are from southern Ontario, although it is a rare vagrant to the southeastern United States. The bright red and black male is particularly distinctive, and Mr. Crowell was able to rule out any confusion with the Scarlet Tanager.

Great Crested Flycatcher

Myiarchus crinitus (Linnaeus)

Status Uncommon transient, rare in summer. Breeds. It was first recorded on 30 May 1931 at New Minas, Kings County. It generally first appears in small numbers in the second half of May (average 22 May, earliest 10 May), and a few scattered pairs or individuals may be found in mainland counties during summer. Fall sightings are not common, but most are seen from late August through September, with last sightings routinely in October (average 25 October, latest 13 November). Two December 1973 records did not provide sufficient detail to eliminate the possibility of confusion with the Ash-throated Flycatcher.

Description *Length:* 20.5-23 cm. *Adults:* Throat and breast pearl-gray; belly sulphur-yellow; upperparts (except tail) brown washed with olive-green; tail rufous; outer primaries margined with pale rufous.

Breeding *Nest:* A cavity in a tree, a natural cavity being used as commonly as one excavated by a woodpecker. It is copiously lined with grass, sometimes twigs, and often with a piece of cast snakeskin or, more frequently in recent years, plastic wrapping. *Eggs:* 4-6; creamy white, streaked and blotched with chocolate-brown. It was first found nesting at Prince's Lodge, near Halifax, on 5 August 1956, as reported by Lloyd B. Macpherson, who watched three well-fledged young being fed by a parent; he also saw a pair at Rockingham, Halifax County, in the early 1960s showing much interest in a man-made nest box. At Milton, Queens County, J. Roy Gordon had two nests (1963 and 1966) in the same natural cavity of an old apple tree on his property. The nests were about 50 cm below the entrance and their contents were not visible; the birds scolded vociferously in mid-June when the nest tree was first approached, but by the end of June, by which time they were carrying food to the young, they were shy and would disappear when he approached the nest. On 18 July 1967 a pair was seen feeding on the Gordon premises but there was no nesting that year.

Range Breeds from east-central Alberta to Nova Scotia, and south to Florida and Texas. Winters in Florida and Cuba and from Mexico to Colombia.

Remarks This rare bird might be confused with the somewhat less rare Western Kingbird. The tail of the Great Crested Flycatcher is bright chestnut but that of the kingbird is almost black, with conspicuously whitish outer feathers.

A greater possibility of misidentification is with the Ash-throated Flycatcher, *Myiarchus cinerascens,* of the southwestern United States, which is an occasional late-fall vagrant in the northeastern United States. In appearance it is like a small Great Crested Flycatcher, but its upperparts are more grayish and its underparts are much paler. Two birds suspected of being this species have been seen in Nova Scotia, but too briefly for positive identification.

This bird's habit of lining its nest with cast snakeskins is unique among Nova Scotia birds. One theory is that this is a ruse to frighten off would-be predators.

Western Kingbird

Tyrannus verticalis Say

Status Uncommon vagrant. The first record of this species was of one rescued from a cat at Lower West Pubnico, Yarmouth County, on 26 October 1935 (I.J. Pothier). Another 15 were recorded up to 1960, all in the southwestern counties. Since then it has become annual in occurrence, at times in some numbers during autumn, again mostly in the southwestern counties. Our only spring records are of individuals on Sable Island on 10 April 1971 and in Shelburne County on 5 June of the same year. An unseasonal wanderer was on Cape Sable on 23 June 1973, and others on Long Island,

Digby County, on 28 July 1976 and on Sable Island on 20 July 1982 seemed too early to be normal fall migrants. The first Western Kingbirds in fall normally appear in September or October (average 20 September, earliest 27 August), and the last ones are seen routinely in November and occasionally in December (average 10 November, latest 20 December). Most startling was one at the feeder of Mrs. Douglas Harlow at Sable River, Shelburne County, 20-23 February 1962 (H.F. Lewis), probably the victim of a preceding gale.

Remarks This kingbird of the western plains resembles our native Eastern Kingbird only in size, shape and behaviour, for its plumage markings are distinctly different. It is grayish green on the back, pale gray on the breast, white at the chin, sulphur-yellow on the belly, and its tail feathers are black, except the white-edged outer feathers. It is most likely to be confused with the Great Crested Flycatcher (see that species for distinctions).

Eastern Kingbird   PLATE 25

Tyrannus tyrannus (Linnaeus)

Status Fairly common in summer. Breeds. In recent years the vanguard of this species seems to have been arriving earlier. Among those arriving after mid-April, which might be taken as normal migrants, the average date of first appearances has been 9 May. In addition, there have been a few individuals and some small groups in the first half of April during six springs since 1968, the earliest on 3 April 1977 at Cape Forchu, Yarmouth County. Kingbirds are found commonly in summer only in agricultural areas. Outbound migration begins in early August, when birds appear on our coasts and islands, but main movements occur in late August and early September. Latest migrants are generally in September or October, occasionally later (average 1 October, latest 26 November). Very late individuals were recorded on Christmas Bird Counts at Yarmouth on 29 December 1973 and at Halifax East on 14 December 1974.

Description *Length:* 21.5-23 cm. *Adults:* Upperparts slate-black; tail broadly tipped with white; red-orange crown patch (usually concealed); underparts white, tinged with gray on breast. *Immatures:* No crown patch.

Breeding *Nest:* Well built and usually quite compact, made of twigs, weed stems and coarse grasses, lined with fine grass or often fine rootlets only; rarely a few feathers will be used for lining. A strong preference is shown for apple trees in orchards, where the nest is saddled on a horizontal limb 2.5-5 m from the ground. Another favoured site is a bush or small tree growing on the bank of a stream that meanders through an open meadow, the nest very often placed directly over the water. An unusual nest location was the concave top of a medium-sized dead stump which protruded 2.5 m above the surface of Black River Lake, Kings County, about 100 m from the shore. The female would alight on the stump and then suddenly drop from sight. She left when the stump was tapped, and scolded from a perch nearby. *Eggs:* 3-4, usually 3; white, spotted and blotched with shades of brown. Laying begins early in June. A nest examined on 28 June 1895 at Gaspereau, Kings County, held three fresh eggs; this was evidently a second nesting attempt, the first having failed. I have no evidence that more than a single brood is raised each year. An abnormally late nesting occurred in 1969 at Gaspereau, when the young from a nest in Cyril Coldwell's orchard did not leave until 27 August.

Range Breeds from central British Columbia, southern Mackenzie Valley, southern Quebec, and Nova Scotia, south to the southern states. Winters in South America.

Remarks Like other members of the flycatcher family, a high percentage of the kingbird's food consists of insects taken on the wing, but on occasion it also eats fruit. One collected by W. Earl Godfrey in early September 1930 had just devoured several raspberries, and W.A. Brown saw one feeding on chokecherries in early July 1935.

The ferocity displayed by both sexes when defending their nesting territory against crows and other larger birds is remarkable.

The Eastern Kingbird's call is a high-pitched metallic chirp, often prolonged into a chatter. The conspicuous, broad white terminal band across an otherwise black tail is perhaps its best field mark.

Gray Kingbird

Tyrannus dominicensis (Gmelin)

Status Two sight records. Evelyn Richardson (1965) gives a precise description of the appearance and behaviour of a Gray Kingbird she saw many years earlier on Bon Portage Island, but without recalling the date. An individual on Sable Island on 20-23 October 1973 was closely observed and accurately described by Alban Richard.

Remarks This large, pale, heavy-billed kingbird breeds from South Carolina south to northern South America but occasionally wanders up the Atlantic coast.

Scissor-tailed Flycatcher

Tyrannus forficatus (Gmelin)

Status Five records. Evelyn Richardson (1965) reported a sighting by Morrill Richardson of one feeding on kelp flies on Bon Portage Island on a November day "around 1950." On 19 November 1978 the Sidney Smith family captured and photographed one on Cape Sable. In 1982, two were seen: on 11 May at Seaforth, Halifax County, by Suzanne Carmilleri and on 4 September at Central Chebogue,

Yarmouth County, by Charles R.K. and Blanche Allen. An individual discovered by Damian Welsh on 1 December 1984 at Hazel Hill, Guysborough County, delighted several subsequent observers and was well photographed by June Jarvis.

Remarks This beautiful flycatcher from the south-central United States has a reputation as a wanderer, perhaps because of its conspicuous appearance and habits.

Fork-tailed Flycatcher

Tyrannus savana Vieillot

Status Three records. The first was seen in Dartmouth on 26 September 1970 by Ian McLaren, later that day joined by Eric Mills and Willett J. Mills. Photographs by Eric Mills were sent to the National Museum, where W. Earl Godfrey confirmed the identification. The second was on Seal Island from 24 to 26 August 1976, seen by the McLaren family and photographed by Ian McLaren. The third was photographed on Cape Breton Island on 25 June 1984 by John Peebles of Richmond, Virginia.

Remarks The Fork-tailed Flycatcher is a species whose appearance makes it self-identifying. It is a South American native and, although the Dartmouth bird was a first Canadian record, the species has strayed surprisingly often to North America, with about 40 occurrences up to 1980, mostly in the northeastern United States.

Family Alaudidae

Horned Lark   PLATE 36

Eremophila alpestris (Linnaeus)

Status Common transient, uncommon in summer and winter. Breeds. In winter it is found mainly along the coastal lowlands, but in summer it frequents the sandy plains and large open fields that it invariably selects for nesting. Spring migrants arrive in March, with heavier concentrations towards the end of the month. Numbers are much greater in the fall movements which start in mid-September and peak towards the end of October when flocks of over 100 are not uncommon. Subsequently, numbers appear to drop off or perhaps merely dissipate into many smaller flocks. During the winter months these small flocks occur in suitable habitats, often in company with Lapland Longspurs. Cape Sable Island is one of their favoured wintering areas.

Description *(Eremophila alpestris alpestris) Length:* 18-20 cm. *Adult male:* Throat and line over eye pale yellow; patch on breast and patch from bill to eye and down side of throat black; crown, back of head and rump cinnamon to light brown; back similar but feathers edged with black, giving striped appearance; wing coverts bright cinnamon;

lower breast and belly white; sides light brown; "horns" (feather tufts) on top of head black and inconspicuous; tail black, outer feathers margined with white. *Adult female:* Similar but markings less sharply defined and general appearance duller. *Eremophila alpestris praticola:* Slightly smaller; back more grayish; throat more whitish; eyebrow stripe usually white.

Breeding *Nest:* On the ground with little if any attempt at concealment; usually composed of dried grass and always in open fields or sandy plains. *Eggs:* 4; greenish white, covered with fine specks of light brown over entire surface. A nest on White Rock Mountain, Kings County, on 28 May 1941 contained four newly hatched young; another at Aldershot Military Camp, near Kentville, contained young on 25 June 1942. A young lark barely able to fly was brought to me on 6 May 1955 by Donald Harvey, who caught it on the Grand Pré meadows in Kings County. Another at the same stage of development was seen by Alban Brown at Telford, Pictou County, on 28 July 1921. This bird is one of the first migrants to arrive in the spring and, considering the wide spread in dates of breeding records, it seems probable that a third brood may be raised if the pair is successful with their first and second.

Range Breeds from the shores of the Arctic Ocean south to northern South America. Also occurs widely in the Old World. Winters from southern Canada southward.

Remarks Two subspecies occur here seasonally. The arctic and subarctic *E. a. alpestris* is a fairly common winter visitor from mid-October to early April in coastal districts but is uncommon to rare in the interior.

Highly gregarious, these little foragers from the north country sometimes travel in flocks of their own kind, but perhaps as often in flocks mingled with Snow Buntings. Commonly called "shore larks," they are usually seen along the coast during early winter; thereafter, as the snows become deeper, they commonly frequent higher ground. It is pleasing, particularly to an agriculturalist, to watch a flock industriously work over a patch of pigweed *(Chenopodium)* in a garden or orchard as though striving to glean every seed.

Horned Larks are strictly ground dwellers; when one is seen at rest off the ground, its perch is usually a post or fence rail, not a tree. These birds usually fly at very low levels. When disturbed on the ground, they spring into the air with a sharp whistling note and hurry away.

The breeding subspecies, *E. a. praticola,* is a relative newcomer to Nova Scotia. This more western subspecies has reached Nova Scotia through a natural expansion of its range. The first record of its occurrence was a bird collected on 2 September 1918 on a sandy plain just west of Auburn, Kings County. Since then its range in Nova Scotia has extended broadly and it is now a locally common summer resident from early March to late October, with stragglers in winter. One seen at Auburn on 3 March 1955 in full song and one collected at Grand Pré on 16 October 1928, occurred at normal seasonal extremes. Two were reported by Eva Urban at her feeder in Avonport, Kings County, on 1 February 1960; one was collected on that date and sent to the National Museum in Ottawa.

Family Hirundinidae

Purple Martin   PLATE 23

Progne subis (Linnaeus)

Status Uncommon transient, rare in summer. Breeds. During migration, martins occur all over the province. The normal spring arrival is after mid-April (average 29 April, earliest 6 April). There are two records from Shelburne County of abnormally early martins: an adult male that killed itself against a window on 2 March 1958, and another that was picked up exhausted on 27 March 1969 (both H.F. Lewis). Of our summer birds that return regularly in spring to their favoured nesting grounds, regrettably the Purple Martin is among the rarest. At the beginning of the twentieth century there were a few relatively small and isolated colonies nesting regularly at Windsor; Shubenacadie, Hants County; Truro; Amherst; Oxford, Cumberland County; and probably a few intermediate points. From time to time these small isolated populations were subject to rather severe setbacks, but recovery or partial recovery always took place within one or two years. About 1950 it was reported that none had nested in Windsor for several years; later it was learned that Truro, too, had no martins. In June 1958 a survey was made of all districts where martins were once known to nest and none were found except in Amherst and Oxford (R.W. Tufts): in Amherst, about 10 pairs were established on the premises then owned by Percy C. Black; in Oxford, R.J. Lunn was caring for a colony of about 30 pairs. Both of these gentlemen felt compelled to resort to firearms at nesting time to protect the martins from the more numerous and covetous European Starlings and House Sparrows. At other points on the survey martin houses were no longer in place, it being considered useless to put them out in spring because of the prevalence of the pugnacious starlings. In 1984 there were two martin colonies in Amherst and eight houses (with 16 nest holes in each house) thriving at Oxford. A new colony of two composite houses was established at Collingwood (17 km from Oxford) in 1983. Fall migrants occur widely during August and are rarely seen after September (average 12 September; latest 28 October 1969 on Sable Island).

Description *Length:* 19-21.5 cm. *Adult male:* Glossy purplish black; wings duller. *Adult female:* Upperparts similar to those of male but duller; wings and tail blackish brown; throat, breast and sides mottled light and dark gray; belly white.

Breeding *Nest:* Usually in houses erected for their use; at other times in cavities of various sorts. The nest is composed of twigs, grass, bits of cloth and other refuse, with a lining of grass and feathers to which are added, as nesting progresses, pieces of green leaves, those from pear trees seemingly being preferred. On 28 June 1928 at Windsor the top branches of a lone pear tree that grew near an occupied martin house on the premises of Basil Colbran were almost denuded of leaves. Other trees were growing nearby but the birds' attention, year after year, had been focussed on this particular pear tree. Whole leaves were not taken, but strips were neatly torn from them, giving the treetop a ragged appearance. *Eggs:* 5; dull white. On 20 June 1928 a nest at Windsor contained five slightly incubated eggs, and on 6 July 1925 two nests at Truro each contained five partly fledged young.

Range Breeds from southern British Columbia, central Alberta, southern Manitoba, southern Ontario, southern Quebec, and Nova Scotia, south to central Mexico. Winters in South America.

Remarks The homing instinct of these birds is well developed, as illustrated by an unusual incident: On the night of 6 July 1925, I undertook to transplant two entire families of Martins, two pairs of adults and their respective broods of five each, from Truro to Wolfville. They were transported by auto, each family in its own compartment of a double nest box. On arrival at Wolfville about midnight the whole contraption was placed on a prearranged pole in my garden. The stoppers were then removed from the two entrances, all being quiet inside during that part of the operation. Next morning, considerably after daylight, the four adults emerged, circled about the garden a few times as though getting their bearings, and then disappeared and did not return to their nests. About two hours later a long-distance call from Truro informed me that two pairs of Martins were then circling madly about the top of the old nest pole and scolding vociferously. Seemingly without hesitation they had abandoned their helpless offspring in obedience to a blind urge to return home.

Birds sometimes do strange things. In early spring 1928, Mr. Colbran took down his martin house in Windsor to get it ready for its tenants, expected any day. It contained eight nests from the previous year. Seven nests were composed of the usual materials, but the eighth was composed almost entirely of rusty nails of various sizes, some straight and some bent, with a mere suggestion of grass mixed in with them. He cleared all the rooms and replaced the house, and soon all compartments were occupied. The following spring the cleaning-out process was repeated and again he found one nest composed of rusty nails.

Tree Swallow   PLATE 25

Tachycineta bicolor (Vieillot)

Status Common in summer. Breeds. Tree Swallows are the first swallows to arrive in spring (average 6 April, earliest 22 March), but a dying bird in Halifax on 3 March 1968 and two lively ones at Cape Sable on 28 February 1976 clearly were not normal migrants. In summer they are widespread and common in towns and along watercourses. Local birds and transients form large gatherings from mid-August through early September. A few remain much later, and last sightings are routine in November (average 6 November, latest 27 November). Birds seen after 11 December four times since 1969—the latest sightings being on the Halifax East Christmas Bird Count on 20 December 1969 (seven birds) and on the count at Port L'Hebert, Shelburne County, on 20 December 1981 (two birds)—had probably been brought back north by storms.

Description *Length:* 13-15 cm. *Adult males:* Upperparts iridescent blue to green; underparts pure white; tail slightly notched. *Adult females:* Not infrequently, lack the iridescence on back which may be dull olive-brown. *Immatures:* Upperparts dull olive-brown.

Breeding *Nest:* Usually in a hollow tree or man-made nest box. It is composed of coarse vegetable matter with a profuse lining of feathers, placed so they curl up over the eggs. In selecting feathers for nest lining, the bird refuses black or even dark ones, insisting that they be white or light gray—at least that has been my experience. If feeding conditions are particularly favourable over a terrain without conventional nest sites (such as is the situation on one of the Mud Islands off the coast of Yarmouth), it will nest on the ground under a flat stone or in a hole it excavates in the ground (Langille 1892). *Eggs:* 4-6, usually 5; white. Laying normally commences at the beginning of June. Usually a single brood is raised, but there are exceptions. Harold F. Tufts observed a pair raising two broods in his garden at Port Mouton, Queens County, during summer 1960. The first young bird of a brood of five left the nest during the last days of June, as is normal. Within a few days a parent was seen carrying nesting material to another box nearby, which a brood of four eventually left on July 31. Dr. Tufts mentioned that this had not been the first time a pair of Tree Swallows had reared two families in one season on his premises. An unusual incident occurred in 1953. On 7 July the last of five young left one of my nest boxes, but a parent bird continued to enter and leave repeatedly thereafter. On the morning of 9 July, I opened the box and found two newly hatched young. They were cared for normally and flew on 27 and 31 July. The only tenable explanation is that the female (or another) laid the two eggs while brooding was in progress, the necessary warmth for successful incubation being provided by the parent and young at night and by the fledglings during the daytime. It was noted that only one bird, presumably the female, cared for the young from 9 to 31 July. Why these eggs had not been trampled and broken during the development of five husky young swallows remains a mystery.

Range Breeds from north-central Alaska to Newfoundland and, in the east, south to North Carolina. Winters on the Gulf Coast, in northern Mexico south to Guatemala, and occasionally north to Massachusetts and New York State.

Remarks The practice of providing nest boxes for these birds has become prevalent. This is unquestionably a boon to the swallows, but these boxes are also coveted by House Sparrows, and competition is often very keen, with the ruffians usually taking over. There are several ways to assist the swallows at such times without resorting to the use of firearms. It is helpful if the entrance hole is elliptical, the vertical measurement being not over 2.4 cm. The horizontal measurement is not important. If made 5-7.5 cm wide it will provide sufficient elbow-room for several little yellow-lined mouths, instead of the usual one, to compete for the food brought during the final days of their confinement. A hole this size discourages the sparrows but is not totally effective. However, if the hole is any smaller the swallows have difficulty entering. So two other suggestions are offered. Suspend the box close to a window, close enough that it is within reach when the window is opened. If that is not feasible, hang it 1.5-2 m off the ground, being careful not to place it where a cat can reach it.

It is always pleasing to have the swallows come back in early spring, but an early arrival does not always work well for the swallows, as happened in April 1940. They were first seen on the 18th, when the weather was delightful. On the 21st it turned cold and snow began falling and continued to do so, intermittently, through the 23rd. Over 30 cm of snow covered much of the ground and temperatures slightly below freezing prevailed. At Gaspereau, Kings County, 100 or more Tree Swallows were seen near a sheltered embankment by the river on the 23rd; those still alive sat dejectedly on the trees, their wings drooping, many so weak from starvation and cold that handling was possible, while others were strewn about on the snow either dead or too weak to fly. Other migrants arrived later but the species appeared to be reduced in numbers that summer.

Tree Swallow feeding young

Violet-green Swallow

Tachycineta thalassina (Swainson)

Status One sight record. A bird believed to be of this species was seen by John and Rachel Erskine on 30 October 1965 at Crescent Beach, Lunenburg County, hawking about over a salt marsh, at times within a few metres of them. Mr. Erskine had been familiar with the species when he had lived in Oregon some years earlier and he clearly saw "the white spots on the sides of the bird's rump."

Remarks The Violet-green Swallow is a very rare vagrant east of the mid-western part of the continent. The only other record in the general region was in New Hampshire in mid-September of the same year.

Northern Rough-winged Swallow

Stelgidopteryx serripennis (Audubon)

Status Rare vagrant. The first record was of a bird seen on Sable Island on 27 August 1964 by Christel and Norman Bell; they also saw three there on 15 August 1966 and two on 4 August 1969. Since then the birds have been reported (and some photographed) each year except for 1981, 1982 and 1983, mostly on Brier, Sable, Seal and Cape Sable islands, but also in Halifax, Lunenburg, Pictou, Queens and mainland Shelburne counties. There have been 18 reports of about 30 birds in spring (8 May to 6 June) and 11 reports of about 19 fall migrants (18 July to 12 October). An extraordinarily early individual was closely observed on Cape Sable on 17 March 1971 by Norman Cunningham.

Remarks This swallow may be distinguished from the similarly brown-backed Bank Swallow and young Tree Swallow by its dusky throat and breast. As it nests a relatively short distance away to the west and southwest of Nova Scotia, its occurrence here is not unusual.

Bank Swallow   PLATE 25

Riparia riparia (Linnaeus)

Status Common in summer. Breeds. It normally appears in the first half of May (average 8 May, earliest 20 April), but migrant flocks are still evident in early June. It is abundant locally in the immediate vicinity of its breeding colonies during nesting season, after which it scatters widely and is seen less commonly up to the time of gatherings of migrants in the second half of August. Stragglers are regular throughout September, and very late birds have occurred during four years in November, the latest one on Sable Island on 21 November 1968.

Description *Length:* 13-14 cm. *Adults:* Upperparts grayish brown without iridescence; grayish brown band across breast; throat and belly white.

Breeding *Nest:* At the end of a tunnel in a sand or gravel bank or a steep-sided sawdust pile and always in colonies. The burrows are always near the top of a bank and extend 60-95 cm into it. The cavity at the end is lined with grass and feathers. *Eggs:* 4-6, usually 5; white. Laying begins about 1 June and nesting operations continue through the first week of August. When the last of the young have flown, the colony locations are forsaken. On 11 June 1917, three nests were examined at a colony of about 200 pairs at Evangeline Beach, Kings County; all contained five fresh eggs.

Range Breeds from northern Alaska to southern Labrador and Newfoundland and, in the east, as far south as some of the southern states. Winters in South America. Found also in the Old World.

Remarks This swallow is distinguished from the others that occur here by its smaller size, brown back and grayish brown band that crosses an otherwise white breast.

Nest burrows are close together and, when the colony is large and space perhaps limited, often arranged in tiers of two or more. Watching a large colony when parents are feeding their young, one is impressed by their ability to tell which nest is their own and by the general lack of confusion and animosity that prevails in the midst of much activity.

I have stated that the nest excavations are "always" near the top of a bank. Perhaps "usually" would have been a better word, but I have yet to note an exception. Positioned as they are at about grass-roots level, they are vulnerable to predators, including inquisitive children who with little effort can dig down or reach from the top of the embankment. If the holes were 2 m or more lower on the perpendicular wall, the nest cavities would be difficult to reach. But the swallows continue to do as they have done for uncounted generations and seem quite capable of maintaining their numbers under the traditional arrangement. Lloyd B. Macpherson suggests that Bank Swallows may choose the top of an embankment because the earth there is more readily excavated than at lower elevations where the compressed subsoil makes digging more difficult.

Cliff Swallow   PLATE 23

Hirundo pyrrhonota Vieillot

Status Uncommon in summer. Breeds. The first Cliff Swallows generally appear in early May (average 6 May, earliest 21 April). In summer, they are common only in the immediate vicinity of their widely scattered nesting colonies. The number of this species breeding in the province appears to have declined in recent decades. Late birds are routinely seen in small numbers after most have departed in August (average 7 October, latest 9 November). Other even later reports from earlier years include three found by Israel J. Pothier on 28 November 1948 at Lower Wedgeport, Yarmouth County; he continued to see one or two daily until the snowy 13th of December, when the last was seen weakly flying from a pig-pen.

Description *Length:* 13-15 cm. *Adults:* Above, except rump and nape, dark iridescent blue; rump buffy orange; forehead buffy white; cheek and throat chestnut; breast and nape grayish fawn with a dark bluish black patch on upper breast; belly white; end of tail nearly square.

Breeding *Nest:* Made of mud pellets and grass, lined with soft grass and feathers and usually attached to the outside wall under the overhanging eaves of a barn or other building. Occasionally a single nest is attached to the outside of a porch or building, but generally the bird nests in colonies. I have never known this species to nest inside a building, but it is said to do so on occasion (Palmer 1949). *Eggs:* 4-5; white, with small spots of cinnamon-brown loosely covering the entire surface. Laying begins about 1 June. On 20 May 1951 at Black River, Kings County, one was seen gathering mud, and on 9 June 1913 two nests containing four fresh eggs each were examined at Albany, Annapolis County.

Range Breeds from central Alaska to northern Nova Scotia, south over much of the United States to central Mexico. Winters from Brazil southward.

Remarks Many in our farming districts believe the House Sparrow is primarily responsible for the decline in the Cliff Swallow population in recent years. The aliens are said to be showing increasing aggressiveness in usurping mud nests, at times taking them over by sheer pugnacity even before the swallows have started to lay.

To those so fortunate as to have these valuable and attractive birds still nesting about their buildings it is suggested that, during dry spells in early summer when nest construction is under way, a bucket of water be dumped from time to time on clay-like soil, to create a muddy spot near the birds' building operations. The pleasure of watching the birds as they gather the mud pellets and carry them to their nests amply compensates one for the slight labour involved.

A novice could confuse this swallow with a Barn Swallow. However, a Barn Swallow has a deeply forked tail, and this bird's is nearly square. Their respective plumage markings are also quite distinctive, the buff rump patch worn by the Cliff Swallow being a good field mark; the Barn Swallow's rump is blue-black.

Our breeding Cliff Swallows are of the subspecies *Hirundo pyrrhonota pyrrhonota*. Twice in fall (in Halifax County on 4 October 1971, and on Seal Island on 8 October 1973) and once in spring (Seal Island on 6 June 1979) there have been reports by several observers of individual swallows with the very pale rump characteristic of *Hirundo pyrrhonota hypopolia* of central and northwestern North America. Vagrants from that region are not unexpected, especially in late fall.

Cave Swallow

Hirundo fulva Vieillot

Status Five records. In 1968 on Sable Island, Christel and Norman Bell noticed five swallows on 11 May and nine on 17-19 May that seemed "odd." Later that month Ian A. McLaren saw "Cliff Swallows" with pale throats and on 21 June he found a dead bird identifiable as a Cave Swallow. The following year, up to five birds were seen on Sable Island from 13 to 30 June, at times perched on a clothesline with other swallows, including Cliff Swallows (the Bells and E. Garvey). Since then there have been three more records. On 16 May 1971 Ian A. McLaren and party collected one on Seal Island. In summer 1982 there were two well-documented sight records: one was among Cliff Swallows at Louisbourg on 9 July, seen by a party of birding tourists led by Bret Whitney and David Wolf, and the other was at Cherry Hill Beach, Lunenburg County, on 14 August, where it was spotted by Lisë and Shirley Cohrs amongst a flock of Barn Swallows eating beach flies.

Remarks The normal range of this bird lies far south of Nova Scotia in the extreme southern United States, Mexico, parts of South America, and islands in the Caribbean Sea. It is distinguished from our Cliff Swallow by its pale throat and dark forehead and rump. Both specimens appear to be attributable to the Cuban subspecies, *Hirundo fulva cavicola* (W.E. Godfrey, letter to I.A. McLaren, 16 August 1971). How these birds, otherwise unrecorded on the east coast north of Florida, came to be here is a mystery; perhaps they became associated with migrant flocks of Cliff Swallows.

Barn Swallow PLATE 25

Hirundo rustica Linnaeus

Status Common in summer. Breeds. Barn Swallows generally arrive in the second half of April (average 23 April, earliest 10 April). They are found throughout the province in summer, especially in farming districts. Gatherings of migrants are often seen from mid-August through mid-September, but stragglers are frequent in this species, routinely last seen in November (average 14 November, latest 30 November). One on the Halifax East Christmas Bird Count on 19 December 1981 was well beyond these limits, and a bird on Sable Island on 9 February 1969 was thoroughly unexpected.

Description *Length:* 15-19 cm. *Adult male:* Upperparts iridescent blue-black; forehead, throat and upper breast rufous chestnut; rest of underparts buff; tail deeply forked, with white spots near tip of all but central feathers. *Adult female:* Similar but underparts paler and tail less forked.

Breeding *Nest:* Made of mud pellets and grass cemented together, lined with grass and feathers, and varying in shape to suit its location in a barn or other building. Usually it nests inside a barn, high up on the top rafters, but quite frequently lower sites will be chosen. It is not uncommon to find a nest outdoors under the protection of the roof of a house verandah, but such locations, for obvious reasons, are not always tolerated. *Eggs:* 4-6; white, spotted rather uniformly with light brown. Nesting begins during the second half of May; one was seen gathering mud pellets on 20 May 1951 at Black River, Kings County. If the pair is successful, at least two broods are raised each year; and considering the lateness of some nestings, one wonders if they do not sometimes raise three. For instance, on 3 September 1952 at Black River a nest containing young was noted high up on the rafters in a barn; six days later, four young Barn Swallows were seen perched on a telephone wire in front of the barn, all with traces of natal down. On 12 September 1967 Cyril Coldwell watched four young leave a nest in his barn at Gaspereau, Kings County. They perched on the rafters and the parents fed them there all that day. One plausible explanation for these very late nestings is that they followed unsuccessful second nestings.

Range Breeds from central Alaska to Labrador and Newfoundland, south to the southern United States and northern Mexico. Winters from Mexico to Argentina. Found also in the Old World.

Remarks Evidence that migration is well under way by mid-August is provided by the following observation made on the late afternoon of 17 August 1939 at Moore's Meadows, just west of Kentville. An immense congregation of swallows was seen swarming over the mosquito-infested marsh. Their numbers were simply incredible; the air was filled with them. Of the hundreds that circled near enough for identification, all were Barn Swallows. They were feeding actively over an area of 200 ha, and as the shadows lengthened they began dropping into the clumps of alders that bordered the meadow, where they presumably spent the night. Late in the afternoon of the following day this marsh was revisited, but no swallows were to be found.

The Barn Swallow is readily distinguished from our other swallows by its deeply forked tail and its cinnamon-brown underparts.

Family Corvidae

Gray Jay PLATE 26

Perisoreus canadensis (Linnaeus)

Status Uncommon resident. Breeds. Fairly common in coniferous woodlands of the interior, decidedly uncommon along the North Mountain range bordering the Bay of Fundy and practically absent in the Annapolis Valley. Fairly common throughout Cape Breton Island but only where evergreen forests are dominant. Although sedentary in its habits and usually seen in pairs (or family groups particularly during May and June), it does on rare occasions gather into flocks that wander aimlessly about the countryside, showing up in places where it has not been seen in years. In September and October small flocks often appear from the New Brunswick-Nova Scotia border, around the Bay of Fundy to Yarmouth. In 1982 there was a particularly large influx of jays at Cape Sable Island and down the entire South Shore during October.

Description *Length:* 28-33 cm. *Adults:* Plumage soft neutral gray, loose and fluffy; crown brownish gray; forehead, throat and face white; tail medium gray, slightly tipped with lighter gray. *Immatures:* Plain sooty gray, darkest on head, paler toward tail; tip of tail brownish white.

Breeding *Nest:* A compact, bulky, well-built structure of twigs, beard lichen and many beakfuls of decayed wood, thickly lined with hair and feathers. It is placed 1-4 m up in firs or spruces in open woods. *Eggs:* 2-4, usually 3; white, distinctly or obscurely spotted with light olive-brown over entire surface. Nest construction takes place leisurely during March and laying begins in early April. I examined many nests, and found Ruffed Grouse feathers used for nest lining far more often than any others. Rotten wood is invariably used in nest construction, presumably as insulation. When their nests are endangered, most bird species show anxiety and anger through behaviours ranging from mild scolding to overt acts of hostility, such as displayed by Goshawks. In so doing they tell the world their nest is nearby. The canny jays take a different approach. An incubating jay will sometimes sit and allow a human intruder to stroke its back while its mate, which may be perched close by, will not emit a sound or show the slightest concern. The jays have probably learned through the millennia that such behaviour is the best way to avoid nest detection.

Range Breeds from Alaska to northern Labrador and Newfoundland, north to the limit of trees and south to Nova Scotia, New Hampshire, northern Michigan and northern California. Winters mainly in its breeding range, occasionally wandering somewhat south of it.

Remarks None of our wild birds is more bold or impudent than the Gray Jay. It will commonly enter a camp to steal food when the owner's back is turned, and the trapper despises it because it steals the bait from his traps. However, its confiding and trustful nature and friendliness, even if gastronomically inspired, has endeared it to all who enjoy the outdoors and the wildlife they find there.

Blue Jay   PLATE 26

Cyanocitta cristata (Linnaeus)

Status Common resident. Breeds. In summer it is found more commonly in wooded areas where it breeds, remote from human settlement. In fall and winter it is much more evident to man, having left its summer haunts in search of better feeding grounds—cornfields are particularly attractive to it. In winter it often comes to feeding stations, where it competes greedily with other birds. Although Blue Jays are generally considered nonmigratory, there is a definite trend southward at winter's approach that is more pronounced in some years than others, which explains why Blue Jays vary in local abundance from winter to winter.

Description *Length:* 28-31 cm. *Adults:* Head with conspicuous blue crest; back purplish blue; tail blue, barred with black, all but two central feathers broadly tipped with white; wings blue with bold white and black bars; belly grayish white; face and throat white; a narrow black collar passes around neck and over the breast.

Breeding *Nest:* A rough, fairly compact framework of twigs lined with fine rootlets, usually built in conifers but not infrequently in apple and other deciduous trees or in thick ornamental shrubbery. *Eggs:* 3-6, usually 4 or 5; showing considerable variation in size, the colour ranging from olive-green to brownish gray, thickly marked with distinct spots of various shades of cinnamon-brown. Nest construction usually begins during the second half of April and laying starts about 1 May. In spring 1950 a pair built a nest in a climbing rose within 50 cm of my window, affording an excellent opportunity to view its progress: the first twigs were placed early on 18 May; the first egg was laid on 22 May about 10 a.m. and thereafter one was laid daily through 25 May; the first egg hatched on the morning of 10 June, and all were hatched by 8 p.m. that evening; the first youngster left the nest on 30 June and by the morning of 1 July all had left and were seen about my garden that day; on 2 July and thereafter neither young nor adults were seen again.

Range Breeds from central Alberta to Newfoundland, south to Florida, the Gulf Coast and Texas. Winters throughout most of its breeding range.

Remarks Noisy and conspicuous most of the year, Blue Jays are quiet and secretive while nesting, behaving much like their cousins the Gray Jays.

In addition to the familiar *jay-jay-jay,* they have a variety of calls, some most pleasing.

Bird-banding has shed light on the Blue Jay's life span. One was tagged and raised as a pet in June 1921; it was released repeatedly but always returned, and remained a pet until its death on 30 June 1936 at the age of 15 years. Another wild bird was captured and banded on 2 January 1922, and retaken on 17 November 1933, making it at least 12 years old.

Black-billed Magpie

Pica pica (Linnaeus)

Status One record. A bird on Brier Island on 18 May 1973 was discovered by Wickerson Lent and photographed by Wayne Neily. The Shelburne *Coastguard* of 7 December 1961 said another had visited the property of Anita Hopkins in Shelburne that autumn, but details of date and exact circumstances are lacking.

Remarks This large (50 cm), flashy black-and-white bird is a resident of central and western North America. Birds seen in the east are often assumed to have escaped from captivity, and although the Brier Island bird was clearly "wild" when it was seen, it could have come from such an event.

Jackdaw

Corvus monedula Linnaeus

Status Three records. An individual found on Brier Island on 6 May 1984 by Nancy Blair and John Kearney was also seen by Roger Foxall and photographed by Ian A. McLaren as a first Canadian record. On 20 May of the same year Roger Foxall found a Jackdaw about 90 km away, on Bon Portage Island, which he felt was a different individual. It remained and was seen by several birders until 24 May. On 15 December 1984 another Jackdaw was discovered in Halifax, subsequently seen by many other observers. It should also be noted that Sylvia Fullerton observed very briefly what she took to be a Jackdaw at Cherry Hill Beach in spring 1983. Because the sighting seemed so improbable, she did not report it for publication, although she mentioned it to a number of friends.

Remarks The Jackdaw is a small, black, gray-naped Eurasian crow. The 1984 records were among the first of a number of occurrences in eastern North America, evidently representing a natural, transoceanic vagrancy (Smith 1985).

American Crow   PLATE 26

Corvus brachyrhynchos Brehm

Status Common resident. Breeds. Crows can be abundant to very common throughout agricultural and coastal areas but uncommon to rare in interior wooded regions, especially in winter. They are most commonly seen in autumn. Some are resident, others show migratory tendencies, more so in some years than in others, perhaps depending upon the severity of the winter or other less obvious factors. A marked increase in numbers noted in Kings County on 5 March 1939 suggested an influx of spring migrants. A movement of 100 or more was recorded on 13 November 1981 at Petite Riviere, Lunenburg County, and 100-150 birds per day were moving through Seal Island on 10-15 October 1982.

Description *Length:* 43-53 cm. *Adults:* Entire plumage black, only slightly iridescent; underparts duller.

Breeding *Nest:* Composed of sticks and coarse weed stalks, lined with beard lichen, sheep's wool or the matted hair of other animals. Usually placed high up in tall trees but occasionally in lower ones; a marked preference is shown for conifers but often nests are built in deciduous trees. Construction begins as early as late March; birds were first seen carrying nesting material on 28, 27, 20 and 23 March in the years 1944-1947 respectively. *Eggs:* 4-7; usually 5; bluish green, thickly marked and washed with various shades of dark brown. Laying begins in the second half of April and continues well into May. An unusually located nest that contained five fresh eggs was seen on the Grand Pré meadows in Kings County on 30 April 1954, built not over 6 m up in a stunted apple tree in the open, about half a kilometre from any other tree. At a distance of 150 m or so, the bird left silently and flew out of sight; it did not reappear while I was at the nest. On 29 April 1902 a set of five fresh eggs was collected from a nest approximately 13 m up in a large spruce. In this case, both birds circled overhead, scolding vociferously.

Range Breeds across Canada from Newfoundland to British Columbia (except along the Pacific coast) and south to Florida, the Gulf Coast and California. Winters from southern Canada southward.

Remarks Few persons have anything good to say of this bird. Its common call is discordant; it is known to steal eggs and young from the nests of valuable songbirds; it plagues the farmer by pulling his newly planted corn and has been found guilty of picking holes in ripening pears and apples and of devouring cherries. Yet all of this crow's deeds are by no means "bad" as judged by human standards. He destroys innumerable meadow voles and great quantities of grasshoppers, crickets, other noxious insect pests—this is what he is doing when seen on the farmer's fields in summer and fall. These beneficial activities often pass unnoticed. Crows are not given protection by law anywhere in Canada but they require none, being well able to fend for themselves despite man's hostility toward them.

It is commonly believed that our winter crows are immigrants from further north that arrive to replace our summer residents, which by then have moved south. This may be true to some extent, but at least some members of our winter population remain to breed, as established by the following incident: On 17 February 1936 one was trapped at Gaspereau, Kings County, banded and released; on 4 June 1941 the same bird was shot at its nest at Lower Canard, Kings County.

The vocal performance of this bird is more varied and meaningful than many people realize. The two notes most commonly heard are the familiar *caw* and what might be described as a brief rattle. This second note, most frequently heard during nesting season, is its "song" and is believed to be part of the bird's courtship behaviour. Its ability to express different emotions when it *caws* is apt to be underestimated. On a duck-hunting expedition on the Grand Pré meadows, I saw a pair of black ducks alight in a slough. As I stalked them, a passing crow stopped and circled overhead, giving vent to several loud, sharply enunciated *caws* that clearly indicated alarm. Its cry was interpreted by the ducks as a danger signal, for they immediately flushed, even though they were still well out of my range. When a crow discovers any one of the larger owls asleep in the daytime, it will begin cawing on a note that seems to indicate anger. When heard by other crows, this call gets an immediate response, for they come on rapidly beating wings from all directions to take part in mobbing their common enemy. At other times the *caw* seems to be given in a conversational manner.

Fish Crow

Corvus ossifragus Wilson

Status Three sight records. Mrs. Betty June Smith saw a Fish Crow at Cape Sable near the light station on 23 February 1966. Her attention was attracted by its strange call, "a broken, two-syllabled cry." The bird was in company with American Crows, allowing her to observe that it was decidedly smaller. Another small, thin-beaked, "smoother" crow, its voice a distinctly nasal *"ca-ar,"* was seen on Sable Island on 12 January 1967. It was very tame (unlike the few Common Crows resident on the island), allowing Christel and Norman Bell to approach within 3 m of it. On 23 September 1978, Shirley Cohrs, already familiar with the species in Florida, saw a calling Fish Crow at Cheticamp, Inverness County.

Remarks Although these sight records cannot be taken as confirmation of the species in Nova Scotia, they are strongly suggestive. The species has in recent years occurred in southern Maine but is not notably migratory. Observers should be alert to field marks other than its distinctive call—its glossier and more iridescent plumage and its habit of hovering—but probably only specimen records would be completely convincing.

Common Raven   PLATE 26

Corvus corax Linnaeus

Status Fairly common resident. Breeds. Ravens occur over the entire province and are usually seen in isolated pairs or alone throughout the year. Sometimes they are common during fall and winter in the restricted localities to which they are drawn by unusually good feeding conditions.

Description *Length:* 53-67 cm. *Adults:* Entire plumage black, with bluish iridescence; feathers on throat narrow and elongated; long wedge-shaped tail.

Breeding *Nest:* Made of coarse sticks, reeds and decayed vegetable matter, lined with soft materials such as sheep's wool, beard lichen, fur and grass. A pair tends to use the same nest site year after year, with new material being added by way of repair each spring. The nests are built in large trees or on cliffsides at elevations of 3-20 m or more. Of 21 nests examined, 10 were in hemlocks, 4 in spruces, 3 on ledges on cliffs, 2 in Yellow Birches, 1 in a poplar and 1 in a beech. *Eggs:* 4-7, usually 4 or 5; pale bluish green or olive-green, dashed or blotched with dark olive-brown more densely about the larger end. Nest construction or repair starts in early March; a raven was seen at Cambridge, Kings County, on 8 March 1944 carrying a stick at least 30 cm long in its beak. On 17 March 1946 at Gaspereau, Kings County, one was seen gathering sheep's wool for nest lining; this nest was later discovered and the five eggs it contained hatched on 18 April. Early in March 1950 at Gaspereau, Cyril Coldwell saw one pull wool from the rump of a live sheep and fly off with a beakful to a nest in the farm woodlot; the young flew from this nest on 11 May. Of the 21 nests examined, 2 held clutches of seven eggs; 5 held six; 6 held five; 7 held four; and 1 on a cliffside contained three fresh eggs, probably an incomplete set.

Range Circumpolar. In North America, breeds from northwestern Alaska, the Canadian Arctic and Greenland, south to Maine, northern Georgia, northern Michigan, North Dakota and through the western United States and Mexico to Nicaragua. Winters in most of its breeding range.

Remarks In addition to its much larger size, its long and wedge-shaped tail distinguishes it from a crow. Its raucous croak is quite different from the softer caw of the smaller bird. Taverner (1934) says of this bird: "The Raven holds aloof from the haunts of man. As civilization has advanced into the primeval vastnesses, the Raven has retired and is still today what he was in the beginning, a bird of the wilderness." While the foregoing may be true of ravens in other parts of Canada, it certainly does not apply here. None of the 21 nests referred to above was remote from agricultural development, and the large majority of them were built in close proximity to farming communities.

Ravens seem to possess uncanny powers, not only to detect food, but to pass the word along to others of their kind widely separated from one another. This is borne out by an incident recounted to me by a deer hunter: After dressing a deer he had killed the first morning out from camp, he hung it in a clump of thick spruces and placed boughs over the carcass to conceal it from any raven that might pass that way. None was seen at that time. Returning two days later to pick it up, he found the carcass picked almost clean and, perched on boulders and trees in close proximity to the cache, 40-50 heavily glutted ravens.

During May 1916 a pair was seen carrying food to their young in a nest. Unfortunately, the female was shot late in the afternoon. In order to determine whether the male would carry on alone or desert the young, the nest was visited about nine o'clock the following morning. On reaching the site, it was surprising and pleasing to find two ravens caring for the young just as though nothing had happened. Possibly, the male had quickly located a new mate to share his domestic responsibilities, or possibly he had located a "helper"—among the Corvidae, "helpers" at the nest are sometimes recruited from the offspring of previous years.

PLATE 25
all adults

Barn Swallow
Page 296

Bank Swallow
Page 293

Tree Swallow
Page 290

Eastern Kingbird
Page 285

Olive-sided Flycatcher
Page 274

Yellow-bellied Flycatcher
Page 277

r Tory Peterson —

Roger Tory Peterson

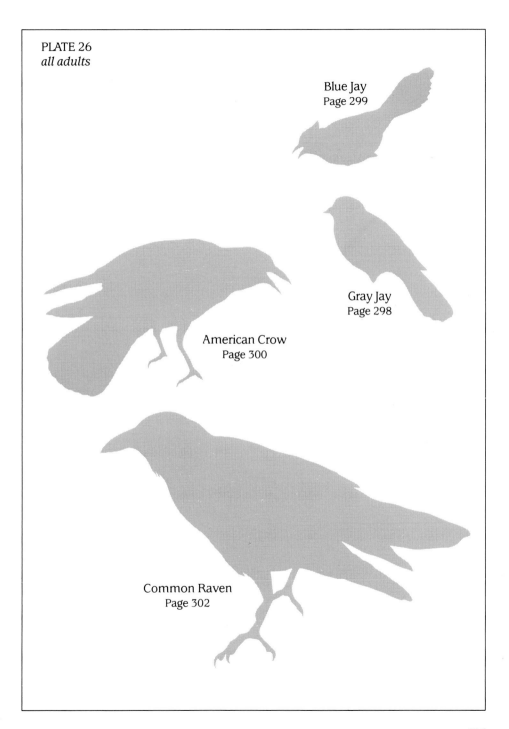

PLATE 26
all adults

Blue Jay
Page 299

Gray Jay
Page 298

American Crow
Page 300

Common Raven
Page 302

305

Although crows regularly congregate at roosts at night, this must be an uncommon practice for ravens because only twice have such gatherings come to my attention. The first was at Coldbrook, Kings County, where on 4 December 1943 I watched ravens coming in from all directions until, as darkness began to fall, an estimated 1,000 birds had gathered in a pine grove close to Highway 1. During the late afternoon of 24 June 1965 I watched hundreds flocking to a roost located somewhere on North Mountain, directly north of Waterville, Kings County. All came from the south and passed high overhead in a steady line that extended for a considerable distance.

At several places in Kings County, refuse from poultry processing plants dumped regularly during late fall and winter attracts many scavengers, including hundreds of ravens, which are very commonly seen during that period over a wide area around the dumping sites.

The most commonly known call of the raven is its coarse croak but it has other notes, some far from discordant. One is a bell-like call, rich and pleasing to the ear, often given while the bird is high in flight and appears to be turning somersaults (righting itself without turning over completely), an acrobatic feat apparently done in play.

Ravens do not wander far from where they were raised. To collect information regarding their range and other aspects of their everyday lives, Cyril Coldwell undertook a study that produced data of great interest and value. Between 1965 and 1970 he captured, banded and released no fewer than 2,006 ravens, using an ingeniously constructed trap device set up on his farm at Gaspereau, Kings County. The trapping was done intermittently regardless of season as availability of bait (the viscera of slaughtered cattle) permitted. Birds that re-entered the traps before three months had elapsed were classed as "repeats" and not recorded. The many taken after a three-month interval were recorded as "returns." The accompanying map graphically portrays the places where 146 bands were recovered up to 1970 from birds killed or found dead. Most were recovered in Kings or nearby counties, but individuals wandered as far afield as Prince Edward Island, Cape Breton Island and Yarmouth County.

Coldwell also compiled data which support the long-held belief that ravens mate for life. No fewer than five pairs (presumably mated) entered the trap together and were later retaken at the same time, a strong indication that they have travelled together during the interim: a pair banded on 27 March 1967 was trapped again on 11 September of that year; a pair taken on 2 December 1967 was retaken on 10 February 1968; a pair taken on 22 November 1966 was trapped again on 21 August 1968; a pair trapped on 18 October 1969 was retrapped on 20 January 1970; and a pair taken on 30 November 1969 was retaken on 14 May 1970.

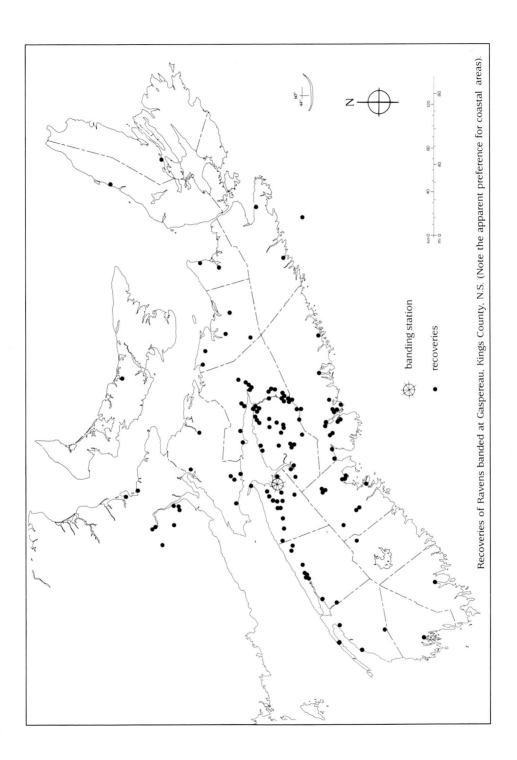

banding station

recoveries

Recoveries of Ravens banded at Gaspereau, Kings County, N.S. (Note the apparent preference for coastal areas).

Family Paridae

Black-capped Chickadee PLATE 27

Parus atricapillus Linnaeus

Status Common resident. Breeds. This familiar bird is present throughout the year and evenly distributed over the province. The winter population varies from year to year, fall emigration presumably being more pronounced in some years than in others. It is seen in the vicinity of towns and settled areas more in winter than in summer; the winter feeding stations provided by householders undoubtedly encourage this pattern.

Description *Length:* 12-14 cm. *Adults:* Entire top of head and throat black; sides of head white; back bluish gray; wings and tail feathers delicately margined with white; breast and belly white; sides buff.

Breeding *Nest:* In holes in dead trees, usually not over 3 m up. Nest boxes are rarely used. The nest cavity is lined with soft, dry moss, on which is placed a thick layer of matted small-mammal fur; rarely, plant down is used, presumably when fur is not available. Nests are most often in open woodland regions but sometimes close to human dwellings. *Eggs:* 5-9, usually 7 or 8; white, spotted with bright cinnamon-brown. On 4 May 1913 near Wolfville, one was busily excavating its nest. On 12 May 1918 at Black River, Kings County, one was seen carrying lining for the nest. Laying begins about mid-May. On 21 May 1913 at Albany, Annapolis County, a nest 1 m up in a dead birch stub contained seven fresh eggs, and on 26 May 1915 at Margaretsville, Annapolis County, a nest 3 m up in a dead birch contained eight fresh eggs. On 10 June 1917 at Sunken Lake, Kings County, a nest held newly hatched young. I have no evidence that more than a single brood is raised, but if the first nest is destroyed the pair will try again.

Range Breeds from Newfoundland, central Manitoba, southeastern Mackenzie Valley and central Alaska, south to northern New Jersey, Indiana and northwestern California. Winters in most of its breeding range.

Remarks This bird's common call proclaims its identity: *chik-a-dee-dee.* It has another call, heard more frequently in spring, a sweet two-toned whistle, *fee-bee,* given slowly and deliberately on a descending scale. This note should not be mistaken for that of a Phoebe, which does not whistle but merely utters *fee-be* explosively, with a strong accent on the first syllable.

The only species in Nova Scotia with which the Black-capped Chickadee might be confused is the Boreal Chickadee, but the latter has a brown instead of black cap and its general colouring is more brownish than grayish.

The Black-capped Chickadee is a favourite about feeding stations in winter. The acrobatic feats it performs when feeding provide endless amusement, and the trust it displays in sometimes alighting on the hand that feeds it endears it to all so favoured.

Birds are sometimes thirsty, even in winter. A row of icicles of varying sizes hung from the roof of my kitchen porch. Despite the cold of a normal day in February, the warmth of the noontime sun on the ice formation made drops of water slowly form and fall at regular intervals. A Black-capped Chickadee appeared from nowhere, hovered hummingbird-like at the tip of the icicle long enough to suck in a single drop of water as it formed and then flew off.

Boreal Chickadee   PLATE 27

Parus hudsonicus Forster

Status Fairly common resident. Breeds. Less common than the Black-capped Chickadee, it is largely restricted to coniferous woods. Occasionally, it wanders in winter and is seen at feeding stations in towns and villages remote from its normal habitat, showing particular interest in suet and peanut butter. The winter population fluctuates from year to year, perhaps the result of wandering movements induced by food shortages at irregular intervals.

Description *Length:* 13-14 cm. *Adults:* Top of head and back of neck dark brownish gray; rest of upperparts lighter brownish gray; sides pale rufous; tail and wings grayish brown; breast, belly and sides of head white; throat black; tail much more deeply notched than that of the Black-capped Chickadee.

Breeding *Nest:* Similar to that of the Black-capped Chickadee but generally located at lower heights and far more often in damp, well-shaded coniferous woods. *Eggs:* 5-7; practically indistinguishable from those of the Black-capped Chickadee but clutch size averages slightly smaller. Laying begins about 20 May and continues to about the end of the month. On 9 May 1913, on Wolfville Ridge, one was seen excavating a nest. On 30 May 1913, another nest containing seven slightly incubated eggs was examined, and on 1 June 1914 another contained seven fresh eggs; both nests were also on Wolfville Ridge, both in open woodland pastures, in natural cavities within a metre from the ground in dead stumps and with entrances from the top. The cavities are invariably lined with a layer of dry moss covered with a pouch-shaped nest of soft, matted fur.

Range Breeds in the coniferous forest of northern North America from the limit of trees, south to northern New York State, northwestern Montana and northern Washington State. Winters in most of its breeding range and irregularly further south.

Remarks The common call of this little woodland acrobat, unlike the clean-cut, well enunciated *chick-a-dee-dee* of its black-capped cousin, is a very husky rendition of *sick-a-dee-dee,* with the accent strongly on the *sick,* giving the listener the impression that the performer is suffering from a bad head cold. It also has a soft warbling song that is rarely heard, and a chattering call.

In summer they are usually seen in pairs, or in small flocks that may well be family groups. In winter they commonly associate with Golden-crowned Kinglets, Black-capped Chickadees and Red-breasted Nuthatches, all foraging together through snow-laden branches and thickets in search of the tree-infesting insects and their eggs that make up a large part of their winter fare; I have never seen any evidence of quarrelsome competition for these morsels. Watching these feathered mites on a bitterly cold day with a blizzard raging through the creaking forest, I have marvelled at how they are able to survive such adverse conditions.

Family Sittidae

Red-breasted Nuthatch   PLATE 27

Sitta canadensis Linnaeus

Status Common resident. Breeds. It is common some years, uncommon to rather rare in others and seldom seen far from coniferous woods at any season. It was common in Kings County during the winters of 1935-36 and 1945-46. It is partial to stands of immature spruce in open woods, where it spends much time working among the cones, extracting the seeds they bear in fruitful years. Large migrations of Red-breasted Nuthatches—numbers estimated sometimes in the thousands occurred in 1967, 1969, 1972, 1975 and 1981—frequently pass through the southwestern end of the province in early September, especially on Brier and Seal islands.

Description *Length:* 11-12 cm. *Adult male:* Back and wings bluish gray; crown and stripe through eye to hindneck glossy black; conspicuous white line over eye; tail feathers black with white spots near tip; throat and cheek white; rest of underparts bright cinnamon-rufous. *Adult female:* Similar but colours somewhat subdued.

Breeding *Nest:* In a hole excavated by the bird in a very rotten stub, at relatively low heights, in open coniferous woods. The cavity is lined with dry grass on which is placed a mat of fur, and the entrance is invariably smeared with sticky balsam. *Eggs:* 5-7; white, speckled with cinnamon, light brown and lavender. Excavating sometimes begins in early April, but several weeks may elapse after completion of these early nests before eggs are laid. On 10 April 1945 at White Rock, Kings County, one was seen excavating about 4 m up in a rotten stub in open evergreen woods. When the nest was visited 10 days later, the birds were not in evidence and the nest appeared to be deserted. On 20 May, a month later, it was visited again and both birds were seen carrying food to the young. On 4 May 1913 on Wolfville Ridge, two nests were being excavated; on 24 May they each contained sets of five fresh eggs. A nest at Starrs Point, Kings County, 4.5 m up in a spruce stub, contained seven fresh eggs on 24 May 1929; the nest was typical, the mat of fur in this instance from a red squirrel.

Range Breeds from southeastern Alaska, southern Yukon, southeastern Mackenzie Valley, central Quebec, and Newfoundland, south to North Carolina, northern Michigan and southern California. Occurs irregularly further south in winter.

Remarks When seen in fall and winter it is usually hobnobbing with chickadees and kinglets, all foraging in loose association through the evergreens, each member incessantly giving its call, a practice followed, presumably, to enable strays and laggards to keep in touch with the roving band.

Many writers have referred to this bird's strange custom of plastering the entrance to its nest with sticky balsam, but few have attempted to explain why it is done. There is no doubt that the bird transports the stuff in its slender bill; frequently I have been within a metre of one at nesting time and noted that the feathers nearest its bill were dark and gummed up.

Its call, *ank-ank-ank*, is similar to that of the slightly larger White-breasted Nuthatch, but higher pitched and more nasal. Its song, seldom heard except at nesting time, is a rapidly repeated series of pleasing half-musical notes.

White-breasted Nuthatch   PLATE 30

Sitta carolinensis Latham

Status Uncommon resident. Breeds. Uncommon to rare throughout the year, distribution being general. Under natural conditions it is most frequently seen from August to late October. However, those who maintain feeding stations in winter frequently attract one or more that remain throughout the season as regular patrons, thus giving the erroneous impression that this bird is a common winter resident. There was an increase in the numbers reported in the mid-1970s, peaking in 1977-78. Since then sightings have decreased once more.

Description *Length:* 13-15 cm. *Adult male:* Upperparts pale bluish gray, except top of head and nape, which are glossy black; white patches near tip of otherwise black outer tail feathers; middle tail feathers bluish gray; underparts, including sides of head, white; undertail coverts rufous. *Adult female:* Similar but top of head bluish gray and nape glossy black.

Breeding *Nest:* In a hole in tree or stump or some other cavity; composed of dry grass and dead leaves, with a lining of soft grass and sometimes feathers. Nests are sometimes located in towns and other settled areas but usually are in wooded regions far from human habitation. *Eggs:* 4-8; creamy white, evenly spotted with various shades of rufous and lavender. The first nest found in Nova Scotia, at Wolfville, was located in a natural cavity in an apple tree about 3 m up and contained four slightly incubated eggs on 26 May 1929 (A.L. Rand). Another Wolfville pair used a small opening in the wainscoting under the eaves of a house for its nest site, which the young left on 10 June 1950 (Mrs. G.R. Forbes). Other nests in recent years have been in both artificial and natural sites.

Range Resident from southern interior British Columbia across southern Canada to Nova Scotia and Prince Edward Island, south to Mexico and the Gulf States.

Remarks The nuthatch is a dapper, busy little creature that never seems at ease but is always eagerly running up and down and over the trunks and larger limbs of trees as though searching for something and determined to find it.

Nuthatches, like woodpeckers, are adept at climbing. When woodpeckers move downward, they hitch down in an awkward, jerky manner, always tail first, but the "upside-down" birds, as nuthatches are sometimes called, race down head first.

Its common call is a nasal *yank-yank-yank,* given by both male and female. Another note that is heard occasionally, mostly in spring, is a more pleasing *ha-ha-ha-ha-ha-ha,* the syllables given in rapid succession.

The only other species with which it is likely to be confused are the Red-breasted Nuthatch and the Black-capped Chickadee. The Red-breasted Nuthatch is distinguished by its black eyestripe and its bright cinnamon underparts, and the chickadee has a black bib which nuthatches lack.

Family Certhiidae

Brown Creeper   PLATE 27

Certhia americana Bonaparte

Status Fairly common resident. Breeds. Its numbers fluctuate somewhat from year to year. Distribution seems to be fairly even throughout woodland areas and it is seldom seen elsewhere. Occasionally in late fall or winter a wanderer appears at a feeding station in town or village, attracted by suet. Migratory movements do occur within its range, both in spring and fall. Ninety were counted on Seal Island on 21 April 1973 and flocks of 7-25 were passing through Seal Island daily on 13-23 October 1980.

Description *Length:* 12.5-13.5 cm. *Adults:* Upperparts brown, streaked with white and buff; tail rather long, with feathers stiff and sharply pointed; a partly hidden white area in wing; bill disproportionately long and curved; underparts white.

Breeding *Nest:* Made of twigs, moss, wood fibre, strips of bark, hair and sometimes a few feathers, and placed under and ingeniously fastened to an apron-like slab of dead bark hanging at a low height from stumps of fir or spruce in damp coniferous woods. *Eggs:* 4-8, usually 6; white, spotted with cinnamon-brown, heavier around the larger end. Laying begins about the first week in May. On 18 May 1927 two nests were found in Kings County: one at Albany held six fresh eggs, and the other, found by Austin L. Rand at Gaspereau, contained six slightly incubated eggs. The Albany nest was typically constructed and placed about 3 m up under a slab of hanging bark on a dead spruce stump in damp, mossy woods; the female was incubating, and it was the persistent singing of the male in the immediate vicinity of the nest that led to its discovery.

Range Breeds from southeastern Alaska, the central Prairie Provinces, central Ontario, southern Quebec, and Newfoundland, south to the southern Appalachian Mountains and eastern Nebraska, and in the western mountains to Central America. Winters from southern Canada southward.

Remarks This slender bird with a mottled brown back blends well with the bark over which it climbs in the course of its daily routine. When feeding, Brown Creepers have a characteristic habit of starting at the base of a tree and working upward, always going around and around as though ascending a spiral staircase. When the desired height is reached, they suddenly drop to the bottom of another tree nearby and start their diligent quest for food all over again.

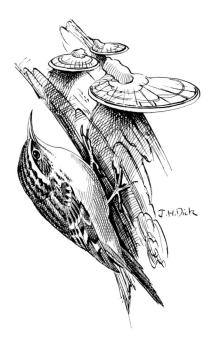

Brown Creeper

Family Troglodytidae

Rock Wren

Salpinctes obsoletus (Say)

Status One record. On 4 October 1980 on Seal Island an individual was found by John Kearney and Nancy Blair. It was subsequently seen by others and photographed by Bruce Mactavish.

Remarks This large, grayish wren of semiarid regions of western North America has strayed to Massachusetts but has been found nowhere else in Canada east of southern Ontario.

Carolina Wren

Thryothorus ludovicianus (Latham)

Status Three sight records. Four individuals have been reported, all on Seal Island: one on 6 October 1974 by John and Shirley Cohrs, two on 15 October 1975 by Charles R.K. Allen and one on 16 May 1984 by Eric Cooke and Sylvia Fullerton.

Remarks This large, rusty and buff wren with a strong white eyestripe is resident in the eastern United States, and wanders routinely as far north as Maine and southern Quebec. Our records indicate that it has a tendency to move during the normal migration season of other birds.

House Wren

Troglodytes aedon Vieillot

Status Rare vagrant, very rare in summer. Since the first edition of this book (1961), when only six records had occurred since 1932, over 150 House Wrens have been reported in the province. A few have been in spring (15 birds from 8 April to 3 June), the rest mostly in fall (between 5 September and 28 November) and all but five were in southwestern Nova Scotia — in Queens, Shelburne, Yarmouth and Digby counties. The majority were on Seal and Cape Sable islands, although nine were seen on Brier Island on 5 October 1975. During the same year, one or two were seen each day on Seal Island from 26 to 29 September; the following year, 34 individuals were recorded on Seal Island between 10 September and 7 November. In addition to these migration-season records, there have been four reports since 1950 of summer birds, three of them singing males engaged in nesting activities.

Remarks This bird's normal breeding range lies south and west of Nova Scotia, but it would not be surprising if one day someone discovers it nesting here. It normally nests in tree cavities but readily accepts a man-made box. Males are known to build several nests to attract one or more females.

I watched one wren's typical behaviour for some time on 28 June 1967 in Mrs. Houghton White's garden in Liverpool, Queens County, where it had first appeared a few days earlier. Presumably a male, it sang almost incessantly while I was there. It was seen lugging twigs into not only one but two (unoccupied) Tree Swallow nest boxes and flying from one to the other as though declaring its ownership of both. A male House Sparrow alighted on one of these boxes but didn't remain long because it was immediately attacked by the wren and was last seen beating a hasty retreat with its diminutive, irate assailant in hot pursuit. The wren was obviously waiting for a mate to show up but none came that season.

Winter Wren   PLATE 27

Troglodytes troglodytes (Linnaeus)

Status Uncommon in summer, rare in winter. Breeds. Spring arrivals are readily detected in places where none had wintered, usually in the second half of April (average 20 April, earliest 31 March). It occurs regularly from late April to November throughout the coniferous wooded areas, particularly those with damp, mossy terrain, and it is also partial to slashings in clearings and forest openings. Winter records are numerous, with single birds seen on many Christmas Bird Counts and several records of lingering wrens in January. The latest date is 6 February 1975 at Lockeport, which suggests that few survive the height of winter, but birds on Bon Portage Island on 6 March 1960 and 30 March 1961 could have survived in that densely forested site.

Description *Length:* 11-12 cm. *Adults:* Upperparts cinnamon-brown; wings and short, stubby tail barred with blackish gray; back also barred with faint gray; a light buff line over the eye; underparts light buff, the flanks and belly heavily barred with blackish gray.

Breeding *Nest:* Bulky and compact, composed of fine twigs, moss and strips of bark, lined with fine grasses and feathers. Usually placed under the roots of an old stump or hidden in the mossy bank of a sluggish stream or other wet places. *Eggs:* 5-7; white or creamy white, finely and sparingly speckled with reddish brown. Piers (1892b) describes a nest and set of six eggs he collected at Kidston Lake in Halifax County on 22 May 1891. It was embedded in the damp sphagnum moss on a boulder over which water was dripping, and sparingly lined with grass and feathers. On 11 June 1894 another nest that contained young was found close to the same location (Piers 1897). Near Fisher Lake, Annapolis County, Rand (1930) located a nest among the upturned roots of a hemlock in well shaded, moss-grown woods on 3 August 1928; the late date suggests a second or even third nesting attempt.

Range Breeds from the Aleutian Islands, southern Alaska, northern British Columbia, northern Ontario, central Quebec, and Newfoundland, south to the southern Appalachians, central Michigan and central California. Winters mainly in the United States south to Florida and the Gulf Coast; in the west from the Aleutian Islands to southern California. Found also in the Old World.

Remarks This little brown bird is far more often heard than seen. A denizen of wet, mossy, tangled undergrowth, he pours forth a song remarkable for its volume, duration and variation, coming as it does from so small a throat. When the song is heard in its fullness the listener may try to find the performer but will seldom succeed because, at his approach, the song stops. A fairly long interlude will occur and then the song will be heard again, coming from another part of the bird's tangled retreat, the invasion of which the singer seems to fear. This tiny, dark brown bird has a stubby tail which it holds straight up. Its smaller size, shorter tail and more heavily barred belly distinguish it from the rare House Wren.

Sedge Wren

Cistothorus platensis (Latham)

Status Rare vagrant. The first record was a specimen collected by Charles R.K. Allen on Seal Island on 2 October 1967. On 18 November of the same year a second bird visited the feeding station of Evelyn Richardson at Villagedale, Shelburne County. Since then, 15 individuals have been documented in the province: five individuals have been in spring, four on Seal Island between 18 and 24 May and one on Brier Island on 26 May 1971; six have been on Seal Island in fall between 22 September and 10 October; very late birds were at Hartlen Point, near Dartmouth, on 5 December 1982 (J. Cohrs), and on the Christmas Bird Count at Broad Cove, Lunenburg County, on 31 December 1976 (several observers); most unusual were two singing males resident in a sedge marsh in the Town of Yarmouth during July 1975 (several observers and photographs).

Remarks The Sedge Wren, formerly known as "Short-billed Marsh Wren," is readily distinguished from the Marsh Wren by its lack of a prominent eyestripe. It evidently has nested in small numbers in New Brunswick (Squires 1976), but its normal range lies largely further west of Nova Scotia.

Marsh Wren

Cistothorus palustris (Wilson)

Status Rare vagrant, very rare in summer. Breeds. The first recorded in Nova Scotia was collected by Harold F. Tufts near Port Joli, Queens County, on 15 November 1949. It was one of three, all of which he described as being active and noisy among a stand of tall reeds *(Phragmites communis)*. The next was taken near Wallace, Cumberland County, by Lloyd Duncanson on 3 November 1953, and another was collected by

Charles R.K. Allen, at East Lawrencetown, Halifax County, on 15 February 1958. Since 1958, the Marsh Wren has been a "regular rarity," with vagrants appearing mostly on Seal Island but also consistently in the area from Cole Harbour to Chezzetcook in Halifax County. Since 1979 they have begun to nest in small numbers close to the New Brunswick border. Away from that area there are only two spring records: Brier Island on 17 May 1971 and Seal Island on 21 May 1982. Fall occurrences—35 records of about 64 birds—have been mainly in September (earliest 18 September) and October, with a few in November and December. They have appeared on Halifax East Christmas Bird Counts in 1968, 1974, 1979 and 1982, and one lingered on Cape Sable until 10 January 1967.

Description *Length:* 12-14 cm. *Adults:* Black cap and a prominent white line over the eye; back black with narrow white stripes; remainder of upperparts rufous; wings and tail grayish brown banded with dark gray; flanks buffy gray; underparts white.

Breeding *Nest:* A large egg-shaped structure with a hole on one side, woven of reeds, lined with finer material and fastened to upright cattails. Although no nests have been discovered to date in Nova Scotia, at least two singing males were found in the Amherst Point Bird Sanctuary during July and August 1979, and the next year two groups of four or five fledged young each were found there being tended by adults on 23 August (C. Desplanque). *Eggs:* 5-7; dull brown, with darker brown spots.

Range Breeds from central British Columbia, northern Alberta, southern Ontario and southeastern New Brunswick, south to the southern United States. Winters in the United States and Mexico.

Remarks It was formerly known as the "Long-billed Marsh Wren." As its name suggests, it frequents marshy places where tall aquatic vegetation predominates. To establish racial identity, three birds collected between 1949 and 1958 were sent to the Carnegie Museum, where they were examined by Kenneth C. Parkes. The result of his examination is somewhat surprising. He found that the Port Joli bird (1949) belongs to the nominate race *Cistothorus palustris palustris,* that normally inhabits the Atlantic coastal strip from New York State to Virginia, which suggests that it was probably carried to Nova Scotia by strong southerly gales. The Wallace specimen (1953) is closest to *C. p. palustris* but shows evidence of intergradation with *Cistothorus palustris waynei.* According to Parkes, this indicates that the bird was a stray from the population along the Virginia coast, where these races meet. The East Lawrencetown bird (1957), on the other hand, is definitely of the race *Cistothorus palustris dissaeiptus,* the form that breeds in New Brunswick and New England. In the field, observers might be able to distinguish the white-breasted coastal birds *(C. p. palustris)* from the buffy-breasted inland birds *(C. p. dissaeiptus),* but the possibility of other races in the province complicates matters.

Family Muscicapidae

Subfamily Sylviinae

Golden-crowned Kinglet   PLATE 27

Regulus satrapa Lichtenstein

Status Common resident. Breeds. It is widely distributed throughout coniferous woodlands, where its numbers vary from year to year, but in some localities it is uncommon to rare during an entire breeding season. It becomes more evident in fall and winter. During September, fall migrants are encountered in large flocks moving through the woods and over the offshore islands. There were hundreds on Seal Island on 8-23 October 1980, and 500 or more were on Brier Island on 10 October 1983. Many remain during winter, when they are often the only bird encountered in deep woods, their "sleigh bell" calls betraying their presence in the tall spruces. Return migration in spring is evident in records from mid-April to mid-May on Sable Island.

Description *Length:* 9-10 cm. *Adult male:* A broad stripe of bright orange on top of head with stripes of yellow and black bordering it; back olive-green, wings and tail darker; two grayish white wing bars; underparts whitish gray. *Adult female:* Similar but orange on crown replaced with bright yellow. *Both sexes:* White eyebrow lines.

Breeding *Nest:* Pensile from near the end of a long branch of a large spruce, well concealed among thick clusters of drooping twigs to which it is attached, at heights of 2-12 m or more, in evergreen woods. It is ingeniously constructed, the foundation being of green moss, strips of fine bark, wood fibre, plant down, hairs and lichens, all compactly interwoven, with a lining of feathers exquisitely arranged so as to curl up and over the entrance, which is on the top. Feathers from the Ruffed Grouse are most commonly used, but I recall one nest that was beautifully lined with feathers from the back of a Blue Jay. The interior is comparatively large and spherical, but the opening is small, an arrangement necessary to accommodate the large family it is destined to hold. *Eggs:* 8-10, usually 9; white or creamy white, lightly specked and wreathed principally around the larger end with light brown or pale lavender. Of 34 nests I have recorded, 22 contained nine eggs, 9 had ten, and 3 held sets of eight; laying was complete in all, but the last 3 were delayed nesting attempts. The earliest date in my records for the beginning of nest construction is 10 April but 16 April is average. Laying begins about 1 May. My earliest record for a complete set is 12 May 1913, when four sets of 10 eggs and one of 9 were examined on Wolfville Ridge, all the eggs being fresh. If the first and second nests are lost, the pair will attempt a third. If the third is lost, they will sometimes start construction of a fourth nest, but this one probably will not be finished. Two third nests in which laying was complete, with eight fresh eggs each, were examined on 30 June 1915 and 29 June 1917. These two nests were not typical, however; they were loosely constructed as though put together in haste.

Range Breeds in coniferous forests from southern Alaska, the southern Yukon, northern Alberta, central Manitoba, southern Quebec, and Newfoundland, south to North Carolina in the mountains, northern Michigan, and southern California. Winters in southern Canada, the United States and Mexico.

Remarks The female appears to do all the incubating, while the male spends his time wandering about in a desultory manner and without animation within about 50 m of the nest tree, his notes low and subdued as though he were talking to himself. But with amazing timing the female leaves the nest about every 15 minutes and hurries to join him. Then his whole manner changes. His notes become spirited and, when they meet, he immediately offers her food, which she accepts with fluttering wings suggestive of a fledgling. During his search for more food she trails close behind, and both are extremely noisy. He feeds her four or five times in the manner described and then suddenly the excitement subsides and she is off in a bee-line to her nest, where she remains for another 15 minutes, after which the performance is repeated. Whether this pattern continues to be followed during the inclemency of a rain storm, I am unable to say.

The song, like a cut-short song of a Ruby-crowned Kinglet, is quieter and descends toward the end in tone and volume.

Ruby-crowned Kinglet   PLATE 27

Regulus calendula (Linnaeus)

Status Fairly common in summer, very rare in winter. Breeds. It appears among the early spring migrants (average 19 April, earliest 7 April); a bird on Cape Sable on 28 March 1964 was unusually early. In summer it is widely distributed throughout evergreen woodlands. It leaves in September and October, numbers generally peaking during the first two weeks of October. Individuals may linger throughout November and into December, having been recorded on Christmas Bird Counts on occasion. There are also a number of January records, and one came regularly to a feeder in Brooklyn, Queens County, until at least early February 1966.

Description *Length:* 9-10 cm. *Adult male:* Partially concealed ruby patch on crown; upperparts olive-green; tail and wings darker; wing with two grayish white bars; underparts grayish white. *Adult female:* Similar but lacks ruby mark on crown. *Both sexes:* White eye ring but no eyebrow stripe.

Breeding *Nest:* Usually semi-pensile, otherwise similar in appearance and construction to that of the Golden-crowned Kinglet, but in a different location. This bird usually places its nest near the top of a thick, slender spruce, close to the trunk, 5-10 m from the ground, in coniferous woods or open groves sometimes close to human habitation. *Eggs:* 5-9, usually 8; pale buff or creamy white, spotted very indistinctly with specks of light brown chiefly about the larger end. Nest construction begins about 1 May, and sets are complete by 24 May, on which date in 1929, an

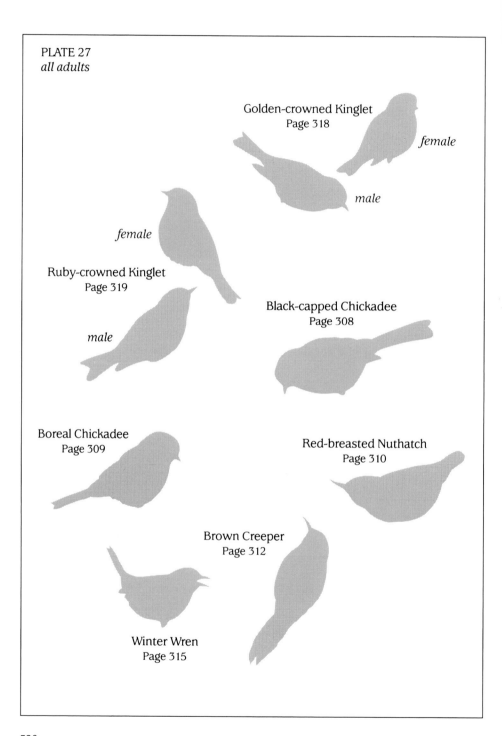

PLATE 27
all adults

Golden-crowned Kinglet
Page 318

female

male

female

Ruby-crowned Kinglet
Page 319

Black-capped Chickadee
Page 308

male

Boreal Chickadee
Page 309

Red-breasted Nuthatch
Page 310

Brown Creeper
Page 312

Winter Wren
Page 315

er Tory Peterson

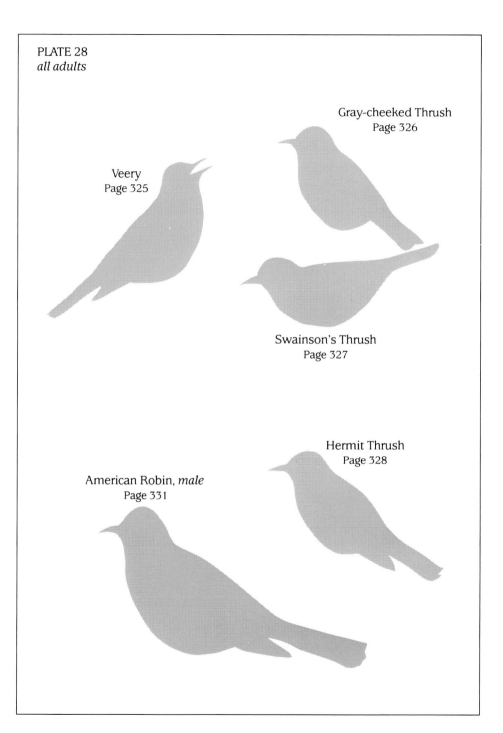

PLATE 28
all adults

Gray-cheeked Thrush
Page 326

Veery
Page 325

Swainson's Thrush
Page 327

Hermit Thrush
Page 328

American Robin, *male*
Page 331

unusually located nest containing eight fresh eggs was examined near Wolfville. It was partly pensile and partly saddled on a large spruce limb about 3 m out and about 6 m from the ground, and admirably concealed among a thick cluster of twigs to which it was loosely fastened. The female had been seen carrying nesting material to this nest on 5 May. On 7 June 1916 a female was seen carrying nesting material to her second nest on Wolfville Ridge; the first had been destroyed by a red squirrel.

Range Breeds in coniferous forests from northern Alaska to Newfoundland, south to northern Maine, southern Ontario and southern California. Winters from New Jersey (occasionally further north) and British Columbia to Mexico.

Remarks The outstanding characteristic of this little male monarch is its song. There are other birds whose songs are just as sweet and varied, but considering the size of the performer, none can match it for volume. Few people know this extremely active and nervous little bundle of energy, next in size to our hummingbird, by sight, but many have heard its song, perhaps caught a glimpse of it high in the top of a conifer and marvelled at its torrent of song. The full song has three distinct parts, but one must be close and there must be no wind if one is to have the benefit of the full rendition. It starts with a low, nervous *tse-tse-tse,* and continues with a more spirited *chirr-chirr-chirr* followed by a gay, rollicking and far-flung *liberty-liberty-liberty,* as though it were proclaiming its ecstasy to the whole world. The final notes are the loudest, and often, because of distance or wind, they are the only part of the song that is heard. Should one wander too close to its well-hidden nest, it will scold with a monotonous *chir-r chir-r chir-r.*

Blue-gray Gnatcatcher

Polioptila caerulea (Linnaeus)

Status Rare vagrant. It was first seen by Donald H. Giffin in August 1938 at Goldboro, Guysborough County. Second and third sightings were by Israel J. Pothier (two on 10 October 1957 at Melvern Square, Annapolis County) and Gordon MacLeod (one on 30 August 1958 at Wine Harbour, Guysborough County). Since 1964 it has been reported in most years. Nine were seen on Seal Island on 25 May 1975, but most sightings are of single birds from throughout the province. Among them have been 13 reports of about 23 birds in spring and early summer (23 April to 28 June) and 30 or more reports of about 50 birds from late summer to early winter (2 August to 27 December). Several have been photographically documented. An unprecedented shower of gnatcatchers descended on Nova Scotia in the fall of 1984, when at least 20 were seen.

Remarks It is an active, diminutive creature, about the size of a kinglet. It has a very long tail, trimmed with white, which it uses proficiently in its gyrations as it whirls about in pursuit of gnat-size insects. It breeds as far north as Massachusetts and northern Vermont but appears to be extending its range northward.

Subfamily Turdinae

Northern Wheatear

Oenanthe oenanthe (Linnaeus)

Status Rare vagrant. The 12 records, some confirmed by photographs, are as follows: 16 August 1969 at Five Islands, Colchester County (W. and P. Hemeon); 11 August 1972 at Sydney (I. MacGregor); 19 September 1973 at Moser River, Halifax County (B. Sabean); 26 May 1975 on Sable Island (I.A. McLaren et al.); 26 September 1975 on Seal Island (several observers); 18-24 June 1977 on Sable Island (H. Ross); 17 September 1977 at Matthews Lake, Shelburne County (G. Perry and R. Turner); 25 September to 4 October, 1981 on Brier Island (several observers); 12 October 1982 at Argyle Head, Yarmouth County (C.R.K. Allen and P.R. Dobson); 23-25 May 1983 on Seal Island (several observers); 14 October 1983 on Seal Island (E. Cooke and S. Fullerton); and early October 1984 on Sable Island (E. Dobson).

Remarks This Eurasian species also breeds in arctic and subarctic Canada, from which it normally migrates to Europe. Breeding males are pale gray above and buff below, with a black mask, black wings, a white rump and a black tail with white basal patches. Females and winter males are dull brown above, with a white eye stripe, and buff below, but retain the white rump and black and white tail. It has been most often seen here along open shorelines, flitting from place to place, then pausing in upright posture with much "teetering," in the manner of a Spotted Sandpiper.

Eastern Bluebird   PLATE 30

Sialia sialis (Linnaeus)

Status Rare transient, very rare in summer. Formerly bred. When it was regular, it arrived during the second half of March and remained until the second half of October, with stragglers later. It was more frequent then near human habitation. During recent decades its numbers have markedly decreased in Nova Scotia and throughout its range in North America. This decrease is attributed to its inability to compete successfully with the more aggressive European Starling which covets and fights for the available nest sites needed by the gentler bluebird. The last nesting record was at Loch Broom, Pictou County, in 1957 (C. Graham), and since 1960 it has been unusual to have more than four or five reports each year. Among these, about 100 have been seen in spring, the earliest on 30 March and the latest (three birds) on Brier Island on 24 June 1962. Individuals between 18 and 20 July 1968 in Shelburne County and on 17 July 1975 at Yarmouth might have been resident in the region. Otherwise, only about 65 fall migrants have been recorded since 1960, between 3 August and 22 November. On 26 September 1981 Frank Hennessey came across 12 bright males in a field near Springhill, Cumberland County, but this is most unusual. On 26 December 1961, one was reported during the Christmas Bird Count at Paradise, Annapolis County.

Description *Length:* 16.5-19 cm. *Adult male:* Bright, rich blue above; breast and sides bright cinnamon-brown; belly white. *Adult female:* Similar but much paler.

Breeding *Nest:* In tree cavities or nest-boxes; composed of dry grass and occasionally supplemented with feathers. When nesting in a hollow tree, it uses the excavations of other hole-nesting species as well as natural cavities. *Eggs:* 3-6; usually pale blue (rarely, white) and unmarked. On 5 May 1937 near Barrington, Shelburne County, a pair took over a nest box after driving off House Sparrows and Tree Swallows that had been competing for it (M. Hopkins). A pair was seen examining a nest site, an excavation formerly used by flickers, near Wilmot, Annapolis County, on 20 May 1939. On 12 June 1928 at Yarmouth, a nest in a bird box contained five young that left that day. On 24 June 1921 a nest in the natural cavity of an apple tree at Margaretsville, Annapolis County, contained three blue eggs that were about one-half incubated. The small number of eggs and the late date suggest a second nesting.

Range Breeds from southwestern Saskatchewan across southern Canada to Nova Scotia (at least formerly), and south to the southern United States and Central America. Winters in the United States and southward.

Remarks A bluebird's favourite perch is an overhead wire along a highway. From such a vantage point in early summer, it drops to the ground after a grasshopper, cricket or other large insect, which it had detected with its keen vision at surprisingly long range. Later in the season the bird adds fruit to its diet.

Elsewhere in eastern North America, progress has been made in restoring populations of Eastern Bluebirds through the extensive provision of suitable nest boxes in rural areas. The same sort of program possibly would entice a few of our spring birds to remain and nest in Nova Scotia. However, we have always been at the edge of the bird's geographical range and probably cannot expect the species to become common here.

Townsend's Solitaire

Myadestes townsendi (Audubon)

Status Three records. One was seen at Wolfville by Sherman Bleakney on 28 December 1975. The second appeared in Tony Lock's garden in Halifax on 2 January 1979, where it stayed until at least 28 February, allowing a large number of birders to view and photograph it. The third solitaire, on Seal Island on 6 November 1980, was recorded by Bruce Mactavish.

Remarks This slender, gray, western thrush breeds throughout the western mountains and is an occasional vagrant to the east coast.

Veery PLATE 28

Catharus fuscescens (Stephens)

Status Fairly common in summer. Breeds. It generally arrives in early May (average 14 May, earliest 25 April); one at Amherst on 19-20 April 1964 was exceptionally early (E. Lowerison). It is common in hardwood areas in southern parts of the province and uncommon elsewhere. Migratory movements have been recorded in early September, but it often goes unreported in fall. Latest sightings were on 11 October 1975 and 1978.

Description *Length:* 16.5-19 cm. *Adults:* Entire upperparts uniform cinnamon-brown; sides of throat and breast buff with delicate or indistinct fine brown spots; centre of throat and belly white; flanks faintly washed with gray; no eye ring.

Breeding *Nest:* On the ground or on very low branches of bushes or small trees, usually in damp or wet places. Composed of fern stalks and other coarse vegetation, with a lining of fine rootlets. *Eggs:* 3-4; greenish blue, unmarked. On 22 June 1965, a nest containing two eggs was found at Crousetown, Lunenburg County, by Nellie Snyder. It was about 60 cm from the ground, placed out on the limb of a short spruce and composed of coarse plant stems and leaf membranes, with a lining of fine rootlets; the nest tree was located in a clump of alders in open woodland. Joseph Johnson found a nest at Karsdale, Annapolis County, on 17 June 1966. It was placed on fallen branches about 60 cm from the ground, contained four eggs, was composed of bark strips and maple leaves and located on the edge of an alder swamp along a woods road.

Range Breeds from southern British Columbia, the central Prairie Provinces, southern Quebec and southwestern Newfoundland, south to Oregon, Ohio and New Jersey, and in the mountains to Georgia. Winters in South America.

Remarks The Veery is one of our best woodland songsters. When heard at twilight in summer, its melodious notes ring out in clear descending cadences that delight the ear. It sings considerably later in the evening than most other birds. On the evening of 23 July 1952 I heard one at Lumsden Lake, Kings County, singing at 9:30 p.m., some time after the last American Robin and White-throated Sparrow had quieted down for the night. It shows a marked preference for thickets of deciduous growth, particularly those where the land is damp and boggy, or near water.

Our nesting birds are of the subspecies *Catharus fuscescens fuscescens.* Darker birds (like that in the colour plate) that have been seen on Sable Island and elsewhere may be *Catharus fuscescens fuliginosa,* which nests in Newfoundland.

Gray-cheeked Thrush   PLATE 28

Catharus minimus (Lafresnaye)

Status Uncommon transient, rare in summer. Breeds. First spring sightings are in late April or early May (average 10 May, earliest 25 April), but birds are still moving through in early June, with reports from Sable Island to mid-June. It was discovered nesting on Seal Island during the nineteenth century (Langille 1884) and in 1922 was still common there and at Cape Forchu, Yarmouth County, and other islands and headlands along the coast (R.W. Tufts). By 1938 it had disappeared from Seal Island (R.W. Tufts), but a bird found in mid-July 1983 (I.A. McLaren) suggests that it still nests there and perhaps elsewhere along the Southwestern Shore. It probably summers with greater frequency on Cape Breton Island than elsewhere in the province. James Bond found it there on 6 July 1949 on French Mountain, Inverness County, and J.E. Victor Goodwill found two on Kidston Island, off Baddeck, on 4 August 1946, and another on the same small island on 21 June 1947. There have been a few more recent sightings from the Cape Breton highlands. A major movement was reported on Brier Island on 6 September 1971, and a number were seen there and at several locations on Cape Breton Island on 22-24 September 1978. Otherwise, autumn reports are generally of ones or twos, the latest in October or November (average 29 October, latest 24 November 1960 at a feeder near Yarmouth).

Description *Length:* 16.5-19 cm. *Adults:* Entire upperparts olive-gray to gray; sides of head lighter gray; throat and belly white; breast may be tinged with buff, with small, wedge-shaped blackish dots; sides gray or brownish gray; eye ring pale gray and rather indistinct.

Breeding *Nest:* Like that of Swainson's Thrush but bulkier, much decayed wood being used in the framework and considerably more beard lichen being added. The location of nests is also similar, but those of the Gray-cheeked Thrush are much better concealed; whether this is by design or the result of the thicker, dwarfed and stunted tree growth in which it is placed, is open to question. The nests are lined with fine, soft dead grass and usually placed about a metre from the ground. *Eggs:* 3-4, usually 3; similar to those of Swainson's Thrush but slightly greener and more speckled than blotched. Laying begins about the end of the first week in June. Five nests discovered on Seal Island are the only ones for which I have data. Three of these were found by Harold F. Tufts, two on 13 June and one on 14 June 1907, all of which contained complete sets of three fresh eggs. I found the other two, one on 19 June 1922 which contained four newly hatched young, and the other on 23 June 1922 which held two young, a few days hatched, and one infertile egg. The construction of all these nests was strikingly similar; all were very bulky, apparently designed to protect the young from the cold and dampness which prevails on Seal Island even in summer. They were situated at heights of 50 cm to 7 m. Three were in low stunted spruces close to the trunks and extremely well hidden by luxuriant beard lichen on all sides. An exceptionally placed nest was about 7 m up in the very thick top of a spruce. The fifth was saddled on the trunk of a fallen spruce, hidden by the moss-grown broken branches and about 50 cm from the ground.

Range Breeds north to the limit of trees from northeastern Siberia, Alaska and across Canada to northern Labrador and Newfoundland, south to New York State in the mountains, northern Ontario, northern Manitoba and northern British Columbia. Winters in the West Indies and South America.

Remarks Why these fragile creatures choose such bleak and inhospitable surroundings to raise their young is hard to comprehend. During June 1922, I was stranded on Seal Island through eight days of rain and continuous fog. There was not a moment of sunshine and the Atlantic air was chill and damp, but the birds seemed not to mind it in the least. The clear, sweet calls of the thrushes and the monotonous trills of the ubiquitous Blackpoll Warblers could be heard on all sides, even when it was raining.

Birds nesting in southwestern Nova Scotia and probably elsewhere in the province are of the small, browner subspecies *Catharus minimus bicknelli*, which also nests near the tree line in New England's mountains. The subspecies *Catharus minimus minimus* of Newfoundland and *Catharus minimus aliciae* of northern Canada presumably migrate through the province, and very gray individuals photographed on Sable Island probably belong to one of these two forms.

Swainson's Thrush   PLATE 28

Catharus ustulatus (Nuttall)

Status Common in summer, very rare in winter. Breeds. First arrivals are generally in early May, occasionally in late April (average 8 May, earliest 18 April). Large numbers appear in late May, and it is widely distributed during summer in coniferous and mixed woodlands. Migration is evident from late August, and large movements have been recorded through September. Late sightings are routine through November (average 10 November; the latest was a bird closely studied by C.W. Helleiner in Halifax on 13 December 1980). Although winter reports of this species north of the southern United States are often considered suspect because of possible confusion with the Hermit Thrush, we have two well-documented ones by qualified observers: the first came to a feeder on Sable Island on 14-16 January 1969 (C. and N. Bell), and the second appeared in Barrington, Shelburne County, on 31 January 1980 (B.J. Smith).

Description *Length:* 16.5-19 cm. *Adults:* Upperparts uniform olive-brown; throat and breast buff, marked with fine brownish gray spots; belly white; sides washed with light grayish brown; buff eye ring.

Breeding *Nest:* Bulky, composed of dry grass, fern stalks, dry leaves, mosses and lichens, with a lining of fine rootlets and sometimes hair; in low trees, conifers preferred, usually not over 5 m up; in open woodland pastures or along the margins of old wood-roads. Although it is said to nest on the ground at times, all of the many nests I have examined were in trees or bushes at low heights; all were in conifers but one, which was in a low deciduous bush in damp woods of mixed growth. *Eggs:* 3-4;

greenish blue, spotted, sometimes blotched, with cinnamon-brown. Laying begins about the last week in May. Some nest dates: 7 June 1927 at Albany, Annapolis County, with three fresh eggs; 5 June 1922 in the same locality, 1 m up in a slender fir in swampy woods of mixed growth, with four slightly incubated eggs; 5 June 1923 at Black River, Kings County, in a small spruce about 1 m up in damp mossy woods, with four slightly incubated eggs.

Range Breeds from Alaska, the southeastern Mackenzie Valley, northern Manitoba, central Quebec, and Newfoundland, south to the northeastern United States, northern Michigan and California. Winters in South America.

Remarks This retiring bird of open woodlands prefers the lower forest strata and, because of its shy nature, is rather difficult to observe. Though a good songster, its notes like those of the Hermit Thrush, its song lacks that bird's clear, pure tones and might be described as being "throaty" and hurried. Its scolding note is an abrupt *prit,* soft and pleasing to the ear; another note commonly given is a high-pitched *peep.* When one hears it singing, it is useless to approach to observe it more closely, for while one is still at some distance, the song will cease as the bird silently drops to conceal itself in thick underbrush. (For distinguishing differences in the plumages of our most common thrushes, see Remarks under the Hermit Thrush.)

Hermit Thrush   PLATE 28

Catharus guttatus (Pallas)

Status Common in summer, rare in winter. Breeds. This thrush is an early spring migrant, usually first appearing in April (average 15 April, earliest 28 March). Large numbers are present by late April or early May, and it is found throughout the province in mixed woodlands during summer. Migratory peaks are not generally evident again until mid-September and can occur through October. Latest sightings have been occasional on Christmas Bird Counts throughout the province, and there are at least eight January and February records, the latest at East Green Harbour, Shelburne County, on 26 February 1983 (several observers).

Description *Length:* 16.5-19 cm. *Adults:* Upperparts, except tail, olive-brown; tail cinnamon-brown; breast buffy white, finely spotted with black; belly and undertail coverts white; flanks buff.

Breeding *Nest:* On the ground; composed of coarse grass, bracken fronds *(Pteridium)* and lichens, with a lining of dry pine needles or deer hair. It is sometimes concealed under fronds of dead bracken or under tiny spruce seedlings and usually found in open woods or on barrens. *Eggs:* 3-4, usually 3; greenish blue, of a slightly lighter shade than robin eggs. Laying begins about mid-May. Of 23 nests examined, the earliest was on 30 May 1923 at Albany, Annapolis County, and contained three young a few days old.

Twilight song of Hermit Thrush

The latest was found on 3 August 1930 near Kingston, Kings County, and contained three half-incubated eggs. Laying was complete in all of the nests examined; in 15 of these nests, three eggs were laid, and in the other 8 there were four eggs.

Range Breeds from Alaska, the southern Yukon, the southern Mackenzie Valley, central Quebec, and Newfoundland, south to the northeastern United States, northern Michigan, central Saskatchewan and, in the western mountains, to New Mexico and California. Winters south to Guatemala.

Remarks The song of the Hermit Thrush is generally considered to be the finest heard in our northern woodlands. The Gray Catbird and the Winter Wren excel in their variation of melodious notes and the Ruby-crowned Kinglet has no rival for volume in relation to size, but none can match the sweetness and aesthetic appeal of this bird's pure, silvery, fluted notes. Its song is perhaps most inspiring when twilight's stillness encompasses the woods in springtime, but it must be heard at fairly close range to appreciate all of the minor notes. In some rural districts, where it is known solely as the bird that sings so sweetly at twilight, it is called the "nightingale."
  In life it may be difficult to distinguish our three most common thrushes—the Hermit Thrush, Swainson's Thrush and the Veery. However, the back of the Hermit Thrush is olive-brown, and its tail is cinnamon-brown, both the back and the tail of Swainson's Thrush are plain gray-brown, and the back and tail of the Veery are both a uniform cinnamon-brown.

Wood Thrush

Hylocichla mustelina (Gmelin)

Status Rare vagrant. One breeding record. Reports of the Wood Thrush in the nineteenth-century literature seem to represent confusion with the Veery. The first bird recorded in modern times was a singing male at Sable River, Shelburne County, on 31 May 1954 (H.F. Lewis). Since then it has been a regular visitor, annual since 1968. There have been 43 reports of some 75 birds in spring, between 22 April and 20 June. Most have been along the Southwestern Shore and its islands (up to 15 on Seal Island on 9-11 May 1975), with a few on Sable Island and in Annapolis, Kings and Halifax counties, and one in Guysborough County. A few of these have been at least temporarily resident singing males, and on 15 May 1973 a nest was discovered in Kejimkujik National Park by Davis Finch and Rick Howie. A bird at Paradise, Annapolis County, on 19 July 1981 may have summered locally. There have been only 12 reports of 13 fall migrants and stragglers between 11 August and 22 November. Another attended the feeder of Vera and Edwin Sollows in Yarmouth from 17 November 1967 to 7 January 1968, when it died during a cold spell.

Remarks It can be readily distinguished from our regular thrushes—the Hermit, Gray-cheeked and Swainson's Thrushes and the Veery—by noting the pattern of its plumage. This bird's white breast and underparts are boldly marked with large rounded spots of dark brown or black, which contrast sharply with the more delicately marked grayish or buffy white breasts of the others. The Wood Thrush, like a number of other southerners, appears to be extending its range northward. As a songster it is regarded as one of the top performers, and it is hoped that it will come to Nova Scotia in increasing numbers.

American Robin   PLATE 28

Turdus migratorius Linnaeus

Status Common in summer, uncommon in winter. Breeds. Spring arrivals first appear in late March (average 22 March, earliest 13 March, apart from an evidently newly appearing flock in Halifax on 6 March 1980). It is abundant from early April to late October or early November. Dates of fall departure are difficult to determine because stragglers from the last waves of migrants, which pass through in early November, elect to overwinter here in numbers that vary considerably from year to year. It is not unusual to see huge flocks of migrating robins in both spring and fall but particularly in the fall, when thousands sometimes move en masse.

Description *Length:* 21.5-26.5 cm. *Adult male:* Top of head and tail blackish gray, the tail with white spots at tips of outer feathers; small white spots above, below and in front of eye; rest of upperparts brownish gray; underparts bright rufous, except throat which is white, striped with black, and lower belly which is white (in autumn, as early as 1 October, the breast feathers of many are tipped with white); bill bright yellow in spring, dusky yellow in fall. *Adult female:* Very similar but colours generally lighter, showing less contrast; less black on head. *Juvenile:* Light buff breast, sometimes almost white, heavily spotted with black; back brownish gray, spotted with grayish white; throat white and unstreaked.

Breeding *Nest:* The foundation is of coarse grass or twigs, on which rests a cup-shaped form, moulded to shape by the bird's breast, of mud lined with soft grass. Very rarely, I have seen nests that lacked mud, probably so because no mud was available in the nesting territory. Nests are usually placed at various heights in tree crotches but many other locations are chosen. For example, a nest examined on 17 May 1933 at Wolfville was neatly arranged in a slight depression on a level piece of ground between apple trees in an orchard; on 11 May 1934 another was built on the ground within a few metres of the previous year's nest. Despite the vulnerability of these nests, the young in both were successfully raised. The most unusual nesting site was on an iron beam of a railway trestle on a bridge near Middleton, Annapolis County. On 28 May 1915 the sitting bird flushed underfoot from this nest, exposing the usual four eggs. The nest was about 1 m below the rails over which trains roared several times a day. *Eggs:* 3-5, usually 4; greenish blue. Laying begins in late April and continues throughout the summer as successive nestings follow, a pair sometimes raising three broods. An early nesting was noted on 11 April 1951 at Wolfville, when a female was seen gathering material, and a late nesting was observed on 23 August 1955 when a female was seen feeding young about ready to fly. There is a lapse of approximately 10 days from the time the first straw is placed until the completed nest contains the usual four eggs.

Range Breeds in Alaska and all across Canada, north to about the limit of trees and south through the United States to northern Mexico. A few winter in southern Canada but most travel further south.

Remarks The robin is one of the best known and most popular birds of garden, farm and countryside. It competes boldly and effectively with us for cherries during a brief period in the summer, but there are relatively few, aside from commercial growers of small fruits, who are not tolerant of this practice. Its return in spring after the long and dreary winter months is eagerly awaited by young and old, many vying with one another to be the first to see one.

During winter 1954-55, four robins fed regularly on hawthorn berries in my garden. One attempted a feeble song on 28 February. They left on 15 March and were not seen thereafter. The first spring arrival, recognized as such by its behaviour, appeared on 23 March that year. Wickerson Lent reports that, during winter 1964-65, robins were present in larger numbers than usual about Brier Island and were commonly seen feeding along the shoreline in the company of Purple Sandpipers.

Turdus migratorius migratorius is the common breeding subspecies. *Turdus migratorius nigrideus,* the race that commonly breeds in Newfoundland and on the Ungava Peninsula, is slightly larger than *T. m. migratorius,* has a deeper red breast and the dark colouring of its head extends well down its back (*see* PLATE 28). That it passes through Nova Scotia as a transient is substantiated by the number of birds that have been collected here. Occasionally, however, robins with exceptionally dark red breasts and dark backs are found nesting here. Two of these I collected at Wolfville: one taken on 13 June 1943 was sent to Austin L. Rand, and the other, collected on 23 May 1957, went to W. Earl Godfrey. Rand (1948) determined my specimen and a number of other extraterritorial specimens brought to his attention to be "probably *nigrideus*-like variants which occur with breeding populations of *T. m. migratorius.*" Since that pronouncement, however, a significant number of "*nigrideus*-like" robins have been recorded here during the breeding season, and my opinion is that the frequency with which they occur suggests a slight intergradation between the two races.

Varied Thrush

Ixoreus naevius (Gmelin)

Status Nine records. The first provincial record was a male seen on 26 October 1965 by Eileen Cardoza in Digby. On 29 October 1968 another male was seen briefly on Sable Island by Christel and Norman Bell, and another was reported there by several observers during October 1971. One appeared on 12 January 1977 at the birdfeeder of John Cliffe at South Maitland, Hants County, and was observed and photographed by many birders in following weeks. Since then, four more winter visitors have appeared:

on 5 February 1977 at North Range, Digby County; 21 January 1978 at Liverpool; 18 February 1978 at Middleton; and 30 December 1978 at Greenwich, Kings County; most stayed at least a few days to be seen by more than one observer. An unprecedented report is of one that spent part of July 1979 in an area of extensive lawns and gardens around the property of the Scott Killams in Yarmouth.

Remarks This thrush of the western mountains is almost regular as a fall-winter vagrant in a "corridor" to the east coast across southern Canada and the northern United States. It is close in size to the American Robin and the colour of its breast is similar, but otherwise its plumage is entirely different, with bright orange eye lines and wing bars and, in males, a dark breast band.

Family Mimidae

Gray Catbird   PLATE 30

Dumetella carolinensis (Linnaeus)

Status Fairly common in summer, very rare in winter. Breeds. Catbirds first appear in spring during late April or early May (average 1 May, earliest 16 April). They are widespread in shrubby growth on the mainland from late May to the second half of September but are uncommon on Cape Breton Island. Numbers migrate through September, but lingering catbirds are regular in October and November, and occasionally into early December. One attended a feeder at Sydney Mines, Cape Breton County, until 2 January 1972 and other late birds have been recorded on Christmas Bird Counts at Salmon River, Cape Breton County, in 1975; Yarmouth in 1976; and Wolfville in 1979, this last bird surviving until mid-January 1980.

Description *Length:* 21.5-23.5 cm. *Adults:* Entire plumage slate-gray, except black cap and tail, and chestnut undertail coverts.

Breeding *Nest:* Composed of twigs, with a lining of fine rootlets and, sometimes, dry leaves; placed in a thicket where it is well concealed by foliage, always at low heights. All but one of the many nests examined were in deciduous bushes. The exception was a nest placed in a small fir among bushes in a thicket of mixed growth, close to the trunk and about 2 m up. *Eggs:* 3-5, usually 4; rich greenish-blue. Laying begins in early June. On 26 May 1934 a male arrived in my garden in full song. On 10 June nest construction was started in a climbing rose beside a window of my house. Four eggs were laid, all of which hatched on 3 July. The young all left the nest on 16 July and stayed about the premises; by 28 July they were practically indistinguishable from their parents. On 11 June 1924 a nest at Black River, Kings County, well concealed in a blackberry tangle, contained four fresh eggs. On 29 June 1915 another at Wolfville, hidden in an alder thicket, held four fresh eggs.

Range Breeds from southern British Columbia, the central Prairie Provinces, southern Ontario, and Nova Scotia, south to the southern United States. Winters from the Gulf States to Cuba and Panama.

Remarks A most entertaining songster, the male has been credited with the ability to mimic other birds. This may be true, but I have failed to detect any noteworthy imitations when listening to his highly variable singing—and why should he try to imitate the melodies of his neighbours when his own are so good! When agitated he mews like a kitten; the similarity is so striking that one is sometimes at a loss as to whether the sound comes from cat or bird.

There are few nesting birds more desirable and few more discriminating in their choice of nesting locale than the catbird. The first and last requisite is thick shrubbery to hide the nest. If you have this to offer, he will likely appear in late May, announcing his arrival by song. Within a few days a mate will mysteriously appear and nesting will follow in early June. Catbirds usually raise two broods, with a new nest, usually near the first one, built for the second family. Thus the company of these delightful birds is ensured for practically the entire summer.

A Gray Catbird was banded as a juvenile in Pennsylvania on 18 August 1962 and found dead in Shelburne County on 7 October of the same year (H.F. Lewis). This illustrates the phenomenon of reverse fall migration, also evident in southern species that appear on our islands and coasts in autumn. Perhaps many of the very late records of our summer birds that normally winter further south, including Gray Catbirds, result from such reverse migration.

Northern Mockingbird   PLATE 30

Mimus polyglottos (Linnaeus)

Status Uncommon fall and winter visitant, rare in summer. Breeds. The status of this bird is somewhat of an enigma. It is rare in spring and summer, when it should be at peak abundance. One would expect most to leave at the approach of cold weather, but instead it is seen much more frequently during October and November, and numbers of these late fall birds remain throughout the winter. Not storm-borne but apparently here of their own volition, a fairly large portion of these winter waifs become regular patrons at feeding stations and are thus greatly assisted in what must be a struggle for survival. Reports of overwintering Northern Mockingbirds have increased since the mid-1970s but vary from year to year. During fall 1980 about 50 individuals were seen, and 22 were recorded on Christmas Bird Counts that year. In 1981-82, 27 were reported to have wintered, 15 wintered in 1982-83 and 17 wintered in 1983-84.

Description *Length:* 23-25.5 cm. *Adults:* Pale gray above; wings and tail black or brownish black, showing white patches on wings, especially when in flight; outer tail feathers conspicuously white; below very pale gray, almost white.

Breeding *Nest:* In thick bushes at low heights; loosely constructed of twigs and grass stems, and usually lined with rootlets. *Eggs:* 3-5; pale blue to greenish blue, sometimes washed with pink, blotched or spotted with brown of various shades. During June and July 1938 a pair was seen frequently in the vicinity of a vacant lot on Jubilee Road in Halifax. The song of the male, particularly in early morning and late in the day, attracted considerable local attention. Although it was realized by those who recognized the bird that it must be one of a breeding pair, it was not until August that Fred H. Sexton discovered the nest in a hawthorn bush growing on the vacant lot. Perched near the nest were "several" fledglings still showing much natal down, while the parent birds scolded close by (H.F. Munro and F.H. Sexton). This was the only nesting record for Nova Scotia for many years. A second record was of a nest at Debert, Colchester County, in 1957, and a third record was of a nest at Pine Hill College, in the City of Halifax in 1958. A fourth nest was found at Glace Bay in summer 1971, and since 1974 nesting has become regular, with one to three nests reported most years.

Range Breeds regularly in southern Ontario and sporadically in the southern parts of all provinces, except P.E.I., at one time or another. Occurs regularly throughout much of the United States, south to the Greater Antilles, the Gulf of Mexico and Mexico.

Remarks This bird will take various foods in winter: frozen grapes, apples, barberries, climbing-rose and multiflora-rose hips, hawthorn berries, meat scraps, bread crumbs, elderberries, raisins and suet. It is pugnacious at feeding stations and successfully drives off contenders. Its distinctive size and general appearance preclude the likelihood of its being confused with any other species.

Brown Thrasher

Toxostoma rufum (Linnaeus)

Status Uncommon vagrant, rare in winter. It was first recorded in 1943, when Harold F. Tufts reported one in full song in his garden at Port Mouton, Queens County. Since then it has been seen with increasing frequency, as regularly in spring and fall as many of our breeding species. First spring migrants come in late April or early May (average 1 May, earliest 10 April, apart from one on Sable Island on 2 April 1971). Counts of 5-15 birds daily have been made on Brier and Seal islands during May, but there are records from throughout the province. Some continue to appear until June and take up brief residence but do not stay (average of last sightings 1 June, latest on Sable Island on 25-29 June 1971). Two at Sable River, Shelburne County, between 11 and 26 July 1980 suggest possible nesting in the region, as fall migrants are not generally first seen until September (average 18 September, earliest 24 August). Peak estimates of five or more daily have been made from mid-September to mid-October on Seal Island and Cape Sable; on Seal Island there were about 35 birds on 24-26 September 1966 and 50 on 1-3 October 1967. Although latest migrants are generally seen in October, stragglers are regular through November and have occurred almost annually on

Christmas Bird Counts throughout the province. One was still present at Timberlea, Halifax County, on 29 January 1965, and since 1968, individuals have survived, generally at feeders, at least into February during all but five winters; these wintering birds have been in all parts of the province from Yarmouth County to Cape Breton Island.

Remarks This long-tailed, rufous-backed, robin-sized bird breeds from southern Alberta to New Brunswick, south to the southern United States. Its frequent occurrences here suggest that it soon may nest if it has not already done so.

It is a delightful songster, its varied melodies being not unlike those of the catbird and the mockingbird, to both of which it is closely related. Thoreau heard its song coming from a perch nearby while he was planting his garden and remarked that it could be interpreted as *drop-it drop-it cover-it-up cover-it-up pull-it-up pull-it-up pull-it-up.* Each phrase of the song is repeated, and in this respect it differs from that of the catbird.

Like the catbird it shows a marked preference for thick shrubbery. It is not likely to be confused with any other species.

Family Motacillidae

Water Pipit PLATE 36

Anthus spinoletta (Linnaeus)

Status Fairly common transient, rare in winter. Pipits usually first appear in early May (average 11 May, earliest 17 April); a flock on the Grand Pré meadowlands on 29 March 1943 could have wintered locally. Generally flocks are small and few in spring and are last seen in late May or early June (average 23 May, latest 15 June). During the 1960s there were several reports by Betty June and Sidney Smith of summer individuals on Cape Sable (15 August 1963 and 1964, 5 August 1967, and 30 July 1968), and by Christel Bell on Sable Island (3 August 1965, 6 August 1969). These are far too early to be normal autumn transients, which otherwise have first appeared in September (average 12 September, earliest 1 September). Large flocks are seen from mid-September through October, especially in coastal areas. It is generally last seen in November but has turned up regularly in small numbers on Christmas Bird Counts around the province. Two were seen at Lawrencetown, Halifax County, on 2 February 1963, and it is perhaps regular in winter on Cape Sable, where 25 were recorded on 15 January 1969.

Description *Length:* 15.5-18 cm. *Adults in spring:* Grayish brown above; light buff stripe above eye; underparts buff, breast and sides very lightly streaked with dark brown; outer tail feathers white. *Adults in autumn:* Similar but somewhat darker above, underparts more streaked with brown.

Range In North America, it breeds from northern Alaska, the Mackenzie Delta, northern Baffin Island, and Greenland, south to Newfoundland, the Gaspé Peninsula, northern Ontario and, in the western mountains, to Arizona. Winters in the United States and Mexico, casually further north. Also found in the Old World.

Remarks Although fairly common, this bird is not well known to the beginning birder for two reasons. First, its preferred habitat is remote from human habitation, and, second, it is highly terrestrial. When the beginner stumbles on a small flock quietly feeding on the ground, the birds immediately spring into the air as one, with choruses of a sharp high-pitched *dee-dee-dee,* their note of alarm, and hurry off in loose formation so quickly that there is no time to discern their distinctive marks. Its tail-tipping habit and white outer tail feathers are distinctive characteristics.

Family Bombycillidae

Bohemian Waxwing

Bombycilla garrulus (Linnaeus)

Status Irregular winter visitor. Periodically and locally common to rare or absent because of its highly nomadic nature. It was first reported in Nova Scotia during winter 1864-65, when specimens from a flock of about 12 were obtained near Halifax (Downs 1865, 1888). From that date until 1962, only eight records were compiled (none for 1921-58). Even allowing for increased numbers of bird observers, it appears that Bohemian Waxwings have become more regular; since 1958 they have been recorded almost every winter, their numbers varying from a few to many. Some winters are remembered for their large Bohemian Waxwing invasions, when flocks of 10-100 were seen from one end of the province to another: 1968-69, 1971-72 and 1975-76. The best winter of all was 1983-84, when, everywhere in the province, flocks averaged 50-200 birds. They generally arrive in November (earliest 22 October) and are routinely seen until April, although they occasionally linger into May (latest 29 May 1976, a flock of 35 in Halifax). Three on Sable Island on 16 June 1966 and one on 29 June 1968 (C. Bell) were possibly unique for eastern Canada at this time of year.

Remarks Somewhat larger than its close relative, the Cedar Waxwing, which is much better known, this bird is more beautifully marked and richer in general appearance. It nests in the far northwest regions of the continent and, when its domestic responsibilities are ended, it covers great distances in quest of food. It is because of these gypsy-like wanderings, so characteristic of waxwings, that it was given the name Bohemian.

Cedar Waxwing   PLATE 30 (*see* page 367)

Bombycilla cedrorum Vieillot

Status Common in summer, rare and irregular in winter. Breeds. It generally appears in late May (average 28 May, earliest 10 May), so regularly that several flocks in April and early May 1983 stand out as unusual. "Waves" of small flocks (25-50 birds) occur in early June. Fall movements take place from mid-August to late September, when larger flocks of 100 or more are sometimes present. Last sightings are generally in October or November, but it is normal to sight one or two on Christmas Bird Counts around the province. Individuals or nomadic flocks have occurred later in winter during seven winters since 1960.

Description *Length:* 17-19 cm. *Adults:* Back, breast and part of crested head rich cinnamon-brown; forehead, chin and line through eye jet black; wings grayish brown; tail gray, broadly tipped with yellow; end of secondaries often, tail rarely, tipped with small sealing wax-like red beads; belly and flanks washed with pale yellow; undertail coverts white.

Breeding *Nest:* Bulky and loosely constructed of twigs, coarse grass, string, beard lichen when immediately available, and other soft materials, with a lining of soft grass, wool from a sheep or bits of fur; I have never noticed feathers. It is saddled on the horizontal limb, usually of a deciduous tree, but occasionally in a conifer. Nests are located in gardens and orchards or in areas remote from human habitation; proximity of food probably exerts a powerful influence in this regard. *Eggs:* 4-5; pale bluish gray, spotted sparsely but uniformly with black. Nesting is irregular, ranging from June to August. On 4 June 1919 a nest was found under construction in Wolfville. On 28 June 1915, two nests, one containing four and the other containing five fresh eggs, were found; and on the same date in 1916 another nest contained four fresh eggs. All were in elms at heights of 3-6 m. A late nest at Port Mouton, Queens County, located on the low branch of an apple tree on 28 July 1945, contained five fresh eggs. At Albany, Annapolis County, a nest on the low limb of a large hemlock contained four fresh eggs on 4 July 1932; it was constructed almost entirely of beard lichen, which was abundant in the neighbourhood, as were blueberries.

Range Breeds across southern Canada from central British Columbia, Lake Athabaska, central Manitoba, northern Ontario, Newfoundland and the Maritimes, south to the southern United States. Winters from extreme southern Canada southward.

Remarks Except during the short periods when they are nesting, these birds travel over the countryside in small flocks, making brief and unexpected visits to our orchard or shade trees.

The items on its menu range from small caterpillars to apple blossom petals. In late summer much small fruit is devoured, wild varieties such as chokecherries and blueberries being highly favoured. In some localities it is called the "cherry-bird" because of its liking for cultivated fruit.

It shows a preference for cedars where these trees thrive in its range. The name Waxwing is derived from the red sealing wax-like beads that appear on the tips of certain wing feathers of both the male and female. It has not been established why this mark of adornment is worn by some individuals and not by others. It is not acquired with age because it sometimes appears on the wings of young birds. Sometimes, but rarely, it appears on the ends of the tail feathers as well.

It produces a high-pitched sibilant note, difficult to describe, which is heard as often when the bird is in flight as when it is perched.

The only species with which this sleek, well-groomed bird might be confused is the Bohemian Waxwing. That bird is larger, the ends of its inner primaries are boldly tipped with yellowish white and its undertail coverts are bright chestnut-rufous, very different from the white undertail coverts of the Cedar Waxwing.

Family Laniidae

Northern Shrike   PLATE 30

Lanius excubitor Linnaeus

Status Irregular and uncommon in winter. This visitor from the north generally first appears here in October or early November (average 21 October, earliest normal date 22 September). There is uncertainty about some sight identifications in early fall because of possible confusion with the Loggerhead Shrike (see Remarks); one very early Northern Shrike was identified by Charles R.K. Allen on 2 September 1966 at Chebogue Point, Yarmouth County. Numbers reported during most winters from 1974-84 have varied from 13 to 28, but in 1977-78 about 50, and in 1978-79 about 100, were recorded. Latest sightings in spring are generally in April, with stragglers through May (average 11 April, latest 31 May).

Description *Length:* 23-26.5 cm. *Adults:* Back bluish gray, slightly lighter on rump; wings and tail black, the tail feathers tipped with white, the outer ones all white; a broad line from base of bill to ear, running through eye, black; underparts grayish white, delicately barred with fine brown or black lines; bill hooked, lower mandible usually pale at base. *Immatures:* Similar but their general appearance is that of a brownish gray bird, the colours subdued and less contrasting.

Range Breeds in the Northern Hemisphere, in North America from northern Alaska, Mackenzie Delta, northern Ungava, and Labrador, south to central Quebec, northern Manitoba and northern British Columbia. Wanders south in winter as far as the central and southwestern United States.

Remarks Perhaps the most outstanding characteristic of this bird is its ferocity. Hawks and owls are fierce but kill mainly, if not wholly, to satisfy their immediate food requirements.

However, the Northern Shrike will kill more prey than it can immediately eat, and the surplus victims are impaled on barbed wire fences or on the thorns of trees. Not infrequently we find the mummified remains of mice and small birds hanging in this manner, a macabre sight long ago recognized as the work of shrikes. Such remains probably have been forgotten by the bird. The birds it kills are usually sparrow-size or smaller, but on 26 October 1916 I saw one closely pursuing a fleeing robin, a bird about its own size. When last seen, the chase was still in progress.

It hunts in a manner similar to that of the American Kestrel. It finds a suitable perch, the highest part of the tallest tree for instance, looking over wide, open terrain and sits for long periods as if sleeping. Instead, it is scanning the countryside for prey within striking range.

Its flight is undulating; when about to alight it has a characteristic trait of coming in below the perch and then suddenly swerving up to it. It so closely resembles its cousin, the Loggerhead Shrike, that definite identification in the field may be difficult. However, a shrike seen in winter is likely to be of this species, but one seen in summer will be a Loggerhead Shrike. Caution should be used in identifying shrikes in spring and fall. Sometimes the black feathers over the bill of the Loggerhead Shrike are difficult to see, and the pale lower mandible of the Northern Shrike may be black by spring. Perhaps the best distinction is the larger, heavier and more strongly hooked bill of the Northern Shrike compared with the snub-nosed appearance of the Loggerhead Shrike.

Loggerhead Shrike

Lanius ludovicianus Linnaeus

Status Rare transient, very rare in summer and winter. Formerly bred. Among nineteenth-century authors, Jones (1879) included the Loggerhead Shrike as "very rare" and Hickman (1896) reported one seen on 27 June 1895. The first conclusive evidence of occurrence was a specimen shot at Truro on 28 December 1909 (Piers' notes). Since 1960 only 15 spring migrants have been reported, between 1 April and 24 June. Although there was a probable nesting in Kings County in 1942 and a confirmed nesting there in 1969, the bird has not recently been recorded in summer except in the Amherst Point Bird Sanctuary on 7 July 1974 and at Round Hill, Annapolis County, where Walter E. Whitehead recorded one or two July birds in 1974 and also during five consecutive years, 1977-81. Since 1960, 21 fall migrants have been recorded, between 12 August (in 1969 on Brier Island) and 29 November. An unusual winter record is supplied by Benjamin K. Doane, who studied one at very close range for 20 minutes near Port La Tour, Shelburne County, on 28 February 1969 as it repeatedly swooped down from its perch for insects in marsh grass.

Description *Length:* 22-23 cm. *Adults:* Slightly smaller than the Northern Shrike but very similar in colouration; breast, however, is grayish white, without the obvious fine transverse lines; more extensive black mask extends over the base of the bill to varying degrees.

Breeding In trees or thick bushes; rather bulky, composed of twigs and coarse grass stems, with a lining of plant down or other soft materials. *Eggs:* 3-5; dull white, thickly blotched with light brown and lavender. The fact that it has bred in the province is substantiated by a record provided by Austin W. Cameron, who described a nest he found at Petit Etang, about 1.5 km north of Cheticamp, Inverness County, on 29 June 1969, the day its three young left. The family group stayed about the immediate vicinity until 28 July. The nest was placed 1.7 m from the ground in a hawthorn bush *(Crataegus),* one of several dozen forming a copse in open countryside, and composed of weed stems, coarse grasses, rags and bits of string. The pair had been seen in the area since 29 April.

Range Breeds from central Alberta, southern Quebec, and southward in the United States to Mexico; formerly bred in the Maritimes and New England, now rarely if at all. Winters in the United States and Mexico.

Remarks It is less bloodthirsty than its larger cousin, the Northern Shrike, and preys largely on insects such as grasshoppers and crickets. Although there are many species of shrikes throughout the world, the Loggerhead Shrike is the only one restricted to North America. It has become increasingly scarce in eastern North America for unknown reasons.

Family Sturnidae

European Starling   PLATE 34

Sturnus vulgaris Linnaeus

Status Introduced, common resident. Breeds. Abundant, except remote from human settlement in the wooded interior, where it is still rare in summer and absent in winter. Its first recorded appearance in Nova Scotia was on 1 December 1915 when a bird was picked up at Dartmouth. Two days later, another was shot in Dartmouth. Others were collected on 18 December 1919 at Liverpool and on 8 February 1921 at Comeau's Hill, Yarmouth County, but nothing more was heard of them until 1925, after which they became much less a novelty. The first nest was found in Halifax in 1928. In May 1930, four nests were found in Yarmouth and another at Port Maitland, Yarmouth County. On 20 June 1933 a flock of 40-50 birds at Avonport, Kings County, were all birds of that year (R.W. Tufts). Nowadays thousands of these birds are counted at their roosts during Christmas Bird Counts; their phenomenal increase in just short of 70 years is shown in these 1983 figures: Amherst, 1,425; Halifax East, 3,935; Halifax West, 6,514; Wolfville, 5,255; and Yarmouth, 2,275.

Description *Length:* 19-21.5 cm. *Adults in summer:* Plumage iridescent, showing green, blue and purple reflections, except wings and tail, where the feathers are duller, with brown margins; belly black; back and flanks marked with buff spots; bill yellow. *Adults in winter:* Similar but buff spots more numerous above; underparts spotted with white.

Breeding *Nest:* Usually in holes in trees, in apertures under eaves of houses or outbuildings, or in nest boxes; composed of dry grass and other vegetable debris. Three male starlings were shot between late April and early May 1958 while carrying beakfuls of nesting material to a nest site reserved for a pair of Northern Flickers. *Eggs:* 5-6; pale blue. The first recorded nesting for Nova Scotia was at Gorsebrook Golf Club in Halifax on 26 June 1928, when I collected a set of five heavily incubated eggs from a nest about 6 m up in a large chestnut tree; a hole excavated by flickers had been taken over and heavily lined with grass. Nesting starts about mid-April and young fledge by late May. If a pair loses its first nest, determined efforts to build anew are made until late June, when the urge to breed ends rather abruptly.

Range Successfully introduced from the Old World to North America at New York City in 1890, it has now spread to Newfoundland, southern Labrador, northern Quebec, northern Manitoba, the southern Yukon, Alaska and northern British Columbia, south to northern Florida and Mexico. Winters north to southern Canada.

Remarks The earliest recorded effort to introduce the European Starling into North America was made in 1872, when a number were brought over from Europe and released in Ohio. This effort failed, as did a number of subsequent tries there. The next attempt took place on 6 March 1890, when 80 birds were imported and liberated at Central Park, New York City, by Eugene Scheiffer. To help these birds establish themselves, 20 additional pairs were released at the same place on 25 April 1891. For about six years they and their progeny did not stray far from New York City, but gradually the spread began. The hordes of Starlings that now swarm over much of North America unquestionably sprang from these Central Park releases.

Because it is generally disliked for a number of reasons, governments have vied with one another to devise ways to control its numbers or break up the immense roosts that deface public buildings and park groves in many of the larger cities. Innumerable devices, ranging from chemical sprays to two-faced artificial owls and one-eyed cats, have been invented and tried, but to date no one has come up with the right answer. The natural enemies of the starling are limited to the bird-eating hawks; in Nova Scotia we have only two, the Sharp-shinned Hawk and the Merlin, and they are far too uncommon to be effective. Our only hope is that the time may come—and it may have arrived already—when the population will reach a level beyond which natural forces will not permit it to increase.

Studies of this bird's behaviour indicate that it is endowed with a high order of intelligence which it applies to all phases of its family life. There appears to be an intimate understanding and spirit of co-operation between the two parents which has made them highly adaptive and successful wherever conditions are favourable to their survival.

Family Vireonidae

White-eyed Vireo

Vireo griseus (Boddaert)

Status Rare vagrant. First reported by Harrison F. Lewis, who closely observed a male singing its characteristic song at Arnold, Shelburne County, on 26 May 1953. Since 1974 it has been regular as a "reverse migrant" in autumn, with 16 observations of individuals (three photographed) between 3 September and 15 November, but most in early October. The only spring record, aside from the 1953 bird, was of a bird netted and banded by Ross Anderson on Brier Island on 17 May 1970.

Remarks Because the normal range of this species lies only slightly to the south and west of Nova Scotia (nesting north to southern Massachusetts), its occurrence here as a vagrant is not unexpected. Juveniles have dark eyes, but the yellow "spectacles" in all plumages are distinctive.

Solitary Vireo   PLATE 29

Vireo solitarius (Wilson)

Status Uncommon in summer. Breeds. This vireo is found rather sparsely from early May (average 7 May, earliest 23 April) to mid-October (average 20 October, latest 25 November). In addition, there are well-documented records of individuals seen on the Halifax East Christmas Bird Count of 15 December 1984 (J. and S. Cohrs) and on the Halifax West Count on 23 December of that year (J. McLaren et al.). During summer its distribution is general over the province. This is a bird of mixed woodlands and only occurs in gardens and settled districts briefly during migration.

Description *Length:* 13-16.5 cm. *Adults:* Top of head and cheeks bluish gray; throat white; conspicuous white "spectacles"; back olive-green; tail and wings darker, the wings showing two white bars; underparts pure white; sides washed with greenish yellow.

Breeding *Nest:* Wholly pensile from a small forked branch, usually in a fir or hemlock. It is composed of fine smooth grasses, plant down, bark fibre and other pliable materials neatly woven together and covered exteriorly with bits of white birch bark or sometimes with paper torn from a hornet's nest. The lining is of smooth grasses or sometimes dry pine needles. Of more than 30 nests examined, all but three were in conifers, at heights of 1-6 m. The exceptions were one in an old, moss-grown wild apple tree, one in a small poplar and a nest in a small ash; these three were in close proximity to coniferous growth. Eggs: 3-5, usually 4; white, sparsely speckled with black or dark brown chiefly around the larger end. Nest construction normally begins during the second half of May and continues into early June. An exceptionally early nest was found by Harold F. Tufts on 12 May 1905 at Black River, Kings County, about one-half completed. A typical egg date is 4 June 1905 at Black River, where a nest containing five well-incubated eggs was found.

Range Breeds from southern British Columbia, the southeastern Mackenzie Valley, central Manitoba, southern Quebec and southwestern Newfoundland, south in the eastern mountains to Pennsylvania, across to Ohio and Minnesota, and south in the western mountains to Mexico. Winters from the southern United States to Central America.

Remarks Although not endowed with particularly colourful plumage, or outstanding ability as a songster, this bird is a general favourite among those who know it well. Its fearlessness around humans is at times surprising. One sitting on its nest permitted me to approach so near that I was able to reach up and stroke its back. Another pleasing characteristic is the devotion the male shows towards his mate. In spring he not only helps with nest-building but shares in the monotonous task of incubation, often singing while sitting on the eggs, and later helps feed the young. During the nesting season he never wanders far from the nest and his sweet musical notes may be heard from early morning till late in the day as he leisurely wanders about his territory.

Yellow-throated Vireo

Vireo flavifrons Vieillot

Status Rare vagrant. The first record of this rarity was of a male picked up dead at Indian Harbour, Halifax County, on 9 April 1958 by Miriam Wetmore. Another was seen and heard singing at Sable River, Shelburne County, by Harrison F. Lewis on 8 June 1964. Since then about 24 individuals have been reported, 1 each in Halifax, Lunenburg and Queens counties, and the rest on Brier, Sable or Seal islands. Only three have occurred in spring, none as early as the 1958 bird; one of these remained singing on territory near Susie Lake, Halifax County, from 29 May to at least 16 June 1974 (E. Cooke, S. Fullerton et al.). Reverse autumn migrants have occured as early as 21 August and as late as 17 October, and occurrences are about equally divided between September and October.

Remarks The breeding range of this readily identified species lies slightly to the south and west of Nova Scotia, reaching southwestern Maine.

Warbling Vireo

Vireo gilvus (Vieillot)

Status Rare vagrant, very rare in summer. Most nineteenth century reports appear to be in confusion with other species; only Hickman's (1896) report of a "rare" bird at Pictou on 20 June 1895 has some plausibility. The first well-documented report was of a bird seen in a Wolfville garden on 10 June 1954 (R.W. Tufts). Since then, the bird's presence has been established by at least 50 sightings, several photographs and two specimens; generally single birds, sometimes two or three, were involved but six were seen on Seal Island on 1 October 1979. About a dozen reports are for spring, between 15 May and 13 June. A singing bird in Pictou County from 11 May to 13 July 1958 (E. Holdway) suggests some potential for breeding, as do reports of birds singing in Pugwash, Cumberland County, and Middleton, Annapolis County, during summer 1967 (O.E. Devitt). Other birds first seen in July (five reports through the month) could represent post-breeding wanderers. The remaining reports have been of evident reverse fall migrants, between 25 August and 12 November, mostly in September and mostly on Brier and Seal islands.

Remarks Although this bird is readily identified when well seen, observers should be aware that young Red-eyed Vireos have dark eyes, and that the yellow on the breast of Philadelphia Vireos can be quite washed out. A good field mark is the lack of a dark streak in front of the eye of the Warbling Vireo, giving it a blank-faced appearance. As the species nests in southern New Brunswick, its occurrence here as a vagrant is unremarkable, and its establishment as a breeder might be anticipated.

Philadelphia Vireo

Vireo philadelphicus (Cassin)

Status Rare transient, very rare in summer. It was first recorded at Norwood, Yarmouth County, where Allen (1916) collected one on 9 July 1904. It was not reported again until 1956, when Robert Gray saw a bird in Colchester County on 26 May. Since then, records of this bird have come from sources from Cape Breton Highlands National Park to Cape Forchu and the *Lurcher Lightship* off Yarmouth, and from all regions in between. About 22 birds have occurred in spring, between 15 May and 18 June. Over 70 have been fall migrants, from 15 August to 15 November, many of them on Brier and Seal islands, especially in September. Summer records are a bird on 9 July 1963 at North Aspy River, Victoria County (A.J. Erskine); another on 21-22 July 1980 at Wine Harbour, Guysborough County (H. Munro); and, most unusual, a singing male in Yarmouth on 12 July 1960 (C.R.K. Allen).

Description *Length:* 11.5-13 cm. *Adults:* Top of head gray or olive-gray, with a white line over and a dusky brown line through the eye; back, wings and tail gray-brown with olive tinge; underparts pale yellow, usually white on throat and belly.

Range Breeds from central British Columbia to central Quebec and southwestern Newfoundland, south to southern Alberta, northern Minnesota, New Brunswick and central Maine. Winters south of central Mexico.

Remarks The Philadelphia Vireo can be mistaken for a greenish warbler, particularly the Tennessee Warbler. However, it has a thicker bill and is more sluggish than any similar warbler. Its yellowish underparts and unbarred wings are marks which distinguish it from other vireos known to occur in Nova Scotia. It breeds in New Brunswick, may breed here and probably occurs with greater frequency than our records indicate.

The species was first described in the early nineteenth century from a bird which was collected incidentally in Philadelphia, hence its name.

Red-eyed Vireo   PLATE 31

Vireo olivaceus (Linnaeus)

Status Common in summer. Breeds. Widely distributed where there are groves of deciduous trees or where these trees predominate in settled and remote areas. It usually arrives about mid-May (average 18 May, earliest 8 May, not including a bird seen by Betty June and Sidney Smith on Cape Sable on 30 April 1970) and is widespread by the end of May. Latest fall reports are usually in October, with a few late stragglers (average 15 October, latest 14 November).

Description *Length:* 14-16.5 cm. *Adults:* Top of head blue-gray, margined with stripes of black; prominent white line over eye; back, wings and tail light olive-brown, showing a slight lustre; no wing bars; iris red; underparts white. *Immatures:* Iris brown.

Breeding *Nest:* Very similar to that of the Solitary Vireo, but the material used in its construction varies considerably with location, availability probably being the governing factor. Maple, apple and elm trees, in that order, appear to be the favoured nest sites. The nests are placed at heights of 1-6 m or more. *Eggs:* 3-4, usually 3; white, sparsely speckled all over with black. Nest building begins during the second week in June and sets of first laying are complete by the end of the third week in June. Some nesting dates are: 2 July 1898, three eggs about one-half incubated, 6 m up in a maple; 18 June 1913, four fresh eggs about 3 m up in a maple; 12 July 1918, three eggs heavily incubated about 3 m up in a maple; and 20 June 1928, three eggs about one-half incubated in an apple tree, about 1 m from the ground; all were in or near Wolfville. On 10 August 1940, Martin H. Bushell saw an unusually late nest being built in a small birch at Hazel Hill, Guysborough County. On 16 August, it contained two eggs and on 30 August he found three very young vireos being cared for by both parents. From then on he visited the nest daily and saw the young leave on 9 September with both adults; they were not seen again.

Range Breeds from British Columbia, the southeastern Mackenzie Valley, central Manitoba, central Ontario, southern Quebec, and the Maritimes, south to Florida, central Texas and northern Oregon. Winters in South America.

Remarks This is the bird that builds the trim, tightly woven pensile nest that is seen hanging from the branches of our shade trees. The nest is usually so well concealed by the foliage in summer that few know of its presence until the leaves fall in autumn, but from then on and during winter it is very conspicuous. So well known are these nests that in some districts the builders are called "hanging-birds."

The male is an inveterate singer. His monotonous, short song is repeated over and over again during most of the day for most of the summer.

Vireos are sluggish, slow-moving birds, often seen hanging upside-down in midair, clinging to a leaf, apparently finding such incongruous positions the most appropriate for consuming the caterpillars and aphids that rank high on their daily menu.

This is our most common vireo and one of our most common woodland birds. In addition to its red eyes, it may be identified by its black and white eyebrow stripes and its lack of wing bars.

Red-eyed Vireo on nest

Family Emberizidae

Subfamily Parulinae

Blue-winged Warbler

Vermivora pinus (Linnaeus)

Status Rare vagrant. The first record was of a bird identified by Evelyn Richardson on Bon Portage Island on 4 May 1963. Since then there have been three more spring records between 13 and 18 May, and a very early bird on Sable Island on 14 April 1975. Reverse fall migrants have been more frequent: 19 individuals were seen (two collected; photographs) between 25 August and 9 October, most of them on Brier and Seal islands, and most in late August and early September.

Remarks This warbler's plumage is so distinctive that the bird is hard to overlook as an occasional stray among our migrants. The bird nests as near as Massachusetts and has been expanding its range in recent years.

Of interest is a detailed report by Joan R. Kelly of a male "Lawrence's Warbler," the rarer form of hybrid between Blue-winged and Golden-winged Warblers, at Big Bras d'Or, Victoria County, on 7 July 1980.

Golden-winged Warbler

Vermivora chrysoptera (Linnaeus)

Status Rare vagrant. The first record was of a male caught in an outbuilding on Bon Portage Island by Evelyn and Morrill Richardson on 17 May 1961. It was readily identified in the hand and subsequently banded and released. Since then, there have been 10 records. Among them, only two have been in spring, on 23 May 1970 and 26 May 1983, both on Seal Island. The rest have occurred between 25 August and 16 October: four on Seal Island, two on Brier Island and a bird each near Broad Cove, Lunenburg County, and in the City of Halifax.

Remarks Somewhat rarer here than its close relative, the Blue-winged Warbler, this species is suffering a population decline in its breeding range in the northeastern and mid-western United States, where it is to some extent being replaced by the Blue-winged Warbler. When it does occur, its yellow wing patch (or bars), yellow cap, and dark eye mask and throat are virtually unmistakable.

Tennessee Warbler   PLATE 32

Vermivora peregrina (Wilson)

Status Fairly common in summer. Breeds. It was evidently overlooked by nineteenth-century observers prior to Downs (1888), who recorded it as "rather common inland." It is among the later warblers to arrive (average 16 May, earliest 7 May) and can still be found on the move during early June in places where it does not nest. It is particularly common in summer on Cape Breton Island. From limited reports of last sightings, it has largely left the province by early September, but a few stragglers are routine into October (average 12 October, latest 11 November). There is also one record of a bird at a Dartmouth feeder on 2 December 1983 (J.S. Cohrs).

Description *Length:* 11.5-13 cm. *Adult male:* Crown and cheeks pale blue-gray; back and rump bright olive-green; ends of wings and tail dark gray; a conspicuous white line over eye and fine black line through eye; entire underparts dirty white, sometimes tinged with yellow; no wing bars. *Adult female:* Similar to male but crown washed with green, and underparts distinctly washed with yellow.

Breeding *Nest:* On the ground in open woodland, pasture or clearing, and well concealed. Composed of grass and moss, with lining of soft grass and hairs. *Eggs:* 4-5; white, with a wreath of dark brown spots around the larger end. On 7 June 1922 at Albany, Annapolis County, a nest in open bushy pasture near the edge of woods was embedded in the moss on the side of a small mound; it was made of grass, with some deer hairs in the lining (H.F. Tufts). On 22 June 1923 a nest similar in construction and location and containing five newly hatched young was found near Wolfville. On 5 July 1916 at Albany, Annapolis County, a parent was seen carrying food to its young, but the nest was not located.

Range Breeds from southeastern Alaska, central Mackenzie Valley, northern Manitoba, northern Quebec and western Newfoundland, south to the Maritimes, northeastern New York State, southern Manitoba, central Saskatchewan and northwestern Montana. Winters from southern Mexico to northern South America.

Remarks This inconspicuous, vireo-like warbler has a distinct white line over its eye, an excellent field mark if the bird is close enough. During the nesting season, despite its ground-nesting habits and the marked preference it shows for bushy pastures as nest sites, it tends to feed among the treetops, a trait which adds to the difficulty of identifying it positively in life.

Its song is merely a short, rapid, high-pitched twitter, the tones of which have been likened to those of the Chimney Swift's chatter.

Its name is derived from the fact that it was first described from a specimen which by mere chance was collected in Tennessee and is in no way indicative of its distribution.

Orange-crowned Warbler

Vermivora celata (Say)

Status Rare transient, very rare in winter. The first known occurrence was of a bird that competed for suet on a food tray at the home of Mrs. A.D.M. Curry in Halifax between 4 January and 8 February 1951, when it was found dead under the tray. There have been at least 53 other reports since then, mostly of single birds, but occasionally two to six birds have been seen daily in the late fall on our southwestern islands or in the Halifax area. Only 17 birds, all singles, have been reported for spring, between 18 April and 22 June (the latest was on Sable Island, where there have been several June sightings). The majority have occurred as fall migrants. Although first fall sightings are routine in September (average 4 October, earliest 30 August), they have been regularly reported into November and December. None survived at feeders as late as the above-mentioned bird in 1951.

Remarks The Orange-crowned Warbler most resembles the fall Tennessee Warbler, which is similarly yellowish below but has white undertail coverts and lacks any hint of streaking on its breast and sides.

The bird collected in 1951 was assigned to the subspecies *Vermivora celata celata* by W. Earl Godfrey. The species nests from Alaska across Canada to southern Labrador and occasionally winters at feeders north to New England.

Nashville Warbler   PLATE 31

Vermivora ruficapilla (Wilson)

Status Fairly common in summer. Breeds. It arrives generally before mid-May (average 8 May, earliest 29 April) and is widely distributed over the province in summer. A few are routinely found in October (average 12 October, latest 17 November). Stragglers in Halifax on 3 December 1977, and on 2 and 8 December 1984, were at or in the vicinity of birdfeeders.

Description *Length:* 11.5-13 cm. *Adults:* Crown and sides of head gray; patch of chestnut on top of crown (sometimes lacking in female); back and wings olive-green; underparts yellow except lower belly, which is white; conspicuous white eye ring; wings without bars.

Breeding *Nest:* On the ground, similar in construction and location to that of the Tennessee Warbler. *Eggs:* 4-5; white, speckled profusely with cinnamon-brown chiefly around the larger end. A nest collected on 6 June 1922 at Albany, Annapolis County, contained four fresh eggs. It was embedded in the side of a low, mossy bank in partly cleared land near heavy woods of mixed growth. The female was particularly bold, advancing to within 2 m and protesting vehemently while a male, presumably her mate, sang persistently from a neighbouring tree. This nest was rather loosely built of grass placed on a foundation of moss and lined with fine grass, mixed with hair that might have come from a porcupine. Two other nests were found at Caledonia, Queens County, in June 1909; one on the 9th held four eggs and another on the 12th contained five eggs, both sets being about two-thirds incubated. The nests were typical in construction and located in a sparsely wooded pasture. One was lined with black, hair-like rootlets and the other with fine grass mixed with hair from a deer (H.F. Tufts).

Range Breeds from southwestern Newfoundland, southern Quebec, southern Manitoba and southern British Columbia, south to Maryland, northern Illinois, Nebraska and central California. Winters from northern Mexico to Guatemala.

Remarks Nashville Warblers—so-called because the first one was discovered at Nashville, Tennessee—are very active birds that usually feed in bushes and along lower branches. Look for them in summer about old, abandoned farms in the process of being reclaimed by the forest. During migration they become quite sociable and may suddenly appear in our gardens in a mixed throng of warblers, all obeying the same compelling urge. This bird could be confused with the Connecticut Warbler, which also has a white eye ring, but the Connecticut Warbler's throat is gray, not yellow. In fall the Nashville Warbler resembles an immature Magnolia Warbler, but that bird has a yellow rump and two white patches on its tail.

Its characteristic song might be described as a rapidly repeated *sweetly-sweetly-sweetly sit-sit-sit-sit-sit,* with less emphasis on the second part.

Northern Parula   PLATE 31

Parula americana (Linnaeus)

Status Fairly common in summer. Breeds. It arrives in early May (average 6 May, earliest 1 May, besides two abnormally early birds on 17 and 26 April 1969). This species is well distributed during summer in wooded areas throughout the province and often lingers in small numbers in late fall (average 24 October, latest 27 November). A later straggler was noted at the Hawkins' feeder in Wilmot, Annapolis County, on 18 December 1981.

Description *Length:* 11-12 cm. *Adult male:* Head and upperparts mostly grayish blue; patch on centre of back greenish yellow; wings and tail grayish blue, the wings showing two prominent white bars and the tail having white spots on the outer feathers near its end; throat and breast mostly yellow, the breast crossed by a band of bluish black bordered with chestnut; belly white; flanks slightly washed with rufous. *Adult female:* Similar, but patch on back duller and underparts light yellow with breast band generally lacking.

Breeding *Nest:* Constructed inside a mass of hanging beard lichen (or "old man's beard", the lichen *Usnea),* usually with no other lining than that provided by the lichen itself. Sometimes a tree or group of trees well festooned with this lichen will attract

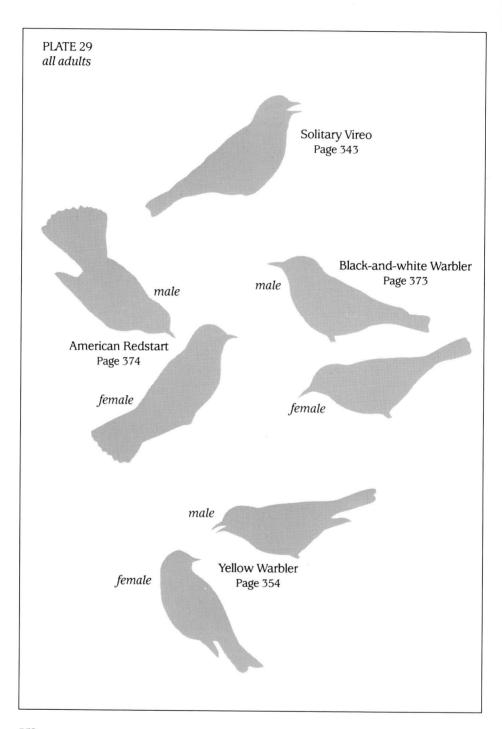

PLATE 29
all adults

Solitary Vireo
Page 343

Black-and-white Warbler
Page 373

male

male

American Redstart
Page 374

female

female

male

Yellow Warbler
female Page 354

Roger Tory Peterson

PLATE 30

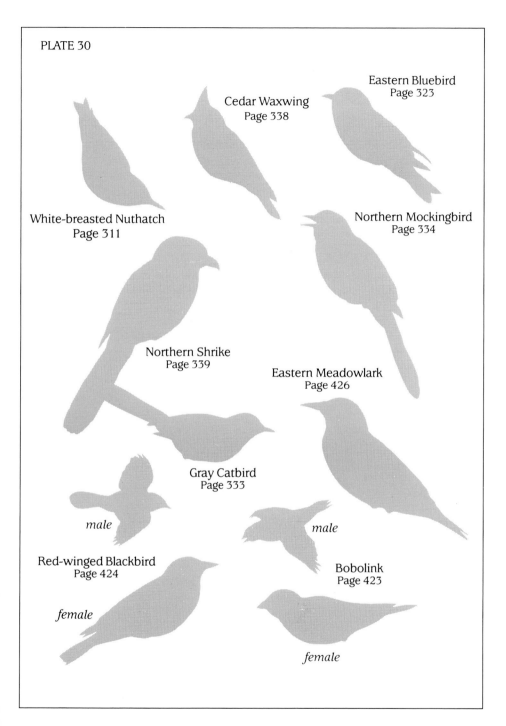

Cedar Waxwing
Page 338

Eastern Bluebird
Page 323

White-breasted Nuthatch
Page 311

Northern Mockingbird
Page 334

Northern Shrike
Page 339

Eastern Meadowlark
Page 426

Gray Catbird
Page 333

male

male

Red-winged Blackbird
Page 424

Bobolink
Page 423

female

female

more than one nesting pair. The nests are built at heights of 1-10 m or more. The suitability of the tree rather than its location appears to be the determining factor in its selection. Quite frequently old apple trees in forested areas are chosen for nest sites, but only if the trees are well decorated with the essential lichen. *Eggs:* 3-5, usually 4; white, with cinnamon specks chiefly around the larger end. Of the 16 complete nests examined, 10 contained four eggs, 4 contained three, and the other 2 held five each. On 22 May 1922 a female was seen pulling at beard lichen and then flying off with fine strands of it in her bill; this indicates that Northern Parulas do not always procure additional lichen from that which grows so profusely on the nest tree itself as they might be expected to do. On 1 June 1909 at Caledonia, Queens County, Harold F. Tufts found a nest containing four slightly incubated eggs and on 12 June of that year he found another nest that contained five fresh eggs. On 1 July 1932 at Albany, Annapolis County, he examined three nests: two contained four eggs and one contained five; all eggs were only slightly incubated, surprising because July is late for first nests; these may have been second nests or renestings.

Range Breeds from central Ontario, southern Quebec, and Cape Breton Island, south to central Florida and the Gulf States. Winters in the West Indies and from southern Mexico to Nicaragua.

Remarks To find these birds during the summer nesting season, one should visit woods where beard lichen flourishes. In such surroundings the distinctive song of the male is most likely to be heard: a sharp twitter ending abruptly on a note with a pronounced rising inflection.

This bird is difficult to study because much of its time is spent among higher branches. When seen to advantage, however, note the small size, the white wing bars, the greenish spot on the back and, in the male, the conspicuous dark band crossing its yellow breast.

The parula is a trusting little bird. Once I climbed to a nest that contained half-grown young. As I was peering into the nest, the female arrived with a bundle of insects for her babies. Instead of scolding like most species, she took slight notice of my proximity, went straight to the nest, quickly unloaded her cargo and left for more.

Yellow Warbler   PLATE 29

Dendroica petechia (Linnaeus)

Status Common in summer. Breeds. An abnormally early individual occurred on Brier Island on 28 March 1965 (W. Lent), and birds on 15 April 1973 on Brier Island and on 14 April 1975 on Sable Island were also unusual. It normally arrives in early May (average 9 May, earliest 26 April) and is widespread in summer, although less common in non-arable areas and almost absent from coniferous woodlands. It is generally last recorded in October (average 15 October, latest 23 November). A bird at Wolfville on 25 November 1929 was possibly a late migrant, but an individual at Yarmouth on 20 December 1964 (C. Higby) was clearly an abnormal laggard.

Description *Length:* 11-13 cm. *Adult male:* Plumage mostly rich yellow but back more olive-yellow; breast streaked with rufous; tail dark olive-green, the inner vanes yellow; wings dark olive-green, the feathers edged with yellow. *Adult female:* Similar but paler; breast plain or slightly striped with rufous.

Breeding *Nest:* Neat and compact, composed of grass, weed stems, pieces of string, cotton wool, plant down and other soft materials, with a lining of plant down, hair and sometimes dandelion "fuzz." Typical nest sites are low bushes, very often in garden shrubbery, but sometimes higher up in deciduous trees. In June 1935 an extraordinary nest site was brought to my attention by Mrs. Fred Burgess. On her verandah at Sheffield Mills, Kings County, rested an isolated and unusually large potted geranium. Securely fastened to its branches was a normally constructed Yellow Warbler nest on which the female was patiently incubating. *Eggs:* 4-5; greenish white, thickly marked with various shades of brown. Nest construction is well underway during the last of May and continues well into June. Sets of first laying are often complete by the end of the first week in June. A nest under construction on 20 May 1942 in a climbing rose in my garden in Wolfville is the earliest I have recorded. Usually only a single brood is raised but there may be exceptions. On 28 June 1949 a female was seen carrying nesting material to a new nest in a lilac bush, although the young from her first nest were still barely able to shift for themselves; my notes do not indicate whether this second nest produced a brood. I have known a pair that, having lost its first and second nests, started building a third but did not complete it.

Range Breeds north to near the limit of trees from Alaska to Labrador and south to northern South America and the West Indies. Winters from Florida and southern California to South America.

Remarks This is one of our most lovable and valuable garden birds. We await its return in May as eagerly as we do that of the robin in March, and we regret its departure in fall. Besides providing enjoyment with its beautiful form, colour and song, it works from morning till night devouring insects that attack our roses and other plants of ornamental and economic importance.

Pairs of some of the larger bird species stay mated for many years if not for life, but this does not hold for smaller species and certainly not for Yellow Warblers. In summer 1925 I banded parent birds that had just finished nesting in a rose bush on my lawn. In 1926 the same male returned, but while nesting operations were under way it was noted that his mate was unbanded. They nested that year close to the old site and later both were trapped; the number on the male was verified and the new female was tagged. In 1927 the male returned for at least a third time but the mate he later chose was not wearing a band. The nest that year was close to where the others had been, and the male was very tame; both members of the pair were again trapped and the new female was banded. Although his return in 1928 was eagerly awaited, the male did not come back.

On 1 June 1939 a nest was started in my garden, the female doing all the work. By 4 June it was about one-half completed. Late that day I saw the male come by, climb into the frail structure, turn and twist about a few times as though testing the workmanship, sing twice while squatting there and then fly off, seemingly well satisfied.

Dendroica petechia aestiva is the southern race which breeds on the mainland, but the northern limit of its breeding range in the province is not definitely known. *Dendroica petechia amnicola* is the northern subspecies whose incidence as a breeding bird in Nova Scotia was established by Godfrey (1958), who collected four specimens at Cape North in 1935, three during the breeding season and one on 10 September. He describes these specimens as intermediate between *D. p. amnicola* and *D. p. aestiva* but with more characteristics of the former. The two races cannot be distinguished from each other in life.

The Yellow Warbler's predominantly yellow colouring sets it apart from all other small Nova Scotia birds.

Chestnut-sided Warbler PLATE 31

Dendroica pensylvanica (Linnaeus)

Status Common in summer. Breeds. Birds generally appear in mid-May (average 14 May, earliest 4 May, apart from a very early bird in Halifax County on 27 April 1966). It is widespread during the summer on the mainland but uncommon on Cape Breton Island. Migration is well underway by mid-September, and last sightings are routine in October but not later (average 11 October, latest 30 October).

Description *Length:* 11.5-13.5 cm. *Adult male:* Entire crown bright yellow; patch on side of head behind eye white; line from base of bill to eye and extending down side of throat black; two yellowish white wing bars; back bright olive-green, streaked with black; tail black with white patches near tip; underparts white, bordered conspicuously along sides with bright chestnut. *Adult female:* Similar but colours duller and area of chestnut more restricted.

Breeding *Nest:* A rather compact affair composed of coarse grass, dry leaves and plant down, with a lining of soft grass and fine rootlets, always (in my experience) placed in the crotch of low deciduous bushes in thickets in open woodland. *Eggs:* 4-5; white, well marked with various shades of brown chiefly about the larger end. Nest construction sometimes begins soon after arrival, a female having been seen gathering material on 25 May 1922 at Albany, Annapolis County. A set of four fresh eggs was examined at Goldenville, Guysborough County, on 23 June 1903 (H.F. Tufts).

Range Breeds from east central Alberta, central Ontario, southern Quebec, New Brunswick and Nova Scotia, south to the northeastern United States (further south in the Appalachians), northern Ohio and eastern Nebraska. Winters in Central America.

Remarks Look for it in new, second-growth thickets of alders and other deciduous bushes growing in scrubby clearings or along the margins of streams, for it shuns deep woods and does not come to our gardens in towns and villages except for brief periods during migration.

The best mark for field identification in spring is its glistening white underparts, bordered on each side with a broad band of sharply contrasting bright chestnut. Fall birds are quite different: greenish above, whitish below, with two yellowish wing bars.

Its song is easily confused with that of our common Yellow Warbler and, to add to the confusion, both birds are often found in the same type of habitat.

Magnolia Warbler   PLATE 32

Dendroica magnolia (Wilson)

Status Common in summer. Breeds. This is one of our commonest warblers. It generally appears before mid-May (average 10 May, earliest 26 April), but the main arrival is later. In summer it is seldom seen about towns and villages or far from wooded areas, its favourite habitat being regions of second growth or bushy pasturelands with conifers. Peak movements are evident through September, but stragglers are routine (average 18 October, latest 5 November). An individual on the Halifax West Christmas Bird Count on 23 December 1973 (D. Welsh) is our only early winter record.

Description *Length:* 12.5-13 cm. *Adult male:* Crown bluish gray; line over eye, two wing bars, and prominent patches across middle of tail white; cheek, nape, and end of tail black; rump yellow; back black, feathers bordered with olive-green; throat yellow; rest of underparts yellow, boldly striped with black. *Adult female:* Similar but colours subdued and stripes on underparts greatly reduced.

Breeding *Nest:* Made of fine twigs and weed stems, with a lining of delicate grasses or fine black rootlets; it is not compact and has a rough exterior but is well built and exceedingly artistic. It is saddled on the limb of a small conifer and usually well out from the trunk, effectively concealed by a bough immediately above it. Favoured locations are in woodland pastures studded with new-growth evergreens and bordered by heavier woods, rather than in well-shaded woods. *Eggs:* 4-5, usually 4; white, beautifully marked with large blotches of various shades and densities of cinnamon, chiefly around the larger end. Nest construction begins about the first week of June and fresh sets have been found as early as 8 June. Of nine nests examined, six contained four eggs, and three held five; all were built at heights of 1-2 m. Harry Brennan, writing from Springville, Pictou County, tells of a fully constructed nest found on 8 June in a small spruce about half a metre from the ground that held five eggs seven days later.

Range Breeds from west-central Mackenzie Valley, central Manitoba, central Quebec, and Newfoundland, south to Virginia in the mountains, central Michigan, central Saskatchewan and central British Columbia. Winters from southern Mexico to Panama.

Remarks The Magnolia Warbler is a sluggish, slow-moving warbler usually found moving about at low heights rather than among the treetops. Though beautifully coloured and a delight to the eye, its song is mediocre: a pleasing little melody translated as *wisha-wisha-wisha,* with the accent on the first syllable.

It is one of three Nova Scotia warblers with a bright yellow rump conspicuous in both sexes and in all plumages. Only the Yellow-rumped and Cape May Warblers share this characteristic. From these it is distinguished by the black band on the end of its otherwise chiefly white tail.

It is called "Magnolia" because the bird from which the species was first described happened to be collected from a magnolia tree.

Cape May Warbler   PLATE 31

Dendroica tigrina (Gmelin)

Status Common transient, uncommon in summer. Breeds. It was called "rare" by nineteenth-century authors and was only occasionally recorded prior to 1960. With the development of spruce budworm epidemics in eastern Canada, it has become much more commonplace during migration and is locally common as a nesting bird on Cape Breton Island. First arrivals are generally in mid-May (average 14 May, earliest 6 May). Migration waves may occur from late August through September, and last sightings are routine in October and beyond (average 23 October, latest 13 December).

Description *Length:* 12-14.5 cm. *Adult male:* Top of head blackish gray; patch about eye chestnut; rump, and patch on neck below ear, yellow; back brownish olive, boldly striped with black; large white area on wing coverts; underparts pale yellow, streaked with blackish. *Adult female:* Quite different; upperparts olive-brown; narrow yellow or white line above the eye; lacks chestnut cheek patch but shows yellow patch on side of neck; underparts dull yellow, with faint brown stripes.

Breeding *Nest:* Placed high up in medium-sized conifers, often among the clusters of cone-bearing branchlets about a metre from the top. Twigs and lichens are used in its construction and its lining is of fur or feathers, or both. *Eggs:* 3-8, usually 6-7; white, with blotches of rufous heaviest around the larger end. The first nesting record for the province was provided by Ward Hemeon who saw a parent bird feeding young at Bass River, Colchester County, on 30 July 1966.

Range Breeds from northeastern British Columbia, the southeastern Mackenzie Valley, northern Alberta, central Manitoba, northern Ontario, northern New Brunswick and Nova Scotia, south to northern New Hampshire, southern Manitoba and central Alberta. Winters in the West Indies.

Remarks Its name is inappropriate, for although the species was first described from a bird collected at Cape May, New Jersey, in May 1811, it seems not to have been recorded there again until September 1920 (Stone 1937).

Although Chapman (1934) and Pough (1949) state, respectively, that the Cape May Warbler lays 3 or 4 eggs, it is now known that larger clutches are laid by this species in response to the rich food supplies available during outbreaks of the spruce budworm.

Field identification is aided by noting its yellow rump, although this mark is obscure on autumn immatures. Only two other warblers known to occur regularly in Nova Scotia—the Magnolia and Yellow-rumped Warblers—have this characteristic; otherwise they are quite different. The Magnolia has conspicuous white patches on its tail which contrasts with a black terminal band, and the Yellow-rumped Warbler's lower breast is white, not yellow.

Black-throated Blue Warbler   PLATE 31

Dendroica caerulescens (Gmelin)

Status Uncommon in summer. Breeds. It generally arrives in mid-May (average 14 May, earliest 28 April); an individual on Brier Island on 11 April 1981 (W. Lent) was clearly not a normal migrant. During the nesting season, this warbler is found mainly in dense hardwoods or mixed growth. Numbers of migrants are seen in September, and stragglers occur through October (average of last sightings 15 October, latest 3 November).

Description *Length:* 12.5-14 cm. *Adult male:* Upperparts slaty blue; throat, breast and sides black; lower breast and belly white; wing has a distinct white spot at base of primary coverts; outer tail feathers show white near ends. *Adult female:* Very different; brownish-olive above; yellowish white stripe over eye; cheek dark brown; underparts buffy or yellowish white; wing shows white patch as in male but reduced in size.

Breeding *Nest:* A beautiful structure of fine grasses, plant down, bits of lichen and shreds of other pliable vegetable matter, neatly and compactly woven together and lined with fine black rootlets. It is covered on the outside with bits of white birch bark held in place by cobwebs. The birch bark gives a ragged effect and probably is placed there as camouflage. I have examined only three nests: all were built in small fir seedlings growing in clumps in well-shaded woods of heavy growth, with conifers predominating, and were within a metre of the ground. *Eggs:* 4; dull white, with brown markings of various densities chiefly around the larger end. The nests cited were all located in a remote area near Black River Lake, Kings County. The first, discovered on 11 June 1905, contained no eggs but had a finished appearance and the female promptly arrived on the scene and scolded. When visited again about a week later, it was still empty, with no bird in attendance, the pair apparently having deserted because of the previous disturbance. On 17 June of that year a nest containing four fresh eggs was found in the same general area; it was collected and later acquired by the National Museum of Canada (H.F. Tufts). The third nest, found on 29 June 1915, contained young being fed by both parents. Harry Brennan found a nest of this species at Springville, Pictou County, on 19 June 1966 in a small fir in well-shaded woods, about 30 cm from the ground. It contained four eggs and, according to custom, was covered exteriorly with bits of white birch bark.

Range Breeds from central Ontario, southern Quebec, and the Maritimes, south in the mountains to northern Georgia, and to southern Ontario and central Minnesota. Winters in the Florida Keys, Bahamas and Greater Antilles.

Remarks There are notable variations in the song of this beautiful woodland warbler, but the one which is perhaps most common is, to my ear, absolutely lacking in melody and unlike that of any other bird found here. It is a short song consisting of three to five (usually three) husky notes, *zee-zee-zee-e-e,* given deliberately and usually with a rising slurred inflection at the end, all notes in the same pitch. Once heard and associated with the sleek little performer, it will be long remembered.

The difference in the colour patterns of the male and female in summer is noteworthy. Though the male in most warbler species is the brighter of the two, there is usually a marked similarity between them, but here we have two birds so unlike in appearance that the casual observer would think they belonged to different species.

The striking plumage of the male in spring is not readily mistaken for that of any other species. Spring females and young in autumn are less distinctive, but usually the white spot at the base of the primary coverts can be seen.

Yellow-rumped Warbler   PLATE 32

Dendroica coronata (Linnaeus)

Status Common in summer, uncommon in winter. Breeds. Arrival of migrants is not difficult to determine in coastal areas, where the birds often arrive in flocks, excitable and noisy, and in bright spring plumage. First arrivals have occurred throughout April (average 19 April, earliest 2 April). Summer birds are widely distributed in coniferous or conifer-dominated woods. Peak numbers of migrants, often in large flocks mixed with other species, have occurred throughout October. Some of these flocks remain into winter in favoured localities, especially in years when bayberries *(Myrica pensylvanica)* are abundant. They are most regular in winter in coastal areas of the Southwestern Shore.

Description *Length:* 13-15 cm. *Adult male:* Top of head, rump, and patch on each side of breast yellow; cheek patch black; throat and belly, and spots near end of outer tail feathers white; back blue-gray, streaked with black; breast and sides black, the feathers tipped with white; two white wing bars. *Adult female:* Similar but much paler and upperparts brown. (See Remarks for a description of "Audubon's Warbler.")

Breeding *Nest:* Fairly compact, and composed of twigs, grass stems, plant down, strips of bark and similar materials, with a lining of hair and feathers. The site most frequently chosen is the limb of a large spruce, on which it is saddled well out from the trunk, partially concealed among the clusters of small shoots; lower heights are most common. Another favoured site is close to the trunk of a small spruce in an open, sunny clearing, such as a woodland pasture. An unusual site was the limb of a large apple tree in an orchard remote from coniferous woods. Another strange location was the thick foliage of an old Virginia creeper *(Parthenocissus quinquefolia)* growing over the wall of a farmhouse at Lower Wolfville; admirably concealed, its discovery was possible only because the bird was seen to enter between the leaves. *Eggs:* 3-5, sets of 4 and 5 being about evenly divided; grayish white, spotted with various shades of brown. Of 24 nests examined, 12 had sets of four, 10 held five, and 2 contained sets of three that were both second attempts. Nest construction begins in early May and complete sets are laid by about the end of the month. There are indications that sometimes two broods are raised.

Range Breeds north to the limit of trees from Alaska to Labrador, and south to Virginia in the mountains, northern Michigan, southern Saskatchewan and Alberta, and south in the western mountains to Guatemala. Winters in the southern United States, coastally from Nova Scotia and British Columbia, south to the Greater Antilles and Panama.

Remarks This warbler's bright yellow rump is conspicuously worn by both sexes, including immatures (except in juvenile plumage), throughout the year. Only two other of our regular warblers have this characteristic: the Cape May and the Magnolia Warblers. However, these two also have strongly streaked yellow underparts which the Yellow-rumped Warbler lacks.

The breeding population in Nova Scotia belongs to the subspecies *Dendroica coronata coronata,* formerly known as the "Myrtle Warbler," as distinct from "Audubon's Warbler," a group of subspecies occupying western North America, which has a yellow rather than white throat, lacks a distinctly darker face patch and shows more extensive white on the male's wing. A bright male "Audubon's Warbler" was closely observed among migrant Yellow-rumped Warblers on Sable Island on 4 May 1967 by Christel and Norman Bell, a first for Atlantic Canada. A second bird, a singing male, was seen briefly but adequately on Seal Island by Ian McLaren on 26 May 1983.

Black-throated Gray Warbler

Dendroica nigrescens (Townsend)

Status Five records. A male foraging in shrubby growth on Sable Island on 9 May 1966 was closely observed by Christel and Norman Bell. Another male came to their window feeder the next year on 1 May. A young male was found on Seal Island on 10 October 1972 by Jean Boulva and Ian A. McLaren, and photographed by Boulva for a first confirmed record. A bird was seen briefly on Brier Island on 1 September 1975 by Lisë and Shirley Cohrs. One discovered and photographed by Ian A. McLaren in the south end of Halifax on 24 November 1984 was later seen by many observers until its disappearance in late December.

Remarks This far-western warbler, whose name is aptly descriptive, has occurred occasionally in the eastern United States and Canada, in both spring and fall.

Townsend's Warbler

Dendroica townsendi (Townsend)

Status One record. A female seen on Sable Island on 9-10 June 1973 by Jean Boulva, Davis Finch and Ian McLaren was photographed by Finch for a first and only provincial record.

Remarks This far-western warbler has occurred only rarely as a vagrant in the eastern United States and Canada. Another individual was found in St. John's, Newfoundland, in late autumn 1983. Its dark mask makes it quite distinct from its close relative the Black-throated Green Warbler, although females of this species have some similarities to the female Blackburnian Warbler.

Hermit Warbler

Dendroica occidentalis (Townsend)

Status Two records. Two females, easily distinguished in several close-up photographs, occurred on Sable Island in spring 1975: the first was found by Davis Finch, Ian McLaren and Edward Miller on 26-27 May and the second was found by Finch on 4 June.

Remarks This is the most western of the vagrant warblers that have appeared in Nova Scotia. Its breeding range extends from Washington State to southern California. The Sable Island birds were the first for Canada, although they have since been recorded in British Columbia, Ontario and Quebec. With its extensive yellow face (including forehead) and gray back, the species, if well seen, cannot be confused with the Black-throated Green Warbler.

Black-Throated Green Warbler   PLATE 32

Dendroica virens (Gmelin)

Status Common in summer. Breeds. It is among the earlier warblers arriving in spring (average 9 May, earliest 3 May), and in summer it is widely distributed in coniferous and mixed growth. Major movements occur in September and occasionally early October, and it is usually last seen in October (average 25 October, latest 16

November). At least one later bird was found by Harrison F. Lewis among a flock of several hundred Yellow-rumped Warblers at Port Joli, Queens County, on 3 December 1950.

Description *Length:* 11.5-13.5 cm. *Adult male:* Back and crown olive-green; face bright yellow; tail black, with white on outer feathers near base; two white wing bars; throat and breast black; belly white; sides striped with black. *Adult female:* Similar but throat and breast mottled black and yellowish white, rather than solid black.

Breeding *Nest:* Composed of fine grass, lichens, moss, plant down and other vegetable matter woven into compact form and usually covered with bits of white birch bark held in place by cobwebs. The lining is of hair or fine black rootlets; no feathers are used. It is usually saddled on a horizontal limb of a large conifer, near the end, and relatively low to the ground. Sometimes a small spruce is selected, but it must be growing in a sunny, open glade or wooded pasture; the nest is placed close to the trunk in such cases. I have found nests in spruce, hemlock and white birch, with frequency in the order named. I know of only one nest built in a very large White Birch and its location was unique. It was constructed inside one of the many tight curls of the old bark. The size of the opening in the curl was such that the nest fit snugly and did not extend above the rim of the curled bark, adding a measure of concealment. *Eggs:* 4-5, usually 4; white, speckled with various shades of brown chiefly around the larger end. Laying begins during the last week in May; two sets of fresh eggs were examined in nests near Wolfville on 2 June 1914. The latest date recorded for fresh eggs is 28 June 1918, and the fact that the nest held a set of five suggests a first nesting.

Range Breeds in east-central British Columbia, northern Alberta, central Saskatchewan, central Manitoba, central Ontario, and Newfoundland, south to central South Carolina, northern Alabama, northern Ohio and Minnesota. Winters from Mexico to Panama and in southern Florida and the West Indies.

Remarks All of our warblers are full of song when they arrive in the spring, but after the cares and responsibilities of domestic life are finished for the year and it has become hot and humid in the woods, most stop singing or sing very little. But this bird is a notable exception, for it is inclined to keep right on. In the spring it is excitedly saying to you, *I-seé-sues-eé* with accents on the *seé* and *eé*, but come the languid days of July and August, its whole manner appears to have changed, for now it is trying to tell you just how it feels as it slowly drawls out a *la—zé—du—dé*. (According to Phyllis Dobson, the sharp, high terminal note *eé* suggests that he is just getting nicely started on his song when someone suddenly steps on his tail.)

Blackburnian Warbler   PLATE 31

Dendroica fusca (Müller)

Status   Uncommon in summer. Breeds. It generally arrives around mid-May (average 14 May, earliest 7 May). During the breeding season, this species is uncommon on the mainland but seen more often on Cape Breton Island. Fall movements have been noted from late August to early October, with latest records generally in October (average 13 October, latest 26 November). Stragglers have been seen on Cape Sable on 14 December 1959, in Yarmouth on 24 December 1969, and in Halifax on 1 December 1973. It is a bird of woodland regions, especially where there are tall spruces or hemlocks, although it may be seen anywhere during migration.

Description   *Length:* 13-14 cm. *Adult male:* Orange stripe through crown; orange band from base of bill, passing above eye to side of neck; throat and breast rich orange; area about eye, back of head, nape, large area of back, and tail black; back has two whitish or buff streaks; outer tail feathers white at base; wing coverts show a white patch; lower breast and belly light buff, lightly streaked with black. *Adult female:* Similar but paler, the colours being diffused and orange being replaced by yellow on breast and face.

Breeding   *Nest:* A rather frail structure of fine twigs and grass or weed stems, with lining of fine rootlets. It is usually saddled on a horizontal branch of a large or medium-sized conifer out near the end and fairly high in the tree. *Eggs:* 4; grayish white, well spotted with various shades of brown, chiefly around the larger end. A typical nest was found by Harold F. Tufts at Black River, Kings County, on 16 June 1905 about 10 m up and saddled well out on the limb of a large spruce in woods of heavy mixed growth.

Range   Breeds from central Alberta, central Ontario, southern Quebec, and Cape Breton Island, south to southeastern New York State, southern Ontario, central Minnesota and in the mountains to western Georgia. Winters mainly in Central and South America.

Remarks   Many species of warblers occur in Nova Scotia and most are brightly coloured. From time to time the question is raised as to which is the most beautiful. Those who know them all in life, and have seen a male Blackburnian in spring plumage, the sun glinting on his flaming throat and breast, with his contrasting colours perhaps against a background of gray poplar buds bursting into leaf, must admit that he merits a place near the top of the list. His song, however, is not in keeping with his fine feathers, for it is little more than a thin, high-pitched, wiry trill, ending with a distinctive twitter.

Yellow-throated Warbler

Dendroica dominica (Linnaeus)

Status Rare vagrant. The first Nova Scotia record was of one noted by Evelyn Richardson on Bon Portage Island on 4 December 1960. Since then there have been about 23 records of 25 individuals. Only three have occurred in spring: on Sable Island on 7 June 1968, and on Brier Island on 30 April 1983 and 6-7 May 1984. Reverse fall migrants have been more regular. A seasonally early bird on Cape Sable on 23 July 1962 was well described by Gerald Smith. The rest have been found between 22 August and 14 December (the last staying until 17 December 1983 near Ben Eoin, Cape Breton County). Apart from the Cape Breton Island bird and one in Dartmouth on 11 November 1980, all our records came from mainland Shelburne County or Sable, Seal, Cape Sable, or Brier islands. The first to be confirmed was photographed by David Higgins on Sable Island on 22 August 1968, and several have been photographed since.

Remarks This warbler breeds in the southeastern United States, north to central Illinois, Ohio and New Jersey. Its face pattern and yellow throat are unmistakable. Both yellow-lored and white-lored birds have been seen and photographed in the province. The white-lored birds are members of the subspecies *Dendroica dominica albilora,* which nests west of the Alleghenies, mainly in the Mississippi Valley, and the yellow-lored birds may be mostly *Dendroica dominica dominica* from the southeastern seaboard of the United States.

Pine Warbler

Dendroica pinus (Wilson)

Status Rare vagrant, very rare in winter. The first record was a specimen collected at Gaspereau, Kings County, on 4 November 1922 (R.W. Tufts). Another three were reported prior to 1960, and since then almost 60 sightings, generally of individuals but sometimes of two or three birds together, have been reported. Several have been confirmed by specimens or photographs. Only nine birds have been reported for spring, between 5 April and 10 June. The rest have appeared as transients or reverse migrants in fall, between 6 August and late December. In recent years they have become almost routine at feeders around Halifax and in the southwestern counties and occasionally elsewhere. A few have survived into January, and fewer still have survived through February.

Remarks The Pine Warbler breeds from southern Manitoba and central Maine southward, and winters successfully north to New England, so its occurrence here as a vagrant is expected. In autumn, females and immatures can be confused with fall

Bay-breasted and Blackpoll Warblers, and identification during that season should be made with caution. The Pine Warbler's unstreaked back and relatively large bill are distinguishing marks.

Prairie Warbler

Dendroica discolor (Vieillot)

Status Uncommon vagrant. Since the first bird was recorded at Louisbourg on 21 September 1964 (J. and G. Lunn), there have been over 100 records of over 200 individuals. Oddly, only one appeared in spring: a bird on Cape Sable on 11-12 May 1979 (B.J. and S. Smith). The rest have been reverse fall migrants. Generally they first appear in August (average 25 August, earliest 26 July). An earlier migrant was captured during a crossing of the ferry *Bluenose* on 22 July 1978 and released near Yarmouth (P.D. Vickery). Latest sightings are routinely through October (average 12 October, latest 31 October). A well-documented straggler was found during the Halifax East Christmas Bird Count near Cow Bay, Halifax County, on 17 December 1983 (F. Lavender).

Remarks It is hard to believe that this conspicuous, yellow, tail-wagging warbler, with its distinctive face and flank markings, could have been completely overlooked prior to 1964. Its present regularity probably reflects its recent range expansion; it now breeds as near as coastal Maine.

Palm Warbler PLATE 33

Dendroica palmarum

Status Fairly common in summer, rare in winter. Breeds. This is one of the first warblers to arrive in spring (average 20 April, earliest 7 April). During the breeding season it is found in bogs and scrubby clearings within the coniferous forest. Migration is obvious in September, but large movements are generally not recorded until October. Small numbers are routine through November, and a few birds have occurred on Christmas Bird Counts around the province. They are much less regular later in winter. Late reports include two near Port Williams, Kings County, on 21 February 1953; one near Halifax on 25 January 1955; and another at Marion Bridge, Cape Breton County, on 20 January 1970. Individuals also have survived the winter on Sable Island on at least two occasions.

Description *Length:* 13-14 cm. *Adults:* Crown chestnut, with border of yellow forming a line over eye; cheek and back brownish olive, brighter on rump; outer tail feathers show white spots near the end, most conspicuous in flight; underparts yellow, with reddish brown stripes on breast and along sides.

Breeding *Nest:* On the ground (rarely in a low bush), usually located on dry, open barrens but sometimes in wet sphagnum bogs and always well concealed. It is composed of grass stems and sections of dry leaves of bracken *(Pteridium)*, with a lining of fine grass, deer hair and invariably feathers, often those of the Spruce Grouse. *Eggs:* 4-5, usually 5; white, with cinnamon-or olive-brown spots or blotches or both, chiefly around the larger end. Nest construction is well under way during the first ten days of May and laying begins about the middle of the month. The earliest date for a complete set is 20 May 1909 at Caledonia, Queens County (H.F. Tufts). With regard to clutch size, a breakdown of the contents of 61 nests reveals that 36 contained sets of five, and 25 sets of four. Feathers used for lining nests have been identified as those of Spruce Grouse, Blue Jay and Robin, given in the order of frequency. The eggs in a set of four examined on 31 May 1909 were practically white, there being but slight trace of any pigmentation. This was an abnormality.

Range Breeds from northeastern British Columbia, southern Mackenzie Valley, northern Manitoba, central Quebec, and Newfoundland, south to Nova Scotia, northern Minnesota and central Alberta. Winters from southeastern United States to Puerto Rico and Yucatan.

Remarks Its song is a monotonous trill with slight variations, some renditions being suggestive of the junco's song. This bird's colour pattern is drab in comparison with those of many of its close relatives. When seen in life, it might best be described as a tawny, yellowish warbler, feeding usually near or on the ground. Its chestnut crown patch is a good mark, as is its habit of constant tail-tipping.

Palm Warbler feeding young Cedar Waxwings

PLATE 31

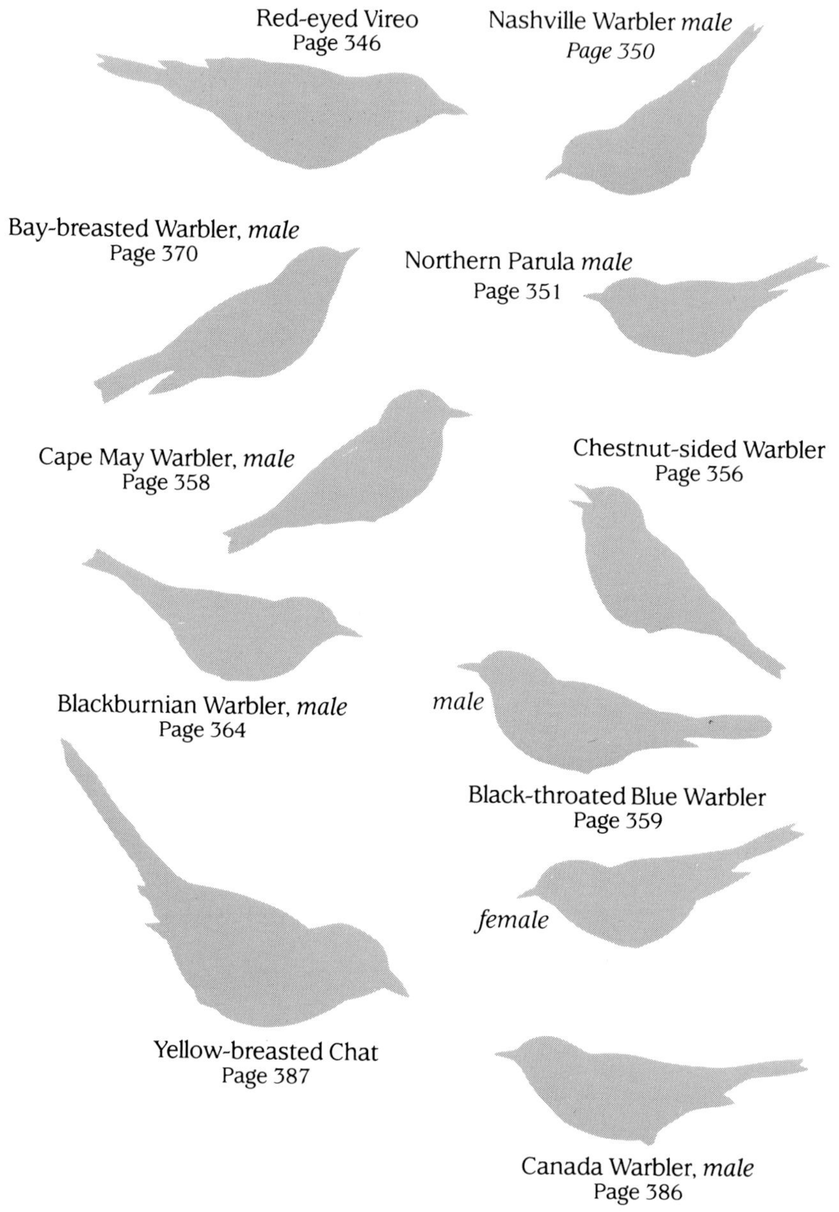

Red-eyed Vireo
Page 346

Nashville Warbler *male*
Page 350

Bay-breasted Warbler, *male*
Page 370

Northern Parula *male*
Page 351

Cape May Warbler, *male*
Page 358

Chestnut-sided Warbler
Page 356

Blackburnian Warbler, *male*
Page 364

male

Black-throated Blue Warbler
Page 359

female

Yellow-breasted Chat
Page 387

Canada Warbler, *male*
Page 386

Crosby

Roger Tory Peterson

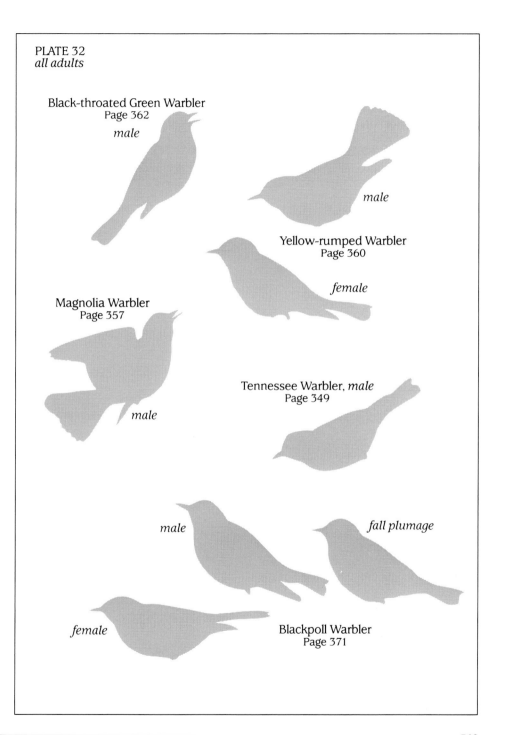

PLATE 32
all adults

Black-throated Green Warbler
Page 362

male

male

Yellow-rumped Warbler
Page 360

female

Magnolia Warbler
Page 357

male

Tennessee Warbler, *male*
Page 349

male

fall plumage

female

Blackpoll Warbler
Page 371

Two incidents of strange behaviour seem noteworthy: Eric Dodge saw one come into his garden in Middleton on 16 August 1949 and offer a small green worm to his pet Cedar Waxwing, which eagerly accepted it. When I was walking over the barrens at Albany, Annapolis County, with Harold F. Tufts on 27 May 1939, one flushed underfoot. Glancing down we saw not only one nest but two, typically under a spruce seedling, but placed so close together that their edges were touching. One contained three warm eggs, the other held two that were cold. The bird had laid her normal complement of five eggs, but why were they not all in one nest? Both had obviously been constructed that season, but the one that held two eggs looked frail and seemed to lack the finishing touches. A plausible explanation is difficult to construct.

The nesting subspecies in Nova Scotia is the "Yellow Palm Warbler," *Dendroica palmarum hypochrysea*. Several observers have reported the "Western Palm Warbler," *Dendroica palmarum palmarum,* among birds in autumn. It is distinguished by a complete lack of yellow on its lower breast and underparts except for the undertail coverts. It nests in western Ontario and beyond, and may be more regular as a migrant here than generally realized.

Bay-breasted Warbler   PLATE 31

Dendroica castanea (Wilson)

Status Fairly common transient, uncommon in summer. Breeds. First spring migrants generally appear in mid-May (average 15 May, earliest 7 May). This warbler favours rather dense coniferous woods for nesting, and in summer is more common on Cape Breton Island. Migratory waves occur from late August through September, and it is generally last seen in October (average 14 October, latest 20 November).

Description *Length:* 12.5-15 cm. *Adult male:* Broad black band extending across forehead, through eye to side of neck; light buff patch on sides of neck; crown and nape rich chestnut (chestnut crown is sometimes largely or wholly lacking); back olive-brown, striped with black; two white wing bars; throat, breast and sides bright rufous; belly grayish white; legs and feet gray. *Adult female:* Similar but duller, throat and breast being largely white and sides only slightly washed with rufous.

Breeding A rough but compact structure of twigs and coarse plant stems, lined with fine black rootlets and soft grasses. The usual site is a medium-sized spruce in open coniferous woods, sometimes close to the trunk or perhaps more often saddled on a limb well out from the trunk, at heights of 2-6 m. *Eggs:* 4-6; white, marked with fine spots of cinnamon-brown of various shades and densities, chiefly around the larger end. On 27 June 1937 I watched a female carrying food to young in a nest at Albany, Annapolis County. The nest was in a large spruce tree about 8 m up, near the end of a long limb, in open evergreen woods. A more recent nest was found in 1969 by John Doyle at Lakelands, Hants County: on 4 June the female had just laid the foundation in a small spruce, close to the trunk, about 2 m up, in open woods; by 10 June the nest was complete but still empty; on 15 June the female was sitting on a full set of four eggs.

Range Breeds from the southeastern Mackenzie Valley, northern Alberta, central Manitoba, south-central Quebec, and Newfoundland, south to central Vermont, northern Michigan and northern Minnesota. Winters in Panama and northern South America.

Remarks This warbler is not normally seen in settled districts except briefly during migration. The male in spring attire with his striking chestnut breast and black face is readily recognized, as is the duller female, but in autumn dress, identification becomes problematic. The adult male still retains traces of brown on his flanks, but females and immatures are quite nondescript and closely resemble immature Blackpoll Warblers. The undertail coverts of the Blackpoll Warbler are pure white but those of the Bay-breasted Warbler are slightly buff. The back and head of the Bay-breasted Warbler are more vivid green.

The song of the Bay-breasted is a series of thin, high-pitched notes, quite devoid of melody, which some field observers find difficult to distinguish from the song of the Cape May Warbler.

Blackpoll Warbler   PLATE 32

Dendroica striata (Forster)

Status Common transient, uncommon in summer. Breeds. First spring arrivals generally occur in mid-May (average 13 May, earliest 1 May). Two earlier appearances must be considered abnormal: 10 near Canso on 18 April 1969 (E. Armsworthy) and 6 at Gardiner Mines, Cape Breton County, on 22 April 1974 (R. Beecher). This warbler nests in coastal and island spruce forests from Yarmouth to Cape Breton Island, and inland is regular in the Cape Breton Highlands. It is among our last summer warblers to depart, with major fall movements evident from mid-September to mid-October. Late birds are routinely seen in November and later (average 5 November, latest 5 December). An individual on Sable Island on 13-15 December 1968 may have been the same bird that frequented a feeder there from 1 January to 4 February 1969 (C. and N. Bell), giving us our only winter record (incorrectly reported as 17 birds in the second edition of this book).

Description *Length:* 13-14.5 cm. *Adult male:* Crown and nape black; cheek white; back gray with black stripes; two white wing bars; underparts white, with bold black stripes along sides; outer tail feathers tipped with white; legs and feet grayish yellow. *Adult female:* Quite different; upperparts, including crown, olive-green to gray-green streaked with dark gray; wing bars yellowish or greenish white; grayish white stripe above eye;

underparts vary from pale olive-yellow to grayish white; sides of head, sides of throat, sides of flanks streaked with dark gray; belly and undertail coverts white; legs and feet similar to those of male.

Breeding *Nest:* Compact and bulky, of coarse twigs, grass stems and lichens, with a lining of fine grass and a profusion of gulls' feathers which curl over the top to conceal the nest contents. It is usually located at low heights in a thick spruce of stunted growth in open woodlands, or in a small spruce growing in a recently cleared area. I have never known it to nest in thick growth or in well-shaded woods. *Eggs:* 4-5; white, rather heavily spotted with various shades of cinnamon-and darker brown, chiefly about the larger end. From 18 to 23 June 1922, six typically placed nests were found on Seal Island. None was over 2 m from the ground and all were saddled on small branches and well concealed by branches growing immediately above. Five nests held eggs and the sixth nest contained newly hatched young. The eggs were two sets of four and three sets of five; incubation of all sets was fairly well advanced, making it apparent that laying begins on Seal Island about the end of the first week in June.

Range Breeds from Alaska to Labrador and Newfoundland, south to Maine, the Catskill Mountains of New York State, central Quebec, northern Manitoba and central British Columbia. Winters in northern South America.

Remarks Blackpolls are more sluggish and slow-moving than most warblers and seem to thrive best in cold damp regions where the stunted, wind-wracked conifers are festooned with beard lichen. Seal Island is such a place. While I was there for eight days in June 1922 there was no respite from the cold and depressing fog that rolled in from the ocean, but these frail creatures seemed not to mind in the least, for they sang continuously.

The novice might confuse spring males with those of the Black-and-White Warbler; however, that bird has a striped rather than solid black crown. In fall, adults and immatures are virtually alike in appearance and are easily confused with fall Bay-breasted Warblers (see Remarks under that species).

Cerulean Warbler

Dendroica cerulea (Wilson)

Status Rare vagrant. References to this species in the nineteenth century are possibly the result of its superficial resemblance of immatures to the Tennessee Warbler, which was not noted until listed by Downs (1888). The first modern record comes from Sable Island, where a male was identified by Christel and Norman Bell on 6 June 1968. Since then, there have been eight spring birds, between 18 May and 14 June, and six fall migrants between 16 August and mid-October. Among these, single individuals occurred at Sable Island, Cape Sable, the inner Tusket Islands and Sydney; one was killed by gulls on Lobster Bay, Yarmouth County; three were on Brier Island; and five were on Seal Island. Only one was photographically documented: a female on Seal Island on 16 August 1983 (I. A. McLaren).

Remarks Cerulean Warblers breed north to southwestern Quebec and northern New Jersey, and their occasional presence as vagrants is not unexpected. Adult males are unmistakable. The bluish and greenish tones, strong white wing bars, pale eyebrow stripe and unstreaked backs of females and immatures are together diagnostic.

Black-and-white Warbler   PLATE 29

Mniotilta varia (Linnaeus)

Status Common in summer, very rare in winter. Breeds. It is generally among the earliest warblers to arrive (average 6 May, earliest 29 April). A bird in a Halifax garden on 2 April 1974 (W.J. Mills) and another (with an equally untimely Hooded Warbler and Northern Waterthrush) on Sable Island on 6 April 1984 were abnormally early. In summer it is widespread in deciduous and mixed woods through the province. Migration peaks are evident in late August and early September, but these birds linger routinely to November (average 5 November, latest 5 December). A bird in Halifax on 21 December 1974 was clearly beyond migrating, and individuals coming to feeders at Amherst on 13 January 1972 (E. and C. Desplanque) and in Yarmouth on 28 January 1964 (M. Higby) showed remarkable tenacity.

Description *Length:* 13-14 cm. *Adult Males:* Upperparts striped black and white, with conspicuous white line down centre of crown bordered with black; cheeks and throat black; upper breast and flanks streaked black and white; lower breast and belly white. *Adult female:* Similar but some markings lighter, brownish gray instead of black; cheeks and throat grayish white.

Breeding *Nest:* On the ground, usually at the base of a small tree and well concealed. Composed of grass, dead leaves and other dry vegetable matter and usually lined with soft hairs of various kinds. *Eggs:* 4; white, speckled with cinnamon-brown of various shades and densities. A nest at North Aylesford, Kings County, examined on 22 June 1945 was hidden at the base of a small birch in an open woodland pasture and contained four practically fresh eggs. One at Black River, Kings County, on 2 June 1922 also was placed at the base of a small birch on the edge of a clearing. It was composed of grass and dry fern fragments, had a lining of deer hair and contained four fresh eggs.

Range Breeds from the central Mackenzie Valley, central Manitoba, north-central Ontario, and Newfoundland, south to the southern United States. Winters from Florida and northern Mexico to northern South America.

Remarks When seen in its natural habitat this bird will likely be creeping actively over logs, under branches and up and down tree trunks, its antics being suggestive of a Nuthatch—because of this characteristic it is not likely to be confused with any other warbler. However, because of the similarity of its colour pattern to that of the Blackpoll Warbler, the novice might mistake one for the other. It should be noted that the Blackpoll Warbler has a solid black crown but this bird has a conspicuous white stripe down the centre of its crown. The Black-and-white Warbler is a bird of the woodlands, occurring in our gardens only during migration.

Black-and-white Warbler

American Redstart   PLATE 29

Setophaga ruticilla (Linnaeus)

Status Common in summer. Breeds. First migrants generally appear before mid-May (average 12 May, earliest 30 April). In summer it is widespread in deciduous growth, even in towns and villages. Fall migration is evident from the first week in August, with peaks occurring through September and occasionally into October. Stragglers are routine into November (average 4 November, latest 3 December).

Description *Length:* 11.5-14 cm. *Adult male:* Upperparts, including head, breast, wings and tail, black; sides of breast and a large central wing patch orange-red; large orange-red patch on each side of tail at base; belly and undertail coverts white. *Adult female:* The orange markings on the male are replaced with lemon yellow; top and sides of head gray; back and wings olive-gray; throat and underparts white.

Breeding *Nest:* Made of grasses, strips of bark, plant down and other soft vegetable materials deftly interwoven, with a lining of fine grass and sometimes hair, the whole structure being neat and compact. It is usually placed in the crotch of a deciduous tree or bush at low heights but sometimes 8-10 m up. Ornamental groves, hedgerows and orchards near human habitation are favoured sites, although it frequently nests in districts remote from human settlement. *Eggs:* 4-5; grayish white, spotted with various shades of brown chiefly around the larger end. Laying begins during the first week of June; a nest found on 30 May 1920 was nearly completed, and two others each held four partially incubated eggs on 14 June 1916.

Range Breeds from southeastern Alaska, the southern Mackenzie Valley, central Manitoba, central Quebec, and Newfoundland, south to Alabama, northern Utah and northeastern Oregon. Winters from Mexico to northern South America and in the West Indies.

Remarks Of all our garden birds, perhaps none is more strikingly beautiful than the male redstart. His brilliant colours of shining black, pure white and flaming orange-red, so charmingly displayed as he whirls about with tail widely fanned in pursuit of small insects, immediately capture one's attention. He is one of the most active and animated warblers, a restless creature, constantly in motion as though rushing to finish whatever needs to be done.

Prothonotary Warbler

Protonotaria citrea (Boddaert)

Status Rare vagrant. An early sight record by James Bouteillier of "several" on Sable Island on 7 September 1903 (McLaren 1981a) is plausible in view of recent occurrences. The next report, well documented by Guy A. Tudor, was of a male aboard MS *Thorshall* about 50 km off Halifax on 13 September 1953. Since then it has been quite regular with about 40 reports of 46 individuals, including several specimens and photographs. More than half have been found on the offshore and southwestern islands, but there are reports from throughout the province, including four from Cape Breton Island. Spring birds include a dozen occurring between 18 April and 9 June; an extraordinarily early one occurred at Cole Harbour, Halifax County, on 6 April 1973 (M. and R. Eaton). The rest have been reverse fall migrants, between 10 August and 28 October, with 12 birds in August, 14 in September and 7 in October.

Remarks This is a brilliantly costumed, golden-yellow warbler with blue-gray wings without wing bars. It nests north to northern New Jersey, central New York State and southern Ontario, and its conspicuousness probably contributes to its relatively frequent detection as a vagrant.

Worm-eating Warbler

Helmitheros vermivorus (Gmelin)

Status Rare vagrant. A male specimen in the American Museum of Natural History was taken on Sable Island on 30 October 1903 but was first reported in the literature by McLaren (1981a). The first modern sighting was also on Sable Island, a closely studied bird on 12 October 1967 (C. and N. Bell). Since then, there have been 10 individual occurrences, including two birds found dead and two photographed; 7 occurrences have been in spring (10-15 May) and 3 in fall (31 August to 14 October). An eleventh bird, aboard ship on Georges Bank on 2 September 1979 was conspicuously off course (D. Amirault).

Remarks This bird's plumage, with bold dark stripes on a bright buff head, is unmistakable. It breeds as nearby as Massachusetts, but its skulking behaviour probably prevents it from being more frequently seen on its occasional visits.

Swainson's Warbler

Limnothlypis swainsonii (Audubon)

Status One record. A weakened bird was found on Seal Island on 9 October 1972 (J. Boulva, I.A. McLaren) and collected for a first Canadian record.

Remarks This is the most southerly of the eastern North American warblers. It does not nest north of southern Illinois, southern Ohio and Delaware and is scarce and shy within its normal range. Its detection here among our more normal vagrants is exceptional.

Ovenbird   PLATE 33

Seiurus aurocapillus (Linnaeus)

Status Fairly common in summer. Breeds. First migrants arrive generally in early to mid-May (average 11 May, earliest 25 April). Individuals on 18 April 1961 on Cape Sable and on 18 April 1971 on Sable Island were unusually early. This bird is widely distributed in deciduous woodlands in summer. It is not abundant during fall migration, which seems to peak in late August and early September. Later records are routine (average 26 October, latest 30 November), but a dying bird in Halifax on 16 December 1974 (J. and S. Cohrs) had stayed at its peril.

Description *Length:* 14-16.5 cm. *Adults:* Centre of crown dull orange, bordered on either side with a narrow dark brown or blackish brown stripe; cheek light olive-gray; white eye ring; rest of upperparts brownish olive. Underparts white, boldly streaked with black, except throat and belly, which are unmarked; no wing bars; legs and feet flesh-coloured.

Breeding *Nest:* On the ground, completely arched over, with entrance at the side. Composed largely of decayed leaves, fern stalks and mosses, and lined with fine rootlets or deer hair. Usually located in shady deciduous woods. *Eggs:* 4; white and well covered with rather large cinnamon-brown spots chiefly around the larger end. Laying begins early in June. On 3 June 1933 one was seen at Albany, Annapolis County, gathering nesting material, and on 11 June 1905 at Black River, Kings County, a nest was found containing four fresh eggs.

Range Breeds from northeastern British Columbia, northern Alberta, central Manitoba, central Quebec, and Newfoundland, south to Georgia, Alabama and Colorado. Winters from the southern United States south to the Lesser Antilles and through Mexico to Colombia.

Remarks This warbler is found most often in shady woodlands, especially where deciduous trees predominate and where a brook or wet, mossy area is near at hand. Its nest is unique among those of our native birds. The roof is cleverly arched over in such a way as to suggest a miniature Dutch oven, hence the name Ovenbird. The colloquial name "teacher-bird" originated from its loud and distinctive song, commonly interpreted as *teacher-teacher-teacher,* given with a marked crescendo ending.
  Unlike most of our songbirds, this bird is a walker, and it constantly tips its tail while it moves with grace and agility over the mossy carpet of its shady woodland retreat. Although it is similar in behaviour to the Northern Waterthrush, with which it might be confused, it has white instead of yellowish underparts (heavily streaked in both birds), lacks the light brown line over the eye that is conspicuous in the Northern Waterthrush and has a dull orange crown patch that the waterthrush lacks.

Seiurus aurocapillus aurocapillus is the summer resident that breeds here. *Seiurus aurocapillus furvior* is the breeding race in Newfoundland that occurs here as a transient. A single *S. a. furvior* was collected by W. Earl Godfrey at Cape North on 30 August 1935. The two races are indistinguishable in the field.

Northern Waterthrush   PLATE 33

Seiurus noveboracensis (Gmelin)

Status Fairly common in summer. Breeds. Normally arrives about mid-May (average 13 May, earliest 6 May); however, five sightings between 4 and 22 April have also been reported. Such very early birds should be carefully observed and documented to avoid confusion with the Louisiana Waterthrush, which migrates earlier than the Northern Waterthrush. It is widely distributed in tangled thickets of deciduous growth in open, wet woodlands. It is generally secretive during the breeding season, but migrants first appear in late August and may build up to considerable numbers by late September. It is generally last recorded in October (average 17 October, latest 1 November).

Description *Length:* 13-15 cm. *Adults:* Upperparts dark olive-brown; pale brown line over eye; underparts pale sulphur yellow, heavily striped with olive-brown or blackish brown, except undertail coverts, which are white; no wing bars.

Breeding *Nest:* On or near the ground in wet, low-lying tangles of usually deciduous growth, well hidden in a mossy bank or the upturned roots of a fallen tree. *Eggs:* 4-5; white, speckled and blotched with various shades of brown. A breeding record is furnished by E. Chesley Allen (1916), who watched a pair feeding young on 4 July 1904 at Carleton, Yarmouth County. Several more nestings have been noted in recent years.

Range Breeds from central Alaska, the southern Mackenzie Valley, northern Quebec, and Newfoundland, south to New England and West Virginia, southern Ontario, central Saskatchewan and western Montana. Winters from southern Florida, the Bahamas and Baja California to northern South America.

Remarks Like the Ovenbird, to which it is closely related, it is a walker. It has a dainty mannerism, similar to that of the Spotted Sandpiper, of pausing now and then in its ambling to teeter a few times. Although called a "waterthrush," it is really a large member of the warbler family disguised as a thrush with a strong preference for wet places.

Its song is clear, loud and melodious. Of the several translations given, *hurry-hurry-hurry-pretty-pretty-pretty,* rapidly enunciated, seems to be most appropriate.

The best field marks are the conspicuous pale line over the eye, the heavily striped yellowish underparts, and its peculiar habit of tipping and teetering while walking.

Louisiana Waterthrush

Seiurus motacilla (Vieillot)

Status Rare vagrant. The first report was of a bird closely studied by Cristel and Norman Bell on Sable Island on the unusual date of 2 July 1966. They reported two more in August 1969, and the next year two more (one photographed by J. Burton) were present there between 6 and 10 August 1970. Since then, individuals have been reported on Sable Island on 27 May 1971, 18-19 May 1977, and 8 September 1978, and on Seal Island on 4 and 23 September 1974, and 31 August 1979.

Remarks This vagrant, nesting as close as southern Maine, is quite common within its normal range, and has probably been underdetected here because of its cryptic appearance and shy behaviour. The best marks by which to distinguish it from the Northern Waterthrush are its pure white eyebrow stripe which broadens, rather than narrows, behind the eye, its larger bill and its buff flanks, which contrast with its dull white underparts.

Kentucky Warbler

Oporornis formosus (Wilson)

Status Rare vagrant. It was first recorded on Sable Island on 1 September 1902 when a bird was collected by James M. Bouteillier (misprinted as J.M. Boutcher in Dwight [1903]). It was not reported again until 14 September 1964, when Benjamin Smith caught one at Cape Sable and was able to examine it in the hand. Since then there have been 12 records (including two birds photographed). Only three birds have been in spring: on 16 May 1976 on Seal Island, and later the same year on Sable Island on 1-4 June and 22-23 June. The others have been reverse fall migrants between 27 August and 2 October, four on Seal Island, and one each on Bon Portage, Brier, Cape Sable and Sable islands; and there was a very late bird on 11 November 1972 on Cape Sable (B.J. and S. Smith).

Remarks Although this bird is strikingly marked with yellow underparts and spectacles and nests north to southern New England, it is a shy dweller in the undergrowth and may easily remain undetected when it occurs as a vagrant.

Connecticut Warbler

Oporornis agilis (Wilson)

Status Rare transient. Reports of a dead bird on Sable Island on 6 October 1901 (Bouteillier 1901) and a sighting there on 15 September 1907 have been questioned (e.g., by Godfrey [1966]), although they are seasonally plausible. Since 1956 there have been reports of 24 individuals. The first was a male studied on Bon Portage Island by Evelyn Richardson on 17 May 1956. Three other spring records include a male at Barrington, Shelburne County, on the unusual date of 12 June 1969, well documented by Mrs. Richardson, and an equally laggard female on Sable Island on 12 June 1975, photographed by Davis Finch. The others have been fall migrants, between 25 August and 20 October, all but two on Bon Portage, Brier, Cape Sable, Sable or Seal islands.

Remarks This bird breeds in west-central Quebec and beyond to the west, and migrates along the Atlantic coast, rarely north of New England. Mourning Warblers can be confused with this species (see Remarks under the Mourning Warbler). Connecticut Warblers are very shy and may easily slip through the province unnoticed.

Mourning Warbler   PLATE 33

Oporornis philadelphia (Wilson)

Status Uncommon in summer. Breeds. This is among the latest warblers to appear in spring (average 26 May, earliest 9 May), and it continues to be found outside of breeding habitat well into June. It is most frequent in the northern parts of the mainland and on Cape Breton Island. Migration peaks have been noted from late August to mid-September, and few remain later (average 23 September, latest 18 October).

Description *Length:* 12.5-14.5 cm. *Adult male:* Head slate-gray; back, wings and tail olive-green; throat and upper breast gray, the feathers margined with black; lower breast to undertail coverts yellow. *Adult female:* Similar but head and breast paler, without black feather margins.

Breeding *Nest:* It nests on or very close to the ground. *Eggs:* Usually 4; white, well speckled with cinnamon-brown. The nest of this bird has not yet been recorded for Nova Scotia, but proof that it breeds here is provided by W. Earl Godfrey, who saw an adult carrying food near Baddeck on 13 July and observed three young just out of the nest near St. Peters, Richmond County, on 29 July 1954. It is probably breeding wherever males are heard singing regularly during June and early July.

Range Breeds from northern Alberta, central Manitoba, central Quebec, and Newfoundland, south to Nova Scotia, southern Michigan, northeastern North Dakota and central Alberta. Winters in Central America and northern South America.

Remarks It was not named for its sad call, like the Mourning Dove, but for the coloration of the male's head and breast, which suggests a dark veil of mourning. The song is not sad but is a bright and spirited twitter, a rapid reiteration of *pécha-pécha-pécha.*

In summer the bird shows a preference for expanses of dense deciduous undergrowth and is seldom found elsewhere.

The species with which it is most likely to be confused is the Connecticut Warbler, but that bird has a conspicuous white eye ring (although autumn female and immature Mourning Warblers have broken eye rings that may be misleading), is larger and has longer undertail coverts which give it a short-tailed appearance. Spring Mourning Warbler males may also be distinguished by the black-scaled appearance of breast and throat; these parts are grayer and much lighter in the Connecticut Warbler.

Common Yellowthroat   PLATE 33

Geothlypis trichas (Linnaeus)

Status Common in summer, very rare in winter. Breeds. Migrants normally appear from early to mid-May (average 11 May, earliest 25 April), and it is widespread in the province in summer. Small peaks of migration begin in September, with larger movements until mid-October and stragglers much later. It has occurred regularly on Christmas Bird Counts in Halifax and occasionally elsewhere, but the only later winter report is of a bird at Cole Harbour, Halifax County, on 20 January 1984 (R. Eaton).

Description *Length:* 11.5-14 cm. *Adult male:* A conspicuous, broad, black facial mask, bordered on crown by a narrow, whitish gray line; rest of upperparts, including wings and tail, olive-green; throat and breast rich yellow; belly white; undertail coverts yellow; flanks washed with brownish gray; no wing bars or white marks on tail. *Adult female:* Similar but lacks the black facial mask; lower breast and belly strongly washed with brownish gray.

Breeding *Nest:* Bulky and outwardly rough, composed of dead leaves, coarse grass and weed stems, with lining of fine black rootlets. It is placed at low heights, often only a few centimetres from the ground in low dense shrubbery, sometimes close to human habitation but usually far from it. *Eggs:* 4-5, more often 4; white, with relatively few speckles of various shades and densities of brown. Laying begins about 1 June; a female was seen carrying nesting material on 25 May 1922 at Albany, Annapolis County. A nest containing four fresh eggs was discovered at Gaspereau, Kings County, on 5 June 1908, and two nests, each containing four fresh eggs, were found by Harold F. Tufts at Caledonia, Queens County, on 20 June 1909.

Range Breeds from southeastern Alaska, the southern Yukon, northern Alberta, central Manitoba, central Quebec, and Newfoundland, south through the United States to Mexico. Winters from the southern United States south to Puerto Rico and Costa Rica.

Remarks This wren-like warbler, with an upturned tail and characteristic jerky flight, inhabits low, dense thickets and shrubbery adjacent to homes and farmlands and in barrens and regenerating logged areas, and is well known by sight and song. Both the male and female have a brilliant yellow throat, and the male has a black mask like that worn by a highwayman.

Its rollicking song has been written as *witchery-witchery-witchery*, with the accent on the "*witch*." Quite frequently the male, as though bursting with excess vitality, leaves his low perch and makes a short, ecstatic flight of 5-6 m up into the air, pauses and then, bubbling over with mixed melodies, flits jerkily back into the thicket's protective cover.

Its shape, coloration, habitat preference and general behaviour preclude its being confused with any other species.

Hooded Warbler

Wilsonia citrina (Boddaert)

Status Rare vagrant. This bird was not recorded until 1959, when a total of five were seen between early August and early September by Evelyn Richardson on Bon Portage Island and by Betty June and Sidney Smith on Cape Sable. Since then, there have been about 45 records of at least 60 birds, including specimens and photographed individuals. Virtually all have occurred on Brier, Bon Portage, Cape Sable, Sable or Seal islands, along with two on the *Lurcher Lightship*. Thirteen have appeared in April (including a very early one on Sable Island on 6 April 1984), six in May, and three in June (latest 14 June 1971, on Sable Island). Three unseasonal birds were seen on Sable Island on 2 July 1967. The rest have been reverse fall migrants, with about twice as many in September as in either August or October. A male was on Cape Sable between 2 and 13 November 1967, and another appeared at Sable River, Shelburne County, on 27 November 1963. The only other non-island record was most unusual: a bird at Ketch Harbour, Halifax County, during the Halifax West Christmas Bird Count on 27 December 1976 (B.K. Doane, E.L. Mills).

Remarks This bird is easy to identify: it is bright yellow below, the male has a black hood surrounding a bright yellow face and the female is distinguished from the similar Wilson's Warbler by her white outer tail feathers. It nests as near as southern New England and is regularly recorded as a vagrant.

Wilson's Warbler   PLATE 33

Wilsonia pusilla (Wilson)

Status Uncommon in summer, fairly common transient. Breeds. Generally appears in spring around mid-May (average 17 May, earliest 12 May). A bird on Sable Island on 18 April 1971 and another in Lunenburg County on 26 April 1974 were considerably ahead of normal dates. It is found throughout the province in summer but not in large numbers. Fall movements are seen from early to mid-September, but it is routine in small numbers much later (average 24 November, latest 12 December). A bird in Dartmouth during the Christmas Bird Count of 20 December 1969 and another at South Bar, Cape Breton County, on 4 January 1982 (H. Hopkins et al.) were noteworthy.

Description *Length:* 11.5-13 cm. *Adult male:* Glossy black cap or crown; rest of upperparts, including wings and tail, olive-green; no wing bars and no white marks on tail; underparts rich yellow. *Adult female:* Similar but lacking the black cap, though sometimes showing a slight trace of it.

Breeding *Nest:* Composed wholly of grass, the lining being of very fine quality; placed on the ground, usually embedded and well concealed in the side of a mossy hummock in open, boggy barrens with scattered growths of stunted trees and scrubby bushes. *Eggs:* 4; white, lightly marked with fine specks of cinnamon-brown in a delicate wreath around the larger end. Although a nest has not yet been recorded here, evidence that this warbler does breed here is provided by Allen (1916), who mentions having seen parents with young at Deerfield, Yarmouth County, on 10 and 13 August 1908.

Range Breeds from northern Alaska, Mackenzie Delta, central Quebec, and Newfoundland, south to Nova Scotia, Vermont, southern Manitoba and, in the mountains, to California. Winters from northern Mexico to Panama.

Remarks Look for this warbler in birch, alder and other deciduous thickets growing in the open sunny glades that occur in wet and swampy low-lying areas. In such places the chattering song of the male may be heard from late May to early July; once heard it is not soon forgotten.

The male's most distinctive mark is his neat, black skullcap. Females and immatures lack this mark and bear resemblance to Hooded and Yellow Warblers, but these two species have tail spots not found on Wilson's Warblers.

Like its many relatives, it feeds largely on insects. Its manner of feeding, however, is like that of a flycatcher, for it commonly sallies forth to take insects in the air—a characteristic shared by other members of its genus of "flycatching warblers."

PLATE 33
all adults

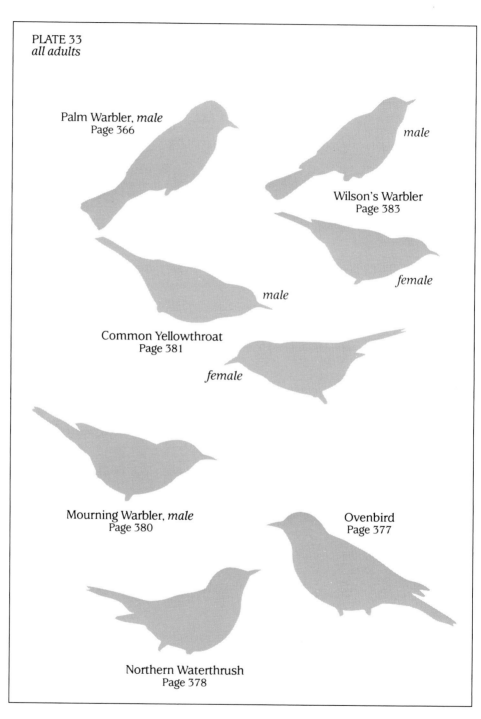

Palm Warbler, *male*
Page 366

male

Wilson's Warbler
Page 383

female

male

Common Yellowthroat
Page 381

female

Mourning Warbler, *male*
Page 380

Ovenbird
Page 377

Northern Waterthrush
Page 378

PLATE 34

House Sparrow
Page 452

male

adult, summer

female

European Starling
Page 341

female

juvenile

Rusty Blackbird
Page 428

male

Common Grackle
Page 431
male

Canada Warbler   PLATE 31

Wilsonia canadensis (Linnaeus)

Status Fairly common in summer. Breeds. This is one of the later warblers to appear in spring (average 19 May, earliest 12 May). It is widespread in summer in suitable habitats. Fall migration starts in mid-August, is well underway in early September and birds generally do not tarry (average last sighting 23 September, latest 18 October).

Description *Length:* 12.5-14.5 cm. *Adult male:* Entire upperparts slaty gray, with crown showing faint black speckles; slender line in front of eye, and eye ring, yellow; underparts yellow, with a broken band of black spots across upper breast in the form of a necklace; undertail coverts white; no wing bars. *Adult female:* Similar but colours paler, particularly the breast markings.

Breeding *Nest:* On or near the ground, composed of decayed leaves, grass, lichens and moss, with a lining of black rootlets. It is invariably located in wet, swampy places in woods of mixed growth, particularly where large trees have long since been uprooted by gales, leaving a tangled mass of decaying debris. *Eggs:* 4-5; white, speckled with cinnamon and brown of various shades chiefly around the larger end. A nest containing two fresh eggs, with two broken ones below it, was found at Caledonia, Queens County, by Harold F. Tufts on 29 June 1909 neatly embedded among the roots of a large upturned spruce in swampy woods. On 9 July 1956 a pair at Black River, Kings County, was disturbed while feeding young in the nest. The bills of both parents were laden with small caterpillars and the two flitted about anxiously. So dense was the tangle of fallen trees in this piece of wet, boggy woods that, in the time at my disposal, I was unable to find the nest, though its location was narrowed down to within a few square metres; another attempt two days later proved fruitless, for no Canada Warblers were seen there, the young presumably having flown in the interim.

Range Breeds from northern Alberta, central Manitoba and southern Quebec, south to the northeastern states (to Tennessee in the mountains) and central Minnesota. Winters in South America.

Remarks To locate a pair of these birds in summer, one should look for the nesting habitats I have described and seek out the wettest and most tangled spots. If one is familiar with the male's rich song, the task of locating the nest is greatly simplified, for during the entire nesting season he will be found close to his doorstep.
   The Canada Warbler is not readily confused with any other warbler. Note the lack of any white marks on its wings or tail, its clear lemon-yellow breast with a black necklace across it (absent in the young and indistinct in the female), its yellow eye ring and its bluish gray upperparts.

Yellow-Breasted Chat   PLATE 31

Icteria virens (Linnaeus)

Status Uncommon vagrant, very rare in winter. Although this bird was not recorded until 20 December 1951, when a dead bird was found at Port Mouton, Queens County, by Herbert Leslie, it has become one of our most regular vagrants since then. There were a dozen more reports by 1960, 100 or more by 1970, and over 200 reports representing hundreds of individuals by the end of 1984. These occurrences have been rather evenly distributed by month from September through November, with about half as many in August and December. Six have stayed or survived into January, and single birds have survived until 1 February 1967 and 4 February 1976, both in Halifax. A bird at Ingomar, Shelburne County, on 22 April 1961 (Mrs. A.P. Hamilton) and another during early July 1965 at Lower Ohio, Shelburne County (H.F. Lewis), are the only exceptions to this autumn-winter pattern of occurrences. Almost all reports have come from the southwestern half of mainland Nova Scotia, though there are records from virtually all counties of the province.

Remarks The largest of our warblers, this bird has neither the appearance nor the behaviour of any other members of its family. Its greenish back, white eye ring and bright yellow throat, breast and upper belly are warbler-like. However, it is considerably larger than a Song Sparrow, has a large, heavy bill instead of the dainty bill characteristic of other warblers, and behaves somewhat like a Gray Catbird. Its normal range in summer is only slightly to the southwest of Nova Scotia, so it is not surprising that it has found its way here; but why so many have reached our shores recently is a question for which a satisfactory answer has not yet been found.

Subfamily Thraupinae

Summer Tanager

Piranga rubra (Linnaeus)

Status Rare vagrant. Chamberlain (1887a) cites an undated specimen from Halifax, and Downs (1888) noted "one or two instances—spring." A bird collected on 25 April 1898 (Piers' notes) was characteristically early. There were only about 10 more records up to 1960, but since then it has been seen much more often. Among these recent occurrences there have been 6 birds in April (earliest on 3 April 1964 at Digby), 24 in May, and 3 in June (latest 21 June 1964 at Rockingham, Halifax County). It has been less frequent in autumn, with two in August (earliest on 19 August 1964 on Sable Island), three in September, and nine in October. A later male was seen in Yarmouth County on 9 November 1951, and a very late female visited the feeder of the Donald Robertsons in Shelburne on 1 December 1957. Only about half of these occurrences have been on the southwestern islands and Sable Island; the rest have been widely scattered from Yarmouth to Glace Bay.

Remarks The adult male remains bright rose-red all year, but the female is olive-green tinged with yellow, and can be confused with the darker-winged and greener females of the Scarlet Tanager. The Summer Tanager does not nest north of southern New Jersey but is now one of the most regular of the birds that "overshoot" their normal ranges in spring to land in Nova Scotia.

Scarlet Tanager

Piranga olivacea (Gmelin)

Status Uncommon vagrant, very rare in summer. This bird is so regular, with over 250 reports since 1957 about equally in spring and fall, that it might almost be best to accord it transient, rather than vagrant, status. McKinlay (1885) wrote of its occurrence in numbers near Pictou in May about 20 years earlier, and Chamberlain (1881) documented a flight to Brier Island on 15 April 1881. Evidently the bird was straying beyond its normal limits in spring then as today. Most such records today are from the southwestern part of the province, especially the islands, but there are reports from all regions, including Cape Breton Island. An adult male seen by Harrison F. Lewis at Sable River, Shelburne County, on 20 March 1963 was extraordinarily early. Most first spring reports are for May, although occasionally in April (average 13 May, earliest 1 April). Migrants may still be found on our islands and elsewhere into June (average of last spring records 28 May, latest 19 June). A half-dozen reports since 1965 from Annapolis, Halifax, Queens and Shelburne counties of birds in late June through July, including singing males, suggest that the species may breed in small numbers. Fall migrants generally reappear first in late August (earliest 5 August) and are usually last seen in October (average 15 October, latest 11 November). A very late male was on Sable Island on 6 and 7 December 1969. One at the feeder of Isabel Cossitt, at Smith's Cove, Digby County, after a heavy ice storm on 28 February 1979, seems unlikely to have wintered in the region.

Remarks The outstanding characteristic of this species is the brilliance of the adult male's plumage in spring and summer, which contrasts sharply with the dullness of the female's plumage. Its name is descriptive, for the male's head and body are brilliant scarlet and his wings and tail are jet black. The female is olive-green and blends so well with the summer foliage that her presence is apt to pass unnoticed. The food of tanagers is largely the insects found among the trees in which they spend most of their time. In spring they sometimes present a striking sight when hunting for insects in the seaweed stranded on our shores.

Western Tanager

Piranga ludoviciana (Wilson)

Status Seven records. It was first recorded in Digby, where a bright-plumaged male appeared in the garden of John Russell about 26 November 1957. It stayed in the vicinity until 5 December, when it was killed by a cat. A wing was salvaged and sent to W. Earl Godfrey, who confirmed the bird's identity. The next bird appeared at the home of Samuel Chivers at Sable River, Shelburne County, on 30 October 1960 (H.F. Lewis). A bird near Tusket, Yarmouth County, in late August 1962 was satisfactorily described by Adele Hurlburt. Other well described birds have been at Lower Ohio, Shelburne County (E. Harris), Cranberry Head, Yarmouth County, on 14 September 1976 (M. Hilton, A. Hurlburt) and at West Pubnico, Yarmouth County, on 27 December 1979 (D. d'Entremont). A female caught in a mist net set by Ross Anderson on Brier Island on 22 August 1980 was photographed, banded and released.

Remarks On 4 December 1957 I saw the Digby bird at close range and it appeared to be in good condition and in typical winter plumage, its face showing only traces of the crimson so conspicuously displayed in summer. In general appearance it suggested an over-sized American Goldfinch in summer plumage. The normal range of the Western Tanager is in the western mountains of Canada and the United States in summer, and from Oregon to Panama in winter, so our vagrants have been hopelessly lost birds.

Subfamily Cardinalinae

Northern Cardinal

Cardinalis cardinalis (Linnaeus)

Status Rare resident. Breeds. Jones (1879) reported that a female, in the company of a male, was shot in Halifax on 31 January 1871 and noted that "nothing in its appearance denoted the probability of its having escaped confinement." The species was not reported again until 31 January 1957, when a female continued to come to the feeder of Louise Daley in Digby until 4 March. On 6 January of the next year, another female appeared in the same place. One or two birds were seen during most subsequent years until an "invasion" occurred in winter 1973-74. Thirty were noted in Yarmouth County, 13 in Shelburne County, 3 in Digby County and 2 in Queens County; in late June 1974 there were still seven reports from Yarmouth County, and individuals were present more widely—a pair nested on the Edgar Hamilton property in Pubnico, Yarmouth County, and remained for several years. In 1976 a pair nested in Yarmouth and remained in the vicinity for three consecutive years. Since then, sightings have diminished, but birds have occurred regularly in the southwestern counties, in the Halifax area, occasionally elsewhere on the mainland and once on Cape Breton Island (two birds on 29 July 1980 at St. Esprit, Richmond County).

Description *Length:* 19-23 cm. *Adult male:* An all-red bird with a crest and black face patch around a heavy, red bill. *Adult female:* Brown with some red on wings and tail; black face; crest and heavy, red bill still distinctive.

Breeding *Nest:* Located in bushes or small trees, composed of loosely arranged twigs, bark, weeds and grasses, and lined with fine rootlets and hair. *Eggs:* 2 to 4; white or greenish white, finely marked with various tones of brown usually scattered over the surface.

Range Resident from Nova Scotia, southern Quebec and Ontario, and South Dakota, south to Florida and Guatemala.

Remarks The Northern Cardinal has been expanding its range northeastward for many years, and it is perhaps surprising that it did not establish a beachhead in Nova Scotia earlier than it did. That it is not loathe to cross water in its excursions is shown by the several records from Brier and Seal islands.

Rose-Breasted Grosbeak   PLATE 37

Pheucticus ludovicianus

Status Fairly common in summer, very rare in winter. Breeds. In some years birds arrive in numbers during the second half of April, in other years not until May (average 1 May, earliest 12 April). Females in Dartmouth on 8 April 1982 and at Canso on 4 April 1984 were abnormally early. The bird is widely distributed in deciduous woods in mainland Nova Scotia and less common on Cape Breton Island. Migratory peaks may occur from late August to late September, but stragglers are frequent (average 19 October, latest 15 November). It has been recorded in late December a half-dozen times in localities from Cape Breton Island to Yarmouth County; one bird wintered at Ralph Johnson's feeder in Liverpool in 1955-56, and another wintered at Beulah Berman's feeder in Barrington Passage, Shelburne County, in 1975-76.

Description *Length:* 18-21.5 cm. *Adult male:* Head, chin and back black; rump white; wings black, conspicuously marked with white; breast and lining of wings bright rose; rest of underparts white; bill grayish white; tail feathers black, the outer three on each side with large white areas on inner webs. *Adult female:* Upperparts brown, the feathers edged with buff; line through centre of crown buff; white line over eye; wings and tail brown with white markings; lining of wings yellowish brown; bill yellowish white.

Breeding *Nest:* Usually composed wholly of twigs, those used for lining being more delicate than the rest, though sometimes there will be fine rootlets in the lining. It is a fragile affair sometimes seeming to be barely strong enough to serve its purpose. The usual location is the upright crotch of a small deciduous tree or bush, often in hedgerows along the open countryside. It is placed at low heights, usually within 5 m of the ground. Because of the thick foliage, the nests are difficult to find in summer but are quite conspicuous after the leaves have fallen and readily distinguished by their general appearance of fragility. That the bird is accustomed to returning to the same immediate area for nesting year after year is suggested by the frequency of traces of old nests being seen near new nests. *Eggs:* 3-5; light blue, marked irregularly with spots of brown of various shades and densities. One nest near Kentville on 20 July 1936 contained four newly hatched young. It was in a thicket of deciduous growth about 2 m from the ground. One at Springville, Pictou County, reported by Harry Brennan, was exceptionally placed, in a fir tree, close to the trunk, about 5 m up.

Range Breeds from northern British Columbia, northern Alberta, central Manitoba, southern Quebec, and Nova Scotia, south to eastern Kansas, central New Jersey, and the mountains of Georgia. Winters from southern Mexico to Venezuela and Ecuador, occasionally to the northern United States at feeders.

Remarks Many people have heard this bird's song and mistaken it for that of a robin. The songs of these two birds are very similar but the cautious listener will detect a slight difference, this bird's notes being more hurried than those of the robin.

The male should not present any problem in identification, but the female, entirely different in plumage markings, suggests an overgrown sparrow or finch. The size and shape of her bill, however, will indicate her identity as a grosbeak. By elimination, her species can then be determined, for her plumage bears little resemblance to that of Pine or Evening Grosbeak females.

Black-headed Grosbeak

Pheucticus melanocephalus (Swainson)

Status Eight records. An adult male of this species was identified in her garden at Digby by Louise Daley on 31 October 1965. She was able to study it closely under excellent light conditions. A young male appeared at Beulah Berman's feeder at Barrington Passage, Shelburne County, in early November 1973; it stayed until at least 15 November and was seen by several observers and photographed by Ian A. McLaren. Another bird was seen by Edgar Spalding at Economy, Colchester County, on the unusual date of 18 May 1977. His description leaves little doubt that this was a near-adult male. Individuals seen by Alban Richard on Sable Island on 18-19 September 1978 and by Robert Turner at Sable River on 3 October 1980 were in the unmistakable adult male plumage. From their descriptions, birds documented as females on 10 August 1977 at Amherst (C. Desplanque), 15 October 1977 at West Pubnico, Yarmouth County (T. D'Eon), and on 13 October 1979 in Dartmouth (J.S. Cohrs, J. McLaren) could also have been young, richly coloured males, but in none was the diagnostic yellow on the belly noted.

Remarks This western relative of the Rose-breasted Grosbeak is occasional in the east. Adult Black-headed Grosbeak males are unmistakable, and young males are a far richer orange-buff below than either male or female Rose-breasted Grosbeaks. However, Black-headed Grosbeak females and immature males can be confusing—look for yellow on the lower breast or belly.

Blue Grosbeak

Guiraca caerulea (Linnaeus)

Status Uncommon vagrant. The first recorded bird was collected at Bedford, Halifax County, in the spring, about 1880 (Piers' notes). It was not reported again until 1961, when individuals appeared between 13 and 15 April at bird feeders in Waverley, Halifax County, and in Lydgate and West Middle Sable, Shelburne County. Since then there have been over 70 reports of this bird from all parts of the province, mostly from the southwestern counties and the Halifax area. Some 70 of these birds were seen in spring: about 30 in 1983, 12 in 1984 and the rest scattered among 10 different years. They often first appear in April (average 29 April, earliest 7 April) and latest spring sightings may extend into June (average 26 May, latest 4 June). Some 50 reverse fall migrants have been evenly distributed over the years since 1961. These have first appeared almost equally in September and October (average 22 September, earliest 1 September) and latest sightings have generally occurred in October (average 9 October, latest 3 December). Individuals have lingered around bird feeders in Halifax until mid-December 1980 and in Dartmouth until 5 January 1984, and a female was seen by Wickerson Lent at Deep Brook, Digby County, on 23 January 1975.

Remarks This species summers in the southern half of the United States, breeding north to New Jersey in the east. However, it continues to expand its range northward. In appearance, both sexes are like overgrown Indigo Buntings but with broad tan or buff wing bars.

Indigo Bunting

Passerina cyanea (Linnaeus)

Status Uncommon vagrant. Several nineteenth-century authors referred to the Indigo Bunting as rare without providing details, and Chamberlain (1881) obtained specimens from a "remarkable flight" to Brier Island on 15 April 1881, an event much like recent ones. In the first three decades of the twentieth century only four sightings were reported, but since then there have been over 150 records, representing hundreds of birds in all, from all parts of the province, but mostly from the southwestern counties. They have arrived virtually every spring, usually first in April (average 19 April, earliest 28 March), with numbers increasing in May. In some years, major "invasions" have been recorded: there were at least 60 individuals in 1963; and over 100 in 1984, including 12 at a feeder on Brier Island and 22 males and 5 females counted by Jerome D'Eon in the Pubnico area of Yarmouth County. Latest sightings have been generally in May (average 24 May; latest 24 June 1962 on Brier Island). The status of occasional singing males in June and of a bird on 5 July 1961 at Bridgetown, Annapolis County, remain uncertain, given the late occurrences of birds that are clearly migrants. It has been less regular and less abundant as a fall migrant, first reports not generally before mid-September (average 2 October, earliest 13 September); a bird on Sable Island on 14 August 1969 was unusually early. Last sightings are routine in late October and occasional in November (average 19 October, latest 30 November). A straggler occurred at Liverpool on 8 December 1960 and another was photographed at Porters Lake, Halifax County, during the Halifax East Christmas Bird Count on 15 December 1979.

Remarks The rich indigo blue of adult males in spring and the plain brown plumages of females and young birds are distinctive. These small sparrow-billed birds breed throughout the eastern United States and southeastern Canada, and rarely to southern New Brunswick. There is something enigmatical about their appearance in Nova Scotia. In the first place, when our April birds began their northward migration, they probably had no intention of coming to Nova Scotia. Brewster (1906) tells us that the normal time of their arrival at Cambridge, Massachusetts, is 15 May, and Palmer (1949) says that they reach Maine, where they breed, between 11 and 18 May. Why then do they come here in fairly large numbers so much earlier and with such regularity? The theory that they are "storm-blown strays" seems at first tenable, but their regularity, year after year, tends to rule out that idea. Storms don't occur with that much regularity! And where do they go after their sojourns here? True, some are picked up dead, but that does not account for the numbers that are seen in April and May. Perhaps many of them are re-oriented and return south.

Painted Bunting

Passerina ciris (Linnaeus)

Status One or two sight records. An adult male perched on a wire at Sable Island on 31 July 1965 was well documented by Christel Bell. A bird described as an all-green finch, the size and shape of an Indigo Bunting, was seen by Eleanor Androschuk on Sable Island in early September 1969.

Remarks Previous Canadian sightings have been considered to be escapees by James et al. (1976). The species does not nest north of Tennessee and southern North Carolina, but vagrants have occurred in New England, including Maine, in recent years. The male is quite unmistakable, and the female is unlike any other finch-like bird.

Dickcissel PLATE 37

Spiza americana (Gmelin)

Status Uncommon vagrant. The first record was of a bird collected on Sable Island on 12 September 1902 (Dwight 1903). The next was of a bird killed by an automobile near North Sydney on 3 December 1929 (Smith 1938). The species was not recorded again until 1952 but has been reported virtually annually since then. It is much less regular in spring. A very early bird at a feeder at the Head of St. Margaret's Bay, Halifax County, on 17 March 1976 (A. Mills) could have wintered somewhere in the region. A dozen others have occurred between 8 April and 7 June, and individuals appeared on Sable Island between 28 June and 1 July 1968 and on 24 June 1970. Over 350 autumn migrants have been reported, generally single birds but sometimes in groups of up to 15. They have routinely appeared first in August (average 7 September, earliest 1 August), but most have occurred in September and October, and a few into December, especially at feeders. They do not appear to tolerate our winters. The latest straggler on the mainland was in Halifax on 3 January 1971. Two birds that appeared on Sable Island on 20-21 February 1970 may have been attempting to winter somewhere in the region.

Remarks It is noteworthy that most of our records are recent. Is this a real increase or merely due to the greater number and abilities of observers? Although yellow-breasted and black-bibbed adult males are distinctive, young birds in autumn are similar to, and often associated with, House Sparrows.

Why so many of these birds appear in Nova Scotia from their breeding range in the mid-western and southern United States is particularly puzzling because the species normally winters from southern Mexico to northern South America.

Subfamily Emberizinae

Green-tailed Towhee

Pipilo chlorurus (Audubon)

Status Three records. A specimen picked up dead near the lighthouse at Cape Sable on 14 May 1955 by Benjamin F. Smith was later acquired by the Nova Scotia Museum. Since then there have been two other records: a bird on Seal Island on 18 May 1974 found by Barbara Hinds and photographed by Bruce Mactavish, and another photographed by Davis Finch on Sable Island on 10-11 June of the same year.

Remarks It is noteworthy that the three individuals of this vagrant from the southwestern United States have appeared in spring. When clearly seen, it is unmistakable, with its olive-green back, gray breast, white throat and rufous cap.

Rufous-sided Towhee

Pipilo erythrophthalmus (Linnaeus)

Status Uncommon vagrant, rare in winter. Although Haliburton (1825) included "Towhee Bird, Pewee or Chewink" in his list of Nova Scotia birds, there seems to be no other more explicit nineteenth-century reference. Piers' well-kept notes, covering many years up to the time of his death in 1940, do not mention it. It was first reported by John Piggot, who saw two at Smiths Cove, Digby County, on 27 September 1936. Up to 1960, another dozen reports were received, eight for October, two for May and one each for September and January. Since then it has become one of our most frequent vagrants, behaving more like a regular transient. Three birds reported for March had probably wintered locally. Otherwise, about 80 of our 100-odd spring birds have appeared in May (average of first sightings 4 May, earliest 7 April). Birds on Sable Island on 11 June 1967 and 15 June 1971 were clearly still on the move, but individuals on the mainland during June, some in song, suggest that a few may try to nest here. One such bird stayed in Dartmouth until 15 July 1957 and another was seen at Sable River, Shelburne County, on 4 July 1967. They are more common as fall migrants: some 230 individuals, sometimes in small groups, have been seen since 1960. Although they have occasionally first appeared in August and September (average 6 October, earliest 21 August) about three-quarters of the birds have occurred in October. They have been equally common as stragglers in November and December, by which time they are generally around birdfeeders. Such individuals have been sustained in small numbers in all parts of the province through the winter cold.

Remarks This large and hardy member of the sparrow family is a fairly common summer resident in New England; it is therefore not surprising that it has found its way to Nova Scotia. In fact, it is rather more surprising that it was so long in doing so. It is a ground feeder and its favourite haunt is a thicket along the open countryside— the type of habitat in which one might expect to find a Gray Catbird.

Its colour pattern is striking. Its upperparts, including head, back and breast, are black; the sides of the white underparts are boldly marked with bright rufous; and the long tail, which it seems to display proudly, is black with white trimmings near the end and very conspicuous in flight.

The bird is called a "towhee" because that is what it seems to say when it gives its common call.

Cassin's Sparrow

Aimophila cassinii (Woodhouse)

Status One record. A bird found on Seal Island on 18-20 May 1974 by Sylvia Fullerton, Barbara Hinds and Bruce Mactavish, was amply photographed by Sylvia Fullerton for a unique Nova Scotia record.

Remarks This drab sparrow from the southwestern United States was the second of its kind to visit Canada, one having appeared at Point Pelee, Ontario, two years earlier. It is a rather large sparrow, grayish, with spots and crescentic marks, rather than streaks, on its back and rump, and with diagnostic barring on the central tail feathers and white tips on the outer tail feathers.

American Tree Sparrow   PLATE 35

Spizella arborea (Wilson)

Status Fairly common transient, uncommon in winter. It generally arrives rather late among fall migrants and transients (average 12 October, earliest 24 September). During winter the American Tree Sparrow is a bird of weed-grown fields, wastelands and roadside thickets and is seldom seen in heavily wooded areas. There may be decided movements of birds in late March and early April, and latest sightings are normally in May (average 7 May, latest 26 May). Two at Gardiner Mines, Cape Breton County, on 10 June 1974 were very late.

Description *Length:* 15-16.5 cm. *Adults:* Crown rufous; nape bluish gray; back rich rufous, striped with black and light gray; wings show two white bars; throat and breast light dove-gray, with an indistinct, but sometimes quite distinct, black dot in centre of breast; sides washed with light or cinnamon-brown.

Range Breeds from northern Alaska, Mackenzie Delta, central Keewatin and northern Quebec, south to central Quebec, northern Manitoba and northern British Columbia. Winters from British Columbia, southern Ontario, and the Maritimes, south to the southern United States.

Remarks It is usually seen flitting among thickets along the highway or busily engaged in gleaning seeds from the taller weeds not yet covered by snow. Sometimes it will be found at feeding stations. Dark-eyed Juncos seem to be its favourite traveling companions.

   It can be best distinguished by its bright chestnut crown patch, its two conspicuous white wing bars and the small black dot on its otherwise unmarked gray-white breast. In general appearance it resembles our common Chipping Sparrow of summer, to which species it is closely related, but the American Tree Sparrow is slightly larger and its markings are definitely brighter and more contrasting, and the Chipping Sparrow lacks the black dot on its breast.

Chipping Sparrow   PLATE 35

Spizella passerina (Bechstein)

Status Common in summer, very rare in winter. Breeds. Spring birds normally arrive in late April or early May (average 3 May, earliest 20 April). Individuals appearing between 30 March and 11 April during four years since 1972 may have wintered in the region. It is found throughout the province in summer but is less common on Cape Breton Island and along the Eastern and Southwestern shores. In autumn it is sometimes abundant in coastal localities and on our islands, with large movements noted in late September and in October. Last sightings are generally in November, but small numbers routinely attempt to winter. For example, Austin L. Rand took a specimen at Wolfville on 19 January 1925, and there have been three January reports and one February report of one or two birds each since 1970.

Description *Length:* 12.5-14.5 cm. *Adults:* Crown chestnut; conspicuous white line over eye, margined by black line that runs through eye; cheek and rump grayish blue; back light brown, streaked with black; wings light brown, shading to gray on primaries, and with indistinct white bars; underparts grayish white, lighter on throat and belly.

Breeding *Nest:* Composed of fine twigs and grass stems, and usually lined with horse hair but sometimes with rootlets only. It is usually saddled on the low limb of a deciduous or an evergreen tree, without apparent preference; quite often the site chosen will be a climbing rose or other vine growing in dooryards. It occurs most commonly in agricultural areas; in the Annapolis Valley, apple trees in orchards are highly favoured nest sites. *Eggs:* 4; blue, with dark brown or black markings around the larger end in the form of a wreath. Nest construction begins about mid-May and continues throughout the month; a bird was seen carrying nesting material on 28 May 1951. Of many nests examined at North Aylesford, Kings County, only one was placed on the ground: it was a normal-looking nest which contained the usual four eggs; in spite of its vulnerable position, the young left it successfully.

Range Breeds from the southern Yukon, the southeastern Mackenzie Valley, central Ontario, southern Quebec and southern Newfoundland, south to Georgia, Mississippi and Central America. Winters from the central United States southward.

Remarks This gentle, friendly litle bird is most frequently found in close association with humans. It is tame and the location of its nest site often proclaims its trustfulness. One built its nest in a climbing rose on a trellis by a front door in Wolfville where many persons passed daily within a metre, but the parent birds showed no alarm. Usually the nest is well built, but an exception was noted in early June 1956. The nest was discovered while still being constructed. A day or two later, when still obviously unfinished, the female laid an egg, and construction then ended. On the day following the laying of the fourth egg, all the eggs fell to the ground through a gaping hole in the bottom of the loosely constructed nest.

Beginners may have difficulty identifying juvenile birds, which are extensively streaked below and lack any hint of the reddish caps of the adults (for distinctions, see Remarks under the American Tree Sparrow).

Clay-colored Sparrow

Spizella pallida (Swainson)

Status Rare vagrant. The first record was of two birds seen by Betty June and Sidney Smith on Cape Sable on 5 October 1973. On 18-19 May 1975, Bruce Mactavish and Stuart Tingley photographed a bird on Seal Island. Since then it has been almost annual, with 16 reports of 19 individuals, including some photographed. Of these, only 2 have been in spring, on 15 May 1976 and 15-16 May 1983, both on Seal Island; the other 17 have occurred between 6 September and 18 November, 11 of them in October. Most have been on Seal Island, with single sightings from Bon Portage Island, Cape Sable, and, on the mainland, from Amherst Point Bird Sanctuary, Dartmouth, and Hartlen Point, Halifax County.

Remarks This mid-western and prairie bird has been expanding its range eastward, with casual nestings to southern Quebec. Because of its resemblance to the Chipping Sparrow, it may have been overlooked as an occasional vagrant in earlier times. Fall Clay-coloured Sparrows are particularly distinctive, with their buffy white breasts, contrasting gray napes and white whisker marks.

Field Sparrow

Spizella pusilla (Wilson)

Status Uncommon vagrant, very rare in winter. Jones (1879), Downs (1888) and Hickman (1896) all asserted that it nested in the province. Although these assertions were probably based on misidentifications, it is difficult to determine which other species might have been involved because these authors list all the present-day breeding species as well. A report of "several" near Sydney on 8 June 1902 (Macoun and Macoun 1909) might be doubted. "Several" on Sable Island on 4 October 1902 (McLaren 1981a) and one near Yarmouth on 14 November 1907 (Allen 1916) are seasonally plausible. The bird was not noted again until 9 May 1954, when Evelyn Richardson found two on Bon Portage Island. Since then it has occurred annually, with over 150 reports of almost 600 individuals: most on Seal Island, some on other frequently visited islands and a few distributed elsewhere in the province (only one on Cape Breton Island); many have been photographically documented. Because they are northeast of their breeding range, they are given vagrant status, although they come and go more regularly than some transient or summer-resident sparrows. About 100 birds have been seen in spring, with first sightings regular in April (average 2 May, earliest 7 April) and last sightings in June (average 20 May, latest 10 June). There are no records of summering birds, and earliest fall migrants usually do not appear until October (three individuals between 21 August and 5 September; average of all other reports 12 October, earliest 22 September). As many as 40 were seen on Seal Island on 18 October 1981. They are not generally seen after mid-November (average 30 October, latest 19 November), but there are six records of birds on Christmas Bird Counts; two were seen on 10 February 1974 at a feeder at Porters Lake, Halifax County; and one wintered until 24 April 1975 at a feeder in Lower Eel Brook, Yarmouth County (P. Dobson).

Remarks The Field Sparrow nests north to southwestern Quebec and southern New Brunswick, so its frequent occurrence here as a vagrant is not surprising. The rusty crown (streaked with gray in young and autumn adults) is shared by several other species. Its most distinctive field marks are its pinkish bill and its indistinctly marked face which, together with its eye ring, gives it a blank-faced appearance. It has a lovely song, which is occasionally heard here in spring.

Vesper Sparrow PLATE 37

Pooecetes gramineus (Gmelin)

Status Uncommon in summer, rare in winter. Breeds. It was formerly fairly common and prior to 1960 the average date of arrival was 22 April. Since then, probably because it is less often encountered, it has been first detected somewhat later (average 3 May, earliest 18 April). In summer it is found locally in dry agricultural areas, largely in the Annapolis Valley. Fall occurrences are more widespread (including three Cape Breton Island records), and a few counts of 10 or more birds have been made from late September through October. Latest departures are difficult to determine, as birds after mid-November will probably attempt to winter. They have been occasional on Christmas Bird Counts (15 at Wolfville on 27 December 1967) and there are January and February reports of 1-7 birds during five winters since 1955.

Description *Length:* 14-16.5 cm. *Adults:* Crown and back light brown, streaked with black and buff; tail dark brown, the outer feathers showing white conspicuously; lesser wing coverts bright rufous; distinct pale eye ring; underparts grayish white, streaked with dark brown with tinge of buff.

Breeding *Nest:* On the ground, composed of coarse grass lined with fine grass, sometimes hair. This bird shows a preference for open pastures or fields where the grass is short and sparse as a result of poor soil. There it places its nest in the open, without the slightest attempt at concealment. *Eggs:* 4-5; usually bluish white, sometimes pinkish white, speckled with various browns. A nest found at Gaspereau, Kings County, on 19 May 1900 contained four fresh eggs. It was placed in an open field, entirely exposed, and composed wholly of grasses. Another found at New Minas, Kings County, on 11 June 1922 contained four slightly incubated eggs. It was similar in construction and location but liberally lined with horse hairs.

PLATE 35
all adults

Savannah Sparrow
Page 403

Song Sparrow
Page 410

Lincoln's Sparrow
Page 411

American Tree Sparrow
Page 396

Chipping Sparrow
Page 397

Swamp Sparrow
Page 413

400

PLATE 36

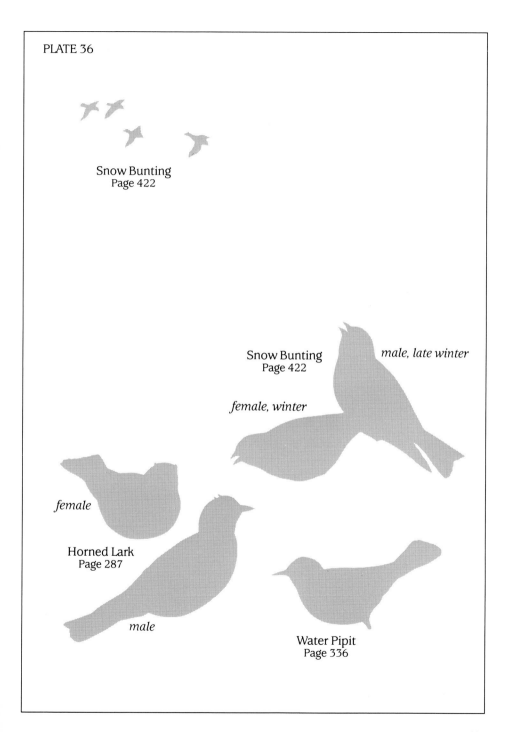

Snow Bunting
Page 422

Snow Bunting
Page 422

male, late winter

female, winter

female

Horned Lark
Page 287

male

Water Pipit
Page 336

Range Breeds from middle British Columbia, northern Alberta, central Ontario, southern Quebec, and Nova Scotia, south to North Carolina, Colorado and central California. Winters in the central and southern United States and Mexico.

Remarks This grayish brown, rather large member of its subfamily seldom comes to a feeding tray in winter but often is seen feeding on weed seeds in roving bands of Dark-eyed Juncos and Tree Sparrows. Its outstanding field mark is the white on the outer feathers of its tail, conspicuous in flight. The junco has similar markings but is a darker, slate-coloured bird.

Usually seen at low elevations, the Vesper Sparrow's favourite perch is a fence rail or post, from which the clear, pure and plaintive notes of its lovely song are impressive, especially when heard close at hand on a calm evening in early spring.

Lark Sparrow

Chondestes grammacus (Say)

Status Rare vagrant. It was first recorded from Sable Island (Dwight 1903), the specimen labelled 4 September 1902. Several were reported to have occurred on the island later that year, on 10 October (McLaren 1981a). It was not reported again until 1956 when one was seen on 9 August and another on 7 September by Evelyn Richardson on Bon Portage Island. Since then it has been virtually annual, with about 80 records of some 100 individuals, some photographically documented. Only four of these have been in spring: on Brier Island on 1 June 1963; at Wilmot, Annapolis County, on 13 June 1966; on Sable Island on 18 May 1970; and on Brier Island on 5 May 1973. Almost all fall birds have been reported from our regularly visited islands or from the southern counties, although there is one record from Inverness County. Two in mid-July 1963 near Yarmouth (the W. Lents) were exceptional, but it is an early fall migrant, normally first appearing in August (average 27 August, earliest 3 August) but not beyond October (average 24 September, latest 26 October); one very late bird was at Italy Cross, Lunenburg County, on 1 December 1984 (J. and S. Cohrs).

Remarks It is about the size of a House Sparrow, decorated with a long fan-shaped tail, handsomely trimmed with white corners that are conspicuous in flight. Its otherwise pure white breast is marked with a single black dot, and it has bright chestnut cheek patches. It should present no identification problem if observed under favourable conditions.

This western sparrow of open country formerly nested east to New York State and now seems to be extending its range eastward.

Lark Bunting

Calamospiza melanocorys Stejneger

Status Rare vagrant. It was first seen by Harrison F. Lewis and Willett J. Mills at Brier Island on 13 September 1955. Since then there have been 10 occurrences of 14 individuals. Spring males have occurred on Brier Island on 27 May 1967 (collected, W. Lent); at Granite Village, Shelburne County, on 7 May 1968 (Mrs. M. Allen); and on Brier Island on 25 May 1980 (R. Denton, A.R. Glavin). Fall birds have been seen at Lansdowne Station, Pictou County, on 28 October 1958 (two birds); on Cape Sable Island on 12 October 1959; on 4 September 1967 at Conrad Beach, Halifax County; and photographed at Seal Island on 4-5 September (two birds) and 1-3 October 1977. A late individual was identified at Conrad Beach by John Comer on 29 December 1959, and Harrison F. Lewis reported that three attended the feeding station of the Donald Robertsons at Shelburne in early January 1968.

Remarks This prairie bird is known as a rare wanderer to the east coast, from Newfoundland south. Spring males, almost solid black with large, white wing patches, could not be confused with any other bird that comes to Nova Scotia. Autumn birds are streaked brownish gray, like many of our sparrows, but their large size and stocky build (like a Bobolink) and whitish or buffy wing patches are helpful marks.

Savannah Sparrow   PLATES 35 & 37

Passerculus sandwichensis (Gmelin)

Status Common in summer, uncommon in winter. Breeds. Although first spring migrants are difficult to identify because this species routinely overwinters, the main arrival of the mainland-nesting subspecies *Passerculus sandwichensis savanna* generally begins after mid-April. Early April reports of these birds are sometimes misidentifications of the "Ipswich Sparrow," *Passerculus sandwichensis princeps,* the subspecies that nests on Sable Island. Migrant "Ipswich Sparrows" may first appear in late March (average 31 March, earliest 21 March) and peak numbers occur along the Eastern Shore from early to mid-April. In summer the mainland subspecies is common and widespread in meadows, coastal dunes, bogs and barrens. A few "Ipswich Sparrows" can be found in most summers mated with mainland birds in the coastal dunes of Halifax County. Migrant and transient Savannah Sparrows have largely gone by October, at which time the first migrant "Ipswich Sparrows" arrive on the mainland (average 8 October, earliest 27 September). Both Savannah Sparrows and "Ipswich Sparrows" winter in small numbers in coastal regions. Estimates of up to 27 of the former and 10 of the latter have been made on Halifax East Christmas Bird Counts. Some "Ipswich Sparrows" winter on Sable Island; as many as 100 were counted there in winter 1969-70.

Description *Length:* 12-15 cm. *Adults:* Crown dark brown with light brown median line, bordered by a buff line over eye; pale yellow mark in front of eye and (sometimes indistinct) on bend of wing; back and tail dark brownish gray with buff streaks; wings brown, the outer webs of the feathers edged with buff; underparts white, breast and flanks heavily streaked with dark brown or black. *P. s. princeps* ("Ipswich Sparrow"): Similar but larger (15-17 cm) and generally much paler; particularly distinctive, even in darker-backed individuals, are the narrower and paler brown breast streaks.

Breeding *Nest (P. s. savanna):* On the ground and composed wholly of grass; usually in hayfields, dunes, or grassier parts of bogs and barrens, rarely in salt marshes, just above the level of the highest tides. *Eggs:* 4-5; bluish white, thickly blotched or washed with cinnamon-brown of various densities. Laying begins in the latter part of May. Of eight first nests near Wolfville between 27 May and 16 June, four contained five eggs and four contained four eggs. *P. s. princeps* ("Ipswich Sparrow"): The nest and eggs are similar but slightly larger.

Range Breeds from northern Alaska, Mackenzie Delta and northern Quebec, south to northeastern and southwestern United States. Winters from Nova Scotia, southern Ontario and southern Alaska to Guatemala and Cuba.

Remarks This little sparrow, commonly called "gray-bird" on the mainland, is an inconspicuous and unobtrusive bird whose usual perch is a weed stalk in a meadow and seldom anything higher than a fence post. Its song is a weak, buzzy trill scarcely loud enough to gain the attention of the average person.

Although this bird bears some resemblance to the Song Sparrow, it is grayer than its browner and slightly larger cousin, and its tail is shorter and slightly notched, that of the Song Sparrow being somewhat rounded. Furthermore, the Song Sparrow lacks any yellow in front of its eye. "Ipswich Sparrows" are as large as Song Sparrows, but their pale plumage and Savannah Sparrow form are distinctive.

Welsh (1972) studied Savannah Sparrows on Martinique Beach, Halifax County. Extensive studies of the breeding biology and population dynamics of the "Ipswich Sparrow" were made by Ian A. McLaren and his students (Stobo and McLaren 1975; Ross 1980a, 1980b; Ross and McLaren 1981), to which the reader is referred for details on this uniquely Nova Scotian subspecies. In addition to their larger size and paler plumage (clearly adapted to their dune-grass habitat), "Ipswich Sparrows" migrate earlier in spring and later in fall, have more successive broods (three routinely and occasionally four, compared with two routinely among mainland birds) and tend to be more frequently polygynous (males often with two, and occasionally more, females in their territories).

In addition to the two breeding subspecies, *Passerculus sandwichensis labradorius* also occurs as a spring and fall transient with unknown frequency. W. Earl Godfrey collected an individual at Cape North, Victoria County, on 5 September 1935, and another was taken by Robie W. Tufts at Spa Springs, Annapolis County, on 8 October 1942. Although generally darker than *P. s. savanna,* with blackish streaks on its back and breast, it is not definitely distinguishable in life.

Grasshopper Sparrow

Ammodramus savannarum (Gmelin)

Status Rare vagrant. It was first recorded on Seal Island, where one was collected by Charles R.K. Allen on 4 October 1964. It has been almost annual since, with about 50 occurrences involving some 170 birds. Only two birds have come in spring: one between 17 and 21 May 1977 on Seal Island and another carefully studied by Robert B. Dickie at Russell Lake, Dartmouth, on the unusual date of 20 June 1982. Most of our fall migrants have been on Seal Island; a few have occurred on the coast or on other islands of the Southwestern Shore. Apart from individuals on Brier Island on 31 August 1975 and at Matthews Lake, Shelburne County, on 29 August 1980, they have not appeared before late September (average 6 October, earliest 23 September). Some remarkable counts have been made on Seal Island during migration peaks: 11 on 18 October 1974, 11 on 11 October 1976, and 9 on 13 October 1980. Although late migrants are not normally seen after November (average 26 October, latest 14 November), a straggler remained at Economy, Colchester County, 18 November-14 December 1972 and four later birds (two photographed) have been reported from Christmas Bird Counts (Broad Cove, Lunenburg County; Cape Breton Highlands National Park; and two on the Halifax East count).

Remarks This little sparrow from the United States and extreme southern Canada has nested in nearby southern Maine. It is distinctly flat-headed, with a prominent eye ring, a short tail and a generally buffy appearance. As this sparrow prefers to run or hide in the grass, it presents a challenge for discovery and identification.

The absence of earlier records and its recent regularity probably reflect increases in the numbers of skilled observers rather than an increase in vagrancy by the bird. In fact, it has greatly decreased in numbers as a breeding bird in the northeastern part of its range in recent years.

Henslow's Sparrow

Ammodramus henslowii (Audubon)

Status Two sight records. These sightings have been accompanied by convincing details: a bird seen on Seal Island by Bruce Mactavish and Stuart Tingley on 10-12 October and (the same bird?) 23 October 1976, and another seen there by Mactavish on 9 October 1978.

Remarks This species, which nests in the northeastern and mid-western United States, north to southwestern Quebec, is as elusive as the Grasshopper Sparrow, and clearly much rarer here. It is more olive about the head, darker billed, and striped on the breast.

Le Conte's Sparrow

Ammodramus leconteii (Audubon)

Status One record. This bird was carefully identified on Seal Island on 6 October 1974 by Bruce Mactavish (who also photographed it), Ross Anderson and Pierre Béland.

Remarks This mid-western Canadian bird nests as far east as central Quebec and may be a more regular transient than our single record suggests. Like other *Ammodramus* species, it is secretive. It is distinguished by its rich buff face and breast, dark bill, darkly striped flanks and, above all, by the distinct "tick" mark at the posterior end of its gray face patch.

Sharp-tailed Sparrow   PLATE 37

Ammodramus caudacutus (Gmelin)

Status Fairly common in summer, rare in winter. Breeds. Birds usually arrive in numbers during the first two weeks of June, but a few may appear earlier (average 31 May, earliest 6 May). It is found in summer about salt marshes, occasionally in freshwater marshes along all our coasts and sometimes well inland on tidal rivers. Last sightings are usually in October (average 26 October, latest 5 December). Stragglers have occurred on Christmas Bird Counts: at Broad Cove, Lunenburg County, in 1972, and on most Halifax East counts since 1979. A bird at Cole Harbour, Halifax County, on 4 February 1964, two there on 1 March 1981 and up to five there in January 1982 and two there on 1 March 1981 all indicate regular overwintering in small numbers.

Description *Length:* 12.5-15 cm. *Adults:* Upperparts brownish or grayish olive, the back with obscure, paler stripes; broad, bluish gray line through centre of crown; cheeks gray, margined with two broad, buff lines, one over the eye and the other below the cheek; tail feathers narrow and pointed at ends, the outer ones shorter than the central ones; breast and sides cream-coloured, sparsely and indistinctly streaked with dull gray; throat grayish white; belly white.

Breeding *Nest:* On the ground in tall, rank grassland that has not been plowed for several years, preferably never; small and deep, composed of soft grass, with lining of smooth fine grass, and fastened to the stems of new grass so that the base of the nest is about flush with the ground surface (rarely it is slightly elevated above the ground). There is some indication that these birds may be colonial in their nesting. Seldom is a pair seen isolated from others of its kind. I have found two nests within about 12 m of each other, and four nests in a 0.5 ha field where additional males were singing close at hand. Such group nesting may result from a shortage of suitable grassland. It has been noted repeatedly that a field growing hay for only one year does not attract them. They insist upon sites where the ground is covered with thick, dead grass of past years, perhaps because this condition provides better nest concealment. The foregoing is based on observations made on the dykeland meadows near Wolfville but is believed applicable to other locations where this bird nests in the province. *Eggs:* 4-6, sets of 4 and 5 about equally divided, 6 being unusual; pale greenish blue, speckled with various shades of light brown. Of 36 nests I have examined, 18 held four eggs, 17 held five, and 1 contained six. My earliest date for eggs is 17 June 1942, when two nests were found with complete sets of fresh eggs. Herbert Brandt and Albert Dixon Simmons found a nest at Port La Tour, Shelburne County, on 12 June 1942, which contained five fresh eggs. Brandt wrote (letter to R.W. Tufts) "This nest was evidently an early effort for the bird in an early spring, for we carefully 'dragged' the square mile without finding further indications. About 15 pairs were observed in this wide meadow." Rand found a nest at Wolfville on 16 July 1925 that contained five young about ready to fly. The validity of Lewis's (1920) record of a nest containing fully fledged young on 12 June 1920 near Yarmouth was questioned by Rand (1929) because of its date, the appearance of the young, and the nest site. The latest date for fresh eggs of first laying is 1 July 1926 and 1927. A total of three nests were found on these dates: one contained five fresh eggs and the other two each held four slightly incubated eggs.

Sharp-tailed Sparrow

Range Breeds in meadows adjacent to salt marshes in James Bay, the St. Lawrence River and the Magdalen Islands, south to North Carolina; also in freshwater marshes of the prairie provinces. Winters in coastal marshes (casually in Nova Scotia) from Massachusetts to Florida and Texas.

Remarks Although this bird nests fairly commonly in many districts, even those who know the more common local birds may mistake it for a Savannah Sparrow without a second glance. The two do resemble each other and associate closely at nesting time, but a careful observer, even without the aid of binoculars, will detect the difference. This bird is smaller and has a slightly tawny appearance that the Savannah Sparrow does not, its breast is much less distinctly striped and its flight is more "buzzy." When it takes off to skim over the tall grass, its wings beat so rapidly that they appear as a blur; the wing-beats of the Savannah Sparrow are slower.

Its song is short and distinctive: it starts with a husky, lisping twitter and ends in what to me sounds like *t-h-r-u-s-hlup,* all sung in about a second. At the height of nesting season, the male sometimes will climb into the air at a rather sharp angle, on fluttering wings, to a height of 3-5 m and then float down on set wings, gushing with song as he drops out of sight into the long grass.

Our breeding birds belong to the subspecies *Ammodramus caudacutus subvirgatus,* found in northern Maine, the Maritimes and along the lower St. Lawrence River. Two birds seen by Fulton Lavender at Russell Lake, Dartmouth, in mid-October 1980 were believed to be of the prairie race *A. c. nelsoni,* as were individuals at Cole Harbour on 9 January 1982 and 15 January 1984 (I.A. McLaren, J. Kearney, E.L. Mills et al.). Colour slides of the last bird suggest that it could equally well be of the James Bay race, *A. c. altera.* Both inland subspecies, especially *A. c. altera,* are regular in New England, and it is possible that unusually early spring migrants belong to these populations. They can be distinguished by their much brighter, buffier breasts and heads, strong white stripes on much browner backs, and absence (or obscurity on *A. c. altera)* of breast streakings.

Seaside Sparrow

Ammodramus maritimus (Wilson)

Status Rare vagrant. A sparrow believed to have been this species was seen by Robie W. Tufts on the Grand Pré meadows on 29 November 1952. On 4 February 1962, a specimen was collected at East Lawrencetown, Halifax County, by Charles R.K. Allen and Lloyd B. Macpherson. Since then there have been 16 occurrences of at least 19 birds. The only spring sighting was on Sable Island on 10 May 1971 (D.W. Welsh). The earliest fall migrant was at Eastern Passage, Halifax County, on 16 August 1979 (F.L. Lavender), and another bird was at Economy, Colchester County, on 27 September 1972. Most others have been seen from October through December (including Christmas Bird Counts) at Brier Island, Seal Island, Cole Harbour, Halifax County (three years; a total of four birds), and Economy (four years). One at Cole Harbour in

December 1979 was seen there until 10 February 1980. An individual at Conrad Beach, Halifax County, on 29 January 1967, and up to three there in mid-January 1974 were only detected after the freezing of the salt marshes drove them to the margins.

Remarks This dark, short-tailed sparrow, with a very long, pointed bill, nests in coastal marshes from Massachusetts south. Birds that arrive here in fall and attempt to winter are clearly misoriented. The 1962 specimen, and the January 1974 birds photographed by Ian A. McLaren, appear to be of the northernmost subspecies, *Ammodramus maritimus maritimus*. A bird McLaren photographed at Cole Harbour dyke on 2 January 1980 had strong blackish streaks dorsally and broad, dark streaks on its breast and sides. Its appearance suggested one of the more southern subspecies, perhaps *Ammodramus maritimus macgillivraii*, which nests from North Carolina to Georgia.

Fox Sparrow   PLATE 38

Passerella iliaca (Merrem)

Status Uncommon in summer, fairly common transient, rare in winter. Breeds. In spring it usually appears in late March (average 27 March, earliest 19 March), with main movements in the first half of April. Although usually it is briefly common in central and northern counties, it is scarce in some years in southern parts (see Remarks). In summer it may be found on spruce-clad islands from Bon Portage Island northward along the Southwestern and Eastern shores, on the coast proper from northeastern Halifax County northward, and in more barren inland areas of Guysborough County and Cape Breton Island. Fall transients outside breeding areas generally appear rather late (average 14 October, earliest 1 October). Several in Dartmouth on 19 August 1967 (M. Clayden) were highly anomalous. Stragglers over winter are usually seen at feeding stations. In some years considerable numbers remain: they were recorded on 10 of 24 Christmas Bird Counts in 1965-66.

Description *Length:* 17-19 cm. *Adults:* Upperparts rufous brown, the feathers edged with bluish gray; rump and tail bright rufous; underparts white, heavily streaked and spotted with dark to reddish brown; middle of belly white.

Breeding *Nest:* On the ground or in low bushes, in sparsely wooded areas; composed of coarse grass lined with fine grass, mosses and feathers. *Eggs:* 4-5; pale blue or greenish blue, speckled and blotched with varying shades of brown. Although the beautiful singing of males in their territories had long been known to occur in summer on our smaller Atlantic coast islands and on Cape Breton Island, nesting has only been confirmed in recent years. Kempton (1891) described a nesting, but the indefinite locality and questionable habitat description render the record suspect. An adult was seen carrying food on middle Halibut Island, Halifax County, on 25 June 1966 by John Comer and Barbara Hinds. Since then, three nestings have been detailed for the Maritimes Nest Records Scheme.

Range Breeds from northern Alaska, northwestern Mackenzie, southern Keewatin, northern Quebec, and Labrador, south to southwestern Nova Scotia, and in the mountains south to California. Winters from southern British Columbia and the central United States to the southern United States.

Remarks Regarding the erratic pattern of this bird's migration through Nova Scotia, Harrison F. Lewis suggests that the birds may follow a preferred route along the south shore of New Brunswick until they can cross the upper Bay of Fundy or come in over land through Cumberland County. "In those springs we see few Fox Sparrows in Shelburne County," he remarks. "But there are springs when, at the time of their migration, the snow still lies deep on the route above mentioned. When so confronted, the migration turns southward from eastern Maine or from Grand Manan and passes through southwestern Nova Scotia and Fox Sparrows are then common there."

This bird is most likely to be confused in life with the Hermit Thrush, which also has a conspicuous rufous tail. However, the thrush has a slender bill quite unlike that of any sparrow, and its underparts are more lightly spotted.

Song Sparrow   PLATE 35

Melospiza melodia (Wilson)

Status Common in summer, uncommon in winter. Breeds. Spring arrivals can readily be noted, in localities (e.g., Cape Sable) where no wintering birds have been present, in the second half of March (average 23 March, earliest 8 March). Larger numbers appear in early April, when migrant groups of 50 or more are often seen. One banded in Knox County, Maine, on 29 March 1960 appeared 10 days later in Shelburne County. Song Sparrows are widespread in summer in relatively open habitats with adequate brushy cover. Major movements have been recorded from mid-September to late October, but many attempt to winter, making late migrants difficult to record. Estimates of over 100 have been made on Christmas Bird Counts at Broad Cove, Lunenburg County (1976), Halifax West (1976, 1977, 1984), and Wolfville (1976, 1979). Song Sparrows attend feeding stations in winter but are by no means dependent on them.

Description *Length:* 14-16 cm. *Adults:* Gray line through centre of rich brown crown; light gray line over eye; rufous line extending from eye to behind ear; feathers on back streaked with black and various shades of brown or buff; no wing bars; tail rufous, the outer feathers shorter than central ones; belly white; breast and sides boldly striped with black or brown, merging into a conspicuous spot on centre of breast. *Juveniles:* No breast spot.

Breeding *Nest:* Composed of weed stems and coarse grass with lining of fine grass, hair or both. Early nests are usually placed on the ground and always well concealed. Later in the season, nests are perhaps more often built low in trees and bushes, concealed by the foliage. Nests are placed in a variety of sites, such as in vines, brush piles and natural cavities in tree trunks, but a most unusual one was at Melanson, Kings County, on 23 July 1939, where I saw a Song Sparrow with food in its bill enter a Tree Swallow nest box. *Eggs:* 4-5, usually 4; bluish white, speckled all over or sometimes blotched with rufous brown so heavily as to conceal the ground colour. The earliest date for a complete set is 20 April 1894, when a nest was found containing four slightly incubated eggs. One nest containing five eggs, found on 3 July 1915 near Wolfville, was probably a second nesting, and another found there containing newly hatched young on 6 August 1932 was probably a third nesting.

Range Breeds from the Aleutian Islands, southern Alaska, southeastern Mackenzie Valley, northern Manitoba, southern Quebec and southern Newfoundland, south to northwestern South Carolina, northern Arkansas and in the mountains to Mexico. Winters from Nova Scotia, southern Ontario and southern Alaska south to the southern United States.

Remarks Perhaps the best known of our sparrows, this bird is as much at home about our dooryards and orchards as it is in areas far removed from habitation. It is a persistent songster in the breeding season, beginning with weaker and less melodious efforts as early as January and occasionally uttering a new fragmentary song well into autumn.

In summer its food consists largely of insects but on occasion it will eat fruit. On 16 July 1949, one was seen in a chokecherry tree at Black River, Kings County, competing with Purple Finches for the ripe fruit. In winter it is practically dependent upon seeds.

When a Song Sparrow enters a birdbath in summer, it scratches one or both ears at least once, usually several times during the operation.

An incident worthy of note is told by Norman MacRae. On 3 April 1952 his cat brought home a live Song Sparrow to his farm in Lower Wolfville. A casual examination revealed no injury. When released, he expected it to take off in haste, but instead it flew to the nearest branch overhead, shook itself vigorously and burst into song.

In their respective plumages, which show considerable variation with age and season, the Song, Lincoln's, Savannah and Swamp Sparrows can present identification problems.

Lincoln's Sparrow   PLATE 35

Melospiza lincolnii (Audubon)

Status Uncommon in summer. Breeds. It arrives generally by mid-May (average 14 May, earliest 27 April). Two on Brier Island on 22 April 1973 (W.P. Neily) were well ahead of schedule. In summer it is fairly common in Pictou, Antigonish and Guysborough counties and on Cape Breton Island, but elsewhere uncommon to rare. It is most often encountered in fall migration, with movements of from a few to 50 or more recorded for late September and the first half of October. Latest sightings are normally in October or November (average 24 October, latest 1 December). Two were found in late December 1957 on Bon Portage Island, and other individuals have turned up on the Pictou Christmas Bird Count on 28 December 1967 and on Halifax East counts on 15 December 1979 and 19 December 1981; one was seen at Economy, Colchester County, on 13-14 December 1981.

Description *Length:* 13.5-15 cm. *Adults:* Crown brown with gray median line; eye stripe and area behind ear also gray; rest of upperparts crown to tail, buffy olive, streaked with black; tail feathers narrow and somewhat pointed; wing mainly rusty brown; underparts mainly white, breast and sides finely streaked with black; broad band of buff across breast and down sides; buff stripes on sides of throat.

Breeding *Nest:* On the ground, well concealed, usually in wet, bushy pasture land. *Eggs:* 4-5; pale green or buff, sometimes almost white, thickly spotted with reddish brown and lavender. Austin W. Cameron discovered a nest on 29 June 1970 at South Lake Ainslie, Inverness County. It was well concealed in debris from felled trees on a steep hillside immediately above a wooded marshy area. The bird did not flush until underfoot; when flushed it was nervous and evasive but stayed nearby chipping excitedly. Another, presumably the mate, was singing close by. The nest contained three young, recently hatched. A nest discovered at Whycocomagh, Inverness County, on 3 July 1965 by S.D. Whitman, contained four young only a few days old (Maritime Nest Records Scheme). On 22 June 1949 at Harrigan Cove, Halifax County (near the border of Guysborough County), George Boyer saw a bird carrying food. Look for the nest in wet swales wherever males are regularly heard singing in June.

Range Breeds from Alaska, northern Manitoba, central Quebec, and Newfoundland, south to Nova Scotia, northern New York State, northern Minnesota, and California. Winters from the southern United States to Guatemala.

Remarks Lincoln's Sparrow is known to few beginning bird students, even those from areas where the bird nests and occurs commonly. There are perhaps two reasons for this: First, it resembles several other members of its drab-coloured subfamily, and thus is readily overlooked in the field. Second, it is shy and elusive by nature, adept in the art of keeping out of sight. When the open, wet bogs studded with dwarfed spruces and alders it favours for nesting grounds are invaded, it usually stops singing as a precautionary measure, and from then on its presence is known only by glimpses gained of a nervous, furtive little bird, constantly chipping in an almost frenzied manner as it flits about, rarely still for a second.

It has a delightful song but, in order to hear it, one must wait patiently, quiet and out of sight. Even if heard once, it may take some time before the listener is rewarded with a repetition of the song, for its normal singing pattern is irregular and spasmodic.

It mixes with other sparrows during fall migrations and is readily overlooked.

Its buffy brown breast band, fine breast stripes and grayish brown face are marks to distinguish it from other sparrows. Song and Swamp Sparrows in juvenile plumages also have buffy suffusions across the breast but are darker overall than young Lincoln's Sparrows.

Swamp Sparrow   PLATE 35

Melospiza georgiana (Latham)

Status Fairly common in summer, rare in winter. Breeds. Migrants first arrive in April (average 15 April, earliest 6 April) but are most commonly reported in May. In summer it is locally common throughout the province in suitable habitat such as wet, marshy areas with thick growths of reeds or other dank vegetation. Fall migration is most evident in late September to mid-October, but latest migrants cannot be distinguished from those few that intend to winter. Estimates of 12-23 birds have been made on five Halifax East Christmas Bird Counts since 1973. Small numbers seem to survive through winter, occasionally at feeders, but 20 around Russell Lake, Dartmouth, on 25 January 1983 were unusual.

Description *Length:* 13-14 cm. *Adults:* Crown chestnut; dark line behind eye and light line over it; back reddish brown, broadly streaked with black; side of neck slate-coloured; rump light brown; throat and belly white; flanks buffy brown; breast gray and unstreaked.

Breeding *Nest:* Composed of coarse weed stems with lining of fine soft grass, placed among weeds or low bushes in wet or marshy ground. It is sometimes fastened to the stems of cattails or other coarse water plants, a few inches above water. *Eggs:* 4; bluish white, well speckled, blotched and washed with rufous. Laying begins during the second week in May. A nest found on 18 May contained four slightly incubated eggs and was lined with soft grass and fastened to the stems of coarse weeds about 30 cm above ground in a bushy swale near Wolfville. Another nest at Albany contained four fresh eggs on 22 May 1925; it was located on the margin of a sluggish stream, fastened to weed stems and slightly above ground. A rather late date for fresh eggs is 28 May 1905, when a set of four was examined near Wolfville. The nest was in a cattail swamp, fastened to the stalks, about 20 cm above water. The exterior was rough but the lining was of very fine grasses.

Range Breeds from southwestern Mackenzie Valley, northern Manitoba, central Quebec, and Newfoundland, south to New Jersey, West Virginia and northeastern North Dakota. Winters from the southern part of its breeding range to the Gulf Coast and Texas.

Remarks Good field marks for this bird at close range are its dark chestnut crown patch; gray, unstreaked breast; and dark appearance. The Chipping Sparrow has similar marks, but the Swamp Sparrow is more robust and lacks the black line through the eye and white one above that the Chipping Sparrow displays; furthermore, the habitats of these two birds are very different. When in juvenile plumage, it is readily mistaken for Lincoln's Sparrow. As its name suggests, this bird is at home in swampy places, especially those where cattails flourish.

Its song is a rapid, monotonous repetition of *tweet-tweet-tweet,* and may be confused with those of other sparrows.

Melospiza georgiana georgiana is the summer resident that breeds here. *Melospiza georgiana ericrypta,* a more northerly race (described by Oberholser in 1938), occurs here as a transient with unknown frequency. W. Earl Godfrey collected four specimens of this bird on Cape Breton Island in 1935: three at Cape North, Victoria County (one each on 5, 6 and 11 September), and one at Margaree Valley, Inverness County, on 6 October. One also was taken at East Lawrencetown, Halifax County, on 15 February 1957 by Charles R.K. Allen. It may be that all or most wintering Swamp Sparrows belong to this second subspecies; the two races are indistinguishable in life.

White-throated Sparrow   PLATE 38

Zonotrichia albicollis (Gmelin)

Status Common in summer, uncommon in winter. Breeds. Spring arrivals can be detected readily in localities where birds have not wintered. They may first appear at any time during April (average 16 April, earliest 28 March), evidently influenced by weather patterns and seasonal conditions. Large numbers normally occur widely in late April and the first half of May. In summer it is found in woodland regions, both on the fringe of settlement and as far removed from human abode as geography permits. In fall, small flocks and, occasionally, very large movements may be recorded from mid-September through October, sometimes into November. Many attempt to winter—1,044 were recorded on the Broad Cove, Lunenburg County, Christmas Bird Count on 29 December 1976. Wintering birds come frequently to feeding stations, especially during snowy periods.

Description *Length:* 16-17 cm. *Adults:* White or tan stripe through centre of crown, bordered with wide black stripes; a yellow spot before the eye; a white or tan stripe on side of head; back rich brown, streaked with black, bordered with light gray; wing with two narrow white bars; underparts gray, whiter on belly; throat patch pure white.

Breeding *Nest:* Made of coarse grass, mosses and fern stalks, lined with soft grass, hair or both; on the ground in open glades or bushy pasturelands, well concealed among brakes, under the edge of brush or under slash left by loggers. *Eggs:* 3-5, usually 4; pale blue or bluish green, evenly speckled or sometimes washed or blotched with various shades of brown. Laying begins about mid-May and continues into early June. I have examined 16 nests with laying completed. Twelve contained 4 eggs, two held 5 and the other two had 3 each. The earliest date for a full set is 18 May. In the past, when nests were located near settlement, their lining was usually horse hair; in areas remote from habitation, deer hair was commonly used. The nests mentioned above were all located in Kings and Annapolis counties.

Range Breeds from central Mackenzie Valley and southeastern Yukon, northern Manitoba and central Quebec, south to the northeastern United States, southern Ontario and central Alberta. Winters from southern Manitoba to Nova Scotia, south to the Gulf Coast and northeastern Mexico.

Remarks Of all bird songs heard in our woods, probably none is more widely known than the white-throat's, yet relatively few people know the name of the performer when they hear him. This bird's song is its outstanding characteristic: It is sweet and plaintive, with perhaps a touch of melancholy. The scale is highly variable but usually begins with two long, flute-like notes followed by a series of clear, whistled cadences, tremulous and vibrating, which gradually weaken at the end. The most fitting translation of its song seems to be *I love Canada-Canada-Canada,* by which it has come to be known as the "Canada-bird." Other listeners, influenced by another interpretation of the song, call it "Old Sam Peabody."

Its summer food is largely insects, but winter stragglers are almost wholly dependent on seeds.

It resembles the White-crowned Sparrow, but that bird lacks the yellow spot before the eye and the conspicuous white throat patch that mark the White-throated Sparrow.

Golden-crowned Sparrow

Zonotrichia atricapilla (Gmelin)

Status Two records. An adult was closely observed by Christel and Norman Bell on Sable Island on 9 May 1967. Another adult was discovered and photographed by the Norman Bowers at Caledonia, Queens County, on 8 May 1977; it remained about their feeder for about a week, giving ample opportunity for many visitors to see it.

Remarks This beautiful far-western sparrow, somewhat like a White-crowned Sparrow but with a black-margined yellow crown, has occurred about a half-dozen times in the northeastern United States. Our two records are the only Canadian records east of Ontario.

White-crowned Sparrow   PLATE 38

Zonotrichia leucophrys (Forster)

Status Uncommon transient, rare in winter. It is very uncommon but regular in spring, generally first appearing in late April or early May (average 6 May, earliest 22 April) and last seen in early June (average 31 May, latest 15 June). Although it is not known to nest, there are two intriguing reports of birds on 22 July 1977 at Wine Harbour, Guysborough County (G. and O. MacLeod), and in early July 1983 near Boularderie, Victoria County (R. Fraser); parts of Guysborough County and Cape Breton Island do have terrain resembling its breeding grounds further north. Fall migrants normally first appear in late September (average 28 September, earliest 10 September); most are seen in October when, after a strong northwesterly atmospheric flow, large numbers may occur in southern parts of the province—over 400 were present on Seal Island on

PLATE 37

Northern Oriole, *male*
Page 437

Rose-breasted Grosbeak
Page 390

male

female

American Goldfinch
Page 449

male

female

male

female

Evening Grosbeak
Page 450

Brown-headed Cowbird
Page 434

female

male

Sharp-tailed Sparrow
Page 406

Dickcissel, *male*
Page 394

Vesper Sparrow
Page 399

Savannah ("Ipswich") Sparrow
Page 403

Roger Tory Peterson

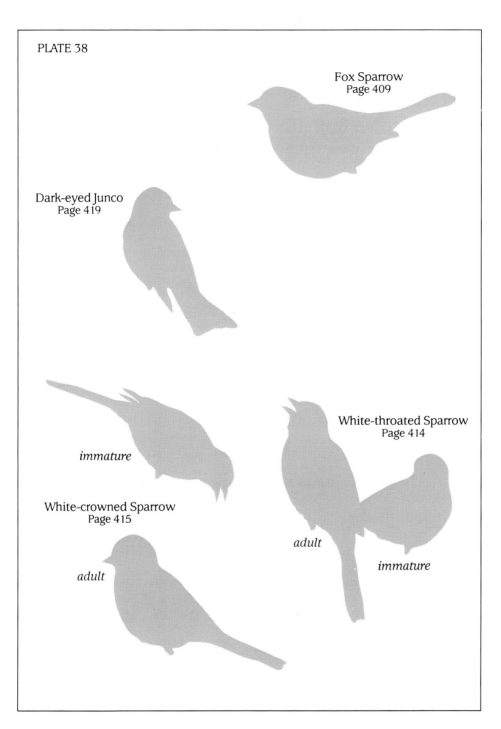

PLATE 38

Fox Sparrow
Page 409

Dark-eyed Junco
Page 419

immature

White-throated Sparrow
Page 414

White-crowned Sparrow
Page 415

adult

adult

immature

417

23 October 1980. They are generally last seen in November (average 3 November, latest 25 November). However, in recent years they have begun to winter in small numbers. The first to do so stayed at feeders on Sable Island and at Glencoe, Pictou County, in 1968-69. At least 10 have been recorded since on Christmas Bird Counts and another dozen or so have survived the winter at feeders in the southwestern half of the province.

Description *Length:* 17-19 cm. *Adults:* White stripe through centre of crown, bordered by wide black stripes; white stripe on side of head, bordered by black stripe from eye or in front of it; back gray with dark brown stripes; wing with two narrow, white wing bars; underparts gray, belly and throat whiter. *Young birds:* Similar but with chestnut and buff replacing the black and white on the head.

Range Breeds from northwestern Alaska to central Keewatin and northern Quebec, south to northern Saskatchewan, south-central Quebec and northern Newfoundland, and south in the west to southern California and New Mexico. Winters from British Columbia in the west and Virginia in the east (casually further north) to the Caribbean islands and Mexico.

Remarks This bird is a close relative of the White-throated Sparrow, which it resembles in size and plumage markings. However, the white crown on this bird is larger and more conspicuous than that of the White-throated Sparrow, which has a yellow spot before the eye and a conspicuous white throat, both lacking in the White-crowned Sparrow. Immatures in autumn with their chestnut caps superficially resemble large American Tree Sparrows.

The main migration of this aristocrat of sparrows lies to the west of Nova Scotia, but the bird is regularly reported here, especially when westerlies prevail in fall.

Almost all our birds are of the eastern subspecies, *Zonotrichia leucophrys leucophrys.* However, a number of individuals of *Z. l. gambelii,* which breeds from Hudson Bay to Alaska, have been recorded. Adults of this subspecies can easily be recognized by their yellow, rather than pink, bills and by their black eye stripes which start from the eye, rather than from the base of the bill; the first, on Sable Island from 25 May to early June 1969, was photographically documented by David Higgins. Another spring bird was seen in Dartmouth in late May 1975 and at least eight birds (two confirmed by photographs) have been recorded on Seal Island during autumn since 1972.

Harris' Sparrow

Zonotrichia querula (Nuttall)

Status Four records. The first was an autumn bird that visited Cape Sable about 1952, observed by Betty June and Sidney Smith. An immature bird appeared at Evelyn Richardson's feeder in Barrington, Shelburne County, on 26 October 1969. An adult found by Barbara Hinds on Seal Island on 29 September 1973 was seen by others over the next two days and was photographed by Sylvia Fullerton. Another adult arrived at Thelma Hawkins' feeder at Wilmot, Annapolis County, on 16 December 1981, and stayed through most of the winter and was observed and photographed by many visitors.

Remarks This large, black-throated relative of our white-throat breeds only in northwestern Canada and winters mostly in the south-central United States. However, vagrants occasionally wander to the east coast.

Dark-eyed Junco   PLATE 38

Junco hyemalis (Linnaeus)

Status Common in summer, fairly common to uncommon in winter. Breeds. First arriving juncos can be detected on islands and other locations generally in late March (average 25 March, earliest 12 March) and they appear in large numbers during April. In summer they are widespread in mixed and coniferous woods, requiring open areas as well. In fall, large movements can be observed: for example, 1200 were seen on Seal Island on 23 October 1980 and 5000 were seen on Brier Island on 10 October 1983. Christmas Bird Count estimates of 500-1000 individuals each have come in recent years from Broad Cove, Lunenburg County; Halifax East; and Wolfville. It remains fairly common in the southwestern counties in winter, but numbers vary elsewhere from year to year. During the coldest season, it is often found around human habitations— on 18 January 1940 a flock of over 200 was seen feeding in Cyril Coldwell's orchard in Kings County and on 11 February 1977 Don MacDougall estimated that 475 were feeding along plowed roadsides near Middle Musquodoboit, Halifax County.

Description *Length:* 15-16.5 cm. *Adult male:* Upperparts, throat and breast dark slate-gray; lower breast and belly white; sides suffused with gray; outer tail feathers conspicuously white; bill grayish pink. *Adult female:* Similar to male but paler. (See Remarks for a description of the western subspecies group known as "Oregon Juncos.")

Breeding *Nest:* Composed of coarse grass lined with finer grass often mixed with hair. It is usually placed on the ground but occasionally in the crevice of a stump or some other opening 1-2 m above ground, and is always well concealed. It may be located in a garden terrace, along the road in a sparsely settled district, or in an area remote from settlement. *Eggs:* 4-5, usually 4; white or bluish white, with fine specks of light brown or cinnamon, chiefly around the larger end, in the form of a wreath. Of 23 nests examined, 20 contained sets of four eggs, only 3 had sets of five. Laying begins about mid-May; the earliest complete set was found on 18 May 1927.

Range Breeds from northern Alaska and northern Quebec, south to central Alberta, northern Minnesota and the mountains of Georgia, and south in the mountains to the southwestern United States. Winters from the southern parts of its breeding range south to the southern United States and northern Mexico.

Remarks This is one of our most common and best known birds. To some it is known as the "black snow-bird"; because of its slaty plumage, others miscall it a "bluebird."

Its song is a weak trill like that of the Chipping Sparrow, but slower and more musical. In summer, juncos feed mainly on insects but in winter their staple fare is weed seeds.

The junco is most readily identified in life by its white outer tail feathers, conspicuous in flight. Though other species of similar size (the Vesper Sparrow, Water Pipit, and Lapland Longspur, for example) also have white outer tail feathers, their general appearance is quite unlike that of a junco and none should be confused with it.

The subspecies nesting in Nova Scotia is *Junco hyemalis hyemalis,* once known as the "Slate-colored Junco." From time to time vagrant individuals of the group of subspecies once recognized as a separate species, the "Oregon Junco," have been reported here and elsewhere in eastern North America. The first two such birds appeared in 1959, one at the Basil C. Silvers' feeder in Bedford, Halifax County, 9-12 January, and another at Mrs. Frank White's feeder in Dartmouth on 9 and 10 January. Since then, 16 individuals have been reported from Halifax, Hants, Lunenburg, Shelburne and Yarmouth counties, all during fall (earliest 29 September) or winter. One collected by Lloyd B. Macpherson on 27 January 1968 at Maitland, Hants County, proved to be of the subspecies *Junco hyemalis montanus.* Other reported birds appear to have been of this dark-hooded, brown-backed, brown-sided race, which is widespread in western Canada. A bird on Sable Island on 16 and 17 October 1975 (I.A. McLaren) had a pale gray head (except around the eyes), dull-brown back and bright pinkish brown sides characteristic of the subspecies *Junco hyemalis mearnsi,* the "Pink-sided Junco," which breeds from southwestern Saskatchewan and southward in the western United States.

Lapland Longspur

Calcarius lapponicus (Linnaeus)

Status Fairly common transient, uncommon in winter. It was unreported in most nineteenth-century lists and rated as "rare" by Jones (1879), who obtained only one specimen; this is probably not indicative of its true status then. Its numbers today show considerable irregularity from year to year. Fall migrants appear generally in late September or early October (average 6 October, earliest 10 September). In winter look for it in low exposed areas along the coast. Flocks of more than 100 have been reported from Grand Pré, Kings County, and from marshes in the Amherst area, but fewer and smaller flocks have been seen on the Cape Breton Island, Eastern and Southwestern shores. Latest spring sightings are normally in April, with several May reports from Sable Island (average 16 April, latest 21 May).

Description *Length:* 15-18 cm. *Adult male in winter:* Crown and back streaked with black, buff and rufous, the crown with a poorly defined buffy median stripe; nape and hindneck chestnut, veiled by brownish feather tips; tail dark brown, the outer feathers showing white marks; underparts white tinged with buff; breast with black obscured by whitish feather tips; flanks streaked with black. *Adult female in winter:* Similar but paler.

Range Circumpolar. In North America, breeds in Greenland, the arctic islands and northern Alaska, south to the edge of forest. Winters from southern Canada to Virginia, southern Texas and the southwestern United States.

Remarks It is often seen in flocks of Snow Buntings and Horned Larks. It is a darker bird than the Snow Bunting. It is more likely to be confused with the Horned Lark, but its facial pattern is different and it lacks the solid black breast band and the black and yellow face markings of the lark.

Smith's Longspur

Calcarius pictus (Swainson)

Status Two sight records. A bird at Skir Dhu, Victoria County, on 6 August 1981, was reported in detail as an adult male Smith's Longspur by Eleanor Waldron, a visiting birder from Martha's Vineyard, Massachusetts, who was first alerted by its "staccato rattle" call (letter to I.A. McLaren). She studied it in good light with binoculars at ranges as close as 10 m. Its striking black-and-white face pattern, white "shoulder-patches" and bright buff underparts were obvious, and she noted (correctly) that its legs were paler than in standard field-guide illustrations. Another bird seen more briefly by Shirley Cohrs on 1 October 1983 appeared to have diagnostic features of an immature or female of this species. It was on Cherry Hill Beach, Lunenburg County, where there were Lapland Longspurs for comparison. It was bright buff ("almost yellow") below, with "merely an impression of triangular mark" on the face. When the bird flew, it showed white outer tail feathers more conspicuous than those of Lapland Longspurs, described as more like those of a Vesper Sparrow.

Remarks Although both these sightings were by single observers, they were reported in convincing detail. The species nests in Alaska and extreme northwestern Canada and normally winters in the south-central United States, but there have been a few autumn and winter records from the east coast from Massachusetts south. The date of the Cape Breton Island bird is particularly unexpected.

Chestnut-collared Longspur

Calcarius ornatus (Townsend)

Status Five records. The first was a male on Bon Portage Island on 29 May-1 June 1962, reported in detail by Evelyn Richardson. Another male was collected on Cape Sable on 28 May 1964 by Norman Cunningham for the National Museum of Canada. A third male was closely observed on Cape Sable by Sidney Smith on 21 April 1967 and, on 8 May 1967, another was found at Port La Tour, Shelburne County, as reported to Harrison F. Lewis by Mrs. Gerald Smith. The most recent record was a female-plumaged bird observed and heard giving a distinctive two-syllabled call by Howard Ross on Sable Island on 9 June 1977.

Remarks Males of this species are unmistakable, with their black breasts, yellow faces and chestnut collars. Females and immatures have distinctive tail patterns and call notes, among other features. It is striking that all of Atlantic Canada's records for this bird, which nests on the central prairies and winters in the southwestern United States, are for spring.

Snow Bunting   PLATE 36

Plectrophenax nivalis (Linnaeus)

Status Common in winter. They usually first arrive from the north in October (average 18 October, earliest 23 September). From late October to late March large flocks may be found, usually in low-lying coastal regions but sometimes inland in agricultural areas. A massive flock of about 1,000 birds was seen on the Grand Pré dyke on 5 and 6 February 1984. Generally, large flocks are not seen after mid-April; an exception was a large movement near Dingwall, Victoria County, on 12-13 May 1977, during a late snowstorm. Latest birds are normally in April, but stragglers occur in May (average 24 April, latest 21 May, on Sable Island).

Description *Length:* 15-18.5 cm. *Adult male in winter:* Crown patch, ear patch, rump and sides cinnamon in various saturations; mark on wing below shoulder black; primaries black, basally white; black mark on outer tail feathers largely white, inner ones black; back cinnamon, dotted with black; rest of plumage white. *Adult female in winter:* Similar but more black in tail and more cinnamon on back, wings and flanks.

Range Circumpolar. In North America, breeds from northern Alaska, Prince Patrick Island, northern Ellesmere Island and northern Greenland, south to northern Quebec, central Keewatin, central Mackenzie Valley and northern British Columbia. Winters in southern Canada and the northern and central United States.

Remarks During open winters when snowfall is light they remain on the coastal lowlands throughout the season and, because such areas are usually remote from human thoroughfares, few people know of their presence. When storms of mid-winter bring heavy snow they suddenly appear about our withered gardens and weed-infested fields, where they feed on the seeds of taller plants that protrude above the snow. At such times their coming never fails to excite comment from observers who, assuming that the "snow-birds" have just flown here from the northland, marvel at how they so accurately time their arrival with that of the heavy snow.

When seen in flight they are usually in loose flocks drifting over the countryside like scattered snowflakes, often mingled with Horned Larks, from which they are distinguishable by their lighter colours and the large area of white on their wings.

The buntings moult their buff and white winter plumage during their journey north. By the time they reach the treeless wastes of the arctic tundra to breed under the glare of continuous daylight, their plumage has changed to a sharply contrasting black and white.

Subfamily Icterinae

Bobolink   PLATE 30

Dolichonyx oryzivorus (Linnaeus)

Status Locally common in summer. Breeds. The Bobolink normally arrives in May (average 8 May, earliest 28 April), but very early individuals have been seen on Cape Sable on 17 April 1974; at Lower West Pubnico, Yarmouth County, on 8 April 1982 (2 birds); and at West Lawrencetown, Halifax County, on 20 April 1983. In the past it was found in summer largely about the meadowlands of Annapolis, Kings, Hants, Cumberland and Colchester counties but in recent years has been seen increasingly in coastal meadowlands and on Cape Breton Island. Gathering migrants are found in August, and it occurs in numbers on the islands off southwestern Nova Scotia during September. Latest sightings are usually in October (average 18 October, latest 18 November), but stragglers were found on Christmas Bird Counts at Yarmouth on 28 December 1969, and at Chezzetcook (Halifax East Count) on 15 December 1973 (and for 3 days thereafter).

Description *Length:* 16.5-20 cm. *Adult male:* Nape creamy buff; rest of head and underparts black; scapulars, lower back and rump white; wings and tail black, the tail feathers with pointed tips, the feathers edged with brown; back black, with buff streaks. *Adult female:* Above light olive, streaked with dark brown or black; centre of crown has a broad buff stripe, bordered with dark brown or black stripes; light buff below with indistinct spots or faint lines of dark brown along flanks; tail feathers pointed at tips.

Breeding *Nest:* Composed entirely of soft dry grass; usually on the ground in hayfields left unmown for a year or longer. *Eggs:* 4-6, usually 5; grayish white, spotted and blotched with various shades and densities of brown and lavender. Laying begins early in June and most sets are complete by 15 June. Of three nests examined on the dykelands below Wolfville, one contained five fresh eggs on 16 June 1904; one had six slightly incubated eggs on 20 June 1915; and an early one held five young about a week old on 22 June 1942.

Range Breeds from southwestern Newfoundland, central Ontario, southern Alberta and southeastern British Columbia, south to Pennsylvania, Colorado and northeastern California. Winters in South America south to Argentina and Paraguay.

Remarks The Bobolink is a very desirable and popular bird. It is well worth a trip to a male bird's domain on a fine day in June to hear the outpouring of his wonderful song as he flies slowly on quivering wings over the daisy-decked meadow where his drably coloured mate patiently guards the nest. As soon as his domestic duties for the year are completed, he exchanges his bright summer garb for one closely resembling that of his mate, and his song is no longer heard. This plumage change occurs about mid-August; one seen at Antigonish on 16 August 1920 was in the process of changing, making him appear mottled and strange. By mid-August Bobolinks gather in flocks and the first leave us soon thereafter.

Like many of our smaller migrants, the males arrive first in spring, often in flocks. On 12 May 1923 about 25 males were perched in a small tree near the edge of the meadows at Canard, Kings County, all singing in chorus; the medley they produced could be heard for a considerable distance.

The striking and distinctive summer plumage of the male is not easily mistaken for that of other summer birds. The sparrow-like plumage of the female may cause confusion but her larger size will distinguish her from the sparrows which may share her habitat in summer.

Red-winged Blackbird PLATE 30

Agelaius phoeniceus (Linnaeus)

Status Common in summer, uncommon in winter. Breeds. It was considered a great rarity in the nineteenth century. Nevertheless, it may have nested, as Downs (1888) states that it was a rare summer resident "in the western part of the province." The first reported nesting was in 1914 in Antigonish County (Lewis 1914). By 1928 it was found nesting in Kings County and has since spread over much of the province. Spring migrants first appear on almost any date in March (average 24 March, earliest 4 March, in localities where the species had not wintered). Although it chooses more diverse habitats elsewhere, in Nova Scotia it primarily breeds in cattail marshes, especially large ones. Large gatherings of these blackbirds are seen during September, and migratory movements are generally most prominent in October. Flocks may be sustained through winter in agricultural districts, but elsewhere only scattered birds remain, generally around bird feeders. Generally fewer are reported from late winter; these winter residents are sometimes found singing in nesting habitats during February thaws, in advance of the arrival of migrants.

Description *Length:* 19-24 cm. *Adult male:* Glossy black all over, except shoulder, which is fiery red with border of buff. *Adult female:* Above dark blackish brown streaked with buff; lines over eye and chin buff; rest of underparts grayish white, striped with dark brown; sometimes a suggestion of red on shoulder.

Breeding *Nest:* Composed of reed stalks, coarse grass and other vegetable matter, lined with finer grass and usually attached to the stems of aquatic plants but sometimes in low bushes in or near swampy land. *Eggs:* 4-5; light blue, marked with blotches of dark brown and lavender of various shades and densities. On 28 May 1932 two nests were found near Windsor, one containing five, and the other four, slightly incubated eggs. Both were fastened to the stems of cattails growing in shallow water (B. Colbran).

Range Breeds from central British Columbia, southeastern Mackenzie Valley, central Manitoba, central Ontario, southern Quebec and southwestern Newfoundland, south to central Mexico. Winters from British Columbia, southern Ontario and Nova Scotia, south to Costa Rica.

John H. Dick

Red-winged Blackbird

Remarks It is customary to find the first spring male already dwelling among the cattails where his nest will soon be located. A large marsh attracts more than one nesting pair, creating rivalry over territorial nesting rights. Each male defends his territory zealously, and this explains why he is so often seen at nesting time in hot pursuit of a would-be trespasser. When the redwings return in spring, the cattail swale, a dreary, deserted waste since the birds' departure the summer before, comes to life once more. Over the lush new growth the dark-coloured males appear here and there, each proclaiming ownership of his particular homesite with an often-repeated *konk-kar-ree, konk-kar-ree,* the notes ending in an ascending trill. To bird-lovers living nearby, the redwing's return to its summer home is a pleasing event.

No one could easily mistake a male Red-winged Blackbird for any other bird, but the sombre-coloured female is less easily recognized. However, no other similar species has her well-defined stripes on its underparts.

Eastern Meadowlark   PLATE 30

Sturnella magna (Linnaeus)

Status Rare and local in summer, uncommon in winter. Breeds. It was rarely recorded in the nineteenth century but is more regular now. A few spring migrants or transients appear in late March or early April (average 11 April, earliest 24 March); a bird appearing on Sable Island on 5 March 1977 had probably been wintering in the region. It is found nesting only in the Annapolis Valley in a relatively small, restricted area of meadowland adjacent to the Annapolis River at Belleisle, a few kilometres west of Bridgetown, Annapolis County, where a few pairs of Meadowlarks have bred for the past several decades. There are few reports from elsewhere of this species during the summer months, but larger numbers appear in autumn. First arrivals since the mid-1950s have generally been in October (average 13 October, earliest 11 September). These birds occur throughout the province, although largely in the southwestern counties, especially in coastal dunes and salt marshes. Many attempt to winter; since the mid-1950s there have been reports of 3 birds in September, about 118 in October, 70 in November, 46 in December, 52 in January and 14 in February. These numbers indicate that not all survive the onslaught of winter.

Description *Length:* 23-28 cm. *Adult male:* Narrow buff line through centre of crown, bordered by black lines on either side which in turn are bordered by a buff line over eye; yellow spot in front of eye; black line running from eye to neck; back, wings and tail mottled with black and browns of various shades and densities; tail feathers pointed, the outer four on either side mostly white; throat and upper breast rich yellow; black crescent-shaped patch on the upper breast; belly rich yellow; sides of breast and flanks grayish white, streaked with black and dark brown. *Adult female:* Paler; black patch on breast somewhat smaller.

Breeding *Nest:* On the ground in hayfields; composed wholly of grass. *Eggs:* 4-6, usually 5; grayish white, spotted and blotched with various shades and densities of brown and purple. Laying begins early in June. On 2 July 1967 Eric Morris found a nest on the Belleisle meadows at a point about 3 km west of Bridgetown, on the north side of the Annapolis River. It contained four eggs about ready to hatch. Fraser Caldwell found three fledglings in the same area in late July 1964. Two seen at Canard, Kings County, on 11 June 1956 were definitely mated, as were two reported by Rundall M. Lewis at Upper Canard on 15 June 1945.

Range Breeds from Nova Scotia, southern Quebec, southeastern Ontario and northern Minnesota, south to Florida, southern Texas and Mexico. Winters mainly in the southern United States, casually in southeastern Canada.

Remarks The Eastern Meadowlark is no more a lark than the Common Nighthawk is a hawk—both are misnomers. This bird, along with orioles and the Bobolink, is closely related to blackbirds. When seen in flight, particularly when flushed, it is best identified by its conspicuously white outer tail feathers and its peculiar manner of propulsion, which consists of a few jerky wing beats alternated with moments of sailing on outspread wings.

In summer its food is largely insects but in winter it normally eats seeds.

The curious imbalance between normal summer and normal winter populations is without explanation. Some wintering birds are found in distress, but others appear well satisfied with their lot. One I collected on the bleak, exposed salt marsh at Boot Island, Kings County, on 7 January 1916 during forbidding weather conditions was actually fat. It had been feeding on seeds of the sea lavender *(Limonium nashii),* a coarse marsh plant growing there in profusion.

The species shows a marked preference for coastal, low-lying districts and I cannot recall having seen one far inland.

Western Meadowlark

Sturnella neglecta (Audubon)

Status One sight record. A meadowlark found by Eric Cooke and Sylvia Fullerton at Cherry Hill Beach, Lunenburg County, on 1 January 1982 uttered the characteristic call note of this species.

Remarks The Western Meadowlark is very difficult to distinguish from the Eastern Meadowlark by plumage characteristics, except at extremely close ranges. However, its call note is diagnostically different: a blackbird-like *chuck,* lower than the rough *dzert* of the Eastern Meadowlark. It is possible that this bird, which dwells on the western plains and occurs casually further east, is a more regular vagrant here than our single record suggests.

Yellow-headed Blackbird

Xanthocephalus xanthocephalus (Bonaparte)

Status Rare vagrant, very rare in winter. The first occurrence for Nova Scotia was on 5 October 1901 (Bouteillier 1901) and another was seen there the next year on 16 September. Piers considered these records as unlikely (Piers' notes), but they are in keeping with other island records (McLaren 1981a). The next to appear were individuals on or about 9 September 1956, one on Bon Portage Island (E. Richardson) and the other at Cape Sable light (B.F. Smith). Since then almost 80 have been reported. Seven have been in spring between 17 April and 10 June. The rest have been autumn migrants, annual since 1975. They can first appear surprisingly early in the season (average 28 August, earliest 13 August; the exact date of a July 1980 bird at Lower West Pubnico, Yarmouth County, was not published). Most have been recorded in September (11 in August, 29 in September, 10 in October, 3 each in November and December) and a number have tarried into or through the winter, generally at feeding stations (2 have been first seen in January, 6 in February, 21 on 2 March and 1 on 22 March). Many of these sightings have been on our well-monitored islands, but others have been seen from Yarmouth County to Cape Breton Island, and a few have been photographically documented.

Remarks This western blackbird is unmistakable in any plumage, although we rarely see fully yellow-headed adult males. It has been expanding its range and now breeds sporadically in the Great Lakes region. It is one of the more regularly reported western vagrants on the Atlantic coast.

Rusty Blackbird   PLATE 34

Euphagus carolinus (Müller)

Status Uncommon in summer, fairly common transient, rare in winter. Breeds. Migrants normally arrive in March (average 26 March, earliest 7 March), and numbers are generally seen from late March through mid-April. During the breeding season it is usually found about still waters or sluggish streams, more often in the interior than along the coast and, as a rule, somewhat remote from human settlements. In autumn, main migratory movements have been recorded between late September and early November, especially in early October. Stragglers have been found almost annually since 1960 on Christmas Bird Counts from Yarmouth to Cape Breton Island (24 on the Count at Bridgetown, Annapolis County, on 17 December 1977). A few have been reported from widely scattered localities during January and February, mostly at feeders, and some very early March birds (e.g., at Kejimkujik National Park on 4 March 1976) had probably wintered locally.

Description *Length:* 21.5-24 cm. *Adult males:* Entire plumage black with greenish iridescence; eye straw-yellow. *Adult female:* Dark slaty gray, with slight iridescence on back. Fall and winter birds show rufous or rust-coloured edges on their feathers.

Breeding *Nest:* Composed of twigs and coarse vegetable matter, usually cemented with mud (rarely, no mud is used), to which is added beard lichen, with lining of smooth, green swamp grass. Nests are usually placed low in small spruces near water. *Eggs:* 4-5, usually 5; grayish or greenish blue, blotched and spotted with various densities of brown and lavender, mostly around the larger end. Of 32 nests in which laying had been completed, 24 contained sets of five eggs, and 8 held sets of four. Laying begins during the first week in May; a set of five fresh eggs was examined at Gaspereau, Kings County, on 12 May 1905. If the first nest is destroyed, another will be built near the site of the first, and a pair has been known to rebuild its nest and lay five eggs within 11 days. On 21 May 1915 at Black River Lake, a nest containing five eggs was collected. Just 20 days later, a new nest found within about 5 m of the first contained four newly hatched young.

Range Breeds from Alaska, northwestern Mackenzie Valley, northern Manitoba and northern Quebec, south to northern New England, southern Ontario and central British Columbia. Winters in the United States from New Jersey and the Ohio River Valley southward.

Remarks Because its preferred summer habitat is mainly in unfrequented regions of the interior, this bird may be unfamiliar to the beginning birder. It is known to woodsmen and country folk by the name "black robin."

It is the earliest spring migrants to reach the habitat it favours, and from the time it arrives until the end of the nesting season it will be seen in scattered pairs that keep well within their own nesting territory.

It should not be confused with the Common Grackle, which is considerably larger and characterized by its conspicuously long and ungainly tail. The Rusty Blackbird is neat and well-groomed in appearance, and in summer the two species do not normally share the same habitat.

All summer the male wears a shiny coat of greenish black, but in fall he changes to a new one with rufous or rusty feather edgings, hence the bird's name. He will appear all winter as a rusty-coloured blackbird, but when he returns in spring the brownish feather edges have worn off and he is once again a shiny, black bird.

Brewer's Blackbird

Euphagus cyanocephalus (Wagler)

Status Rare vagrant. The first reports of this species came from Harrison F. Lewis, who observed three males associating with Common Grackles and Rusty Blackbirds at a Shelburne feeder in mid-February 1957, and from Robie W. Tufts, who saw what he believed to be a male Brewer's Blackbird near Digby on 7 December of the same year.

Since then there have been 13 reports involving 15 individuals, including the more readily distinguished females. Spring birds were reported on Cape Sable on 29 March 1961 and 7 May 1979 (B.J. and S. Smith) and on Seal Island between 14 and 29 May 1978 (two birds, several observers). The others have appeared in fall and winter: four in September (earliest 23 September), two each in October and November, one each in January and February, and one on Sable Island between 30 November 1969 and early March 1970; other than the Sable Island bird, these have occurred at Dartmouth (two birds), Lockeport, Shelburne, Cape Sable, Economy (Colchester County) and on Brier (two birds) and Seal islands. Females were diagnostically photographed by Ian A. McLaren at Dartmouth on 13 November 1971 and by Russel Crosby at Lockeport during January 1977.

Remarks Brewer's Blackbird is a western and mid-western species whose breeding range has been expanding eastward. It is a regular vagrant to the east that may be overlooked because of its similarity to the Rusty Blackbird. Males, unlike those of the Rusty Blackbird, show glossy purple on the head and do not develop rusty feather edgings in winter. Females are brownish gray, with darker wings and backs and without any rusty tones; the best mark is their dark brown eye (but note that juvenile Rusty Blackbirds may also have dark eyes). Careful comparisons also reveal the relatively longer tail and more conical bill of the Brewer's Blackbird.

Great-tailed Grackle

Quiscalus mexicanus (Gmelim)

Status One confirmed record. On 17 November 1983 a large, partly brown grackle appeared at the A.P. Munt's feeder at Lake LaRose, Annapolis County. Many birders came to see it, and photographs taken by Ian A. McLaren, Eric Mills and others confirmed it as a female Great-tailed Grackle. It was last seen during February 1984. Three earlier sight records of large grackles remain problematic as a result of the more recent splitting of the former Boat-tailed Grackles into the very similar Boat-tailed and Great-tailed species (see Remarks). The first was a male seen by Christel and Norman Bell on Sable Island between 7 and 10 May 1968. The second was closely viewed at Glace Bay on 5 August 1969 and for several days thereafter by several observers, including Sarah MacLean and the Arthur Spencers. Finally, a bird that from its description could only have been a female of one of these large grackles was seen by Gerald Forbes on Sable Island on 1 November 1982.

Remarks The Great-tailed Grackle is resident from the southwestern United States to Central Mexico but is rapidly spreading northward. The Boat-tailed Grackle, *Quiscalus major,* is a largely coastal bird from New York State to central Texas. They are similar in appearance, but throughout most of its range the Boat-tailed is dark-eyed and the Great-tailed is light-eyed. However, Boat-tailed Grackles along the Atlantic coast are pale-eyed. Thus detailed descriptions of size, tail and bill shape, iridescence patterns in males and coloration of back and breast in females are required to discriminate the two species. None of the pre-1983 records can be used to do this, although the description of the 1982 female on Sable Island seems to fit best a Great-tailed Grackle.

Common Grackle   PLATE 34

Quiscalus quiscula (Linnaeus)

Status Common in summer, uncommon in winter. Breeds. The species was considered rare in several nineteenth-century accounts. However, Hickman (1896) listed it as breeding and "very common" about Pictou, and it had become common in Kings County by about 1910 (R.W. Tufts). Today, in areas where they have not wintered, they generally appear in the second half of March (average 26 March, earliest 6 March) and are widespread by April. In summer the population is largely restricted to urban and agricultural areas, but after the nesting season large flocks forage widely in the countryside. Migrants become conspicuous on the coasts and islands of the southwestern counties between mid-September and mid-November, but some large flocks remain into winter. For example, over 1,000 were recorded on the Christmas Bird Count at Kingston, Kings County, on 22 December 1974, and 50-100 or more have been observed on other Christmas Counts and also somewhat later in winter in farm districts and towns from Cumberland and Halifax counties to Yarmouth County. In addition, individuals and small flocks have wintered at feeders throughout the province.

Description *Length:* 28-33 cm. *Adult male:* Iridescent sheen on head, neck and upper breast varies from green or blue to purple; bronze sheen on back; rest of plumage black with less iridescence, generally bronze in tone; eye straw-colour. *Adult female:* Smaller and duller, iridescence showing slightly on head, neck and breast.

Breeding *Nest:* Made of coarse grass and other rough vegetable matter, often cemented with mud and lined with fine grass; usually built in tall spruce trees, sometimes singly but often in colonies of various sizes. This occasional tendency toward colonial nesting may be induced by a scarcity of the most desirable nesting sites, such as the hedges of tall, thick-growing spruces that are often isolated throughout farming districts. It is unusual to see grackles nesting in districts even slightly remote from habitation. *Eggs:* 4-7, usually 5-6; greenish blue, marked rather heavily with blotches and spots of dark brown or black. Laying begins during the second half of April. A nest containing seven fresh eggs was collected at Wolfville on 10 May 1928 and another containing five which were slightly incubated was taken by Basil Colbran at Windsor on 26 May 1927. A most unusual nest at Gaspereau, Kings County, on 13 June 1965 was in a hole originally made by a flicker in a decayed apple-tree limb. It contained young about ready to fledge, and both parents protested my intrusion.

PLATE 39

Pine Siskin, *adult*
Page 448

female

Common Redpoll
Page 446

male

female

Pine Grosbeak
Page 439

female

Purple Finch
Page 441

male

male

PLATE 40

Red Crossbill
Page 443

female

juvenile

subadult male

male

White-winged Crossbill
Page 445

female

juvenile

male

Range Breeds from east central British Columbia, southwestern Mackenzie Valley, northern Manitoba, southern Quebec, and Nova Scotia, south to the southern United States. Winters mainly in the middle and southern United States; casually further north.

Remarks Primarily a ground feeder, the grackle has greatly benefitted from man's development of land for agricultural purposes. Ornamental spruce hedgerows and groves are also used as nesting sites. Its food is largely insects during summer, but later it relies partially upon waste grain and wild fruits. Its habit of devouring the eggs and young of songbirds in spring is a black mark against it. Like the crow, it probably has fewer friends than enemies among mankind.

Inexperienced observers sometimes mistake this bird for a starling. When seen in the field, the most obvious difference is in the tails, the tail of the grackle being long, that of the starling being particularly short; the grackle is considerably larger, its manner of flight is slower and more deliberate and at close range the marked difference in plumages becomes apparent.

Brown-headed Cowbird   PLATE 37

Molothrus ater (Boddaert)

Status Fairly common resident. Breeds. Blakiston and Bland (1856) reported it as "occasional" and Jones (1879) reported it as "rare", but there was no subsequent nineteenth-century reference to it. The first record for Kings County was in 1922 (R.W. Tufts). It remained a rare summer resident prior to 1950, when one was reported on 31 December at Lower Wedgeport, Yarmouth County (I. Pothier). It is now much more common in winter, and the main spring movements are generally from late March to mid-April. It is widespread in summer, and has even parasitized nests of "Ipswich Sparrows" on Sable Island (Stobo and McLaren 1975). After the nesting season it becomes highly gregarious and is often seen mixed with flocks of European Starlings and Red-winged Blackbirds. Large migratory movements generally occur in October and November, but many stay in settled areas into winter (an estimated 3,300 were seen on the Christmas Bird Count at Kingston, Kings County, on 22 December 1975). These birds remain around cattle feedlots, grain-storage facilities and bird feeders, often in association with other blackbirds, House Sparrows and European Starlings.

Description *Length:* 18-20 cm. *Adult male:* In spring and summer, entire head and upper breast glossy seal-brown, rest of plumage black with greenish blue iridescence; in the fresh plumage of fall and winter, brown on head and breast is much darker, giving the bird an appearance of being all black; by the first of March, head and breast have regained their seal-brown colour. *Adult female:* Dull gray, somewhat lighter on throat, faintly and finely streaked below. *Young birds:* Buffy gray, somewhat streaked below.

Breeding *Nest:* None of its own, eggs being laid in the nests of other birds. The eggs are dropped during June and July, and the Yellow Warbler, in my experience, is the species most frequently victimized. *Eggs:* 1 per female cowbird per nest; more found in a single nest are thought to be laid by additional cowbirds; grayish white, covered evenly with fine, dark brown speckles.

On finding a cowbird's egg in her nest, the rightful owner will sometimes attempt to get rid of it by adding a new, false bottom to the nest, completely covering the egg (and sometimes her own eggs) with nesting material. In order to restore the original depth of the nest, the bird builds the walls higher, giving the whole structure a distorted appearance. However, usually the egg is accepted and hatched along with the rest.

Since the mid-1970s, Bernard L. Forsythe has carried on a study of birds nesting on Wolfville Ridge, Kings County, and vicinity. He has found cowbird eggs or young in nests of the following small birds:

Alder Flycatcher
Veery
Solitary Vireo
Red-eyed Vireo
Northern Parula
Yellow Warbler
Chestnut-sided Warbler
Magnolia Warbler
Black-throated Blue Warbler
Yellow-rumped Warbler
Blackburnian Warbler

Black-and-white Warbler
American Redstart
Ovenbird
Common Yellowthroat
Canada Warbler
Chipping Sparrow
Song Sparrow
White-throated Sparrow
Dark-eyed Junco
American Goldfinch
Purple Finch

It seems probable that any small passerine bird will be victimized if its nest is suitable and available to the cowbird.

Range Breeds from central British Columbia, southeastern Mackenzie Valley, central Manitoba, southern Quebec, and Nova Scotia, south to Mexico. Winters mainly in the middle and southern United States and Mexico, less abundantly north to southern Canada.

Remarks By human standards, the female cowbird is not only a born sneak but a shiftless parasite as well. She builds no nest of her own but goes snooping about the shrubbery until she locates one of another bird smaller and weaker than herself; she lays her egg in it and goes merrily on her way, never bothering to call around to see how her offspring is faring under the care of its foster parents. And how does it get along? It gets along far too well, for being larger than its fellow nestlings it gluttonously grabs most of the food brought by the victimized parents. Because of its unfair advantage, the baby cowbird is sometimes the only nestling to survive, the weaker ones being suffocated or pushed out of the nest as the little monster gradually takes over the entire space.

Why the species is parasitic is a mystery that science has not solved. Neither is there an answer to this conundrum: Having been raised by a warbler or some other bird, why does it immediately leave its foster parents and join the cowbird throng? In other words, how does it know it's a cowbird?

The cowbird is recorded as having parasitized the nests of over 250 species, at times removing the eggs of the rightful owner, presumably to give its own egg a better chance of survival.

The plumage of the male cowbird is distinctive, but that of the female may lead to confusion with Red-winged and Rusty Blackbird females and immature starlings. The Rusty Blackbird female is larger and has straw-coloured eyes; the Red-winged Blackbird female is boldly striped and, like immature starlings, has a long, pointed bill. The cowbird female has dark eyes, her plumage is mainly plain, with only faint streaks on her underparts, and her bill is short and stubby.

Black-cowled Oriole

Icterus dominicensis (Linnaeus)

Status One sight record. An oriole seen by Benjamin K. Doane on Seal Island on 24 May 1971 was believed to have been a male of this species (Doane 1971).

Remarks This species is resident in Mexico, Central America and the West Indies. From the plumage described by Doane (1971), the bird could have belonged to the migratory subspecies of the Bahamas. It is perhaps not merely coincidental that a Cuban Cave Swallow had appeared on Seal Island on the previous weekend.

Orchard Oriole

Icterus spurius (Linnaeus)

Status Rare vagrant. The first report of this species in Nova Scotia was of a female collected at Three Fathom Harbour on 6 September 1890 (Piers 1894). Saunders (1902) collected a young male on Sable Island on 15 May 1901. It was not reported again until 1958, when Ralph S. Johnson repeatedly saw an adult male about his garden in Liverpool from 25 May to 5 June. Since then, it has been reported quite regularly. Most birds have come in spring, for which there are some 40 reports of 52 individuals. The earliest was on 15 April 1971 in Yarmouth County (L. Delaney) and the latest among several June records from Sable Island was on 22 June 1975. A male at Lower Ohio, Shelburne County, on 28 June 1966 (B. Harris) was perhaps a would-be breeder, as were a pair that spent two days in an orchard near Wallace, Cumberland County, in June 1982 (R.S. Bidwell). Fall vagrants are not as regular, with 14 reports of 18 individuals between 20 August and 3 October. This species has been recorded from

Glace Bay to Yarmouth and around the southwestern end of the province to Digby and Annapolis counties, but not yet further up the Annapolis Valley or beyond, except for the above-mentioned report from Cumberland County.

Remarks This oriole breeds from southern Saskatchewan to southern Ontario and northern Massachusetts, south to Mexico. It is slightly smaller than the Northern Oriole, and the rich orange that glorifies the males of that species is replaced by chestnut in the Orchard Oriole. Females and young males are olive-green above and yellowish below, the young males with a distinctive black bib.

Northern Oriole   PLATE 37

Icterus galbula (Linnaeus)

Status Uncommon transient, rare in summer and winter. Breeds. There are no nineteenth-century reports other than Chamberlain's (1887b) record of one collected near Halifax in September 1886. During the past 50 years the status of this species has changed from rare to generally uncommon in all parts of the province. Spring birds generally appear in early May (average 6 May, earliest 17 April). Sometimes these are seen in large numbers, especially along the southwestern coast and islands; however, only a few remain to breed. There are nesting reports from the southwestern part of the province, including Halifax and Kings counties. This small summer population is augmented by fall transients, easily detectable where the species does not nest, which generally first appear in late August (average 27 August, earliest 16 August). Daily estimates of 10-20 birds are routine on Brier and Seal islands in September—on 1-3 October 1967 an estimated 150 were on Seal Island. During late November and early December, Northern Orioles often appear in rural and urban gardens, and they occur regularly on Christmas Bird Counts throughout the province. A few have been sustained at feeders into January, and two birds in Halifax remained at feeders into spring.

Description *Length:* 18-20 cm. *Adult male:* Head, neck, throat, upper back, scapulars and central tail feathers black; wings black, the wing coverts tipped with white; rest of plumage bright orange. *Adult female:* Crown, back and tail yellowish brown, mottled with black; rump and underparts dull orange, brighter on breast; wings dark blackish brown with white bars, the feathers edged with buff.

Breeding *Nest:* Composed of fine grasses, fine strips of pliable bark, plant fibres, string and similar materials interwoven neatly and securely. The nest is wholly pensile from near the end of a long limb, usually of an elm, at heights of 3-12 m or more. The 16 nests that have come to my attention were all close to human habitation and in elms, except one in a maple. *Eggs:* 4-6; grayish white with strange, scroll-like markings and blotches of black and dark brown. Some nest dates are: 18 June 1938 at Berwick, Kings County, both birds feeding young in nest; 16 June 1939, a pair at Digby nesting in a maple tree (L. Daley); and 21 June 1954, a pair building in an elm tree at Mill Village,

Queens County. In the last instance the female was in charge of construction but the male was often in close attendance and on occasion brought her choice pieces of material to work into the nest. The pair was last seen feeding young in this nest on 12 August (L. Mack). Nestings have been reported more widely since.

Range Breeds from southern British Columbia, central Alberta, southern Manitoba and southwestern Quebec, south to Georgia, Louisiana and into Mexico in the west. Winters from southern Mexico to northern South America, occasionally further north at feeders.

Remarks This bird is sometimes called a "golden robin," a tribute to the striking brilliance of the male's plumage. It feeds largely on insects and is known to be partial to tent caterpillars and potato beetles making it economically, as well as aesthetically, valuable.

The nest is so ingeniously interwoven and so securely fastened that it often will withstand gales and storms for several years before the last vestige of material is blown away. In summer it is well concealed among leaves and difficult to find, but in winter, when the branches are bare, it is conspicuous as it sways in the wind.

The behaviour of some birds in late fall indicates that their migratory urge has expired. For many years, Louise Daley, a well-known bird-lover in Digby, cared for some of these stranded waifs. She first enticed them into a simple box-trap and then placed them in a cage, where she fed them fresh grapes and bird foods procured from pet shops. Long before their release in spring, it was not uncommon for the male orioles to be in full song.

Northern Oriole nest in December

The breeding orioles of Nova Scotia belong to the subspecies *Icterus galbula galbula,* the "Baltimore Oriole," as distinguished from the western "Bullock's Oriole," *Icterus galbula bullocki,* and related subspecies. Some birds appearing here in late fall have been identified as "Bullock's Orioles." The first was kept alive at a feeding station in Halifax in December 1969 and January 1970. It was said to be an intergrade, although largely *bullockii* (W.E. Godfrey, personal communication with I.A. McLaren, 1970). A few "Bullock's"-like females have been seen since, with gray backs without dark streaks, gray bellies, and yellow, rather than orange, breasts and undertail coverts. A more distinctive immature male, again with a gray back and a black throat and eyeline, was seen on Seal Island on 8 October 1978 (several observers) and one was photographed at Ian A. McLaren's feeder in Halifax in late December that year. One of the even more distinctive adult males came to Margaret Clark's feeder in Halifax during November 1982. An immature male on Seal Island on 26 May 1982 was well described by Michael Crowell and James McLaren.

Family Fringillidae

Subfamily Fringillinae

Brambling

Fringilla montifringilla Linnaeus

Status One record. An adult male appeared in the early evening of 18 May 1983 at Don Lightbody's feeder at Lake Echo, Halifax County; Mr. Lightbody secured excellent photographs, and other observers were Kay and Dorothy Lightbody and Sheila Connell. The bird was very timid and left at about 8:30 p.m., never to reappear.

Remarks This Old World species has occurred with sufficient frequency throughout North America that records of the bird are now believed to represent true vagrancy, rather than escapes from captivity. It has been seen in the northeastern United States, but the only other Canadian records to date are from British Columbia and Manitoba.

Subfamily Carduelinae

Pine Grosbeak   PLATE 39

Pinicola enucleator (Linnaeus)

Status Irregularly fairly common resident. Breeds. In summer it is generally found in boggy coniferous woodlands remote from human habitation. Although this species still comes to settled areas in winter, it is not seen as commonly or as regularly as it was 70 years ago, when it fed on maple and ash seeds along town streets. It was then a regular winter bird whose arrival was anticipated as the arrival of robins is now anticipated in March. Nowadays in winter it is seen usually in small flocks scattered over the rural countryside. Pine Grosbeaks reported on Christmas Bird Counts around the province have seldom numbered more than 100, although over 200 were noted on the Wolfville Count in 1977 and on the Halifax West Count in 1978.

Description *Length:* 23-25 cm. *Adult male:* Head, rump and underparts rose-red, becoming gray on belly; wings and tail black, the wings with two white bars; back dark gray, the feathers margined with rose-red. *Adult female:* Gray, with crown and rump olive-yellow and wings and tail black, the wings with two white bars.

Breeding *Nest:* Composed of twigs and beard lichen, with a lining of fine vegetable matter mixed with fur; usually placed close to the trunk of a dwarfed, spindly spruce that grows in open, boggy woods where sphagnum flourishes. *Eggs:* 3-4; pale green, flecked with various shades of lavender and brown. It is a late nester, construction usually being delayed until about 1 June. A nest found on 16 June 1910 at Jordan Falls, Shelburne County, contained three partially incubated eggs. On 20 June of that year another was found in the same district. It contained one egg, but when visited three days later, a red squirrel was sitting on the edge of the empty nest. The composition and location of these two nests, both found by Harold F. Tufts, were typical. On 18 August 1928, Rand (1930) collected a fully feathered immature male at Fisher Lake, Annapolis County, and saw several bob-tailed young there in 1927 and 1928. Near Ingonish, Victoria County, Austin W. Cameron saw a male feeding a young bird barely able to fly on 17 July 1945; and W. Earl Godfrey collected a female on 24 June 1954 at Cape North with an egg in her oviduct. An early, half-completed nest was discovered by Harry Brennan near Springville, Pictou County, on 11 May 1967. It was placed close to the trunk of a small spruce in open woodland, about 3 m up, and the male was in full song nearby. On 17 May it contained one egg; three days later, it held a complete set of three eggs.

Range Breeds in the northern forests of the Northern Hemisphere; in North America from Alaska and northern Ungava, south to Nova Scotia, northern New Hampshire, central Manitoba and, in the western mountains, to New Mexico and California. Winters in southern parts of its breeding range and south to Pennsylvania, Iowa, Nebraska and occasionally further.

Remarks In my boyhood days these birds regularly came at the beginning of winter, having a prominence then like that held now by Evening Grosbeaks. I recall that they began to come less regularly and to dwindle in numbers about the time the Evening Grosbeaks began to appear more numerously and with increased regularity. Coincidental perhaps, but the two species do compete for the same winter foods. On 11 December 1968, for instance, three Pine Grosbeaks suddenly appeared in my back yard in Wolfville and joined a group of House Sparrows feeding on "scratch" (a mixture of grains) on the ground. At the same time, 25-30 Evening Grosbeaks were assembled on my food tray eating sunflower seeds, 5-6 m away. The Pine Grosbeaks soon left and were not seen again, but the Evening Grosbeaks continued to come daily and often. In former days, the Pine Grosbeaks would have fed at the food tray.

At the turn of the twentieth century, boys in Wolfville commonly pelted Pine Grosbeaks in the trees along Main Street with snowballs and catapults. It was customary to focus attention on the brightest rosy male and, because the birds were unwary, apparently having had little contact with humans, direct hits were frequently scored. Today, such senseless, open molestation of beautiful and harmless birds would not be tolerated.

The bright rosy males seen in the small winter flocks of Pine Grosbeaks are usually conspicuously outnumbered by the drabber females and immature males.

Purple Finch   PLATE 39

Carpodacus purpureus (Gmelin)

Status Fairly common in summer, uncommon in winter. Breeds. Spring birds generally appear in April (average 11 April, earliest 14 March; appearances in February and early March may represent locally wintering birds). Large arrivals may occur through April and into May. In summer Purple Finches may be found almost anywhere but particularly in coniferous, especially spruce, woodlands. Main fall movements occur in September and October, after which the birds appear intermittently at feeding stations. During autumn they also eat wild berries and are especially fond of the multiflora rose.

Description *Length:* 14-16 cm. *Adult male:* Head, back and breast rose red, brighter on rump; wings and tail dark brown, feathers edged with red; lower breast paler red, shading to white on belly. (This plumage is not acquired until the male is about two years old.) *Adult female:* Upperparts light olive-brown, streaked with dark brown; underparts white, boldly streaked with dark olive-brown, shading to white on belly.

Breeding *Nest:* Composed of twigs and grass stems, rough exteriorly, lined variously with hair, fine rootlets, beard lichen when available, and occasionally wool from a sheep; usually placed near the top of a small or medium-sized spruce or fir in open woodland, sometimes so high as to be among the cone-bearing branchlets. Rarely it nests in deciduous trees, the nest saddled on a horizontal branch; apple trees in an orchard have been the only kind of deciduous tree used by this finch for nesting that I have noted. *Eggs:* 4-6, usually 5; blue, spotted sparsely about the larger end with black. These birds are rather late nesters, normally not laying until late May. Nest construction was noted on 12 May at Wolfville, and the earliest date for a complete set of fresh eggs is 30 May 1914. Of 13 nests examined, 7 contained five eggs, 5 contained four, and 1 held a set of six. The latest date for a set of first laying is 17 June 1913, the eggs slightly incubated. A nest discovered on Wolfville Ridge on 31 May 1915 contained five fresh eggs and was attended by what appeared to be two protesting females; it was later learned that one of them was a male in subadult plumage, an indication that first-year males breed.

Range Breeds from northern British Columbia, northern Alberta, central Manitoba, southern Quebec, and Newfoundland, south to northern New Jersey, central Minnesota, southern Alberta and along the Pacific coast to Baja California. Winters from Nova Scotia, southern Ontario and southern British Columbia to the southern United States.

Remarks The male Purple Finch's song and bright red plumage are notable characteristics. The name "Purple" is a misnomer, for the male is rose-coloured. His song in its fullness is a rich, rapidly enunciated, loud ecstatic warble, sometimes poured out in a torrent of melody as he hovers on outspread trembling wings. I heard one male attempt to sing very early in spring, but its tremulous, feeble rendition bore little resemblance to the song just described.

At nesting time some bird species show a preference for locations close to human habitation—Tree Swallows and Yellow Warblers, for instance—but others have a strong opposite preference. The Purple Finch is quite impartial in this regard, building its nest just as often in our gardens as in remote forested areas.

There is little justification for confusing the male of this species with any of our other birds, except possibly the House Finch, but the female is a different matter. She is a heavily striped, grayish brown, sparrow-sized bird with a conspicuous whitish line extending back from above her eye.

House Finch

Carpodacus mexicanus (Müller)

Status Rare vagrant and possible resident. The species first appeared in 1978 when an adult male arrived at Beulah Berman's feeder in Barrington Passage, Shelburne County, on 13 April. On 15 April a male and a female, later joined by another female, came to the feeders kept by Eric and Barbara Ruff and by Dorothy Kirk in Yarmouth. The birds stayed for weeks to be admired by many, and the bird at Barrington Passage was photographically confirmed (photographs were sent to National Museum of Canada). Another female appeared on 24-26 May 1978 at West Pubnico, Yarmouth County (Ted D'Eon et al.). Since then, there have been 23 reports involving some 47 individuals (not counting probable "repeats"), among which about 15 have been in Yarmouth, 8 in the Pubnicos, 4 in the Halifax area, 8 on Seal Island, 5 on Brier Island, 3 in Tatamagouche, Colchester County, 2 in Paradise, Annapolis County, and 1 each from Barrington, Shelburne County, and Wolfville. These birds have been seen in all months of the year, but most have first appeared in April or late autumn.

Remarks This finch is easily recognized. The male has a deep red bib, forehead and rump, and the striped female lacks the distinct eyebrow and dark face patch of female Purple Finches.

House Finches have spread in eastern North America since their release in New York City in 1940. As Austin (1961) describes it: "In 1940 cage-bird dealers in southern California shipped numbers of these birds, caught illegally in the wild, to New York dealers for sale as 'Hollywood finches.' Alert agents of the Fish and Wildlife Service spotted this violation of the International Migratory Bird Treaty and quickly put an end to the traffic. To avoid prosecution the New York dealers released their birds. The species was soon noted in the wild on nearby Long Island, and it has slowly been increasing its range ever since."

A bird on Seal Island on 2-3 November 1980 (B. Mactavish) was evidently a "pale variant" male, the red replaced by bright buff.

Red Crossbill   PLATE 40

Loxia curvirostra Linnaeus

Status Irregular, uncommon resident. Breeds. For an unknown number of years prior to 1920, the Red Crossbill was seasonally regular in the Annapolis Valley and presumably over the province generally, particularly during late May and early June, apparently attracted by the elm seeds which ripen at that time. About 1921 it practically disappeared, and from then until the early 1960s it was a rare bird throughout Nova Scotia. From 1962 on, numbers increased, with 12 seen that year in mid-May at Liverpool, and similar flocks seen on 19 April 1963 at Lower Ohio, Shelburne County, and on 3 June 1963 at Bridgewater. A peak number of more than 100 Red Crossbills was recorded on 26 November 1967 at Conrad Beach, Halifax County, by Charles R.K. Allen. By 1972 the Red Crossbill was common in small flocks provincewide and, during Christmas Bird Counts that year, 138 were counted at Broad Cove, Lunenburg County, 36 in Cape Breton Highlands National Park and 48 in the Dartmouth area. Another 100 of these birds were noted on 2 September 1975 at Belleville, Yarmouth County. Since that time numbers have again declined, with small numbers seen through all seasons in widely scattered areas, 1-10 birds per sighting.

Description *Length:* 13.5-16.5 cm. *All plumages:* Mandibles crossed at tips. *Adult male:* Body dark red, brighter on rump; wings and tail dark brown; tail well forked. *Adult female:* Crown and rump yellowish orange; wings and tail grayish brown; rest of body olive-green.

Breeding *Nest:* Because its nesting season extends from midwinter to midsummer, two types of nests are necessarily constructed, those for winter use being more substantially built to withstand the cold than summer nests. Winter nests are composed of twigs, weed stems, decayed wood fibre (worked into the exterior) and beard lichen. Summer nests are made of soft vegetable matter and lined with the silken down or tassels of fireweed *(Epilobium angustifolium)* seedpods; sometimes feathers are added, probably as often as procurable at that time of year. A nest I examined in August was fragile, without dead wood fibre and much less compact. Nests are placed in a variety of sites, the most usual spot being in a large spruce, near the end of a long bushy limb, saddled among a cluster of twigs that help conceal it from below while overhanging branches protect it from above. Sometimes nests are hidden among the thick growths of beard lichen found on dead trees. A few nests have been found in the thick tops of small or medium-sized firs growing in dense, coniferous woods; others have been found in hemlocks, well hidden among clusters of small twigs or sprouts that grow where the branch leaves the trunk. The woodland chosen by the birds may be wholly coniferous or of both hard and soft growth; it may be in dry upland or low, boggy land, the prime requisite being an ample supply of seed-bearing cones. Nests have been found at heights of 3-10 m or more. *Eggs:* 3-4; pale blue-green with spots of various shades of brown and lavender, chiefly around the larger end. Nesting begins early in January and may continue through July or later. My first nest was found on 4 August 1896. It was about 6 m up, saddled far out on the limb of a large spruce growing in an ornamental grove in Wolfville. The bird was brooding four half-fledged young. Three nests were found on 31 January 1906 by Harold F. Tufts (1906). Two contained newly hatched young and the third held three partially incubated eggs. On 25 February of that year I found two nests with fresh eggs; the first held four eggs, the other, three. Two nests were found in March 1906, one on the 13th and the other on the 31st; they contained three and four fresh eggs, respectively. All these 1906 nests were found in Kings County, in wooded areas adjacent to farmlands. Complete sets of three and four eggs were about evenly divided. In each instance the females did all the incubating. The males were observed a number of times at very close range when feeding their mates by regurgitation. On one occasion, at temperatures below -20°C, I watched this feeding operation at a distance of about 1 m. The food substance passing from his throat to hers looked like a stream of thick cream, but it was actually a mass of small whitish seeds from the spruce and hemlock cones on which he had been feeding. Nests were located by watching males carrying food to sitting females or by watching females carrying nesting material. One partly finished nest was visited later and found to contain four fresh eggs, all of which had cracked as a result of having been frozen, and no birds were in evidence. One 8 ha block of open, second-growth coniferous woods contained one dozen or more pairs of nesting Red Crossbills from January to March 1906, and perhaps half as many nesting White-winged Crossbills. The birds continued to nest there late in the winters of 1902, 1906 and 1913, but I have no record of more recent nestings.

Range Breeds in both the New and Old Worlds; in North America from southern Alaska, Manitoba, central Ontario, and Newfoundland, south to the northern United States and, in the western mountains, to Mexico and Guatemala.

Remarks The two species of crossbills are easy to distinguish. The Red Crossbill displays plain dark wings, but the wings of the White-winged Crossbill, as its name suggests, are conspicuously marked with double bars of white.

On 1 June 1969, Cyril Coldwell collected two birds from a mixed flock of crossbills, at Gaspereau, Kings County, to determine their subspecific status. The specimens were sent to the National Museum of Canada in Ottawa where W. Earl Godfrey identified them as *Loxia curvirostra minor,* the race found breeding here. *Loxia curvirostra pusilla* has been recorded here only once. Several specimens collected in late February 1932 near Wolfville by W. Earl Godfrey and Roland W. Smith were later examined by Harry C. Oberholser, who identified them as belonging to *L. c. pusilla,* the breeding subspecies of Newfoundland.

White-winged Crossbill   PLATE 40

Loxia leucoptera Gmelin

Status Irregular, fairly common resident. Breeds. It has two distinct breeding seasons: early January to late April and early July to late September. Although it occurs most often during those months, wandering flocks may be seen at any time of year. It shows a strong preference for coniferous forests but is occasionally seen elsewhere. James C. Morrow saw a flock of 10-12 White-winged Crossbills feeding on tiny caterpillars on an infested oak in Halifax on 3 June 1951. From 1955 on, flocks of 20-150 birds were commonly seen. One very large invasion occurred on 23 February 1963, when Charles R.K. Allen and Lloyd B. Macpherson came upon "many thousands" of White-winged Crossbills eating white spruce seeds and later recounted that "the sound of the scales dropping all around was like a heavy rain." Such a flock has not occurred here since, but the species is still present and widely scattered over the province; flocks of 10-50 birds have been found during all seasons but most often in the winter months.

Description *Length:* 15-17 cm. *All plumages:* Mandibles crossed at tips. *Adult male:* Wings and tail black, the wings boldly marked with two white bars; rest of plumage rose-red, brighter on rump. *Adult female:* Gray suffused with olive-green, brighter on crown and rump; wings and tail dark gray, the wings boldly marked with two white bars; underparts less greenish, and lightly striped with dark gray.

Breeding *Nest:* Winter nests are similar to those built by Red Crossbills and better constructed than summer nests, which consist of a few insecurely placed conifer twigs, with a liberal quantity of beard lichen on top. The moss is roughly moulded into the shape of a nest, and remains in that form until the young are hatched; but after they are about a week old, it becomes depressed and finally is completely flattened. Two nest sites were quite different from those selected by Red Crossbills: a small slender spruce growing in open woodland pasture near heavy coniferous woods; and the top of a small spruce about 5 m high, growing in a thicket of its own kind so dense that only the topmost branchlets were green. *Eggs:* 3-4; practically indistinguishable from those of the Red Crossbill. The first of the two fairly well defined breeding seasons, which begins in midwinter and continues throughout April, is, I believe, far less regular in Nova Scotia than the second, which begins in late July and continues well into September. However, I have no evidence either to suggest a particular pair nests more than once a year or that it does not. The following are typical nesting dates. Winter nesting: 8 February 1906, three slightly incubated eggs; 26 February 1906, four eggs in similar condition; 1 April 1906, three fresh eggs; 26 April 1906, four fresh eggs; all in Kings County. On 19 April 1925 four eggs about one-half incubated were located at Seal Island. Summer nesting: A female collected at Seabright, Halifax County, on 12 July 1916 was soon to lay eggs (L.R. Bishop). On 25 August 1931 a nest at Albany, Annapolis County, contained four young, which flew on 8 September. In the same locality on 30 August 1938, a male was seen feeding three young that were barely able to fly. A singing male collected in Inverness County on 17 July 1940 had the greatly enlarged testes of a bird that was breeding or about to breed. At Bear River, Annapolis

County, Lloyd Duncanson collected a breeding pair on 19 July 1950. At Albany three young flew from a nest when the tree was shaken on 30 August 1950, and at the same place on the following day a male was seen feeding a young bird well able to fly. All nests were in coniferous forests remote from habitation.

Range Breeds in both the Old and New Worlds. Breeds in North America north to the limit of trees and south to Nova Scotia, northern New York State, the Prairie Provinces and southern British Columbia. Wanders irregularly further south in winter.

Remarks Unlike its red cousin, this bird does not seem to relish elm seeds but appears to be more a forest species and is seldom seen on other than cone-bearing trees.

The White-winged Crossbill's song is rich and full and closely resembles that of the American Goldfinch. At times the male is seen pouring forth a torrent of melody while circling overhead on slowly flapping wings, a sure sign that nesting is in progress or about to begin.

While busily tearing apart seed cones, a task for which their peculiar bills are perfectly adapted, these birds usually betray their presence with a monotonous half-musical chattering. However, sometimes they work in absolute silence like a flock of miniature parrots.

The White-winged Crossbill is similar in colour to the Pine Grosbeak, which also has white wing-bars, but the grosbeak is robin-size and the crossbill is more nearly sparrow-size.

Common Redpoll   PLATE 39

Carduelis flammea (Linnaeus)

Status Irregularly common in winter. Abundant some years, occasionally rare to absent other years. Whether this irregularity is the result of availability of food, prevailing winds at times of migration or to other less obvious factors is not known. Fall birds generally first appear in October or November (average 30 October, earliest 4 October); an exceptionally early bird was seen at Cape Sable on 8 September 1965 (B.J. and S. Smith). Numbers build by late December, when estimates of 100-1000 or more Common Redpolls have been made on Christmas Bird Counts around the province. The latest reports are generally in April (average 11 April, latest 4 May). Two later spring birds at St. Esprit, Richmond County, on 10 June 1982 (R. and M. Meyerowitz) were unusual but reports from Sable Island in 1968 were quite startling: following a sighting of three birds between 8 and 10 June, three of these little northerners were seen on 6 July, one on 12 July, one on 26 July, and one on 2 August (C. and N. Bell, I.A. McLaren). Winter 1935-36 was a "redpoll winter." They were common from December to April and for the two weeks of mid-April the local winter population, augmented by northbound transients, swarmed over parts of the Annapolis Valley. On 18 April, C.A. Borden had "millions of small birds" come out of the sky and settle all about him while he was pruning the trees in his apple orchard at Sheffield Mills, Kings County. The birds were seemingly unconscious of his presence, alighting close by and chattering excitedly. In all his years of orcharding he had never seen anything like it. They stayed a few minutes and then suddenly the entire flock rose into the air as one bird and whirled away in a cloud. Nothing so dramatic has been reported in recent years but redpolls were very common in the winters of 1959-60, 1968-69 and 1981-82.

Description *Length:* 13-14 cm. *All plumages:* Bill short and sharply pointed. *Adult male:* Crown bright satiny red; rump and breast delicately suffused with pink; back streaked brown and gray; wings and tail dark brown, the wings with two light gray bars, and the tail well notched; belly white; flanks and rump streaked with brown. *Adult female:* Similar but without pink on rump or breast; underparts and rump more heavily streaked with brown.

Range Breeds in the northern parts of the Northern Hemisphere. In North America, breeds south to Newfoundland, central Quebec, northern Manitoba and northern British Columbia, and winters south to the central United States.

Remarks Redpolls are closely related to Pine Siskins and American Goldfinches, both of which they resemble in size, manner of flight and feeding habits. In winter these three species commonly fly together in mixed flocks, but as the time in spring for northward migration approaches, great numbers of redpolls often congregate and travel by themselves. On 17 April 1942 I saw one of these great mass migrations in progress near Wilmot, Annapolis County. The branches of a small roadside apple orchard were so thickly covered with redpolls that the trees presented a leaden-gray appearance. The ground below was so thickly covered that it looked like a gray carpet in motion, as thousands of individuals hopped about. The centre of this great flock was not more than 30 m away, and the din of birds' combined twitterings was impressive, as though each one in its excitement was trying to out-twitter the others. When flushed by a blast from my car's horn, the roar of their wings was like a sudden gale of wind. As they wheeled into the sky in dense formation, twisting and turning as though uncertain of the proper course to follow, they looked like an immense swarm of giant bees. Never before or since have I seen so many redpolls at one time.

Hoary Redpoll

Carduelis hornemanni Holboll

Status Rare in winter. Hoary Redpolls have been reported in Nova Scotia only since 1959, when a "frosty-looking" bird was seen in a large flock of Common Redpolls at Lower Canard, Kings County, on 27 December (R.W. Tufts). Three such birds were seen at Gaspereau, Kings County, on 13 March 1960, and one collected there on 15 March was confirmed by W. Earl Godfrey as a Hoary Redpoll. The next four were seen on 18 January 1969 near Halifax by Jean Boulva and Robert Gauthier; and on 22 February 1969 Charles R.K. Allen saw one at Kennetcook, Hants County. Since then, individuals have been reported, sometimes as "probables" but with convincing details, on 18 May

1977 on Sable Island (McLaren 1981a); 27 December 1977 at Fenwick, Cumberland County (R. Burrows); 26 March 1978 at Green Bay, Lunenburg County (C. Cohrs); and, in Halifax, on 4-5 January 1981 (M. Clark) and 1-2 March 1982 (probably two birds, S. Cohrs and I.A. McLaren).

Remarks Common Redpolls are sometimes misidentified as Hoary Redpolls by the overenthusiastic, but the frosty appearance and plain white rump, unstreaked in the centre, are distinctive, although the rump is readily seen only when the birds fly off at close range. Another good mark is the Hoary Redpoll's smaller bill, which gives its face a "squashed-in" appearance. The Hoary Redpoll is a rarer, more northern bird than its more common cousin. Recent work casts some doubt on its status as a distinct species.

Pine Siskin   PLATE 39

Carduelis pinus (Wilson)

Status Irregularly common resident. Breeds. Nomadic in nature, its numbers fluctuate from year to year and from season to season. As a rule, wandering flocks come, remain for indefinite periods and disappear. When this bird is common or rare in any particular part of the province at any specified time, it should not be assumed that similar conditions prevail elsewhere. This bird has been noted in every month of the year but most often from April through June and from October through December, and least often in August—the largest number for that month was recorded on 27 August 1977 at Sydney Forks, Cape Breton County, and the Grand Anse River valley, Inverness County, when over 100 were counted at both localities. This was one of the years when the Pine Siskin was common throughout the province, with flocks of up to 200 from Cape Breton Island to Antigonish and down both the Annapolis Valley and the Southwestern Shore to Yarmouth.

Description *Length:* 11.5-13 cm. *Adults:* Upperparts buff, streaked with blackish brown; tail deeply notched, dark brown at end, outer feathers edged with yellow at the base; wings dark brown with yellow bases on the primary and secondary feathers making yellow patches of varying brightness on the folded wing; underparts mostly whitish, tinged with buff and streaked with dark brown; bill short and sharply pointed.

Breeding *Nest:* Made of twigs, coarse grass or weed stems, beard lichen (when available), lined with hair or moss or both. It is usually saddled on the horizontal limb of a spruce or a large pine; if on a pine, usually high and far out on the limb. Nests are located in coniferous forests remote from habitation or, perhaps as often, in ornamental groves of conifers in towns and other settled districts, usually fairly high in the tree. *Eggs:* 3-4; pale bluish white, lightly speckled with various shades of brown. Its nesting is as irregular as its occurrence, as the following dates show. A nest examined on 4 August 1898 contained four fresh eggs; two other nests, on 6 and 10 June 1910, each held fresh sets of four and three eggs, respectively; all three were in large white pines in ornamental groves in Wolfville and placed well out from the trunks at heights of 6-12 m. Three nests under construction were found on 18 April 1915 on Wolfville Ridge, saddled on the branches of medium-sized spruces in open coniferous woods; two were later robbed by a natural predator, but the third contained a full set of three fresh eggs on 27 April.

Range Breeds from southern Alaska, central Manitoba, southern Quebec, and Newfoundland, south to the northern United States and, in the western mountains, to Mexico. Winters from southern Canada to the southern United States and Mexico.

Remarks The outstanding characteristic of this bird is the general irregularity of both its comings and goings and its nesting habits.

On 13 September 1968 Phyllis Dobson and Charles R.K. Allen observed one in full song at St. Andrews, Colchester County, suggesting that it was nesting or about to do so.

It is not difficult to distinguish this species in the mingled flocks of goldfinches and redpolls with which it commonly associates in winter. The goldfinch is unstreaked; redpolls have bright red caps, inconspicuous black bibs, lighter underparts and breasts less streaked than those of siskins.

American Goldfinch   PLATE 37

Carduelis tristis (Linnaeus)

Status Fairly common resident. Breeds. Goldfinches are widely distributed in summer, perhaps more often seen in agricultural areas than in areas remote from human habitation. In winter their numbers vary from common to rather rare, perhaps according to the availability of the many kinds of seeds they depend on during the lean months. Flocks range about the countryside in search of these seeds, usually gleaned from weeds and other low-growing plants. At other times they may be seen busily extracting seeds from the cones of scrub spruces, and in recent years they have become regular at bird feeders in winter. Goldfinches normally appear on Christmas Bird Counts, on which estimates of 100 or more have been made throughout the province. A record high count of 989 was made on the Halifax East Count in 1982.

Description *Length:* 13-14 cm. *Adult male:* Crown and tail black; wings black with white bar and yellow lesser coverts; uppertail coverts white; rest of plumage bright canary-yellow. *Adult female:* Upperparts buff with yellowish tinge; no black crown patch; wings and tail lighter than summer male's; underparts buff washed with pale yellow; two white wing bars.

Breeding *Nest:* Composed of grass, plant down, strips of pliable bark and other materials, neatly and compactly interwoven and usually lined with dandelion "fuzz" or thistledown. It is placed in trees, sometimes bushes, of deciduous varieties; apple trees in orchards are favoured sites. The nests are usually at fairly low heights. *Eggs:* 4-7, usually 5; pale bluish white, rarely with a few specks of brown scattered irregularly over the surface. The American Goldfinch is a late nester: the birds usually begin to lay about mid-July and continue as late as early September, but occasionally nest construction is under way in early June. A female was gathering cotton wool, from a supply placed in my garden for the convenience of various species at nesting time, on 8 June 1955; on 14 July 1960 a young male, able to flutter only a short distance, was brought to me by children; the nest from which it had flown was obviously of early June construction. Some late nesting records: On 13 August 1960 a female was seen carrying nesting material. A nest in an apple tree in a Wolfville orchard contained four eggs on 6 September 1948, and the last fledglings left on 24 September. Another nest at Blomidon, Kings County, contained half-grown young on 3 September 1952. On 16 September a young bird just out of a nest was calling lustily and incessantly for food near Wolfville.

Range Breeds from southern British Columbia, the middle parts of the prairie provinces, central Ontario, southern Quebec and southwestern Newfoundland, south to northern Georgia, southern Colorado and Baja California. Winters from southern Canada to Mexico.

Remarks It is widely known as "thistle-bird" and "wild canary," both names not inappropriate because it is often seen feeding on thistle seeds in late summer and its bright colours and general appearance resemble those of the cagebird.

In late summer the male loses his brilliant plumage and, until early the following April, closely resembles his drab mate, whose plumage changes little from season to season. Because the male's plumage is so dull in winter, many people do not recognize the bird at that season.

The goldfinch's flight is notably undulating and often, if not usually, accompanied by a vocal *per-chick-o-ree,* repeated at every dip as it swings over the countryside. The male's song is a sweet, spirited melody he pours forth usually while perched but sometimes while flying on outstretched, slowly flapping wings high overhead.

The male bears no marked similarity to any other species that occurs in Nova Scotia. The Yellow Warbler, which approximates it in size, is yellow all over and lacks the black wings and cap of the goldfinch; the bill of the warbler is slender, that of the goldfinch is short and stubby.

Evening Grosbeak   PLATE 37

Coccothraustes vespertinus (Cooper)

Status Uncommon in summer, irregularly common in winter. Breeds. A first major invasion of New England and eastern Canada took place in winter 1889-90, but the species did not occur in Nova Scotia until 1913 (Lewis 1913). This bird was not reported again until early March 1926, when a small flock was observed at Annapolis Royal by J.L. DeVany. On 28 January 1928, one that had been killed by a cat was brought to a taxidermist at Truro (Piers' notes). On 24 April 1929 a specimen collected at Windsor by Victor Gould was presented to Acadia University. The next recorded appearance was on 25 January 1932 when John W. Piggott saw a small flock in Bridgetown, Annapolis County; 3 males and 20 females were recorded at Windsor on 5 April (Mrs. R. Curry). In 1938 the Evening Grosbeak was coming regularly, arriving in early November and leaving in April, with stragglers into June. It is now one of the most familiar winter birds at feeders in town and countryside. The first summer occurrence was in July 1947, when C.S. Eaton saw a male feeding on cherries at Wolfville; on 9 September of that year Merritt Gibson reported two males and a female eating sumac berries on the Wolfville Ridge. By 1984 it was widely established as a breeding bird, especially on Cape Breton Island.

Description *Length:* 16.5-21.5 cm. *Adult male:* Forehead, line extending over eye, back, rump and belly bright yellow; top of head, wings and tail black; wing coverts and half of secondaries conspicuously white; nape, sides of head, and chin dark seal-brown; breast brown, shading into yellow; legs and feet reddish brown; bill pale whitish gray in late fall and winter, changing to pale greenish gray in early spring. *Adult female:* Above olive-brown, with yellowish wash on nape and sides of breast; scapulars grayish white; rest of wing black; tail black, the feathers tipped with white; throat white to upper breast; rest of underparts gray suffused with yellow.

Breeding *Nest:* Made of coarse twigs, with lining of fine roots and mosses; at heights of 5-10 m or more, a preference being shown for pine trees. *Eggs:* 3-5; greenish blue, blotched with brown of varying shades. For years the only proof of breeding was parent birds seen feeding "bob-tailed" young. The first incidence of this occurred at Ingonish Beach, Victoria County, on 1 August 1958 (S. Bleakney); such observations have since come from almost every county in the province. The first nest with young was found by Murray A. Bent on Wolfville Ridge in spring 1971.

Range Breeds in central British Columbia, central Saskatchewan, northern Michigan and central Ontario, New Brunswick and Nova Scotia, and south in the western mountains to southern Mexico. Wanders widely in winter.

Remarks Many Evening Grosbeaks have been trapped and banded at feeding stations over a wide area in recent years, shedding light on the interesting habits of these nomadic creatures. It appears, for instance, that small flocks have some sort of affinity that holds them together in their wanderings. Two birds trapped at Wolfville, from a small flock, wore bands with similar dates, placed on them at a station in New Hampshire. Two individuals banded by me at Wolfville on 6 December 1954 were recaptured together by Willett J. Mills at Halifax on 13 February 1955; obviously they had been together during the interim. That these birds travel on some sort of schedule is suggested by the behaviour of one I banded on 8 March 1952 which, having wandered hither and yon for a whole year, was recaptured on my tray on 4 March 1953.

When they come to us in the fall their beaks vary in colour from horn to very pale pinkish white. These shades are retained until late March, when they gradually change to a greenish tinge, which becomes slightly more pronounced during the following weeks until they forsake our feeding trays, usually in early May.

This bird was first discovered in 1823 and named "Evening Grosbeak" because, coincidentally, it was then heard to sing only in the evening. Chapman (1934) describes the song as a wandering, jerky warble, beginning low, suddenly increasing in power and then suddenly ending as though the performer were out of breath.

Evening Grosbeaks

Family Passeridae

House Sparrow   PLATE 34

Passer domesticus (Linnaeus)

Status Introduced, locally common resident. Breeds. Most abundant in cities, towns, and communities where agriculture flourishes. Its numbers are conspicuously lower in more sparsely populated districts and reach the vanishing point in heavily forested areas and open, barren country. Just when this alien reached Nova Scotia is unrecorded, but Piers noted that, "In the '50's, somewhere about 1856 or 1857, Charles and Rupert Eaton, of Lower Canard (Kings County), large potato growers and exporters, imported a number of English Sparrows from New York or Mass. (not sure which) and set them free, and soon R.W. Starr found others among his orchard at

Starr's Point." Coues (1890) states that it first appeared on Cape Breton Island in November 1889, coincidentally with the completion of the Cape Breton railroad. House Sparrows rapidly spread over Nova Scotia and increased in number up to the early 1900s, but with the advent of the motor car replacing the horse (the spilled grain from feed bags and in stables and the undigested grain in the horses' droppings were significant food sources), and the closing of many small farms, numbers began to fall. For example, on Christmas counts from Halifax West, 2500 were recorded in 1958, but only about 1700 in 1982 even with twice as many observers; in Yarmouth, 263 House Sparrows were reported on the 1968 Christmas count, but only about half that number in 1984 although there were 30 observers instead of two. In contrast, the small population of these birds on Brier Island has remained fairly constant in recent years at 50-70 individuals. It is not widely recognized that the House Sparrow shows migratory tendencies. For example, transients have appeared twice in spring and twice in fall on Sable Island, since a small breeding population there became extirpated in 1971 (McLaren 1981a). In addition, many have been recorded since 1970 during five springs and seven autumns on Seal Island, 10-15 km from the nearest mainland sources.

Description *Length:* 12.5-16 cm. *Adult male:* Crown gray; chestnut stripe extending from eye to nape and broadening over sides of neck; wing coverts chestnut, with single bar of white; cheek grayish white; chin and breast black; lower breast and belly dirty or grayish white, the flanks washed with darker gray. *Adult female:* Above buffy gray, darker on crown; light buff line over eye; wing bar buff; chin light gray; breast darker gray; belly lighter gray.

Breeding *Nest:* Composed of coarse grass, weed stems and trash, lined with fine grass and copiously with feathers, usually from the nearest poultry yard. Nest sites vary greatly, though holes in trees, Tree Swallow nest boxes, crevices about buildings and the mud nests from which they have driven the Cliff Swallows that built them are commonly used. *Eggs:* 4-7, usually 5-6; white to brownish white, finely marked with olive over the entire surface. Probably three broods are raised when nothing interferes with the success of the first and second. Evidence of early nesting activity was noted on 18 February 1946 at Wolfville, when a male and female took turns going in and out of a swallow nest box. On 4 March 1941 a female was seen gathering grass for her nest. A nest containing seven fresh eggs was examined on 29 June 1927 at Wolfville.

Range Introduced to North America about 1850, it now occurs in most settled parts of the continent.

Remarks Chapman (1934) mentions that it was liberated at Brooklyn, New York, about 1850-52, and was largely confined to the cities of the Atlantic states as late as 1870. These dates tend to support those already cited from Piers' notes, and point to New York City as the probable source of the birds the Eatons imported.

Although over a century has passed since it was first liberated in North America, it has never shown complete independence of man. Its greatest density of population occurs in towns and villages, and in rural districts it makes its headquarters about farm buildings, seldom foraging far beyond the limits of cultivated lands.

This bird's general unpopularity has been brought about by some of the undesirable traits it exhibits. For example, this bird's habit of fighting with much-loved swallows for possession of the nest boxes placed to attract the swallows to gardens in spring has made it unpopular. Despite this, the House Sparrow is a beneficial bird because its food in summer is largely insects that plague the farmer.

Appendix 1: Hypothetical Species

In previous editions of this book some species were presented as "hypothetical" when evidence for their occurrence was based on sight records alone. In this edition, we have referred to these as "sight records" whenever there seemed to be little or no doubt about the correctness of the identifications; dubious or questionable sight records have been excluded. However, a number of other species have been reported as occurring in the province but about which information is not wholly satisfactory. Some reports lack data on the exact time or place of occurrence. Some reports show a lack of discrimination among two or more possible vagrants—a problem that has not been resolved by observations or specimens. Some birds have undoubtedly been correctly identified but almost certainly represent individuals that have escaped from captivity, although not necessarily in Nova Scotia. The following gives a brief account of such species.

Bulwer's Petrel *Bulweria bulwerii* (Jardine and Selby)
An all-dark petrel seen off Yarmouth on 13 August 1982 was reported as this species, but the possibility that it was one of the all-dark petrels from the Indo-Pacific cannot be excluded.

Scarlet Ibis *Eudocimus ruber* (Linnaeus)
At least two birds were seen by many observers in summer 1981. All such North American reports are considered by authorities (American Ornithologists' Union 1983) to represent escaped birds.

Roseate Spoonbill *Ajaia ajaja* (Linnaeus)
A secondhand source reported one seen on Sable Island in summer 1948, but the observer evidently did not believe that such sight records merited publication (McLaren 1981a).

Black Rail *Laterallus jamaicensis* (Gmelin)
Sanford et al. (1903) mention a mounted specimen said to be from Halifax, but no data are given on place or date of capture (see previous editions of this book).

Spotted Redshank *Tringa erythropus* (Pallas)
A bird on 2 January 1960 was considered by observers to be a Common Redshank *(Tringa totanus)* and was included as such in the earlier editions of this book. However, in some respects the description suggests a Spotted Redshank, although the critical differences in wing pattern were not noted. The Common Redshank has not been recorded in North America, whereas the Spotted Redshank is rare but regular. The record is treated as hypothetical and probably Spotted Redshank by American Ornithologists' Union (1983). Two other reports of "redshanks" have not been sufficiently detailed for discrimination of species.

Green Sandpiper *Tringa ochropus* Linnaeus
Although Brewer (1878) quotes a letter to the effect that a skin sent to London, England, was from a bird taken in Halifax, no details are given on date or place of collection.

South Polar Skua *Catharacta maccormicki* (Saunders)
See Remarks under Great Skua.

Thayer's Gull *Larus thayeri* Brooks
See Remarks under Iceland Gull.

Groove-billed Ani *Crotophaga sulcirostris* Swainson
Reports of an ani in Guysborough County in fall 1975 and of another at Debert, Colchester County, on 7-8 December 1980, did not include enough details for discrimination from the Smooth-billed Ani, *Crotophaga ani,* although this species is less prone to wander.

Tropical Kingbird *Tyrannus melancholius* Vieillot
A bird was identified as this species by R.W. Tufts at Wolfville on 18 July 1976. However, it was seen only briefly and, since the species cannot be separated on appearance from Couch's Kingbird, *Tyrannus couchii,* which is also prone to wander, the identification is uncertain.

Bahama Swallow *Tachycineta cyaneoviridis* (Bryant)
Although her description is convincing, no date is given by Evelyn Richardson (1965) for a bird seen by her one May on Bon Portage Island.

Fieldfare *Turdus pilaris* Linnaeus
Two Fieldfares were reported by two separate observers to have been seen on the barrens near Louisbourg during October 1971, and another person reported having seen two there in October 1972. These were passed on to the Nova Scotia Museum, but unfortunately no details were given on names of observers or exact dates of sightings.

Bachman's Sparrow *Aimophila aestivalis* (Lichtenstein)
The species is listed for Cape Sable (Smith and Smith 1972), but no details on date of occurrence were kept. The bird also has been tentatively identified on Seal Island.

Boat-tailed Grackle *Quiscalus major* Vieillot
See Remarks under Great-tailed Grackle.

European Goldfinch *Carduelis carduelis* (Linnaeus)
A convincing sight record on 11 September 1970 (see second edition of this book) presumably represents an escaped captive.

Appendix 2: Unsuccessful Introductions

The following is a list of species whose attempted introduction to Nova Scotia has failed:

Common Capercaillie *Tetrao urogallus* Linnaeus
Five pairs were liberated on 7 October 1929 at South Brookfield, Queens County, by F.B. McCurdy, who imported them from Sweden. They are believed to have lived only a few days (Tufts 1930).

Black Eurasian-Grouse *Lyurus tetrix* (Linnaeus)
Ten pairs were released with the Capercaillie and met the same fate.

Chukar *Alectoris chukar* (Gray)
Several pairs were released in different areas in summer 1957 by the Nova Scotia Department of Lands and Forests, but all are believed to have perished before winter.

Wild Turkey *Meleagris gallopavo* Linnaeus
Several pairs were released with the Chukars in 1957 with the same results.

Northern Bobwhite *Colinus virginianus* (Linnaeus)
Fifty pairs were imported from southern Ontario in 1950 by the Kings County Fish and Game Association. They were liberated in the Canard area of Kings County on 6 April but were evidently annihilated by persistent low temperatures and snowstorms in the days following. During 1952 considerably larger numbers were released in the same area. These were birds of the year that had been raised in the Provincial Wildlife Park at Shubenacadie, Hants County. During early fall 1953 several large flocks were seen, and in spring 1954 the distinctive calls of the cocks were commonly heard throughout the district. Few, however, survived the following winter (1954-55) and none was reported from the areas of liberation in 1956. Single birds in Kings and Yarmouth counties in 1976 and flocks in Lunenburg County in 1981 and 1982 may have been unauthorized releases or escapes from stocks kept for dog-training purposes (N. Van Nostrand).

Literature Cited

Allen, E.C.
1916. Annotated list of birds of Yarmouth and vicinity, southwestern Nova Scotia. *Proc. Trans. Nova Scotian Inst. Sci.* 14: 67-95.

Allen, E.G.
1939. Nicolas Denys, a forgotten observer of birds. *Auk* 56: 283-285.

American Ornithologists' Union
1983. *Check-List of North American Birds.* 6th ed. American Ornithologists' Union.

Audubon, J.J.
1839. *The Birds of America,* vol. 7. George R. Lockwood, New York.

Austin, O.L., Jr.
1961. On the American status of *Tiaris canora* and *Carduelis carduelis. Auk* 80: 73-74.

Austin-Smith, P.J., and G.E. Dickie.
1985. Nesting success and productivity of Bald Eagles *(Haliaeetus leucocephalus)* in Nova Scotia 1984. [N.S.] *Lands and Forests Technical Note* No. 28.

Austin-Smith, P.J. and G. Rhodenizer.
1983. Ospreys, *Pandion haliaetus,* relocate nests from power lines to substitute sites. *Canadian Field-Nat.* 97: 315-319.

Bagg, A.M.
1967. Factors affecting the occurrence of the Eurasian Lapwing in eastern North America. *The Living Bird* 1967: 87-122.

Bagg, A.M., and R.P. Emery.
1966. Regional reports, fall migration. Northeastern Maritime region. *Audubon Field-Notes* 20: 7-19.

Banks, R.C.
1977. The decline and fall of the Eskimo Curlew, or why did the curlew go extaille? *Amer. Birds* 31: 127-134.

Bartlett, C.O.
1960. American Widgeon and Pintail in the Maritime Provinces. *Canadian Field-Nat.* 74: 153-155.

Bayley, I.A.
1925. The birds of Bird Islands, Nova Scotia. *Canadian Field-Nat.* 39: 183-187.

Bent, A.C.
1919. Life histories of North American diving birds. *U.S. Nat. Mus. Bull.* 107.
1923. Life histories of North American wild fowl. Part 1. *U.S. Nat. Mus. Bull.* 126.
1925. Life histories of North American wild fowl. Part 2. *U.S. Nat. Mus. Bull.* 126.
1927. Life histories of North American shore birds. Part 1. *U.S. Nat. Mus. Bull.* 142.
1937. Life histories of North American birds of prey. Part 1. *U.S. Nat. Mus. Bull.* 170.
1938. Life histories of North American birds of prey. Part 2. *U.S. Nat. Mus. Bull.* 174.

Bierregaard, R.O., A.B. David, T.D. Baird, and R.E. Woodruff.
 1975. First Northwest Atlantic breeding record of the Manx Shearwater. *Auk* 92: 145-147.

Blakiston, T., and R.E. Bland.
 1856. A list of the birds of Nova Scotia, as far as ascertained, compiled mostly from actual observations, in the years 1852-3-4 and 5. Land Birds. *Naturalist* (London) 6: 268-271.
 1857. A list of the birds of Nova Scotia, as far as ascertained, compiled mostly from actual observations, in the years 1852-3-4 and 5. Waterbirds. *Naturalist* (London) 7: 103-106.

Bouteillier, J.[1]
 1906. Bird migration, 1905. Observations made on Sable Island, Nova Scotia. *Ottawa Nat.* 20: 127-129.

Bouteillier, R.[1]
 1901. Autumn notes on birds, Sable Island, N.S. *Ottawa Nat.* 15: 199-200.

Brewer, T.M.
 1878. Changes in our North American fauna. *Bull. Nuttall Ornithol. Club* 3: 50-51.

Brewster, W.
 1906. The birds of the Cambridge region. *Mem. Nuttall Ornithol. Club,* No. 4.
 1909a. Something more about Black Ducks. *Auk* 26: 173-179.
 1909b. Occurrence of the Whimbrel *(Numenius phaeopus)* off the coast of Nova Scotia. *Auk* 26: 190-191.

Brooks, Alan.
 1933. Notes on short trip to Nova Scotia and New Brunswick. *Canadian Field-Nat.* 47: 70-72.

Brown, R.G.B.
 1980. A second Canadian Record of Audubon's Shearwater *Puffinus lherminieri. Canadian Field-Nat.* 94: 466-476.

Brown, R.G.B., D.I. Gillespie, A.R. Lock, P.A. Pearce, and G.H. Watson.
 1973. Bird mortality from oil slicks off eastern Canada, February-April 1970. *Canadian Field-Nat.* 87: 225-234.

Brown, R.G.B., D.N. Nettleship, P.Germain, C.E. Tull, and T. Davis.
 1975. *Atlas of Eastern Canadian Seabirds.* Canadian Wildl. Serv., Envir. Canada, Ottawa.

Bryant, H.
 1857. A list of birds observed at Grand Manan and at Yarmouth, N.S., from June 16 to July 8, 1856. *Proc. Boston Soc. Nat. Hist.* 6: 114-123.

Cairns, W.E., and I.A. McLaren.
 1980. The status of the Piping Plover in eastern North America. *Amer. Birds* 34: 206-208.

Chamberlain, M.
 1881. Remarkable flight of birds. *Ornithologist and Oologist* 6: 53.
 1887a. A *Catalogue of Canadian Birds with Notes on the Distribution of the Species.* J. & A. McMillan, Saint John, N.B.
 1887b. The Baltimore Oriole *(Icterus galbula)* in Nova Scotia. *Auk* 4: 258.
 1891. A *Popular Handbook of the Ornithology of the United States and Canada, based on Nuttall's Manual.* 2 vols. Little, Brown, and Co., Boston.

Champlain, Samuel de.
 1922. *The Works of Samuel de Champlain,* ed. H.P. Biggar. Vol. 1. The Champlain Society, Toronto, Ontario.

Chapman, F.M.
 1934. *Handbook of Birds of Eastern North America.* D. Appleton and Co., New York.

---

[1]Some of the papers in the previous edition under R. and J. Bouteillier were attributed to the wrong Bouteillier when published, and their name was variously misspelt. The papers are here given under the correct authorships. See clarification in McLaren (1981a).

Collins, J.W.

1884. Notes on the habits and methods of capture of various species of sea birds that occur on the fishing banks off the eastern coast of North America, and which were used as bait for catching codfish by New England fishermen. *U.S. Bur. Fisheries, Ann. Rep. U.S. Comm. Fisheries,* 1882: 311-338.

Cooke, W.W.

1910. Distribution and migration of North American shorebirds. *U.S. Dept. Agric. Biol. Surv. Bull.* 185, 47 pp.

1915. Bird migration. *U.S. Dept. Agric. Bull.* 185.

Coues, W.P.

1890. *Passer domesticus* in Cape Breton. *Auk* 7: 212.

Deane, R.

1879. The Frigate Pelican in Nova Scotia. *Bull. Nuttall Ornithol. Club* 4: 64.

Dewar, J.M.

1912. The evolution of waders. *The Zoologist,* 4 Ser., 16: 161.

Doane, B.K.

1971. A Black-cowled Oriole? *Nova Scotia Bird Soc. Newsletter* 13: 79-81.

Downs, A.

1865. On the land birds of Nova Scotia. *Proc. Trans. Nova Scotian Inst. Sci.* 1 (3): 38-51.

1866. On the land birds of Nova Scotia. *Proc. Trans. Nova Scotian Inst. Sci.* 1 (4): 130-136.

1886. Pied or Labrador Duck. *Proc. Trans. Nova Scotian Inst. Sci.* 6: 326-327.

1888. A catalogue of the birds of Nova Scotia. *Proc. Trans Nova Scotian Inst. Sci.* 7: 142-178.

Dutcher, W.

1891. The Labrador Duck: a revised list of the extant specimens in North America with some historical notes. *Auk* 8: 201-214.

1894. The Labrador Duck—another specimen, with additional data respecting extant specimens. *Auk* 11: 4.

Dwight, J.

1895. The Ipswich Sparrow *(Ammodramus princeps)* and its summer home. *Mem. Nuttall Ornithol. Club* No. 1.

1897. A species of Shearwater *(Puffinus assimilis* Gould) new to the North American fauna. *Proc. Biol. Soc. Washington* 11: 69-70.

1903. Some new records for Nova Scotia. *Auk* 20: 439-440.

Erskine, A.J.

1968. Northern birds summering in eastern Canada. *Nova Scotia Bird Soc. Newsletter* 10: 128-130.

1971. Bird communities in and around Cape Breton Wetlands. *Canadian Field-Nat.* 85: 129-140.

1977. Birds in boreal Canada: communities, densities and adaptations. *Canadian Wildl. Serv. Rep. Ser.* 41.

1978. The first ten years of the co-operative breeding bird survey in Canada. *Canadian Wildl. Serv. Rep. Ser.* 42.

Finch, D.W.

1972. The nesting season. Northeastern Maritime region. *Amer. Birds* 26:832-837.

Forbush, E.H.

1916. *A History of the Game Birds, Wild-fowl and Shore Birds of Massachusetts and Adjacent States.* 2nd ed. Comm. of Massachusetts, Boston, Mass.

Freedman, B., C. Beauchamp, I.A. McLaren and S.I. Tingley.

1981. Forestry Management practices and populations of breeding birds in a hardwood forest in Nova Scotia. *Canadian Field-Nat.* 95: 307-311.

Gates, A.D.

1975. The tourism and outdoor recreation climate of the Maritime Provinces. *Publ. Appl. Meteorol. Envir. Canada, Atmosph. Envir. Ser.* REC-3-73.

Gesner, A.
1842. Birds of Nova Scotia and New Brunswick. Pp. 41-46 in *Synopsis of the Contents of Gesner's Museum of Natural History at Saint John, N.B.* Henry Chubb, Saint John, N.B.

Gibbon, R.S.
1964. Studies and observations of the Black-backed Three-toed Woodpecker near Stewiacke. *Nova Scotia Bird Soc. Newsletter* 6(3): 5-13.

Gilpin, J.B.
1872. On the eagles of Nova Scotia. *Proc. Trans. Nova Scotian Inst. Sci.* 3: 202-209.
1880. On the semi-annual migration of sea fowl in Nova Scotia. *Proc. Trans. Nova Scotian Inst. Sci.* 5: 138-151.
1881. On the birds of prey of Nova Scotia. *Proc. Trans. Nova Scotian Inst. Sci.* 5: 255-268.
1882a. Shore birds of Nova Scotia. *Proc. Trans. Nova Scotian Inst. Sci.* 5: 376-387.
1882b. Rare birds in Nova Scotia. *Ornithologist and Oologist* 7: 122-123.

Gochfield, M.
1964. An exotic hummingbird. *Nova Scotia Bird Soc. Newsletter* 6 (3): 11-12.

Godfrey, W.E.
1958. Birds of Cape Breton Island, Nova Scotia. *Canadian Field-Nat.* 72: 7-27.
1959a. Notes of the Great Auk in Nova Scotia. *Canadian Field-Nat.* 73: 175.
1959b. The Common Scoter on Cape Breton Island—a correction. *Canadian Field-Nat.* 73: 184.
1966. The Birds of Canada. *Nat. Mus. Canada Bull.* 203, *Biol. Ser.* 73.
1984. A tribute to Robie Wilfred Tufts, 1884-1982. *Canadian Field-Nat.* 98: 513-518.

Goss, N.S.
1885. Wilson's Plover in Nova Scotia. *Auk* 2: 221-222.

Grieve, S.
1885. *The Great Auk, or Garefowl* (Alca impennis, Linn.), *its History, Archeology, and Remains.* Thomas C. Jack, London and Edinburgh.

Gross, A.O.
1937. Birds of the Bowdoin-MacMillan Arctic Expedition 1934. *Auk* 54: 12-42.

Hakluyt, R.
1600. The *Principal Navigations Voyages Traffiques and Discoveries of the English Nation . . . . . .* Vol. 3, p. 162. London.

Haliburton, T.C.[2]
1825. *A General Description of Nova Scotia, Illustrated by a New and Correct Map.* Royal Acadian School, Halifax, N.S.

Hickman, W.A.
1896. List of birds observed at Pictou, Nova Scotia, from first of January to first of July, 1895. *Ottawa Nat.* 9: 231-235.

James, R.D., P.L. McLaren, and J.C. Barlow.
1976. Annotated checklist of the birds of Ontario. *Life Sci. Misc. Publ. Royal Ont. Mus.* 1976.

Johnson, R.A.
1940. Present range, migration and abundance of the Atlantic Murre in North America. *Bird-Banding* 11: 1-17.

Jones, J.M.
1868. On some of the rarer birds of Nova Scotia. *Proc. Trans. Nova Scotian Inst. Sci.* 2: 70-73.
1870. Rare birds in Nova Scotia. *Amer. Nat.* 4: 253.
1879. List of the birds of Nova Scotia—land birds. *Forest and Stream* (N.Y.) 12: 65-66, 105-106, 205, 245.
1885. Water birds of Nova Scotia. *Forest and Stream* (N.Y.) 25: 43-44, 83, 123.

---

[2]Inferred author.

Kempton, A.C.
1891.   Fox Sparrow in Nova Scotia. *Forest and Stream* (N.Y.) 34: 412.
Kennard, F.H.
1902.   The Yellow-crowned Night Heron *(Nycticorax violaceus)* in Nova Scotia. *Auk* 19: 396-397.
Kortright, F.H.
1942.   *The Ducks, Geese, and Swans of North America.* Amer. Wildlife Inst., Washington, D.C.
Langille, J.H.
1884.   Bicknell's Thrush. *Auk* 1: 268-270.
1892.   *Our Birds in their Haunts.* Orange Judd Co., New York.
Lewis, H.F.
1913.   The Evening Grosbeak in Nova Scotia. *Bird-lore* 15: 1973.
1914.   Breeding of the Red-winged Blackbird *(Agelaius phoeniceus phoeniceus)* in Nova Scotia. *Auk* 31: 537-538.
1920.   Notes on the Acadian Sharp-tailed Sparrow *(Passerherbulus nelsoni subvirgatus). Auk* 37: 587-589.
1929.   The *Natural History of the Double-crested Cormorant* (Phalacrocorax auritus auritus). Ru-Mi-Lou Books, Ottawa.
1957.   Report on official investigation of cormorants in Nova Scotia in 1956 and 1957. *Nova Scotia Mus. Sci. Newsletter* 2 (2): 28-32.
Lloyd, H.
1920.   The duck specimens recorded as Labrador Duck in Dalhousie College, Halifax, Nova Scotia. *Canadian Field-Nat.* 34: 155-156.
1927.   European Widgeon crosses from Iceland. *Canadian Field-Nat.* 41: 171.
Lock, A.R., and R.K. Ross.
1973.   The nesting of the Great Cormorant *(Phalacrocorax carbo)* and the Double-crested Cormorant *(Phalacrocorax auritus)* in Nova Scotia in 1971. *Canadian Field-Nat.* 87: 43-49.
MacArthur, R.H., and E.O. Wilson.
1967.   *The Theory of Island Biogeography.* Princeton Univ. Press, Princeton, N.J.
MacLellan, C.R.
1958.   The role of woodpeckers in control of the Codling Moth in Nova Scotia. *Canadian Entomol.* 40: 21.
Macoun, J.
1903.   *Catalogue of Canadian Birds.* Part 2. Geological Survey of Canada, Ottawa.
Macoun, J. and J. M. Macoun
1909.   *Catalogue of Canadian Birds.* Geological Survey of Canada, Ottawa.
Majka, C.G., B.L. Roscoe, and M.V. MacKinnon.
1976.   The first nest record of the Greater Yellowlegs *(Tringa melano leuca)* in Nova Scotia. *Canadian Field-Nat.* 90: 200-201.
May, J.B.
1935.   The *Hawks and Owls of North America.* Amer. Wildl. Inst., Washington, D.C.
McAtee, W.L.
1945.   *Branta c. hutchinsi* on the Altantic coast. *Auk* 62: 461-462.
McKinlay, J.
1885.   Field notes from Pictou County, Nova Scotia. *Auk* 2: 39-43.
1899.   The Corn Crake in Nova Scotia. *Auk.* 14: 75-76.
McLaren, I.A.
1981a. The birds of Sable Island, Nova Scotia. *Proc. Trans. Nova Scotian Inst. Sci.* 31: 1-84.
1981b. The incidence of vagrant landbirds on Nova Scotian islands. *Auk* 98: 243-257.
1985.   Survey of nineteenth century ornithology in Nova Scotia. Part I. Annotated list of unusual records. *Nova Scotia Birds* 27 (2): 46-54; (3): 65-71.
1986.   Survey of nineteenth century ornithology in Nova Scotia. Part II. Annotated bibliography. *Nova Scotia Birds* 28 (2): 71-79.

McLaren, I.A., and A. MacInnis.
1977. A Zone-tailed Hawk in Nova Scotia. *Canadian Field-Nat.* 91: 310-311.

McLeod, R.R.
1903. *Markland or Nova Scotia, its History, Natural Resources and Native Beauties.* J.L. Nichols, Ltd., Toronto, Ont.

McNeil, R. and J. Burton.
1971. First authentic North American record of the British Storm Petrel *(Hydrobates pelagicus). Auk* 88: 671-672.

Mendall, H.L.
1944. Food of hawks and owls in Maine. *J. Wildl. Management* 8: 198-208.

Miller, E.H..
1985. Parental behaviour in the Least Sandpiper *(Calidris minutilla) Canadian J. Zool.* 63: 1593-1601.

Milton, G.R., and P.J. Austin-Smith.
1983. Changes in abundance and distribution of Double-crested *(Phalacrocorax auritus)* and Great Cormorants *(P. carbo)* in Nova Scotia. *Colonial Waterbirds* 6: 130-138.

Morrell, C.H.
1899. Some winter birds of Nova Scotia. *Auk* 16: 250-253.

Mousley, H.
1939. Nesting behaviour of Wilson's Snipe and Spotted Sandpiper. *Auk* 56: 129-133.

Murphy, R.C., and W. Vogt.
1933. The Dovekie influx of 1932. *Auk* 50: 325-349.

Oberholser, H.C.
1938. The bird life of Louisiana. *Louisiana Dep. Conserv. Bull.* 28.

Ouellet, H., McNeil, R., and Burton, J.
1973. The Western Sandpiper in Quebec and the Maritime Provinces. *Canadian Field-Nat.* 87: 291-300.

Palmer, R.S.
1949. Maine birds. *Bull. Mus. Comp. Zool.* 102: 1-656.

Palmer, R.S., (ed.)
1976. *Handbook of North American Birds.* Vol. 2,3. *Waterfowl* . Yale Univ. Press, New Haven and London.

Peters, H.S.
1941. Ring-necked Ducks breeding in Prince Edward Island and Nova Scotia. *Auk* 58: 401-402.

Piers, H.
1890. Notes on Nova Scotian zoology. *Proc. Trans. Nova Scotian Inst. Sci.* 8: 467-474.
1892a. Notes on Nova Scotia zoology: No. 2. *Proc. Trans. Nova Scotian Inst. Sci.* 8: 175-184.
1892b. On the nidification of the Winter Wren in Nova Scotia. *Proc. Trans. Nova Scotian Inst. Sci.* 8: 203-207.
1894. Notes on Nova Scotian zoology: No. 3. *Proc. Trans. Nova Scotian Inst. Sci.* 8: 395-410.
1897. Notes on Nova Scotia zoology: No. 4. *Proc. Trans. Nova Scotian Inst. Sci.* 9: 255-267.
1898. Remarkable ornithological occurrences in Nova Scotia. *Auk* 15: 195-196.
1915. The occurrence of European birds in Nova Scotia. *Proc. Trans. Nova Scotian Inst. Sci.* 13: 228-239.
1927. Accidental occurrence in Nova Scotia of the Rock Ptarmigan *(Lagopus rupestris welchi* or *L. rupestris rupestris):* with remarks on the status of *L. welchi* as a specific name. *Proc. Trans. Nova Scotian Inst. Sci.* 16: 1-8.

Pitelka, F.A.
1950. Geographic variation and the species problem in the shorebird genus *Limnodromus. Univ. Calif. Publ. Zool.* 50: 1-108.

Pough, R.H.
1949. *Audubon Bird Guide. Small Land Birds.* Doubleday and Co., Garden City, N.Y.

Prevost, Y.A., R.R. Bancroft, and N.R. Seymour.

    1978.   Status of the Osprey in Antigonish County, Nova Scotia. *Canadian Field-Nat.* 92: 294-297.

Quinney, T.E., and P.C. Smith.

    1980.   First breeding record of Black-crowned Night Heron in Nova Scotia. *Canadian Field-Nat.* 94: 463.

Rand, A.L.

    1929.   Natal down and juvenal plumage of the Sharp-tailed Sparrow. *Auk* 46: 243-244.

    1930.   Notes on the summer birds of the interior of western Nova Scotia. *Canadian Field-Nat.* 44: 95-96.

    1948.   Distributional notes on Canadian birds. *Canadian Field-Nat.* 62: 175-180.

    1950.   An abnormally colored Woodcock *(Philohela minor). Canadian Field-Nat.* 64: 153.

Richardson, E.

    1965.   *Living Island.* Ryerson, Toronto, Ontario.

Richardson, W.J.

    1982.   Northeastward reverse migration of birds over Nova Scotia, Canada, in Autumn. A radar study. *Behav. Ecol. Sociobiol.* 10: 193-206.

Roland, A.E.

    1982.   *Geological Background and Physiography of Nova Scotia.* Nova Scotian Inst. of Science, Halifax.

Ross, H.A.

    1980a. The reproductive rates of yearling and older Ipswich Sparrows, *Passerculus sandwichensis princeps. Canadian J. Zool.* 58: 1557-1763.

    1980b. Growth of nestling Ipswich Sparrows in relation to season, habitat, brood size, and parental age. *Auk* 97: 721-732.

Ross, H.A., and I.A. McLaren.

    1981.   Lack of differential survival among young Ipswich Sparrows. *Auk* 98: 495-502.

Rowe, J.S.

    1972.   Forest regions of Canada. *Canadian Forestry Serv. Bull.* 1300.

Sandford, L.C., L.B. Bishop, and T.S. Van Dyke.

    1903.   *The Waterfowl Family.* Macmillan, London and New York.

Saunders, W.E.

    1902.   Birds of Sable Island, N.S. *Ottawa Nat.* 16: 15-31.

Scott, D.M.

    1959.   Observations on marine birds of southwestern Nova Scotia. *Canadian Field-Nat.* 73: 15-20.

Shortt, T.M.

    1943.   Correlation of bill and foot coloring with age and season in the Black Duck. *Wilson Bull.* 55: 3-7.

Simmons, M., D. Davis, L. Griffiths, and A. Muecke.

    1984.   *Natural History of Nova Scotia.* 2 Vols. Nova Scotia Dept. Education and Dept. Lands and Forests, Halifax.

Smith, B.J. and S. Smith.

    1972.   [List of birds of Cape Sable, Nova Scotia]. *Nova Scotia Bird Soc. Newsletter* 14: 74-78.

Smith, P.W.

    1985.   Jackdaws reach the New World. *Amer. Birds* 39: 255-258.

Smith, R.W.

    1938.   Noteworthy records for Nova Scotia. *Auk* 55: 548-550.

Solman, V.E.F.

    1974.   Harrison Flint Lewis, 1893-1974. *Canadian Field-Nat.* 88: 507-516.

Squires, W.A.

    1976.   The birds of New Brunswick. *New Brunswick Mus. Monogr. Ser.* No. 7.

Stobo, W.T., and I.A. McLaren.

    1975.   The Ipswich Sparrow. *Proc. Trans. Nova Scotian Inst. Sci.* 27 (suppl 2): 1-105.

Stone, W.
  1937.   *Bird Studies at Old Cape May.* 2 Vols. Delaware Valley Ornithol. Club., Acad. Nat. Sci., Philadelphia.
Storey, A.E., and J. Lein.
  1985.   Development of the first North American Colony of Manx Shearwaters. *Auk* 102: 395-401.
Taverner, P.A.
  1934.   Birds of Canada. *Nat. Mus. Canada Bull.* 72.
Tothill, J.D.
  1918.   Diving habit of the Spotted Sandpiper. *Ottawa Nat.* 32: 56.
Townsend, C.W.
  1906.   Notes on the birds of Cape Breton Island. *Auk* 23: 172-179.
  1915.   Notes on the Rock Dove. *Auk* 22: 306-316.
  1922.   The summer birds of Advocate, Cumberland County, Nova Scotia. *Canadian Field-Nat.* 36: 44-46.
Tuck, L.M.
  1961.   The Murres: their distribution, populations and biology—a study of the genus *Uria. Canadian Wildl. Serv. Monogr. Ser.* No. 1.
Tufts, H.F.
  1898.   Notes on the birds of Kings Co., Nova Scotia. *Ottawa Nat.* 12: 173-177.
  1899.   Notes on the birds of Kings Co., Nova Scotia. *Ottawa Nat.* 12: 229-233, 359-362.
  1906.   Nesting of crossbills in Nova Scotia. *Auk* 23: 339-340.
  1907.   Notes on some Seal Island (Yarmouth County, Nova Scotia) birds. *Ottawa Nat.* 21: 93-95.
Tufts, R.W.
  1915.   Wilson's Snipe wintering in Nova Scotia. *Auk* 32: 368.
  1925.   Record of the Sooty Tern for Nova Scotia. *Canadian Field-Nat.* 39: 64.
  1930.   Black Grouse and Capercaillie liberated in Nova Scotia. *Canadian Field-Nat.* 44: 214.
  1949.   First record for White Pelican in Nova Scotia. *Canadian Field-Nat.* 63: 116.
  1955.   Rare and unusual birds observed during 1955. *Nova Scotia Mus. Sci. Newsletter* 1(2): 5.
Welsh, D.A.
  1975.   Savannah Sparrow breeding and territoriality on a Nova Scotia dune beach. *Auk* 92: 235-251.
White, H.G.
  1891.   Migration of the Red Phalarope *(Crymophilus fulicarius). Auk* 8: 233-235.
Willis, J.R.
  1859.   List of birds of Nova Scotia. Compiled from notes made by Lieutenant Blakiston, R.A., and Lieutenant Bland, R.E., made in 1858. *Ann. Rep. Board Regents Smithsonian Inst.* 1858: 280-286.

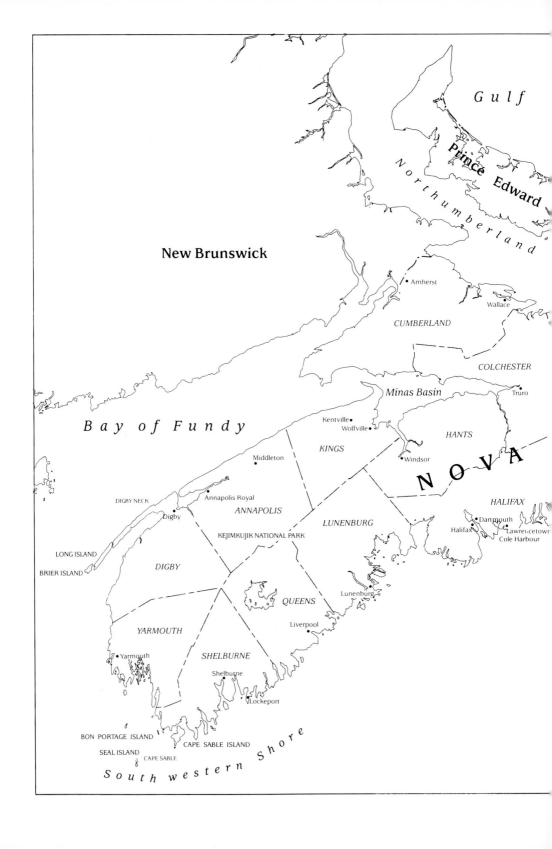

Gulf

Prince Edward

Northumberland

New Brunswick

• Amherst

Wallace

CUMBERLAND

COLCHESTER

Minas Basin

Truro

Kentville •
Wolfville •

HANTS

B a y   o f   F u n d y

Middleton •

KINGS

• Windsor

N O V A

DIGBY NECK

• Annapolis Royal

HALIFAX

Digby •

ANNAPOLIS

• Dartmouth

Halifax •
Lawrencetown

Cole Harbour

LUNENBURG

LONG ISLAND

KEJIMKUJIK NATIONAL PARK

BRIER ISLAND

DIGBY

QUEENS

Lunenburg •

• Liverpool

YARMOUTH

• Yarmouth

SHELBURNE

Shelburne •

Lockeport

BON PORTAGE ISLAND

CAPE SABLE ISLAND

SEAL ISLAND   CAPE SABLE

S o u t h   w e s t e r n   S h o r e

of St. Lawrence

ST. PAUL ISLAND

Cabot Strait

CAPE NORTH

CAPE BRETON HIGHLANDS NATIONAL PARK

Island

Inverness

VICTORIA

Baddeck

Glace Bay

Sydney

Strait

INVERNESS

Cape Breton Island

SCATARIE ISLAND

Louisbourg

Bras d'Or Lake

Pictou

New Glasgow

Antigonish

RICHMOND

Cape Breton Shore

PICTOU

ANTIGONISH

Port Hawkesbury

SCOTIA

Arichat

Strait of Canso

Guysborough

Canso

GUYSBOROUGH

Sheet Harbour

Eastern Shore

SABLE ISLAND

Atlantic Ocean

Index

All common and scientific names appearing in the text are indexed below. The page number facing the plate which carries the coloured illustration of the bird is given in boldface after its common name.